Volume II

The Van de Walle Professional Mathematics Series

Teaching Student-Centered Mathematics

Developmentally Appropriate Instruction for Grades 3–5

Second Edition

John A. Van de Walle
Late of Virginia Commonwealth University

Karen S. Karp
University of Louisville

LouAnn H. Lovin
James Madison University

Jennifer M. Bay-Williams
University of Louisville

PEARSON

Boston   Columbus   Indianapolis   New York   San Francisco   Upper Saddle River
Amsterdam   Cape Town   Dubai   London   Madrid   Milan   Munich   Paris   Montréal   Toronto
Delhi   Mexico City   São Paulo   Sydney   Hong Kong   Seoul   Singapore   Taipei   Tokyo

Vice President, Editor in Chief: Aurora Martínez Ramos
Executive Editor: Linda Bishop
Senior Development Editor: Christina Robb
Editorial Assistant: Laura White
Marketing Manager: Christine Gatchell
Production Editor: Karen Mason / Cynthia DeRocco
Editorial Production Service: Electronic Publishing Services Inc.
Manufacturing Buyer: Megan Cochran
Electronic Composition: Jouve
Interior Design: Electronic Publishing Services Inc.
Cover Designer: Laura Gardner

Image Credits: Chapter Opener Images: Left blocks, J. McPhail/Shutterstock; Middle tangrams, David Crehner/Fotolia; Right blocks, Sergey Galushko/Fotolia. Teaching Tip Icon: Koya79/Fotolia. Standards for Mathematical Practice Icon: Xuejun Li/Fotolia

Cover Image: Paulrommer/Shutterstock

Credits and acknowledgments borrowed from other sources and reproduced, with permission, in this textbook appear on the appropriate page within text.

Library of Congress Cataloging-in-Publication Data

Van de Walle, John A.
Teaching student-centered mathematics. Developmentally appropriate instruction for grades 3–5.—[Second edition] / John A. Van de Walle, Late of Virginia Commonwealth University, Jennifer M. Bay-Williams, University of Louisville, Karen S. Karp, University of Louisville, LouAnn H. Lovin, James Madison University.
    pages cm.—(Volume II of the Van de Walle professional mathematics series)
  Includes bibliographical references and index.
  ISBN-13: 978-0-13-282487-3
  ISBN-10: 0-13-282487-6
  1. Mathematics—Study and teaching (Elementary)   I. Bay-Williams, Jennifer M. II. Karp, Karen S. III. Lovin, LouAnn H. IV. Title.
QA13.V34 2014
372.7—dc23   2012039984

10 9 8

ISBN 10: 0-13-282487-6
ISBN 13: 978-0-13-282487-3

About the Authors

The late **John A. Van de Walle** was a professor emeritus at Virginia Commonwealth University. He was a mathematics education consultant who regularly gave professional development workshops for K–8 teachers in the United States and Canada. He visited and taught in elementary school classrooms and worked with teachers to implement student-centered math lessons. He co-authored the Scott Foresman-Addison Wesley Mathematics K–6 series and contributed to the Pearson School mathematics program, enVisionMATH. In addition, he wrote numerous chapters and articles for the National Council of Teachers of Mathematics (NCTM) books and journals and was very active in NCTM, including serving on the Board of Directors, as the chair of the Educational Materials Committee, and as a frequent speaker at national and regional meetings.

Karen S. Karp is a professor of mathematics education at the University of Louisville (Kentucky). Prior to entering the field of teacher education she was an elementary school teacher in New York. Karen's research interest centers on teaching mathematics to diverse populations. She is also co-author of *Elementary and Middle School Mathematics: Teaching Developmentally, Growing Professionally: Readings from NCTM Publications for Grades K–8, Developing Essential Understanding of Addition and Subtraction for Teaching Mathematics in Pre-K–Grade 2*, and numerous book chapters and articles. She is a former member of the Board of Directors of NCTM and a former president of the Association of Mathematics Teacher Educators (AMTE). She continues to work in classrooms to support teachers of students with disabilities in their mathematics instruction.

LouAnn H. Lovin is a professor of mathematics education at James Madison University (Virginia). She co-authored the first edition of the *Teaching Student-Centered Mathematics* Professional Development Series with John A. Van de Walle as well as *Teaching Mathematics Meaningfully: Solutions for Reaching Struggling Learners* with special educators David Allsopp and Maggie Kyger. LouAnn taught mathematics to middle and high school students before transitioning to pre-K–grade 8. Over the last 15 years, she has worked in pre-K through grade 8 classrooms and engaged with teachers in professional development as they implement a student-centered approach to teaching mathematics. She has published articles in NCTM's *Teaching Children Mathematics* and *Mathematics Teaching in the Middle School* and has served on NCTM's Educational Materials Committee. LouAnn's research interest is investigating ways to develop teachers' mathematical knowledge needed to teach for understanding.

Jennifer M. Bay-Williams is a professor of mathematics education at the University of Louisville (Kentucky). Jennifer has published many articles on teaching and learning in NCTM journals. She has also coauthored numerous books, including *Mathematics Coaching: Resources and Tools for Coaches and Leaders, K–12; Developing Essential Understanding of Addition and Subtraction for Teaching Mathematics in Pre-K–Grade 2; Math and Literature: Grades 6–8; Math and Nonfiction: Grades 6–8;* and *Navigating through Connections in Grades 6–8*. Jennifer taught elementary, middle, and high school in Missouri and in Peru, and continues to work in classrooms at all levels with students and with teachers. Jennifer served as member of Board of Directors for TODOS: Equity for All, as president of AMTE, and as editor for the 2012 NCTM Yearbook.

Brief Contents

Contents

Part II: Teaching Student-Centered Mathematics

10 Developing Whole-Number Place-Value Concepts 151

11 Building Strategies for Whole-Number Computation 171

12 Exploring Fraction Concepts   202

13 Building Strategies for Fraction Computation 231

14 Developing Decimal and Percent Concepts and Decimal Computation 256

15 Promoting Algebraic Thinking 282

Preface

All students can learn mathematics with understanding! It is through the teacher's actions that every student, in his or her own way, can come to believe this important truth. We believe that teachers must create an environment in which students are trusted to solve problems and work together using their ideas to do so. Instruction involves posing tasks that will engage students in the mathematics they are expected to learn. Then, by allowing students to interact with and struggle with the mathematics using *their* ideas and *their* strategies—a student-centered approach—the mathematics they learn will be connected to other mathematics and to their world. Students will see the value of mathematics and feel empowered to use it. The title of this book, *Teaching Student-Centered Mathematics: Developmentally Appropriate Instruction for Grades 3–5*, reflects this vision. This vision is so critical to the learning of mathematics that, in this second edition, we start with a new Part I that addresses how to build a student-centered environment in which students can become mathematically proficient.

What Are Our Goals for the Professional Math Series?

Creating a classroom in which students design their solution pathways, engage in productive struggle, and connect mathematical ideas is complex. Questions arise, such as, "How do I get students to wrestle with problems if they just want me to show them how to do it? What kinds of tasks lend themselves to this type of engagement? Where can I learn the mathematics content I need in order to be able to teach in this way?" With these and other questions firmly in mind, we have three main objectives for the series:

1. Illustrate what it means to teach mathematics in a student-centered, problem-based manner.

2. Serve as a reference for all of the mathematics content suggested for grades pre-K–2, 3–5, and 6–8 as recommended in the *Common Core State Standards* and the *Curriculum Focal Points* (CCSSO, 2010; NCTM, 2006), as well as research-based strategies concerning how students learn this content.

3. Present a practical resource of robust, problem-based activities and tasks that can engage students in the mathematics that is important for them to learn.

These are also goals of *Elementary and Middle School Mathematics: Teaching Developmentally*, a comprehensive resource for teachers in grades K–8, which has been widely used in universities and in schools.

There is some overlap of both the text and activities between the comprehensive K–8 book and this Professional Series. However, we have adapted the Professional Series to be more useful for a practicing classroom teacher by focusing the content on specific grade bands and adding additional information on creating an effective classroom environment, engaging families, and aligning teaching to the new standards. We've also included more activities and lessons. We hope you will find that this is a valuable resource for teaching and learning mathematics!

Why Revise the Professional Math Series?

Since the writing of the first edition of this book began nearly a decade ago, many developments in mathematics education have occurred—from the publication of NCTM's *Curriculum Focal Points* (2006) to the development and implementation of the *Common Core State Standards* (CCSSO, 2010). Research has provided new information about how students learn particular mathematical ideas. We have also received great feedback from readers about what they liked about the first edition and what they wished would be in the second edition. It was time to incorporate these ideas into the book to ensure classroom teachers had access to strong support aligned with the latest developments in mathematics education.

What's New to the Second Edition of the Professional Math Series?

We made numerous significant changes to the Professional Series. They include:

- **A New Part I: Establishing a Student-Centered Environment.** The second edition is divided into *two* parts. Part I consists of seven chapters (all new) that address important ideas for creating a classroom environment in which all students can succeed. Part I focuses on what it means to teach mathematics *through* problem solving and how to differentiate instruction to meet the needs of *all* students. The final chapter in Part I expands the focus of mathematics education beyond the classroom, offering ideas for working with families, principals, and the community. These chapters focus on important "hot" topics that teachers and reviewers requested and that are important in making mathematics accessible to all learners. They are, by design, shorter in length than the content chapters in Part II, but are full of effective strategies and ideas. The intent is that these chapters can be used in professional development workshops, book study, or professional learning community (PLC) discussions. This new part replaces Chapter 1 in the first edition, which provided briefer attention to some of these topics. Part I includes:

  - A more in-depth definition of what we mean by *understanding*, using the eight mathematical practices identified in the *Common Core State Standards* (CCSSO, 2010), the five strands of mathematical proficiency from *Adding It Up* (NCTM, 2001), and NCTM's process standards (2000) (Chapter 1).

  - A discussion of what it means to teach mathematics *through* problem solving (as compared to teaching mathematics *for* problem solving). We include a discussion about criteria to use in the selection of problem-based tasks, and we present a set of recommendations for facilitating effective classroom discourse (Chapter 2).

  - Information on various formative assessment strategies, including observations, diagnostic interviews, and tasks, as well as creating and using rubrics (Chapter 3).

  - Strategies to support the diverse range of learners in your classroom (Chapters 4–6).

  - Concrete ideas about how to communicate and engage with a variety of stakeholders to ensure students receive the support they need to be successful in mathematics (Chapter 7).

- **Connections to the *Common Core State Standards*.** A priority in preparing the second edition was to align the material to the *Common Core State Standards*. This has resulted in important changes:

  - Connections to the eight Standards for Mathematical Practice, critical components of the CCSSO recommendations, are highlighted in the text through marginal notes that focus readers' attention on examples in the nearby text of what these eight practices look like across content areas and grade levels.

- Chapters have been reorganized and updated to reflect the CCSSO recommendations and present a more coherent progression of mathematical ideas and student learning. Explicit and specific attention is given to grade-level positioning of content throughout the discussion within each content chapter.

- **Increased Attention to Student Diversity.** A new emphasis on diversity can be seen with the addition of chapters on differentiating instruction (Chapter 4) as well as planning, teaching, and assessing culturally and linguistically diverse students (Chapter 5) and students with exceptionalities (Chapter 6). Additional strategies for supporting students with special needs and English language learners are included in Part II chapters, are highlighted in several activities in each chapter (noted with icons), and are incorporated into the revised expanded lessons at the end of each Part II chapter.

- **Coverage of Technology.** Since the first edition was published, technology has changed drastically. Now there is an increased availability of high-quality websites, applets, freeware, and so on. Throughout each chapter we identify effective, free technology that can help make content more visible, relevant, and interesting to students. To locate these examples, look for the Technology Notes in Part II.

- **Revised, Updated Expanded Lessons.** Every Part II chapter still has a lesson at the end, but they have all been revised. Lessons have been added or revised to explicitly focus on concepts central to intermediate elementary school mathematics. All lessons now include (1) NCTM and CCSSO grade-level recommendations, (2) adaptation suggestions for English language learners and students with special needs, and (3) formative assessment suggestions for what to observe and what questions to ask students.

 **What's New to Volume II?**

The most noteworthy changes to Volume II *(Developmentally Appropriate Instruction for Grades 3–5)* are related to the content. The recent movement to the *Common Core State Standards* has resulted in major shifts in what mathematics is taught in the intermediate grades in the elementary school. There is a considerable emphasis on fractions and algebraic thinking as related to number and operation. You will also note that the probability chapter in the first edition has been eliminated. We made this decision based on the recommendations from NCTM's *Curriculum Focal Points* and the *Common Core State Standards*, in which probability concepts are delayed until middle school. Instead, at the request of many reviewers, a chapter has been added on place value. The detailed table of contents provides a good indication of all of these changes. Among those many changes includes differences in coverage of:

- **Basic Facts.** In Chapter 9 there is an increased focus on the research-based developmental model of developing basic facts, and new activities and games to support basic fact mastery. Although there is a discussion of addition and subtraction facts, given that Volume I of the series addresses these topics heavily the focus here shifts to building strength in multiplication and division facts.

- **Fractions.** Chapter 12 has been changed considerably, using recommendations from the document *Developing Effective Fractions Instruction for Kindergarten through 8th Grade: A Practice Guide* (IES, 2010), which emphasizes the notions of partitioning and iterating. In addition, more attention is given to length models (bar diagrams) and to common student misconceptions.

- **Computation with Fractions, Decimals, and Percents.** We have expanded attention to operations with rational numbers across Chapters 13 and 14 with an emphasis on how to teach them conceptually and effectively (and using appropriate terminology). Each operation section concentrates on the importance of estimation and on understanding why the standard algorithms work.

- **Algebra.** Chapter 15 may be the most unrecognizable. It is now organized by important areas of algebra, as described in recent literature on teaching algebraic thinking. The chapter includes significantly more attention to content described in the *Common Core State Standards*, including generalizing arithmetic, use of symbols, structure in the number system, and functional thinking.

- **Measurement.** The structure of Chapter 16 has changed. Previously the development of all the measurement formulas was shared at the end of the chapter; now the formulas are integrated with the corresponding measurement topic (e.g., area or volume).

- **Geometry.** Chapter 17 now includes a section on van Hiele's levels of geometric thought, with an increased focus on moving toward level 2 thinking within the discussion on each topic. The geometry topics of composing and decomposing shapes received increased attention as aligned with the standards in the intermediate elementary level curriculum. In addition, as requested by reviewers, topics that are emphasized in the middle school, such as transformations, receive less consideration in this edition.

- **Data.** Chapter 18 has also has undergone dramatic change. It now is organized around the process of doing statistics as described in the *Guidelines for Assessment and Instruction in Statistical Education (GAISE) Report* (American Statistical Association, 2005). Changes include new and revised sections on posing questions, data collection (both numerical and categorical), data analysis, and interpreting results, as well as an emphasis on the shape of data and variability. The chapter includes shifts consistent with topics in the CCSS (e.g., the emphasis on line plots and the use of circle graphs as a means to support learning of fractions in grades 3–5).

▲ What Special Features Appear in the Professional Series?

Throughout the Book

New! Teaching Tips.　Teaching Tips identify practical take-away ideas that can support the teaching and learning of specific chapter content being addressed. These might be an instructional suggestion, a particular point about language use, a common student misconception, or a suggestion about a resource.

Stop and Reflect.　Reflective thinking is the key to effective learning. This is true not only for our students but also for ourselves as we continue to learn more about effective mathematics teaching. Keep your eye out for these sections that ask you to solve a problem or reflect on some aspect of what you have read. These Stop and Reflect sections do not signal every important idea, but we have tried to place them where it seemed natural and helpful for you to slow down a bit and think. In addition, every chapter in Part I ends with a Stop and Reflect section. Use these for discussions in professional learning communities or for reflection on your own.

Blackline Master Icons.　Blackline Masters are used in some of the activities and Expanded Lessons. Look for the icon in the margin alerting you to the Blackline Masters. In Appendix C, you will find a thumbnail version of all Blackline Masters. A PDF version of each full-sized Blackline Master is available on the PDToolkit site.

Additional Features in Part II

Big Ideas.   Much of the research and literature espousing a developmental approach suggests that teachers plan their instruction around "big ideas" rather than isolated skills or concepts. At the beginning of each chapter, you will find a list of the key mathematical ideas associated with the chapter. These lists of learning targets can help you get a snapshot of the mathematics you are teaching.

Activities.   Numerous problem-based tasks are presented in activity boxes. Additional ideas are described directly in the text or in the illustrations. They are designed to engage your students in doing mathematics (as described in Chapter 2). Most of these activities are presented in the numbered activity boxes and many have new adaptation and accommodation suggestions for English language learners and students with special needs. These are denoted with icons for easy reference. Following this Preface, you will find the Activities at a Glance table, which lists all the named and numbered activities with a short statement about the mathematical goal for each.

It is important that you see these activities as an integral part of the text that surrounds them. The activities are inserted as examples to support the development of the mathematics being discussed and how your students can be supported in learning that content. Therefore, we hope that you will not use any activity for instruction without reading carefully the full text in which it is embedded.

Formative Assessment Notes.   Assessment should be an integral part of instruction. As you read, we want you to think about what to listen and look for (assess) in different areas of content development. Therefore you will find Formative Assessment Notes that describe ways to assess your students' developing knowledge and understanding. These Formative Assessment Notes can also help improve your understanding about how to help your students through targeted instruction.

New! Technology Notes.   Integrated throughout the book are Technology Notes, which provide practical information about how technology can be used to help your students learn the content in that section. Descriptions include open-source software, interactive applets, and other Web-based resources—all of which are free.

New! Standards for Mathematical Practice Notes.   Connections to the eight Standards of Mathematical Practice from the *Common Core State Standards* are highlighted in the margins. The location of the note indicates an example of the identified practice in the nearby text.

Expanded Lessons.   The activities in the book are written in a brief format so as to provide many activities for the content without detracting from the flow of ideas. At the end of each Part II chapter, we selected one activity and expanded it into a complete lesson plan, following the *Before, During, After* structure described in Chapter 2. These Expanded Lessons provide a model for converting an activity description into a full lesson that can engage students in developing a strong understanding of the related concept. In this new edition, all lessons are now aligned with NCTM and CCSSO grade-level recommendations and include adaptation suggestions for English language learners and students with disabilities.

New! *Common Core State Standards Appendixes.* The *Common Core State Standards* outline eight Standards for Mathematical Practice (Appendix A) that help students develop and demonstrate a deep understanding of and capacity to do mathematics. We initially describe these practices in Chapter 1 and highlight examples of the mathematical practices throughout the content chapters in Part II. We used the *Common Core State Standards* (CCSSO, 2010) as a guide to determine the content emphasis in each volume of the series. Appendix B provides a list of the critical content areas for each grade level discussed in this volume.

New! *PDToolkit.* The PDToolkit for *Teaching Student-Centered Mathematics: Developmentally Appropriate Instruction*, Second Edition (Volumes I, II, and III), together with the book, offers the tools you need to teach student-centered, problem-based mathematics.

The following resources are currently available:

- Video examples
- Virtual manipulatives
- Full-size, printable versions of the Blackline Masters from Volumes I, II, and III

In the future, we will continue to add additional resources.

To access the PDToolkit, go to http://pdtoolkit.pearson.com and enter the following code: PDTOOL-CLONK-LOSSY-SAVVY-HIGHS-LINES

Acknowledgments

We would like to begin by acknowledging *you:* the reader, the teacher, the leader, and the advocate for your students. The strong commitment of teachers and teacher leaders to always strive to improve how we teach mathematics is the reason this book was written in the first place. And, because of ongoing input and feedback, we endeavored to revise this edition to meet your changing needs. We have received input from so many teachers and reviewers, and all of it has informed the development of this substantially revised second edition!

In preparing the second edition, we benefited from the thoughtful input of the following educators who offered comments on the first edition or on the manuscript for the second: Alanna Arenivas, Dallas Independent School District; Lakita Combs, Klein Instructional Center; Susan Faller-Mitchell, Southern Oregon University; Kelly Herman-Roberts, Jones County Schools; and Susan E. Mast, Kyrene School District. The reviewers' comments helped push our thinking on many important topics and many specific suggestions offered by these reviewers found their way into this book. We offer our sincere appreciation to these individuals for their suggestions and constructive feedback.

As we reviewed standards, research, and teaching articles; visited classrooms; and collected students' work samples, we were continually reminded of the amazing mathematics instruction going on in our profession. From the mathematics educators and mathematicians working on standards documents, to the mathematics discussions occurring in pre-K–grade 8 classrooms that are then shared with others, we see great hope and vision in preparing all students to be mathematically proficient. It is for this broad commitment to mathematics education on the part of so many that we are so grateful, as well as the particular teachers with whom we have worked in recent years.

As authors, we also want to acknowledge the strong support of our editorial team throughout the process, from the first discussions about what a second edition might include, through the tedious editing at later stages in the development. Without their support, the final product would not be the quality resource we hope you find it to be. Specifically, we thank Kelly Villella-Canton for helping us envision our work, Linda Bishop for seeing this vision through, and both of them for their words of encouragement and wisdom. Working on three volumes of a book simultaneously is quite an undertaking! Christina Robb found a way to keep us organized and provided timely and much-needed feedback throughout our writing. We are grateful for Dana Weightman and the team at Pearson who patiently walked us through the permissions process. We also wish to thank Karla Walsh and the rest of the production and editing team at Electronic Publishing Services Inc.

Even with the support of so many, researching and writing takes time. Simple words cannot express the gratitude we have to our families for their support, patience, and contributions to the production of these books. Briefly we recognize them by name here: Karen thanks her husband, Bob Ronau, and her children and grandchildren, Matthew, Tammy, Josh, Misty, Matt, Christine, Jeff, Pamela, Jessica, Zane, Madeline, Jack, and Emma. LouAnn thanks her husband, Ramsey, and her two sons, Nathan and Jacob. Jennifer thanks her husband, Mitch, and her children, MacKenna and Nicolas.

The origin of this book began many years ago with the development of *Elementary and Middle School Mathematics: Teaching Developmentally* by John A. Van de Walle. What began as a methods book spread to the teaching community because it offered content support, activities, and up-to-date best practices for teaching mathematics. The series was developed as a way to focus on and expand the specific grade-level topics. John was adamant that all children can learn to reason and make sense of mathematics. We acknowledge his enduring vision, his commitment, and his significant contributions to the field of mathematics education. His ideas continue to inspire the work you see in this new edition.

The response to the first edition has been amazing. We hope the second edition will be received with as much interest and enthusiasm as the first and continue to be a valuable support to your mathematics teaching and your students' learning.

Activities at a Glance

This table lists the named and numbered activities in Part II of the book. In addition to providing an easy way to find an activity, the table provides the main mathematical goal or objective for each activity, stated as succinctly as possible. You should see the table only as a listing of the named activities, and not as an index of instructional ideas.

Rather than a book of activities, this is a book about teaching mathematics. Many practical and effective activities are used as examples. Every activity should be seen as an integral part of the text that surrounds it. Therefore, it is extremely important not to take any activity as a suggestion for instruction without reading carefully the full text in which it is embedded.

1

Teaching Mathematics for Understanding

An understanding can never be "covered" if it is to be understood.

Wiggins and McTighe (2005, p. 229)

Teachers generally agree that teaching for understanding is a good thing. But this statement begs the question: What is *understanding?* Understanding is being able to think and act flexibly with a topic or concept. It goes beyond knowing; it is more than a collection of information, facts, or data. It is more than being able to follow steps in a procedure. One hallmark of mathematical understanding is a student's ability to justify why a given mathematical claim or answer is true or why a mathematical rule makes sense (CCSSO, 2010). Although students might *know* their multiplication basic facts and be able to give you quick answers to questions about these basic facts, they might not *understand* multiplication. They might not be able to justify the correctness of their answer or provide an example of when it would make sense to use this basic fact. These tasks go beyond simply knowing mathematical facts and procedures. Understanding must be a primary goal for all of the mathematics you teach.

Understanding and Doing Mathematics

Procedural proficiency, a main focus of mathematics instruction in the past, remains important today, but conceptual understanding is an equally important goal (CCSSO, 2010; National Research Council, 2001; NCTM, 2000). Numerous reports and standards emphasize the need to address skills and understanding in an integrated manner; among these are the *Common Core State Standards* (CCSSO, 2010), a state-led effort coordinated by the National Governors Association Center for Best Practices (NGA Center) and the Council of Chief State School Officers (CCSSO) that has been adopted by nearly every state

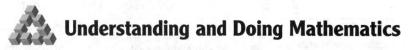

and the District of Columbia. This effort has resulted in attention to *how* mathematics is taught, not just *what* is taught.

The National Council of Teachers of Mathematics (NCTM, 2000) identifies the process standards of problem solving, reasoning and proof, representation, communication, and connections as ways to think about how students should engage in learning mathematics content as they develop both procedural fluency and conceptual understanding. Students engaged in the process of *problem solving* build mathematical knowledge and understanding by grappling with and solving genuine problems as opposed to completing routine exercises. They use *reasoning and proof* to make sense of mathematical tasks and concepts and to develop, justify, and evaluate mathematical arguments and solutions. Students create and use *representations* (e.g., diagrams, graphs, symbols, and manipulatives) to reason through problems. They also engage in *communication* as they explain their ideas and reasoning verbally, in writing, and through representations. Students develop and use *connections* between mathematical ideas as they learn new mathematical concepts and procedures. They also build *connections* between mathematics and other disciplines by applying mathematics to real-world situations. By engaging in these processes, students learn mathematics by *doing* mathematics. Consequently, the process standards should not be taught separately from but in conjunction with mathematics as ways of learning mathematics.

Adding It Up (National Research Council, 2001), an influential research review on how students learn mathematics, identifies the following five strands of mathematical proficiency as indicators that someone understands (and can do) mathematics:

- *Conceptual understanding:* Comprehension of mathematical concepts, operations, and relations
- *Procedural fluency:* Skill in carrying out procedures flexibly, accurately, efficiently, and appropriately
- *Strategic competence:* Ability to formulate, represent, and solve mathematical problems
- *Adaptive reasoning:* Capacity for logical thought, reflection, explanation, and justification
- *Productive disposition:* Habitual inclination to see mathematics as sensible, useful, and worthwhile, coupled with a belief in diligence and one's own efficacy (Reprinted with permission from p. 116 of *Adding It Up: Helping Children Learn Mathematics*, 2001 by the National Academy of Sciences, Courtesy of the National Academies Press, Washington, D.C.)

This report maintains that the strands of mathematical proficiency are interwoven and interdependent—that is, the development of one strand aids the development of others (Figure 1.1).

Building on the NCTM process standards and the five strands of mathematical proficiency, the *Common Core State Standards* (CCSSO, 2010) outline the following eight Standards for Mathematical Practice (see Appendix A) as ways in which students can develop and demonstrate a deep understanding of and capacity to do mathematics. Keep in mind that you, as a teacher, have a responsibility to help students develop these practices. Here we provide a brief discussion about each mathematical practice.

Figure 1.1

Interrelated and intertwined strands of mathematical proficiency.

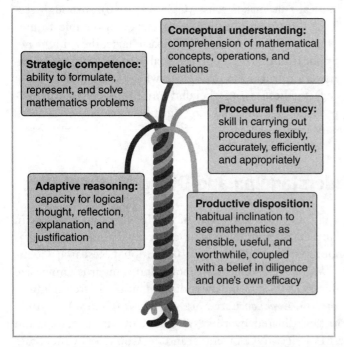

Strategic competence: ability to formulate, represent, and solve mathematics problems

Conceptual understanding: comprehension of mathematical concepts, operations, and relations

Procedural fluency: skill in carrying out procedures flexibly, accurately, efficiently, and appropriately

Adaptive reasoning: capacity for logical thought, reflection, explanation, and justification

Productive disposition: habitual inclination to see mathematics as sensible, useful, and worthwhile, coupled with a belief in diligence and one's own efficacy

Source: Reprinted with permission from Kilpatrick, J., Swafford, J., & Findell, B. (Eds.), *Adding It Up: Helping Children Learn Mathematics.* Copyright 2001 by the National Academy of Sciences. Courtesy of the National Academies Press, Washington, D.C.

1. *Make sense of problems and persevere in solving them.* To make sense of problems, students need to learn how to analyze the given information, the parameters, and the relationships in a problem so that they can understand the situation and identify possible ways to solve it. One way to help students analyze problems is to have them create bar diagrams to make sense of the quantities and relationships involved. Once students learn various strategies for making sense of problems, encourage them to remain committed to solving them. As they learn to monitor and assess their progress and change course as needed, they will solve the problems they set out to solve!

2. *Reason abstractly and quantitatively.* This practice involves students reasoning with quantities and their relationships in problem situations. You can support students' development of this practice by helping them create representations that correspond to the meanings of the quantities and the units involved. When appropriate, students should also learn to represent and manipulate the situation symbolically. Encourage students to find connections between the abstract symbols and the representation that illustrates the quantities and their relationships. For example, when fourth graders draw a bar diagram showing one tree as being four times the height of another tree, encourage them to connect their representation to the expression $4 \times h$, where h is the height of the shorter tree. Ultimately, students should be able to move flexibly between symbols and other representations.

3. *Construct viable arguments and critique the reasoning of others.* This practice emphasizes the importance of students' using mathematical reasoning to justify their ideas and solutions, including being able to recognize and use counterexamples. Encourage students to examine each others' arguments to determine whether they make sense and to identify ways to clarify or improve the arguments. This practice emphasizes that mathematics is based on reasoning and should be examined in a community—not carried out in isolation. Tips for supporting students as they learn to justify their ideas can be found in Chapter 2.

4. *Model with mathematics.* This practice encourages students to use the mathematics they know to solve problems from everyday life. For third graders, this could mean writing a multiplication or division equation to represent a given situation or using their measurement sense to determine whether a rug advertised in the newspaper would fit in a designated location in their classroom. Be sure to encourage students to determine whether their mathematical results make sense in the context of the given situation.

5. *Use appropriate tools strategically.* Students should become familiar with a variety of problem-solving tools and they should learn to choose which ones are most appropriate for a given situation. For example, fifth graders should experience using the following tools for computation with decimals: base-ten manipulatives, decimal grids, pencil and paper, calculators, and number lines. Then, if these students are asked to find the sum of 3.45 and 2.9 and provide their reasoning, they could use base-ten manipulatives or decimal grids to illustrate the meaning of each decimal and how the decimals were combined.

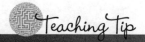
Teaching Tip

> Research suggests that students, in particular girls, may tend to continue to use the same tools because they feel comfortable with the tools and are afraid to take risks (Ambrose, 2002). Look for students who tend to use the same tool or strategy every time they work on a task. Encourage all students to take risks and to try new tools and strategies.

6. *Attend to precision.* In communicating ideas to others, it is imperative that students learn to be explicit about their reasoning. For example, they need to be clear about the meanings of operations and symbols they use, to indicate units involved in a problem, and to clearly label diagrams that accompany their explanations. As students share their ideas, emphasize this expectation and ask clarifying questions that help make the details of their reasoning more apparent. Teachers can further encourage students' attention to precision by introducing,

highlighting, and encouraging the use of accurate mathematical terminology in explanations and diagrams.

7. *Look for and make use of structure.* Students who look for and recognize a pattern or structure can experience a shift in their perspective or understanding. Therefore, set the expectation that students will look for patterns and structure and help them reflect on their significance. For example, help students notice that the order in which they multiply two numbers does not change the product—both 4×7 and 7×4 equal 28. Once students recognize this pattern in other examples, they will have a new understanding and use of a powerful property of our number system: the commutative property of multiplication.

8. *Look for and express regularity in repeated reasoning.* Encourage students to step back and reflect on any regularity that occurs in an effort to help them develop a general idea or method to identify shortcuts. For example, as students begin multiplying numbers, they will encounter situations in which a number is multiplied by 0. Over time, help them reflect on the results of multiplying any number by 0. Eventually they should be able to express that when any number is multiplied by 0, the product is always 0.

Like the process standards, the Standards for Mathematical Practice should not be taught separately from the mathematics. Instead, teachers should incorporate these practices as ways for students to learn and do mathematics. Students who learn to use these eight practices as they engage with mathematical concepts and skills have a greater chance of developing conceptual understanding. Note that learning these mathematical practices and developing understanding take time. So the common notion of simply and quickly "covering the material" is problematic. The opening quotation states it well: "An understanding can never be 'covered' if it is to be understood" (Wiggins & McTighe, 2005, p. 229). Understanding is an end goal—that is, it is developed over time by incorporating the process standards and mathematical practices and striving toward mathematical proficiency.

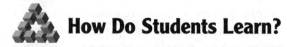 How Do Students Learn?

Let's look at a couple of research-based theories that can illustrate how students learn in general: constructivism and sociocultural theory. Although one theory focuses on the individual learner while the other emphasizes the social and cultural aspects of the classroom, these theories are not competing; they are actually compatible (Norton & D'Ambrosio, 2008).

● Constructivism

At the heart of constructivism is the notion that learners are not blank slates but rather creators (constructors) of their own learning. All people, all of the time, construct or give meaning to things they perceive or think about. Whether you are listening passively to a lecture or actively engaging in synthesizing findings in a project, your brain is applying prior knowledge (existing schemas) to make sense of the new information.

Constructing something in the physical world requires tools, materials, and effort. The tools you use to build understanding are your existing ideas and knowledge. Your materials might be things you see, hear, or touch, or they might be your own thoughts and ideas. The effort required to construct knowledge and understanding is reflective thought.

Through reflective thought, people connect existing idea to new information and thus modify their existing schemas or background knowledge to incorporate new ideas. Making these connections can happen in either of two ways—*assimilation* or *accommodation*. Assimilation occurs when a new concept "fits" with prior knowledge and the new information expands an existing mental network. Accommodation takes place when the new concept does not "fit" with the existing network, thus creating a cognitive conflict or state of confusion that causes what theorists call *disequilibrium*. As an example, some students assimilate fractions into their existing schemas for whole numbers. When they begin to compare fractions, they treat the numerators and denominators separately, as if they represented two whole numbers that have no relationship to each other. Such a student might mentally compare $\frac{2}{3}$ and $\frac{3}{4}$ by explaining that since $2 < 3$ (the numerators) and $3 < 4$ (the denominators), $\frac{2}{3} < \frac{3}{4}$. This student might initially confirm this erroneous thinking by using an area model that corresponds to a part-whole fraction to illustrate that $\frac{2}{3} < \frac{3}{4}$ because $\frac{2}{3}$ has less area than $\frac{3}{4}$. A teacher could then challenge this student to compare the fractions $\frac{1}{2}$ and $\frac{2}{5}$. This student's overgeneralization of whole-number ideas (e.g., $1 < 2$ and $2 < 5$, and so $\frac{1}{2} < \frac{2}{5}$) is then called into question when he or she approaches the area model illustrating that $\frac{1}{2} > \frac{2}{5}$. To settle the dissonance, the student eventually has to accommodate his or her schema for comparing fractions. It is through the struggle to resolve the disequilibrium that the brain modifies or replaces the existing schema so that the new concept fits and makes sense, resulting in a revision of thought and a deepening of the person's understanding.

For an illustration of what it means to construct an idea, consider Figure 1.2. The gray and white dots represent ideas, and the lines joining the ideas represent the logical connections or relationships that develop between ideas. The white dot is an emerging idea—one that is being constructed. Whatever existing ideas (gray dots) are used in the construction are connected to the new idea (white dot) because those are the ideas that give meaning to the new idea. The more existing ideas that are used to give meaning to the new one, the more connections will be made.

Each student's unique collection of ideas is connected in different ways. Some ideas are well understood and well formed, while others are less so. Students' prior experiences help them develop connections and ideas about whatever they are currently learning.

Understanding exists along a continuum (Figure 1.3), from an instrumental understanding—knowing something by rote or without meaning (Skemp, 1978)—to a relational understanding—knowing what to do and why. Instrumental understanding, at the left end of the continuum, shows that ideas (e.g., concepts and procedures) are learned, but in isolation (or nearly so) to other ideas. Here you find ideas that have been memorized. Due to their isolation, these often poorly understood ideas are easily forgotten and are unlikely to be useful for constructing new ideas. At the right end of the continuum is relational understanding. Relational understanding means that each new concept or procedure (white dot)

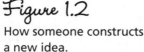

Figure 1.2

How someone constructs a new idea.

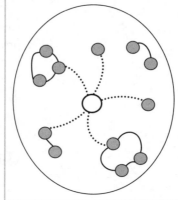

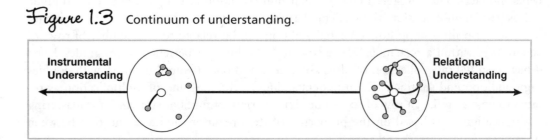

Figure 1.3   Continuum of understanding.

is not only learned, but is also connected to many existing ideas (gray dots), so there is a rich set of connections.

A primary goal of teaching for understanding is to help students develop a relational understanding of mathematical ideas. Because relational understanding develops over time and becomes more complex as a person makes more connections between ideas, teaching for this kind of understanding takes time and must be a goal of daily instruction.

◈ Sociocultural Theory

Like constructivism, sociocultural theory not only positions the learner as actively engaged in seeking meaning during the learning process, but it also suggests that the learner can be assisted by working with others who are "more knowledgeable." According to sociocultural theory, every learner has a unique zone of proximal development, which is a range of knowledge that may be out of reach for the individual to learn alone, but is accessible if the learner has the support of peers or more knowledgeable others (Vygotsky, 1978). For example, when students are learning about perimeter and area, they do not necessarily recognize that two rectangles can have the same perimeter but different areas. A more knowledgeable person (a peer or teacher) will know that if students explore creating different rectangles that have the same perimeter, the examples they generate will suggest this relationship between a rectangle's perimeter and area.

The most effective learning for a given student occurs when the activities of the classroom lie within his or her zone of proximal development. Targeting that zone helps teachers provide students with the right amount of challenge while avoiding boredom on the one hand and anxiety on the other when the challenge is beyond the student's current capability. Consequently, classroom discussions based on students' own ideas and solutions are "foundational to children's learning" (Wood & Turner-Vorbeck, 2001, p. 186).

◬ Teaching for Understanding

◈ Teaching toward Relational Understanding

To explore the notion of understanding further, let's look into a learner-centered fourth-grade classroom. In learner-centered classrooms, teachers begin *where the students are*—with *the students'* ideas. Students are allowed to solve problems or to approach tasks in ways that make sense to them. They develop their understanding of mathematics because they are at the center of explaining, providing evidence or justification, finding or creating examples, generalizing, analyzing, making predictions, applying concepts, representing ideas in different ways, and articulating connections or relationships between the given topic and other ideas.

For example, in this fourth-grade classroom, students have already reviewed double-digit addition and subtraction computation and have been working on multiplication concepts and facts. They mastered most of their multiplication facts by the end of third grade but as part of an extension, the students have used contexts embedded in story problems. They are also illustrating how repeated addition can be related to the number of rows of square tiles within a rectangle. These students' combined experiences from grades 3 and 4 have resulted in a collection of ideas about tens and ones (from their work with double-digit addition and subtraction), an understanding of the meaning of multiplication as related to unitizing (i.e., a row of six as one six), a variety of number strategies for mastering multiplication facts based on the properties of the operation, and a connection between multiplication and arrays and area.

The teacher sets the following instructional objectives for her students: (1) Begin development of computational strategies for multiplication with multidigit numbers based on place value and the properties of operations. (2) Illustrate and explain multiplication calculations using equations and arrays and/or area models.

The lesson begins with a task that is designed to set the stage for the main part of the lesson. On a projector, the teacher shows a 6×8 rectangle made of square tiles. The bottom row of eight tiles is shaded to draw students' attention to it (see Figure 1.4). The students quickly agree that adding up 6 eights will tell how many squares are in the rectangle. The teacher asks, "But if we didn't remember that 6 rows of 8 is 48, could we slice the rectangle into two parts where we know the multiplication fact and use that to get the total mentally?" Students are given a few minutes to think of at least one way to slice the rectangle, to share the idea with a partner, and to prepare to share with the class. The students offer four ideas:

- "We sliced one row off the bottom. The top part is 5 by 8, so 40 tiles. Forty plus the 8 tiles on the bottom row makes 48 tiles."

- "We cut the rectangle in half top to bottom. Each smaller rectangle is 6 by 4; 24 and 24 is 48." The teacher asks, "How did you add the two 24s?" One of the students from the group explained, "We used double 25 and took 2 off." A student from a different group noted, "You could also add 20 and 20 to get 40, and then add on 4 and 4 to get 48."

- "Our strategy was the same idea, but we sliced the rectangle in half the other way and got 3 times 8 or 24, and then we doubled it to get 48."

- "We used doubles. If you take 2 columns of 6, that's 12. Then double that will give you 4 columns, or 24. And then double 24 is 48."

The teacher passes out centimeter grid paper. On the board she sketches a large rectangle, labels the dimensions 8 and 24, and tells the students that she wants each of them to construct an 8- by 24-cm rectangle on the grid paper. She explains that the students' task is to figure out how many square tiles are in the rectangle without counting them. Instead, they are to slice the rectangle into two or more parts—like they did with the 6 by 8 example—and use the smaller parts to figure out how many tiles are in the entire rectangle. As is the norm in the class, the teacher expects the students to be prepared to explain their reasoning and to support it with words, numbers, and drawings.

Stop and Reflect

Before reading further, solve this problem by finding two or more ways to slice the 8- by 24-cm rectangle into two or more parts. Draw a sketch for each way you can think of. Then check to see if your ways are alike or different from those that follow. ∎

The students work in pairs for about 15 minutes. The teacher listens to different students talk about the task and offers a hint to a few students who are stuck: "What multiplication facts related to 8 do you know? How could you use those facts to slice the rectangle?" Soon the teacher begins a discussion by having students share their ideas and answers. As the students report, the teacher records their ideas on the board. Sometimes the teacher asks questions to help clarify ideas for others. She makes no evaluative comments, though she asks the students who are listening if they understand or have any questions to ask the presenters. The following solution strategies are common in classes where students are regularly asked to generate their own approaches. Figure 1.5 shows sketches for three of these methods.

Figure 1.4

A 6 by 8 rectangle split into 5 by 8 and 1 by 8 rectangles to make it easier to find the number of square tiles.

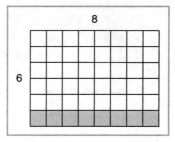

Figure 1.5

Three different ways to slice a rectangle into smaller parts to make it easier to find its area.

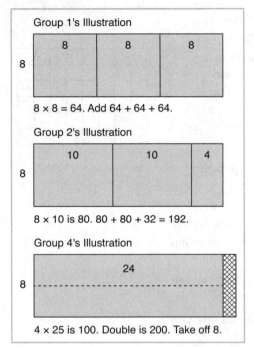

Group 1's Illustration

8 × 8 = 64. Add 64 + 64 + 64.

Group 2's Illustration

8 × 10 is 80. 80 + 80 + 32 = 192.

Group 4's Illustration

4 × 25 is 100. Double is 200. Take off 8.

- Group 1: "We know that 24, the top dimension, divided by 3 is 8, so we made three 8 by 8 squares. We know 8 times 8 is 64. We added 64 plus 64 plus 64." There is a brief discussion about how the students added the 64s mentally.

- Group 2: "We used groups of ten along the side that is 24 cm long. We sliced 2 sections of 10, and then there were 4 left at the end. Eight times 10 is 80. That makes 160 in the 2 big sections, and then the last section is 8 by 4. We added 160 and 32 in our heads."

- Group 3: "Our method was sort of like that, but we just used 8 times 20, which is 160. Then you add the 32 at the end."

- Group 4: "We didn't really slice the rectangle. Instead, we added an extra column of 8 at the end and made it 8 by 25. Then we knew that 4 rows of 25 is like a dollar, or 100. That makes 200 squares in all. But then we had to take off the 8 from the extra column that we added."

Stop and Reflect

What ideas did you learn from those shared in this example? Try using some of these ideas to find the product of 6 and 38. These numbers may make you think of a method not used in the task just discussed. ■

This vignette illustrates that when students are encouraged to solve a problem in their own way (using their own particular set of gray dots, or ideas), they are able to make sense of their solution strategies and explain their reasoning. This is evidence of their development of mathematical proficiency.

During the discussion periods in classes such as this one, ideas continue to grow. The students may hear and immediately understand a clever strategy shared by a classmate that they could have used but that did not occur to them. Others may begin to create new ideas to use that build from thinking about their classmates' strategies over multiple discussions. Some students in the class may hear excellent ideas from their peers that do not make sense to them. These students are simply not ready or do not have the prerequisite concepts (gray dots) to understand these new ideas. In future class sessions there will be similar opportunities for all students to grow at their own pace based on what they already understand.

Teaching toward Instrumental Understanding

In contrast to the lesson just described, in which students are developing concepts (understanding multidigit multiplication) and procedures (the ability to multiply flexibly) and seeing the relationships between these ideas, let's consider how a lesson with the same basic objective (multidigit multiplication) might look if the focus is on instrumental understanding.

In this classroom, the teacher distributes centimeter grid paper and asks students to draw the 8- by 24-cm rectangle on their paper. On the board the teacher draws a rectangle and writes the multiplication problem 8 × 24 beside it. The teacher directs the students to count over to the right 20 squares and to draw a vertical line in the rectangle as she demonstrates the process on the board. Then the teacher uses a series of questions to guide students through each step in the U.S. standard algorithm for multidigit multiplication. Students record the steps on their own paper at the same time.

- The teacher points to the small section of the rectangle and asks, "What is 8 times 4?"
- Students respond, "Thirty-two."
- The teacher notes, "We want to record the 32 in our problem." (She demonstrates how to write a 2 beneath the line in the problem and carry the 3. She also writes "32" in the small portion of the rectangle.)
- The teacher asks, "What is 8 times 2?" (Attention is directed to the 8 by 20 portion of the rectangle.)
- Students respond, "Sixteen."
- The teacher explains, "Because we are multiplying 8 by 20, we just add 0 to get 160 or 16 tens." (The teacher writes "16 tens" in the large portion of the rectangle.)
- The teacher continues the process: "We already have three tens. How much is 16 and 3?"
- Students respond, "Nineteen."
- The teacher continues the algorithm: "We record the 19 tens below the line. The final answer is 192." (See Figure 1.6.)

Figure 1.6

The U.S. standard algorithm is modeled using a rectangle partitioned into tens and ones.

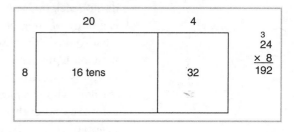

Next, the students are given five similar multiplication problems. For each problem they are to sketch a small rectangle on their paper and show how it is partitioned into tens and ones. Then they record the two products in the rectangle and complete the computation on the side. The teacher circulates and helps students who are struggling by guiding them through the steps that were modeled in the first example.

In this lesson, the teacher and students use an area model on centimeter grid paper to illustrate the various partial products in the problem. After engaging in several similar lessons, most students are likely to remember, and possibly understand, how to multiply multidigit numbers by using the standard algorithm. Using an area model to illustrate the multiplication algorithm can build toward relational understanding; however, when the expectation is for all students to use one method, students do not have opportunities to apply other strategies that may help them build connections between multiplication and place value; multiplication and addition; or multiplication and estimation—connections that are fundamental characteristics of relational understanding. It is important to note that this lesson on the standard algorithm, in combination with other lessons that reinforce other approaches, *can* build a relational understanding, as it adds to students' repertoire of strategies. But if this lesson represents the sole approach to multiplying multidigit numbers, then students are more likely to develop an instrumental understanding of mathematics.

● The Importance of Students' Ideas

Let's take a minute to compare these two classrooms. By examining them more closely, you can see several important differences. These differences affect what is learned and who learns. Let's consider the first difference: Who determines the procedure to use?

In the first classroom, each student looks at the numbers in the problem, thinks about the relationships between the numbers, and then chooses a computational strategy that is based on these ideas or a preference on the facts that the student knows. They are developing several different strategies to solve multiplication problems by exploring numbers (taking numbers apart and putting them together differently); using various representations, such as arrays and area models; and thinking about connections between addition and multiplication. The students in the first classroom are being taught mathematics for understanding—relational understanding—and are developing the kinds of mathematical proficiency described earlier.

In the second classroom, the teacher provides one strategy for how to multiply—the standard algorithm. Although the standard algorithm is a valid strategy, the entire focus of the lesson is on the steps and procedures that the teacher has outlined. The teacher solicits no ideas from individual students about how to combine the numbers. She can only find out who has or has not been able to follow her directions. And even more problematic is that the teacher shares a commonly taught "rule" that does not always work: when you multiply by 10 you just "add" a zero. (For example, consider when you multiply 14.5×10.)

When students have more choice in determining which strategies to use, as in the first classroom, they can learn more content and make more connections. In addition, if teachers do not seek out and value students' ideas, students may come to believe that mathematics is a body of rules and procedures that are learned by waiting for the teacher to tell them what to do. This view of mathematics—and what is involved in learning it—is inconsistent with mathematics as a discipline and with the learning theories described previously. Therefore, it is a worthwhile goal to transform your classroom into a mathematical community of learners who interact with each other and with the teacher as they share ideas and results, compare and evaluate strategies, challenge results, determine the validity of answers, and negotiate ideas. The rich interaction in such a classroom increases opportunities for productive engagement and reflective thinking about relevant mathematical ideas, and students develop a relational understanding of mathematics.

A second difference between the two classrooms is the learning goals. Both teachers might write "understand multidigit multiplication" as the objective for the day. What is captured in the word *understand* is very different in each setting, however. In the first classroom, the teacher's goals are for students to connect multiplication to what they already know and to see that two numbers can be multiplied in many different ways. In the second classroom, understanding is connected to being able to carry out the standard algorithm supported by a singular approach using grid paper. The learning goals and, more specifically, how the teacher interprets the meaning behind the learning goals, impact what students learn.

These lessons also differ in terms of how accessible they are—and this, in turn, affects who learns the mathematics. The first lesson is differentiated in that it meets students where they are in their current understanding. When a task is presented as "solve this in your own way," it has multiple entry points, meaning it can be approached in a variety of ways, some more sophisticated than others. Consequently, students with several different levels of prior knowledge or learning strategies can figure out a way to solve the problem. This makes the task accessible to more learners. Then, as students observe strategies that are more efficient than their own, they develop new and better ways to solve the problem. This approach also requires that the students, rather than the teacher, do the *thinking*.

In the second classroom, everyone has to do the problem in the same way. The students do not have the opportunity to apply their own ideas or to see that there are numerous ways to solve the problem. This may deprive students who need to continue working on the development of basic ideas of tens and ones, as well as students who could easily find one or more ways to do the problem if only they were asked to do so. The students in the second classroom are also likely to use the same method to multiply all numbers instead of looking for more efficient ways to multiply numbers based on the relationships between numbers. For example, they are likely to multiply 4×51 using the standard algorithm instead of thinking, "That would be 4×50 and then 4 more." Recall the importance of building on prior knowledge and learning from others. In the first classroom, student-generated strategies, multiple approaches, and discussions about the problem represent the kinds of strategies that enhance learning for a range of learners.

Students in both classrooms will eventually succeed at finding products of multidigit numbers, but what they learn about multiplication—and about doing mathematics—is quite different. Understanding and doing mathematics involves generating strategies for solving problems, applying those approaches, seeing if they lead to solutions, and checking to see if answers make sense. These activities were all present in the first classroom but not in the second. Consequently, students in the first classroom, in addition to successfully finding products of multidigit numbers, will develop richer mathematical understanding, become more flexible thinkers and better problem solvers, remain more engaged in learning, and develop more positive attitudes toward learning mathematics.

Mathematics Classrooms That Promote Understanding

Three of the most common types of teaching are direct instruction, facilitative methods (also called a *constructivist approach*), and coaching (Wiggins & McTighe, 2005). With direct instruction, the teacher usually demonstrates or models, lectures, and asks questions that are convergent or closed-ended in nature. With facilitative methods, the teacher might use investigations and inquiry, cooperative learning, discussion, and questions that are more open-ended. In coaching, the teacher provides students with guided practice and feedback that highlights ways to improve their performances.

You might be wondering which type of teaching is most appropriate if the goal is to teach mathematics for understanding. Unfortunately, there is no definitive answer because there are times when it is appropriate to engage in each of these types of teaching, depending on the instructional goals, the learners, and the situation. Some people believe that all direct instruction is ineffective because it ignores the learners' ideas and removes the productive struggle or opportunity to learn. This is not necessarily true. A teacher who is striving to teach for understanding can share information via direct instruction as long as that information does not remove the need for students to reflect on and productively struggle with the situation at hand. In other words, regardless of instructional design, the teacher should not be doing the thinking, reasoning, and connection building; it must be the students who are engaged in these activities.

Regarding facilitative or constructivist methods, remember that constructivism is a theory of learning, not a theory of teaching. Constructivism helps explain how students learn—by developing and modifying ideas (schemas) and by making connections between these ideas. Students can learn as a result of different kinds of instruction. The instructional approach chosen should depend on the ideas and relationships students have already constructed. Sometimes students readily make connections by listening to a lecture (direct instruction). Sometimes they need time to investigate a situation so they can become aware of the different ideas at play and how those ideas relate to one another (facilitative). Sometimes they need to practice a skill and receive feedback on their performance to become more accurate (coaching). No matter which type of teaching is used, constructivism and sociocultural theories remind us as teachers to continually wonder whether our students have truly developed the given concept or skill, connecting it to what they already know. By shedding light on what and how our students understand, assessment can help us determine which teaching approach may be the most appropriate at a given time.

The essence of developing relational understanding is keeping students' ideas at the forefront of classroom activities by emphasizing the process standards, mathematical proficiencies, and the Standards for Mathematical Practice. This requires that the teacher create a classroom culture in which students can learn from one another. Consider the following features of a mathematics classroom that promotes understanding (Chapin, O'Conner, &

Anderson, 2009; Hiebert, Carpenter, Fennema, Fuson, Wearne, Murray, Olivier, & Human, 1997; Hoffman, Breyfogle, & Dressler, 2009). In particular, notice who is doing the thinking, the talking, and the mathematics: students.

Teaching Tip

Listen carefully to students as they talk about what they are thinking and doing as they engage in a mathematical task. If they respond in an unexpected way, try to avoid imposing your ideas onto their ideas. Ask clarifying questions to try to make sense of the sense your students are making.

- *Students' ideas are key.* Mathematical ideas, expressed by students, are important and have the potential to contribute to everyone's learning. Learning mathematics is about coming to understand the ideas of the mathematical community.

- *Opportunities for students to talk about mathematics are common.* Learning is enhanced when students are engaged with others who are working on the same ideas. Encouraging student-to-student dialogue can help students think of themselves as capable of making sense of mathematics. Students are also more likely to question each other's ideas than the teacher's ideas.

- *Multiple approaches are encouraged.* Students must recognize that there is often a variety of methods that will lead to a solution. Respect for the ideas shared by others is critical if real discussion is to take place.

- *Mistakes are good opportunities for learning.* Students must come to realize that errors provide opportunities for growth as they are uncovered and explained. Trust must be established with an understanding that it is okay to make mistakes. Without this trust, many ideas will never be shared.

- *Math makes sense.* Students must come to understand that mathematics makes sense. Teachers should resist always evaluating students' answers. In fact, when teachers routinely respond with "Yes, that's correct," or "No, that's wrong," students will stop trying to make sense of ideas in the classroom and discussion and learning will be curtailed.

To create a climate that encourages mathematics understanding, teachers must first provide explicit instruction on the ground rules for classroom discussions. Second, teachers may need to model the type of questioning and interaction that they expect from their students. Direct instruction would be appropriate in such a situation. The crucial point in teaching for understanding is to highlight and use students' ideas to promote mathematical proficiency.

Most people go into teaching because they want to help students learn. It is hard to think of allowing—much less planning for—the students in your room to struggle. Not showing them a solution when they are experiencing difficulty seems almost counterintuitive. If our goal is relational understanding, however, the struggle is part of the learning, and teaching becomes less about the teacher and more about what the students are doing and thinking.

Keep in mind that you too are a learner. Some ideas in this book may make more sense to you than others. Others may create dissonance for you. Embrace this feeling of disequilibrium and uneasiness as an opportunity to learn—to revise your perspectives on mathematics and on the teaching and learning of mathematics as you deepen your understanding so that you can help your students deepen theirs.

Stop and Reflect

Look back at the chapter and identify any ideas that make you uncomfortable or that challenge your current thinking about mathematics or about teaching and learning mathematics. Try to determine why these ideas challenge you or make you uncomfortable. Write these ideas down and revisit them later as you read and reflect further. ■

2

Teaching Mathematics through Problem Solving

By inviting . . . children to solve problems in their own ways, we are initiating them into the community of mathematicians who engage in structuring and modeling their "lived worlds" mathematically.

Fosnot and Jacob
(2007, p. 25)

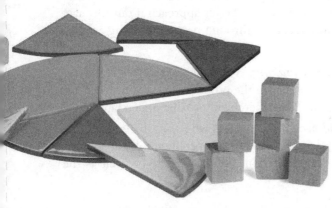

Teaching mathematics *through* problem solving is a method of teaching mathematics that helps students develop relational understanding. With this approach, problem solving is completely interwoven with learning. As students *do* mathematics—make sense of cognitively demanding tasks, provide evidence or justification for strategies and solutions, find examples and connections, and receive and provide feedback about ideas—they are simultaneously engaged in the activities of problem solving and learning. Teaching mathematics through problem solving requires you to think about the types of tasks you pose to students, how you facilitate discourse in your classroom, and how you support students' use of a variety of representations as tools for problem solving, reasoning, and communication.

Teaching through Problem Solving: An Upside-Down Approach

For many years and continuing today, mathematics has been taught using a teaching-*for*-problem-solving approach: The teacher presents the mathematics, the students practice the skill, and finally, the students solve word problems that require using that skill. Unfortunately, this "do-as-I-show-you" approach to mathematics teaching has not been successful for helping many students understand or remember mathematics concepts (e.g., Pesek & Kirshner, 2002; Philipp & Vincent, 2003).

Teaching mathematics *through* problem solving generally means that students solve problems to learn new mathematics rather than just apply mathematics after it has been learned. Students learn mathematics through real contexts, problems, situations, and models that allow them to build meaning for the concepts (Hiebert, Carpenter, Fennema, Fuson, Wearne, Murray, Olivier, & Human, 1997). So teaching *through* problem solving might be described as "upside down" from the traditional approach of teaching *for* problem solving because the problem is presented at the beginning of a lesson and skills and ideas emerge from working with the problem. An example of teaching through problem solving might have students explore the following situation before they know the standard algorithm of adding fractions by using common denominators.

Tatyana needs $\frac{1}{2}$ foot and $\frac{1}{3}$ foot of ribbon for a school project. Figure out the total length of ribbon she will need.

The teacher would explain to the class that there is more than one correct strategy to solve this problem and that they are to find as many different strategies as they can. As students work on the problem, they may use fraction strips, they may choose to draw the ribbon lengths, or they may simply use numbers to capture their ideas.

Stop and Reflect

Find a way to determine how long the ribbon will be without using the standard algorithm of finding common denominators to add the fractions. ■

Through this context and exploration students would be led to develop the standard algorithm for adding fractions. This problem also generates opportunities for students to improve their fraction sense as they find ways to model fractions and their equivalents. The ribbon provides a context for thinking of fraction of a length, expanding on student understanding of fraction of an area. It also emphasizes the meaning of the part–whole fraction relationship as students investigate how they might combine different sized fractional parts.

Teaching *through* problem solving requires a paradigm shift, which means that teachers are doing more than just tweaking a few things about their teaching; they are changing their philosophy of how they think students learn best and how they can best help them learn. At first glance, it may seem that the teacher's role is less demanding because the students are doing the mathematics, but the teacher's role is actually more demanding in such classrooms. Here are some of the important teacher responsibilities:

- Select high-quality tasks that allow students to learn the content by figuring out their own strategies and solutions.

- Ask high-quality questions that allow students to verify and relate their strategies.

- Listen to students' responses and examine their work, determining in the moment how to extend and formalize their thinking through targeted feedback.

There is no doubt that teaching mathematics through problem solving can be challenging, but the results are worth the effort! It promises to be a better approach if our ultimate goal is deep (relational) understanding because teaching through problem solving accomplishes these goals:

- *Focuses students' attention on ideas and sense making.* When solving problems, students are necessarily reflecting on the concepts inherent in the problems. Emerging concepts are more likely to be integrated with existing ones, thereby improving understanding.

- *Emphasizes mathematical processes and practices.* Students who are solving problems will engage in all five of the processes of doing mathematics—problem solving, reasoning, communication, connections, and representation (NCTM, 2000), as well as the eight mathematical practices outlined in the *Common Core State Standards*, resulting in mathematics that is more accessible, more interesting, and more meaningful. Note that the first Standard for Mathematical Practice is "Make sense of problems and persevere in solving them" (CCSSO, 2010).

- *Develops students' confidence and identities.* Every time teachers pose a problem-based task and expect a solution, they implicitly say to students, "I believe you can do this." When students are engaged in problem solving and discourse in which the correctness of the solution lies in the justification of the process, they begin to see themselves as capable of doing mathematics and see that mathematics makes sense.

- *Provides a context to help students build meaning for the concept.* Using a context facilitates mathematical understanding, especially when the context is grounded in an experience familiar to students and when the context uses purposeful constraints that potentially highlight the significant mathematical ideas (Fosnot & Dolk, 2001).

- *Allows entry and exit points for a wide range of students.* Good problem-based tasks have multiple paths to the solution so each student can make sense of and solve the task by using his or her own ideas. Furthermore, students expand their ideas and grow in their understanding as they hear, critique, and reflect on the solution strategies of others.

- *Allows for extensions and elaborations.* Extensions and "what if" questions can motivate advanced learners or quick finishers, resulting in increased learning and enthusiasm for doing mathematics.

- *Engages students so there are fewer discipline problems.* Many discipline issues in a classroom are the result of students becoming bored, not understanding the teacher directions, or simply finding little relevance in the task. Most students like to be challenged and enjoy being permitted to solve problems in ways that make sense to them, giving them less reason to act out or cause trouble.

- *Provides formative assessment data.* As students discuss ideas, draw diagrams or use manipulatives, defend their solutions and evaluate those of others, and write reports or explanations, they provide the teacher with a steady stream of valuable information that can be used to inform subsequent instruction.

- *Is a lot of fun!* Students enjoy the creative process of problem solving and sharing how they figured something out. After seeing the surprising and inventive ways that students think and how engaged students become in mathematics, very few teachers stop using a teaching-*through*-problem-solving approach.

Using Problems to Teach

When teachers teach mathematics through problem solving, students learn the desired content through problems (tasks or activities). A *problem* is defined here as any task or activity for which students have no prescribed or memorized rules or methods, and for which they do not have a perception that there is a specific "correct" solution method (Hiebert et al., 1997). In other words, the task or activity is a genuine problem.

Features of a Problem

Problems that can serve as effective tasks or activities for students to solve have common features. Use the following points as a guide to assess whether a task or an activity has the potential to be a genuine problem.

- *The problem should engage students where they are in their current understanding.* Students should have the appropriate ideas to begin engaging with the problem and to solve the problem, and yet should still find it challenging and interesting.

- *The problematic or engaging aspect of the problem must be a result of the mathematics that the students are to learn.* In solving the problem or doing the activity, students should be concerned primarily with making sense of and developing their understanding of the mathematics involved. Any context or external constraints used should not overshadow the mathematics to be learned.

- *The problem must require justifications and explanations for answers and methods.* In a high-quality problem, neither the process nor the answer is straightforward, so justification is central to the task. Students should understand that the responsibility for determining whether answers are correct and why they are correct rests on their mathematical reasoning, not on the teacher telling them that they are correct.

⬢ Examples of Problems

Problems can be used to develop both concepts and procedures, as well as the connection between concepts and procedures. In the following examples, the first two problems focus on concepts and the third problem focuses on a procedure.

CONCEPT: Area as related to multiplication and addition (grade 3)

Sam wants to make an outside pen for his dog. He bought 36 square stones, with sides 1-foot long, to use for the floor. If Sam wants to have a rectangular floor in the dog pen, how can he arrange the 36 square stones? Can you find more than one way? How many ways do you think there are? Why?

CONCEPT: Equality (grade 5)

$$6 \times p = 3 \times p + 18$$

Find a number p so that the equation is true. Is there more than one number for p that will make the equation true? Why or why not?

Note that a task in the form of a story problem does not automatically make the task a problem. A story problem can be "routine" if students read it and know right away that it is a multiplication problem and multiply to answer it. Conversely, an equation with no words, as in the second example above, is not necessarily routine and can actually be a rich problem to investigate.

PROCEDURE: Multiplying two-digit whole numbers (grade 4)

Solve this problem in two different ways: 32×17 _____
For each way, explain how you solved it.

The third example, although focused on a procedure, is a problem because students must figure out *how* they are going to approach the task (assuming they have not been taught the standard algorithm at this point). Students are also challenged to find more than one way to solve the problem. Implicit is the challenge to determine how the two solution strategies are different. The third example is important because it illustrates that virtually all mathematics concepts and procedures can be taught through problem solving.

◆ Selecting Worthwhile Tasks

As noted earlier in the three features of a problem, a task must engage students where they currently are in their understanding and simultaneously must be problematic for the students. In selecting such a task, consider the level of cognitive demand, the potential of the task to have multiple entry and exit points, and the relevancy of the task to students.

Level of Cognitive Demand

Research supports the practice of engaging students in productive struggle to develop understanding (Bay-Williams, 2010; Hiebert & Grouws, 2007). Both words in the phrase *productive struggle* are important. Students must have the tools and prior knowledge to solve a problem, and not be given a problem that is out of reach because otherwise they will struggle without being productive; however, students should not be given tasks that are straightforward and trivial because they will not struggle with mathematical ideas and further develop their understanding. When students know that struggle is an expected part of the process of doing mathematics, they embrace the struggle and feel success when they reach a solution (Carter, 2008).

Figure 2.1 shows a useful framework for determining whether a task has the potential to challenge students (Smith & Stein, 1998). The framework distinguishes between tasks that require low levels and high levels of cognitive demand. Tasks that have low-level cognitive demand are routine and straightforward and do not engage students in productive

Figure 2.1 Levels of cognitive demand.

Low-Level Cognitive Demand Tasks	High-Level Cognitive Demand Tasks
Memorization • Involve producing previously learned facts, rules, formulas, or definitions for memorizing • Are routine in that they involve exact reproduction of a previously learned procedure • Have no connection to related concepts	**Procedures with Connections** • Focus students' attention on the use of procedures for the purpose of developing deeper levels of understanding of mathematical concepts and ideas • Suggest general procedures that have close connections to underlying conceptual ideas • Are usually represented in multiple ways (e.g., visuals, manipulatives, symbols, problem situations) • Require that students engage with the conceptual ideas that underlie the procedures in order to successfully complete the task
Procedures without Connections • Use of procedures is specifically called for • Are straightforward, with little ambiguity about what needs to be done and how to do it • Have little or no connection to related concepts • Are focused on producing correct answers rather than developing mathematical understanding • Require no explanations, or the explanations only focus on listing or restating the steps of the procedure	***Doing* Mathematics** • Require complex and non-algorithmic thinking (i.e., non-routine—without a predictable, known approach) • Require students to explore and to understand the nature of mathematical concepts, processes, or relationships • Demand self-monitoring or self-regulation of students' own cognitive processes • Require students to access relevant knowledge in working through the task • Require students to analyze the task and actively examine task constraints • Require considerable cognitive effort

Source: Adapted with permission from Stein, M., Smith, M., Henningsen, E. and Silver, E. (2009). *Implementing Standards-Based Mathematics Instruction: A Case for Professional Development,* copyright 2009 by the National Council of Teachers of Mathematics. All rights reserved.

struggle. Tasks with high level of cognitive demand not only engage students in productive struggle, but they also challenge students to make connections between concepts and to other relevant knowledge. Although there are appropriate times to use low-level cognitive demand tasks, a heavy or sole emphasis on these types of tasks will not lead to relational understanding of mathematics. As an example of different levels of tasks, consider the degree of reasoning required if you ask fourth grade students to find the product of three given numbers versus if you ask them to find three numbers whose product is 108. The first task only requires students to multiply three numbers. The second task requires them to use number sense to generate three reasonable numbers that will result in a given product. As a consequence of working on this second task, students have potential opportunities to think about and use number relationships while they work on their computational skills for multiplication.

Multiple Entry and Exit Points

A problem or task that has multiple entry points has varying degrees of challenge within it or it can be approached in a variety of ways. One of the advantages of a problem-based approach is that it can help accommodate the diversity of learners in every classroom because students are encouraged to use a strategy that makes sense to them instead of using a predetermined strategy that they may or may not be ready to use successfully. Some students may initially use less-efficient approaches, such as guess and check or counting, but they will develop more advanced strategies through effective questioning by the teacher and by reflecting on other students' approaches. For example, for the task of finding three numbers whose product is 108, one student may use a guess and check approach, listing three numbers and multiplying them to see if their product is 108, whereas another student may use a more systematic approach, such as dividing 108 by 2 and then splitting the resulting 54 into two factors. Still another student may readily know that 3 is a factor of 108 because of his or her knowledge of divisibility by 3, and use that information and the fact 108 is an even number to find two more factors.

Tasks should also have multiple exit points or various ways that students can demonstrate an understanding of the learning goals. For example, students might draw a diagram, write an equation, use manipulatives, or act out a problem to demonstrate their understanding.

Consider the opportunities for multiple entry and exit points in the following tasks for third grade.

TASK 1:

(The teacher draws a 4 inch × 7 inch rectangle on the board and labels the sides.) What is this polygon called? What is the perimeter of this polygon?

TASK 2:

(The teacher gives each student a sheet of grid paper.) On your grid paper, draw, describe, and name a polygon that has the following side lengths: 4 units, 4 units, 7 units, and 7 units. Can you make more than one polygon with these same dimensions?

Stop and Reflect

To what degree do these tasks offer opportunities for multiple entry and exit points? ■

With the first task students will gain some experience calculating perimeter but they will miss any opportunity to think deeply about the situation or the concept. Although perimeter is more implicit in the second task, it offers more opportunity for students to engage with the notion of perimeter and polygons in a variety of ways, which also offers the teacher more information about each student's level of understanding. For example, if a student initially thinks that only one polygon (a rectangle) can be made, this is informative. As students create new polygons, do they calculate the perimeter each time? Do they think that the area is the same for all the polygons with the same perimeter? Clearly, the second task offers many more opportunities for all students to engage in the task in a variety of ways.

Relevant and Well-Designed Contexts

One of the most powerful aspects of teaching through problem solving is that the problem that begins the lesson can get students excited about learning mathematics. Compare the following two fourth-grade introductory tasks on multiplying 2 two-digit numbers. Which one do you think would more interesting to students?

> *Teaching Tip*
>
> Before giving a selected task to your class, anticipate several possible student responses to the task, including possible misconceptions, and think about how you might address these responses. Anticipating the responses gives you time to consider how you will respond to various approaches, and it also helps you to quickly recognize different strategies and misconceptions when students are working on the task.

Classroom A: "Today we are going to use grid paper to show the sub-products when we multiply 2 two-digit numbers."

Classroom B: "The school is planning a fall festival and our grade level is in charge of selling drinks. The principal said we had 14 cases of bottled water in the storage closet. I went into the storage closet to see how many bottled waters we have. I could see 4 cases, each having 28 bottles in 7 rows of 4, at the front of the closet, but the others were in the back where I could not see them so I could not count them all. We need to figure out a way to determine how many bottles of water we have."

Familiar and interesting contexts increase students' engagement. Your goal as a teacher is to design problems that provide specific parameters, constraints, or structure that will support the development of the mathematical ideas you want students to learn. In the context used in Classroom B above, the situation involves 14 cases of drinks that are separated into 4 cases and 10 cases. The teacher is aware that some of her students will find it difficult to work with double digits, so she structures the context to subtly suggest a way to partition the numbers into smaller numbers. She is also aware that a few of her students still tend to count large amounts by ones, but the constraint that each case has 4 drinks in 7 rows again subtly suggests skip counting by fours as a way to determine how many bottles are in each case. This constraint begins to incrementally move these students toward more efficient ways of counting (i.e., multiplication). Also, the fact that each case is almost 30 bottles may lead some students to use computational estimation to round the amount to 30 as they grapple with how to determine how many drinks are in 14 cases. For those students who have already mastered their basic facts for multiplication, the two groupings of cases help them move toward multiplying with two-digit numbers. By building in such structure through constraints and parameters, teachers can support students in developing more sophisticated strategies that honor where the students currently are in their understanding (Fosnot & Dolk, 2001).

Orchestrating Classroom Discourse

Classroom discourse refers to the interactions between all the participants that occur throughout a lesson—in a whole-class setting, in small groups, between pairs of students, and with the teacher. The purpose of discourse is not for students to state their answers and get validation from the teacher but to engage all learners and keep the cognitive demand high (Breyfogle & Williams, 2008-2009; Kilic, Cross, Ersoz, Mewborn, Swanagan, & Kim, 2010; Smith, Hughes, Engle, & Stein, 2009).

Classroom Discussions

The value of student talk throughout a mathematics lesson cannot be overemphasized. As students describe and evaluate solutions to tasks, share approaches, and make conjectures, learning will occur in ways that are otherwise unlikely to take place. As they listen to other students' ideas, they come to see the varied approaches in how problems can be solved and see mathematics as something that they can do. Questions such as those that ask students if they would do it differently next time, which strategy made sense to them (and why), and what caused problems for them (and how they overcame them), are critical in developing mathematically proficient students. Orchestrating discourse after students have worked on problems is particularly important because it is this type of discussion that helps students connect the problem to more general or formal mathematics and make connections to other ideas.

Implementing effective discourse in the classroom can be challenging. Finding ways to encourage students to share their ideas and to engage with others about their ideas is essential to productive discussions. Consider the following research-based recommendations that can be useful in a whole-class setting, in small groups, and in peer-to-peer discussions (Chapin, O'Conner, & Anderson, 2009; Rasmussen, Yackel, & King, 2003; Stephan & Whitenack, 2003; Wood, Williams, & McNeal, 2006; Yackel & Cobb, 1996).

- *Clarify students' ideas in a variety of ways.* You can restate students' ideas as questions in order to verify what they did as well as what they mean to confirm what you've heard or observed. You can also apply precise language and make significant ideas more apparent. Paying attention to students' ideas sends the message that their ideas are valued and, therefore, is a key step to encouraging the participation of individual students. In addition, modeling how to ask clarifying questions demonstrates to students that it is OK to be unsure and that asking questions is appropriate. It is important to keep in mind that although you may understand a student's ideas and reasoning, there may be students in the class who do not. Therefore, look for opportunities to ask clarifying questions even if you do not need clarification. You can also ask students to restate someone else's ideas in their own words in order to ensure that ideas are stated in a variety of ways and to encourage students to listen to one another. This strategy of clarification is important for English language learners (ELLs) because it reinforces language and enhances comprehension.

- *Emphasize reasoning.* Ask follow-up questions, whether the answer is right or wrong, to place an emphasis on the reasoning process. Your role is to understand students' thinking, not to lead them to the correct answer and move on. Therefore, follow up with probes to learn more about their answers and their reasoning. Sometimes you will find that what you assumed they were thinking is not correct. Also, if you only follow up on wrong answers, students quickly figure this out and get nervous when you ask them to explain their thinking. In addition, move students to more conceptually based explanations when appropriate. For example, if a student says that he knows $\frac{3}{4}$ is more than $\frac{2}{3}$, ask him (or another student) to explain or illustrate how he knows this is true.

Figure 2.2 Examples of teacher prompts for supporting classroom discussions.

Clarify Students' Ideas	"You used the red trapezoid as your whole?" "So, first you recorded your measurements in a table?" "What parts of your drawing relate to the numbers from the story problem?" "Who can share what Ricardo just said, but using your own words?"
Emphasize Reasoning	"Why does it make sense to start with that particular number?" "Explain how you know that your answer is correct." "Can you give an example?" "Do you see a connection between Julio's idea and Rhonda's idea?" "What if . . . ? " "Do you agree or disagree with Johanna? Why?"
Encourage Student–Student Dialogue	"Who has a question for Vivian?" "Turn to your partner and explain why you agree or disagree with Edwin." "Talk with Yerin about how your strategy relates to hers."

You can also ask students what they think of the idea proposed by another student or ask if they see a connection between two classmates' ideas or between a classmate's idea and a concept previously discussed.

- *Encourage student–student dialogue.* You want students to think of themselves as capable of making sense of mathematics so that they do not always rely on the teacher to verify the correctness of their ideas. Encouraging student-to-student dialogue can help build this sense of self. Students are also more likely to question one another's ideas rather than the teacher's ideas. When students have different solutions, ask them to discuss one another's solutions. Or ask someone to rephrase another student's ideas or to add something further to someone else's ideas. Provide opportunities that allow students to share their ideas in small groups or with a peer. This will ensure that all students are able to participate in sharing because not all students will be able to share during every whole-class discussion. Before a whole-class discussion, students can practice their explanations with a peer; this is one way to support ELLs and students with special needs during mathematical discussions. See Chapters 5 and 6 for other ideas about how to support these particular groups of students in mathematical discussions. Figure 2.2 offers examples of teacher prompts that can support classroom discussions.

Make sure to explain to students that after they hear a question or a prompt they will have time to think so that silence in the classroom does not feel uncomfortable. For example, you can say, "This question is important. Let's take some time to think about it." There will be times when no one responds to your question or prompt. If the situation gets awkward, make sure students understand the question or prompt; then ask them to talk with a partner and try the discussion again.

◆ How Much to Tell and Not to Tell

When teachers teach mathematics *through* problem solving, one of the most perplexing dilemmas is how much, if anything, to tell. On one hand, telling can diminish what is learned and lower the level of challenge in a lesson. On the other hand, telling too little can sometimes leave students floundering, or unproductively struggling. Following are four things that you need to tell students about:

- *Introduce mathematical conventions.* Symbols, such as × and ≤, are conventions. Terminology is also a convention. As a rule of thumb, symbolism and terminology should be introduced after concepts have been developed and then specifically as a means of expressing or labeling ideas.

- *Discuss alternative methods.* If an important strategy does not emerge naturally from students, then you should propose the strategy, being careful to identify it as "another" way, not the only or the preferred way.

- *Clarify students' methods.* You should help students clarify or interpret their ideas. For example, suppose a student explained that she solved 1000 − 369 by "adding one to 369 to get 631." You might be familiar with this strategy and therefore understand the student's reasoning, although it is incomplete. So that other students will better understand her reasoning, help the student be more explicit about why she added one to 369 and how she ended up with 631. For example, start by simply asking the student why she added 1 to 369. The reason is to make the numbers easier to work with—it's easier to subtract 1000 − 370 than 1000 − 369. Ask the student to describe her reasoning after she changed the problem to the easier problem, 1000 − 370. She may explain it like this: "I subtracted 1000 − 300 to get 700 and then subtracted 70 to get 630. Then I added one to get 631." Here again, probe the student for why she added 1 instead of subtracted 1. She may explain, "When I subtracted 370 instead of 369, I subtracted one more than I really needed to. So I needed to add 1 back in. So that makes the answer 631."

- *Make connections between ideas.* You should also look for opportunities to highlight a significant idea in students' methods and point out related concepts. For example, sometimes students are uncertain what is actually being measured when they measure angles. If you think about moving or rotating through an angle, the movement can help focus students' attention to the attribute of the angle being measured. Suppose, because of the context you have used, a student describes moving or turning through an angle as he is determining its measure. Stop and point out this significant idea. In addition, relate this idea to how you move through an interval on a ruler as you use it to measure the length of an object. The notion of moving through an interval or rotating through an angle is an important measurement concept that highlights the attribute being measured. Drawing everyone's attention to this connection can help students see the connection, which in turn can enhance their understanding.

Representations: Tools for Problem Solving, Reasoning, and Communication

A representation can be thought of as a kind of tool, such as a diagram, graph, symbol, or manipulative, that expresses a mathematical idea or concept. Representations are not ends in themselves to be learned for the sake of learning, but are valuable tools in problem solving, reasoning, and communicating about mathematical ideas. Representations can help students think through a problem and better communicate their ideas to another person. When a student solves a problem, how he or she represents the ideas in the problem will likely influence the solution process. In fact, the representations that students choose to use can provide valuable insight into their ways of interpreting and thinking about the mathematical ideas at hand.

Models or representations, whether they are conventional or not, give learners something they can use to explore, reason, and communicate as they engage in problem-based tasks. The goal of using representations is so that students can manipulate ideas, not manipulate symbols in a rote manner. By using personally meaningful representations to manipulate and communicate about mathematical ideas, students will make connections between mathematical ideas (relational understanding) and move toward mathematical proficiency.

◈ Tips for Using Representations in the Classroom

Because different representations can illuminate different aspects of a mathematical idea, multiple representations should be explored and encouraged. The more ways students are given to think about and test an emerging idea, the better they will correctly form and integrate it into a rich web of concepts and thereby develop a relational understanding. Figure 2.3 illustrates various representations for demonstrating an understanding of any topic. Students who have difficulty translating a concept from one representation to another also have difficulty solving problems and understanding computations (Clement, 2004; Lesh, Cramer, Doerr, Post, & Zawojewski, 2003; NCTM, 2000). Strengthening the ability to move between and among representations improves students' understanding and retention of ideas.

The following are rules of thumb for using representations in the classroom:

- Introduce new representations or tools by showing how they can represent the *ideas* for which they are intended. Keep in mind that because representations are not the *concepts*, some students may not "see" what you see.

- Allow students (in most instances) to select freely from available tools to use in solving problems.

- Encourage students to create their own representations. Look for opportunities to connect these student-created representations to more conventional representations.

- Encourage the use of a particular representation when you believe it would be helpful to a student having difficulty.

- Ask students to use representations such as diagrams and manipulatives when they explain their thinking. This will help you gather information about students' understanding of the idea and also their understanding of the representations that have been used in the classroom. It can also be helpful to other students in the classroom who may be struggling with the idea or the explanation being offered.

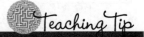

Teaching Tip

Pay attention to students' choices of representations and use those representations as starting points for dialogues with them about their thinking. What they find important may be surprising and informative at the same time.

Figure 2.3

Mathematical understanding can be demonstrated through these different representations of mathematical ideas. Translations between each can help students develop new concepts and demonstrate a richer understanding.

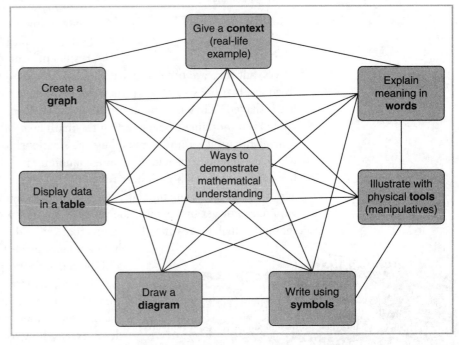

- In creating tasks and when facilitating classroom discussions, focus on making connections between the different representations used (and make sure each is understood). Helping students make these connections is very important to their learning.

Note that problems can start with one representation (e.g., a story problem) and ask the student to translate the information to another representation (e.g., an equation); yet a student might get to the final representation by working through other representations (e.g., creating a table or drawing a picture to get to an equation). These representations, whether student-created or more conventional, are critical in supporting students' reasoning and actually progressing toward more abstract symbolic representations.

◆ Manipulatives

Let's turn to one kind of representation that is commonly used to support students' learning of mathematics—manipulatives or concrete objects. Any time a concept is new, regardless of the ages of the students, manipulatives can help make the concept visual, concrete, and connected to other ideas students have learned. Used wisely, they can be a positive factor in students' learning. Only using manipulatives, however, particularly in a rote manner, does not ensure that students will understand. It is important to consider how manipulatives can help, or fail to help, students construct mathematical knowledge.

First of all, manipulatives alone have no inherent meaning. A person has to impose meaning on them. The manipulative is not the concept. Figure 2.4 shows fraction bars commonly used to represent different fractional quantities. If a student is able to identify the first bar as three-thirds and the second bar as four-fourths, does this mean the student has constructed the concepts of fractions and now can compare fractions using these manipulatives? No, all you know for sure is that the student has learned the names typically assigned to the manipulatives. Some students can identify fractions using fraction manipulatives, but they are not sure what they are supposed to pay attention to when they compare fractions. Is it the size of the pieces, the number of the pieces in the bar, or how much of the bar is shaded? They may be uncertain as to whether the length of the bar (i.e., the size of the whole) is important. Understanding the mathematical concept that four-fourths is larger that four-eighths relies on understanding the relationship between the size of the pieces and the whole in each fraction, and then understanding that when comparing fractions they have to be from the same size whole. These relationships must be created by students in their own minds and imposed on the manipulative or the model used to represent the concept. For a student who does not yet understand the relationship, the model does not illustrate the concept for that individual. Over time, discussions that explicitly focus on the mathematical concepts can help students make the connections between manipulatives and the related concepts.

Second, the most widespread misuse of manipulatives occurs when teachers tell students, "Do exactly as I do." There is a natural temptation to get out the materials and show students exactly how to use them. Students mimic the teacher's directions, and it may even look as if they understand, but

Figure 2.4

Objects and names of objects are not the same as mathematical ideas and relationships between objects.

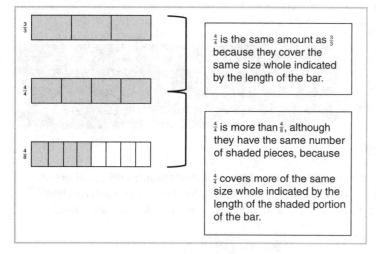

$\frac{4}{4}$ is the same amount as $\frac{3}{3}$ because they cover the same size whole indicated by the length of the bar.

$\frac{4}{4}$ is more than $\frac{4}{8}$, although they have the same number of shaded pieces, because

$\frac{4}{4}$ covers more of the same size whole indicated by the length of the shaded portion of the bar.

Teaching Tip

It is incorrect to say that a manipulative or object "illustrates" or shows a concept. Manipulatives can help students visualize the relationships and talk about them, but what they see are the manipulatives, not concepts.

they could be just following what they see. A rote procedure with a manipulative is still just that—a rote procedure.

A third and related misuse of manipulatives occurs when teachers always tells students which manipulative to use for a given problem. Students need opportunities to choose their own representations to use when reasoning through a problem (Mathematical Practice 5, "Use appropriate tools strategically") and when communicating their ideas to others.

Visuals and Other Tools

There are other ways for students to represent and illustrate mathematical concepts. Drawings are one option and are important for a number of reasons. First, when students draw, you learn more about what they do or do not understand. For example, when students are comparing $\frac{4}{5}$ and $\frac{2}{3}$ with their own drawings, you can observe whether they understand that the wholes for each of the fractions must be the same size to compare them. Second, manipulatives can sometimes restrict how students can model problems, whereas drawings allow students to use any strategy they want. Figure 2.5 shows an example of a fifth grader's solution for adding $\frac{2}{3}$ and $\frac{3}{5}$. This example illustrates how student-generated drawings can provide significant information about students' understanding. What common misconception does this student's work highlight? Look for opportunities to use students' representations during classroom discussions to help students make sense of the more abstract mathematical symbols and computational procedures. Furthermore, as students use different representations to solve a problem, have them compare and contrast the various ways.

Figure 2.5
A fifth grader shows her incorrect thinking about how to add $\frac{2}{3}$ and $\frac{3}{5}$.

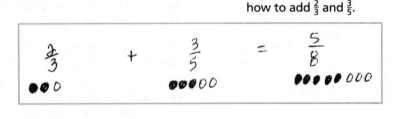

Representations generated and manipulated through technology can also support students as they reason about and communicate their mathematical ideas. Changes can usually be made to situations more quickly using a computer than using physical manipulatives or student-generated drawings, leaving more time for exploration. For example, dynamic geometry software allows students to explore shapes, making and testing conjectures about their properties by changing the shapes on the computer screen (see, for example, www.nctm.org/standards/content.aspx?id=25040). Virtual manipulatives can help students link manipulatives to symbols. For example, some websites display decimals using numerals and computerized base-ten blocks. As changes are made to the base-ten blocks, students can see the results of the actions they take on the numeral representation of the decimal (e.g., go to http://nlvm.usu.edu/en/nav/grade_g_2.html and click on Base Blocks Decimals). This dynamic link between these two representations helps students make sense of their activity as well as the numbers. An added bonus with technology is that sometimes the language displayed on the computer program can be changed for ELLs.

Meaningful contexts help students make sense of mathematical ideas. Using real objects, pictures, drawings, and virtual manipulatives can help students relate to and better understand a context, especially one that is unfamiliar. This is particularly important in supporting ELLs or students with disabilities.

A Three-Phase Lesson Format

A three-phase lesson format (*Before, During, After*) provides a structure for teaching mathematics through problem solving (see Table 2.1). *Before* refers to the time before students start work on the problem, *During* refers to the time during which students work on the problem, and *After* refers to the discussion that takes place after students work on the problem.

Table 2.1 Three-Phase Lesson Structure

Lesson Phase		Teacher Actions in a Teaching Mathematics through Problem-Solving Lesson
Before	Activate prior knowledge.	Begin with a simple version of the task; connect to students' experiences; brainstorm approaches or solution strategies; estimate or predict whether tasks involve a single computation or are aimed at the development of a computational procedure.
	Be sure the problem is understood.	Have students explain to you what the problem is asking. Go over vocabulary that may be troubling. Caution: This does not mean that you are explaining how to do the problem, just that students should understand what the problem is about.
	Establish clear expectations.	Tell students whether they will work individually, in pairs, or small groups, or if they will have a choice. Tell them how they will share their solutions and reasoning.
During	Let go!	Although it is tempting to want to step in and "help," hold back and enjoy observing and learning from students.
	Notice students' mathematical thinking.	Base your questions on students' work and their responses to you. Use prompts like: Tell me what you are doing; I see you have started to [multiply] these numbers. Can you tell me why you are [multiplying]? [substitute any process/strategy]; Can you tell me more about . . . ? Why did you . . . ? How does your diagram connect to the problem?
	Provide appropriate support.	Look for ways to support students' thinking and avoid telling them how to solve the problem. Ensure that students understand the problem (What do you know about the problem?); ask the student what he or she has already tried (also, Where did you get stuck?); suggest that the student use a different strategy (Can you draw a diagram? What if you used cubes to act out this problem? Is this like another problem we have solved?); create a parallel problem with simpler values (Jacobs & Ambrose, 2008).
	Provide worthwhile extensions.	Challenge early finishers in some manner that is related to the problem just solved. Possible questions to ask are: I see you found one way to do this. Are there any other solutions? Are any of the solutions different or more interesting than others? Some good questions for extending thinking are, What if . . . ? or Would that same idea work for . . . ?
After	Promote a community of learners.	You must teach your students about your expectations for this part of the lesson and how to interact respectfully with their peers. Role play appropriate (and inappropriate) ways of responding to each other. The "Orchestrating Classroom Discourse" section provides strategies and recommendations for how to facilitate discussions that help create a community of learners.
	Listen actively without evaluation.	The goal here is noticing students' mathematical thinking and making that thinking visible to other students. Avoid judging the correctness of an answer so students are more willing to share their ideas. Support students' thinking without evaluation by simply asking what others think about a student's response.
	Summarize main ideas and identify future problems.	Formalize the main ideas of the lesson, helping to highlight connections between strategies or different mathematical ideas. In addition, this is the time to reinforce appropriate terminology, definitions, and symbols. You may also want to lay the groundwork for future tasks and activities.

The lesson may take one or more math sessions, but the three-phase structure can also be applied to shorter tasks, resulting in a 10 to 20 minute minilesson.

 Before

In the *Before* phase of the lesson you are preparing students to work on the problem. As you plan for this stage, analyze the problem you will give to students in order to anticipate students' approaches and possible misinterpretations or misconceptions (Wallace, 2007). This can inform the questions you ask in the *Before* phase of the lesson to clarify students' understanding of the problem (i.e., knowing what the problem means rather than how they will solve it).

◆ During

In the *During* phase of the lesson, students explore the problem (alone, with partners, or in small groups). This is one of two opportunities you will get in the lesson to find out what your students know, how they think, and how they are approaching the task you have given them (the other is in the discussion period of the *After* phase). You want to convey a genuine interest in what students are doing and thinking. This is not the time to evaluate or to tell students how to solve the problem. When students ask whether a result or method is correct, ask students, "How can you decide?" or "Why do you think that might be right?" or "How can we tell if that makes sense?" Use this time in the *During* phase to identify different representations and strategies students used, interesting solutions, and any misconceptions that arise that you will highlight and address during the *After* phase of the lesson.

◆ After

In the *After* phase of the lesson your students will work as a community of learners, discussing, justifying, and challenging various solutions to the problem that they have just worked on. It is critical to plan for and save ample time for this part of the lesson. Twenty minutes is not at all unreasonable for a good class discussion and sharing of ideas. It is not necessary to wait for every student to finish. Here is where much of the learning will occur as students reflect individually and collectively on the ideas they have explored. This is the time to reinforce precise terminology, definitions, or symbols. After students have shared their ideas, formalize the main ideas of the lesson, highlighting connections between strategies or different mathematical ideas.

What Do I Do When a Task Doesn't Work?

Sometimes students may not know what to do with a problem you pose, no matter how many hints and suggestions you offer. Do not give in to the temptation to simply tell them. When you sense that a task is not moving forward, don't spend days just hoping that something wonderful may happen. You may need to regroup and offer students a simpler but related task that prepares them for the one that proved too difficult. If that does not work, set it aside for the moment. Ask yourself why it didn't work well. Did the students have the prior knowledge they needed? Was the task too advanced? Consider possible ways to step back or step forward in the content in order to support and challenge students. Nonetheless, trust that teaching mathematics through problem solving offers students the productive struggle that will allow them to develop understanding and become mathematically proficient.

Stop and Reflect

Describe in your own words what is meant by "teaching mathematics *through* problem solving." What do you foresee to be some opportunities and challenges to implementing problem-based mathematics tasks effectively in your classroom? ■

3

Assessing for Learning

I realize how valuable a well-designed, research-based probe can be in finding evidence of student understanding. Also how this awareness of children's thinking helped me decide what they (students) actually knew versus what I thought they knew.

A teacher from the Vermont Mathematics Partnership*

Assessment That Supports Instruction

In a problem-based approach, teachers often ask, "How do I assess?" The Assessment Principle in the *Principles and Standards for School Mathematics* (NCTM, 2000) stresses two main ideas: (1) assessment should enhance students' learning, and (2) assessment is a valuable tool for making instructional decisions.

Assessment is not separate from instruction and in fact should include the critical mathematical practices (CCSSO, 2010) and processes (NCTM, 2000) that occur in the course of effective problem-based instructional approaches. The typical approach of an end-of-chapter test of skills may have value, but it rarely reveals the type of data that can fine tune instruction so that it is tailored to improving the performance of individual students. In fact, Daro, Mosher, and Corcoran (2011) state that "the starting point is the mathematics and thinking the student brings to the lesson, not the deficit of mathematics they do not bring" (p. 48). Stiggins (2009) goes further to suggest that students in the upper elementary grades should be informed partners in understanding their progress in learning and how to enhance their growth in understanding concepts. They should begin to use their own assessment results to move forward as learners as they see that "success is always within reach" (p. 420). Using carefully selected assessment tasks allows us to integrate assessment into instruction and make it part of the learning process.

Assessments usually fall into one of two major categories: summative or formative. *Summative assessments* are cumulative evaluations that might generate a single score, such as an end-of-unit test or a standardized test that is used in your state or school district. Although the scores are important for schools and teachers, used individually they often do not help shape teaching decisions on particular topics or identify misunderstandings that may hinder students' future growth.

Formative assessments are those assessments that are used to determine the point-in-time status of students' understanding, to preassess, or to attempt to identify students' naïve understandings or misconceptions. The information is interpreted and used to provide feedback and make decisions about the next instructional steps (Wiliam, 2010). Wiliam goes on to note three key processes in formative assessment: "1) Establishing where the learners are in their learning, 2) Establishing where they are going and 3) Working out how to get there" (p. 45). As Wiliam states, "To be formative, assessment must include a recipe for future action" (slide 41).

For example, a formative assessment for a third-grade class could be to have a group of students solve the following word problem: "If Lindy has 34 shells in her collection and Jesse has 47, how many shells are in both collections?" Immediately the teacher observes one student quickly jotting down a straight line on the paper, making a hash mark with a 34 underneath and using small arcs to jump up four times to 74 and then makes one jump of six and another jump of one and indicates 81 with a hash mark (see Figure 3.1). Another student selects from a collection of base-ten materials in the center of the table, models each number, groups the tens together, then combines the ones and trades 10 of the ones for an additional ten piece, getting 81 as an answer. Observing a different student, the teacher notes he is using counters but is counting by ones. First he counts out the 34, then the 47, and then recounts them all to reach 78 (miscounting along the way). The information gathered from observing these three students reveals very different paths the teacher should take for the next steps. This teacher is at the first step in Wiliam's three key processes, noting where students are in their learning. Moving into the second step, the teacher notes that one student should move to more challenging tasks while two students need to move closer to the CCSS standard of representing and solving addition and subtraction problems within 100 through more targeted instruction.

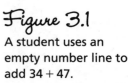

Figure 3.1
A student uses an empty number line to add 34 + 47.

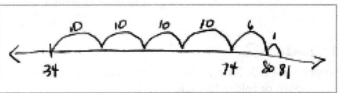

If summative assessment can be described as a digital snapshot, formative assessment is like streaming video. One is a picture of what a student knows that is captured in a single moment of time, and the other is a moving picture that demonstrates active student thinking and reasoning. In the following pages and throughout Part 2 of this book in the Formative Assessment Notes feature, we focus on a variety of formative assessment approaches that include Piaget's three broad categories of formative assessments: observations, interviews, and tasks (Piaget, 1976).

◆ Observations

All teachers learn useful bits of information about their students every day. When the three-phase lesson format (suggested in Chapter 2) is followed, the flow of evidence about student performance increases dramatically, especially in the *During* and *After* portions of lessons. If you have a systematic plan for gathering this information while observing and listening to students, at least two very valuable results occur. First, information that may have gone unnoticed is suddenly visible and important. Second, observation data gathered systematically can be combined with other data and used in planning lessons, providing feedback to students, conducting parent conferences, and determining grades.

Depending on the information you are trying to gather, several days to two weeks may be required to complete a single observation of how a whole class of students is progressing on a standard. Shorter periods of observation will focus on a particular cluster of concepts or skills or on particular students. Over longer periods, you can note growth in mathematical processes or practices, such as the development of problem solving, representation, or reasoning. To use observation effectively, you should take seriously the following maxim: Only try to collect data on a reasonable number of students in a single class period.

Anecdotal Notes

One system for recording observations is to write short notes either during or immediately after a lesson in a brief narrative. One possibility is to have a card for each student taped on the top edge to a clipboard (see Figure 3.2). Another option is to write anecdotal notes on an electronic tablet and store them in a spreadsheet. In either case, focus your observations on approximately five students a day. The students selected may be members of one or two cooperative groups or a group previously identified as needing additional support.

Checklists

To cut down on writing and to help focus your attention, a checklist duplicated for each student with several specific processes or content objectives can be devised (see Figure 3.3). As you build your checklist, include a place for comments. These comments should focus on big ideas and conceptual understanding rather than small skills. For example you will prob-

Figure 3.2

Preprinted cards for observation notes can be taped to a clipboard or folder for quick access.

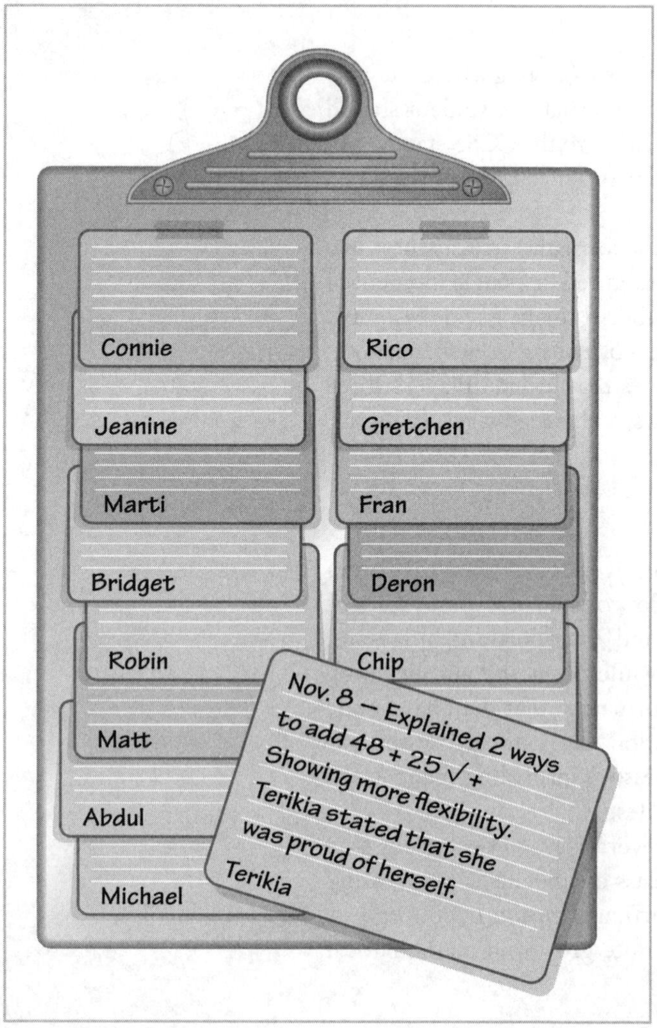

Figure 3.3

A focused checklist and rubric that can be printed for each student.

NAME: *Sharon V.*

FRACTIONS	NOT THERE YET	ON TARGET	ABOVE AND BEYOND	COMMENTS
Understands numerator/ denominator		✓		
Area models		✓		*Used pattern blocks to show $\frac{2}{3}$ and $\frac{3}{6}$*
Set models	✓			
Uses fractions in real contexts	✓			
Estimates fraction quantities		✓		*Showing greater reasonableness*
MATHEMATICAL PRACTICES				
Makes sense of problems and perseveres		✓		*Stated problem in own words*
Models with mathematics	✓			*Reluctant to use abstract models*
Uses appropriate tools		✓		

Figure 3.4 A full-class observation checklist used for a long-term objective or for a short-term objective covered over several days.

Topic: *Mental Computation Adding 2-digit numbers* **Names**	**Not There Yet** *Can't do mentally*	**On Target** *Has at least one strategy*	**Above and Beyond** *Uses different methods with different numbers*	**Comments**
Lalie		✓ *3-18-2013 3-21-2013*		
Pete	✓ *3-20-2013*	✓ *3-24-2013*		*Difficulty with problems requiring regrouping*
Sid			✓ + *3-20-2013*	*Flexible approaches used*
Lakeshia		✓		*Counts by tens, then adds ones*
George		✓		
Pam	✓			*Beginning to add the group of tens first*
Maria		✓ *3-24-2013*		*Using a posted hundreds chart*

ably find a note such as "is beginning to see how multiplication facts can be related, such as using 10×7 to think about 9×7" more helpful than "knows the easy multiplication facts but not the hard ones."

Another format involves listing all students in a class on a single page or not more than a few pages (see Figure 3.4). Across the top of the page are specific abilities or common misconceptions to look for. (These can be based on learning progressions or trajectories.) Pluses and minuses, checks, or codes can be entered in the grid. A full-class checklist is more likely to be used for long-term objectives. Topics that might be appropriate for this format include problem-solving processes, communication skills, and such skill areas as basic fact fluency or computational estimation. Dating entries or noting specifics about observed performance is also helpful.

Questioning

Observations do not have to be silent. Probing into student thinking through the use of questions can provide better data and more insights to inform instruction. As you circulate around the classroom to observe and evaluate students' understanding, your use of questions is one of the most important ways to formatively assess in each lesson phase. Keep the following questions in mind (or on a clipboard, index cards, or a bookmark) as you move about the classroom to prompt and probe students' thinking:

- What can you tell me about [today's topic]?
- How can you put the problem in your own words?
- What did you do that helped you understand the problem?
- Was there something in this problem that reminded you of another problem we've done?
- Did you find any numbers or information you didn't need? How did you know that the information was not important?
- How did you decide what to do?
- How did you decide whether your answer was right?
- Did you try something that didn't work? How did you figure out it was not going to work?
- Can something you did in this problem help you solve other problems?

Getting the students used to responding to these questions (as well as accustomed to asking questions about their thinking and the thinking of others) helps prepare them for the more intensive questioning used in diagnostic interviews.

◆ Diagnostic Interviews

A diagnostic interview uses what we know about students' cognition to design an assessment (Huff & Goodman, 2007). The interview is usually a one-on-one investigation of a student's thinking about a particular concept or the processes that are being used to solve problems. The interview usually lasts from three to ten minutes. The challenge of diagnostic interviews is that they are assessment opportunities, not teaching opportunities. It is hard to listen when students are making errors and not respond immediately. Instead, the interviews are used to listen and probe and to discover both strengths and gaps in understanding, which will lead to more targeted instruction.

Examples of diagnostic interviews include tasks such asking students to state which is greater—$\frac{4}{8}$ or $\frac{4}{4}$. You could also ask a student to solve a mixed number subtraction such as $6\frac{1}{4} - 2\frac{3}{4}$. The task should be aligned to recent work or your attempts to pinpoint underlying foundational gaps in understanding.

Diagnostic interviews have the potential to provide information that you simply cannot get in any other way. Think of interviews as a formative assessment tool to be used for only a few students at a time, not for every student in the class. You can briefly interview a single student while the rest of the class is working on a task. For example, if the whole class is working in groups on a task, you can explain to the class that you will be interviewing some of them while they work in order to better understand their thinking. Some teachers work with the student at an interactive whiteboard and record the whole conversation and any written work.

The most obvious reason to consider an interview is that you need more information about a particular student and how he or she is constructing concepts or using a procedure. In fact, these dialogues can be considered intense error analysis. Remediation will be more successful if you can pinpoint why a student is having difficulty before you try to fix the problem.

A second reason for conducting an interview is to gather information either to plan your next instructional steps or to assess the effectiveness of your instruction. In an examination of hundreds of research studies, Hattie (2009) found that the feedback that teachers received from students on what they knew and did not know was critical in improving students' performance. That is precisely what diagnostic interviews are designed to do!

For example, are you sure that your students have a good understanding of place value, or are they just doing the exercises according to rote procedures? Let's look at an actual classroom situation.

> Ms. Marsal was working with George, a student with disabilities who was displaying difficulty with calculating multidigit numbers. George also exhibited unreasonable estimates to computation, in some cases thinking the answer to a problem would result in tens when it was in the hundreds. To get George to reveal where his thinking was in terms of what he understood and where some gaps might be, Ms. Marsal planned a diagnostic interview. Using an adaptation of a task modeled at a conference presentation (Griffin & Lavelle, 2010), she asked the student to write the number that goes with 3 ones, 1 hundred, and 5 tens. Although base-ten materials were on the table, they went untouched. George responded by writing 315 (writing in the order he heard the numbers, without attention to the place values). Then Ms. Marsal resisted the temptation to immediately correct the student, as is necessary in these interviews, and instead probed further by asking George to take out 3 ones, 1 hundred, and 5 tens using the base-ten materials. Showing fluency with the values of base-ten materials,

George took out the correct amounts and placed them on the table, but in the order given in the problem, not in place value order. Then when offered a place value mat, George said, "I get it," and placed them in the correct positions. When asked to write the number that corresponded with the materials, George wrote the number (153) as seen in Figure 3.5. Ms. Marsal asked why he got two different numbers and which number he thought was correct. George quietly pondered and then pointed to the second number and said, "This one is right; I think you were trying to trick me."

Figure 3.5

Student's work on a diagnostic interview task.

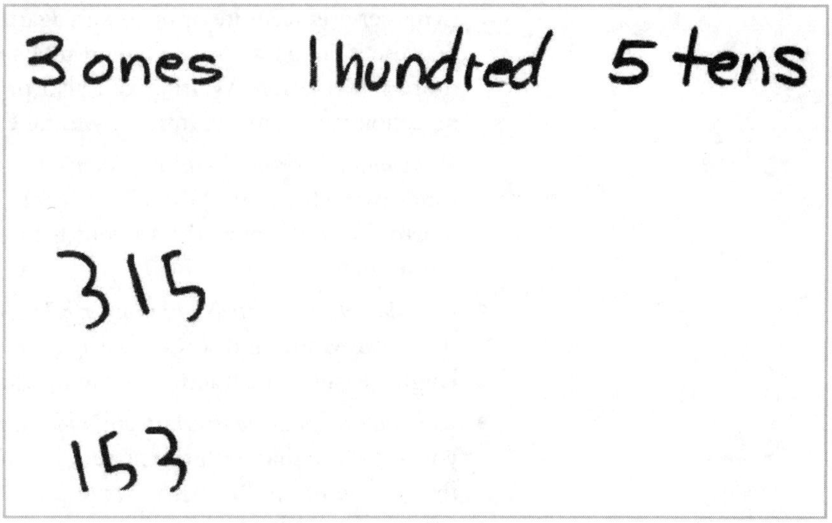

3 ones   1 hundred   5 tens

315

153

Although this interview revealed that the student had a good grasp of the value of the base-ten materials, it did reveal that there were lingering gaps in his understanding the place value concepts. Yet, this is a case in which the diagnostic interview was an actual learning experience. Notice that the teacher linked the assessment to the classroom instruction through the use of concrete materials and the structured semiconcrete support of the place value mat. This connection provided a way for the student to think about the number rather than just the individual digits. In addition, the cognitive dissonance caused by the difference in the two numerical outcomes, one responding to just the words alone and the other with concrete materials, enabled more connected ideas to emerge. Planning could then begin for future instruction based on actual evidence from the student.

There is no one right way to plan or structure a diagnostic interview. In fact, flexibility is a key ingredient. You should, however, have an overall plan that includes an easier task and a more challenging task in case you have misjudged your starting point. Also, did you notice that the teacher in the vignette had instructional materials ready for the student to use? Be sure you have materials available that match those students have used during instruction and that will provide insights into what the student understands.

Begin by asking the student to complete the first task you've planned. When the opening task has been completed, ask the student to explain what was done. "How would you explain this to a second grader (or your younger sister)?" and "What does this (point to something on the paper) stand for?" and "Tell me why you did this that way." You may want to ask, "Can you show me what you are thinking with the materials?" If the student gets two different answers, as in the previous scenario, ask, "Why do you think you got two different answers? Which one do you think is correct? If you tried to do this problem again, which approach would you try first?" In each case, it is important to explore whether the student can use models to connect actions to what he or she wrote or explained earlier.

Consider the following suggestions as you implement your diagnostic interview:

- *Avoid revealing whether the student's answer is right or wrong.* Often your facial expressions, tone of voice, or body language can give a student clues that the answer he or she gave is correct or incorrect. Instead, use a response such as "Can you tell me more?" or "I think I know what you are thinking." If a student asks whether the answer is right, you can say, "That's interesting" or "I see what you are doing."

- *Avoid asking leading questions.* Comments such as "Are you sure about that?" or "Wait, is that what you mean?" may indicate to students that they have made a mistake and cause them to reconsider their answers. This can hinder your ability to discover what they know and understand.

- *Wait silently for the student to give an answer.* Give ample time to allow the student to think and respond. Only then should you move to rephrasing the question or probing for a better understanding of the student's thoughts. After the student gives a response (whether it is accurate or not), wait again! This second wait time is even more important because it encourages the student to elaborate on his or her initial thought and provide more information. Waiting can also provide you with more time to think about the direction you want the interview to take.

- *Remember that you should not interject clues or teach.* The temptation to do so is sometimes overwhelming. Watch and listen. Your goal is to use the interview not to teach but to find out where the student is in terms of conceptual understanding and procedural fluency.

- *Let students share their thinking freely without interruption.* Encourage students to use their own words and ways of writing things down. Interjecting questions or correcting language can be distracting to the flow of students' thinking and explanations.

- *Ask students to demonstrate their understanding in multiple ways.* For example, ask, "Can you show me that with the materials?" or "Can you draw a picture to help think about this problem?" or "Can you write a word problem to go with that equation?" or "Can you explain what you just did?"

The benefits of the diagnostic interview become evident as you plan instruction that capitalizes on students' strengths while recognizing possible weaknesses and confusion. Also, unlike large-scale testing, you can always ask another question to find out more when the student is taking an incorrect or unexpected path. These insights are invaluable in moving students to mathematical proficiency.

◆ Tasks

The category of tasks refers to written products, including performance-based tasks, journal entries, student self-assessments, and tests. Good assessment tasks for either instructional or formative assessment purposes should permit every student in the class, regardless of mathematical ability, to demonstrate his or her knowledge, skill, or understanding.

Problem-Based Tasks

When problem-based tasks are used for assessment and evaluation, the intent is to find what students do know, rather than just identify what they do not know (e.g., they can't add mixed numbers). The result is a broad description of the ideas and skills that students possess. For example, "Adam can identify fractions given a regional model, but has difficulty placing fractions on a number line, particularly fractions greater than one."

Problem-based tasks have several critical components that make them good tasks for assessment. They:

- Focus on a central mathematics concept or skill aligned to valued learning targets

- Stimulate the connection of content a student knows to new content

- Allow multiple solution methods or approaches with a variety of tools

- Offer opportunities along the way for students to correct themselves

- Confront common student misconceptions

- Encourage students to use reasoning and explain their thinking

- Create opportunities for observing students' use of mathematical processes and practices
- Generate data for instructional decision making as you "listen" to your students' thinking

Problem-based tasks can be written products (e.g., journal entries, student self-assessments, or tests) or they can be performance-based tasks. Notice that the following examples of performance-based tasks are not elaborate, yet when followed by a discussion, each can engage students for most of a class session. What mathematical ideas and practices are required to successfully respond to each of these tasks? Will the task help you determine how well students understand the ideas?

THE WHOLE SET (GRADES 3–4)

Learning targets: (1) Determine a whole, given a fractional part (using a set model). (2) Make sense of quantities and their relationships in context.

Mary counted 15 cupcakes left from the whole batch that her mother made for the picnic. "We've already eaten two-fifths," she noted. How many cupcakes did her mother bake?

IN BETWEEN (GRADES 4–5)

Learning targets: (1) Estimate double-digit multiplication problems. (2) Use reasoning and regularity of patterns to identify a solution.

Write a multiplication problem that has an answer that falls between the answers to these two problems:

$$\begin{array}{r} 49 \\ \times 25 \\ \hline \end{array} \qquad \begin{array}{r} 45 \\ \times 30 \\ \hline \end{array}$$

Write an explanation of how you came up with your solution.

CLOSE DECIMALS (GRADES 4–5)

Learning Targets: (1) Compare two decimals by reasoning about their size. (2) Analyze and critique the reasoning of others.

Alan tried to make a decimal number as close to 50 as he could using the digits 1, 4, 5, and 9. He arranged them in this order: 51.49. Jerry thinks he can arrange the same digits to get a number that is even closer to 50. Do you agree or disagree? Explain.

Translation Tasks

One important option for a task is what we refer to as a *translation task*. Using seven representations for concepts (see Figure 2.3), students are asked to more than one representation (e.g., words, tools, and numbers) to demonstrate understanding of a single problem. As students move between these representations, there is a better chance that a concept will be formed correctly and integrated into a rich web of ideas.

So what is a good way of structuring a translation task? With use of an adaptation of a template for assessing concept mastery from Frayer, Fredrick, and Klausmeier (1969) (see Figure 3.6), you can give students a computational equation and ask them to:

- Write a word problem that matches the equation
- Illustrate the equation with materials or drawings
- Explain their process of arriving at an answer

In particular, students' ability to communicate how they solved a problem is critical for open-response questions on state assessments (Parker & Breyfogle, 2011).

Figure 3.6

Translation task template with example task.

Equation/Written Symbols	Word Problem/Real-World Situation
Manipulatives/Illustration	**Explanation**

Translation tasks can be used for whole-class lessons or for individual or small-group diagnosis. For example, fifth-grade students may be given a 10×10 grid with 75 squares shaded, as in the section titled "Manipulatives/Illustration" in Figure 3.6. Their task could be to write the percent of the square that is shaded in the "Equation/Written Symbols" area, describe a real-world situation in which that percentage is used in the "Word Problem" area, and explain to another person in writing what percent means in the "Explanation" area. Students could also be asked to write the percentage as both a fraction and a decimal (showing their ability to make translations within written symbols) in the "Equation/Written Symbols" area.

Think about using translation tasks when you want to find out more about a student's thinking. If a student represents ideas in various forms and can explain why these representations are similar or different, you can use this valuable information to recognize misconceptions he or she may have and then identify the type of activity you can provide to advance the student's learning. Following are two other options for tasks that can be used with the translation task template to assess student understanding. Remember, a translation task can start in any section of the template and then the student proceeds to fill in the other three sections. Consider the following two starters.

In the "Word Problem" area, write "One side of the rectangle is 6 cm. The area is 48 square centimeters. How long is the other side?"

Students make a corresponding drawing, write an equation (e.g., $6 \times \underline{} = 48$ or $48 \div 6 = \underline{}$), and explain how they solved the problem.

In the "Equation/Written Symbols" area, write "$3\frac{1}{2} + 2\frac{1}{4} = ?$" Then in the three other sections, the student should write a corresponding word problem, make an illustration to demonstrate the solution to this problem, and explain to a friend how he or she should approach this problem.

In some instances, the real value of a task is in what it can reveal about students' understanding. That will come primarily through discussion in the *After* phase of your lesson. It is important that you help your students develop the habits of adding justifications to their answers and listening to and evaluating the explanations of others. As illustrated here, do not always start with the same section, because sometimes students can translate one way but not in reverse.

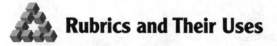

Rubrics and Their Uses

Appropriate assessment tasks yield an enormous amount of information that must be evaluated by examining more than a simple count of correct answers. A *rubric* consists of a scale based on predetermined criteria with two important functions: (1) It permits the student to see what is central to excellent performance, and (2) it provides the teacher with scoring guidelines that support analysis of students' work. In a teaching-through-problem-solving approach, you will often want to include criteria and performance indicators such as the following:

- Solved the problem(s) accurately and effectively
- Justified and explained strategy use or arguments
- Used logical reasoning
- Expressed a grasp of numerical relationships and structure
- Incorporated multiple representations and/or multiple strategies
- Demonstrated an ability to appropriately select and use tools and manipulatives
- Communicated with precise language and accurate units
- Identified general patterns of ideas that repeat, making connections from one big idea to another

Rubrics are usually built from the highest possible score. By describing what an outstanding performance would be on a given standard or learning target, you are then able to set the benchmarks for the other levels.

◆ Generic Rubrics

Generic rubrics identify categories of performance instead of specific criteria for a particular task and therefore can be used for multiple assignments. The generic rubric allows a teacher to score performances by first sorting into two broad categories, as illustrated in the four-point rubric shown in Figure 3.7. The scale then allows you to separate each category

Figure 3.7

With a four-point rubric, performances are first sorted into two categories. Each performance is then considered again and assigned to a point on the scale.

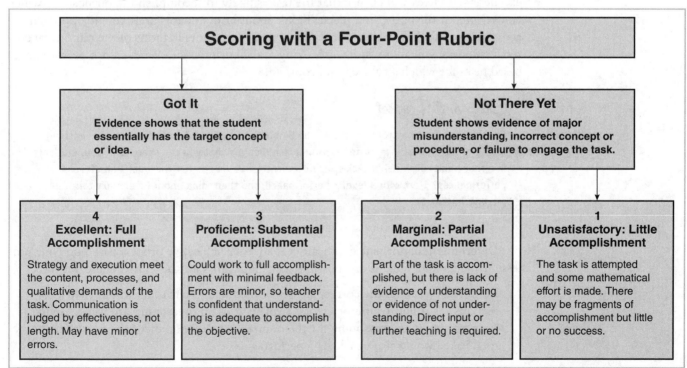

Scoring with a Four-Point Rubric

Got It
Evidence shows that the student essentially has the target concept or idea.

Not There Yet
Student shows evidence of major misunderstanding, incorrect concept or procedure, or failure to engage the task.

4
Excellent: Full Accomplishment

Strategy and execution meet the content, processes, and qualitative demands of the task. Communication is judged by effectiveness, not length. May have minor errors.

3
Proficient: Substantial Accomplishment

Could work to full accomplishment with minimal feedback. Errors are minor, so teacher is confident that understanding is adequate to accomplish the objective.

2
Marginal: Partial Accomplishment

Part of the task is accomplished, but there is lack of evidence of understanding or evidence of not understanding. Direct input or further teaching is required.

1
Unsatisfactory: Little Accomplishment

The task is attempted and some mathematical effort is made. There may be fragments of accomplishment but little or no success.

Figure 3.8

A rubric used during an activity or for a single topic over a period of several days.

Observation Rubric Making Whole Given Fraction Part (3/17)		
Above and Beyond Clear understanding. Communicates concept in multiple representations. Shows evidence of using idea without prompting. *Fraction whole made from parts in rods and in sets. Explains easily.*	*Sally* *Latania* *Greg*	 *Zal*
On Target Understands or is developing well. Uses designated models. *Can make whole in either rod or set format (note). Hesitant. Needs prompt to identify unit fraction.*	*Lavant (rod)* *Julie (rod)* *George (set)* *Maria (set)*	*Tanisha (rod)* *Lee (set)* *J.B. (rod)* *John H. (rod)*
Not There Yet Some confusion or misunderstands. Only models idea with help. *Needs help to do activity. No confidence.*	*John S.*	*Mary*

into two additional levels. Note that a rating of 0 is given for no response or effort, or for responses that are completely off task. The advantage of the four-point scale is the relatively easy initial sort into the "Got It" or "Not There Yet" categories.

Another possibility is to use your three- or four-point generic rubric on a reusable form, as in Figure 3.8. Include space for content-specific indicators and another column for jotting down the names of students. A quick note or comment may be added to a name. This method is especially useful for planning purposes.

◆ Task-Specific Rubrics

Task-specific rubrics include specific statements, also known as *indicators*, that describe what performance looks like at each level of the rubric and, in so doing, establish criteria for acceptable performance. Initially, when you create a task-specific rubric, it may be difficult to predict what student performance at different levels will or should look like. Your decision about performance levels will depend on several criteria: your own knowledge and experience with students at that grade level, the students who are working on the same task, and your own insights about the task or mathematical concept. One important part of setting performance levels is predicting students' common misconceptions or the expected thinking or approaches to the same or similar problems.

To facilitate writing performance levels, write out indicators of "proficient" or "on target" performances before you use the task in class. This excellent self-check will ensure that the task is likely to accomplish the purpose for which you selected it for in the first place. Think about how students are likely to approach the activity. If you find yourself writing performance indicators in terms of the number of correct responses, you are most likely looking at drill or practice exercises, not performance-based tasks for which a rubric is appropriate.

Stop and Reflect

Consider the fraction problem titled "The Whole Set" on page 35. Assume you are teaching fourth grade and want to write performance indicators that you can share with your students in a four-point rubric. What task-specific indicators would you use for level 3 and level 4 performances? Start with a level 3 performance, and then think about level 4. Try this before reading further. ■

Determining performance indicators is always a subjective process based on your professional judgment. Here is one possible set of indicators for the "The Whole Set" task:

Level 3: Determines the correct answer or uses an approach that would yield a correct answer if not for minor errors. Explanations and reasoning are weak. Giving a correct result and reasoning for the number eaten but an incorrect result for the total baked would also be a level 3 performance.

Level 4: Determines the total number baked and uses words, pictures, and numbers to explain and justify the result and how it was obtained. Demonstrates knowledge of fractional parts and their relation to the whole.

Indicators such as these should be shared with students ahead of time. Sharing indicators before working on a task clearly conveys what is valued and expected.

What about level 1 and level 2 performances? Here are suggestions for the same task:

Level 2: Uses some aspect of fractions appropriately (e.g., divides the 15 into 5 groups instead of 3) but fails to illustrate an understanding of how to determine the whole. Shows evidence that he or she does not understand that a fraction is a number. (The student may believe it is two whole numbers.)

Level 1: Shows some effort but little or no understanding of a fractional part relative to the whole.

Unexpected methods and solutions happen. Don't limit students to demonstrating their understanding only as you thought or hoped they would when there is evidence that they are accomplishing your objectives in different ways. Such occurrences can help you revise or refine your rubric for future use.

Students' Self-Assessment with Rubrics

In the beginning of the year, post your rubric prominently and discuss it with the class. Many teachers use the same rubric for all subjects; others prefer to use a specialized rubric for mathematics. In your discussion, let students know that as they do activities and solve problems, you will sometimes look at their work and listen to their explanations and provide them with feedback in the form of a rubric, rather than a letter grade or a percentage.

Make it a habit to discuss students' performance on tasks in terms of the rubric. You might also have students use the rubric to self-assess their work, giving reasons for the rating. You can have class discussions about a completed task by talking about what might constitute "on target" and "above and beyond" performance. Also share student work (anonymously) as a way to highlight excellent responses as well as responses that need more detail or work shown. Use these work samples to get students to talk about what could make an answer stronger and better aligned with the rubric. This process of critiquing others' work is included in the Standards for Mathematical Practice and therefore is recognized as an essential element to mathematical proficiency.

A rubric reveals much more than a grade. It is a meaningful way to communicate feedback to students (and parents). It should let students know how well they are doing and encourage them to work harder by giving specific areas for improvement. When their performance is not progressing satisfactorily, students should understand that there are specific things they can work on. Your task is to target the follow-up instruction in response to their gaps and misunderstandings as well as their identified strengths.

You do not need to use rubrics with every task, nor is it necessary to reserve rubrics for assessments that you want to grade. If you are using the four-point rubric just described, the language of the rubric can be used informally with your students: "Maggie, the rubric states to get a 4 you need to solve the problem with two different methods and explain your thinking. Is that what you did?"

Teaching Tip

When you return papers, review the indicators with students, including examples of correct answers and successful responses. This will help students understand how they could have done better. Often it is useful to show work from classmates (anonymously) or from a prior class. Let students decide on the score for the anonymous student. Importantly, students need to see models of what a level 4 performance looks like.

The rubric scale can also be used in recording observations of student performance. If you describe the task across the top of a class checklist, and list the students' names down the left side, then it is useful to record a 1, 2, 3, or 4 next to each name. You may want to leave space for writing detailed comments for some students so that they can be grouped in follow-up instruction according to common misunderstandings.

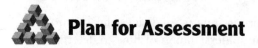 ## Plan for Assessment

"An assessment system designed to help steer the instruction system must give good information about direction as well as distance to travel. A system that keeps telling us we are not there yet is like a kid in the back seat whining 'are we there yet?'" (Daro et al., 2011, p. 51). Instead we need a system in which teachers do the following:

- Establish where students are in their learning
- Identify the learning destination
- Carefully plan a route
- Begin the learning journey
- Make regular checks on progress along the way
- Make adjustments to the course as conditions dictate (Wiliam, 2010)

Then, assessments can more easily be translated into tools that inform instruction and support students' growth.

Stop and Reflect

How can sharing samples of students' work (both strong and weak responses) support all students' ability to generate more in-depth responses? ■

4

Differentiating Instruction

[Differentiation] moves us away from seeing and teaching students as a unit toward reflecting on and responding to them as individuals.

Sousa and Tomlinson
(2011, p. 9)

All fourth graders do not learn the same thing, in the same way, and at the same rate. Every classroom at every grade level contains a range of students with varying abilities and backgrounds. Perhaps the most important work of teachers today is to be able to plan (and teach) lessons that support and challenge *all* students to learn important mathematics.

Differentiation and Teaching Mathematics through Problem Solving

Teachers have for some time embraced the notion that students vary in reading ability, but the idea that students can and do vary in mathematical development may be new. Mathematics education research reveals a great deal of evidence demonstrating that students vary in their understanding of specific mathematical ideas. Attending to these differences in students' mathematical development is key to differentiating mathematics instruction for your students.

Interestingly, the problem-based approach to teaching is the best way to teach mathematics while attending to the range of students in your classroom. In a traditional, highly directed lesson, it is often assumed that all students will understand and use the same approach and the same ideas as determined by the teacher. Students not ready to understand the ideas presented by the teacher must focus their attention on following rules or directions without developing a conceptual or relational understanding (Skemp, 1978). This, of course, leads to endless difficulties and can leave students with misunderstandings or in need of significant remediation. In contrast, in a problem-based classroom, students are expected to approach problems in a variety of ways that make sense to *them*, bringing to each problem the skills and ideas that they own. So, with a problem-based approach to teaching mathematics, differentiation is already built in to some degree.

To illustrate, let's consider a third-grade classroom in which the teacher posed the following task to students.

In the school library there are 489 books. 215 of the books are about different kinds of mammals. How many of the books are not about mammals?

She asked the students to be ready to explain how they got their answers. Following are some of the students' explanations:

Edwin: I used an open number line. I started at 215 and counted up 5 to get to 220, then added 80 to get to 300, then 100 to get to 400, and then 89 to get to 489 [see Figure 4.1]. I knew I needed to add $5 + 80 + 100 + 89$, but it was easier to add $5 + 80 + 100 + 90$ to get $185 + 90$, which is 275. But since I added one to 89 to make the addition easier, I needed to subtract one from my answer. So my answer is 274.

Jeana: I started at 489 and went backwards to 215, but I did not use a number line. I did it in my head. I knew I needed to subtract 89 to get down to 400. Then I jumped down to 300 by subtracting 100. Then I subtracted 80 to get to 220 and then 5 more to get to 215. So I added $89 + 100 + 80 + 5$, which is 274, to find out how much I subtracted.

Carmen: I added 11 to each number in the problem so I had $500 - 226$. Then I subtracted $500 - 200$ to get 300 and then $300 - 20$ to get 280. Then all I had to do was subtract 6 more to get to 274.

Sam: My way was like Carmen's, but I subtracted something from each number. I subtracted 15 from each number so that I had $474 - 200$. Then I could see that the answer was 274.

Figure 4.1

Edwin's strategy to find $489 - 215$.

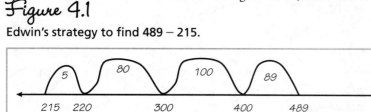

Some students recognized they can add or subtract the same amount to both numbers in a subtraction problem and maintain the difference. Others used an adding up strategy supported with a number line. Still others used mental math and subtracted quantities in chunks that made sense to them. If the teacher had expected all students to use a number line, then many of the students may have been using a method that did not make sense to them or a less-efficient method than they would have independently used. Also, the cognitive demand of the task would have been lowered. If the teacher had expected all the students to recognize that you can add or subtract the same quantity from the numbers to create easier numbers to work with while maintaining the difference, then some students may have been confused because they are not ready for this strategy. Instead, the teacher allowed the students to use their own ideas to determine how many books were about topics other than mammals. This expectation and the recognition that different students will approach and solve the same problem in various ways honors students' varying mathematical development and sets the stage for differentiated mathematics instruction. In addition, by listening to how different students approached the task, the teacher has acquired important information that can be used to plan subsequent instruction that meets a variety of students' needs.

The Nuts and Bolts of Differentiating Instruction

Differentiation is an instructional approach that requires a shift from focusing on the "middle-of-the-road" students to attending to all students. As overwhelming as this may sound, differentiation does not require a teacher to create individualized lessons for each and every student in the classroom. Rather, it requires emphasizing three basic ideas:

- Planning lessons around meaningful content, grounded in authenticity
- Recognizing each student's readiness, interest, and approach to learning
- Connecting content and learners by modifying content, process, product, and the learning environment (Sousa & Tomlinson, 2011)

Planning Meaningful Content, Grounded in Authenticity

Before you begin to think about differentiation, you first need to know where you want students to "be" at the end of the learning experience. You must be explicitly aware of the content that students should know, understand, and be able to do after engaging in a given lesson or sequence of lessons. This awareness enables you to effectively guide students' learning by varying or differentiating instruction. If you do not have a clear idea about the specific learning outcomes, identifying how and when to differentiate can be difficult. In fact, Tomlinson (1999) claims that "If the 'stuff' [content] is ill conceived, the 'how' [differentiation] is doomed" (p. 16).

Note that the content must be authentic and grounded in important mathematics that emphasize the big ideas in ways that require students to develop relational understanding. Authentic content engages students in the heart of mathematics by requiring them to be problem solvers and creators of knowledge. Through this kind of engagement, students also develop a productive disposition toward mathematics and see it as sensible, useful, and worthwhile.

Recognizing Students as Learners

Knowing each student in the context of learning requires finding out who he or she is as an individual on traits such as readiness, interests, and learning profile. *Readiness* refers to a student's proficiency with the knowledge, understanding, and skills embedded in specific learning goals. *Interest* means a student's attraction to particular topics, ideas, and events. Using contexts that are interesting and familiar to students enhances their attention and motivation to engage and achieve (Sousa & Tomlinson, 2011). A *learning profile* identifies how a student approaches learning—how each student prefers to learn (e.g., in groups, alone); process and reason about information (e.g., by listening, observing, participating, or through talking; by thinking about details first and then the big picture or vice versa; by doing one task at a time or multitasking); and use or demonstrate what has been learned (e.g., writing, verbalizing, drawing). By using students' preferences for learning to structure the environment, tasks, and assessments, you are greatly facilitating the learning process.

Information about your students' traits can inform how you might modify different elements of the classroom (Sousa & Tomlinson, 2011; Tomlinson, 2003). You can gather information pertaining to students' readiness by using preassessments several days before a given unit so that you have time to analyze the evidence and assess each student's readiness for the unit. You can also use surveys, typically at the beginning and midpoint of the year, to gather information about students' interests and learning profiles. Interest surveys give

Figure 4.2 Learning profile inventory.

When working on a task I like to . . .	I like to work . . .	When working I like the room to be . . .	When working I like . . .	When learning about new ideas I like to . . .	When sharing information, I like to . . .
☐ sit at my desk	☐ with a partner	☐ warm	☐ quiet	☐ hear about it	☐ talk
☐ sit somewhere other than my desk	☐ in a small group	☐ cool	☐ noise	☐ read about it	☐ show
☐ stand	☐ alone	☐ darker, lights off	☐ music	☐ see visuals about it	☐ write
☐ lie on the floor	☐ other	☐ brightly lit	☐ other	☐ use materials to explore	☐ other
☐ other		☐ other		☐ talk about it	
				☐ other	

students opportunities to share personal interests (e.g., what they like to do after school, on the weekends, and during the summer; what school subjects they find most interesting and why) and information about pets, siblings, and extracurricular activities. Use your students' interests to provide contexts for the mathematics they are learning to increase their motivation and engagement. Learning profile surveys or questionnaires also help students think about what helps them learn and what does not, such as preferring to work in pairs versus alone, being able to work with background noise, and needing to process ideas verbally (see Figure 4.2). Teacher observation can also provide valuable insights into student learning profiles. By recording students' information on index cards, you can quickly refresh your memory by looking through the cards as you plan lessons. You can also sort the cards to help you create groups based on interests or learning profiles.

◆ Connecting Content and Learners

A critical component of differentiated lesson planning is determining how to modify four classroom elements to help the learner better connect with the content (Tomlinson, 2003). These four classroom elements are content, process, product, and the learning environment.

Content: What You Want Each Student to Learn

Generally, what is learned (the big ideas) should be relatively the same for all students. However, content can still be differentiated in terms of depth (level of complexity) and breadth (connecting across different topics) (Murray & Jorgensen, 2007; Small, 2009). Students' readiness typically informs the level of complexity or depth at which the content is initially presented for different groups of students. Interest and learning profiles tend to inform differentiation geared toward breadth.

An example of a depth adaptation for developing understanding and skill with organizing, representing, and interpreting data is a minilesson in which all students organize and represent data and answer questions based on the data. Some students may have a smaller set of data to deal with or they may be asked to answer given questions about the data, while others, who are ready for more sophisticated content, are asked to generate their own questions about the data. An example of a breadth adaptation for the same objective is to allow students a choice in terms of the kind of data with which they will work. For example, based on their interests, students might choose to work with data pertaining to sports, books, science, gaming, or pets. By working with data from various contexts, students not only learn something about those contexts, but they can also begin to see the broader applications of organizing, representing, and interpreting data.

Process: How Students Engage in Thinking about the Content

Although the big ideas of a learning experience remain relatively stable when differentiating, how students engage with and make sense of the content—the *process*—changes. Tomlinson (1999) described the process as students "taking different roads to the same destination" (p. 12). You can use different strategies or encourage students to take different "roads" to increase access to the essential information, ideas, and skills embedded in a lesson (Cassone, 2009; Tomlinson, 2003). For example, the use of manipulatives, games, and relevant and interesting contextual problems provides different ways for students to process their ideas while engaging with content.

The process standards in the *Principles and Standards for School Mathematics* (NCTM, 2000), which served as a basis for the Standards for Mathematical Practice in the *Common Core State Standards* (CCSSO, 2010), lend themselves well to

Teaching Tip

Be sure that the tasks you ask students to do are closely aligned with the learning objectives of the lesson.

differentiating how students engage with and make sense of content. In particular, the representation process standard emphasizes the need to think about and use different ways to represent mathematical ideas, which can help students make connections between concepts and skills. With the communication process standard, students can use verbal or written communication as they share their reasoning, depending on their strengths. In addition, the problem-solving process standard allows for differentiation because of the myriad of strategies that students can use—from drawing a diagram or using manipulatives to solving a simpler problem and looking for patterns.

Due to their different levels of readiness, it is imperative that students be allowed to use a variety of strategies and representations that are grounded in their own ideas to solve problems. You can facilitate students' engagement in thinking about the content through a variety of methods. For example, teachers may

- Use visuals or graphic organizers to help students connect ideas and build a structure for the information in the lesson.
- Provide manipulatives to support students' development of a concept.
- Provide different manipulatives from those previously used with the same content.
- Use an appropriate context that helps students build meaning for the concept and that employs purposeful constraints that can highlight the significant mathematical ideas.
- Share examples and nonexamples to help students develop a better understanding of a concept.
- Gather a small group of students to develop foundational knowledge for a new concept.
- Provide text or supplementary material in a student's native language to aid understanding of materials written or delivered in English.
- Set up learning centers or a tiered lesson (a lesson that offers learners different pathways to reach a specific learning goal).

Product: How Students Demonstrate What They Know, Understand, and Are Able to Do after the Lesson Is Over

The term *product* can refer to what a student produces as a result of completing a single task, or to a major assessment after an extended learning experience. The products related to a single task would be consistent with the ways students share their ideas in the *After* portion of a lesson, described in Chapter 2, which could include students explaining their ideas with manipulatives, through a drawing, in writing, or simply verbally. The products related to an extended experience can take the form of a project, portfolio, test, write-up of solutions to several problem-based inquiries, and so on. An important feature of any product is that it allows a variety of ways for students to demonstrate their understanding of essential content.

Learning Environment: The Logistics, Physical Configuration, and Tone of the Classroom

Consider how the physical learning environment might be adapted to meet students' needs. Do you have a student who prefers to work alone? Who prefers to work in a group? Who can or cannot work with background noise? Who prefers to work in a setting with brighter or dimmer lighting? Attending to these students' needs can affect the seating arrangement, specific grouping strategies, access to materials, and other aspects of the classroom environment. In addition to the physical learning space, establishing a classroom culture in which students' ideas and solutions are respected as they explain and justify them is an important aspect of a differentiated classroom. Refer to the recommendations provided in Chapter 2 pertaining to facilitating effective classroom discussions and establishing a supportive and respectful learning environment.

Examples of Differentiated Instruction

Differentiated Tasks for Whole-Class Instruction

One challenge of differentiation is planning a task focused on a target mathematical concept or skill that can be used for whole-class instruction while meeting a variety of students' needs. Let's consider two different kinds of tasks that can meet this challenge: parallel tasks and open questions (Murray & Jorgensen, 2007; Small, 2009).

Parallel Tasks

Parallel tasks are two or three tasks that focus on the same big idea but offer different levels of difficulty. The tasks should be created so that all students can meaningfully participate in a follow-up discussion with the whole class. You can assign tasks to students based on their readiness, or students can choose which task to work on. If they choose a task that is too difficult, they can always move to another task. Consider how the following parallel tasks emphasize the big idea of division but at different levels of difficulty.

TASK 1:

There are 48 fourth graders on the playground. They want to form 4 teams with an equal number of students on each team. How many students will be on each team?

TASK 2:

There are 1080 fourth graders in our school system. There are the same number of fourth graders at each of the 5 elementary schools. How many fourth graders would be at each school?

Stop and Reflect

Which of the two tasks do you think would be more difficult and why? ■

Both tasks provide opportunities for students to work with division, but the size of the numbers in the second task increases the level of difficulty. If students need to use manipulatives to fairly share the 48 students among 4 teams, the numbers in the first task still allow for their use. On the other hand, the numbers in the second task would be too cumbersome for students to model using single cubes, but they could use base-ten materials to equally distribute 1080 into 5 groups. If you want to encourage students to move beyond using manipulatives, only offer the single cubes with the second task. Students will then have an incentive to think about using another strategy. Even if students use the long division or partial quotients algorithm, the size of the numbers in the second task still makes it more challenging.

You can facilitate a whole-class discussion by asking questions that are relevant to both tasks. For example, with respect to the previous two tasks, you could ask the following questions of the whole class:

- How did you determine how many students were in each group?

- Some of you indicated that you split up the total number of students based on place value and then thought about how to share those amounts across your equal groups. Why does that strategy make sense?

- Suppose there were one more fourth grader. How would that change your answer?

- Suppose the number of students in each group increased by one. How many more fourth graders would there be?

Although students work on different tasks, because the tasks are focused on the same big idea, these questions allow them to extend their thinking as they hear others' strategies and ideas.

For many problems involving computation, you can simply insert multiple sets of numbers to vary the difficulty. In the following problem, students are permitted to select the first, second, or third number in each set of brackets. Giving a choice increases motivation and helps students become more self-directed learners (Bray, 2009; Gilbert & Musu, 2008).

LEARNING OBJECTIVE: Represent and solve problems involving multiplication (grade 3)

Mark had [2, 5, 8] markers in [6, 7, 12] boxes. How many markers does Mark have?

The following parallel tasks for fifth graders focus on the big idea of division.

TASK 1:

Create a word problem that can be solved by dividing a whole number by a unit fraction.

TASK 2:

Create a word problem that can be solved by dividing two multidigit whole numbers.

With the first task, the teacher provides an option for students who are ready to deal with problems that involve division with unit fractions. The parallel task still offers an opportunity for students to think about division, but without them having to deal with the increased challenge of fractions.

In thinking about how to create parallel tasks, once you have identified the big idea you wish to focus on, consider how students might differ in reasoning about that idea. The size of the numbers involved, the operations students can use, and the type of measurement with which students are most familiar are just a few differences to consider. Start with a task from your textbook and then modify it to make it suitable for a different developmental level. The original task and the modified task will serve as the parallel tasks offered simultaneously to your students. If you number the parallel tasks and allow students to choose the task they will work on, be sure there are instances in which the more difficult task is the first one. This randomness will ensure that students consider both options before they choose their task.

Open Questions

A question is open when it can be solved in a variety of ways or when it can have different answers. Following are two examples of open questions. Both questions can have different answers and can also be solved in a variety of ways.

I measured an object in the classroom and found that it weighed 10 grams. What could the object be?

The product of three numbers is 1200. What could the three numbers be?

Stop and Reflect

How would you solve each of these tasks? Can you think of at least two different strategies or answers for each task? ∎

Open questions have a high level of cognitive demand, as described in Chapter 2, because students must use more than recall or do more than merely follow steps in a procedure. As such, there are ample opportunities for them to approach the problems at their own level, which means open questions automatically accommodate for student readiness. Consequently, when given an open question, most students can find something appropriate to contribute, which helps to increase their confidence in doing mathematics and can inform you of their level of understanding.

A variety of strategies can be used to create open questions (Small, 2009; Sullivan & Lilburn, 2002), including the following:

- Give the answer and ask for the problem.
- Replace a number in a given problem with a blank or a question mark.
- Offer two situations or examples and ask for similarities and differences.
- Create a question that can generate a range of possible answers so that students have to make choices.

The two previous examples of open questions illustrate the first strategy of giving an answer and asking for the problem. Following are other examples that show how to use the other strategies to convert standard questions to open questions.

Strategy: Replace a number in a given problem with a blank or question mark.

Standard Question	Open Question
23 × 68	?3 × 6?

Strategy: Offer two situations or examples and ask for similarities and differences.

Standard Question	Open Question
Write the decimal 34.562 in expanded form.	How are the decimals 34.562 and 43.265 similar and how are they different?

Strategy: Create a question that can generate a range of possible answers so that students have to make choices.

Standard Question	Open Question
List two equivalent fractions for $\frac{1}{2}$. Explain why they are equivalent.	The numerator of one fraction is 1 and the numerator of an equivalent fraction is 3. What could the denominators of the equivalent fractions be? Explain why they are equivalent.

Facilitating follow-up discussions is also important when you use open questions. While students work on an open question, walk around and observe the variety of strategies and answers students are finding. During this time, plan which students you will ask to share their ideas during the follow-up discussion to ensure multiple strategies and answers are examined. During the discussion, look for opportunities to help students make connections between different ideas that are shared. For example, in the previous task in which students are looking for similarities and differences between the decimals 34.562 and 43.265, one student might say that the two decimals have the same number of digits and another student might say that both numbers use the same place values. You could ask the class, "If two decimals have the same number of digits, does it always mean they will also use the same place values?" Asking questions that challenge students to clarify similarities or patterns they find can help them build connections, support those who need additional help, and also challenge students to extend their understanding.

◈ Learning Centers

Sometimes a mathematical concept or topic can be explored by having students work on different tasks at various classroom locations called *learning centers*. Students can work on concepts or topics in learning centers as an initial introduction, as a midpoint exploration, or as a follow-up task that provides practice or allows extension. Because you can decide which students will be assigned to which centers, you can differentiate the content at each center. For example, each center can use a different representation of the concept, requiring students to use different approaches to solve a problem, or centers can vary in terms of the difficulty of the task (e.g., different centers can use different numbers that change the level of difficulty).

A good task for a learning center is one that can be repeated multiple times during one visit. This allows students to remain engaged until you are ready for them to transition to another center or activity. For example, at one center students might play a game in which they take turns describing to each other various two-dimensional figures based on the kind and number of angles and the presence or absence of parallel or perpendicular lines. Technology-enhanced tasks on the computer or interactive whiteboard that can be repeated can provide the focus of a center, but these tasks must be carefully selected. Among other aspects, you will want to choose technology-based tasks that require students to engage in reflective thought. For example, "Exploring Properties of Rectangles and Parallelograms" in the NCTM online resources (at www.nctm.org/standards/content.aspx?id=25040) offers students opportunities to explore geometric relationships using dynamic software. The dynamic nature of the software allows students to stretch, shrink, and rotate rectangles and parallelograms as they think about what features remain the same even with these changes. They can also reflect on the commonalities and differences between rectangles and parallelograms. Another example, "Playing Fraction Tracks" (at www.nctm.org/standards/content .aspx?id=26975), provides a game setting in which students have opportunities to reason about how various fractions relate to a whole, to compare different fractional quantities, and to work with equivalent fractions.

You may want students to work at centers in small groups or individually. Therefore, for a given topic, you might prepare four to eight different activities (you can also use the same activity at two different learning centers). However, be sure to keep the centers focused on the same topic or concept so that you can help students build connections across the centers.

To ensure greater student success at the centers, review with your whole class any instructions you have provided at each center on cards. For students with disabilities who have difficulty reading, provide audio-recorded directions at each center. If necessary, model or teach again any necessary skills. After students have had time to work in several centers, follow up with individual or class discussions to ensure that students are learning the essential ideas and connections that the centers are meant to elicit.

◆ Tiered Lessons

In a tiered lesson, you set the same learning goals for all students, but different pathways are provided to reach those learning goals, thereby creating the various tiers. First you need to decide which category you wish to tier: content, process, or product. If you are new to preparing tiered lessons, tier only one category until you become more comfortable with the process. Once you decide which category to tier, determine the challenge of each of the defined tiers based on student readiness levels, interests, and learning profiles (Kingore, 2006; Murray & Jorgensen, 2007; Tomlinson, 1999). Murray and Jorgensen (2007) suggest starting with creating three tiers to make the process more manageable: a regular tier or lesson, an extension tier that provides extra challenge, and a scaffolding tier that provides more background or support. Once you have this framework, you can design as many tiers as needed to meet your students' needs. All tiered experiences should have the following characteristics (Sousa & Tomlinson, 2011):

- Address the same learning goals
- Require students to use reasoning
- Be equally interesting to students

We have already considered some ways to tier the content by using parallel tasks and open questions. However, varying the degree of challenge is not just about the content. You can also tier lessons using any of the following four aspects (Kingore, 2006):

- *Degree of assistance.* If some students need additional support, you can partner students, provide examples, help them brainstorm ideas, or provide a cue sheet (Figure 4.3).
- *Structure of the task.* Some students, such as students with disabilities, benefit from highly structured tasks. However, gifted students often benefit from a more open-ended structure.
- *Complexity of the task.* Make tasks more concrete or more abstract and/or include more difficult problems or applications.

• *Complexity of the process.* As you think about your learners, ask yourself these questions: How quickly should I pace this lesson? How many instructions should I give at one time? How many higher-level thinking questions are included as part of the tasks?

Consider how the following original task is adapted to change the level of challenge. Assume that the students do not know the standard algorithm for changing mixed numbers to fractions to complete the computation.

ORIGINAL TASK (GRADE 4):

Elliot is making birdhouses. He has $3\frac{1}{4}$ gallons of paint. He used $2\frac{3}{4}$ gallons to paint the birdhouses he has made. How much paint does Elliot have left? Explain how you know.

The teacher has distributed fraction circles to students to model the problem and paper and pencils to illustrate and record how they solved the problem. He asks them to model the problem and be ready to explain their solution.

ADAPTED TASK (GRADE 4):

Elliott had some paint. He uses some of it to paint birdhouses. How much paint does Elliot have left? Explain how you know.

The teacher asks students what is happening in this problem and how they might solve the problem

Figure 4.3 Problem solving cue sheet.

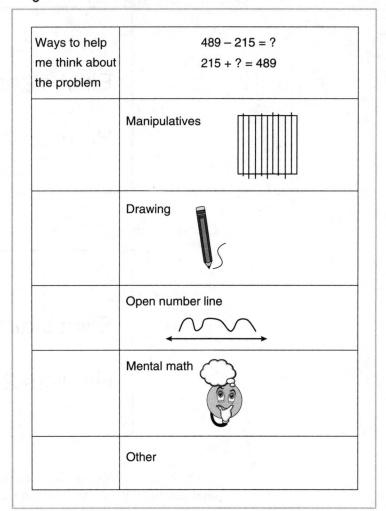

and what tools might help them solve the problem. Then he distributes task cards that indicate how much paint Elliot started with and how much he used. The teacher has varied the difficulty of the tasks by considering whether the student will need to break up the first quantity to determine the amount left. He also offers the more advanced students fractional amounts with unlike denominators.

Card 1 (easier)

Elliot starts with $3\frac{3}{4}$ gallons.

He uses $2\frac{1}{4}$ gallons.

Card 2 (middle)

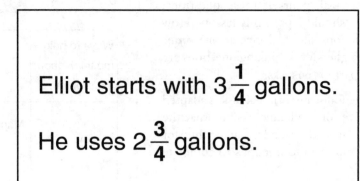

Elliot starts with $3\frac{1}{4}$ gallons.

He uses $2\frac{3}{4}$ gallons.

Card 3 (advanced)

Elliot starts with $3\frac{1}{2}$ gallons.

He uses $2\frac{1}{4}$ gallons.

In each case, students must use words, pictures, models, or numbers to show how they figured out the solution. Various tools are provided (fraction circles, fraction bars, and grid paper) for students' use.

Stop and Reflect

Which of the four aspects that change the challenge of tiered lessons was addressed in the adapted task? ■

You would preassess your students to determine the best ways to use these task cards. One option is to give students only one card, based on their current academic readiness (e.g., easy cards to those who struggle with subtraction of mixed numbers). A second option is to give out cards 1 and 2 based on readiness, then use card 2 as an extension for those who successfully complete card 1, and card 3 as an extension for those who successfully complete card 2. In each of these cases, you will need to record at the end of the lesson which students were able to model and explain the various levels of the problems so that the next lesson can be appropriately planned. Notice that this tiered lesson addresses both the complexity of the task (difficulty of different cards) and the process (instructions are broken down by first starting with the no-numbers scenario).

The following example illustrates how to tier a lesson based on structure. Notice that the different tasks vary in how open-ended the work is, yet all tasks focus on the same learning goal of identifying properties of parallelograms.

LEARNING OBJECTIVE: Classify parallelograms according to their properties (grade 5)

Students are given a collection of parallelograms including squares and rectangles as well as nonrectangular parallelograms. The following tasks are distributed to different groups, based on their learning needs and prior knowledge of quadrilaterals:

- Group A: Explore the set of parallelograms. Use your ruler and protractor to measure the parallelograms. Make a list of the defining properties that you think are true for every parallelogram. (open-ended)
- Group B: Measure the parallelograms' angles and sides using your ruler and protractor. Record any patterns related to sides, angles, and diagonals that are true for all of the parallelograms. (slightly structured)
- Group C: First, sort the parallelograms into rectangles and non-rectangles. Use a ruler to measure the sides and a protractor to measure the angles of the parallelograms. Look for patterns in your measurements that define the shapes as parallelograms. Use the following suggestions and questions to work through the problem:
  1a. What pattern do you notice about the measures of the *sides* of all the parallelograms in the *non-rectangle* set?
  1b. What pattern do you notice about the measures of the *sides* of all the parallelograms in the *rectangle* set?
  2a. What pattern do you notice about the measures of the *angles* of all the parallelograms in the *non-rectangle* set?
  2b. What pattern do you notice about the measures of the *angles* of all the parallelograms in the *rectangle* set? (most structured)

> *Teaching Tip*
>
> Make sure students understand the vocabulary used in tasks before they begin working independently. For instance, one of the tasks in the tiered lesson example uses the word *property*. Before they start the task, have a group discussion with students who are assigned that task about the meaning of the term.

The three tiers in this lesson reflect different degrees of difficulty in terms of task structure. However, all students are working on the same learning objective and they all must engage in reasoning about the properties of two-dimensional shapes to complete their tasks.

In Chapter 6 you will read about response to intervention (RtI), a multitier student-support system that offers struggling students increasing levels of intervention. We want to distinguish between the tiers in RtI and tiered lessons used in differentiation. In RtI the tiers refer to the different degrees of intervention offered to students as needed—from the first tier that occurs in a general education setting and involves the core instruction for all students based on high-quality mathematics curriculum and instructional practices to the upper tier that could involve one-on-one instruction with a special education teacher. Tiered lessons used in differentiation would be an avenue to offer high-quality core instruction for all students in the first tier or level of RtI.

◆ Flexible Grouping

Allowing students to collaborate on tasks supports and challenges their thinking and increases their opportunities to communicate about mathematics and build understanding. In addition, many students feel that working in groups improves their confidence, engagement, and understanding (Nebesniak & Heaton, 2010). Even students who prefer to work alone need to learn the life skill of collaboration and should be provided opportunities to work with others.

Determining how to place students in groups is an important decision. Avoid continually grouping by ability. This kind of grouping, although well-intentioned, perpetuates low levels of learning and actually increases the gap between more and less dependent students. Instead, consider using *flexible grouping* in which the size and makeup of small groups vary in a purposeful and strategic manner (Murray & Jorgensen, 2007). When coupled with the use of differentiation strategies, flexible grouping gives all students the chance to work successfully in groups.

Flexible groups can vary based on students' readiness, interests, language proficiency, and learning profiles, as well as the nature of the tasks. For example, sometimes students can work with a partner because the nature of the task best suits two people working together. At other times, flexible groups might be created with four students because their assigned task has enough components or roles to warrant a larger team. Note that it can be effective to occasionally place struggling learners with more capable students who are likely to be helpful. However, consistently pairing struggling learners with more capable students is not helpful for either group. The idea behind flexible grouping is that groups can and do easily change in response to all students' readiness, interests, and learning profiles and the nature of the task they will be doing.

Regardless of how you group your students, the first key to successful grouping is individual accountability. Although the group is working together on a task, individuals must be able to explain the content, the process, and the product. Second, and equally important, is building a sense of shared responsibility within a group. At the start of the year, it is important to engage students in team-building activities and to set expectations that all group members will participate in the assigned group tasks and that all group members will be responsible for ensuring that the entire group understands the concept.

Reinforcing individual accountability and shared responsibility may create a shift in your role as the teacher. When a member of a small group asks you a question, pose the question to the whole group to find out what the other members think. Students will soon learn that they must use teammates as their first resource and seek teacher help only when the whole group needs help. Also, when you are observing groups, rather than asking a student what she is doing, ask another student in the group to explain what the first student is doing. Having all students participate in the oral report to the whole class also builds individual accountability. Letting students know that you may call on any member to explain what the group did is a good way to ensure that all group members understand what they did. In addition, having students individually write and record their strategies and solutions is important. Using these techniques will increase the effectiveness of grouping, which in turn will help students learn mathematical concepts more successfully.

Stop and Reflect

Why is teaching mathematics through problem solving (i.e., a problem-based approach) a good way to differentiate instruction and reach all students in a classroom? ■

5

Planning, Teaching, and Assessing Culturally and Linguistically Diverse Students

One of the aims of schools should be to produce citizens who treat one another with respect, who value the contributions of those with whom they interact irrespective of race, class, or gender, and who act with a sense of social justice.

Boaler (2006, p. 74)

Culturally and Linguistically Diverse Students

We are lucky to be in a country in which people from all over the world bring us rich diversity in cultural practices and languages. Students' native languages are not only an important part of their cultural heritage, but students also think, communicate, and learn in their native languages. Since 1980, the number of school-aged children who speak a language other than English at home has risen from 4.7 million to 11.2 million (National Center for Education Statistics, 2011).

Jo Boaler's quote captures the essence of the equity principle from *Principles and Standards for School Mathematics:* "Excellence in mathematics education requires equity—high expectations and strong support for all students" (NCTM, 2000, p. 12). Teaching for equity is much more than providing students with an equal opportunity to learn mathematics. Attention to language and culture, two interrelated and critical considerations, is important in planning, teaching, and assessing students from diverse backgrounds. Students who are given instructional tasks that are well-supported and thought provoking—rather than low-level tasks with short-term gains—can reach higher levels of mathematical proficiency.

◆ Funds of Knowledge

Students from different countries, regions, or experiences, including those who speak different languages, are often viewed as challenges to a teacher or school. Rather, students' varied languages and backgrounds should be seen as a resource in teaching (Gutierrez, 2009). Valuing a person's cultural background is more than a belief statement; it is a set of intentional actions that communicates to the student, "I want to know about you, I want you to see mathematics as part of your life, and I expect that you can do high-level mathematics." In getting to know students, we access their funds of knowledge (the essential knowledge or information students use to survive and thrive) (Gonzáles, Moll, & Amanti, 2005). Instead of teaching English language learners (ELLs) from a deficit model (lack of knowledge and experience), we can connect their experiences at home and with family to those of the mathematics classroom. The more we enhance learning for all students, regardless of their places of birth, the more enriched the opportunities for learning become.

◆ Mathematics as a Language

Mathematics is commonly referred to as a *universal language*, but this is not entirely true. Conceptual knowledge (e.g., division) is universal. Procedures (e.g., how you divide) and symbols are culturally determined and are not universal. Treating mathematics as universally

 Table 5.1 Steps and Thought Processes of Division Algorithm Common in France, Spain, and Central and South America

Step in the Algorithm	Explanation or Think Aloud for the Step
2144 ⌐ 32	What number times 32 is close to 214? 6 is close because 6 times 2 is twelve and 18 and 1 is 19. 7 is too big since 7 times 2 is 14 and 21 plus 1 is 22, so it must be 6.
2144 ⌐ 32 ⟍ 6	6 times 32 is 192.
192 ⟍ 2144 ⌐ 32 ⟍ 6	214 minus 192 is 22, and bring down the 4.
192 ⟍ 2144 ⌐ 32 ⟍ 224 6	What number times 32 is close to 224? 7. 7 times 32 is 224.
224 ⟍ 192 ⟍ 2144 ⌐ 32 ⟍ 224 67	224 minus 224 is 0.
224 ⟍ 192 ⟍ 2144 ⌐ 32 ⟍ 224 67 ⟍ 0	The answer is 67.

the same can lead to inequities in the classroom. For example, the division process in France, Spain, Honduras, Cuba, and other countries varies from that used in the United States, as does the language and notation that is used to describe the process (Perkins & Flores, 2002; Secada, 1983) (see Table 5.1).

Another example is simplifying expressions such as $2(8 + 15 - 11)$ (*Common Core State Standards* content for fifth grade). In the United States, students are typically instructed to simplify inside the parentheses first (order of operations). But in Mexican textbooks, the expression is evaluated by using the distributive property, $2(8 + 15 - 11) = 2 \times 8 + 2 \times 15 - 2 \times 11 = 16 + 30 - 22 = 24$ (Perkins & Flores, 2002). Notice that both ways are equivalent and accurate. Making the connection between these two approaches explicit (1) honors different cultural approaches and (2) aligns with the vision in the *Common Core State Standards*—to teach mathematics with deep understanding.

How we do mathematics is also influenced by culture. For example, mental mathematics is highly valued in many countries, whereas in the United States recording every step is valued. Compare the following two division problems from a fourth-grade classroom (Midobuche, 2001):

Can you follow what the first student did? If you learned division in the United States, this is likely easy to follow. But, if you learned division in another country, you may wonder why the first solution has so many steps. Can you follow the second example? It is, in effect, the same thinking process, only the multiplication and related subtraction are done mentally. The critical equity question, though, is not just whether you can follow an alternative approach, but how you will respond when you encounter a student using such an approach.

- Will you require the students to show their steps (disregarding the way they learned it)?
- Will you ask students to elaborate on how they did it?
- Will you have students show other students their way of thinking?

The latter two responses communicate to students that you are interested in their way of knowing mathematics and that there are many ways in which different people and different cultures approach mathematics. Supporting invented strategies for algorithms is an important way to show that you value students as individuals and a good way to gain insights into useful and interesting culturally influenced strategies.

Teaching Tip

Instead of requiring students to write all their steps, ask them to think aloud as they solve a problem or ask how they did it in their head.

⬥ Culturally Responsive Instruction

Culture and language are interwoven and interrelated. Therefore, teaching strategies that support diverse learners often support both cultural diversity and language. For example, if you invite students to talk to a partner before sharing with the whole class, you not only provide ELLs with an additional speaking opportunity to support language development, but you also distribute the sharing, listening, and teaching, so you are sharing power within the classroom community.

Culturally responsive mathematics instruction is not just for recent immigrants; it is for all students, including students from different ethnic groups, different socioeconomic levels, and so on. It includes consideration for content, relationships, cultural knowledge, flexibility in approaches, use of accessible learning contexts (i.e., contexts familiar or interesting to students), a responsive learning community, and working in cross-cultural partnerships (Averill, Anderson, Easton, Te Maro, Smith, & Hynds, 2009). As described in Chapter 4, differentiation can be accomplished by adapting the content, process, product, and the classroom environment (Tomlinson, 2003). Following are four strategies for differentiating that address the specific needs of linguistically and culturally diverse students. These ideas are also presented in an at-a-glance format in Table 5.2.

Table 5.2 At-a-Glance Focus on Culturally Relevant Mathematics Instruction

Aspect of Culturally Relevant Instruction	Reflection Questions to Guide Teaching and Assessing
Communicate high expectations.	Does the content include a balance of procedures and concepts? Are students expected to engage in problem solving and generate their own approaches to problems? Are connections made between mathematics topics?
Make content relevant.	In what ways is the content related to familiar aspects of students' lives? In what ways is prior knowledge elicited/reviewed so that all students can participate in the lesson? To what extent are students asked to make connections between school mathematics and mathematics in their own lives? How are student interests (events, issues, literature, or pop culture) used to build interest and mathematical meaning?
Communicate the value of students' identities.	In what ways are students invited to include their own experiences within a lesson? Are story problems generated from students and teachers? Do stories reflect the real experiences of students? Are individual student approaches presented and showcased so that each student sees his or her ideas as important to the teacher and peers? Are alternative algorithms shared as a point of excitement and pride (as appropriate)? Are multiple modes to demonstrate knowledge (e.g., visuals, explanations, models) valued?
Model shared power.	Are students (rather than just the teacher) justifying the correctness of solutions? Are students invited to (and expected to) engage in whole-class discussions in which students share ideas and respond to each other's ideas? In what ways are roles assigned so that every student feels that he or she contributes to the class and learns from other members of the class? Are students given a choice in how they solve a problem or in how they demonstrate knowledge of the concept?

Focus on Important Mathematics

Too often, our first attempt to help ELLs is to simplify the mathematics or remove the language from the lesson. Simplifying or removing language can take away opportunities to learn. Culturally responsive instruction stays focused on the big ideas of mathematics (i.e., based on standards such as the *Common Core State Standards*) and helps students engage in and stay focused on those big ideas. For example, in a lesson on perimeter and area of nonstandard shapes, a recording sheet might begin with definitions of each term and then a drawing or photograph added to illustrate the situation (Murrey, 2008). The teacher can incorporate opportunities for students to share their definitions and to discuss the meaning of the task prior to engaging in solving it. In this way, ELLs are able to use appropriate mathematical language and focus on finding a solution.

Make Content Relevant

There are really two components to making content relevant. One is to think about the mathematics: "Is the mathematics itself presented meaningfully and is it connected to other content?" The second is to contextualize the content so that it is grounded in familiarity.

Mathematical Connections.

Helping students see that mathematical ideas are interrelated will fill in or deepen their understanding of and connections to previously taught content. For example, consider the following fifth-grade problem:

Melissa is making braided bracelets. To prepare one she needs six strands of colored rope, each of them $1\frac{1}{4}$ feet long. She wants to make 8, one for each of her friends who are coming to her party. How much rope does she need to have?

You may recognize that this task includes adding and multiplying fractions. Although the mathematics is already presented in a conceptual and meaningful manner, it is important to connect whole number and fraction operations. For example, to find how much rope is needed for 8 people ($6 \times 1\frac{1}{4}$ feet, or $7\frac{1}{2}$ feet per person, then $8 \times 7\frac{1}{2}$ to find total amount of rope), a student may use addition because of the fraction, not recognizing that multiplication can be used. Asking questions such as, "How did you solve it?" or "How did you decide to [add/multiply]?" and "Are these ways equivalent?" helps students make meaningful connections between whole numbers and fractions and between addition and multiplication.

Context Connections.

Making content relevant is also about contexts. The context of creating bracelets grounds student thinking in something familiar so they can focus on reasoning about the mathematical relationships. Using problems that connect students to developmentally appropriate social or peer connections is one way to contextualize learning. Another is to make connections to historical or cultural contexts. Seeing mathematics from various cultures provides opportunities for students to "put faces" on mathematical contributions. For example, the Mayan place-value system can be introduced as a way to think about the structure of our base-ten system. Students can then apply this understanding to large numbers (grades 3 through 5) and decimal fractions (grade 4). Or you can have students create freedom quilts, which tell stories about the Underground Railroad (Neumann, 2005) and can be used to develop *Common Core State Standards* goals such as discovering that shapes can be partitioned into different shapes that each have the same area (grade 3) or classifying shapes based on properties (grades 3 through 5).

Incorporate Students' Identities

Incorporating students' identities in the mathematics they do overlaps with the previous category, but it merits its own discussion. Students should see themselves in mathematics and see that mathematics is a part of their culture. The classroom environment should incorporate students' cultural practices. For example, students from some countries may not feel comfortable challenging an approach used by another student in a classroom discussion.

Both researchers and teachers have found that telling stories about their own lives, or asking students to tell stories, makes the mathematics relevant to students and can raise student achievement (Turner, Celedón-Pattichis, Marshall, & Tennison, 2009). Table 5.3 provides ideas for making mathematics relevant to a student's home and community.

The following teacher's story illustrates one way to incorporate family history and culture by reading *The Hundred Penny Box* (Mathis, 1986). In Mathis's story, a 100-year-old woman remembers an important event in every year of her life as she turns over each of her 100 pennies. Each penny is more than a piece of money; it is a "memory trigger" for her life.

> Taking a cue from the book, I asked each student to collect one penny from each year they were alive starting from the year of their birth and not missing a year. Students were encouraged to bring in additional pennies their classmates might need. Then the students consulted with family members to create a penny time line of important events in their lives. Using information gathered at home, they started with the year they were born, listing their birthday and then recording first steps, accidents, vacations, pets, births of siblings, and so on.

Students in grades 3 through 5 can prepare time lines too, determining the important events that happened each year since their birth. The number line is an important model to use in teaching fractions and this context helps students build meaning of fractions on the number line. For example, you can ask students "What events happened in the first $\frac{1}{4}$ of your life?"

Table 5.3 Where to Find Mathematics in Students' Homes and Community

Where to Look	What You Might Ask Students to Record and Share (and Mathematics That Can Be Explored)
Grocery store or market place	• Cost of an item of which they bought more than one (multiplication) • Cost of an item that came with a quantity (e.g., dozen eggs) (division) • Better buy of two different-sized items (division) • Shapes of different containers (geometry) • Different types/brands of foods they select, such as what kind of bread) (data)
Photographs	• Of a person they admire (data) • Of a favorite scene (geometry, measurement) • Of 2-D and 3-D shapes in their home or neighborhood (geometry) • Of a flower (multiplication with number of petals, algebraic thinking)
Artifact (game or measuring device) from their culture or that is a favorite	• The game likely involves mathematics. • Measuring devices can be used to explore fractions and decimals.

or "What has happened in the most recent $\frac{1}{6}$ of your life?" or "If you had a sister born when you were 2, in what fraction of your life have you had that sister?"

Ensure Shared Power

When we think about creating a positive classroom environment, one in which all students feel as if they can participate and learn, we are addressing considerations related to power. The teacher plays a major role in establishing and distributing power, whether it is intentional or not. In many classrooms, the teacher has the power—telling students whether answers are right or wrong (rather than having students determine correctness through reasoning), demonstrating processes for how to solve problems (rather than giving choices for how students will engage in the problem), and determining who will solve which problems (rather than allowing flexibility and choice for students). The way that you assign groups, seat students, and call on students sends clear messages about who has power in the classroom.

Teaching Culturally and Linguistically Diverse Students

Creating effective learning opportunities for ELLs involves integrating the principles of bilingual education with those of standards-based mathematics instruction. When learning about mathematics, students may be learning content in English for which they do not know the words in their native language (e.g., *numerator* and *denominator* in the study of fractions). In addition, story problems are difficult for ELLs, not only due to the language but also to the fact that sentences in story problems are often structured differently from sentences in conversational English (Janzen, 2008). Teachers of English to Speakers of Other Languages (TESOL), a professional organization focused on the needs of ELLs, argues that ELLs need to use both English and their native language to read, write, listen, and speak as they learn appropriate content—a position similarly addressed in NCTM standards documents and position statements. The strategies discussed in this section are the ones that appear most frequently in the literature as critical to increasing the academic achievement of ELLs in mathematics classrooms

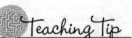
Teaching Tip

Any one of the categories in Table 5.4 could be the focus of a lesson study, discussions with colleagues, or the basis for individual reflection. The importance lies not in the specific suggestions, but in the concept of having an eye on language development and mathematics content.

(e.g., Celedón-Pattichis & Ramirez, 2012; Echevarria, Vogt, & Short, 2008). Table 5.4 offers reflective questions related to instructional planning for and the teaching of ELLs.

◆ Focus on Academic Vocabulary

ELLs enter the mathematics classroom from homes in which English is not the primary language of communication. Although a person may develop conversational English language skills in a few years, it takes as many as seven years to learn *academic language*, which is the language specific to a content area such as mathematics (Cummins, 1994). Academic language is harder to learn because it is not used in a student's everyday world. In addition, there are unique features of the language of mathematics that make it difficult for many students, in particular those who are learning English. Teaching the academic language of mathematics evolves over time and requires thoughtful and reflective instructional planning.

Honor Use of Native Language

Valuing students' native languages is one of the ways you value their cultural heritage. In a mathematics classroom, students can communicate in their native language while continuing

Table 5.4 Reflective Questions for Planning and Teaching Mathematics Lessons for ELLs

Process	Mathematics Content Considerations	Language Considerations
Reflective Questions for Planning		
1. Determine the mathematics.	• What mathematical concepts (aligned to grade-level standards) am I teaching? • What student-friendly learning objectives will I post? • How does this mathematics concept connect to other concepts students have learned?	• What language objectives might I add (e.g., include reading, writing, speaking, and listening)? • What visuals or words will I use to communicate the content and language objectives?
2. Consider students' needs.	• How can I connect the content to be taught to content that students have learned? Or, how will I fill in gaps if students don't have prerequisite content needed for the lesson?	• What context or models might I select that are a good match to students' social/cultural backgrounds and previously learned vocabulary?
3. Select, design, or adapt a task.	• What task can I use that addresses the content identified in item 1 and the needs of my students identified in item 2? • How might I adapt a task so that it has multiple entry and exit points (i.e., is challenging and accessible to a range of students)?	• What context might I use that is meaningful to the students' cultures and backgrounds? • What language pitfalls does the task have? Which of these will I eliminate and which of these need explicit attention? • Which words or phrases, even if familiar to students, take on new meaning in a mathematics context (e.g., homonyms, homophones, and words such as *degree, table, find*)?
Reflective Questions for Teaching		
1. Introduce the task (the *Before* phase).	• How will I introduce the task in a way that elicits prior mathematics knowledge needed for the task? • Is a similar task needed to build background related to the content (or would such a preview take away from the purpose or challenge of the task)?	• How can I connect the task to students' experiences and to familiar contexts? • What key vocabulary do I want to introduce so that the words will be used throughout the lesson? (Post key vocabulary in a prominent location.) • What visuals and real objects can I use that bring meaning to the selected task? • How can I present the task in visual, written, and oral formats? • How will I be sure that students understand what they are to do in the *During* phase?
2. Work on the task (the *During* phase).	• What hints or assists might I give students as they work that will help them focus without taking away their thinking? • What extensions or challenges will I offer for students who successfully solve the task? • What questions will I pose to push the mathematics identified in the learning goals?	• Have I grouped students for both academic and language support? • Have I encouraged students to draw pictures, make diagrams, and/or use manipulatives? • Have I used strategies to reduce the linguistic demands without hindering the problem solving (e.g., using a graphic organizer, sentence starters such as "I solved the problem by. . . .", recording tables, and concept maps).

Table 5.4 (Continued)

Process	Mathematics Content Considerations	Language Considerations
3. Debrief and discuss the task and the mathematics (the *After* phase).	• How will students report their findings? • How will I format the discussion of the task? • What questions will I pose to push the mathematics identified in the learning goals?	• What ways can I maximize language use in nonthreatening ways (e.g., think-pair-share)? • How can I encourage and reinforce different formats (multiple exit points) for demonstrating understanding of the lesson content? • How might I provide advance notice, language support, or rehearsal to ELLs so that they will be comfortable speaking to their peers? • Am I using appropriate "wait time"?
Formative Assessment		
Throughout lesson and unit	• What questions will I ask during the lesson, or what will I look for in students' work as evidence of learning the objectives (*During* and *After* phases)? • What follow-up might I provide to students who are not demonstrating understanding of the mathematics?	• What words will I use in my questions to be sure the questions are understood? How might I use a translator to assist in assessment? • If a student is not succeeding, how might I diagnose whether the problem is with language, mathematics content, or both? • What accommodations can I provide to be sure I am accessing what the students know?

their English language development (Haas & Gort, 2009; Moschkovich, 2009; Setati, 2005). For example, a good strategy for students working in small groups is having students discuss the problem in their preferred language. If a student knows enough English, then the presentation in the *After* phase of the lesson can be shared in English. If the student knows little or no English and does not have access to a peer who shares his or her native language, then a translator, use of a web-based dictionary, or a self-made mathematics-focused dictionary can be a strong support. Students within the small group can be coached to use visual aids and pictures to communicate. Teachers can look up the essential terms in a student's native language to assist students. Bilingual students will often code-switch, moving between two languages. Research indicates that this practice of code-switching supports mathematical reasoning because students select the language from which they can best express their ideas (Moschkovich, 2009).

Certain native languages can support learning mathematics words. Because English, Spanish, French, Portuguese, and Italian all have their roots in Latin, many mathematics words are similar across languages (Celedón-Pattichis, 2009; Gómez, 2010). For example, *aequus* (Latin), *equal* (English), and *igual* (Spanish) are cognates. See whether you can figure out the English mathematic terms for the following Spanish words: *división*, *hexágano*, *ángulo*, *triángulo*, *álgebra*, *circunferencia*, and *cubo*. Students may not make this connection if you do not point it out, so it is important to explicitly teach students to look for cognates.

Use Content and Language Objectives

If students know the purpose of a lesson, they are better able to make sense of the details when they are challenged by some of the oral or written explanations. When language expectations are explicitly included, students will know that they will be responsible for reaching certain language goals alongside mathematical goals and will be more likely to attempt to learn those skills or words. Here are two examples of dual objectives:

1. Students will analyze properties and attributes of three-dimensional solids. (mathematics)

2. Students will describe in writing and orally a similarity and a difference between two different solids. (language and mathematics)

Explicitly Teach Vocabulary

Intentional vocabulary instruction must be part of mathematics instruction for all students. This includes attention to terms within a lesson and additional opportunities to develop academic language. These additional opportunities can reinforce understanding as they help students learn the terminology. Examples include the following:

- Self-made dictionaries that link concepts and terms with drawings or clip art
- Foldables of key words for a topic
- Games focused on vocabulary development (e.g., Pictionary or $10,000 Pyramid)
- Interactive word walls, including visuals and translations

In addition, many websites provide translations students can use to create cards with terms and their translations and to build personal mathematics dictionaries (Kersaint, Thompson, & Petkova, 2009).

Teaching Tip

> Not all vocabulary should be "previewed" because the term (and its concept) can sometimes be better understood after some exploration has occurred.

All students benefit from an increased focus on language; however, too much emphasis on vocabulary can diminish the focus on mathematics. It is important that the language support be *connected* to the mathematics and the selected task or activity.

As you analyze a lesson, you must identify terms related to the mathematics and to the context that may need explicit attention. Consider the following grade 4 short constructed response item (medium level of difficulty) from the 2009 National Assessment of Educational Progress (NAEP) (National Center for Education Statistics, n.d.):

Sam did the following problems.

$$2 + 1 = 3$$
$$6 + 1 = 7$$

Sam concluded that when he adds 1 to any whole number, his answer will always be odd. Is Sam correct? _____
Explain your answer.

In order for students to engage in this task, the terms *even* and *odd* must be understood. Both terms may be known for other meanings beyond the mathematics classroom (*even* can mean level and *odd* can mean strange). *Concluded* is not a math word, but also must be understood if an ELL student is to understand the meaning of the problem. Finally, you must give guidance on how students will explain their answers—do they need to use words, or can they use pictures or diagrams?

Stop and Reflect

Odd and *even* are among hundreds of words whose meanings in mathematics are different from everyday usage. Other terms include *product, mean, sum, factor, acute, foot, division, difference, similar,* and *angle.* Can you name five others? ■

◆ Lesson Considerations

Support for academic language use is a significant part of lesson considerations. In addition, facilitating discourse that provides access to ELLs is critical. This includes (1) efforts to ensure ELLs understand and have the background for engaging in the focus tasks and (2) the need to put structures in place for student participation throughout the lesson.

Build Background

Similar to building on prior knowledge, building background also takes into consideration native language and culture as well as content (Echevarria, Vogt, & Short, 2008). If possible, use a context and appropriate visuals to help students understand the task you want them to solve. This is a nonthreatening and engaging way to help students make connections between what they have learned and what they need to learn.

Some aspects of English and mathematics are particularly challenging to ELLs (Whiteford, 2009/2010). For example, teen numbers sound a lot like their decade number—if you say *sixteen* and *sixty* out loud, you can hear how similar they are. Emphasizing the *n* sound helps ELLs hear the difference. The *th* sound for decimal place values also needs emphasis so that students hear the difference between hundreds and hundredths. Remember, too, that the U.S. measurement system, in particular conversions between units (e.g., from inches to feet), may be unfamiliar to ELLs. When encountering content that may be unfamiliar or difficult for ELLs, devote additional time to build background so that students can engage in the mathematical tasks without also having to navigate language and background knowledge.

Use Comprehensible Input

Comprehensible input means that the message you are communicating is understandable to students. Modifications include simplifying sentence structures and limiting the use of nonessential or confusing vocabulary (Echevarria, Short, & Vogt, 2008). Note that these modifications do not lower expectations for the lesson. Sometimes unnecessary words and phrases in questions make them less clear to nonnative speakers. Compare the two sets of teachers' instructions:

NOT MODIFIED:

You have a worksheet in front of you that I just gave out. For every situation, I want you to determine the total area for the shapes. You will be working with your partner, but each of you needs to record your answers on your own paper and explain how you got your answer. If you get stuck on a problem, raise your hand.

MODIFIED:

Please look at your paper. (Holds paper and points to the first picture.) You will find the area of each shape. What does area mean? (Allows wait time.) How can you calculate area? (*Calculate* is more like the Spanish word *calcular,* so it is more accessible to Spanish speakers.) Talk to your partner. (Points to mouth and then to a pair of students as she says this.) Write your answers. (Makes a writing motion over paper.) If you get stuck (shrugs shoulders and looks confused), raise your hand (demonstrates).

Notice that three things have been done: sentences have been shortened, confusing words have been removed, and related gestures and motions have been added to the oral directives. Also, notice the wait time the teacher gives. It is very important to provide extra time after posing a question or giving instructions to allow ELLs time to translate, make sense of the request, and then participate.

Another way to provide comprehensible input is to use a variety of tools to help students visualize and understand what is verbalized. In the preceding example, the teacher models the instructions. Effective tools include manipulatives, real objects, pictures, visuals, multimedia, demonstrations, and children's literature (Echevarria, Vogt, & Short, 2008). Students should be expected to include various representations of their understandings such as drawing and writing to explain what they have done. Doing so helps to develop students' understanding and language while giving the teacher a better idea of what they do and do not understand. For example, if you are teaching volume of rectangular solids, show different kinds of cubes (e.g., 1-inch cubes, 1-centimeter cubes, number cubes). Ask students, "How many same-sized cubes will fill the rectangular container?" And, as you ask, physically move some cubes into the container to illustrate. Review terms for the container (base, length, width, height) and label a container for reference. Students should be expected to include multiple representations of their understandings such as drawing, writing, and explanation of what they have done.

Engage Students in Discourse That Reflects Language Needs

Discourse, or the use of classroom discussion, is essential for the learning of *all* students, but is particularly important for ELLs who need to engage in productive language (writing and speaking) as well as receptive language (listening and reading). As noted in the *Application of Common Core State Standards for English Learners,*

> ELLs are capable of participating in mathematical discussions as they learn English. Mathematics instruction for ELL students should draw on multiple resources and modes available in classrooms—such as objects, drawings, inscriptions, and gestures—as well as home languages and mathematical experiences outside of school. Mathematical instruction should address mathematical discourse and academic language." (CCSSO, 2011, p. 2)

There are strategies you can use in classroom discourse that help ELLs understand and participate. As described in the preceding quote, the use of gestures and visuals is critical to learning English and mathematics. For example, *revoicing* is a research-based strategy that helps ELLs hear an idea more than once and hear it restated with the appropriate language applied to concepts. But, because ELLs cannot always explain their ideas fully, don't rush to call on someone else; instead, patiently press for details. Pressing for details is not done just so the teacher can decide whether the idea makes sense; it also allows other students to make sense of the idea too (Maldonado, Turner, Dominguez, & Empson, 2009). Because practicing language is important for ELLs, having opportunities for students to practice phrases or words through think-pair-share or choral response also is effective. Finally, students from other countries often solve or record problems differently, so inviting ELLs to share how they solved the problem can enhance the richness of discussion around different approaches to problems.

Teaching Tip

Making the strategies of ELLs public and connecting these strategies to others is interesting and supports the learning of all students while building the confidence of ELLs.

Plan Cooperative/Interdependent Groups to Support Language

The use of cooperative groups is a valuable way to differentiate instruction. For ELLs, groups provide the opportunity to use language, but only if the groups are carefully formed in a way that considers students' language skills. Placing an ELL with two English-speaking students may result in the ELL being left out. On the other hand, grouping all Spanish speakers together prevents these students from having the opportunity to hear and participate in mathematics in English. Consider placing a bilingual student in a group with a student with limited English, or place students that have the same first language together with native speakers so that they can help each other understand and participate (Garrison, 1997; Khisty, 1997).

◆ Implementing Strategies for ELLs

The strategies just described are subtle moves in teaching. As you read the following vignette, look for strategies that the teacher applies to provide support for ELLs while keeping expectations high.

Ms. Steimer is teaching a third-grade lesson that involves the concepts of estimating length (in inches) and measuring to the nearest half inch. The task asks students to use estimation to find three objects that are about 6 inches long, three objects that are about 1 foot long, and three objects that are about 2 feet long. Once identified, students are to measure the nine objects to the nearest half inch and compare the measurements with their estimates.

Ms. Steimer has several English language learners in her class, including a student from Korea who knows very little English and a student from Mexico who speaks English well but is new to U.S. schools. These two students are not familiar with the measurement units of feet or inches. Ms. Steimer knows they will likely struggle in trying to estimate or measure in inches and will not have measured using fractions. She takes time to address the language and the increments on the ruler to the entire class. Because the word *foot* has two meanings, Ms. Steimer decides to address that explicitly before launching into the lesson. She begins by asking students what a "foot" is. She allows time for them to discuss the word with a partner and then share their answers with the class. She explains that today they are going to be using the measuring unit of a foot (while holding up the foot ruler). She asks students what other units can be used to measure. In particular, she asks her English language learners to share what units they use in their countries of origin, having metric rulers to show the class. She asks students to study the ruler and compare the centimeter to the inch by posing these questions: "Can you estimate about how many centimeters are in an inch? In 6 inches? In a foot?"

Moving to the lesson objectives, Ms. Steimer draws a large line on the board to represent an inch on the ruler. She marks the halfway point and labels the ends of the giant inch as 18 inches and 19 inches. Below it she draws a snake whose length ends at the $18\frac{1}{2}$ inch mark. Then she asks students how long the snake is and writes the measurement $18\frac{1}{2}$ inches on the board. Next, she asks students to tear a paper strip that they estimate is 6 inches long. Students then measure their paper strips using their rulers, writing down their measurement to the nearest half inch. Now she has them ready to begin estimating and measuring.

Stop and Reflect

What specific strategies to support ELLs can you identify? ■

There are a number of strategies in the vignette that provide support for ELLs: recognizing the potential language confusion around the word *foot*, as well as lack of familiarity with U.S. measurement; using the think-pair-share technique; and looking at the ruler to compare measurement systems. Using concrete models (the ruler and the torn paper strip) to build on students' prior experiences (use of the metric system in Korea and Mexico) and visuals (illustrating on the board how to read the $\frac{1}{2}$ on the ruler with a giant inch) provide support. Most important, Ms. Steimer did not diminish the challenge of the task with these strategies. If she had altered the task—for example, not expecting the ELLs to estimate since they didn't know how to measure using an inch—she would have lowered her expectations. Conversely, if she had simply posed the problem without taking time to have students study a ruler or provide other visuals, she might have kept her expectations high but failed to provide the support that would enable her students to succeed. Finally, by making a connection for all students to the metric system, she showed respect for the students' cultures and broadened the horizons of other students regarding measurements in other countries.

◆ Assessment Considerations

Throughout the discussion of strategies for supporting ELLs are opportunities for assessment. Formative assessment, as described in Chapter 3, is embedded in instruction and informs instructional decisions. For example, the use of visuals and gestures is important in helping ELLs to

- Understand the instructions and mathematical ideas (comprehensible *input*)
- Participate in the lesson (small groups or discussion)
- Communicate their own understanding (formative assessment).

The use of native language is also important for assessment. Research shows that ELLs perform better when a test is given in their native language (Robinson, 2010). If a teacher wants to understand what a student knows about mathematics, then the student should be able to communicate that understanding in a way that is best for the student, even if the teacher may need a translation.

Several strategies can assist teachers in using formative assessments with ELLs, including tasks with multiple entry and exit points, diagnostic interviews, tasks that limit linguistic load, accommodations, and self-assessments.

Select Tasks with Multiple Entry and Exit Points

An aspect of teaching mathematics through problem solving that is important, particularly for ELLs, is to select tasks carefully. If a problem can be solved in multiple ways, an ELL is more likely to be able to design a strategy that makes sense and then illustrate that strategy. Inviting students to show and/or explain their strategies provides options for ELLs to use words and pictures to communicate their thinking.

Use Diagnostic Interviews

Chapter 3 provides a strong foundation on diagnostic interviews, which are critical for ELLs because of the insights they can provide related to language and mathematical understanding.

When ELLs do not get a correct answer or cannot explain a response, teachers tend to think it is a lack of mathematical understanding rather than a language issue. This is particularly true with ELLs who have a pretty strong ability to communicate in everyday English (as opposed to academic English). Before drawing conclusions about what mathematics a student does and does not understand, it is important to observe whether it is content or language that is causing a problem. This dilemma is nicely illustrated in the problem presented in Figure 5.1 (Fernandez, Anhalt, & Civil, 2009).

Stop and Reflect

Before reading further, review Figure 5.1 and consider what you think might have prevented students from answering the problem correctly. ∎

As you reviewed the problem, you may have considered numerous reasons that students might have struggled with this problem, including a lack of understanding the mathematical concept of perimeter, or the terminology of perimeter, square, or triangle. What did the diagnostic interviews reveal? Students struggled with what the question was asking. The word *if* stumped one student because she did not understand the "if . . . then" meaning in mathematics (a challenge for native English speakers as well). Once the word *if* was removed from the sentence, she was able to solve the problem. Most of the students interviewed could solve the problem once they understood it.

This perimeter problem reminds us of how important it is to follow up with students when they are not successful on a task in order to figure out why. The fact that there are many possible reasons why a student might not be able to solve a task, some related to language and others to mathematics, is a strong argument for using diagnostic interviews. If we misdiagnose the reason for a student's struggles, our interventions will be misguided.

Diagnostic interviews also can be used prior to instruction in order to assess the mathematical and language needs of students. Hearing an ELL's interpretation of a problem and seeing how she approaches the problem provide valuable insights that you can incorporate into your planning and teaching.

Limit Linguistic Load

If you are trying to assess student understanding, look for language that can interfere with students' understanding the situation (e.g., unneeded elaboration in a story, difficult or unfamiliar vocabulary). Consider the perimeter problem in Figure 5.1. It is important for students to learn the meaning of "if . . . then" phrases, but it would have been more clear if the problem had been stated as: "The square and the triangle have the same perimeter. What is the length of one side of the square?" Removing pronouns like *they*, *this*, *that*, *his*, *her*, and using actual names can assist ELLs in understanding some problems. For example, recall the bracelet problem:

Melisa is making braided bracelets. To prepare one she needs six strands of colored rope, each of them $1\frac{1}{4}$ feet long. She wants to make 8, one for each of her friends who are coming to her party. How much rope does she need to have?

Figure 5.1

An NAEP-released item posed to 15 fourth-grade ELL students in an after-school setting.

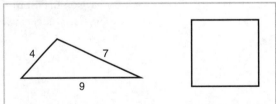

If both the square and the triangle above have the same perimeter, what is the length of each side of the square?

a. 4

b. 5

c. 6

d. 7

Source: Fernandez, Anhalt, & Civil (2009)

Rewritten, it might read:

Melisa is making bracelets. She needs six strands of rope to make one bracelet. Each strand is $1\frac{1}{4}$ feet long. Melisa wants to make 8 bracelets for her friends. How many feet of rope does Melisa need?

Notice that it is not only reducing the language, but also adding specific referents that makes the meaning of the story more clear. Of course, this particular problem could be adapted further by using illustrations and removing even more of the context, which may be more appropriate depending on the language proficiency of the ELLs.

Another way to reduce the linguistic load is to pick a context and stay with it for an entire lesson or series of lessons. This allows students to focus their thinking on the mathematics without getting bogged down in the various contexts that might be on an assessment.

Provide Accommodations

In assessing, providing accommodations refers to strategies for making sure that the assessment itself is accessible to students. This might mean being able to hear the question (students often can understand spoken English better than written English), shortening the assessment, or extending the time (Kersaint, Thompson, & Petkova, 2009). In addition, you can provide sentence starters so that the ELLs know what type of response you want. For example, "My equation fits the story because. . . ."

Incorporate Self-Assessment

It may take time to help students learn what it means to self-assess. Creating a list of content from a unit and asking students to rate how well they know it can be one way to gather information on what students know. Similarly, after a lesson, quiz, or test, students can rate or describe how hard they thought the lesson, quiz items, or test items were. This is valuable not only for you in the formative assessment process, but also for students as they learn to self-monitor and look for ways to measure their own improvement.

Stop and Reflect

The goal of equity is to offer all students access to important mathematics. What might you have on the list of things to do (and things not to do) that provide culturally and linguistically diverse students with the opportunity to learn mathematics? ∎

6

Planning, Teaching, and Assessing Students with Exceptionalities

Most low achievers in mathematics are probably "instructionally disabled," not cognitively or "learning disabled."

Baroody (2011, p. 31)

Talented [mathematics] students need teachers who can move beyond the traditional "teacher role" of a dispenser of information to that of a role model who is passionate about learning, able to translate that passion into action, aggressively curious, and comfortable with this change of role.

Greenes, Teuscher, and Regis (2010, p. 80)*

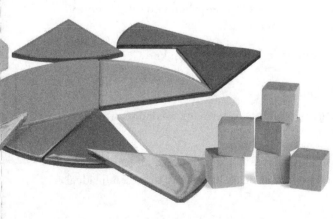

Instructional Principles for Diverse Learners

The NCTM *Principles and Standards for School Mathematics* state, "All students, regardless of their personal characteristics, backgrounds, or physical challenges must have opportunities to study—and support to

* Reprinted with permission from *Preparing Teachers for Mathematically Talented Middle School Students*, p. 80. Copyright 2010 by the National Council of Teachers of Mathematics. All rights reserved.

learn—mathematics" (NCTM, 2000, p. 12). Within the same document and as previously noted in Chapter 5, the equity principle states, "Excellence in mathematics education requires equity—high expectations and strong support for all students" (NCTM, 2000, p. 12). We know that teaching for equity is much more than providing students with an equal opportunity to learn mathematics; instead, it attempts to attain equal outcomes for all students by being sensitive to individual differences.

Many achievement gaps are actually instructional gaps or expectation gaps. It is not helpful when teachers establish low expectations for students, such as when they say, "I just cannot put this class into groups to work; they are too unruly" or "My students with disabilities can't solve word problems—they don't have the reading skills." Operating under the belief that some students cannot do mathematics ensures that they won't have ample opportunities to prove otherwise. Instead, we suggest you consider Storeygard's (2010) mantra for teachers, which proclaims "My kids can!"

As can be gleaned from the opening quotations, there is a spectrum of learners who need to be considered if we intend to have equity in our instruction. Figuring out how you will maintain equal outcomes (high expectations) while providing for individual differences (strong support) can be challenging. Equipping yourself with an ever-growing collection of instructional strategies for a variety of students is critical. A strategy that works for one student may be completely ineffective with another, even for a student with the same exceptionality. Addressing the needs of *all* students means providing access and opportunity for:

- Students who are identified as struggling or having a disability
- Students who are mathematically gifted
- Students who are unmotivated or need to build resilience

You may think, "I do not need to read the section on mathematically gifted students because they will be pulled out for math enrichment." Students who are mathematically talented need to be challenged in the daily core instruction, not just when they are participating in a program for gifted students.

The goal of equity is to offer all students access to important mathematics during their regular classroom instruction. Yet inequities exist, even if unintentionally. For example, if teachers do not build in opportunities for student-to-student interaction in a lesson, they may not be addressing the needs of girls, who are often social learners, or English language learners, who need opportunities to speak, listen, and write in small-group situations. It takes more than just wanting to be fair or equitable; it takes knowing the strategies that accommodate each type of learner and making every effort to incorporate those strategies into your teaching. "Equity does not mean that every student should receive identical instruction; instead, it demands that reasonable and appropriate accommodations be made as needed to promote access and attainment for all students" (NCTM, 2000, p. 12).

Across the wonderful and myriad diversities of your students, all students learn mathematics in essentially the same way (Fuson, 2003). The authors of *Adding It Up* (National Research Council, 2001) conclude that all students are best served when you give attention to the following three principles:

1. Learning with understanding is based on connecting and organizing knowledge around big conceptual ideas.
2. Learning builds on what students already know.
3. Instruction in school should take advantage of students' informal knowledge of mathematics.

These principles, also reflected in the tenets of constructivist theory, apply to all learners and therefore are essential in making decisions about how you can adapt instruction to meet individual learners' needs through accommodations and modifications. An *accommodation* is a response to the needs of the environment or the learner; it does not alter the task. For example, you might write down directions for a student instead of just presenting them orally. A *modification* changes the task, making it more accessible to the student. For example, if the task is finding the area of a compound shape, you might break the shape up into two rectangles and ask the student to find the area of each shape and combine. Then have the student attempt the next shape without the modification. When modifications result in an easier or less-demanding task, expectations are lowered. Modifications should be made in a way that leads back to the original task, providing scaffolding or support for learners who may need it. In the sections in this chapter, we share research-based strategies that reflect these principles while providing appropriate accommodations and modifications for the wide range of students in your classroom.

◈ Multitiered Systems of Support

In many areas, a systematic process for achieving higher levels of performance for all students often includes a multitiered system of support sometimes called *response to intervention* (RtI). This approach commonly emphasizes ways for struggling students to get immediate assistance and support rather than waiting for students to fail before they receive help. This same multitiered support system can also be used to identify students who are far exceeding standards and need additional challenges. Multitiered models are basically centered on three interwoven elements: high-quality curriculum, instructional support (interventions), and formative assessments that capture students' strengths and weaknesses. These systems of support were designed to determine whether low achievement is due to a lack of high-quality mathematics (i.e., "teacher-disabled students") (Baroody, 2011; Ysseldyke, 2002) or due to an actual learning disability. They can also help determine more intensive instructional options for students who need to catch up or those who may need to have additional advanced mathematical challenges beyond what other students study.

Response to Intervention

RtI is a multitiered student support system that is frequently represented in a three-tier triangular format. As you move up the tiers, the number of students involved decreases, the teacher–student ratio decreases, and the level of intervention increases. As you might guess, there is a variety of RtI models in use as states and districts structure their unique approaches to meet local needs. Each tier in the triangle represents a level of intervention with corresponding monitoring of results and outcomes, as shown in Figure 6.1. The foundational and largest portion of the triangle (tier 1) represents the core instruction for all students based on a high-quality mathematics curriculum, instructional practices (i.e., manipulatives, conceptual emphasis, etc.), and progress monitoring assessments. For example, if using a graphic organizer in tier 1 core instruction, the following high-quality practices would be expected in the three phases of the lesson—*Before, During,* and *After*:

𝓕𝓲𝓰𝓾𝓻𝓮 6.1

Multitiered systems of support—using effective strategies to support all students.

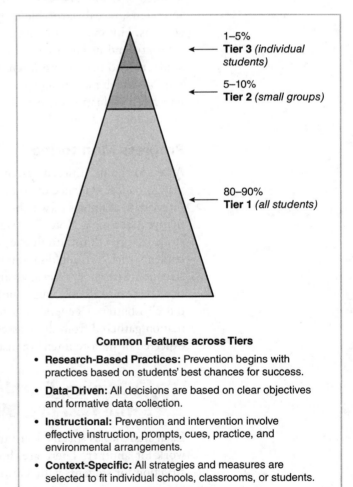

1–5%
← **Tier 3** *(individual students)*

5–10%
← **Tier 2** *(small groups)*

80–90%
← **Tier 1** *(all students)*

Common Features across Tiers

- **Research-Based Practices:** Prevention begins with practices based on students' best chances for success.
- **Data-Driven:** All decisions are based on clear objectives and formative data collection.
- **Instructional:** Prevention and intervention involve effective instruction, prompts, cues, practice, and environmental arrangements.
- **Context-Specific:** All strategies and measures are selected to fit individual schools, classrooms, or students.

Source: Based on Scott, T., and Lane, H. (2001). *Multi-Tiered Interventions in Academic and Social Contexts.* Unpublished manuscript, University of Florida, Gainesville.

- *Before:* States purpose, introduces new vocabulary, clarifies concepts from the prior knowledge in a visual organizer, and defines tasks of group members if groups are being used
- *During:* Displays directions in a chart, poster, or list; provides a set of guiding questions in a chart with blank spaces for responses
- *After:* Facilitates a discussion to highlight or make more explicit the significant concepts or skills and then presents summary and list of important concepts as they relate to one another

Tier 2 represents students who did not reach the level of achievement expected during tier 1 instructional activities. Students in tier 2 should receive supplemental targeted instruction (interventions) outside the core mathematics lessons that uses more explicit strategies with systematic teaching of critical skills and concepts, more intensive and frequent instructional opportunities, and more supportive and precise prompts (Torgesen, 2002). The National Council of Teachers of Mathematics Position Statement on Interventions (2011a) states, "Although we do not specifically state the precise interventions, we endorse the use of increasingly intensive and effective instructional interventions for students who struggle with mathematics." Interventions are "reserved for disorders that prove resistant to lower levels of prevention and require more heroic action to preclude serious complications" (Fuchs & Fuchs, 2001, p. 86).

Identifying and using these supplemental interventions is a flexible process that can be adapted or tailored based on how students respond. If further assessment, such as diagnostic interviews, reveals favorable progress, the students are weaned from the extra intervention sessions. However, if difficulties and struggles remain, the interventions can be adjusted in intensity, and in rare cases, students are referred to the next tier of support. Tier 3 is for students who need more intensive periods of instruction, sometimes with one-on-one attention, which may include comprehensive mathematics instruction or a referral for special education evaluation or special education services. Instructional strategies for the three tiers are outlined in Table 6.1.

Progress Monitoring

A key to the multitiered system of support is the monitoring of students' progress. One way to collect evidence of student knowledge of concepts is through the use of diagnostic interviews, examples of which are described throughout the book in a feature called "Formative Assessment Notes," marked with the following icon 📄. Another approach is to assess students' growth toward fluency in basic facts, an area that is a well-documented barrier for students with learning disabilities (Mazzocco, Devlin, & McKenney, 2008). Combining instruction with short daily assessments to monitor students' knowledge of number combinations that were already taught proved that the students were not only better at remembering but also better at generalizing to other facts (Woodward, 2006). The collection of information gathered from these assessments reveals whether students are making the progress expected or if more intensive instructional approaches need to be put in place.

◆ Planning, Teaching, and Assessing Students with Learning Disabilities

Each student has specific learning needs, and strategies that work for one student may not work for another. There are, however, some general ideas that can help as you plan instruction for students with learning disabilities. The following questions should guide your planning:

1. What organizational, behavioral, and cognitive skills are necessary for the students with disabilities to derive meaning from this activity?
2. Which students have known weaknesses in any of these skills or concepts?

3. How can I provide additional support in these areas of weakness so that students with learning disabilities can focus on the conceptual task in the activity? (Karp & Howell, 2004, p. 119)

Each phase of the lesson evokes specific planning considerations for students with disabilities. Some strategies apply throughout a lesson. The following discussion is not

Table 6.1 Interventions for Teaching Mathematics in a Multitiered System of Support

Tiers	Interventions
Tier 1	A highly qualified regular classroom teacher: • Incorporates high-quality rigorous curriculum and has expectations for all students to be challenged • Builds in *Common Core State Standards* Mathematical Practices and NCTM process standards • Commits to teaching the curriculum as defined • Supports students' use of multiple representations such as manipulatives, visual models, and symbols • Monitors progress to identify struggling students and students who excel at high levels • Uses flexible student grouping • Fosters active student involvement • Communicates high expectations
Tier 2	A highly qualified regular classroom teacher, with possible collaboration from a highly qualified special education teacher: • Works with students (commonly in small groups) in supplemental sessions outside of the core instruction • Conducts individual diagnostic interviews to target strengths and weaknesses • Collaborates with special education, gifted, or English language learner (ELL) teachers • Creates lessons that emphasize the big ideas (focal points) or themes • Incorporates the CSA (concrete/semi-concrete/abstract) approach • Shares thinking in a think-aloud to show students how to make problem-solving decisions • Incorporates explicit systematic strategy instruction (summarizes key points and reviews key vocabulary or concepts before the lesson) • Models specific behaviors and strategies, such as how to handle measuring materials or geoboards • Uses mnemonics or steps written on cards or posters to help students follow problem-solving steps • Uses peer-assisted learning, in which another student can provide help to a student in need • Supplies families with additional support materials to use at home • Encourages student use of self-regulation and self-instructional strategies such as revising notes, writing summaries, and identifying main ideas • Teaches test-taking strategies (allows the students to use a highlighter on the test to emphasize important information) • Slices back (Fuchs & Fuchs, 2001) to material from a previous grade level to ramp back up to grade-level curriculum
Tier 3	A highly qualified special education teacher: • Works one-on-one with students • Uses tailored instruction based on specific areas of weakness • Modifies instructional methods, motivates students, and further adapts curricula • Uses explicit contextualization of skills-based instruction

exhaustive, but it should provide you with specific suggestions for offering support to students throughout the lesson while you maintain the challenge.

1. Structure the environment
   - *Centralize attention.* Move the student close to the board or teacher. Face students when you speak to them and use gestures. Where possible, remove competing stimuli.
   - *Avoid confusion.* Word directions carefully and ask the student to repeat them. Give one direction at a time. Use the same language for consistency. For example, talk about base-ten materials as ones, tens, and hundreds (or when teaching decimals as ones, tenths, and hundredths), rather than interchanging those names with "flats," "rods," or other words about their shape rather than their value.
   - *Create smooth transitions.* Ensure that transitions between activities have clear directions and that there are limited chances to get off task.

2. Identify and remove potential barriers
   - *Find ways to help students remember.* Recognize that memory is often not a strong suit for students with disabilities and develop mnemonics (memory aids) for familiar steps or write directions that can be referred to throughout the lesson. For example, STAR is a mnemonic for problem solving: **S**earch the word problem for important information; **T**ranslate the words into models, pictures, or symbols; **A**nswer the problem; **R**eview your solution for reasonableness (Gagnon & Maccini, 2001).

Teaching Tip

Note that searching the word problem for important information is different from identifying key words because the use of a key word approach is not effective.

   - *Provide vocabulary and concept support.* Give explicit attention to vocabulary and symbols throughout the lesson. Preview essential terms and related prior knowledge/concepts, create a math wall of words and symbols to provide visual cues, and connect symbols to their precise meanings.
   - *Use "friendly" numbers.* Instead of using $6.13, use $6.00 to emphasize conceptual understanding rather than mixing computation and conceptual goals. Incorporate this technique when computation and operation skills are *not* the lesson objective.
   - *Vary the task size.* Students with learning disabilities can become frustrated by the enormity of the task. One way to address this problem is to assign students with disabilities fewer problems to solve.
   - *Adjust the visual display.* Design assessments and tasks so that there is not too much on a single page. The density of words, illustrations, and numbers on a page can be overwhelming for students with disabilities. Find ways to put only one problem on a page, increase the font size, or reduce the visual display by not putting too many figures or unrelated clip art on a single page.

3. Provide clarity
   - *Reiterate the time frame.* Give students additional reminders about the time left for exploring materials, completing tasks, or finishing assessments. This helps students with time management.
   - *Ask students to share their thinking.* Use the think-aloud method or the think-pair-share strategy.
   - *Emphasize connections.* Provide concrete representations, pictorial representations, and numerical representations. Have students connect them through carefully phrased questions. Also, connect visuals, meanings, and words. For example, as you fold a strip of paper into fourths, point out the part–whole relationship with gestures as you pose a question about the relationship between $\frac{2}{4}$ and $\frac{1}{2}$.
   - *Adapt delivery modes.* Incorporate a variety of materials, images, examples, and models for visual learners. Some students may need to have the problem or assessment read to them or generated with voice creation software. Provide written instructions in addition to oral instructions.

- *Emphasize the relevant points.* Some students with disabilities may inappropriately focus on the color of a cube instead of the quantity of cubes when filling a prism to measure the volume.
- *Use methods for organizing written work.* Provide tools and templates so that students can focus on the mathematics rather than on the creation of a table or chart. Also use graphic organizers, picture-based models, and paper with columns or grids.
- *Provide examples and non-examples.* To define rhombuses, give examples of rhombuses as well as shapes that are not rhombuses. Help students focus on the characteristics that differentiate the examples from the non-examples.

4. Consider alternative assessments
   - *Propose alternative products.* Provide options for how to demonstrate understanding (e.g., a verbal response that is written by someone else, voice recorded, or modeled with a manipulative). Use voice recognition software or word prediction software that can generate a whole menu of word choices when students type a few letters.
   - *Encourage self-monitoring and self-assessment.* Students with learning disabilities often are not good at self-reflection. Asking them to review an assignment or assessment to explain what was difficult and what they think they got right can help them be more independent and take greater responsibility for their learning.
   - *Consider feedback charts.* Help students monitor their growth by charting progress over time.

5. Emphasize practice and summary
   - *Help students bring ideas together.* Create study guides that summarize the key mathematics concepts and support students as they review key concepts. Students can begin to develop their own study guides by identifying, summarizing, and coordinating the big ideas.
   - *Provide extra practice.* Use carefully selected problems (not a large number) and allow the use of familiar physical models.

Not all of these strategies will apply to every lesson and to every student with special needs, but as you are thinking about a particular lesson and certain students in your class, you will find that many of these will apply and will allow your students to engage in the task and accomplish the learning goals of the lesson.

◆ Implementing Interventions

NCTM (2007) has gathered a set of effective, research-based approaches for teaching students with difficulties in mathematics (such as students needing interventions in tier 2 or tier 3 of a support system such as RtI), highlighting the use of several key strategies that are also suggested by Gersten, Beckmann, Clarke, Foegen, Marsh, Star, and Witzel (2009). These strategies include systematic and explicit instruction, think-alouds, concrete and visual representations of problems, peer-assisted learning activities, and formative assessment data provided to students and teachers. These interventions, proven to be effective for students with disabilities, may represent principles quite different from those at tier 1. The strategies described here are interventions for use with the small subset of students for whom the initial core instruction was ineffective.

Explicit Strategy Instruction

Explicit instruction is often characterized by highly structured, teacher-led instruction on a specific strategy. When engaging in this explicit instruction you do not merely model the strategy and have students practice it; instead, you try to illuminate your decision making—a process that may be troublesome for these particular learners. In this instructional strategy, after you assess the students so you know what to model, you use a tightly scripted sequence that goes from modeling to prompting students through the model to practice. Your instruction is highly organized in a step-by-step format and involves teacher-led explanations of concepts and strategies, including building critical connections and meaning that help learners relate new knowledge to concepts they know. Let's look at a classroom teacher who is using explicit instruction:

> As you enter Mr. Logan's classroom, you see a small group of students seated at a table listening to the teacher's detailed explanation and watching his demonstration of equivalent fraction concepts. The students are using manipulatives, as prescribed by Mr. Logan, and moving through carefully selected tasks. He tells the students to take out the red one-fourth pieces and asks them to check how many one-fourth pieces will exactly cover the blue one-half piece. Mr. Logan asks, "Is *equivalent* a word you know?" Then, to make sure they don't allow for any gaps or overlaps in the pieces, he asks them to talk about their reasoning process with the question, "What are some things you need to keep in mind as you place the fourths on the half?" Mr. Logan writes their responses on the adjacent board as $\frac{2}{4} = \frac{1}{2}$ and also as "two-fourths is the same as one-half" to connect the ideas that they are looking for how many fourth pieces cover one half piece. Then he asks them to compare the brown eighths and the yellow sixths to the piece representing one-half and records their responses. The students are taking turns answering these questions out loud. During the lesson Mr. Logan frequently stops the group, interjects points of clarification, and directly highlights critical components of the task. For example, he asks, "Are you surprised that it takes more eighths to cover the half than fourths?" Vocabulary words, such as *whole*, *numerator*, and *denominator*, are written on the math word wall nearby and the definitions of these terms are reviewed and reinforced throughout the lesson. At the completion of the lesson, students are given several similar examples of the kind of comparisons discussed in the lesson as independent practice.

A number of aspects of explicit instruction can be seen in Mr. Logan's approach to teaching fraction concepts. He employs a teacher-directed format, carefully describes the use of manipulatives, and incorporates a model-prompt-practice sequence. This sequence starts with verbal instructions and careful demonstrations with concrete models, followed by prompting, questioning, and then independent practice. The students are deriving mathematical knowledge from the teacher's oral, written, and visual clues.

As students with disabilities solve problems, explicit strategy instruction can help guide them in carrying out tasks. First, ask the students to read and restate the problem; draw a picture; develop a plan by linking this problem to previous problems; write the problem in a mathematical sentence; break the problem into smaller pieces; carry out operations; and check answers with a calculator, hundreds chart, or other appropriate tools. These self-instructive prompts, or self-questions, structure the entire learning process from beginning to end. Unlike during more inquiry-based instruction, the teacher models these steps and explains the components with terminology that is easily understood by students with disabilities—students who did not discover them independently through initial tier 1 or tier 2 activities. Yet, consistent with what we know about how all students learn, students are still developing an understanding of concepts and engaged in problem solving (not just in skill development).

Concrete models can support explicit strategy instruction. For example, when you demonstrate a multiplication array with cubes, you might say: "Watch me. Now make a rectangle with the cubes that looks just like mine." In contrast, a teacher with a more inquiry-oriented approach might say: "Using these cubes, how can you show me a representation for 4 × 5?" Although initially more structured, the use of concrete models will provide students with disabilities with greater access to abstract concepts.

There are a number of possible advantages to using explicit strategy instruction for students with disabilities. This approach helps you make more explicit the covert thinking strategies that others use in mathematical problem solving. Although students with disabilities hear other students' thinking strategies in the *After* phase of each lesson, they frequently cannot keep up with the rapid pace of the sharing. Without extra time to reprocess the conversation, students with disabilities may not have access to these strategies. More explicit approaches are also less dependent on the students' ability to draw ideas from past experience or to operate in a self-directed manner.

Explicit strategy instruction can also have distinct disadvantages for students with disabilities. Some aspects of this approach rely on memorizing, which can be one of their weakest skills. Taking a known weakness and building a learning strategy around it is not productive. There is also a concern that approaches that are highly teacher controlled promote long-term dependency on teacher assistance. This is of particular concern for students with disabilities because many are described as passive learners.

Students learn what they have the opportunity to practice. Students who are never given opportunities to engage in self-directed learning (based on the assumption that this is not an area of strength) will be deprived of the opportunity to develop skills in this area. In fact, the best explicit instruction is scaffolded, meaning it moves from a highly structured, single-strategy approach toward multiple models, including examples and nonexamples. It also includes immediate error correction followed by the fading of prompts to help students move to independence. Explicit instruction, to be effective, must include making mathematical relationships explicit (so that students, rather than only learning how to do that day's mathematics, make connections to other mathematical ideas). Because making connections is a major component in how students learn, it must be central to instructional strategies for students with disabilities.

Concrete, Semi-Concrete, Abstract (CSA)

The CSA (concrete, semi-concrete, abstract) intervention has been used in mathematics education in a variety of forms for years (Heddens, 1964; Witzel, 2005). Based on Bruner's reasoning theory (1966), this model reflects a sequence that begins with an instructional focus on concrete representations (manipulative materials) and tools, then moves to semi-concrete representations (drawings or pictures) and abstraction (using only numerals or mentally solving problems) over time. Built into this approach is the return to visual models and concrete representations as needed or as students begin to explore new concepts or extensions of concepts previously learned. As students share reasoning that shows they are beginning to understand the mathematical concept, there can be a shift to semi-concrete representations. This is not to say that this is a rigid approach that moves to abstraction only after the other phases. Instead, it is essential that there be parallel modeling of number symbols throughout this approach to explicitly relate concrete models and visual representations to the corresponding numerals and equations.

CSA also includes modeling the mental conversations that go on in your mind as you help students articulate their own thinking. Again, as you articulate your thought processes using an appropriate model for a student, your choice of a reasoning strategy and model should be based on evidence from the student's performance on targeted assessments. In the last component of CSA, students are capable of working with abstract aspects of the concepts without an emphasis on concrete or semi-concrete images.

Peer-Assisted Learning

Students with special needs also benefit from other students' modeling and support (Fuchs, Fuchs, Yazdian, & Powell, 2002). The basic notion is that students learn best when they are placed in the role of an apprentice working with a more skilled peer or "expert." Although the peer-assisted learning approach shares some of the characteristics of the explicit strategy instruction model, it is distinct because knowledge is presented on an as-needed basis as opposed to a predetermined sequence. The students can be paired with older students or peers who have a more sophisticated understanding of a concept. At other times, tutors and tutees can reverse roles during the tasks. Having students with disabilities "teach" others is an important part of the learning process, so giving students with special needs a chance to explain concepts to another student is valuable.

Think-Alouds

When you use a think-aloud as an instructional strategy, you demonstrate the steps to accomplish a task while verbalizing the thinking process and reasoning that accompany the steps. Remember, don't start with where your thinking is; assess and start where the student's thinking is. The student follows this instruction by imitating your process of talking through a solution on a different, but parallel, task. This is similar to the model in which "expert" learners share strategies with "novice" learners.

Consider a problem in which fourth-grade students are given the task of determining how much paint will be needed to cover the walls of their classroom. Rather than merely demonstrating, for example, how to use a ruler to measure the distance across a wall, the think-aloud strategy would involve talking through the steps and identifying the reasons for each step while measuring the space. As you place a mark on the wall to indicate where the ruler ended in the first measurement, you might state, "I used this line to mark off where the ruler ends. How should I use this line as I measure the next section of the wall? I know I have to move the ruler, but should I repeat what I did the first time?" All of this dialogue occurs prior to placing the ruler for a second measurement. Often teachers share alternatives about how else they could have carried out the task. When you use this metacognitive strategy, try to talk about and model possible approaches (and the reasons behind these approaches) in an effort to make your invisible thinking processes visible to students.

Although you can choose any of these strategies as needed, your goal is always to work toward a high level of student responsibility for learning. Movement to higher levels of understanding of content can be likened to the need to move to a higher level on a hill. For some, formal stair steps with support along the way is necessary (explicit strategy instruction); for others ramps with encouragement at the top of the hill will work (peer-assisted learning). Other students can find a path up the hill on their own with some guidance from visual representations (CSA approach). All people can relate to the need to have different support during different times of their lives or under different circumstances, and it is no different for students with special needs (see Table 6.2). Yet, these students must eventually learn to create a path to new learning on their own, as that is what will be required in the real world after formal education ends. Leaving students knowing only how to climb steps with support and face hills with constant assistance and encouragement from others will not help them attain their life goals.

◆ Adapting for Students with Moderate or Severe Disabilities

Students with moderate or severe disabilities often need extensive modifications and individualized supports to learn mathematics. This population of students may include those with severe autism, sensory disorders, limitations affecting movement, cerebral palsy, processing disorders such as intellectual disabilities, and combinations of multiple disabilities.

Originally, the curriculum for students with severe disabilities was called *functional*, in that it often focused on life skills such as managing money, telling time, using a calculator, measuring, and matching numbers to complete such tasks as entering a telephone number or identifying a house number. Now directives and assessments have broadened the curriculum to address the content strands that were specifically delineated by grade level in the *Common Core State Standards* (CCSSO, 2010).

Table 6.2 Common Stumbling Blocks for Students with Disabilities

Stumbling Blocks	What Will I Notice?	What Should I Do?
Student has trouble forming mental representations of mathematical concepts.	• Can't interpret a number line with fractional intervals • Has difficulty going from a story about a garden plot (to set up a problem on finding area) to graph or dot paper	• Explicitly teach the representation— for example, exactly how to draw a diagram (e.g., partition the number line) • Use larger versions of the representation (e.g., number line or grid paper) so that students can move to or interact with the model
Student has difficulty accessing numerical meanings from symbols (issues with number sense).	• Has difficulty with basic facts; for example, doesn't recognize that 3×5 is the same as 5×3 • Does not understand the meaning of the equal sign • Can't interpret whether an answer is reasonable	• Explicitly teach multiple ways of representing a number showing the variations at exactly the same time • Use a number balance to support understanding of the equal sign • Use multiple representations for a single problem to show how it would appear in a variety of ways (base-ten blocks, illustrations, and numbers) rather than using multiple problems
Student is challenged to keep numbers and information in working memory.	• Gets confused when other students share multiple strategies during the *After* portion of the lesson • Forgets how to start the problem-solving process	• Record (in writing) the ideas of other students during discussions • Incorporate a chart that lists the main steps in problem solving as an independent guide or make bookmarks with questions the students can ask themselves as self-prompts • Use word labels with each numeric value
Student lacks organizational skills and the ability to self-regulate.	• Misses steps in a process • Writes computations in a way that is random and hard to follow	• Use routines as often as possible or provide self-monitoring checklists to prompt steps along the way • Use graph paper to record problems or numbers • Create math word walls as a reference
Student misapplies rules or overgeneralizes.	• Applies rules such as "always subtract the smaller from the larger" too literally, resulting in errors such as $35 - 9 = 34$ • Mechanically applies algorithms—for example, adds $\frac{7}{8}$ and $\frac{12}{13}$ and generates the answer $\frac{19}{21}$	• Always give examples and counterexamples to show how and when "rules" should be used and when they should not • Tie all rules into conceptual understanding; don't emphasize memorizing rote procedures or practices

At a beginning level, students develop number sense, use measuring tools, compare graphs, explore place-value concepts (sometimes linked to money use), use the number line, and compare quantities. When possible, the content should be connected to life skills and features of jobs. Shopping skills and activities in which food is prepared are both options for mathematical problem solving. At other times, you can link mathematical learning objectives to everyday events in a practical way. For example, when the operation of division is studied, figuring how candy can be equally shared at Halloween or how game cards can be dealt would be appropriate. Students can also undertake a small project such as constructing a box to store different items as a way to explore shapes and measurements.

Do not believe that all basic facts must be mastered before students with moderate or severe disabilities can move forward in the curriculum. Students can learn geometric or measuring concepts without having mastered all basic facts. Geometry for students with

Table 6.3 Activities for Students with Moderate or Severe Disabilities

Content Area	Activity
Number and operations	• Create a list of supplies that need to be ordered for the classroom or a particular event and calculate the cost. • Calculate the number of calories in a given meal. • Compare the cost of two meals on menus from local restaurants.
Algebra	• Show an allowance or wage on a chart to demonstrate growth over time. • Write an equation to show how much the student will earn in a month or a year.
Geometry	• Use spatial relationships to identify a short path between two locations on a map. • Tessellate several figures to show how a variety of shapes fit together. Using tangrams to fill a space will also develop important workplace skills such as packing boxes or organizing supplies on shelves.
Measurement	• Fill differently shaped items with water, sand, or rice to assess volume, ordering the containers from least to most. • Take body temperature and use an enlarged thermometer to show comparison to outside temperatures. • Calculate the amount of paint needed to cover the walls or ceiling of the classroom, using area. • Estimate the amount of time it would take to travel to a known location using a map.
Data analysis and probability	• Survey students on favorite games (either electronic or other) and use the top five as choices for the class. Make a graph to represent and compare the results. • Examine the outside temperatures for the past week and estimate the temperatures for the next 3 days.

moderate and severe disabilities is more than merely identifying shapes; it is critical for being oriented in the real world through interpreting maps of the local area. Students who learn to count bus stops and judge time can be helped to navigate their world successfully.

Table 6.3 offers ideas across the curriculum that are appropriate for teaching students with moderate to severe disabilities.

◆ Planning for Students Who Are Mathematically Gifted

Students who are mathematically gifted include those who have high ability or high interest. Some may be gifted with an intuitive knowledge of mathematical concepts, whereas others have a passion for the subject even though they may have to work hard to learn it. Many students' giftedness becomes apparent to parents and teachers when they grasp and articulate mathematics concepts at an earlier age than expected. They are often found to easily make connections between topics of study and frequently are unable to explain how they quickly got an answer (Rotigel & Fello, 2005). Many teachers have a keen ability to spot talent when they notice students who have strong number sense or visual/spatial sense (Gavin & Sheffield, 2010). These teachers are not pointing to students who are fast and speedy with their basic facts, but those who have the ability to reason and make sense of mathematics.

Do not wait for students to demonstrate their mathematical talent; instead, develop it through a challenging set of tasks and inquiry-based instruction (VanTassel-Baska & Brown, 2007). Generally, as described in the RtI model described previously, high-quality core instruction is able to respond to the varying needs of diverse learners, including the talented and gifted. Yet, for some of your gifted students, the core instruction proves not to be enough of a challenge. The curriculum for these advanced learners should be adapted to consider level, complexity, breadth, depth, and pace (Assouline & Lupkowski-Shoplik, 2011; Renzulli, Gubbins, McMillen, Eckert, & Little, 2009; Saul, Assouline, & Sheffield, 2010).

There are four basic categories for adapting mathematics content for gifted mathematics students: acceleration, enrichment (depth), sophistication (complexity), and novelty (Gallagher & Gallagher, 1994; Ravenna, 2008). In each category, your students should apply, rather than just acquire, information. The emphasis on implementing and extending ideas must overshadow the mental collection of facts and concepts.

Acceleration

Acceleration recognizes that your students may already understand the mathematics content that you plan to teach. Some teachers use "curriculum compacting" (Reis & Renzulli, 2005) to give a short overview of the content and assess students' ability to respond to mathematics tasks that would demonstrate their proficiency. Another option is to reduce the amount of time these students spend on aspects of the topic, or moving to more advanced content at the next grade level or beyond. Allowing students to increase the pace of their own learning can give them access to curriculum different from their grade level while demanding more independent study. But moving students to higher mathematics (by moving them up a grade, for example), will not succeed in engaging them as learners if the instruction is still at a slow pace. Research reveals that when gifted students are accelerated through the curriculum they become more likely to explore STEM (science, technology, engineering, and mathematics) fields (Sadler & Tai, 2007).

Enrichment

Enrichment activities go beyond the topic of study to content that is not specifically a part of your grade-level curriculum but is an extension of the original mathematical tasks. For example, while studying place value both in very large numbers and decimals, mathematically gifted students can stretch their knowledge to study other bases such as base five, base eight, or base twelve. This provides an extended view of how our base-ten numeration system fits within the broader system of number theory. Other times the format of enrichment can involve studying the same topic as the rest of the class while differing on the means and outcomes of the work. Examples include group investigations, solving real problems in the community, writing letters to outside audiences, and identifying applications of the mathematics learned.

Sophistication

Another strategy is to increase the sophistication of a topic by raising the level of complexity or pursuing greater depth of content, possibly outside of the regular curriculum or by connecting mathematics to other subject areas. Frequently, gifted students explore topics similar to those of their classmates but focus on higher-level thinking or on more complex or abstract ideas. This can mean exploring a larger set of ideas in which a mathematics topic exists. For example, while studying a unit on place value, mathematically gifted students can deepen their knowledge to study other numeration systems such as Roman, Mayan, Egyptian, Babylonian, Chinese, and Zulu. This study provides a multicultural view of how our numeration system fits within the historical number systems (Mack, 2011). In the algebra strand, when studying sequences or patterns of numbers, mathematically gifted students can learn about Fibonacci sequences and their appearances in the natural world in shells and plant life.

Novelty

Novelty introduces completely different material from the regular curriculum and frequently occurs in after-school clubs, out-of-class projects, or collaborative school experiences. In collaborative experiences, students from a variety of grades and classes may volunteer for special mathematics projects, with a classroom teacher, principal, or resource teacher taking the lead. The novelty category includes having students explore topics that are within their developmental grasp but outside the curriculum. For example, students may look at mathematical "tricks" using binary numbers to guess classmates' birthdays or solve reasoning problems using a logic matrix. They may also explore topics such as topology through the creation of paper "knots" called *flexagons* (see www.flexagon.net) or large-scale investigations of the amount of food thrown away at lunchtime. A group might create tetrahedron kites or find mathematics in art. Another aspect of the novelty approach provides different options for students in culminating performances of their understanding, such as demonstrating their knowledge through inventions, experiments, simulations, dramatizations, visual displays, and oral presentations.

Strategies to Avoid

There are a number of ineffective approaches for gifted students that find their way into classrooms. Following are five common ones:

1. *Assigning more of the same work.* This is the least appropriate way to respond to mathematically gifted students and the most likely to result in students hiding their abilities. This approach is described by Persis Herold as "all scales and no music" (quoted in Tobias, 1995, p. 168).

2. *Giving free time to early finishers.* Although students find this rewarding, it does not maximize their intellectual growth and can lead to hurrying to finish a task.

3. *Assigning gifted students to help struggling learners.* Routinely assigning gifted students to teach students who are not meeting expectations that they have mastered does not stimulate their intellectual growth and can place them in a socially uncomfortable and/or undesirable situation. Consistently using this approach puts mathematically talented students in a constant position of tutoring, rather than allowing them to create deeper and more complex levels of understanding.

4. *Providing gifted pull-out opportunities.* Unfortunately, generalized gated programs are often unrelated to the regular mathematics curriculum (Assouline & Lupkowski-Shoplik, 2011). Although it can benefit students, add-on experiences are not enough. Gifted students need adaptations to the instruction in their mathematics classroom. Learners with a high level of ability shouldn't get one-stop shopping in a gifted program that focuses on all academic subjects; they need individual attention to develop depth and more complex understanding of mathematics.

5. *Offering independent enrichment on the computer.* This practice often does not engage students with mathematics in a way that will enhance conceptual understanding and support their ability to justify their thinking to others. However, there are some excellent enrichment opportunities on the Internet.

Sheffield (1999) writes that gifted students should be introduced to the "joys and frustrations of thinking deeply about a wide range of original, open-ended, or complex problems that encourage them to respond creatively in ways that are original, fluent, flexible and elegant" (p. 46). Accommodations, modifications, and interventions for mathematically gifted students must strive for this goal.

Stop and Reflect

How is equity in the classroom different from teaching all students equitably? ■

7

Collaborating with Families, Community, and Principals

With students, parents and teachers all on the same page and working together for shared goals, we can ensure that students make progress each year and graduate from school prepared to succeed in college and in a modern workforce.

CCSSO (2010)

Parental and Community Support for Mathematics

Teaching mathematics developmentally, addressing the increased content demands articulated in the Common Core State Standards Initiative (CCSSO, 2010), and ensuring that students are mathematically proficient requires everyone's commitment. Numerous studies have found a positive relationship between the level of parental involvement and their child's achievement in school (e.g., Aspiazu, Bauer, & Spillett, 1998; Henderson et al., 2002). We often hear educators make statements such as "You must have the principal's support" and "You need to get parents on board," and we nod our heads in agreement. But knowing what this support looks like and recognizing how to get the support are less clear. In this chapter, we discuss ideas for developing a collaborative community that understands and is able to support high-quality mathematics teaching and learning for every student.

Parents know the importance of mathematics for their child's future. They participate in their child's learning by doing such things as supporting homework, volunteering at the school, and meeting with teachers, even if they may recall unpleasant experiences or difficulties with school mathematics from their own schooling. Understanding that memories of mathematics classes are not always pleasant for parents and appreciating parental support prepares us to suitably identify for parents the mathematics goals that students should be experiencing in the twenty-first century. Communication with parents is key to encouraging their support and involves using one-way, two-way, and three-way communication strategies (see Figure 7.1).

Figure 7.1 Ways to communicate with families.

One-Way Communication Strategies	Letters sharing the goals of a unit	Websites where resources and curriculum information are posted	Newsletters
Two-Way Communication Strategies	Log of student work (signed or commented on by parents)	PTA meetings, open house	One-on-one meetings, class or home visits
Three-Way (or More) Communication Strategies	Family math nights	Conferences (with parent and child)	Log or journal of student learning with input from student, parent, and teacher

◆ Communicating Mathematics Goals

Every year parents need opportunities to get information directly from the school leaders and teachers about their child's mathematics program, including the kind of instruction that might differ from what they experienced in their own schooling. For example, even if your school has been engaged in implementing a mathematics program that reflects the NCTM *Principles and Standards for School Mathematics* and now the *Common Core State Standards*, the program will still be new to the parents of your students. Changes to the mathematics curriculum—new textbooks, new technologies, new philosophies—are all perfect reasons for communicating with parents. This interaction is one of the most important components of successfully implementing a standards-based mathematics curriculum such as the *Common Core State Standards* (Bay, Reys, & Reys, 1999). Without such opportunities for communication, parents may draw their own conclusions about the effectiveness of the mathematics curriculum, develop frustrations and negative opinions about what is happening in their child's classroom or school, and communicate this apprehension to other parents. Table 7.1 highlights common questions parents ask about standards-based mathematics programs. Providing a forum for parents around mathematics highlights the importance of the subject and gives parents confidence that your school is a great place for preparing their children for middle school and beyond.

Be proactive! Don't wait for concerns or questions to percolate. Some early action strategies include engaging parents in family and community math nights, positive homework practices, and parent coaching sessions, as well as sharing where to find mathematics-related resources for their children (e.g., websites and manipulatives). Let's discuss each.

◆ Family and Community Math Nights

There are many ways to conduct a family or community mathematics event, such as including a math component in a back-to-school night, discussing it in a PTA meeting, or a hosting a showcase for a new mathematics program. Critical to this plan is providing opportunities for parents to be learners of mathematics so they experience what it means to *do mathematics* (just like their children).

Teaching Tip

Welcome back or family math nights are a great time to have parent–child teams experience working together on math tasks.

Table 7.1 Categories of Parent Questions Related to Standards-Based Mathematics

Category	Types of Questions
Pedagogy	• Why isn't the teacher teaching? (And what is the point of reinventing the wheel?) • Are students doing their own work when they are in groups? Is my child having to do the work of students who don't understand the work? • Why is there so much reading and writing in math class? • Why is my child struggling more than in previous years?
Content	• Is my child learning the basic skills? • Why is my child learning different ways than what I learned for doing the operations? • Will my child be on-track for Algebra I in eighth grade? Ninth grade? • Where are the math topics I am used to seeing, and why are there topics I never learned? • Is my child learning mathematics or just doing activities?
Evidence	• Is there any evidence that this approach or curriculum is effective? • Will my child do better on state/national standardized tests with this new approach? • Will this prepare my child for middle school, high school, college, and beyond?
Understanding	• Why is mathematics teaching changing? • How can I help my child [with homework; to be successful]? • Where can I learn more about the *Common Core State Standards*?

Source: Adapted from Bay-Williams, J. M., & Meyer, M. R. (2003). What Parents Want to Know about Standards-Based Mathematics Curricula. *Principal Leadership, 3*(7), 54–60. Copyright 2003 National Association of Secondary School Principals. For more information on NASSP products and services to promote excellence in middle level and high school leadership, visit www.nassp.org.

When choosing mathematical tasks to use with parents, be sure the tasks focus on content that really matters to them and relates to what they already know is a part of the grades 3 through 5 curriculum (e.g., a task about fractions and a measurement activity are good ideas). Tasks throughout this book are ideal for a math night. Figure 7.2 contrasts two third-grade problems for learning about perimeter—one that is straightforward and lends to a procedural approach (add up the sides), and one that is designed for a teaching-through-problem-solving experience (explore and find different perimeters for a given area).

Stop and Reflect

What distinctions do you notice between the two tasks in Figure 7.2? What is valued as "doing mathematics" in both of the problems? ■

The contrasting perimeter problems are ideal for discussing with parents what it means to do mathematics because they (1) offer a familiar context, (2) require minimum prior knowledge, (3) have multiple solution strategies, (4) involve using manipulatives (color tiles and/or grid paper), and (5) (in the first example) connect the mathematical ideas of area, perimeter, rectangles, and squares, as well as addition and multiplication. Another good choice is a fraction problem because not only are they central to the grades 3 through 5 curriculum, but also because understanding fractions is essential to be successful in algebra in middle school. They also bring to the forefront how teaching conceptually is better than the

Figure 7.2 Problems to explore at a parent or community night.

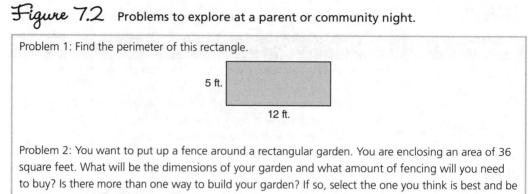

Problem 1: Find the perimeter of this rectangle.

5 ft.

12 ft.

Problem 2: You want to put up a fence around a rectangular garden. You are enclosing an area of 36 square feet. What will be the dimensions of your garden and what amount of fencing will you need to buy? Is there more than one way to build your garden? If so, select the one you think is best and be ready to justify your choice.

procedural approach the parents had when they were students. See Chapter 13 and Chapter 14 for more excellent activities related to fractions.

The potential each of these problems has to support and challenge students in making sense of mathematics should be made explicit during a discussion with parents. After giving parents time to do both tasks and discussing solution strategies (as you would with students), ask participants to consider the learning opportunities in the two contrasting tasks. Ask questions such as the following:

- What skills are being developed in each problem?
- Which problem gives more opportunity to make connections between mathematics and the real world?
- Which task would your child be most motivated to solve? Why?

Help parents identify the depth of the mathematics in the teaching-through-problem-solving task. Remind them that in grades 3 through 5, students are building important foundations for algebraic thinking—looking for patterns, reasoning, and generalizing. Help parents see these aspects in this measurement problem. Share the *Common Core State Standards* and the NCTM standards (in parent-friendly language), and focus on the goal of having students becoming mathematically proficient as described in those standards. Ask parents, "Where do you see these proficiencies being supported in the two tasks we did?"

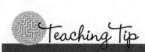

Teaching Tip

Provide copies of the appropriate *Common Core State Standards* Introduction and Overview pages (the first two pages for each grade) and allow parents time to think about each "Critical Area."

Address any or all of the questions in Table 7.1 that apply to your setting. One way to do this is to have parents write their questions on note cards and collect them so you can identify common questions and decide the order in which to discuss each question. The sections that follow provide possible responses to questions that parents (or community members) commonly ask.

Pedagogy

When parents ask questions that point to their belief that mathematics is best learned through direct instruction —just as they learned it—remind them of the experiences they had in *doing* mathematics with the perimeter task. Point to the difference between being *shown* how to do something (e.g., "This is how you find perimeter; now practice this") and *developing* an understanding of something (e.g., "What different fence options do you have when trying to enclose 12 square meters for a garden and *how* did you calculate the perimeter?"). You can help parents identify the skills and concepts that are developed through these two experiences. Ask, "Where do you see the concept of perimeter? Where do you see the development of the procedure?" Point out that skills are (still) important, and students benefit by generating their own procedures and connecting those procedures to a solid understanding. Explicitly promote the fact that a developmental approach to learning mathematics provides the means for students to: (1) use prior knowledge, (2) make connections, (3) use alternative strategies and reasoning, (4) apply mathematical ideas to new situations, and (5) develop positive dispositions about being able to do mathematics.

Role of the Teacher

Similarly, address the role of the teacher as *organizer* (organizes a worthwhile mathematical task), *facilitator* (facilitates student interaction), and *questioner* (asks questions to help students make connections or to deepen their understanding). Remind parents that just because the teacher is not telling their child what to do does not mean that the teacher is not teaching. The teacher is orchestrating the class so that each student develops the ability to solve problems independently.

Cooperative Groups

Parents may also wonder about the frequency of their child working in cooperative groups because this may differ from their own mathematics learning experiences. Help parents see the role of others in their learning as they solved the problems and as they heard solutions from those who were working at other tables. Connect that experience to the value of cooperative learning. You can do this in a variety of ways:

1. *Share the one-page parent overview from the NCTM Families Ask department titled "Cooperative Learning" (Coates & Mayfield, 2009).* Families Ask, a feature posted on the NCTM website at www.nctm.org/resources/content.aspx?id=9292, provides over 20 excellent, written-for-parents discussions on a range of topics appropriate for grades 3 through 5.

2. *Include a feature in your parent newsletter.* Early in the year, you can feature cooperative learning, addressing its importance across content areas. In mathematics, this can include the following benefits: hearing different strategies, building meaning, designing solution strategies, and justifying approaches, all of which are essential to building a strong understanding of mathematics and important life skills.

3. *Send home letters introducing math units of study.* If you are about to teach a unit on adding and subtracting fractions, a letter can help parents know the important aspects of the content. This is a great time to mention that students will work in groups so that they can see different ways to illustrate fractions with pictures, and explain the meaning of the procedure.

4. *Do a cooperative learning mathematics activity at a family math night or back-to-school event.* Use a task that lends itself to assigning roles to different members of the group and won't take long to solve. Have parents work with two to three others to solve the task.

5. *Invite parents to assist in a mathematics group assignment.* Seeing firsthand the dialogue and thinking that happens in cooperative groups can go a long way in illustrating how valuable cooperative groups can be!

Parents may initially worry that students working in groups are simply copying from other students and not learning. Share strategies you use to build in individual accountability and shared responsibility. For example, teachers may ask each student to record explanations in his or her notebook. At other times, you may assign specific roles to each member of the group.

Teaching Tip

Being proactive about communicating the benefits of cooperative learning, as well as how you build in individual accountability and shared responsibility, will go a long way toward converting parent concerns into parent support.

Use of Technology

Parents may be avid users of technology yet still have concerns about their child using calculators and computers in grades 3 through 5 when they haven't yet mastered their basic facts for multiplication or learned procedures for fractions and decimal computation. Even though research overwhelmingly finds that students using calculators achieve at least as much as those not using calculators, calculators are widely blamed for students' lack of reasoning and sense making. Reassure parents that students will learn the basic facts and procedures, and the calculator can support that learning. The calculator is used when it is appropriate to support the mathematical goals of the day. For example, students can use calculators when the goal is learning volume versus not using the calculator when the goal is how to multiply. Share an example. In a lesson on volume (fifth grade), students might bring boxes from home and measure them two ways. First, they see how many centimeter cubes fit in the box. Second, they measure the length, width, and height to the nearest centimeter and calculate the volume. These two ways are compared. In this case, the calculator helps keep the focus on volume, rather than on calculations with decimals.

An important message to parents is that mastery of basic facts should *not* be a prerequisite to using a calculator. Instead, students (and teachers) should be making good decisions about whether a calculator supports or detracts from solving a particular problem (and learning the intended mathematics).

Practice and Problem Solving

Parents may also wonder why there are fewer skill or practice problems and more story problems in the curriculum. Effective mathematics learning environments are rich in language. Real mathematics involves more word problems and far fewer "naked number" skill problems. In contrast to when the parents went to school, skills are now less needed in the workplace because of available technology, but the importance of number sense, reasoning, and being able to solve real problems has increased. Because some students struggle with reading and/or writing, share strategies you use to help them understand and solve story problems (see Figure 7.3).

Parents may worry when they see their child struggle with a single mathematics problem because they may believe that fast means successful. But faster isn't smarter. Cathy Seeley's book with this same title (2009) is a great read on this topic written for families, educators, and policymakers. Seeley offers 41 brief messages, many of which can address parent questions about mathematics (e.g., "A Math Message to Families: Helping Students Prepare for the Future," "Putting Calculators in Their Place: The Role of Calculators and Computation in the Classroom," and "Do It in Your Head: The Power of Mental Math"). Explain that engaging students in productive struggle is one of the two most effective ways teachers can develop conceptual understanding in students (the other is making connections between mathematical ideas) (Bay-Williams, 2010; Hiebert & Grouws, 2007). Rather than presenting a series of simpler problems for students to practice, standards-based curricula characteristically focus on fewer tasks, each of which provides students with an opportunity for higher-level thinking, multiple-strategy solutions, and more time focused on math learning. Share the first standard from Standards for Mathematical Practice in the *Common Core State Standards* (see Figure 7.4) and ask the parents what they notice. Focus on the importance of *perseverance*. This is true in mathematics and in life. Reassure parents that some tasks take longer because of the nature of the task, not because their child lacks understanding. Mathematics is not nearly as much about speed and memorization as it is about being able to grapple with a novel problem, try various approaches from a collection of options, and finally reach an accurate answer.

Figure 7.3

Share with parents how you support reading and problem solving.

Reading Strategies for Math Problems
- Read aloud (whole class)
- Read a math problem with a friend
- Find and write the question
- Draw a picture of the problem
- Act out the problem
- Use a graphic organizer (recording page with problem solving prompts)
- Discuss math vocabulary
- Play math vocabulary games

Figure 7.4   Standard 1 from the Standards for Mathematical Practice.

---

1. Make sense of problems and persevere in solving them.

Mathematically proficient students start by explaining to themselves the meaning of a problem and looking for entry points to its solution. They analyze givens, constraints, relationships, and goals. They make conjectures about the form and meaning of the solution and plan a solution pathway rather than simply jumping into a solution attempt. They consider analogous problems, and try special cases and simpler forms of the original problem in order to gain insight into its solution. They monitor and evaluate their progress and change course if necessary. Older students might, depending on the context of the problem, transform algebraic expressions or change the viewing window on their graphing calculator to get the information they need. Mathematically proficient students can explain correspondences between equations, verbal descriptions, tables, and graphs or draw diagrams of important features and relationships, graph data, and search for regularity or trends. Younger students might rely on using concrete objects or pictures to help conceptualize and solve a problem. Mathematically proficient students check their answers to problems using a different method, and they continually ask themselves, "Does this make sense?" They can understand the approaches of others to solving complex problems and identify correspondences between different approaches.

Source: CCSSO (Council of Chief State School Officers). (2010). *Common Core State Standards,* p. 6. Retrieved from http://corestandards.org. The *Common Core State Standards* are © Copyright 2010. National Governors Association Center for Best Practices and Council of Chief State School Officers. All rights reserved.

Mathematics Content

A common concern of parents is that their children are not learning their basic facts and standard algorithms or the procedures they remember using when in elementary school. You must address (at least) two points related to these related issues. First, the skills that parents are looking for (e.g., long division procedures) are still there; they just look different because they are presented in a way based on understanding, not just memorization. Standard algorithms are still taught, but they are taught *along with* alternative (or invented) strategies that build on students' number sense and reasoning. Let parents experience that both invented and standard algorithms are important in being mathematically proficient by inviting them to solve the following problems.

$$69 + 47 = \underline{\qquad} \qquad 309 - 288 = \underline{\qquad}$$
$$487 + 345 = \underline{\qquad} + 355$$

Ask for volunteers to share the ways that they thought about the problems. For the subtraction problem, for example, the following might be shared:

- 300 take away 288 is 12, then add the 9 back on to get 21
- 288 up to 300 is 12 and up 9 more is 21
- 309 to 300 is 9, then down to 290 is 10 more (19), and then to 288 is 2 more (21)

These invented strategies, over numerous problems, reinforce place value concepts and the relationship between addition and subtraction. Noticing that these values are both near 300 helps to select a strategy. This bird's-eye view of the problem is important in doing mathematics, rather than always doing the same thing no matter what the numbers. This is very evident in the third example, which can be solved with no computation if the relationship between the numbers is noticed first.

Second, what is "basic" in the twenty-first century is much more than computation and number skills. Many topics in the upper elementary curriculum were not a part of the curriculum a generation ago (for example, fraction computation and the connections of algebra to the operations). Looking together through the essential concepts in the *Common Core State Standards* or the NCTM *Curriculum Focal Points* helps parents see that the curriculum is not just an idea generated from their child's school, but the national consensus on what elementary school students need to learn.

Student Achievement

At the heart of parents' interest in school mathematics is wanting their child to be successful—not only in the current classroom, but also at the next level of school and later on in the high-stakes assessments like the ACT or SAT for college entrance. If your state has implemented the *Common Core State Standards*, you can share that the standards are for K–12 and are designed to prepare students for college and future careers. The *Common Core State Standards* website (http://corestandards.org) has an increasing number of resources for parents to help them ensure that their child is college and career ready.

Another approach to inform parents about student achievement is to share research on the *ineffectiveness* of the traditional U.S. approach to teaching mathematics. The Trends in International Mathematics and Science Study (TIMSS), an international study conducted regularly that includes many countries, continues to find that U.S. students achieve at an average level in fourth grade and then score lower in mathematics than international students from that point on. Discuss the implications of unpreparedness for students who want to seek higher paying jobs on what is now an international playing field.

Parents may be more interested in how your specific school is doing in preparing students for the future. Share evidence from your school of mathematics success, including stories about individual children (anonymously) or the success of a particular classroom, like the following one received by a principal:

> I was worried at the start of the year because my son has never liked math and was coming home with pretty complicated problems to solve. But, now he is coming home telling me all about the math problems he is doing at school (more like projects than practice!). As an aside, I am also learning a lot—I didn't learn this way, but I am finding the homework problems are really interesting as we figure them out. I wish I could have learned math this way when I was in school! I am just curious if this is something he will get to do again in fourth grade, or if this is just something the teacher is doing just for this year.

Such communications help parents see that there is a transition period and that in the end a standards-based approach helps engage students and build their understanding over time.

◆ Homework Practices and Parent Coaching

The way in which parents are involved in homework can make a difference in student attitudes and learning, particularly at the elementary level (Cooper, 2007; Else-Quest, Hyde, & Hejmadi, 2008; Patall, Cooper, & Robinson, 2008). For example, students perform better when parents provide a quiet environment and establish rules about homework completion. Also, a parent's emotions are connected to the student's emotions, and positive emotions are connected to better performance (Else-Quest et al., 2008). Therefore, parents who exhibit positive interest, humor, and pride in their student's homework support their child's mathematics learning.

You may have heard parents say, "I am not good at math" or "I don't like solving math problems." Parents may feel this way and, given the research just described, it is particularly important to redirect parents to portray mathematics in a positive light. For example, "Even though math can be hard, stick with it and you will figure it out." Teaching parents how to help their children has also been found to make a difference in supporting student achievement (Cooper, 2007).

How do you effectively encourage students and their families to support mathematics learning at home? Here we break down the many possible ways into four categories: (1) parent participation, (2) homework support, (3) resources for parents, and (4) beyond homework experiences.

Parents' Participation

If parents can witness first hand your questioning and the many ways that problems can be solved, they will have a vision of how they can support learning at home. For example, they may notice that you encourage students to select their own strategy and explain how they know it works. Parents will also pick up on the language that you are using and will be able to reinforce that language at home. You can even provide a note-taking template that includes categories such as the following: What is the big idea of the lesson? What illustrations or tools are being used to help students understand? What are some questions the teacher is asking that I could also ask? What does the teacher do when a student is stuck?

Homework Support

Homework can be a positive experience for students, families, and the teacher. Take the following recommendations into consideration when thinking about the homework that you will assign to your students:

1. *Mimic the three-phase lesson model.* Complete a brief version of the *Before* phase of a lesson to be sure the students understand the homework before they go home. At home, students complete the *During* phase. When they return with the work completed, apply the sharing techniques of the *After* phase of the homework. Students can even practice the *After* phase with their family if you encourage this through parent or guardian communications. Some form of written work must be required so that students are held responsible for the task and are prepared for the class discussion.

2. *Use a distributed-content approach.* Homework can address content that has been taught earlier in the year as practice, that day's content as reinforcement, or upcoming content as groundwork. Interestingly, research has found that distributed homework that combines all three components is more effective in supporting student learning (Cooper, 2007). The exception is students with learning disabilities, who perform better when homework focuses on reinforcement of skills and current class lessons.

3. *Promote an "ask-before-tell" approach with parents.* Parents may not know how best to support their child when he or she is stuck or has gotten a wrong answer. One important thing you can do is to ask parents to implement an "ask-before-tell" approach (Kliman, 1999). This means that before parents explain something, they should ask their child to explain how he or she did it. The child may self-correct (a life skill), and if not, at least the parents can use what they heard from their child to provide targeted assistance.

4. *Provide good questioning prompts for parents.* Providing guiding questions for parents or guardians supports a problem-based approach to instruction as they help their children. Figure 7.5 provides guiding questions that can be included in the students' notebooks and shared with families. Translating questions for parents who are not native speakers of English is important. Often a child can help you with this task.

Homework of this nature communicates to families the problem-based or sense-making nature of your classroom and might help them see the value in this approach. A final note: A little bit goes a long way— if students are to spend time solving meaningful problems, then just a few engaging problems a night can accomplish more than a long set of practice problems.

Teaching Tip

Providing specific guidance to families makes a big difference in what they do (and do not do) to help their children learn mathematics and be confident in doing mathematics.

Figure 7.5 Questions for families to help their children with homework.

These guiding questions are designed to help your child think through his or her math homework problems. When your child gets stuck, ask the following:

- What do you need to figure out? What is the problem about?
- What words are confusing? What words are familiar?
- Did you solve problems like this one in class today?
- What have you tried so far? What else can you try?
- Can you make a drawing or chart to help you think about the problem?
- Does your answer make sense?
- Is there more than one answer?
- What math words or steps do you use in class?

Resources for Families

Parents will be better able to help to their child if they know where to find resources. The Internet can provide a wealth of information, but it can also be an overwhelming distraction.

 *Teaching Tip*

Don't forget the value of your own website as the first site for parents to visit for support. Post your unit letters to families, newsletters, access to homework assignments, possible strategies for doing the homework, and even successful student solutions.

Help families locate the good places to find math support. First, check whether your textbook provides websites with online resources for homework. These resources can include tutorials, video tutoring, videos, connections to careers and real-world applications, multilingual glossaries, audio podcasts, and more. Second, post websites that are good general resources. Here are some examples:

- *Figure This! Math Challenges for Families* (www.figurethis.org/index.html). This website has a teacher corner and a family corner. It offers outstanding resources to help parents understand standards-based mathematics, help with homework, and engage in *doing* mathematics with their children. It was originally designed for middle school, but the family corner provides general guidance and many of the challenges address content now in grades 3 through 5 (e.g., on fractions). It is also available in Spanish.

- *National Council of Teachers of Mathematics (NCTM)* (www.nctm.org/resources/families .aspx). This frequently updated site connects families to help on homework, current trends in mathematics, and resources.

- *Math Forum* (http://mathforum.org/parents.citizens.html). This site includes many features for teachers and families. For example, "Ask Dr. Math" is a great homework resource because students can write in their questions and get answers fairly quickly. Parents may also want to read or participate in Math Discussion Groups, read about Key Issues for the Mathematics Community, or download some of the very interesting problems posted here.

- *National Library of Virtual Manipulatives* (http://nlvm.usu.edu/en/nav/vlibrary.html). This site has numerous applets and virtual tools for learning about many mathematics topics.

There are also great websites for specific content. For example, Conceptua Math (www .conceptuamath.com) has excellent applets for exploring fraction operations.

Beyond Homework: Seeing Mathematics in the Home

In the same way that families support literacy by reading books with their children or pointing out letters of the alphabet when they encounter them, families can and should support numeracy. Because this has not been the practice in many homes, it means you have the responsibility to help parents see the connection between numeracy and everyday life. In her article "Beyond Helping with Homework: Parents and Children Doing Mathematics at Home," Kliman (1999) offers some excellent suggestions, which include asking parents to share anecdotes, find mathematics in the books they read, do scavenger hunts, and create opportunities during household chores. Figure 7.6 provides a sample letter home that suggests these four ideas to parents.

Adults constantly use estimation and computation in doing everyday tasks. If you get parents to talk about these instances with their children, imagine how much it can help students learn about mathematics and its importance as a life skill.

◆ Involving **All** Families

Some families are at all school events and conferences; others rarely participate. However, all families want their children to be successful in school. Parents who do not come to school events may have anxiety related to their own school experiences, or they may feel complete confidence that the school and its teachers are doing well by their child and that

Figure 7.6 Sample letter to parents regarding ways to infuse mathematics into their interactions with their child.

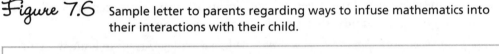

Making Math Moments Matter (M⁴)

Dear Families:
As a fifth grader, your child is increasingly aware of what is going on in the world. In that world is a lot of math! In our class this year we are working on **fractions** and **decimals,** as well as learning about **volume** of different containers. It will really help your child to <u>understand</u> and <u>see the importance</u> of math, if you find ways to talk about "math moments" (on any math topic, but especially fractions, decimals, and volume). We call it Making Math Moments Matter (M⁴ for short). Here are some ways to have fun with M⁴ at home.

Share stories. Share a math moment at dinner (or in the car). When have you used mathematics today (shopping, laundry, budgets, etc.)? Think of the many things you might have estimated—how long it will take to get to work, or to run a series of errands. Take turns sharing stories. We will share family math moments in class!

Connecting to reading. As they tell you about the book they are reading, ask quantity-type questions: What fractions (or percent) of the time is the main character at school? What fraction of the book have you read? What fraction will you read tonight?

Chores. Yes, chores! If it takes $\frac{3}{4}$ of an hour to do a load of laundry, how long will 3 loads take? If you walk the dog for 0.25 hour twice each day, how many hours is the dog walked in a week? A month? If you earn $5 an hour walking dogs, what might you earn in a week?

Scavenger hunts. Riding in the car can be more interesting if there are things to look for. Consider challenging your fifth grader to look for fractions, decimals, or percents on signs. Search for as many 3-D shapes as you can (e.g., a train car is a rectangular solid, a trash can is a cylinder, etc.).

they do not need to participate. In some cultures, questioning a teacher may be perceived as disrespectful. Rodríguez-Brown, a researcher on Hispanic families writes, "It is not that Latino parents do not want to support their children's learning. . . . [They] believe that it is disrespectful to usurp the teachers' role" (2010, p. 352).

Try to find ways to build a strong rapport with all families. Some strategies to consider include the following:

1. *Honor different strategies for doing mathematics.* Although this is a recommendation in standards documents, it is particularly important for students from other countries because they may have learned different ways to do the operations (Civil & Planas, 2010).

2. *Communicate with positive notes and phone calls.* Be sure to find a way to compliment each student's mathematical thinking (not just a good score on quiz) at some point early in the school year.

3. *Host informal gatherings to discuss mathematics teaching and learning.* Having regular opportunities to meet with the parents allows for the development of rapport and trust. Consider hosting events in out-of-school facilities. Schools in high-poverty communities have found that having parent events at a community center or religious institution brings in families that are reluctant to come into a school.

4. *Incorporate homework that involves the family.* When a student brings in homework that tells about his or her family and you provide positive feedback or a personal comment, then you are establishing a two-way communication with the family via homework.

5. *Translate letters that are sent home.* If you are doing a class newsletter (for families) or a letter describing the next mathematics unit, make an effort to translate the letter into the native language of the families represented in your class. If you cannot do this, consider having the first class session include a component in which students write to their families about what they are about to do. Ask them to write in their parents' first language and to include visuals to support their writing. Ask parents to respond (in their language of choice). This is a great practice for helping students know what they need to learn, and it communicates to families that they are an important part of that learning.

6. *Post homework on your webpage.* For parents who are not native speakers of English, posting problems on your site makes it easier for them to take advantage of online translations. Although these translations may not be perfectly accurate, they can aid in helping parents and students understand the language in the problems.

For more suggestions on ensuring that your mathematics tasks and homework are meeting the needs of culturally and linguistically diverse students, see Chapter 5 and read the NCTM Research Brief titled "Involving Latino and Latina Parents in Their Children's Mathematics Education" (Civil & Menéndez, 2010). For suggestions on students with special needs, see Chapter 6.

Principal Engagement and Support

Teachers cite a supportive principal as one of the most essential components in successfully implementing a standards-based curriculum (Bay et al., 1999). Therefore, a principal plays a pivotal role in establishing a shared vision for a problem-based mathematics program. Principals, who have many competing priorities, often cannot take the time to attend the professional development workshops that are designed for teachers who will be teaching the mathematics program. And what they need to know is qualitatively different from what a classroom teacher needs to know.

Since the launch of the *Common Core State Standards*, school administrators, parents, and community members are more aware than ever about mathematics standards. If your state has not adopted the *Common Core State Standards*, there are still state-level standards that are the focus of mathematics goals and assessments. Though it may seem that the need to communicate with administrators is something to simply check off your list, it *must* be a top priority.

Even though principals are hearing more about mathematics standards, higher standards, and the need to ensure that all students are successful, it does not mean they understand what standards-based mathematics curriculum *is* in terms of the content or the related CCSS Standards for Mathematical Practice or NCTM process standards. The principal is likely to get bombarded with broad or specific questions from parents, such as: "Is 'new math' back?" or "Why isn't the teacher teaching the procedures for multiplying and dividing?" or "What are the Standards for Mathematical Practice?" When a principal is asked these questions, he or she needs to give a convincing response that is accurate and that also addresses the heart of the parents' concerns (that their child is going to get a good, sound, research-based mathematics experience).

Meyer and Arbaugh (2008) suggest professional development specifically for principals. Although their focus is on the adoption of standards-based textbooks, the plan they outline applies to all principals who are seeking to be knowledgeable and effective advocates for implementing new standards or mathematics curricula. The following ideas are adapted from their suggested professional development to focus on one-on-one conversations:

1. *Contrast old and new curriculum.* As a first step, it is important to know what is new and different in the mathematics program. One way to start is to provide a set of materials that represent typical *Common Core State Standards*–aligned tasks alongside the previous curriculum. Point out the noticeable similarities and differences or the key features of the curriculum. (Note: It is important to focus on *both* similarities and differences—not everything is being replaced, and this is an important message.)

2. *Discuss how parents and students will respond.* Anticipate what will be noticed by parents (or their children). Which changes might be welcomed? Which changes might be worrisome? How will the welcome aspects be promoted and the worrisome aspects be explained?

3. *Experience the curriculum.* Invite the principal to visit your classroom or other classrooms in which the Standards for Mathematical Practice or the NCTM process standards are being infused. Ask the principal to join a group of students and listen to their discussion of how they are solving a problem. Or organize a lesson in which students actually present their solutions to the principal in the *After* phase. For example, in fourth grade, have students show their different ways for multiplying fractions using visuals and explanations. If possible, ask the principal to solve one of the problems students are doing and share his or her strategy with the class. This first-hand experience can provide the principal with a wonderful story to share with parents and with insights that won't be gained from reviewing standards documents.

4. *Discuss emerging issues.* Plan a regular time to meet with the principal to discuss what he or she has heard from families about the mathematics program. Discuss what you might do to respond to questions (some of their anticipated issues may have already been described in the preceding section on parents' concerns). If there is a question about a problem-based approach, Chapter 2 should be a great read for a principal and contains talking points to share with others.

Finally, keep your principal apprised of successes and breakthroughs. These stories provide the principal with evidence to share when pressed by parents or community members.

Principals are very often your strongest advocate and are in a position to serve as buffers between school mathematics and the community.

▲ Communicating with Stakeholders

A final and critical point is to be careful in how we communicate with stakeholders (e.g., parents, district administrators, other teachers, community partners). Without knowing it, we sometimes say things that, although well intentioned, increase concerns rather than help to ease stakeholder anxiety. Table 7.2 provides three such examples.

Stop and Reflect

Place your hand over the second and third columns in Table 7.2 and ask yourself: "How might a parent respond if he or she heard this statement?" "What might the parent misinterpret?" "How might my principal respond?" Then read the responses in the table to see whether they represent stakeholders like those in your setting. As a rule, it is a good idea to filter your statements through these questions. ◼

Initially the statements may not seem harmful, but they can set off alarms from the lens of a stakeholder. Consider these reactions, and then review the language shift in the third column, which communicates a stronger (and less potentially disconcerting) message. Along these lines, it is very important to convey to stakeholders an excitement for and pride in your mathematics program. Being tentative, reserved, vague, or silent on the mathematics program can only raise concerns in the community. Help stakeholders understand that

Table 7.2 Statements and Possible (Unintended) Interpretations of the Statements

Original Statement	What a Parent or Administrator Might Think	A Stronger, Carefully Composed Statement
"The [mathematics program] still addresses skills, but it also includes concepts."	"Why are they bringing skills up? They must be taking those away. My child/U.S. kids have to know basics. How can I put a stop to this?"	"The skills in the [mathematics program] are expanding from what we once learned and now include . . ."
"It is important for students to learn from one another, so I will be more in the role of facilitator."	"The teacher is not teaching? My child does better when things are explained clearly. When I come see you teach, what am I looking for if you are just letting the kids learn on their own?"	"In our classroom, we learn from one another. I give carefully selected tasks for students to discuss and then we talk about them together so that everyone has a chance to learn the mathematics we are doing, and that approach gives me the chance to work one-on-one as needed."
"This year we are doing a whole new mathematics program that the state has adopted."	"My worst nightmare—an experiment of something new during the years my child is in elementary school. This will cause problems for the rest of his life."	"We are doing some new things in order to make sure your child is well prepared for . . . [or that our program is the best available]. You might have noticed that last year we [added writing as a component to our math program]. This year, here are the big things we hope to accomplish. . . ."

the mathematics program students are experiencing aligns with best practices in education, represents what students need to know in today's world, and prepares them for mathematics at the next level, as well as the mathematics they need for life.

Stop and Reflect

What do you think the parents of your students would most value about teaching mathematics through problem solving? How will you use your response to this question to build strong family support and engagement? Repeat the question for other stakeholders, like your principal. ■

8

Exploring Number and Operation Sense

Big IDEAS

1 Addition and subtraction are connected. Addition names the whole in terms of the parts and subtraction names a missing part. This structure holds true whether students are considering whole numbers or other numbers such as fractions and decimals.

2 Multiplication is related to addition and involves counting groups of like size and determining how many there are in all (multiplicative thinking). Multiplication and division have an inverse relationship.

3 Division can be interpreted as fair sharing or as repeated subtraction. Division names a missing factor in terms of the known factor and the product.

4 Models can be used to solve contextual problems for all operations and to figure out what operation is involved in a problem, regardless of the size of the numbers. Models can also be used to give meaning to number sentences. Representing contextual situations with equations is at the heart of algebraic thinking.

This chapter is about helping students connect different meanings and relationships to the four operations of addition, subtraction, multiplication, and division so that they can accurately and fluently apply these operations in real-world settings. As students think about how many objects they have after changes take place or as they compare quantities, they develop what might be termed *operation sense*, a highly integrated understanding of the four operations and the many different but related meanings these operations take on in real contexts. This is all part of the Operations Core (National Research Council Committee, 2009), in which students learn to see mathematical situations in their day-to-day lives or in story problems and begin to identify and model these situations using words, pictures, manipulatives, and/or numbers (e.g. equations). The Operations Core builds and expands on the NRC's Number Core and Relations Core that are developed in the primary grades and will be extended in the discussion of number sense and place value in Chapter 10.

As you read this chapter, pay special attention to the impact on the development of number sense, basic fact mastery, and computation. As students develop an understanding of operations, they can and should simultaneously be developing more sophisticated ideas about number and ways to think about basic fact combinations.

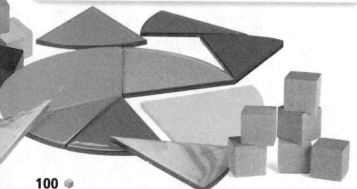

Developing Addition and Subtraction Operation Sense

Although students begin learning about addition and subtraction prior to third grade, which is where this book begins, there are structures that support the learning of additive situations that don't expire. Instead, these same structures can support students' thinking about addition and subtraction with larger whole numbers as well as with fractions and decimals.

Addition and Subtraction Problem Structures

We begin this chapter with a look at three categories of problem structures for additive situations (which include both addition and subtraction), and later explore four problem structures for multiplicative situations (which include both multiplication and division). These categories help students develop a schema to identify important information and to structure their thinking. In particular, researchers suggest that students with disabilities should be explicitly taught these underlying structures so that they can identify important characteristics of the situations and determine when to add or subtract (Fuchs, Fuchs, Prentice, Hamlett, Finelli, & Courey, 2004; Xin, Jitendra, & Deatline-Buchman, 2005). Students' thinking can be supported by identifying whether a problem fits a "join" or "separate" classification. When students are exposed to new problems, the familiar characteristics will assist them in generalizing from similar problems on which they have practiced. Furthermore, teachers who are not aware of the variety of situations and corresponding structures may randomly offer problems to students without the proper sequencing to support students' full grasp of the meaning of the operations. By knowing the logical structure of these problems, you will be able to pose a variety of problem types (within each structure) and help students interpret a variety of real-world contexts. More importantly, you will be able to recognize which structures cause the greatest challenges for students.

Researchers have separated addition and subtraction problems into structures based on the kinds of relationships involved (Verschaffel, Greer, & DeCorte, 2007). These include change problems (join and separate), part–part–whole problems, and compare problems (Carpenter, Fennema, Franke, Levi, & Empson, 1999). The basic structure for each of these three categories of problems is illustrated in Figure 8.1. Each structure involves a number family such as 30, 50, 80. Depending of which of the three quantities is unknown, a different problem type results. Each of the problem structures is illustrated with the story problems that follow. The number family 40, 80, 120 is used in each example problem and can be connected to the structure in Figure 8.1. Note that the problems are described in terms of their structure and interpretation and not as addition or subtraction problems. Contrary to what you may have thought, a joining action does not always mean addition, nor does separate or remove always mean subtraction.

Figure 8.1

Basic structures for addition and subtraction story problem types. Each structure has three numbers and any one of the three numbers can be the unknown.

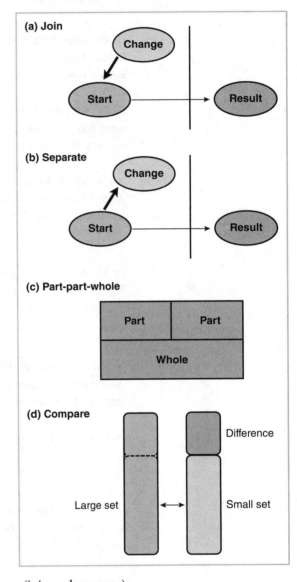

◀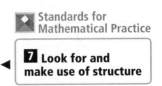

Standards for Mathematical Practice

7 Look for and make use of structure

Examples of Change Problems

Join. For the action of joining, there are three quantities involved: an initial or starting amount, a change amount (the part being added or joined), and the resulting amount (the total amount after the change takes place). In Figure 8.1(a) this is illustrated by the change being "added to" the initial amount. Any one of these three quantities can be unknown in a problem, as shown in these three types of joining problems.

JOIN: Result Unknown

Sandra had a collection of 80 stickers. George gave her 40 more. How many stickers does Sandra have altogether?

JOIN: Change Unknown

Sandra had a collection of 80 stickers. George gave her some more. Now Sandra has 120 stickers. How many stickers did George give her?

JOIN: Start Unknown

Sandra had some stickers. George gave her 40 more. Now Sandra has 120 stickers. How many stickers did Sandra have to begin with?

Separate. In separating problems, the initial amount is the whole or the largest amount, whereas in the joining problems, the result is the largest amount (whole). In separating problems, the change is that an amount is being removed or taken away from the initial value. Again, refer to Figure 8.1(b) as you consider these problems.

SEPARATE: Result Unknown

Sandra had a collection of 120 stickers. She gave 40 stickers to George. How many stickers does Sandra have now?

SEPARATE: Change Unknown

Sandra had 120 stickers. She gave some to George. Now she has 80 stickers. How many stickers did she give to George?

SEPARATE: Start Unknown

Sandra had some stickers. She gave 40 to George. Now Sandra has 80 stickers left. How many stickers did Sandra have to begin with?

Examples of Part–Part–Whole Problems

Part–part–whole problems involve two parts that are combined into one whole, as in Figure 8.1(c). In these situations, either the missing whole, one of the missing parts (unknown), or both parts must be found. The combining may be a physical action, or it may be a mental combination in which the parts are not physically combined (see following examples). This structure links to the idea in the Number Core that numbers are embedded in other numbers. Students can break apart 7 into 5 and 2. Each of the addends (or parts) was embedded in the 7 (whole). This is also true for breaking numbers such as 90 into 35 and 55. There is no meaningful distinction between the two parts in a part–part–whole situation, so there is no need to have a different problem for each part as the unknown. For both possibilities (whole unknown and part unknown), example problems are given. The first problem in each set is a mental combination in which there is no action. The second problem involves a physical action.

PART–PART–WHOLE: Whole Unknown

George has 80 pennies and 40 nickels. How many coins does he have?

George has 80 pennies and Sandra has 40 pennies. They put their pennies into a coin bank. How many pennies did they put into the bank?

PART–PART–WHOLE: Part Unknown

George has 120 coins. Eighty of his coins are pennies, and the rest are nickels. How many nickels does George have?

George and Sandra put 120 pennies into the coin bank. George put in 40 pennies. How many pennies did Sandra put in?

Examples of Compare Problems

Compare problems involve the comparison of two separate quantities. The third amount does not actually exist but is the difference between the two amounts. Figure 8.1(d) illustrates the compare problem structure. There are three ways to present compare problems, corresponding to which quantity is unknown (smaller, larger, or difference). For each of these, two examples are given: One problem in which the difference is stated in terms of more and another in terms of less. Note that the language of "more" will often confuse students and thus presents a challenge in interpretation.

COMPARE: Difference Unknown

George has 120 pennies and Sandra has 80 pennies. How many more pennies does George have than Sandra?

George has 120 pennies. Sandra has 80 pennies. How many fewer pennies does Sandra have than George?

COMPARE: Larger Unknown

George has 40 more pennies than Sandra. Sandra has 80 pennies. How many pennies does George have?

Sandra has 40 fewer pennies than George. Sandra has 80 pennies. How many pennies does George have?

COMPARE: Smaller Unknown

George has 40 more pennies than Sandra. George has 120 pennies. How many pennies does Sandra have?

Sandra has 40 fewer pennies than George. George has 120 pennies. How many pennies does Sandra have?

Stop and Reflect

Go back through all of these examples and match the numbers in the problems with the components of the structures in Figure 8.1. For each problem, do two additional things. First, use base-ten materials to model (solve) the problem as you think students might do. Second, for each problem, write either an addition or subtraction equation that you think best represents the problem as you did it with materials. ■

In most curricula, the overwhelming emphasis is on the easiest problem types: join and separate with the result unknown. These become the de facto definitions of addition and subtraction: Addition is "put together" and subtraction is "take away." The fact is, these are not the only meanings of addition and subtraction.

When students develop these limited put-together and take-away definitions or meanings for addition and subtraction, they often have difficulty later when addition or subtraction is called for but the structure is different from put together or take away. It is important that students be exposed to all forms within these different problem structures.

Teaching Tip

Remember that students often think of the equal sign as an operation sign (meaning to do a computation) rather than a relational sign (indicating a relationship). When you read an equation at the point of the equal sign say "is the same as." This reinforces the meaning of the symbol.

Problem Difficulty

Some of the problem types are more difficult than other problem types. The join or separate problems in which the start part is unknown (e.g., Sandra had some stickers) are often the most difficult, probably because as students try to model the problem they do not know how many materials to put down to begin. Problems in which the change amounts are unknown are also difficult. Compare problems are often challenging because the language often confuses students into adding instead of finding the difference.

Many students will attempt to solve compare problems as part–part–whole problems without making separate sets of counters or materials for the two amounts. The larger quantity is used as the whole and the smaller quantity is used as one of the parts. They need to recognize that the quantities in comparison problems come from different wholes and the quantities in part–part–whole problems come from the same whole.

As students begin to translate a story problem into an equation, they may be challenged to create a matching equation that emphasizes the corresponding operation. This is particularly important as students move into explorations that develop algebraic thinking. The structure of the equations also may cause difficulty for English language learners, who may not initially have the flexibility in creating equivalent equations due to reading comprehension issues with the story situation.

◆ Teaching Addition and Subtraction

So far you have seen a variety of story problem structures for addition and subtraction and you have used base-ten materials to help you think about how these problems can be solved by your students. Combining the use of contexts and models (base-ten materials, drawings, bar diagrams, number lines) is important in helping students construct a deep understanding of these two operations. Let's examine how each approach can be used in the classroom. As you read this section, note that addition and subtraction are taught at the same time to reinforce their inverse relationship.

Contextual Problems

There is more to think about than simply giving students word problems to solve. In contrast with the rather straightforward and brief contextual problems given in the primary grades, you need to set the problems you give in meaningful contexts.

Fosnot and Dolk (2001) point out that in story problems, students tend to focus on getting the answer. "Context problems, on the other hand, are connected as closely as possible to children's lives, rather than to 'school mathematics.' They are designed to anticipate and to develop children's mathematical modeling of the real world" (p. 24). Contextual problems might derive from recent experiences in the classroom, a field trip, a discussion you have been having in art, science, or social studies, or from children's literature. Rich contexts are used to help students construct mathematical ideas, notice patterns, and engage in meaningful discussion. Because contextual problems connect to life experiences, they are important for English language learners, too, even though it may seem that the language presents a challenge to ELLs. To support their comprehension of such stories, the sentences can be structured using present and past tense; the word order can be adapted to noun then verb; terms like *his/her* and *it* can be replaced with a name; and unnecessary vocabulary words can be removed. Having a visual or letting students model this story are also effective strategies for ELLs and students with disabilities.

You may wish to stay with a particular context, which is particularly important for ELLs and students with disabilities, but at the same time allow for variety and differentiation. For example, it might be interesting to compare the populations of cities or counties in your region. Place the names of the cities on cards and either write the population directly on the card or have a corresponding chart for students to refer to. Then give students two cards and word problems that go along with their cities, or you can have students create their own word problems. Students who can handle the larger numbers can work with densely populated locations, while students needing a gentler ramp up to the content can start with two sparsely populated areas. This will give students opportunities to add the combined populations, compare their populations, or use other possible scenarios.

Lessons Built on Context or Story Problems.

What might a good lesson built around word problems look like? The answer comes more naturally if you think about students not just solving the problems but also using words, pictures, and numbers to explain how they went about solving the problem and justifying why they are correct. In a single class period, try to focus on a few problems with an in-depth discussion, rather than a lot of problems with little elaboration. Students should be allowed to use whatever physical materials or drawings they feel they need to help them. Whatever they put on their paper should explain what they did well enough to allow someone else to understand their thinking.

A particularly effective approach is having students correct others' written solutions. For example, you can give the class a set of fictitious students' work with calculations related to a recent fundraiser at the school. By using anonymous students' work, the students in your class can analyze the reasoning used to translate the problem from the situation, mistakes in computation, and errors in copying numbers over.

> ◆ **Standards for Mathematical Practice**
>
> ◀ **3 Construct viable arguments and critique the reasoning of others**

Choosing Numbers for Problems.

When adding and subtracting in grades 3 through 5, it is best to use real-world data to link to students' interests or other subject areas, such as science. One advantage of using this kind of information is that you can differentiate problems in accord with the students' number development, giving them numbers as large as they can conceptually grasp. Word problems can serve as an opportunity to learn about number and computation at the same time. For example, a problem involving the combination of 315 and 420 has the potential to help students focus on sets of hundreds, then sets of tens or ones. They might think "add 300 and 400, and then add 35 more." Invented strategies for computation in addition and subtraction are a focus of Chapter 11.

Figure 8.2

Part–part–whole models for 5 + 3 = 8 and 8 - 3 = 5.

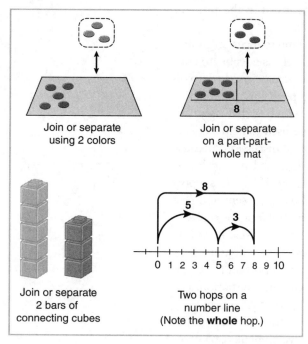

Join or separate using 2 colors

Join or separate on a part-part-whole mat

Join or separate 2 bars of connecting cubes

Two hops on a number line (Note the **whole** hop.)

Model-Based Problems

Many students will use counters, bar diagrams, or number lines (models) to solve story problems. The model is a thinking tool that helps them both understand what is happening in the problem and a means for keeping track of the numbers and steps in solving the problem. Problems can also be posed using models when there is no context involved.

When the parts of a set are known, addition is used to name the whole in terms of the parts. This simple definition of addition serves both action situations (join and separate) and static or no-action situations (part–part–whole). For illustrative purposes, each of the models shown in Figure 8.2 represents 5 + 3 = 8. Some of these are the result of a definite put together or joining action, and some are not. Notice that in every example, both of the parts are distinct, even after the parts are combined. These models will be used with larger numbers in grades 3 through 5, but the structure of the model remains the same. If base-ten materials are used, the two parts should be in different piles or on different sections of a mat. For students to see a relationship between the two parts and the whole, the image must be kept as two separate sets. This helps students reflect on the action after it has occurred. "These 35 base-ten blocks are the ones I started with. Then I added 55 base-ten blocks, and now I have 90 altogether."

The use of bar diagrams (also called *strip* or *tape diagrams*) as semi-concrete visual representations is a central fixture in both Japanese curriculum and what is known as *Singapore mathematics*. As with other tools, they support students' mathematical thinking by generating "meaning making space" (Murata, 2008, p. 399) and are a precursor to the use of number lines (including empty or minimally notated number lines). Murata states, "Tape diagrams are designed to bring forward the relational meanings of the quantities in a problem by showing the connections in context" (2008, p. 396). Here is an example. Note how the matching bar diagram visually connects to the part–part–whole diagram students have been using since the primary grades.

Mary made 686 biscuits. She sold some of them. If 298 were left over, how many biscuits did she sell? (See Figure 8.3.)

Figure 8.3

A bar diagram that supports students' thinking about the problem.

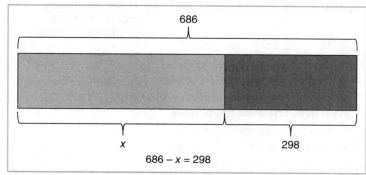

686

x

298

$686 - x = 298$

Source: Solving Algebra and Other Story Problems with Simple Diagrams: a Method Demonstrated in Grade 4–6 Texts Used in Singapore page 42 By Sybilla Beckmann (2004) The Mathematics Educator, Vol. 14, No. 1, 42–46

A number line is also a worthwhile model, but it can initially present conceptual difficulties for children below second grade and students with disabilities (National Research Council Committee, 2009). This is partially due to their difficulty in seeing the unit, which is a challenge when it appears in a continuous line. A number line is also a shift from counting a number of individual objects in a collection to continuous length units. There are, however, ways to introduce and model number lines that support young learners as they learn to use this representation. Familiarity with a number line is essential because third graders will use number lines to locate fractions and add and subtract time intervals, fourth graders will locate decimals and use them for measurement, and fifth graders will use perpendicular number lines in coordinate grids (CCSSO, 2010).

A number line measures distances from zero the same way a ruler does. If you don't actually teach the use of the number line through an emphasis on the unit (length), students may focus on the hash marks or numerals instead of the spaces (a misunderstanding that becomes apparent when their answers are consistently off by one). At first students can build a number path by using a given length, such as a set of Cuisenaire rods of the same color to make a straight line of multiple single units. This will show each length unit is "one unit" and that same unit is repeated over and over (iterated) to form the number line (Dougherty, 2008). Furthermore, if arrows (hops) are drawn for each number in an expression, the length concept is more clearly illustrated. Eventually, the use of a ruler or a scale in a bar graph or coordinate grid will reinforce this model.

t·e·c·h·n·o·l·o·g·y note

There's a free virtual number line at www.eduplace.com/kids/mw that emphasizes the unit. Go into the site, select a grade, select eManipulatives, and then select Number Line. Each grade level focuses on different skills—try grade 4 to work with decimals. The student clicks on the number line at any number to start, and then selects numbers on the keypad at the left to input the unit. The figure will jump forward (for addition) or backward (for subtraction) depending on whether the student selects the left-pointing arrow or right-pointing arrow.

Developing Multiplication and Division Operation Sense

A key component of the third-grade curriculum is to help students develop *operation sense* with respect to multiplication and division. This means facilitating students' connections of the different meanings of multiplication and division to each other, as well as connections to addition and subtraction. Operation sense supports students' effective application of these operations in real-world settings.

◆ Multiplication and Division Problem Structures

Like addition and subtraction, there are problem structures that will help you in formulating and assigning multiplication and division tasks. They will also help your students with generalizing as they identify regularity by solving familiar situations.

Most researchers identify four different classes of multiplicative structures (Greer, 1992): equal groups, comparison, area, and combinations. The term *multiplicative* is used here to describe all types of problems that involve multiplication and division. Of these, the two structures shown in Figure 8.4, equal groups (repeated addition, rates) and multiplicative comparison, are by far the most prevalent in the elementary school. Equal-group problems are the focus in the third grade standards and comparison problems are emphasized in the fourth grade standards (CCSSO, 2010). Problems matching these structures can be modeled with sets of counters, number lines, bar diagrams, or arrays. They represent a large percentage of the multiplicative problems in the real world, but students should have experiences with all four multiplicative structures.

In multiplicative problems, one number or *factor* counts how many sets, groups, or parts of equal size are involved. The other factor tells the size of each set or part. The

Standards for Mathematical Practice

8 Look for and express regularity in repeated reasoning

Figure 8.4

Two of the four basic structures for multiplication and division story problems. Each structure has three numbers. Any one of the three numbers can be the unknown in a story problem.

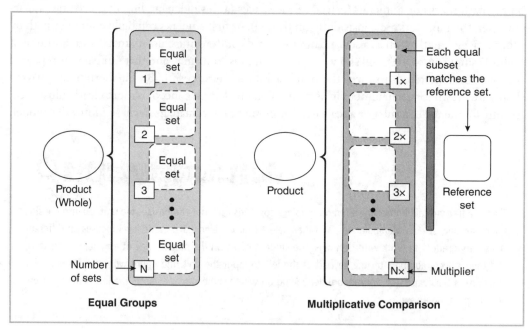

third number in each of these two structures is the *whole* or *product* and is the total of all of the parts. The parts and wholes terminology is useful in making the connection to addition.

Examples of Equal-Group Problems

When the number and size of groups are known, the problem is a multiplication situation. When either the number of sets or the size of sets is unknown, then the problem is a division situation. These division situations, however, are not alike. Problems in which the size of the sets is unknown are called *fair-sharing* or *partition* problems. The whole is shared or distributed among a known number of sets to determine the size of each. If the number of sets is unknown but the size of the equal sets is known, the problems are called *measurement* or sometimes *repeated-subtraction* problems. The whole is "measured off" in sets of the given size. These terms are used with the examples that follow. Use the illustrations in Figure 8.4 as a reference.

There is also a subtle difference between problems that might be thought of as *repeated-addition* problems (e.g., If 3 children have 4 apples each, how many apples are there?) and those that might be termed *rate* problems (e.g., If there are 4 apples per child, how many apples would 3 children have?). In a rate problem, students are working with a composed unit (in this case, apples per child). For each equal-groups category, two examples of rate problems are provided.

EQUAL GROUPS: Product Unknown (Multiplication)
Mark has 4 bags of apples. There are 6 apples in each bag. How many apples does Mark have altogether? (repeated addition)

If apples cost 7 cents each, how much did Jill have to pay for 5 apples? (rate)

Peter walked for 3 hours at 4 miles per hour. How far did he walk? (rate)

EQUAL GROUPS: Size of Group Unknown (Partition Division)

Mark has 24 apples. He wants to share them equally among his 4 friends. How many apples will each friend receive? (fair sharing)

Jill paid 35 cents for 5 apples. What was the cost of 1 apple? (rate)

Peter walked 12 miles in 3 hours. How many miles per hour (how fast) did he walk? (rate)

EQUAL GROUPS: Number of Groups Unknown (Measurement Division)

Mark has 24 apples. He put them into bags containing 6 apples each. How many bags did Mark use? (repeated subtraction)

Jill bought apples at 7 cents apiece. The total cost of her apples was 35 cents. How many apples did Jill buy? (rate)

Peter walked 12 miles at a rate of 4 miles per hour. How many hours did it take Peter to walk the 12 miles? (rate)

Examples of Comparison Problems

In multiplicative comparison problems there are really two different sets, as there were with comparison situations for addition and subtraction. In additive situations, the comparison is an amount or quantity difference. In multiplicative situations, the comparison is based on one group being a particular multiple of the other (multiple copies). With multiplication comparison, there are 3 possibilities for the unknown: The product could be unknown; the group size could be unknown; and the number of groups could be unknown. Two examples of each possibility are provided here.

COMPARISON: Product Unknown (Multiplication)

Jill picked 6 apples. Mark picked 4 times as many apples as Jill. How many apples did Mark pick?

This month Mark saved 5 times as much money as last month. Last month he saved $7. How much money did Mark save this month?

COMPARISON: Group Size Unknown (Partition Division)

Mark picked 24 apples. He picked 4 times as many apples as Jill. How many apples did Jill pick?

This month Mark saved 5 times as much money as he did last month. If he saved $35 this month, how much did he save last month?

COMPARISON: Number of Groups Unknown (Measurement Division)

Mark picked 24 apples, and Jill picked only 6. How many times as many apples did Mark pick as Jill did?

This month Mark saved $35. Last month he saved $7. How many times as much money did he save this month as last?

Stop and Reflect

What you just read is complex yet important. Stop now and get a collection of about 35 counters to model the equal-group examples starring Mark. Match each story with one of the structures modeled in Figure 8.4. How are these problems alike and how are they different? Repeat the exercise for the Jill and Peter problems. Can you see how the problems in each group are alike and how they are related across the problem structures?

When you are comfortable with the equal-group problems, repeat the same process with the multiplicative comparison problems. Again, start with the first problem in all three sets and then the second problem in all three sets. Reflect on how they are the same and different. ∎

Examples of Area Problems

What distinguishes area problems from the others is that the product is literally a different type of unit from the two factors. This is known as a *product of measures* problem. In a rectangular shape, the product of two lengths (length × width) is an area, usually square units.

AREA: Product Unknown (Multiplication)

Lisa's garden measures 4 feet wide and 8 feet long. What is the area?

AREA: Side Dimension Unknown (Division)

A playground has an area of 27 square feet. If one side is 9 feet long, how long is the side next to it?

Figure 8.5 illustrates how different the square units are from the two factors of length: 4 feet times 7 feet is not 28 feet, but 28 square feet. The factors are each one-dimensional entities, but the product consists of two-dimensional units.

Notice how familiarity with the array model can help students bridge to models of area. Although an array represents equal sets, it can be modeled with circular counters or any items. Yet, if you begin to use the small square tiles for the array and push the tiles together, this can be recorded on grid paper and connected more easily to the area problem structure.

Figure 8.5

Length times length equals area.

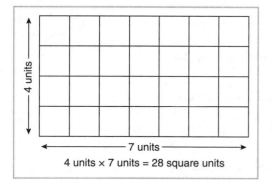

4 units × 7 units = 28 square units

Examples of Combination Problems

Combination problems involve counting the number of possible pairings that can be made between two or more sets.

COMBINATIONS: Product Unknown

Sam bought 4 pairs of pants and 3 jackets, and they all can be worn together. How many different outfits consisting of a pair of pants and a jacket does Sam have?

An experiment involves tossing a coin and rolling a die. How many different possible results or outcomes can this experiment have?

In these two examples, the product is unknown and the size of the two sets is given. It is possible—although rarely—to have related division problems for the combinations concept. Figure 8.6 shows one common method of modeling combination problems with two sets—an *array*. Counting how many combinations of two or more things or events are possible is important in determining probabilities. The combinations concept is most often found in the probability strand.

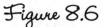

A model for a combination situation.

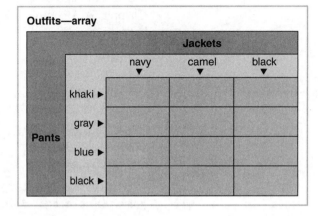

Teaching Multiplication and Division

Multiplication and division are often taught separately, with multiplication preceding division. It is important, however, to combine multiplication and division soon after multiplication has been introduced in order to help students see how they have an inverse relationship. In most curricula, these topics are first presented in grade 2 (as suggested by the *Common Core State Standards*) and then become a major focus in third grade, with continued development in the fourth and fifth grades. "In grades 3–5, students should focus on the meanings of, and relationship between, multiplication and division. It is important that students understand what each number in a multiplication or division expression represents.... Modeling multiplication problems with pictures, diagrams, or concrete materials helps students learn what the factors and their product represent in various contexts" (NCTM, 2000, p. 151).

A major conceptual hurdle in working with multiplicative structures is understanding groups of items as single entities while also understanding that a group contains a given number of objects (Clark & Kamii, 1996). Students can solve the problem "How many apples are in 4 baskets of 8 apples each?" by counting out four sets of eight counters and then counting them all. To think multiplicatively about this problem as four sets of eight requires students to conceptualize each group of eight as a single item to be counted. Experiences with making and counting equal groups, especially in contextual situations, are extremely useful.

Contextual Problems

When teaching multiplication and division, it is essential to use interesting contextual problems instead of more sterile story problems (or "naked numbers"). However, as with addition and subtraction, there is more to think about than simply giving students word problems to solve. Consider the following problems.

George bought 12 packs of game cards with 15 cards each. How many cards did George buy?

Yesterday, as we planned for the school's Fall Festival, we discovered that it took 7 yards of paper to cover the bulletin board in the front lobby of the school. There are 25 more bulletin boards in the hallways and classrooms around the school. How many yards of paper will we need if we cover all the bulletin boards in the school?

The first problem is similar to a typical problem that you could find in a textbook and is rather mundane. The second problem is based on students' recent experience in the classroom and builds on that known context. As stated previously, with a meaningful context students are more likely to exhibit their most spontaneous and meaningful approaches to solving a problem because they have some connection to it.

What might a good lesson look like for a third-, fourth-, or fifth-grade class that is built around problems? The tendency in the United States is to have students solve several problems in a single class period, and the focus of the lesson is getting answers. If the focus of the lesson is sense making, solving several problems in one class period might not be the best approach. Students should be allowed to use whatever physical materials they feel they need to help them, or they can simply draw pictures. Whatever they put on their paper should explain what they did well enough to allow someone else to understand it (allow at least a half page of space for a problem or use the idea of the translation task discussed in Chapter 3). A complete lesson will often revolve around one or two problems and the related discussion.

Formative Assessment Note

The techniques that students use to solve problems provide you with important information concerning their number development, strategies they may be using to determine basic facts, and methods they are using for multidigit computation. Therefore, it is essential that you look at more than the answers students get. Your observations can give you clues as to what numbers to use in problems for the next day. The information can be used to give special number or computation development work to students in need of it. Selected papers showing student work can be saved in folders and used in conferences to show parents how their child is working and progressing.

Suppose that in a diagnostic interview you ask a student to figure out 7 times 26. In response the student adds 26 seven times. The student's use of an additive approach informs you that it might be fruitful to focus on the idea of taking numbers apart in useful ways—part–part–whole ideas. The idea is to look for easier numbers with which to work in multiplication. For example, working with the factor 25 instead of 26 can be easier, especially if one thinks in terms of quarters: 4 quarters make a dollar (or 100 cents) and 8 quarters make two dollars (or 200 cents). Because you only need seven 25s, that is 175. Taking care of the one remaining 7 left from the 26, you now add 175 and 7. If you have been working on benchmarks of 5 and 10, you can observe the student's use of these ideas in adding 175 and 7. Does the student count up from 175 or decompose 7 into 5 and 2 to add more efficiently?

Similarly, you can present whole-class assessments by posing problems involving number concepts or computations that you have not yet explored with your students. How they approach the problems will give you clues as to where that portion of your number curriculum can best begin.

Whenever possible, use vocabulary development strategies such as reviewing key words needed for the task or linking visuals or gestures to the words in the problem to ensure that the situations are comprehensible to ELLs. Then, encourage students to solve problems using whatever techniques they wish, using words, pictures, and numbers to explain their process.

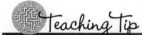 Teaching Tip

To ease the language demands on ELLs, you may want to build lessons around only two or three problems contexts.

Symbolism for Multiplication and Division. When students solve simple multiplication story problems before learning about multiplication symbolism, they will most likely write repeated-addition equations to represent what they did. This is your opportunity to introduce the multiplication sign and explain what the two factors mean.

The usual convention in the United States is that 4×8 refers to four sets of eight, not eight sets of four. There is no reason to be so rigid about this convention that you would mark a student as incorrect. The important thing is that the students can tell you what each factor in their equations represents. In vertical form, it is usually the bottom factor that indicates the number of sets. These conventions allow us to communicate clearly about the problem with each other. It also helps to build toward the commutative property of multiplication (see discussion in "Properties of Multiplication and Division" section).

The quotient 24 divided by 6 is represented in three different ways: $24 \div 6$, $6 \overline{)24}$, and $\frac{24}{6}$. Students should understand that these representations are equivalent. Students often mistakenly read 6)24 as "6 divided by 24," due to the left to right order of the numerals. Generally this error does not match what they are thinking.

Compounding the difficulty of division notation is the unfortunate phrase "goes in to" as in, "6 goes in to 24." This phrase carries little meaning about division, especially in connection with a fair-sharing or partitioning context. The "goes in to" terminology is simply engrained in adult parlance and has not been in textbooks for years. Instead of this phrase, you can use appropriate terminology with students, such as "How many groups of 6 are in 24?"

Choosing Numbers for Problems.

When selecting numbers for multiplicative story problems or activities, there is a tendency to think that large numbers pose a burden to students, or that 3×4 is somehow easier to understand than 4×17. An understanding of products or quotients is not affected by the size of the numbers, as long as the numbers are within your students' grasp. A contextual problem involving 14×8 is very appropriate for third graders. When given the challenge of using larger numbers, students are likely to invent computational strategies (e.g., ten 8s and then four more 8s) or model the problem with manipulatives.

Remainders

More often than not in real-world situations, division does not result in a simple whole number. For example, problems with 6 as a divisor will result in a whole number only one time out of six. In the absence of a context, a remainder can be dealt with in only two ways: It can either remain a quantity left over, or it can be partitioned into fractions. In Figure 8.7, the problem $11 \div 4$ is modeled to show a remainder as a fraction.

In real contexts, remainders sometimes have three additional effects on answers:

- The remainder is discarded, leaving a smaller whole-number answer.
- The remainder can "force" the answer to the next highest whole number.
- The answer is rounded to the nearest whole number for an approximate result.

The following problems illustrate all five possibilities.

1. You have 30 pieces of candy to share fairly with 7 friends. How many pieces of candy will each friend receive?
   Answer: 4 pieces of candy and 2 left over. (left over)

2. Each baby bottle holds 8 ounces of milk. If there are 46 ounces in the pitcher, how many baby bottles can you fill?
   Answer: 5 and $\frac{6}{8}$ baby bottles. (partitioned as a fraction)

3. The rope is 25 feet long. How many 7-foot jump ropes can be made?
   Answer: 3 jump ropes. (discarded)

4. The ferry can hold 8 cars. How many trips will it have to make to carry 25 cars across the river?
   Answer: 4 trips. (forced to next whole number)

5. Six children are planning to share a bag of 50 pieces of bubble gum. About how many pieces will each child get?
   Answer: About 8 pieces for each child. (rounded, approximate result)

Students should not just think of remainders as "R 3" or "left over." Addressing what to do with remainders must be central to teaching about division. In fact, one of the most common

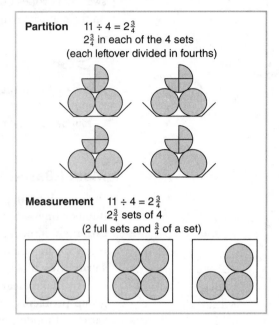

Figure 8.7
Remainders expressed as fractions.

Partition $11 \div 4 = 2\frac{3}{4}$
$2\frac{3}{4}$ in each of the 4 sets
(each leftover divided in fourths)

Measurement $11 \div 4 = 2\frac{3}{4}$
$2\frac{3}{4}$ sets of 4
(2 full sets and $\frac{3}{4}$ of a set)

errors students make on high-stakes assessments is to divide and then no pay attention to the context when selecting their answer. For example, in problem 3 (shown previously), an answer of $3\frac{4}{7}$ ropes doesn't make any sense. Rest assured that it will be a multiple choice option on the state assessment because common errors are used to create possible answers!

Stop and Reflect

It is useful for you to create problems using different contexts. See if you can create division problems for which the contexts would result in remainders dealt with as fractions, remainders rounded up, and remainders rounded down. ■

Model-Based Problems

In the beginning, students will be able to use the same models—sets, bar diagrams, and number lines—for all four operations. A model not generally used for addition, but that is extremely important and widely used for multiplication and division, is the array. An *array* is any arrangement of things in equal groups of rows and columns, such as a rectangle of square tiles, blocks, or circular counters (see Blackline Master 18).

To make clear the connection to addition, early multiplication activities with equal-group problems should also include writing an addition sentence for the same model. A variety of models are shown in Figure 8.8. Notice that the products are not included—only addition and multiplication expressions or equations are written. This is another way to avoid the tedious counting of large sets. A similar approach is to write one sentence that expresses both concepts at once, for example, $9 + 9 + 9 + 9 = 4 \times 9$.

Figure 8.8

Models for equal-group multiplication.

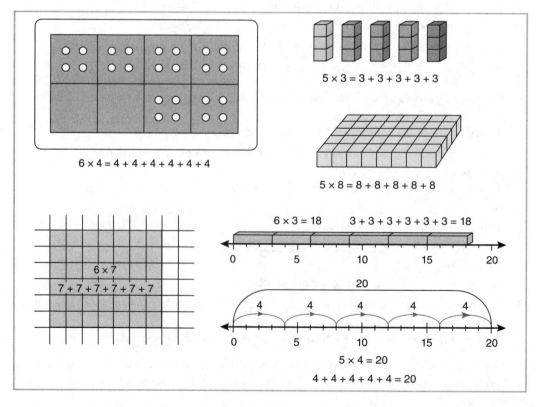

As with additive problems, students benefit from activities with models to focus on the meaning of the operation and the associated symbolism. Activity 8.1 has a good problem-solving spirit.

Activity 8.1 FINDING FACTORS

Start by having students think about a context that involves arrays, such as parade formations, seats in a classroom, or patches of a quilt. Then, assign a number that has several factors—for example, 12, 18, 24, 30, or 36. Have students find as many arrays (perhaps made from square tiles or cubes or drawn on grid paper) and corresponding multiplication expressions as possible for their assigned number. (Students can also use counters and attempt to find a way to separate the counters into equal subsets.) For students with physical disabilities who may have limited motor skills to manipulate the materials, this activity is available as an interactive applet at http://illuminations.nctm.org/ActivityDetail.aspx?id=64.

Be sure to draw students' attention to the dimensions of the arrays. You want students to make the connection that the factors in the multiplication expression they have written indicate the number of rows and columns (the dimensions) in a rectangle that consist of the given number of squares. Your class will undoubtedly want to decide whether a rectangle that is 3 by 8 should be counted differently from one that is 8 by 3. Leave the decision to the class, but take advantage of the opportunity to discuss how 3 rows of 8 are the same amount as 8 rows of 3. Note that if sets rather than arrays are made, 3 sets of 8 look very different from 8 sets of 3. So, as students begin to think about the commutative property of multiplication, array models provide a helpful representation.

The next activity is an extension of "Finding Factors," in that students look for patterns in the factors they find for numbers, such as the number of factors, the type of factors, the shape of the resulting array, and so on. Rather than always assigning numbers that have several factors, this activity suggests including numbers that have only a few factors so that differences between numbers become more distinct.

Activity 8.2 FACTOR PATTERNS

BLM

Tell students that they are going to look for multiplication expressions and the corresponding rectangular array for several numbers (e.g., 1 through 16 or 10 through 25). Their task includes finding all the multiplication expressions and rectangular arrays for each number. Have enough square tiles available that students can use to explore possible arrays. They are to record their rectangles on grid paper (see Blackline Masters 10 and 11) and label each rectangle with the number of squares and a multiplication equation. Students should group together all arrays with the same number of squares. This organization helps when students are comparing arrays across different numbers. After identifying the multiplication expressions and the rectangular arrays, students are to look for patterns in the factors and rectangular arrays. For example, which numbers have the least number of arrays and, therefore, the least number of factors? Which numbers have only a factor of 1 and itself? Which numbers have arrays that form a square? What can you say about the factors for even numbers? Do even numbers always have 2 even factors? What about odd numbers? Encourage students to think about why different patterns occur.

◆ Standards for
Mathematical Practice

**7 Look for and
make use of
structure**

Use this activity to explore the numbers that are prime (only have a factor of itself and 1) and those that are composites (those that can be made with two or more different arrays). Have students continue to consider the patterns that they notice as they classify different numbers into these groupings.

Activities 8.1 and 8.2 can also include division concepts. When students have learned that 3 and 6 are factors of 18, they can write the equations $18 \div 3 = 6$ and $18 \div 6 = 3$, along with $3 \times 6 = 18$ and $6 + 6 + 6 = 18$ (assuming that three sets of six were modeled). The following variation of these activities focuses on division. Having students create word problems to fit what they did with the tiles, cubes, or counters is another excellent elaboration of this activity. Having students explain how they can connect the situation to the models and to the equation is important in demonstrating understanding as described in the use of translation tasks in Chapter 3.

◢ *Activity 8.3* LEARNING ABOUT DIVISION

Using the context of a story about sharing, provide students with an ample supply of counters (beans) and some way to place them into small groups (small paper cups). Have students count out a number of counters to be the whole or total set (you may want to start with a number like 31). They record this number: Next specify either the number of equal groups to be made or the size of the group to be made: "Separate your counters into four equal-sized groups" or "Make as many groups of four as is possible." Next, have the students write the corresponding multiplication equation for what their materials show; under that, have them write the division equation. For ELLs, be sure they know what *groups, equal-sized groups,* and *groups of four* mean. For students with disabilities, consider having them start with a partition approach, in which they share the counters by placing one at a time into each cup.

Be sure to have the class do both types of exercises: number of equal groups unknown and group size unknown. Discuss with the class how these two are different, yet each is related to multiplication and each is written as a division equation. You can show the different ways to write division equations at this time, such as $31 \div 4$, $4\overline{)31}$, and $\frac{31}{4}$. Do Activity 8.3 several times. Make sure to include whole quantities that are multiples of the divisor (no remainders) and situations with remainders. Note that it is technically incorrect to write the answer to a problem like $31 \div 4$ as 7 R 3 because this is not a number (a quotient should be a number). As written, the 3 is not well defined because it is really $\frac{3}{4}$. However, in the beginning, the form 7 R 3 may be the most appropriate to use.

The activity can be varied by changing the model. Have students build arrays using square tiles or blocks or by having them draw arrays on centimeter grid paper. Present the exercises by specifying how many squares are to be in the array. You can then specify the number of rows that should be made (partition) or the length of each row (measurement). How could students model fractional answers using drawings of arrays on grid paper?

Properties of Multiplication and Division

There are multiplicative properties that are useful and, thus, worthy of attention. The emphasis should be on the ideas, not the terminology or definitions.

The applet "Rectangle Division" from the National Library of Virtual Manipulatives website (http://nlvm .usu.edu/en/nav/frames_asid_193_g_2_t_1.html?from=grade_g_2.html) is an interactive illustration of division with remainders. A division problem is presented with an array showing the selected number of squares in the product. The dimensions of the array can be modified, but the number of squares stays constant. If, for example, you model the problem $52 \div 8$, the squares will show an 8 by 6 array with 4 remaining squares in a different color ($8 \times 6 + 4$), as well as any other variation of 52 squares in a rectangular array plus a shorter column for the extra squares. This applet vividly demonstrates how division is related to multiplication.

When modeling multiplicative comparison problems, consider exploring them with the use of a bar diagram. These diagrams are frequently found in the mathematics programs emerging from Singapore (Beckmann, 2004). See Figure 8.9 for a bar diagram related to the following situation:

Zane has 5 small toy cars. Madeline has four times as many cars. How many cars does Madeline have?

Activity 8.4 THE BROKEN MULTIPLICATION KEY

The calculator is a good way to relate multiplication to addition. Students can find various products on the calculator without using the ⊠ key. For example, 6×4 can be found by pressing ⊞ 4 ⊟ ⊟ ⊟ ⊟ ⊟ ⊟. (Successive presses of ⊟ add 4 to the display each time. You began with zero and added 4 six times.) Students can be challenged to demonstrate their result with sets of counters. But note that this same technique can be used to determine products such as 23×459 (⊞ 459 and then 23 presses of ⊟). Students will want to compare to the same product using the ⊠ key. Because the function of using the equal sign on the calculator may be abstract for some students with disabilities, you may need to actually carry out the repeated addition by adding 4 ⊞ 4 ⊞ 4 ⊞ 4 ⊞ 4 ⊞ 4 ⊟ on a scientific calculator so the student can see the full equation and the answer on the same screen.

Figure 8.9

A student's work shows a model for multiplicative comparisons.

Activity 8.5 THE BROKEN DIVISION KEY

Have students work in groups to find methods of using the calculator to solve division exercises without using the divide key. The problems can be posed without a story context. "Find at least two ways to figure out $61 \div 14$ without pressing the divide key." If the problem is put in a story context, one method may actually match the problem better than another. Good discussions can follow different solutions with the same answers. Are they both correct? Why or why not?

Explore Broken Calculators at www.nctm.org/eresources/view_article.asp?article_id=7457&page=11&add=Y and www.fi.uu.nl/toepassingen/00014/toepassing_rekenweb.en.html. These two applets demonstrate the previous activities, allowing for problems at different levels of difficulty.

Stop and Reflect

Can you find three ways to solve 61 ÷ 14 on a calculator without using the divide key? For hints, see the footnote.* ■

Formative Assessment Note

A good way to check on students' understanding of the operations is to provide several story problems with different operations. It is not necessary to do this all on one day. Have students work on two or three problems a day over the course of a week. If your objective is to find out about their understanding of the operations, you can focus on this by not having them actually do the computations. Rather, have them indicate what operations they would use and with what numbers. To avoid guessing, have students draw a picture to explain why they chose the operations that they did.

Figure 8.10

A model for the commutative property for multiplication (a) and an illustration of a problem showing the associative property of multiplication (b).

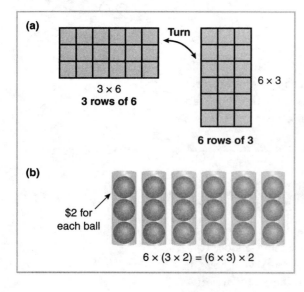

Commutative and Associative Properties of Multiplication.

It is not obvious that 3×8 is the same as 8×3 or that, in general, the order of the numbers makes no difference (the commutative property). A picture of 3 sets of 8 objects cannot immediately be seen as 8 piles of 3 objects. Nor on a number line is 8 hops of 3 noticeably the same as 3 hops of 8. The array, by contrast, is quite powerful in illustrating the commutative property, as shown in Figure 8.10(a). Students should build or draw arrays and use them to demonstrate why each array represents two equivalent multiplication expressions.

As in addition, there is an associative property of multiplication that is fundamental in flexibly solving problems (Ding & Li, 2010). This property allows that when you multiply three numbers in an expression you can multiply either the first pair of numbers or the last pair and the product remains the same. A context is helpful, so here is an example that could be shared with students: "Each tennis ball costs two dollars. Each can has 3 tennis balls. How much will it cost if we need to buy 6 cans?" After analyzing the problem by showing actual cans of tennis balls or illustrations, students should try to consider the problem two ways: (1) find out the cost for each can and then the total cost $6 \times (3 \times 2)$; and (2) find out how

* There are two measurement approaches to find out how many 14s are in 61 (by repeatedly adding or subtracting 14). A third way is essentially related to partitioning or finding 14 times what number is close to 61.

many balls in total and then the total cost $(6 \times 3) \times 2$ (see Figure 8.10(b)) (Ding, personal communication, October 7, 2010).

Zero and Identity Properties.   Factors of 0 and, to a lesser extent, 1 often cause conceptual challenges for students. In textbooks, you may find that a lesson on factors of 0 and 1 has students use a calculator to examine a wide range of products involving 0 or 1 ($423 \times 0, 0 \times 28$, 1536×1, etc.) and look for patterns. The pattern suggests the rules for factors of 0 and 1, but not a reason. In another lesson, a word problem might ask how many grams of fat there are in 7 servings of celery, with 0 grams of fat in each serving. This approach is far preferable to an arbitrary rule because it asks students to reason. Make up interesting word problems involving 0 or 1, and discuss the results. Problems with 0 as a first factor are really strange. Note that on a number line, 5 hops of 0 lands at 0 (5×0). What would 0 hops of 5 be? Another fun activity is to try to model 6×0 or 0×8 with an array. (Try it!) Arrays for factors of 1 are also worth investigating. (Numbers that can only be made with an array with dimensions of 1 and itself are prime numbers!)

Distributive Property.   The distributive property of multiplication over addition refers to the idea that either of the two factors in a product can be split (decomposed) into two or more parts and each part is multiplied separately and then added. The result is the same as when the original factors are multiplied. For example, to find the number of yogurts in 9 six-packs, use the logic that 9×6 is the same as $(5 \times 6) + (4 \times 6)$. The 9 has been split into 5 six-packs and 4 six-packs. The concept involved is very useful in relating one basic fact to another, and it is also involved in the development of two-digit computation. Figure 8.11 illustrates how the array model can be used to demonstrate that a product can be broken up into two parts. The next activity is designed to help students discover how to partition factors or, in other words, learn about the distributive property of multiplication over addition.

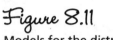

Figure 8.11

Models for the distributive property of multiplication over addition.

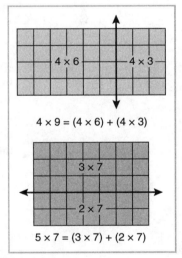

$4 \times 9 = (4 \times 6) + (4 \times 3)$

$5 \times 7 = (3 \times 7) + (2 \times 7)$

◢ *Activity 8.6* **DIVIDE IT UP**

Supply students with several sheets of centimeter grid paper or color tiles to represent a small garden that will be planted with two different kinds of vegetables. Assign each pair of students a product—a garden plot size, such as 6 × 8. Garden sizes (products) can vary across the class to differentiate for varying skill levels or they can all be the same. The task is to find all of the different ways to make a single slice or cut through the rectangle to divide the plot for the two different seeds. For each slice, students write an equation. For a slice that results in one row of 8, students would write $6 \times 8 = (5 \times 8) + (1 \times 8)$. The individual products can be written in the arrays as was done in Figure 8.11. Although the order of operations is not in the CCSS standards until sixth grade, this might be a good time to discuss how grouping symbols should be considered first.

Why Not Division by Zero?   Sometimes students are simply told "Division by zero is not allowed," often because teachers do not fully understand this concept themselves (Quinn, Lamberg, & Perrin, 2008). Some students harbor misconceptions that the answer should be either zero or the number itself. To avoid an arbitrary rule, pose problems to be modeled that involve zero: "Take 30 counters. How many sets of 0 can be made?" or "Put 12 blocks in 0 equal groups. How many in each group?" or "Can you show me how to share 5 oranges with 0 children?" Then move students toward reasoned explanations (Crespo & Nicol, 2006) that consider the inverse relationship of multiplication and division and take the answer and put it back into a multiplication problem as a check. Then, with the orange problem, you would ask, "What, when multiplied by 0, produces an answer of 5?" There is no answer. If you have students think of it as repeated subtraction, they would take 0 from the original 5 oranges, leaving 5 and so forth. Therefore, division by zero is undefined; it just doesn't make sense when we use our definition of division and its inverse relationship to multiplication.

◆ Strategies for Solving Contextual Problems

We have suggested the use of contextual problems or story problems to help students develop meanings for multiplication and division. But often students in grades 3 through 5 (although not exclusively so) are at a loss for what to do. Also, struggling readers or ELLs may need support in understanding the problem. In this section you will learn some techniques for helping them.

Analyzing Context Problems

Consider the following problem:

In building a road through a neighborhood, workers filled large holes in the ground with dirt brought in by trucks. 638 truckloads of dirt were required to completely fill the holes. The average truck carried $6\frac{1}{4}$ cubic yards of dirt, which weighed 7.3 tons. How many tons of dirt were used to fill the holes?

Typically, in fifth-grade books, problems of this type are found as part of a series of problems revolving around a single context or theme. Data may be found in a graph or chart, or perhaps a short news item or story. Students have difficulty deciding on the correct operation and are often challenged to identify the appropriate data for solving the problem. Sometimes students will find two numbers in the problem and guess at the correct operation. Instead, students need tools for analyzing problems. At least two strategies can be very helpful: (1) thinking about the answer before solving the problem, or (2) working a simpler problem.

▣ *Formative Assessment Note*

What do you do if a student is having difficulty solving word problems? The first thing is to find out what is causing the difficulty. If you can't tell from the student's written efforts or from observation, a short diagnostic interview is highly recommended. Prepare some problems written out on paper, one problem to a page. Provide appropriate physical materials (e.g., counters, square tiles, grid paper), but encourage the student to use whatever she wishes in order to solve the problem. Explain that you want to hear what she is thinking so that you will know how to help her. Remember that the purpose of your interview is to gain insight into the student's difficulties and to use this information to prepare problems or other tasks for a later lesson. Do not use the interview as a time to intervene or teach!

When a student does not seem to know what to do with a problem, a simple yet effective suggestion is to have her restate the problem in her own words. Then go through the story problem sentence by sentence. With each sentence, have her describe how the information provided impacts the situation. When reasonable, have her use physical materials or models to act out the problem or a simpler version of the problem with numbers in her comfort range. Have her describe what the physical materials or models stand for. Then ask her to explain with the materials what is happening in the problem. This can help the student with similar analyses when you are not there to make these suggestions.

Standards for Mathematical Practice

1 Make sense of problems and persevere in solving them ▶

Think about the Answer before Solving the Problem. Students who struggle with solving word problems need to spend adequate time thinking about the problem and what it is about. In addition, ELLs need to comprehend both the contextual words (like *dirt*, *filled*, and *road*) and the mathematical terminology (*cubic yards*, *weighed*, *tons*, *how many*). Instead of rushing in and beginning to do calculations, believing that "number crunching" is what solves problems, they should spend time talking about (and later thinking about) what the answer might look like. In fact, one great strategy for differentiation is to pose the problem with the numbers missing or covered up. This eliminates the tendency to number crunch. For our sample problem, it might look like this:

- *What is happening in this problem?* Some trucks were bringing dirt to fill up holes.
- *Is there any extra information we don't need?* We don't need to know about the cubic yards in each truck.
- *What will the answer tell us?* How many tons of dirt were needed to fill the holes. My answer will be some number of tons.
- *Will that be a small number of tons or a large number of tons?* Well, there were 7.3 tons on a truck, but there were a lot of trucks, not just one. It's probably going to be a lot of tons.
- *About how many do you think it will be?* It's going to be a lot. If there were 1000 trucks, it would be 7300 tons. So it will be less than that. But it will be more than half of 7300, so the answer is more than 3650 tons.

In this type of discussion, three things are happening. First, the students are asked to initially focus on the problem and the meaning of the answer, instead of on numbers. The numbers are not important in thinking about the structure of the problem. Second, with a focus on the structure of the problem, students identify the numbers that are important as well as the numbers that are not important. Third, the thinking leads to a rough estimate of the answer and the unit of the answer (tons, in this case). In any event, thinking about what the answer tells and about how large it might be is a useful starting point.

Work a Simpler Problem. The reason that models are rarely used with problems such as the dirt problem is that the large numbers are very challenging to model. Distances in thousands of miles, and time in minutes and seconds—data likely to be found in the upper elementary grades—are difficult to model. The general problem-solving strategy of "try a simpler problem" can almost always be applied to problems with unwieldy numbers.

A simpler-problem strategy has the following steps:

1. Substitute small whole numbers for all relevant numbers in the problem.
2. Model the problem (with base-ten materials, drawings, number lines, arrays) using the new numbers.
3. Write an equation that solves the simpler version of the problem.
4. Write the corresponding equation substituting back the original numbers.
5. Calculate or use a calculator to do the computation.
6. Write the answer in a complete sentence, and decide whether it makes sense.

Figure 8.12 shows how the dirt problem might be made simpler. It also shows an alternative, in which only one of the numbers is made smaller and the other number is illustrated symbolically. Both methods are effective.

Figure 8.12

Two ways students created a simpler problem.

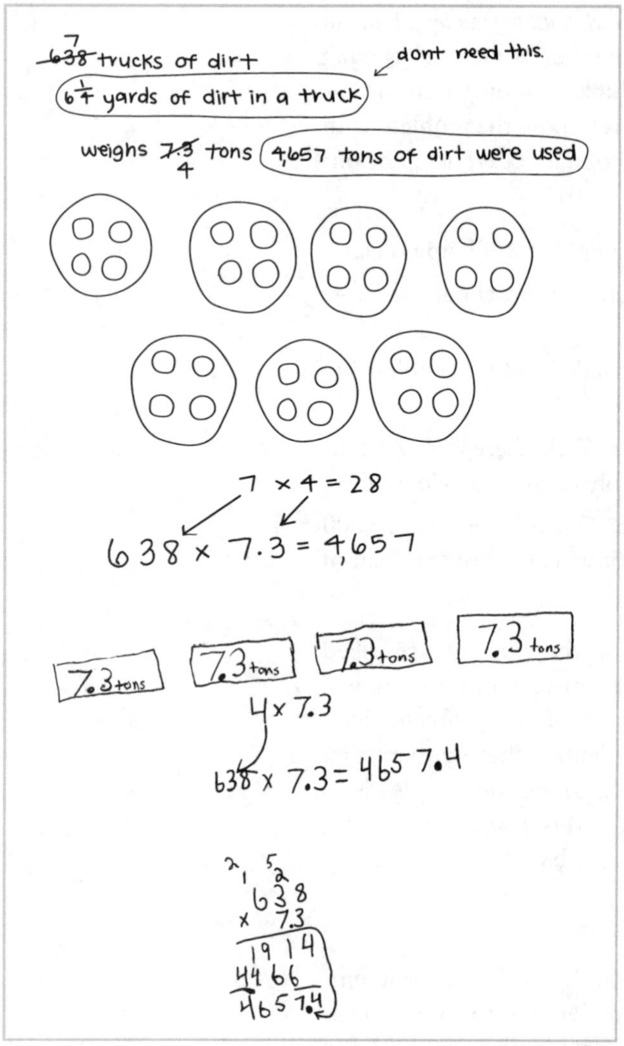

The idea is to provide tools students can consistently use to analyze a problem and not just guess at what computation to do. It is much more useful to have students do a few problems for which they must use a model of a drawing to justify their solution than to give them a lot of problems for which they guess at a solution but don't use reasoning and sense making.

Caution: Avoid the Key Word Strategy! It is often suggested that students should be taught to find "key words" in story problems. Some teachers even post lists of key words with their corresponding meanings. For example, *altogether* and *in all* mean you should add, and *left* and *fewer* indicate that you should subtract. The word *each* suggests multiplication. To some extent, the overly simple and formulaic story problems often found in textbooks reinforce this approach. When problems are written in this way, it may appear that the key word strategy is effective.

In contrast with this belief, researchers and mathematics educators have long cautioned against the strategy of key words (e.g., Clement & Bernhard, 2005; Kenney, Hancewicz, Heuer, Metsisto, & Tuttle, 2005; Sowder, 1988). Here are four arguments against the key word approach:

1. The key word strategy sends a terribly wrong message about doing mathematics. The most important approach to solving any contextual problem is to analyze it and make sense of it. The key word approach encourages students to ignore the meaning and structure of the problem and look for an easy way out. Mathematics is about reasoning and making sense of situations. Sense-making strategies always work!

2. Key words are often misleading. Many times the key word or phrase in a problem suggests an operation that is incorrect. The following problem shared by Drake and Barlow (2007) demonstrates this possibility.

There are three boxes of chicken nuggets on the table. Each box contains six chicken nuggets. How many chicken nuggets are there in all? (p. 272)

Drake and Barlow found that one student generated the answer of 9, using the words "how many in all" as a suggestion to add $3 + 6$. Instead of making sense of the situation, the student used the key word approach as a shortcut in making an operational decision.

3. Many problems have no key words. Except for the overly simple problems found in primary textbooks, a large percentage of problems have no key words. A student who has been taught to rely on key words is left with no strategy.
Here's an example:

Aidan has 28 goldfish. 12 are orange and the rest are yellow. How many goldfish are yellow?

4. Key words don't work with two-step problems or more advanced problems, so using this approach on simpler problems sets students up for failure with more complex problems because they are not learning how to read for meaning.

Multistep Word Problems

Students often have difficulty with multistep problems that begin in the grade 4 standards (CCSSO, 2010). First, be sure they can analyze the structure of one-step problems in the way that we have discussed. The following ideas, adapted from suggestions by Huinker (1994), are designed to help students see how two problems can be linked together to help think about multistep problems.

1. Give students a one-step problem and have them solve it. Before discussing the answer, have the students use the answer to the first problem to create a second problem. The rest of the class can then be asked to solve the second problem. Here is an example:

Given problem: It took 3 hours for the Morgan family to drive the 195 miles to Washington, D.C. What was their average speed?

Second problem: The Morgan children remember crossing the river at about 10:30, or 2 hours after they left home. About how far from home is the river?

2. Make a "hidden question." Repeat the approach above by giving groups of students a one-step problem. Give different problems to different groups. Have them solve the first problem and write a second problem. Then they should write a single combined problem that leaves out the question from the first problem. That question from the first problem is the "hidden question." Here is a simple example:

Given problem: Toby bought three dozen eggs for 89 cents a dozen. How much was the total cost?

Second problem: How much change did Toby get back from $5?

Hidden-question problem: Toby bought three dozen eggs for 89 cents a dozen. How much change did Tony get back from $5?

Have other students identify the hidden question. Because all students are working on a similar task but with different problems (be sure to mix the operations), they will be more likely to understand what is meant by a hidden question.

3. Pose standard multistep problems, and have the students identify and answer the hidden question. Consider the following problem:

The Marsal Company bought 275 widgets wholesale for $3.69 each. In the first month, the company sold 205 widgets at $4.99 each. How much did the company make or lose on the widgets? Do you think the Marsal Company should continue to sell widgets?

4. Begin by considering the questions that were suggested earlier: "What's happening in this problem?" (Something is being bought and sold at two different prices.) "What will the answer tell us?" (How much profit or loss there was.) These questions will get you started. If students are stuck, you can ask, "Is there a hidden question in this problem?" Although the examples given here provide a range of contexts, for ELLs, using the *same* (and familiar) context across this three-step process would reduce the linguistic demands and therefore make the stories more comprehensible—and the mathematics more accessible.

Formative Assessment Note

One of the best ways to assess students' knowledge of the meaning of the operations is to have them generate story problems for a given equation or result (Drake & Barlow, 2007; Whitin & Whitin, 2008). Use a diagnostic interview to see whether your student can flexibly think about an operation using the translation task approach from Chapter 3. Fold a sheet of paper into quarters. Give students an expression, such as 5×7, and ask that they record the question and answer it in the upper left-hand quarter, write a story problem representing the expression in another quarter of the paper, draw a picture (or model) in the third section, and describe how they would tell a younger student how to solve this problem in the last section. (Students with disabilities could dictate the story problem and the description of the solving process while the teacher transcribes.) Students who can ably match scenarios, models, and explanations to the computation will demonstrate their understanding, whereas struggling students will likely reveal areas of weakness. This assessment can be adapted by giving students the result (e.g., "24 cents") and asking them to write a subtraction problem (or a division problem, or any other appropriate type of problem) that will generate that answer, along with models and word problems written in the remaining quarters. Another option is to use a piece of children's literature to write a word problem that emphasizes the meaning of one of the four operations. The student then has to complete the other three sections.

Expanded Lesson

Learning about Division

Content and Task Decisions

Grade Level: 3

Mathematics Goals

- To develop the measurement (repeated subtraction) concept of division

- To connect the measurement concept of division to multiplication and addition

Grade Level Guide

NCTM Curriculum Focal Points	Common Core State Standards
Within the heading of Number and Operations and Algebra, a focal point at third grade is to develop an understanding of division. Students explore the meaning of division of whole numbers through "successive subtraction" (NCTM, 2006, p. 15).	As part of the standards for third-grade students, "Interpret whole-number quotients of whole numbers, e.g., interpret $56 \div 8$ as the number of objects in each share when 56 objects are partitioned equally into 8 shares, or as a number of shares when 56 objects are partitioned into equal shares of 8 objects each" (CCSSO, 2010, p. 23).

Consider Your Students' Needs

Students have explored multiplication concepts, but it is not necessary that they have mastered all of their multiplication facts prior to starting division. This lesson could be used as an introduction to division. For students who have been exposed to division, the lesson can further develop early ideas and help connect the ideas to contextual situations.

For English Language Learners

- Rather than have ELLs write a story, they can illustrate the story.

- Stories about a lot of different topics can be overwhelming for students learning English. Instead, you can ask students to write stories about something specific (for example, apples).

- Be sure that students know the terms *sets* and *groups,* as well as *remainder.*

For Students with Disabilities

- Have students match a story problem with an equation if they are not able to write their own.

Materials

Each student will need:

- 35 counters

- Small paper cups or portion cups that will hold at least 6 counters (alternatively, students can stack counters in piles)

Lesson

Before

Begin with a simpler version of the task:

- Draw 13 counters (dots) on the board. Ask, "How many groups of 3 can we make if we have 13? How many will be left over?" Most students should be able to answer this question mentally. After receiving several answers, have a student come to the board and demonstrate how to verify the answer of four groups of 3 and 1 left. (*Note:* Depending on your students, you may want to precede the first step using a number such as 12 so that there are no remainders. Do not wait too long before remainders are addressed.)

- Ask, "What equation could we write for what we have on the board?" Accept students' ideas. Correct ideas include:

  - $3 + 3 + 3 + 3 + 1 = 13$

  - $4 \times 3 + 1 = 13$ ($3 \times 4 + 1$ technically represents three groups of 4 and 1 more.)

  - $13 \div 3 = 4$ with 1 left over

- Say, "Think of a situation in which someone might have 13 things and wants to find out how many groups of 3. Make up a story problem about your situation." Have several students share their story problems.

Present the focus task to the class:

- Distribute small paper cups or portion cups and counters to students. Pose the two problems:

  - Use 31 counters to see how many groups of 4 you can make.

- Use 27 counters to find out how many groups of 6 you can make.

- Ask students for ideas of how they might use the cups to help them solve the problems.

Provide clear expectations:

- Write the directions on the board:

  1. Find how many groups of 4 you can make using 31 counters.

  2. Write three equations: one addition, one multiplication, and one division.

  3. Write a story problem to go with the division equation.

  4. Repeat steps 1, 2, and 3 using 27 counters to make groups of 6.

During

Initially:

- Observe that each student understands the task and is in the process of attempting to solve the first situation.

- If you find that some students, particularly those with disabilities, are struggling, you may need to start them by supporting them in the placement of 4 counters in the first cup. Then they should be able to use that model to continue.

Ongoing:

- Ask students to explain and show (on the overhead or table) why their equations go with what they did with the counters.

- Focus your questions during the lesson on the connections between the actions of the activity and the corresponding symbolism and the writing of the story problems.

- Challenge early finishers to see whether they can do the same thing for 125 things in groups of 20. However, they will have to figure it out without using counters.

After

Bring the class together to share and discuss the task:

- Ask students to show how they know how many groups of 4 can be made with 31 counters. A picture may be drawn on the board or use counters with a projection device.

- Have several students share their equations. Ask those who have different equations to share theirs as well.

- Have students explain how their equations match what was done with the counters. If students disagree, have them respectfully explain their reasoning. Students should be comfortable with their ideas about the multiplication and addition equations. Because this is an introductory lesson on division, you should correct any misunderstandings about the division equation and what it means.

- Have several students share their story problems. Students should explain how the story situation matches the action of finding how many groups of 4 are in 31. For example: "There were 31 apples in the basket. If each apple tart requires 4 apples, how many tarts can be made?"

- If time permits, repeat with the $27 \div 6$ situation.

Assessment

Observe

- Look for evidence that students see the connection between the action of finding how many equal groups in a given quantity, and the manner in which a multiplication equation and a division equation are connected. Do not be overly concerned about the use of 4×7 instead of 7×4.

- Story problems should indicate the action of measuring equal-sized groups of 4 rather than dividing the quantity into four groups in a process of sharing or partitioning. If students make this error, simply have them discuss whether or not the story fits well with the action. Do not indicate that the story is incorrect. It is also possible that students will create multiplication stories with 31 being the unknown amount. Here, ask students which equation best represents the problem.

Ask

- How are multiplication, division, and addition related?

- How does your story problem connect to the division equation? Is it in any way like subtraction?

9

Helping Students Master the Basic Facts

Big IDEAS

1 Number relationships provide the basis for strategies that help students learn basic facts. For example, when solving 7×8 you can help students think about decomposing the 7 into $2 + 5$. Then $(2 + 5) \times 8$ is the same as $2 \times 8 + 5 \times 8$. Using the distributive property and building off the benchmark of 5 allows students to use the structure and number relationships that continue to help them with larger numbers.

2 All of the facts are conceptually related so students can figure out new or unknown facts using those they already know. For example, "think addition" is a powerful way to think of subtraction facts. Rather than 13 "take away 6," which requires a lot of counting, students can think 6 and what adds to 13. They might add up to 10 (4) and then add 3 more to get 7, or they may think double 6 is 12 so it must be one more or 7. Or in the case of multiplication, 6×8 can be thought of as five 8s (40) and one more 8. It might also be three 8s doubled.

3 Because mastering the basic facts is a developmental process, students move through phases, starting with counting, then more efficient reasoning strategies, and eventually quick recall and mastery. Instruction must help students through these three phases without rushing them to know their facts only through memorization.

4 When students struggle with developing basic fact fluency, they may need to return to foundational ideas. Just providing additional drill will not resolve their challenges and can negatively affect their confidence and success in mathematics.

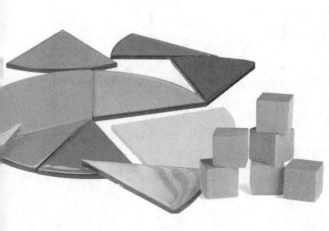

Basic facts for addition and multiplication are the number combinations for which both *addends*, or both *factors*, are less than 10. Basic facts for subtraction and division are the corresponding combinations. Therefore, $15 - 8 = 7$ is a basic subtraction fact because the corresponding addends are less than 10.

Mastery of a basic fact means that a student can give a quick response (in about 3 seconds) without resorting to inefficient means, such as counting by ones. According to the *Curriculum Focal Points* (NCTM, 2006) and the *Common Core State Standards for Mathematics* (CCSSO, 2010), addition and subtraction concepts should be learned in first grade, with quick recall of basic addition and subtraction facts mastered by the end of grade 2.

According to *Curriculum Focal Points*, concepts of multiplication and division should be learned in third grade, with quick recall of the one-digit facts (up through 9×9) mastered in grade 4. In the *Common Core State Standards*, however, the one-digit multiplication facts are to be known by quick recall by the end of grade 3.

Developing quick and accurate recall with the basic facts is a developmental process. It is critical that students know their basic facts well, and teaching them effectively requires much more than flash cards and timed tests. This chapter explains strategies for helping students learn their facts, including instructional approaches to use—and others to avoid. The key point: Focus on number sense! Research indicates that early number sense predicts school mathematics success more than other measures of cognition like reading ability or verbal, spatial, or memory skills (Jordan, Kaplan, Locuniak, & Ramineni, 2007; Locuniak & Jordan, 2008; Mazzocco & Thompson, 2005).

Developmental Nature of Basic Fact Mastery

Even though students in grades 4 to 10 have had ample opportunities to learn their facts, every teacher in those grades knows students who still count on their fingers, make marks in the margins to count on, or simply guess at answers. These students have not mastered their facts because they have not developed efficient methods of producing a fact answer based on number relationships and reasoning. Drilling inefficient methods does not produce mastery!

When teaching basic facts, teachers need to attend to the essential understanding that students progress through stages that will eventually result in "just knowing" that $2 + 7$ is 9 or that 5×4 is 20. Arthur Baroody, a mathematics educator who does research on basic facts, describes three phases in the process of learning facts (2006, p. 22):

1. *Counting strategies*—using object counting (e.g., blocks or fingers) or verbal counting to determine the answer. Example: $4 + 7 =$ _____ . Student starts with 7 and counts on verbally (8, 9, 10, 11), or the student counts 4, counts 7, and then "counts all" over again to reach 11.

2. *Reasoning strategies*—using known information to logically determine an unknown combination. Example: $4 + 7$. Student knows that $3 + 7$ is 10, so $4 + 7$ is one more, 11.

3. *Mastery*—producing answers efficiently (fast and accurately). Example: $4 + 7$. Student quickly responds, "It's 11; I just know it."

Over many years, research supports the notion that basic fact mastery is dependent on the development of reasoning strategies (Baroody, 2003, 2006; Brownell & Chazal, 1935; Carpenter & Moser, 1984; Fuson, 1992; Henry & Brown, 2008). This chapter will focus on effective ways to teach students in grades 3 through 5 to use reasoning strategies and sense making to master the basic facts (phases 2 and 3).

Formative Assessment Note

When are students ready to work on reasoning strategies? Based on the research, they are ready to apply reasoning strategies when they efficiently use counting strategies (start with the largest number and count up, or in the case of multiplication, start with a known fact and count up one more group) and when they are able to decompose numbers (e.g., that 6 can be decomposed into $5 + 1$). Pose basic fact problems to students in a diagnostic interview to see whether they show evidence of these skills. Once they have grasped these needed skills, begin work on reasoning strategies. If they are lacking one skill, provide more experiences to develop it.

◆ Approaches to Fact Mastery

In attempting to help students master the basic facts, three somewhat different approaches can be identified. Although these approaches are all used, not all are equally effective. First is to work on memorization of each fact in isolation. A second approach can be traced at least as far back as the 1970s. Rathmell (1978) suggests that for various groupings of basic facts, teach students a collection of strategies or thought patterns that have been found to be efficient and teachable. The third approach, *guided invention*, also focuses on using strategies to learn facts; however, students generate, or reinvent, the strategies.

Memorization

Unfortunately, some curriculums and teachers move from presenting concepts of addition and multiplication straight to memorization of facts, feeling that developing strategies is not essential in this process (Baroody, Bajwa, & Eiland, 2009). This idea that students can just store the facts when practiced extensively means that students have 100 separate addition facts (just for the various combinations of 0 through 9) and 100 separate multiplication facts that must be repeatedly memorized and practiced. They may even have to memorize subtraction and division facts separately, bringing the total to more than 300 facts! However, many fourth and fifth graders have not mastered addition and subtraction facts, and many middle school students do not know their multiplication facts. This is strong evidence that the memorization method alone simply does not work. You may be tempted to respond that you learned your facts in this manner, as did many others. However, studies as long ago as 1935 (Brownell & Chazal) concluded that students actually develop a variety of different reasoning strategies for answering basic facts apart from the large amounts of isolated drill. Unfortunately, this drill does not support an increased sophistication or refinement of these strategies. Moreover, Baroody (2006, p. 27) notes that this drill approach to basic fact instruction works against the development of the five strands of mathematics proficiency (National Research Council, 2001), pointing out the following limitations:

- *Inefficiency.* There are too many facts to memorize in isolation.
- *Inappropriate applications.* Students misapply the facts and don't check their work for reasonableness.
- *Inflexibility.* Students don't learn flexible strategies for finding the sums or products and therefore continue to count by ones.

Struggling learners and students with disabilities often have difficulty memorizing so many isolated facts and are trapped in phase 1, relying on the use of counting strategies (Mazzocco et al., 2008). In addition, drill often causes unnecessary anxiety and undermines student interest and confidence in mathematics. Connecting new knowledge to what students already know allows all students to master the basic facts. Students who rely on simply counting must learn meaningful alternative approaches that allow for the development of more complex mathematical thinking (Garza-Kling, 2011).

Explicit Strategy Instruction

For approximately three decades, basic fact instruction has focused on explicitly teaching efficient strategies that are applicable to a collection of facts. Students then practice these strategies as they are taught to them. There is strong evidence to indicate that such methods are effective (e.g., Baroody, 1985; Bley & Thornton, 1995; Fuson, 1984, 1992; Rathmell, 1978).

Rather than giving students something new to memorize, explicitly teaching strategies supports student reasoning in choosing strategies that help them get solutions without counting. However, sometimes textbooks or teachers focus on memorizing a particular strategy, connecting it only to the facts that work with the strategy. This approach doesn't work (for the same reason that memorizing isolated facts doesn't work). A recent study found that students whose teachers relied heavily on memorization of basic fact strategies, rather than ones that emphasized reasoning about the strategies, had low number-sense proficiency (Henry & Brown, 2008). This memorization approach should be avoided.

Guided Invention

The third approach (Gravemeijer & van Galen, 2003) connects fact mastery to students' collection of number relationships. Some students may think of 9×4 as "9 times 2 is 18 and double that for 36." Other students note that 10×4 is 40, so you take 4 from the 40 to get 36. Still other students may know 9×5 is 45 and you take 9 from that to get 36. What is important is that students use number combinations and relationships that make sense to them.

Gravemeijer and van Galen call this approach *guided invention* because many of the efficient strategies will not be developed by all students without teacher guidance. That is, you cannot simply place all of your efforts on number relationships and the meanings of the operations and assume that fact mastery will magically occur. Instead, you should design sequenced tasks and problems that will promote students' invention of effective strategies. Then, students need to clearly articulate these strategies and share them with peers. This sharing is often best carried out in think-alouds, in which students talk through the decisions they made and share counterexamples.

◆ Facilitating Strategy Development

To guide your students to use effective strategies, you need to have knowledge of many successful approaches. With this knowledge, you will be able to recognize the emergence of effective strategies as your students develop them and at the same time help others capitalize on their peers' ideas.

Plan experiences that help students move on the trajectory from counting to strategies to mastery and quick recall. One effective approach is to use story problems with numbers selected in such a manner that students are most likely to develop a particular strategy as they solve them. In discussing student strategies, you can focus attention on the methods that are most effective.

If you look at $6 + 7$, you will find some students may count on from 7 (7, 8, 9, 10, 11, 12, 13). Others will use the Up Over 10 strategy (7 to 10 is a jump of 3 and 3 more is 13). Help students who are counting on to see the connections to Up Over 10. This moves students from counting (phase 1) to reasoning strategies (phase 2). To move from reasoning strategies to recall (phase 3), continue to develop story problems that have numbers that go up over 10. Students will build up speed the more they practice this strategy. Eventually, students say "I just knew it" because these mental strategies become fluent.

Story Problems

Story problems provide a context that can help students understand the situation and apply flexible strategies for doing computation. Some teachers may express hesitancy to use story problems with ELLs or students with disabilities because of the additional language or reading required, but because language supports understanding, story problems are important for all students.

Contexts selected must be relevant and understood. Consider, for example, that the class is working on the $\times 3$ facts. The teacher poses the following question:

In 3 weeks we will be going to the zoo. How many days until we go to the zoo?

Suppose that Aidan explains how he figured out 3×7 by starting with double 7 (14) and then adding 7 more. He knew that 6 added onto 14 equals 20 and one more is 21. You can ask another student to explain Aidan's thinking.

This requires students to attend to ideas that come from their classmates. Now explore with the class what other facts might work with Aidan's strategy. Some may notice that all of the facts with a 3 as a factor will work for the "double and add one more" strategy. Others may say that you can always add one more group on if you know the next smaller fact. For example, for 6×8, you can start with 5×8 and add 8. Students with disabilities may be challenged to keep all of their peers' ideas in working memory, so recording the ideas on the board is an effective support.

Posing a daily story problem such as the preceding one, followed by a brief discussion of the various strategies that students used, can improve students' accuracy and efficiency with basic facts (Rathmell, Leutzinger, & Gabriele, 2000). A similar approach is shown in Figure 9.1, which includes a story example intended to support reasoning strategies from grade 4 of *Investigations in Number, Data, and Space* (Russell & Economopoulos, 2008). Research has found that when a strong emphasis is placed on students solving story problems, they not only become better problem solvers but also master more basic facts than students in a drill program (National Research Council, 2001).

Standards for
Mathematical Practice

◀ **3** Construct
viable arguments
and critique the
reasoning of others

Reasoning Strategies

A second approach is to directly model a reasoning strategy. A lesson may be designed to have students examine a specific collection of facts for which a particular type of strategy is appropriate. You can discuss how these facts are all alike in some way, or you might suggest an approach and see whether students are able to use it with similar facts.

Continue to discuss strategies invented by students and plan lessons that encourage conversations about strategies. Don't expect to have a strategy introduced and understood with just one story problem or one exposure. Just as when using story problems, students need lots of opportunities to make the strategies their own, or to use new strategies that their classmates have shared. Many students will simply not be ready to use an idea in the first few days, and then suddenly something will connect and a useful idea will be theirs. No student should be forced to adopt someone else's strategy, but every student should be required to understand strategies that are brought to the discussion.

Figure 9.1

Story problem from the *Investigations in Number, Data, and Space* curriculum to develop basic fact reasoning strategies.

Grade 4, Unit 1: Factors, Multiples, and Arrays

Lesson: Making Arrays

A package of juice boxes has 8 juice boxes.

How many juice boxes are in 3 packages?

How many juice boxes are in 6 packages?

How many juice boxes are in 9 packages?

Source: Van de Walle, John; Karp, Karen S.; Bay-Williams, Jennifer M., *Elementary and Middle School Mathematics: Teaching Developmentally,* 8th ed., © 2013. Reprinted and electronically reproduced by permission of Pearson Education, Inc., Upper Saddle River, New Jersey. Originally in Russell, S. J., & Economopoulos, K. (2008). *Investigations in Number, Data, and Space (Grade 4).* New York: Pearson.

Reasoning Strategies for Addition Facts

Addition facts—the sums through 20—are considered mastery items in the second-grade curriculum (CCSSO, 2010). However, very few third-grade teachers will ever see a new class that has mastered all of these facts, and many teachers of fifth grade and higher have students who still have gaps.

For teachers in grades 3 through 5, the following ideas are important:

- All of the addition facts can be connected to one or more very important number relationships. For students who have not mastered addition facts, time will be saved by devoting attention to those relationships rather than to spending time on drill.

- Students will rarely master a subtraction fact without knowing the corresponding addition fact. That is, if a student knows $12 - 8$, it is almost certain that he or she knows $8 + 4$. Therefore, mastery of addition facts should be seen as a prerequisite to subtraction facts.

- Diagnosis of what facts individual students have mastered and where gaps remain will help you plan a targeted method to help students. Time invested in this analysis will save time in the long run.

The following sections provide a brief look at strategies for addition facts. With this information you can plan effective activities to help students in grades 3 through 5 reach mastery.

One More Than and Two More Than

As students enter third grade there is an expectation that some strategy use and facts are mastered. Because 51 of the 100 addition facts involve a 0, 1, or a 2, these are likely facts that are known. Students who are missing facts with a zero are often holding on to the faulty notion that "addition makes bigger." Therefore, they might answer 8 to $7 + 0$. These facts do not require any strategy, but rather a good understanding of the meaning of zero and addition.

Many students in grades 1 and 2 have been taught to use a counting-on strategy for facts with addends of 1 or 2, as well as those involving a 3. If students are using a counting-on strategy efficiently—and using it only for these small addends—do not try to stop it. However, we strongly suggest that you discourage the use of counting on for all facts. It is difficult for some students to separate counting on for some facts and not for others. Students in grades 3 through 5 who have not yet mastered addition facts are often using counting on for facts such as $8 + 5$, for which that strategy is not efficient.

Activity 9.1 ONE MORE THAN AND TWO MORE THAN WITH DICE AND SPINNERS

Make a die with sides labeled $+ 1, + 2, + 1, + 2$, "one more," and "two more." Use with another die labeled 3, 4, 5, 6, 7, and 8 (or whatever values students need to practice). After each roll of the dice, students should say the complete fact: "Four and two more equals six." Alternatively, roll one die and use a spinner with $+ 1$ on one half and $+ 2$ on the other half. For students with disabilities, you may want to start with a die that just has $+ 1$ on every side and then another day move on to a $+ 2$ die. This will help emphasize and practice one approach.

◆ Make 10

Perhaps the most important strategy for students to know is the Make 10 strategy, which includes the combinations that add to 10. Starting with story problems using two numbers that add to 10, or that ask how many are needed to make 10, can assist this process.

The ten-frame is a very useful tool for creating a visual image for students developing this strategy. Place six counters starting on the upper left corner on one ten-frame and ask, "How many more to make 10?" This activity can be repeated frequently with counters or the little ten-frame cards (see Blackline Masters 3 and 4) until all combinations that make 10 are mastered. Later, display a blank ten-frame to help build the visual image and say a number less than 10. Students start with that number and complete the 10 fact. If you say four, they say "Four plus six equals ten." This can also be done individually or in small groups. This knowledge supports other strategies (described later in this chapter) such as Up Over 10 in addition and Down Over 10 and Take from the 10 in subtraction.

Knowing number combinations that make 10 not only helps with basic fact mastery but also builds up the foundations for working on addition with higher numbers and understanding place-value concepts. Consider, for example, 28 + 7. Using the Make 10 strategy, students can add 2 up to 30 and then 5 more. This strategy can be extended to make 100.

◆ Up Over 10

Thirty-six facts have sums greater than 10, and all of those facts can be solved by using the Up Over 10 strategy. That makes this a very useful strategy. Before using this strategy, be sure that students have learned to think of the numbers 11 to 18 as 10 and some more. Surprisingly many third-grade students have not constructed this relationship.

In this approach, students use their known facts that equal 10 and then add the rest of the remaining addend on to the 10. For example, students solving 6 + 8 can start with the larger number and see that 8 is 2 away from 10; therefore, they take 2 from the 6 to get 10 and then add on the remaining 4 to get 14. This process is also called Break Apart to Make Ten (or BAMT) (Sarama & Clements, 2009).

◢ *Activity 9.2* MOVE IT, MOVE IT

Give students a mat with two ten-frames. Flash cards are placed next to the ten-frames, or a fact can be given orally. The students should first model each number in the two ten-frames with counters to represent the problem (9 + 6 would mean covering nine places on one frame and six on the other). Ask students to move it—that is, to decide a way to group the counters to show (without counting) what the total is. Ask students to explain what they did and connect it to the new equation. For example 9 + 6 may become 10 + 5 by moving the counter up to the first ten-frame. Emphasize strategies that are working for students, such as Make 10 or Up Over 10 (see Blackline Master 1). After students have found a total, have students share and record the equations. Students who are still using counting strategies or students with disabilities may need additional experience or one-on-one time working on this process.

The Up Over 10 strategy is often not emphasized in U.S. textbooks or classrooms (Henry & Brown, 2008) but it is heavily emphasized in high-performing countries (Korea, China, Taiwan, and Japan) in which students learn facts sooner and more accurately. A recent study found that the Make 10 strategy contributed more to developing fluency with Up

Over 10 facts (e.g., 7 + 8) than using doubles (even though using doubles had been empha-sized by teachers and textbooks in the study). Moreover, this strategy can be later applied to adding "up over" 20, 50, or other benchmark numbers. Thus, the long-term utility of this reasoning strategy deserves significant attention.

Activity 9.3 FRAMES AND FACTS

Make little ten-frame cards (Blackline Masters 2 and 3) and display them to the class on a projector. Show an 8 (or 9) card. Place other cards beneath it one at a time as students respond with the total. Have students say orally what they are doing. For 8 + 4, they might say, "Take 2 from the 4 and put it with 8 to make 10. Then 10 and 2 left over is 12." Move to harder cards, like 7 + 6. Ask students to record each equation. Especially for students with disabilities, highlight how they should explicitly think about filling in the little ten-frame starting with the higher number. Show and talk about how it is more challenging to start with the lower number as a counterexample.

◆ Doubles and Near-Doubles

There are only 10 doubles facts, and only seven of these have addends of 3 or greater. However, these seven facts provide useful anchors for other facts. One way to begin devel-oping the doubles is by using a children's literature connection, *Two of Everything* (Hong, 1993). This Chinese folktale is the story of a couple (the Haktaks) who finds a magic pot that doubles everything that is put inside. Using that story as a context, a simple doubling machine can be drawn on the board in the shape of a pot, or students can have a mat with a pot shape. First, concrete items of a given number are deposited in the pot with the question "What amount comes out?" Then cards can be made with an input number on one card and the students have to write the output on another card as it goes through the doubling pot or function machine. A pair of students or a small group can use input/output machines, with one student suggesting the input and the other(s) stating the output.

Activity 9.4 CALCULATOR DOUBLES

For this activity, students work in pairs with a calculator. The students first make their calculator into a "double maker" by pressing 2 ✕ into the calculator. Then one student says a double fact, for example "seven plus seven." The student with the calculator presses 7 ✕ on the calculator, says what the double is, and then presses = to see the double (14) on the display. The students then switch roles. For ELLs who are just learning English, invite them to say the double in their native language and in English. (Note that the calculator is also useful for practicing the + 1 and + 2 facts.)

+	0	1	2	3	4	5	6	7	8	9
0	0	1								
1	1	2	3							
2		3	4	5						
3			5	6	7					
4				7	8	9				
5					9	10	11			
6						11	12	13		
7							13	14	15	
8								15	16	17
9									17	18

The doubles are also useful starting points for another set of facts often referred to as the *near-doubles*: facts such as 6 + 7 or 5 + 4, for which the addends are only one apart. These facts are shown here. The strategy for these doubles-plus-one or doubles-minus-one facts uses a known fact to derive an unknown fact. The strategy is to double the smaller number and add 1, or to double the larger and then subtract 1. Be sure students know the doubles before you focus on this strategy.

Something to be looking for is that some students with weak number concepts might apply double-plus-one incorrectly by beginning with the larger addend rather than the smaller. For example, they may use double 7 plus 1 for 7 + 6. Therefore, it is a good idea to focus especially on the doubling of the smaller addend. To counteract this error, write approximately 10 near-doubles facts on the board. Vary which addend is smaller. Have students solve problems independently, write the answers, and then discuss their ideas for efficient methods of answering these facts. Make sure they share their thinking so others can benefit from their decision-making process. Some students find it easy to extend the idea of the near-doubles to double-plus-two.

Figure 9.2 Near-doubles facts.

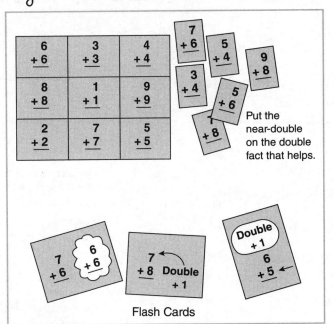

Put the near-double on the double fact that helps.

Flash Cards

 Activity 9.5 **ON THE DOUBLE!**

Create a display that illustrates the doubles (see Figure 9.2). Prepare cards with near-doubles (e.g., 4 + 5). Ask students to find the double that could help them solve the fact they have on the card and place it on that spot. Ask students if there are other doubles that could help.

Reasoning Strategies for Subtraction Facts

Subtraction facts prove to be more difficult than addition. This is especially true when students have been taught subtraction through a *count-count-count* approach—that is, for 13 − 5, count 13, count off 5, count what's left. Counting is the first phase in reaching basic fact mastery, but unfortunately many sixth, seventh, and eighth graders are still counting.

Without opportunities to learn and use reasoning strategies, students will continue to rely on inefficient counting strategies to come up with subtraction facts, which is a slow and often inaccurate approach. Therefore, spend sufficient time working on the reasoning strategies outlined here to help students move to phase 2 and eventually on to mastery (phase 3).

Subtraction as Think-Addition

In Figure 9.3 subtraction is modeled in such a way that students are encouraged to think, "What adds to this part to make the total?" When done in this think-addition manner, students use known addition facts and the inverse relationship of addition to subtraction to produce the unknown quantity or part. If this important relationship between parts and wholes—between addition and subtraction—can be made, subtraction facts and two- and three-digit subtraction problems will be much easier (Peltenburg, van den Heuvel-Panhuizen, & Robitzsch, 2012). When students see 9 − 4, you want them to think spontaneously, "Four and what adds to nine?" By contrast, observe a third-grade student who struggles with this fact. The idea of thinking addition never occurs to the student. Instead, the student counts back from 9 and may or may not end up with 5 as the answer. The value of think-addition to solve subtraction problems cannot be overstated. This means that it is essential that addition facts be mastered first.

Figure 9.3
Using a think-addition model for subtraction.

Connecting Subtraction to Addition Knowledge

1. Count out 13 and cover.

2. Count and remove 5. Keep these in view.

3. Think: "Five and what makes thirteen?" 8! 8 left. 13 minus 5 is 8.

4. Uncover.

8 and 5 is 13.

Figure 9.4 Introducing missing number cards.

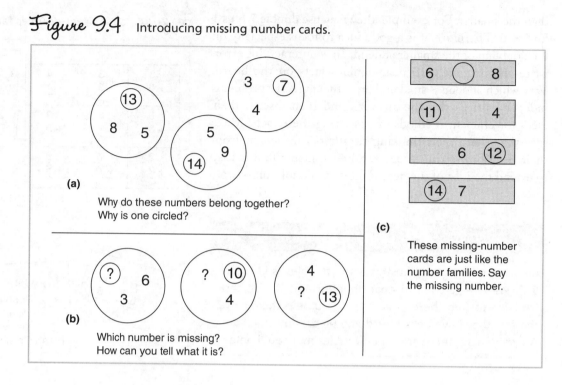

(a)

Why do these numbers belong together?
Why is one circled?

(b)

Which number is missing?
How can you tell what it is?

(c)

These missing-number cards are just like the number families. Say the missing number.

Story problems that promote think-addition are those that sound like addition but have a missing addend: join–start unknown; join–change unknown; and part–part–whole–part unknown (see Chapter 8 for more on these problem structures). Consider this problem:

Jack had 5 fish in his aquarium. Grandma gave him some more fish. Then he had 12 fish. How many fish did Grandma give Jack?

Notice that the action is join, which suggests addition. Students should think, "*Five and how many more adds up to 12?*" In the discussion in which you use problems such as this, your task is to connect this thought process with the subtraction fact $12 - 5$. Students may use an Up Over 10 strategy to solve this problem, just as they did with addition facts ("It takes 5 to get to 10 and 2 more to 12 is 7").

Activity 9.6 **MISSING NUMBER CARDS**

Show students families of numbers with the sum circled as in Figure 9.4a. Ask why they think the numbers go together and why one number is circled. When this number family idea is understood, draw a different card and cover one of the numbers with your thumb, saying, "What's missing?" Ask students how they figured it out. After your modeling, students can do this with partners. Alternatively, you can create cards with one number replaced by a question mark, as in Figure 9.4b.

BLM

When students understand this activity, explain that you have made some missing-number cards based on this idea, as in Figure 9.4c (see Blackline Master 17). Ask students to name the missing number and explain their thinking. Differentiate for students with disabilities by strategically selecting a cluster that emphasizes a particular strategy (see Figure 9.5).

Formative Assessment Note

If you suspect students have not yet mastered their subtraction facts, prepare a page of them and a corresponding page of addition facts. To make the correlation between the addition and subtraction facts easier for you to see, match the facts on the two pages by putting the addition fact $5 + 4$ in the same position (row and column) on the addition page as $9 - 4$ is on the subtraction page.

Ask students to respond only to those facts that they know quickly without having to resort to counting. Explain that you only want to find out what they know so that you can help them with those facts they have yet to master.

If you find that they have not mastered all or nearly all of their addition facts, then that is the place to begin. The paired addition and subtraction facts may give you evidence as to whether students are using addition facts to respond to subtraction facts. If addition facts are known but subtraction facts are not known, then your task is to help students develop a think-addition approach.

Stop and Reflect

Look at the three subtraction facts shown here and try to reflect on what thought process you use to get the answers. Even if you "just know them," think about what a possible approach might be. ■

$$\begin{array}{ccc} 14 & 12 & 15 \\ -\,9 & -\,6 & -\,6 \\ \hline \end{array}$$

◆ Down Over 10

You may have applied a think-addition strategy for any of the problems in the Stop and Reflect. Or, you may have started with the 14 and counted down to 10 (4) and then down 1 more to 9, for a total difference of 5. This reasoning strategy is called Down Over 10. If you didn't already use this strategy, try it with one of the examples.

This reasoning strategy is a derived fact strategy because students use what they know (that 14 minus 4 is 10) to figure out a related fact ($14 - 5$). In the same way as the Make 10 and Up Over 10 strategies, this strategy is also emphasized in high-performing countries (Fuson & Kwon, 1992) and frequently ignored in the United States. One reason this strategy is so useful is that it supports students' number sense while moving them to fact mastery.

One way to develop the Down Over 10 strategy is to write five or six pairs of facts in which the difference for the first fact is 10 and the second fact is either 8 or 9—for example, $16 - 6$ and $16 - 7$ or $14 - 4$ and $14 - 6$. Have students solve each problem and discuss their strategies. If students do not naturally see the relationship, ask them to think about how the first fact can help solve the second. Reinforce the Down Over 10 strategy, by posing story problems such as the following:

Becky had 16 stuffed animals. She gave 7 to a friend. How many does Becky have left?

Figure 9.5

Missing number cards worksheet. The blank version can be used to fill in any sets of facts you wish to emphasize (see Blackline Master 17).

Make-ten facts	Near-doubles	Two fact families (7, 8, 15) (4, 8, 12)
4 ◯ 8	5 6 ◯	4 ⑫
◯ 9 6	⑬ 7	⑮ 8
8 7 ◯	⑮ 8	⑫ 4
⑮ 6	5 ⑪	7 8 ◯
5 ⑬	7 ◯ 15	⑫ 8
8 ⑰	⑨ 4	⑫ 8
6 ◯ 8	⑰ 8	4 ⑫
3 9 ◯	⑪ 6	8 ⑮
9 ◯ 16	5 ◯ 4	⑮ 7
◯ 6 8	3 ⑦	7 ◯ 8
7 ◯ 16	⑨ 5	4 ⑫
3 ◯ 9	6 ⑬	◯ 4 8
8 ◯ 8	⑰ 9	8 ⑮

◆ Take from the 10

This strategy is also consistently used in high-performing countries. It takes advantage of students' knowledge of the combinations that make 10, and it works for all subtraction problems in which the starting value (minuend) is greater than 10. For example, take the problem $16 - 8$. Students decompose the minuend into $10 + 6$. Subtracting from the 10 (because they know this fact), $10 - 8$ is 2. Then they add the 6 back on to get 8. Try it on these examples:

$$15 - 8 = \qquad 17 - 9 = \qquad 14 - 8 =$$

▲ Reasoning Strategies for Multiplication and Division Facts

Using a problem-based approach and focusing on reasoning strategies are just as important for developing mastery of the multiplication and related division facts (Baroody, 2006; Wallace & Gurganus, 2005). Multiplication facts can and should be mastered by relating new facts to existing knowledge. As with addition and subtraction facts, start with story problems and concrete materials as you develop reasoning strategies.

Understanding the commutative property cuts the basic facts to be memorized in half. Therefore, students should completely understand the commutative property. This can be visualized by using arrays. For example, an array to show 2×8 can be described as 2 rows of 8 or 8 rows of 2. In both cases, the answer is 16. For a virtual site to connect arrays to multiplication facts, go to www.haelmedia.com/OnlineActivities_txh/mc_txh3_002.html.

Teaching Tip

Although the numerical answers to 2×8 and 8×2 are the same, the calculations they mean are different: 2×8 means 2 groups of 8; 8×2 means 8 groups of 2. The model you use should help explain the calculation. Although you shouldn't mark a student as incorrect for missing this distinction, you need to be precise in your language and models as you demonstrate representations of the problem in class.

◆ Doubles

×	0	1	2	3	4	5	6	7	8	9
0			0							
1			2							
2	0	2	4	6	8	10	12	14	16	18
3			6							
4			8							
5			10							
6			12							
7			14							
8			16							
9			18							

Facts that have 2 as a factor are equivalent to the addition doubles and should already be known by students by the time you introduce them to multiplication. So the goal is to help students realize that 2×7 is the same as double 7, but so is 7×2. Try story problems in which 2 is the number of sets. For example, have a calendar available and ask, "Our field trip is in 2 weeks. How many days will we need to wait?" (2 groups of 7) Later, use problems in which 2 is the size of the sets. For example have buttons available and ask, "George was making sock puppets. Each puppet needed 2 buttons for eyes. If George makes 7 puppets, how many buttons will he need for the eyes?" (7 groups of 2)

◆ Fives

×	0	1	2	3	4	5	6	7	8	9
0						0				
1						5				
2						10				
3						15				
4						20				
5	0	5	10	15	20	25	30	35	40	45
6						30				
7						35				
8						40				
9						45				

This group of facts includes all that have 5 as the first or second factor, as shown here. Practice skip counting by fives to 100. Connect counting by fives with arrays that have rows of 5 dots (see Figure 9.6). Point out that such an array with six rows is a model for 6×5, eight rows is 8×5, and so on. Connections can be made to counting minutes on a clock too.

◆ Zeros and Ones

Thirty-six facts have at least one factor that is either 0 or 1. These facts, though seemingly easy on a procedural level, sometimes confuse students with rules they may have learned for addition. When you add zero to a number $(6 + 0)$, it does not change the number, but 6×0

Figure 9.6 Fives facts.

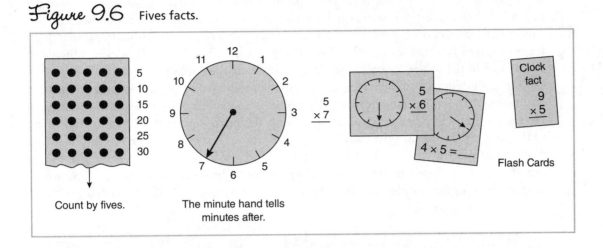

Count by fives.

The minute hand tells minutes after.

Flash Cards

Activity 9.7 CLOCK FACTS

Focus on the minute hand of the clock. When it points to a number, how many minutes after the hour is it? Draw a large clock face, and point to numbers 1 to 9 in random order. Students respond with the minutes after. Now connect this idea to the multiplication facts with 5. In this way, the fives facts become the clock facts.

---

is always zero. The $n + 1$ fact can be thought of as one more or the next number, but $n \times 1$ does not change the number. The concepts behind these facts can be developed best through story problems and an emphasis on the meaning of the operations. Alternatively to story problems, ask students to put words to the equations. For example, say that 6×0 is six groups with zero items in them (or six rows of chairs with no people in each). For 0×6, there are six in the group, but you have zero groups. For example, you worked 0 hours babysitting at $6 an hour. Avoid rules that are strictly procedural, such as "Any number multiplied by zero is zero."

×	0	1	2	3	4	5	6	7	8	9
0	0	0	0	0	0	0	0	0	0	0
1	0	1	2	3	4	5	6	7	8	9
2	0	2								
3	0	3								
4	0	4								
5	0	5								
6	0	6								
7	0	7								
8	0	8								
9	0	9								

◆ Nifty Nines

Facts with a factor of 9 include the largest products but can be among the easiest to learn due to several reasoning strategies and patterns that support students' learning. First, students can derive that 9×7 is the same as 10×7 less one set of 7, or $70 - 7$. Because students can often easily multiply by 10 and subtract from a decade value (if they've mastered their Make 10 combinations), this strategy makes sense. You might introduce a related idea by showing a set of connecting cubes (see Figure 9.7) with only the end cube a different color. After explaining that every bar has 10 cubes, ask students to find a way to figure out how many are light gray.

Second, a table of nines facts includes some interesting patterns that lead to finding the products: (1) the tens digit of the product is always one less than the "other" factor (the factor other than 9), and (2) the sum of the two digits in the product is always 9. For 7×9, 1 less than 7 is 6, and 6 and 3 makes 9, so the answer is 63. In order for students to explore and discover this pattern, ask students to record each fact for nines in order ($9 \times 1 = 9$, $9 \times 2 = 18 \ldots 9 \times 9 = 81$) and write down patterns they notice. After discussing all the patterns, ask students how

×	0	1	2	3	4	5	6	7	8	9
0										0
1										9
2										18
3										27
4										36
5										45
6										54
7										63
8										72
9	0	9	18	27	36	45	54	63	72	81

Figure 9.7
Another way to think of the nines.

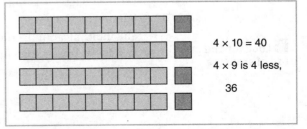

$4 \times 10 = 40$

4×9 is 4 less,

36

Standards for Mathematical Practice

8 **Look for and express regularity in repeated reasoning** ▶

these patterns can be used to figure out a product to a nines fact. (*Warning:* This strategy, grounded in the base-ten system, can be useful, but it also can cause confusion because the conceptual connection is not easy to see.) It is not, however, a rule without reason. Challenge students to think about why this pattern works. The nifty-nine pattern illustrates clearly one of the values of pattern and regularity in mathematics.

Once students have invented a strategy for the nines based on these patterns, a tactile way to help students remember the nifty nines is to use fingers—but not for counting! Here's how: Hold up both hands. Starting with the pinky on your left hand, count over to the finger that matches the factor (other than nine). For example, for 4×9, you move to the fourth finger (see Figure 9.8). Bend it down. Now look at the fingers – those to the left of the folded finger represent tens; those to the right represent ones. You have three tens to the left of the folded finger and six ones to the right—36 (Barney, 1970).

Figure 9.8

Nifty nines using fingers to show 4×9.

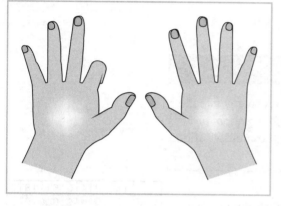

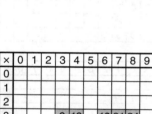

BLM

◆ Using Known Facts to Derive Other Facts

Only 25 multiplication facts remain (actually fewer, due to the commutative property). These 25 facts can be learned by relating each to an already known fact or helping fact. For example, 3×8 is connected to 2×8 (double 8 and 8 more). The 6×7 fact can be related to either 5×7 (5 sevens and 7 more) or to 3×7 (double 3×7). The helping fact must be known, and the ability to do the mental addition must also be there. For example, to go from $5 \times 7 = 35$ and then add 7 for 6×7, a student must be able to efficiently add 35 and 7.

Arrays are powerful models for these strategies. Provide students with copies of the 10×10 dot array (Figure 9.9) (see also Blackline Master 18). The lines in the array make counting the dots easier and often suggest the use of the easier fives facts as helpers. For example, 7×7 is 5×7 plus double 7, or $35 + 14$.

Knowing the doubles strategy is very effective in helping students learn difficult facts (Flowers and Rubenstein, 2010–2011). The Double and Double Again strategy shown in Figure 9.10a is applicable to all facts with 4 as a factor. For example 4×6 is the same as 2×6 doubled. But for 4×8, double 16 is also a difficult addition. Help students with this by noting, for example, that $15 + 15$ is 30, and $16 + 16$ is 2 more, or 32. Adding $16 + 16$ on paper defeats the development of efficient reasoning.

×	0	1	2	3	4	5	6	7	8	9
0										
1										
2										
3				9	12		18	21	24	
4				12	16		24	28	32	
5										
6				18	24		36	42	48	
7				21	28		42	49	56	
8				24	32		48	56	64	
9										

The Double and One More Set strategy shown in Figure 9.10b is a way to think of facts with 3 as one factor. With an array or a set picture, the double part can be circled, and it is clear that there is one more set. Two facts in this group involve more difficult mental additions: 3×8 and 3×9. Using doubling and one more, you can generate any fact.

The Half Then Double strategy can be used if either factor is even. Select the even factor, and cut it in half as shown in Figure 9.10c. If the smaller fact is known, that product is doubled to get the new fact.

Students often use a Close Fact strategy when they add one more set to a known fact, as shown in Figure 9.10d. For example, think of 6×7 as 6 sevens. Five sevens is close: That's 35. Six sevens is one more seven, or 42. When using 5×8 to help with 6×8, the language "6 groups of eight" or "6 eights" is very helpful in remembering to add 8 more and not 6 more. This Close Fact reasoning strategy has no limits—it can be used for any multiplication fact. It also reinforces students' number sense and relationships between numbers. Asking students whether they know a nearby fact to derive the new fact over time will help make this mental process become automatic for students.

Standards for Mathematical Practice

7 **Look for and make use of structure** ▶

Formative Assessment Note

Use word problems as a vehicle for assessing harder facts in a one-on-one diagnostic interview. Consider this problem: *Connie put her old crayons into bags of 7. She was able to make 8 bags with 3 crayons left over. How many crayons did she have?* Or *Carlos and Jack kept their baseball cards in albums with 6 cards on each page. Carlos had 4 pages filled, and Jack had 8 pages filled. How many cards did each boy have?* (Do you see the Half Then Double strategy?)

As the student works to get an answer, encourage her to talk about the strategies she is using. Ask her if she can solve it another way. This push adds to the benefit of the assessment by seeing what methods your student can pull from. Remember, students with disabilities may need arrays and pictures of sets or groups to help interpret the information from the problems and support their thinking about multiplication facts and relationships.

Activity 9.8 IF YOU DIDN'T KNOW

Pose the following task: "If you did not know the answer to 8 × 7 [or any fact that you want students to think about], how could you figure it out without counting?" Encourage students to come up with more than one way, hopefully using the strategies suggested above. ELLs and reluctant learners benefit from first sharing their ideas with a partner and then with the class.

Figure 9.9

An array is a useful model for developing strategies for the hard multiplication facts (see Blackline Master 18).

Figure 9.10

Reasoning strategies for using a known fact to derive an unknown fact.

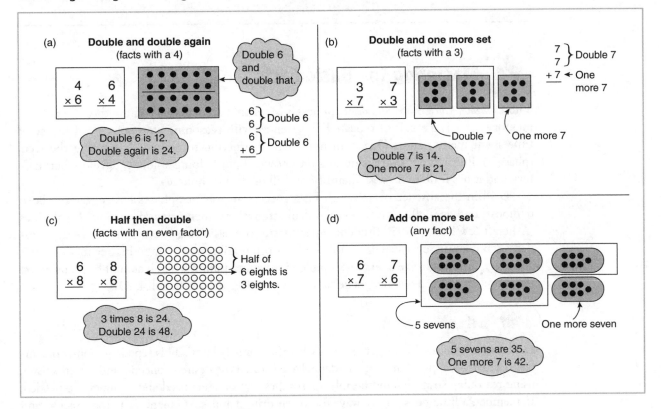

◆ Division Facts

Division fact mastery is dependent on the inverse relationship of multiplication and division. For example, to solve 36 ÷ 9, you tend to think, "Nine times what is thirty-six?" In fact, because of this relationship, the reasoning strategies for division are to (1) think multiplication and then (2) apply a known multiplication fact, as needed. Story problems continue to be a key vehicle to develop this connection.

Exercises such as 50 ÷ 6 might be called *near facts*. Divisions with remainders are much more prevalent in real-life situations than division facts or division without remainders. To determine the answer to 50 ÷ 6, most people mentally review a short sequence of multiplication facts, comparing each product to 50: 6 times 7 (low), 6 times 8 (close), 6 times 9 (high). It must be 8. That's 48 and 2 left over. Students should be able to do these near-fact problems mentally and with reasonable speed.

 **HOW CLOSE CAN YOU GET?**

To practice near facts, try this exercise. Help students develop the process of going through the multiplication facts as was just described. This can be a game for small groups or an activity with the full class.

$$4 \times \square \rightarrow 23, \underline{\hspace{2cm}} \text{ left over}$$

Find the largest factor without going over the target number.

$$7 \times \square \rightarrow 52, \square \text{ left over}$$

$$6 \times \square \rightarrow 27, \square \text{ left over}$$

$$9 \times \square \rightarrow 60, \square \text{ left over}$$

Mastering the Basic Facts

The *Common Core State Standards* precisely state that students will know their facts from memory. This is a result of repeated experiences with reasoning strategies, not because of time spent memorizing. This is an important distinction to make in mastering the facts (phase 3). Fortunately, there is quite a bit known about helping students develop fact mastery, and it has little to do with quantity of drill or drill techniques.

Drill in the absence of accomplishing success at previous phases has repeatedly been demonstrated as ineffective. However, drill strengthens memory and retrieval capabilities (Ashcraft & Christy, 1995). Students must master the basic facts (develop quick recall). Students who continue to struggle with the facts often fail to understand higher mathematics concepts; their cognitive energy gets pulled into computation when it should be focusing on the more sophisticated concepts being developed (Forbringer & Fahsl, 2010).

◆ Effective Drill

Drill can only help students get faster at what they already know. This repetitive non-problem-based activity is appropriate once students have learned the desired concepts and are effectively using reasoning strategies and flexible approaches, but greater speed and accuracy are needed. Remember, a little goes a long way. Too often drill includes too many facts too quickly, and students become frustrated, overwhelmed, and unmotivated. Five multiplication problems targeted to a particular student can be as useful in assessing student understanding as 25 problems.

Therefore, not much is gained from the additional 20 problems. Also, when students are making mistakes, more drill and practice is not the solution—identifying and addressing misconceptions is far more effective. Because students progress at different paces—gifted students tend to be good memorizers, whereas students with intellectual disabilities have difficulty memorizing (Forbringer & Fahsl, 2010)—drilling using the same problems for all students rarely makes sense.

When working on moving students to phase 3 (know from memory), as with strategies, identify a group of facts that are related. Flash cards, for example, are more effective if they are not covering all facts and strategies but are focused on a select group that the student is ready to memorize. For example, if given a stack of × 1 facts, some students will quickly learn these facts, noting the generalizations, but for some students—in particular, students with disabilities—more discussion and illustration are often needed. Because many students need multiple experiences, it is important that instruction is differentiated and engaging.

When students are still struggling with gaps in their knowledge of facts, make sure your temptation to drill is warranted. Before committing to this solution, ask yourself two questions: Will drill build understanding? How is this affecting the student's disposition toward learning? What students often learn from more drill is "Math is full of rules that I don't understand," which leads to not liking mathematics and believing they are not good at it. In reality, when a student is making errors on a procedure, it is usually a conceptual issue (as in misconception). When the problem is conceptual, remediation should include dropping back to activities that strengthen the student's conceptual knowledge.

There is little doubt that strategy development and general number sense (number relationships and operation meanings) are the best contributors to fact mastery. Drill in the absence of these factors has repeatedly been demonstrated as ineffective. However, the positive value of drill should not be completely ignored. Drill of nearly any mental activity strengthens memory and retrieval capabilities.

One important use of technology is in differentiated drill, such as that found in Fun 4 the Brain (www.fun4thebrain.com) and Math Fact Café (www.mathfactcafe.com). These free online programs work to help all students develop fluency with math facts. In short sessions that are customized for individual learners, the software allows you to differentiate instruction based on fact families. Students have the opportunity to earn electronic rewards and then move on to more difficult exercises.

◆ Games to Support Basic Fact Mastery

Playing games and doing activities in which students can choose from the collection of reasoning strategies discussed in this chapter will allow them to become more adept at selecting strategies and more fact fluent. Games and activities provide low-stress approaches to practicing basic facts while helping students move toward quick recall. In addition, games increase student involvement, encourage student-to-student interaction, and improve communication—all of which are related to improved academic achievement (Forbringer & Fahsl, 2010; Kamii & Anderson, 2003; Lewis, 2005).

As noted previously, focus on related clusters of facts and target what individual students need to practice. Also, encourage students to self-monitor—they can create their own game board or game that includes the facts they are working to master.

Table 9.1 offers some ideas for how classic games can be adapted to focus on basic fact mastery, as well as how each can be differentiated.

Table 9.1 Classic Games Adapted to Basic Fact Mastery

Classic Game	How to Use It with Basic Fact Mastery	Suggestions for Differentiation
Bingo	Each bingo card has a fact problem (e.g., 2×3) in each box. The same fact will be on multiple bingo cards but in different locations on each card. You will call out an answer (e.g., 6), and the students will find a matching problem (or more than one problem) on their card.	Create bingo boards that focus on different clusters of facts (e.g., doubles or doubles + 1 on some boards, and Up Over 10 on other boards). Be sure that the answers you call out are an even mix of the clusters so that everyone has the same chance to win.
Concentration	Create cards that have a fact problem (e.g., 3×5) on one half and the answer (e.g., 15) on the other half. Shuffle the cards and turn them face-down in a 6×4 grid. (If you like, you can make the grid larger to use more cards.)	Select cards that focus on a particular cluster of facts (e.g., + 1 and $\times$ 5 facts) for each round of the game. Multiple groups can play the game simultaneously—each group will use the parts of the deck that contain the facts they are working on. Also, consider making cards that show the ten-frames below the numbers to help provide a visual for students.
Dominoes	Create (or find online) dominoes that have a fact on one end and an answer (not to that fact) on the other end. Each student gets the same number of dominoes (around eight). On his or her turn, they can play one of the dominoes in their hand only if they have an answer or a fact that can connect to a domino on the board.	As with other games, select the dominoes that focus on particular clusters of facts.
Four in a Row	Create a 6×6 square game board with a sum (or product) written on each square. Below, list the numbers 0 through 9. Each of the two players has counters of a different color to use as their game pieces. On the first turn, Player 1 places a marker (paper clip) on two addends/factors and then gets to place his or her colored counter on the related answer. (If you have repeated the same answer on different squares of the board, the player only gets to cover one of them.) Player 2 can only move one paper clip and then gets to place his or her colored counter on the related answer. The first player to get four in a row wins.	Rather than list all the values below the chart, just list the related addends or factors. For example, use 1, 2, 6, 7, 8, 9 if you want to work on + 1 and + 2, or use 3, 4, 5, 6 if you are working on these multiplication facts.
Old Maid (retitled as Old Dog)	Create cards for each fact and each answer. Add one card that has a picture of an old dog (or use your school mascot). Shuffle and deal cards. On each player's turn, the player draws from the person on his or her right, sees whether that card is a match to a card in his or her hand (a fact and its answer), and, if so, lays down the pair. Then the person to the left draws from him or her. Play continues until all matches are found and someone is left with the Old Dog. Winner can be the person with (or not with) the Old Dog, or the person with the most pairs.	See Concentration (above).

Consider the following activity that engages students in creatively applying all four operations.

Activity 9.10 BOWL A FACT

In this activity (suggested by Shoecraft, 1982), you draw circles placed in a triangular fashion to look like bowling pins, with the front circle labeled 1 and the others labeled consecutively through 10. For culturally diverse classrooms, be sure that students are familiar with bowling. (If they are not, consider showing an online video clip).

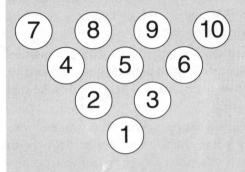

Take three dice and roll them. Students use all three numbers on the three dice to come up with equations that result in answers that are on the pins. For example, if you roll 4, 2, and 3, they can "knock down" the 5 pin with $4 \times 2 - 3$. If they produce equations using these three numbers to knock down all 10 pins, they get a strike. If not, they roll again and see whether the three new numbers used in equations can knock the rest down for a spare. The pins that are left standing are added to get the score. Low score wins. After demonstrating the game, students can play in small groups.

Activity 9.11 SALUTE!

Place students in groups of three and give each group a deck of cards. (Omit face cards and use aces as ones.) Two students draw a card without looking at it and place it on their foreheads facing outward so the others can see it. The student without a card tells the product of the two cards. The first of the other two students to correctly say the factor on their forehead wins the round. For ELLs, students with disabilities, or reluctant learners, speed can increase anxiety and inhibit participation. You can remove speed of response by having the two students write down the card they think they have (within five seconds) and rewarding them one point if they are correct. This activity can be differentiated by including only certain cards (e.g., multiplication facts using only the numbers 1 through 5). The game can also be played with addition facts for students who still need support.

Fact Remediation

Students who have not mastered their basic facts by the fifth grade are in need of something other than more drill. They have certainly seen and practiced facts countless times in previous grades. There is no reason to believe that the drills *you* provide will somehow be more effective than last year's. These students need something better. The following key ideas can guide your efforts to help these older students.

1. *Recognize that more drill will not work*. Students' fact difficulties are due to a failure to develop or to connect concepts and relationships, not a lack of drill. At best, more drill will provide temporary results. At worst, it will cause negative attitudes about mathematics.

2. *Inventory the known and unknown facts for each student in need.* Identify each student's fact profile—what facts are known quickly and comfortably and which are not. Fifth- and sixth-grade students can do this diagnosis for you. Provide sheets of all facts for one operation in random order and have the students circle the facts they are hesitant about and answer all others. Caution them that finger counting or making marks in the margin is not permitted.

3. *Diagnose strengths and weaknesses.* Find out what students do when they encounter one of their unknown facts. Do they count on their fingers? Add up tic marks or numbers in the margins? Guess? Try to use a related fact? Write down times tables? Are they able to use any of the relationships suggested in this chapter? Conduct a 10-minute diagnostic interview with each student in need. Simply pose unknown facts and ask the student how he or she approaches them. Note the connections that are already there.

4. *Provide hope.* Students who have experienced long-term difficulty with fact mastery often believe that they cannot learn facts or that they are doomed to finger counting forever. Let these students know you will provide some new ideas that will help them. Take that burden on, and spare them the prospect of more defeat.

5. *Build in success.* As you begin a well-designed fact program for a student who has experienced failure, be sure that successes come quickly and easily. Begin with easy strategies, and introduce only a few new facts at a time. Exposure to five facts in a three-day period will provide more success than introducing 15 facts in a week. Success builds success! Point out to students how one strategy is all that is required to learn many facts. Use fact charts to show what set of facts you are working on. It is surprising how the chart quickly fills up with mastered facts. Keep reviewing newly learned facts and those that were already known. Success feels good and failures are not as apparent. Short practice exercises can be designed as homework. Explain strategies and build them into the exercises. At the end of the exercises, have students write about which ideas are helpful and which are not. Use this information to design the next exercise.

Your extra effort beyond class time can be motivating to a student to make some personal effort on his or her own time. During class, these students should continue to work with all students on the regular curriculum. You must believe and communicate to these students that the reason they have not mastered basic facts is not a reflection of their abilities. With efficient strategies and individual effort, success will come. Believe!

● What to Do When Teaching Basic Facts

Here are important reminders about effectively teaching the basic facts. This is such an important life skill for all learners that it is imperative that you, as a teacher, use what research suggests are the most effective practices. The following list of recommendations support the development of quick recall of the basic facts.

1. *Ask students to self-monitor.* The importance of this recommendation cannot be overstated. Across all learning, having a sense of what you don't know and what you need to learn is important. It certainly holds true with memorizing facts. Students should be able to identify which facts are difficult for them and continue to work on reasoning strategies to help them derive those facts.

2. *Focus on self-improvement.* This point follows from self-monitoring. If you are working on improving students' quickness at recalling facts, students should only be competing with themselves. Students can keep track of how long it took them to go through their "fact stack," for example, and then, two days later, pull the same stack and see whether they are quicker (or more accurate) than the last time.

3. *Drill in short time segments.* You can project numerous examples of double ten-frames in relatively little time. You can also have each student pull a set of flash cards, pair with another student, and go through each other's set in 2 minutes. Long periods (10 minutes or more) are not effective. Using the first 5 to 10 minutes of the day, or extra time just before lunch, can provide continued support on fact development without taking up mathematics instructional time better devoted to other topics.

4. *Work on facts over time.* Rather than do a unit on fact memorization, work on facts over months and months, working on reasoning strategies, then on memorization, and then on continued review and monitoring.

5. *Involve families.* Share the big plan of how you will work on learning basic facts with students' families. One idea is to have one or two "Take Home Facts of the Week." Ask family members to help students by using reasoning strategies when they don't know a fact.

6. *Make drill enjoyable.* There are many games (not flash cards) designed to reinforce facts that are not competitive or anxiety inducing.

7. *Use technology.* When students work with technology, they get immediate feedback and reinforcement, helping them to self-monitor. Try www.kentuckymathematics.org/resoures/pimser.asp for some ideas.

8. *Emphasize the importance of quick recall of facts.* Without creating pressure or anxiety, highlight to students that in real life and in the rest of mathematics, they will need these facts all the time—they really must learn them and learn them well. Celebrate student successes.

◆ What Not to Do When Teaching Basic Facts

The following list describes strategies that may have been designed with good intentions but work against student recall of the basic facts.

1. *Avoid using lengthy timed tests.* When under the pressure of time, students get distracted and abandon their reasoning strategies. Students also develop anxiety, which works against learning mathematics. Having students self-monitor the time it takes them to go through a small set of facts can help with their speed and avoid the negatives of long timed tests.

2. *Don't use public comparisons of mastery.* You may have experienced bulletin boards that show which students are on which step of a staircase to mastering their multiplication facts. Imagine how the student who is on the step 3 feels when others are on step 6. Or imagine the negative emotional reaction to public competition with flash cards for the half who don't win. Adults often refer to the competitions with flash cards as the moment they started to dislike mathematics, specifically reflecting on a game called "Around the World," in which one student is pitted against another with the loser sitting down. It is great to celebrate student successes, but avoid public comparisons between students.

3. *Don't proceed through facts in order from 0 to 9.* Work on collections of facts based on the strategies and conceptual understanding, and knock out those that students know rather than proceeding in a rigid fashion by going in numerical order.

4. *Don't work on all facts all at once.* Select a strategy (starting with easier ones) and then work on memorization of that set of facts (e.g., doubles). Be sure students really know these facts before moving on. Differentiation is needed! Students should not move to new facts until one set is mastered—otherwise they will become confused and your goal for them to master all the facts will backfire.

5. *Don't move to memorization too soon.* This has been addressed throughout the chapter, but is worth repeating. Quick recall or mastery can be attained only after students are ready, meaning they have a robust collection of reasoning strategies to apply as needed.

6. *Don't use facts as a barrier to important mathematics.* Students who have total command of basic facts do not necessarily reason better than those who, for whatever reason, have not yet mastered facts. Mathematics is not solely about computation. Mathematics is about reasoning and using patterns and making sense of things. Mathematics is problem solving. There is no reason that a student who has not yet mastered all basic facts should be excluded from more advanced mathematical experiences.

7. *Don't use fact mastery as a prerequisite for calculator use.* Insisting that students master the basic facts before allowing them to use a calculator denies them important learning opportunities. For example, if your lesson goal is for students to discover the pattern (formula) for the perimeter of rectangles, then a good lesson would have students building and exploring different-shaped rectangles, recording the length, width, and perimeter, and looking for patterns. A student who has not yet developed fact fluency will be too bogged down in computation without a calculator. With a calculator, the same student can participate and hopefully attain the learning goals of the lesson. But, once students have mastered their facts, fade the use of calculators to compute basic facts. Students should consistently practice their facts to increase their fluency and number sense.

Formative Assessment Note

If there is any purpose for a timed test of basic facts, it may be for diagnostic purposes—to determine which number combinations are mastered and which need to be learned. For it to be diagnostic, the follow-up should include the teacher and the student identifying possible misconceptions or misapplication of strategies, as well as which facts are mastered and which need more practice.

E x p a n d e d   L e s s o n

If You Didn't Know

Content and Task Decisions

Grade Level: 3–4

Mathematics Goals

- To develop student-invented strategies for multiplication facts.
- To develop problem-solving skills in the context of basic multiplication facts.

Grade Level Guide

NCTM *Curriculum Focal Points*	*Common Core State Standards*
In a Focal Point connection under "Number and Operations" in grades 3 and 4, students use properties of multiplication to solve multiplication and division problems involving the basic facts developing quick recall and fluency.	In the domain of Operations and Algebraic Thinking, third grade students multiply and divide within 100 using the properties of multiplication and the inverse relationship between multiplication and division. In grades 3 and 4, students use the four operations with whole numbers to solve problems.

Consider Your Students' Needs

Students understand that multiplication is connected to the process of repeated addition. They are proficient with their addition facts and have mastered the easier multiplication facts. They may still struggle with some of the more difficult multiplication facts.

For English Language Learners

- Be sure that students know the words *equal groups,* which can be acted out (asking students to make or be a part of an equal group).
- As needed, provide translations for the numbers.

For Students with Disabilities

- Use a set of round counters that align with the array on the Blackline Master. These can be used to model the array so that you can use a think-aloud to show and describe how the array is created.

Materials

Each student will need:

- Copy of a 10 × 10 array (see Blackline Master 18) and a cardstock L-shaped piece as is shown in Figure 9.9.

Lesson

Before

Begin with a simpler version of the task:

- Ask students to remember when they were learning addition facts and how knowing 6 + 6 could help them figure out 6 + 7. Elicit student ideas. The point to emphasize is what is meant by a fact that they know (e.g., a fact that they have already mastered and know without counting).
- Ask students to pretend that they do not know 6 × 5 but that they do know 5 × 5. Use a projection of the 10-by-10 dot array and the L-shaped card to illustrate a 6 × 5 array on the overhead. How could they use 5 × 5 to help them determine 6 × 5? Elicit student ideas. For example, 5 × 5 is 25 and one more group of 5 is 30.
- Without using the dot array, ask students to suppose they know 3 × 5 but not 6 × 5. How could they use 3 × 5 to determine 6 × 5? Again elicit student ideas. For example, 3 × 5 is 15 and means 3 groups of 5; 6 × 5 means 6 groups of 5, so just double the 15 to get 30.

Present the focus task to the class:

- If you did not know the answer to 6 × 8, how could you figure it out by using some facts that you do know?

Provide clear expectations:

- Explain to students that their methods should be something that they can do in their heads and should not rely on counting by ones. In other words, they should use a fact that they know and have already mastered.
- Encourage students to come up with more than one way.
- Explain that the 10-by-10 array is only one tool to help them think about different strategies. They do not have to use this tool.

During

Initially:

- If students have difficulty getting started, first ask them what 6 × 8 means in terms of addition (e.g., 6 groups of 8). Suggest they write the six 8s either vertically or horizontally and look for different ways to group the numbers so that they can determine the answer more quickly. Do not press for a particular approach. Alternatively, suggest that they use the 10-by-10 dot array. Is there a part of the array that they can use easily?

Ongoing:

- Encourage students to come up with more than one way to find 6 × 8. You might have to suggest ideas to try.

- As students work, ask them to explain their strategies. You may need to provide guidance in how they can better explain or illustrate their approach to their classmates.

After

Bring the class together to share and discuss the task:

- Use a think-pair-share approach in which students discuss their ideas with a partner before they share them with the class.

- As students share their ways of thinking about how to determine 6 × 8 mentally, they may need to accompany their explanations with drawings or equations so that classmates can follow along. You may need to step in to help students make explicit the particular strategy they are using, such as Half Then Double, add one more set, and so on.

- Help students make connections between symbolic approaches, such as a listing of six 8s and a semi-concrete approach by looking at a portion of the 10-by-10 array.

- Ideas students may use include 3 × 8 and then double, 6 × 4 and then double, 5 × 8 and one more 8, and double-double-double (12, 24, 48). Each of these ideas can be used with other hard multiplication facts as well. For a given strategy, challenge students to find other facts with which they can use the same approach.

Assessment

Observe

- Look for students who only use repeated addition to determine the answer to the multiplication fact. Have these students mastered the easier multiplication facts?

- Some students may need skills with mental addition to make a strategy useful. For example, to use 3 × 8 and then double, a student must be able to double 24 mentally.

Next Steps

- Use word problems as a vehicle for prompting and developing different strategies. For example, to prompt the Double and Double Again approach, pose a word problem such as the following: *Mike and Sarah were making goody bags for the end-of-the-year party. They wanted to put 6 pieces of candy in each student's bag. Mark made 2 bags while Sarah made 4 bags. How many pieces of candy did each person use?*

- For students having difficulty with easier facts, provide meaningful practice with strategies for groups of facts (double, fives, threes, nines) as described in this chapter.

Ask

- How can the Half Then Double strategy help with a more difficult problem like 16 × 2?

10

Developing Whole-Number Place-Value Concepts

**IDEAS**

1 Number sense is flexibly thinking about numbers and their relationships.

2 Numbers are related to each other in a variety of ways. The number 67, for example, is more than 50, 3 less than 70, and composed of 60 and 7 as well as 50 and 17. Each of these forms of 67 may be useful in a variety of situations, from estimation to comparison to computation.

3 Very large numbers possess the same place-value structure as the smaller numbers that students have worked with in earlier grades. But quantities as large as 1000 or more can be difficult to conceptualize because of their size. Very large numbers are best understood in terms of familiar real-world contexts.

Number sense, a rich, relational understanding of number, involves many different ideas, relationships, and skills. We can think of *number sense* as a "good intuition about numbers and their relationships . . . [that] develops gradually as a result of exploring numbers, visualizing them in a variety of contexts, and relating them in ways that are not limited by traditional algorithms" (Howden, 1989, p. 11).

Number sense in grades 3 through 5 should start with larger whole numbers but also be developed beyond whole numbers as other types of numbers—fractions, decimals, and percents—are added to students' repertoire of number ideas. This chapter focuses on number sense with respect to larger whole numbers, whereas Chapter 12 focuses on fraction sense, Chapter 13 on fraction operations, and decimal and percent concepts are discussed in Chapter 14.

Number sense is linked to a complete understanding of place value, including extensions to decimal numeration as it develops across the elementary and middle grades. In grades 3 and 4, students extend their understanding to numbers up to 10,000 in a variety of contexts. In fourth and fifth grades, the ideas of whole numbers are extended to decimals (CCSSO, 2010). A significant part of this development includes students' putting numbers together (composing) and taking them apart (decomposing) in a wide variety of ways as they solve addition and subtraction problems with two- and three-digit numbers. Students' efforts with the invention of their own computation strategies will both enhance their understanding of place value and provide a firm foundation for flexible methods of computation.

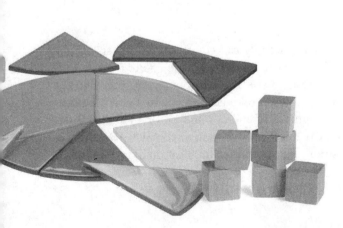

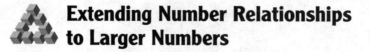

Extending Number Relationships to Larger Numbers

After students learn to count meaningfully, number relationships must become the emphasis to move students away from merely counting and toward developing number sense, a flexible concept of number not completely tied to counting. Students' knowledge of the early number relationships can be built on to extend them to numbers up to and greater than 100. The following three ideas can be demonstrated using the little ten-frames as shown in Figure 10.1a. First refresh prior knowledge and briefly ask students about the relationships of one more than and one less than. Then, in a similar manner, ask them to consider 10 more than and 10 less than a given number. For example, 70 is 10 more than 60 (that is, one more ten-frame) and 50 is 10 less than 60 (one less ten-frame). The second idea is connected to fact strategies. If a student uses the Up Over 10 addition strategy when thinking about adding on to 8 or 9 by first adding up to 10 and then adding the rest, the extension to similar two-digit numbers is quite simple (see Figure 10.1b). Finally, it is a very useful idea to take apart or decompose larger numbers to begin to develop flexibility. Students can think of ways to decompose a multiple of 10 such as 80—maybe into 50 and 30 or into 40 and 40. Once they decompose multiples of 10, the challenge is to think of ways to break apart multidigit numbers that have a 5 in the ones place, such as 25 or 35.

Being able to recognize and generate equivalent representations of the same number is the component of number sense that will serve students well during tasks that require estimation, comparison, or computation. This ability linked to place-value understanding increases students' flexibility in dealing with numbers because they can easily generate equivalent representations that will make their work easier. Challenge students to find as many different ways to represent a given number as possible. The number 67, for example, is 65 and 2 more, 3 less than 70, and composed of 60 and 7, as well as 50 and 17 or 40 and 27. Each of these forms of 67 may be useful in a variety of computational situations. For instance, if you are adding 67 and 56, thinking of 67 as 50 and 17 allows you to add 50 and 50 (from the 56) to get 100. Now add the 17 and 6 to get 23. Combine the 100 and 23 to get 123. Once students are able to think flexibly like this, they will be able to mentally do additions such as 67 and 56 faster than using a pencil-and-paper procedure.

◆ Part–Part–Whole Relationships

Stop and Reflect

Before reading on, get some counters or coins. Count out a set of 18 counters in front of you as if you were a child counting them. ■

Any student who has learned how to count meaningfully can count out 18 objects as you just did. What is significant about the experience is what it did *not* cause you to think about. Nothing in counting a set of 18 objects will cause a student to focus on the fact that the amount could be made of two parts. For example, separate the counters you just set out into two piles and reflect on the combination. It might be 12 and 6, 7 and 11, or 14 and 4. Make a change in your two piles of counters and say the new combination to yourself. Focusing on a quantity in terms of its parts (decomposition) has important implications for developing number sense as well as operation sense.

$\mathcal{Figure}$ 10.1   Extending early number relationships to mental computation activities.

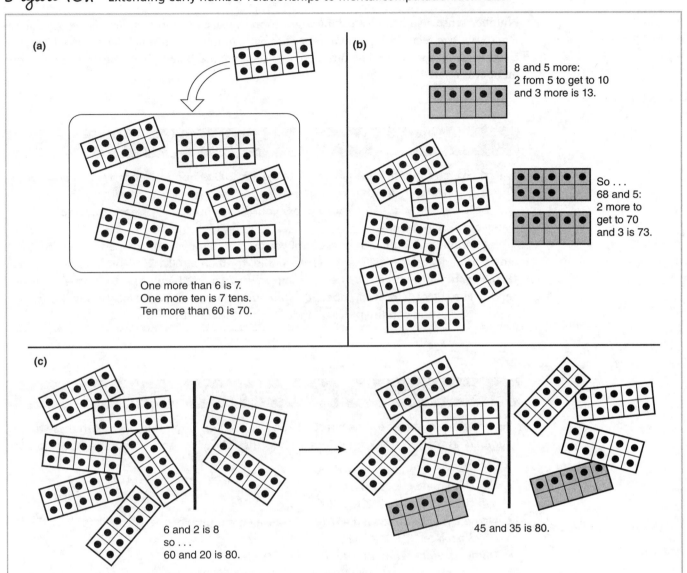

(a)

One more than 6 is 7.
One more ten is 7 tens.
Ten more than 60 is 70.

(b)

8 and 5 more:
2 from 5 to get to 10
and 3 more is 13.

So . . .
68 and 5:
2 more to
get to 70
and 3 is 73.

(c)

6 and 2 is 8
so . . .
60 and 20 is 80.

45 and 35 is 80.

◢ $\mathcal{Activity}$ 10.1   **BUILD IT IN PARTS**

Provide students with one type of material, such as base-ten materials or little ten-frame cards. The task is to see how many different combinations for a particular number, such as 83, students can make using two parts. (If you wish, you can allow for more than two parts.) For each combination, students are challenged to see and read their representation in two parts. Each different combination can be displayed on a small mat, such as a quarter-sheet of construction paper. For each representation, have students write an addition equation that matches the way they identified the parts within the decomposition.

    Writing the combinations encourages reflective thought focused on the part–whole relationship and decomposition of numbers. It also helps make apparent the clear connection between part–whole concepts and addition concepts.

◆ Relative Magnitude

Number sense also includes having a grasp on the size of numbers. *Relative magnitude* refers to the size relationship one number has with another—is it much larger, much smaller, close, or about the same? The next activity uses a number line to help students see how one number is related to another.

▶ *Activity* 10.2 WHO AM I?

Sketch a number line labeled with a 0 and 200 at opposite ends. Mark a point with a question mark that corresponds to your secret number. (Estimate the position the best you can.) Students try to guess your secret number. For each guess, place and label a mark on the line.

Continue marking each guess until your secret number is discovered. As a variation, the endpoints can be different—for example, try 0 and 1000, 200 and 300, or 500 and 800. For students with disabilities, it is important to mark the guesses that have occurred and where they are located. Labeling those numbers at their actual locations will support students' reasoning in the process of identifying the secret number.

▶ *Activity* 10.3 CLOSE, FAR, AND IN BETWEEN

Put any three numbers on the board. If appropriate, use larger numbers. With these three numbers as referents, ask questions such as the following, and encourage discussion of all responses:

- Which two are closest? Why?
- Which is closest to 300? To 250?
- Name a number between 457 and 364. Name a multiple of 25 between 219 and 364.
- Name a number that is more than all of these.
- About how far apart are 219 and 500? 219 and 5000?
- If these are "big numbers," what are some small numbers? Numbers about the same? Numbers that make these seem small?

219   364   457

◆ Connections to Real-World Ideas

Encourage students to see large numbers in the world around them. First, look for numbers around your school: the number of students in each grade level, the number of students who ride the school buses, the number of minutes devoted to mathematics each day throughout the school day (and then each week or year), the number of cartons of chocolate and plain milk served in the cafeteria each year, the number of hours (or minutes) school has been in session since the beginning of the year, or how many hours they've spent in school. Then, you can look at other numbers such as measurements, numbers at home, numbers on a field trip, and so on. All sorts of things can and should be counted and measured to create graphs, draw inferences, create word problems, and make comparisons.

Approximate Numbers and Rounding

The most familiar form of computational estimation is rounding, which is a way of changing the numbers in a problem to others that are easier to compute mentally. Students in grade 3 are expected to use place-value understanding to round numbers to the nearest 10 or 100, and students in grades 4 should be able to round any multidigit whole number to any place value (CCSSO, 2010).

To be useful in estimation, rounding should be flexible and conceptually well-understood. To round a number simply means to select a compatible number. (Note that the term *compatible* is not a mathematical term. It refers to numbers that would make the problem easier to compute mentally.) The compatible number can be any close number and need not be a multiple of 10 or 100, but in many cases students are asked to round to one of these places.

A number line with benchmark numbers highlighted can be useful in helping students select compatible numbers. An empty number line like the one shown in Figure 10.2 can be made using strips of poster board (or cash register tape) taped end to end. Labels are written above the line. The ends can be labeled 0 and 100, 100 and 200, . . . 900 and 1000. Indicate a number above the line that you want to round. Discuss the marks (or compatible numbers) that are close. Teach students the convention that if a number that is being rounded has a 5 in the place being considered, although it is halfway between two numbers, they round up. The number line is a powerful tool for these discussions.

Figure 10.2

An empty number line can be labeled in different ways to help students round numbers.

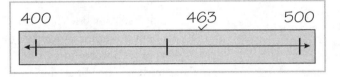

Important Place-Value Concepts

Place-value understanding requires an integration of new and sometimes difficult-to-construct concepts of grouping by tens (the base-ten concept) with procedural knowledge of how groups are recorded in our place-value scheme, how numbers are written, and how they are spoken. Importantly, learners must understand the word grouping. Because the root word *group* is frequently used for instructing students to work together, this different use of the word may cause confusion, particularly for ELLs.

Integration of Base-Ten Grouping with Counting by Ones

Recognizing that students can count out a set of 53, we want to help them see that making groupings of tens and leftovers is a way of counting that same quantity. Each of the sets in Figure 10.3 has 53 tiles, and students can count those sets using three distinct approaches. Each approach helps students think about the quantities in a different way (Thompson, 1990).

1. *Counting by ones*. Younger students usually begin with this method. Initially, a count-by-ones approach is the only way they name a quantity or "tell how many." All three sets in Figure 10.3 can be counted by ones. Students

Figure 10.3

Three equivalent sets of 53 objects.

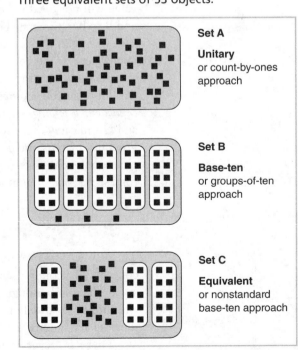

Set A

Unitary
or count-by-ones approach

Set B

Base-ten
or groups-of-ten approach

Set C

Equivalent
or nonstandard base-ten approach

with pre-base-ten understandings (they are not using 10 as a unit) use counting by ones as the only way they are convinced that all three sets are the same.

2. *Counting by groups and singles.* In Figure 10.3 set B, counting by groups and singles would go like this: "One, two, three, four, five groups of 10, and one, two, three singles." Consider how novel this method would be for a student who had never thought about counting a group of objects as a single item (unitizing). Also notice how this approach to counting does not tell directly how many items there are. This counting must be coordinated with a count by ones before it can be a means of telling how many.

3. *Counting by tens and ones.* This is the way adults would probably count set B and perhaps set C: 10, 20, 30, 40, 50, 51, 52, 53. Although this count ends by saying the number of items, it is not as explicit as the second method in counting the number of groups.

Your foremost objective should be helping students integrate the grouping-by-tens concept with what they know about numbers from counting by ones. If they first counted by ones, the question might be, "What will happen if we count these by groups and singles (or by tens and ones)?" If a set has been grouped into tens and ones and counted, then ask, "How can we be really certain that there are 53 things here?" or "How many do you think we will get if we count by ones?" You cannot tell students that these counts will all be the same and hope that will make sense to them—it is a relationship they must construct themselves.

Stop and Reflect

What are some defining characteristics of pre-place-value students and those who understand place value? ■

There is a subtle yet profound difference between students at these stages. Some know that set B is 53 because they understand the idea that five groups of 10 and 3 more is the same amount as 53 counted by ones; others simply say, "It's 53," because they have been told that when things are grouped this way, it's called 53. The students who understand place value will not need to count set B by ones. They understand the "fifty-threeness" of sets A and B to be the same. The students in the pre-place-value stage may not be sure how many they will get if they count the tiles in set B by ones, or if the groups were "ungrouped" how many there would be.

Recognition of the equivalence of sets B and C is another step in students' conceptual development. Groupings with fewer than the maximum number of tens are referred to as *equivalent groupings* or *equivalent representations*. Understanding the equivalence of sets B and C indicates that grouping by tens is not just a rule that is followed, but also that any grouping by tens, including all or some of the singles, can help tell how many. Many computational techniques (e.g., regrouping in addition and subtraction) are based on equivalent representations of numbers.

◆ Integration of Grouping with Words

The way we say a number, such as 53, must also be connected with the grouping-by-tens concept. The counting methods provide a connection. The count by tens and ones results in saying the number of groups and singles separately: 5 tens and 3." Saying the number of tens and singles separately in this fashion can be called *base-ten language*. Students can associate the base-ten language with the standard language: "5 tens and 3—53."

There are several variations of the base-ten language for 53: 5 tens and 3, 5 tens and 3 ones, 5 tens and 3 singles, and so on. Each may be used interchangeably with the standard

Formative Assessment Note

As a third-, fourth-, or fifth-grade teacher, you may not know how much your students understand about place-value concepts. Students are often able to disguise their lack of understanding of place value by following directions, using the base-ten materials in prescribed ways, and using the language of place value.

The diagnostic tasks presented here are designed to help you look more closely at students' understanding and thinking. Designed as diagnostic interviews rather than full-class activities, these tasks have been used by several researchers and are adapted primarily from Labinowicz (1985), Kamii (1985), and Ross (1986).

The first diagnostic interview, referred to as the **digit correspondence task**, has been used widely in the study of place-value development. Take out 36 blocks. Ask the student to count the blocks, and then have the student write the number that tells how many there are. Circle the 6 in 36 and ask, "Does this part of your 36 have anything to do with how many blocks there are?" Then circle the 3 and repeat the question. As with all diagnostic interviews, do not give clues. Based on responses to the task, Ross (1986, 2002) has identified five levels of place-value understanding:

1. **Single numeral.** The student writes 36 but views it as a single numeral. The individual digits 3 and 6 have no meaning by themselves.
2. **Position names.** The student correctly identifies the tens and ones positions, but still makes no connections between the individual digits and the blocks.
3. **Face value.** The student matches six blocks with the 6 and three blocks with the 3.
4. **Transition to place value.** The 6 is matched with six blocks and the 3 with the remaining 30 blocks but not as three groups of 10.
5. **Full understanding.** The 3 is correlated with three groups of 10 blocks and the 6 with six single blocks.

In the next diagnostic interview, write the number 342. Have the student read the number. Then have the student write the number that is 1 more. Next, ask for the number that is 10 more. You may wish to explore further with models. One less and 10 less can be checked the same way. Watch to see whether the student is counting on or counting back by ones, or if the student immediately knows that ten more is 352.

This third diagnostic interview is also revealing. Ask the student to write the number that represents 5 tens, 2 ones, and 3 hundreds. Note that the task does not give the places in order. What do you think will be a common misunderstanding? If the student doesn't write 352, then ask the student to show you the number with base-ten materials.

These assessments will help you identify the knowledge as well as the gaps students have in the area of place value.

name 53. If you have ELLs, however, it is best to select one base-ten approach (e.g., 5 tens and 3 ones) and consistently connect it to the standard approach. Other languages often use the base-ten format (e.g., 11 is "ten and one," 12 is "ten and two," and so on), so this can be a good cultural connection for students.

◆ Integration of Grouping with Place-Value Notation

The symbolic scheme that we use for writing numbers (ones on the right, tens to the left of ones, and so on) must be co-ordinated with the grouping scheme.

Language again plays a key role in making these connections. The explicit count by groups and singles

Teaching Tip

It is important to be precise in your language. Whenever you refer to a number in the tens, hundreds, or thousands (or beyond), make sure you do not just say "six," but instead refer to it with its place value location, such as 6 tens (or 60). Students are confused when numbers are discussed as digits rather than describing their actual value.

Figure 10.4

Relational understanding of place value integrates three components shown as the corners of the triangle.

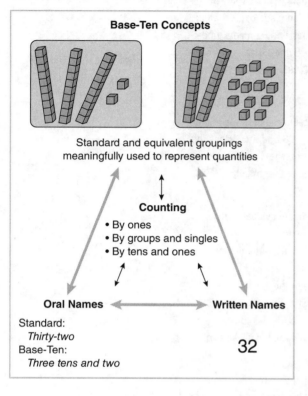

(i.e., 3 tens and 2) matches the individual digits as the number is written in the usual left-to-right manner. A similar coordination is necessary for hundreds and other place values. "Making a transition from viewing 'ten' as simply the accumulation of 10 ones to seeing it both as 10 ones and as 1 ten is an important first step for students toward understanding the structure of the base-ten number system" (NCTM, 2000, p. 33).

Figure 10.4 summarizes the ideas of an integrated place-value understanding that have been discussed so far. Note that all three methods of counting are coordinated as the principal method of integrating the base-ten concepts, the written names, and the oral names.

◆ Base-Ten Models

Physical models for base-ten concepts play a key role in helping students develop the idea of "a ten" as both a single entity and as a set of 10 units. Remember, though, that the models do not show the concept to the students; the students must mentally construct the "10-makes-one relationship" and impose it on the model. A good base-ten model for ones, tens, and hundreds is one that is proportional. That is, a model for ten should be physically 10 times larger than the model for a one, and a hundred model should be 10 times larger than the ten model. Proportional materials allow students to check that ten of any given piece is equivalent to one piece in the column to the left (10 tens equals 1 hundred). Base-ten models can be categorized as groupable and pregrouped.

Groupable Models

Models that most clearly reflect the relationships of ones, tens, and hundreds are those for which the ten can actually be made or grouped from the single pieces. When students put 10 beans in a small cup, the cup of 10 beans literally is the same as the 10 single beans. Plastic connecting cubes also provide a good transition to pregrouped ten rods because they form a similar shape. Bundles of wooden craft sticks or coffee stirrers can be grouped with rubber bands. Examples of these groupable models are shown in Figure 10.5a. These materials provide a good transition to the pregrouped models described next.

Electronic versions of pregrouped base-ten manipulatives (such as the Base Block applet at http://nlvm .usu.edu/en/nav/vlibrary.html) are computer representations of the three-dimensional base-ten blocks, including the thousands piece. With simple mouse clicks, students (including those with disabilities) can place ones, tens, hundreds, or thousands on a virtual place-value mat. If 10 of one type are lassoed by a rectangle, they snap together; if a piece is dragged one column to the right, the piece breaks apart into 10 of that unit. Compared to real base-ten blocks, these virtual materials are free, are easily grouped and ungrouped, can be shown to the full class on a projection device, and are available in endless supply, even the thousands blocks.

Pregrouped Models

Models that are pregrouped are commonly shown in your textbooks and are often used in instructional activities. Pregrouped models, such as those in Figure 10.5b, cannot be taken apart or put together. When 10 single pieces are accumulated, they must be exchanged or traded for a ten, and likewise, tens must be traded for hundreds. With pregrouped models, students should confirm that they understand that a ten piece really is the same as 10 ones. Students combine multiplicative understanding (each place is 10 times the value of the place to the right) with a positional system (each place has a value).

The little ten-frame cards effectively link to the familiar ten frames students used as primary students to think about numbers and, as such, may initially be more meaningful than the concrete versions or paper strips and squares of base-ten materials (see Blackline Masters 2 and 3). This model has the distinct advantage of always showing the distance to the next decade. For example, when 47 is shown with 4 ten cards and a seven card, a student can see that three more will make five full cards, or 50. Although there is a pregrouped cube for one thousand, it is important to group 10 hundred pieces and attach them together as a cube to show how it is formed. Otherwise, some students only count the square units they see on the surface of the six faces and think the cube represents 600.

Nonproportional Models

Nonproportional models can be used by students who fully understand that 10 units make "a ten" and thereby grasp the relationship of the powers of ten. These are models, such as money, for which the ten is not physically 10 times larger than the one. Like a bead frame that has same-sized beads in different columns (on wires) or chips that are given different place values by color, these nonproportional representations are not used for introducing place-value concepts. They are used when students already have a conceptual understanding of the numeration system and may need additional reinforcement. Oftentimes money is a useful tool for students with special needs who understand the relationships between the place values yet need support in developing other mathematical concepts.

Extending Base-Ten Concepts

Now that you have a sense of the important place-value concepts, we turn to activities that assist students in developing these concepts. This section starts with a focus on the top of the triangle of ideas in Figure 10.4. The connections of this most important component with writing numbers and with the way we say numbers—the bottom two corners of the triangle in the same figure—are discussed separately. However, in the classroom, the oral and written names for numbers can and should be developed in concert with conceptual ideas.

Figure 10.5

Groupable and pregrouped base-ten models.

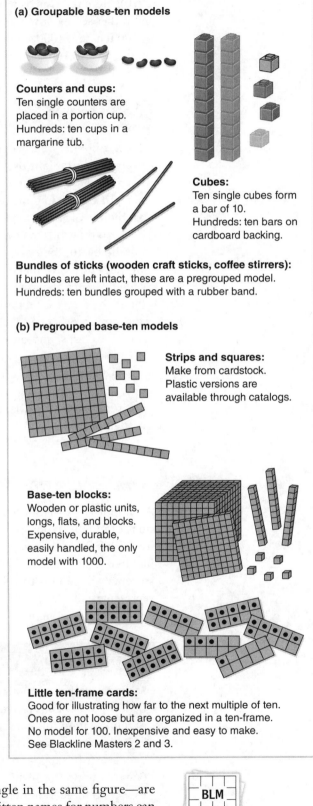

(a) Groupable base-ten models

Counters and cups:
Ten single counters are placed in a portion cup. Hundreds: ten cups in a margarine tub.

Cubes:
Ten single cubes form a bar of 10.
Hundreds: ten bars on cardboard backing.

Bundles of sticks (wooden craft sticks, coffee stirrers):
If bundles are left intact, these are a pregrouped model.
Hundreds: ten bundles grouped with a rubber band.

(b) Pregrouped base-ten models

Strips and squares:
Make from cardstock. Plastic versions are available through catalogs.

Base-ten blocks:
Wooden or plastic units, longs, flats, and blocks. Expensive, durable, easily handled, the only model with 1000.

Little ten-frame cards:
Good for illustrating how far to the next multiple of ten. Ones are not loose but are organized in a ten-frame. No model for 100. Inexpensive and easy to make. See Blackline Masters 2 and 3.

BLM

◆ Grouping Hundreds to Make 1000

As students enter third grade, they are expected to know numbers up to 1000 (CCSSO, 2010). Here the issue is not one of connecting a count-by-ones concept to a group of 1000, but rather seeing how a group of 1000 can be understood as a group of 10 hundreds as well as 100 tens and 1000 single ones. As a means of introducing thousands as groups of 10 hundreds and also 100 tens, consider the following estimation activity.

Activity 10.4 TOO MANY TO COUNT?

Show students a large plastic bag or cardboard box with more than 1000 items. For example, you might use a set of wrapped straws or Styrofoam packing peanuts. First, have students make and record estimates of how many straws are in the bag (they need not put their name on their estimates). Discuss with students how they selected their estimates. Give portions of the straws to pairs or tables of students to count. Suggest early on that they may want to use rubber bands to create bundles of 10 or 100. If they bundle by 10, then ask, "How can we use these groups of 10 to tell how many straws we have? Can we make new groups from the groups of 10? What is 10 groups of ten called?" Once they see a bundle of 100, let them change their estimates if they wish (limit them to a time period to make this change to emphasize that this is an estimate and not an exact count). When all bundles or groups are made, count the thousands, hundreds, tens, and ones separately. Record on the board as 1 thousand + 4 hundreds + 7 tens + 8 ones.

In this activity, it is important to use a groupable model so that students can see how the 10 groups of 100 are the same as the 1000 individual items. This connection is often lost in the rather simple display of a 1000 in a cube in the pregrouped base-ten models.

◆ Equivalent Representations

An important variation of the grouping activities is aimed at the equivalent representations of numbers. For example, ask students who have just completed the preceding activity, "What is another way you can show 1,478 besides 1 group of a thousand, 4 groups of a hundred, 7 tens, and 8 singles? Let's see how many ways you can find." Interestingly, most students will go next to 1,478 singles. The following activities focus on creating equivalent representations.

Activity 10.5 THREE OTHER WAYS

Students work in groups or pairs. First, they show 463 on their desks with base-ten materials in the standard representation. Next, they find and record at least three other ways of representing this number.

A variation of this activity is to challenge students to find a way to show an amount with a specific number of pieces. "Can you show 463 with 31 pieces?" (There is more than one way to do this.) Students in grade 3 can get quite involved with finding all the ways to show a three-digit number.

◤ *Activity* 10.6 **CAN YOU MAKE THE LINK?**

Show a collection of materials that is only partly grouped in sets of 10. For example, you may have 25 chains of 10 paper clips, and about 150 additional unconnected paper clips. Be sure the students understand that each chain has 10 paper clips. Have students count the number of chains and the number of singles in any way they wish to count. Ask, "How many in all?" Record all responses, and discuss how they got their answers. Next, change the groupings (make a ten from the singles, or make hundreds from the tens and repeat). Do not change the total number from one time to the next. Once students begin to understand that the total does not change, ask in what other ways the items could be grouped.

◤ *Activity* 10.7 **BASE-TEN RIDDLES**

Base-ten riddles can be presented orally or in written form. In either case, students should use base-ten materials to help solve the riddles. The examples here illustrate a variety of different levels of difficulty. Have students write new riddles when they complete these.

- I have 23 ones and 4 tens. Who am I?
- I have 4 hundreds, 12 tens, and 6 ones. Who am I?
- I have 30 ones and 3 hundreds. Who am I?
- I am 45. I have 25 ones. How many tens do I have?
- I am 341. I have 22 tens. How many hundreds do I have?
- I have 13 tens, 2 hundreds, and 21 ones. Who am I?
- If you put 3 more hundreds with me, I would be 1150. Who am I?
- I have 23 hundreds, 16 tens, and 2 ones. Who am I?

◢ Oral and Written Names for Numbers

In this section, we focus on helping students connect the bottom two corners of the triangle in Figure 10.4—oral and written names for numbers—with their emerging base-ten concepts of using groups of 10 or 100 as efficient methods of counting. Note that the ways we say and write numbers are conventions rather than concepts. Students must learn these conventions by being told rather than through problem-based activities. It is also worth remembering that for ELL students, the convention or pattern in our English number words is probably not the same as it is in their native language.

◆ Three-Digit Number Names

The approach to three-digit number names starts with showing mixed arrangements of base-ten materials and having students give the base-ten name (4 hundreds, 3 tens, and 8 ones) and the standard name (438). Vary the arrangement from one example to the next by changing only one type of piece. That is, add or remove only ones or only tens or only hundreds. It is important for students with disabilities to see counterexamples, so actively point out that some students wrote 200803 for 283, and ask them whether that is correct. These conversations allow students to explore their misunderstandings and focus on the place-value system more explicitly.

◀ **Standards for Mathematical Practice**

3 Construct viable arguments and critique the reasoning of others

Figure 10.6

Building numbers with a set of cards.

The major difficulty is with modeling numbers involving no number in the tens place, such as 702, or no number in the hundreds place, such as 1046. As noted earlier, the use of base-ten language is quite helpful here. The difficulty of the internal zero is more pronounced when writing numerals. Students frequently incorrectly write 7002 for 702. The emphasis on the meaning in the oral base-ten language will be a significant help. At first, students do not see the importance of zero in place value and do not understand that zero helps us distinguish between such numbers as 203, 23, and 230 (Dougherty, Flores, Louis, & Sophian, 2010). ELLs may need additional time to think about how to say and write the numerals, because they are translating all the terms within the number.

Researchers note that there are significantly more errors with four-digit number names than three-digit numbers, so do not think that students will easily generalize to larger numbers without actually exploring examples and tasks (Cayton & Brizuela, 2007).

◆ Written Symbols

To show how the numbers are built, have a set of 27 cards—one for each of the hundreds (100–900), one for each of the tens (10–90), and ones cards for 1 through 9 (see Figure 10.6). Notice that the cards are made so that the tens card is two times as long as the ones card, and the hundreds card is three times as long as the ones card (you can add thousands cards too, just make them proportionally four times longer than the ones card). As students place base-ten materials for a number (e.g., 457) on the place-value mat, have them also place the matching cards (e.g., 400, 50, and 7) below the materials in the correct column. Then starting with the hundreds card, layer the others on top, right aligned. This approach will show how the number is built while allowing the student to see the individual components of the number. This is especially helpful if there are zero tens. The place-value mat and the matching cards demonstrate the important link between the base-ten models and the written form of the numbers.

The next two activities are designed to help students make connections between all three representations: models, oral language, and written forms. The activities can be done with any multidigit numbers, depending on students' needs.

Activity 10.8 **SAY IT/PRESS IT**

Display models of ones, tens, hundreds (and thousands if appropriate) in a mixed arrangement. Use a projector, virtual manipulatives (they come in endless quantities), or simply draw on the board using a cube-square-stick-dot method (use cubes for thousands, squares for hundreds, sticks for tens, and dots for ones) to represent the base-ten materials. Students say the amount shown in base-ten language ("2 thousands, 4 hundreds, 1 ten, and 5 ones") and then in standard language ("two thousand, four hundred fifteen"). Next, students enter the number into their calculators (or they can use paper to respond). Have someone share his or her display and defend it. Make a change in the materials and repeat. You can also do this activity by saying the standard name for a number. Pay special attention to numbers that have components in the teens (e.g., 317) and those with internal zeros (e.g., 408). ELLs may need additional time to think of the words that go with the numbers, especially as the numbers get larger.

Activity 10.9 DIGIT CHANGE

 Have students enter a specific three- or four-digit number on the calculator. The task is to change one or more of the digits in the number without simply entering the new number. For example, change 315 to 305 or to 295. Changes can be made by adding or subtracting an appropriate amount. Students should write or discuss explanations for their solutions. Students with disabilities may need the visual support of having cards that say "add 10" or "add 100" first to explore how the number changes. They may also need support with base-ten materials to be able to conceptualize the number and then move to more abstract work on the calculator alone.

Patterns and Relationships with Multidigit Numbers

In grades 3 through 5, create tasks that require the use of place-value ideas and place-value models with the goal to promote what is sometimes called *ten-structured thinking*, that is, flexibility in using the structure of tens and hundreds in the number system.

◆ The Hundreds Chart

The hundreds chart (see Blackline Masters 6 and 7) is an important tool for developing ten-structured thinking. The hundreds chart should not be abandoned after grade 2, as is often the case. When students are exploring invented strategies for addition and subtraction, the hundreds chart can be used as a model to support students' thinking and to support the communication of their ideas. The rows of 10 encourage students to think about using strategies based on place value and benchmark numbers—in this case, working with multiples of 10. For example, in adding 47 + 25, students might locate the number 47 on the chart and see that three more counts get them to 50 and then 22 more is easy to compute. Similarly, students might begin with 47 and go down two rows—adding 20—and then count on five more. What is important is not the particular methods that are used, but rather the use of multiples of 10 that is encouraged by the chart.

The hundreds chart is especially useful for exploring patterns created by skip counting. Patterns in skip counts can be observed both in the numbers and in the way that the numbers appear on the chart. For example, skip counts by 3 form diagonal patterns. These patterns point to the regularity of using equal groupings. You may want to see how familiar your students are with these and other hundreds-chart patterns.

In the following activity, number relationships on the hundreds chart are made more explicit by connecting the chart numbers to representations using base-ten models.

Activity 10.10 MODELS WITH THE HUNDREDS CHART

Use any physical model for two-digit numbers with which the students are familiar. Base-ten materials or the little ten-frames are recommended (see Blackline Masters 2, 3, and 4).

- Give students one or more numbers to first make with the models and then find on the chart. Use groups of two or three numbers in either the same row or the same column.
- Indicate a number on the chart. What would you have to change to make each of its neighbors (the numbers to the left, right, above, and below)?

As a first step in moving to higher numbers, continue your hundreds charts to 200. Then a more powerful idea is to extend the hundreds chart to 1000.

Activity 10.11 THE THOUSANDS CHART

Provide students with several sheets of the blank hundreds charts (Blackline Master 5). Assign groups of three or four students the task of creating a 1-to-1000 chart. The chart is to be made by taping 10 charts together in a long strip. Students should decide how they are going to divide up the task with different students completing different parts of the chart. The thousands chart should be discussed as a class to examine how numbers change as you count from one hundred to the next, what the patterns are, and so on. In fact, hundreds chart activities done in the primary grades can all be extended to a thousands chart.

◆ Relationships with Benchmark Numbers

Often in computations it is useful to recognize that a number can be made up of a "familiar" number and some more numbers as an extension of part–part–whole thinking. The familiar numbers part (maybe a multiple of 50 or 100) is dealt with first, and then the smaller left-over piece can be considered.

These familiar numbers also are often broken apart (decomposed) in computations. The next activity is useful for developing the thinking required for counting up or "think-addition" approaches to multidigit subtraction. Have students share their thinking strategies.

Activity 10.12 200 AND SOME MORE

Say a number between 300 and 1000. Students respond with "200 and ____." For 630, the response is "200 and 430." Use other numbers that end in 50 for the first part, such as "450 and some more."

The following activities can be done independently or in pairs, but it is good to do them with the full class so that strategies can be discussed. These activities develop place-value concepts, number sense, or flexible strategies for computation.

Figure 10.7

Compatible-pair searches.

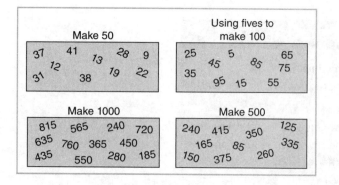

Activity 10.13 COMPATIBLE PAIRS

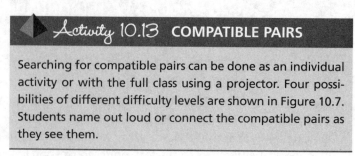

Searching for compatible pairs can be done as an individual activity or with the full class using a projector. Four possibilities of different difficulty levels are shown in Figure 10.7. Students name out loud or connect the compatible pairs as they see them.

◆ Activity 10.14 CALCULATOR CHALLENGE COUNTING

Students press any three digit number on the calculator (e.g., 770), then ⊞ 20. They say the sum before they press ⊟. Then they continue to add 20 mentally, challenging themselves to say the number before they press ⊟. They should see how far they can go before making a mistake.

The constant addend in this activity can be any number, even a three- or four-digit number. After 20 as your constant, try 25. Try 400 and then 480. As an added challenge, after a student has progressed through eight or ten counts, have the student reverse the process by pressing ⊟ followed by the same number, and then pressing ⊟ several times. Have students share their strategies for determining the sum or difference. Discuss patterns that appear.

Numbers beyond 1000

For students to have good concepts of numbers beyond 1000, the place-value ideas that have been carefully developed must be extended. This is sometimes difficult to do because physical models for thousands are not readily available, or you may just have one large cube to show. At the same time, number-sense ideas must also be developed. In many ways, connecting very large numbers to real amounts is just as important as connecting smaller numbers to real quantities.

◆ Extending the Place-Value System

Two important ideas developed for three-digit numbers should be extended to larger numbers. First, the grouping idea should be generalized. That is, 10 in any position makes a single thing (group) in the next position, and vice versa. Second, the oral and written patterns for numbers in three digits are duplicated in a clever way for every three digits to the left. These two related ideas are not as easy for students to understand as adults seem to believe. Because models for large numbers are often difficult to demonstrate or visualize, textbooks frequently deal with these ideas in a predominantly symbolic manner. That is not sufficient!

◆ Activity 10.15 WHAT COMES NEXT?

Use paper models of base-ten strips and squares (see Blackline Master 4). The unit or ones piece is a 1 cm square. The tens piece is a 10 cm × 1 cm strip. The hundreds piece is a square, 10 cm × 10 cm. What is next? Ten hundreds is called a thousand. What shape would a thousand be? Tape together a long strip made of 10 paper hundreds squares. What comes next? (Reinforce the idea of 10 makes 1 that has progressed to this point.) Ten thousand strips would make a square measuring 1 meter on each side, making a paper 10,000 model. Once the class has figured out the shape of each piece, the problem posed to them is "What comes next?" Let small groups work on the dimensions of a 100,000 piece. Ten ten-thousand squares (100,000) go together to make a huge strip. Draw this strip on a long sheet or roll of paper, and mark off the 10 squares that make it up. You will have to go out in the hall.

How far you want to extend this square-strip-square-strip sequence depends on your class. The idea that 10 in one place makes 1 in the next can be brought home dramatically. It is quite possible with older students to make the next 10 meter × 10 meter square using chalk lines on the playground. The next strip is 100 meters × 10 meters. This can be measured out on a large playground with students marking the corners. By this point, the payoff includes an appreciation of both the increase in size of each successive amount as well as the 10-makes-1 progression (powers of ten). The 10 meter × 10 meter square models 1 million and the 100 meter × 10 meter strip is the model for 10 million. The difference between 1 million and 10 million is dramatic. Even the concept of 1 million tiny centimeter squares is impressive.

Try the "What Comes Next?" discussion in the context of these three-dimensional models. The first three shapes are distinct: a cube, a long, and a flat. What comes next? Stack 10 flats and they make a cube, the same shape as the first one, only 1000 times larger. What comes next? (See Figure 10.8.) Ten cubes make another long. What comes next? Ten big longs make a big flat. The first three shapes have now repeated! Ten big flats will make an even bigger cube, and the triplet of shapes begins again. Note that students with disabilities have difficulty interpreting spatial information, which plays into their challenges with interpreting the progression of place-value materials (Geary & Hoard, 2005).

Each cube has a name. The first one is the unit cube; the next is a thousand, the next a million, then a billion, and so on. Each long is 10 cubes: 10 units, 10 thousands, 10 millions. Similarly, each flat shape is 100 cubes.

To read a number, first mark it off in triples from the right. The triples are then read, stopping at the end of each to name the unit (or cube shape) for that triple (see Figure 10.9). Leading zeros in each triple are ignored when the number is read. If students can learn to read numbers like 059 (fifty-nine) or 009 (nine), they should be able to read any number. To write a number, use the same scheme. If first mastered orally, the system is quite easy. Remind students there is a convention to reading numbers, and to maintain clarity they should not use the word "and" when reading a whole number. For example, 106 should be read as "one hundred six," not "one hundred and six." The word "and" is only needed to signify a decimal point. Please make sure you read numbers accurately.

It is important for students to realize that the system does have a logical structure, is not totally arbitrary, and can be understood.

■ **Standards for Mathematical Practice**

7 Look for and make use of structure ▶

$\mathcal{F}igure$ 10.8

With every three places, the shapes repeat.

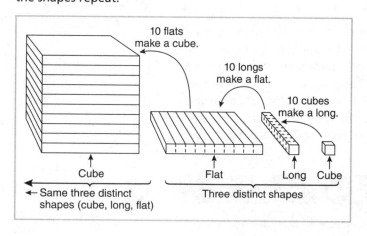

10 flats make a cube.

10 longs make a flat.

10 cubes make a long.

Cube   Flat   Long   Cube

← Same three distinct shapes (cube, long, flat)   Three distinct shapes

$\mathcal{T}eaching\ \mathcal{T}ip$

Although we are using the terms *cube, long,* and *flat* to describe the shape of the materials, students will see the shape pattern made as each gets 10 times larger. In fact, it is still critical to call these "ones, tens, and hundreds," particularly for students with disabilities. We need to name them by the number they represent rather than their shape. This reinforces conceptual understanding and is less confusing for students who may struggle with these concepts.

◆ Conceptualizing Large Numbers

The ideas just discussed are only partially helpful in thinking about the actual quantities involved in very large numbers. For example, in extending the square-strip-square-strip sequence with paper materials, some appreciation for the quantities of 1000 or of 100,000 is included. But it is hard for students to translate quantities of small squares into quantities of other items, distances, or time.

Stop and Reflect

How do you think about 1000 or 100,000? Do you have any real concept of a million? ■

In the following activities, numbers like 1000, 10,000 (see Blackline Master 22), or even 1 million are translated literally or imaginatively into something that is easy or fun to think about. Interesting quantities become lasting reference points for large numbers and thereby add meaning to numbers encountered in real life.

BLM

▶ *Activity* 10.16　**COLLECTING 10,000**

As a class or grade-level project, collect some type of object with the objective of reaching some specific quantity—for example, 1000 or 10,000 bread tabs or bottle caps. If you begin aiming for 100,000 or 1 million, be sure to think it through. One teacher spent nearly 10 years with her classes before amassing a million bottle caps. It takes a small dump truck to hold that many!

▶ *Activity* 10.17　**HOW LONG?/HOW FAR?**

In this activity, talk about real and imagined distances with students by posing investigations for them to consider such as, "How long is a million baby steps?" Other ideas that explore the length of a million objects or people include estimating a line of toothpicks, dollar bills, or candy bars end to end; students holding hands in a line; blocks or bricks stacked up; students lying down head to toe. Standard measures—feet, centimeters, meters— can also be used, with students noting that larger numbers emerge when the smallest units are used.

▶ *Activity* 10.18　**A LONG TIME**

How long is 1000 seconds? How long is a million seconds? A billion? How long would it take to count to 10,000 or 1 million? (To make the counts all the same, use your calculator to do the counting. Just press the ⊟ .) How long would it take to do some task like buttoning and unbuttoning a button 1000 times?

Figure 10.9　The triples system for naming large numbers.

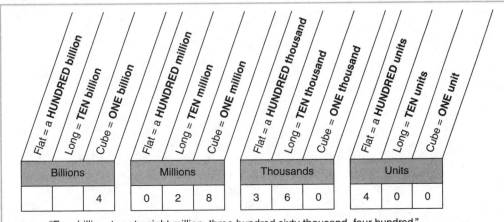

"Four billion, twenty-eight million, three hundred sixty thousand, four hundred."

Activity 10.19 REALLY LARGE QUANTITIES

Ask how many:

- Candy bars would cover the floor of your classroom
- Steps an ant would take to walk around the school building
- Grains of rice would fill a cup or a gallon jug
- Quarters could be stacked in one stack from floor to ceiling
- Pennies could be laid side by side down the entire hallway
- Pieces of notebook paper would cover the gym floor
- Seconds you have lived

Big-number projects need not take up large amounts of class time. They can be explored over several weeks as take-home projects or group projects or, perhaps best of all, be translated into great school-wide estimation contests. The NCTM *Principles and Standards for School Mathematics* also recognize the need for relating large numbers to the real work: "A third-grade class might explore the size of 1000 by skip-counting to 1000, building a model of 1000 using ten hundreds charts, gathering 1000 items such as paper clips and developing efficient ways to count them, or using strips that are 10 or 100 centimeters long to show the length of 1000 centimeters" (NCTM, 2000, p. 149). All these and similar activities help students build number sense with larger numbers so they can flexibly think about these numbers and their relationships.

Expanded Lesson

Close, Far, and in Between

Content and Task Decisions

Grade Level: 3

Mathematics Goals

- To develop number sense through thinking about relative magnitude of numbers
- To develop strategies for mental mathematics

Grade Level Guide

NCTM *Curriculum Focal Points*	Common *Core State Standards*
In third grade in a Focal Point Connection, students develop and build their facility with mental computation by using their estimation skills and flexibility with numbers.	When students are in third grade they are now flexibly adding and subtracting within 1000 using strategies based on place value and the relationship between the operations of addition and subtraction.

Consider Your Students' Needs

Students should have experience decomposing smaller numbers to facilitate adding and subtracting (e.g., to add 18 and 25, they can think, "Take 2 away from 25 and add that to 18 to get 20, then 20 + 23 is 43"). That is, students are familiar with using fives and tens as benchmarks. Students are also familiar with using a number line.

For English Language Learners

- Preview key words that they will need in order to give their explanations: greater than, less than, close to, far, and between.
- Provide opportunities to pair-share explanations before doing whole class explanations.

For Students with Disabilities

- Instead of a number line at the board, use one on the floor so that students can move to the location of the actual number and move to the closest benchmark number. In this way they can experience the shortest distance in a concrete fashion.
- As students move to their desks, have already prepared number lines and possibly problems that ramp up at an easier pace.

Materials

- None

Lesson

Before

Begin with a simpler version of the task:

- Using a projector or board, write the numbers 27, 83, and 62.
- Draw an empty number line on the board and label the points for 0 and 100. Ask a student to come forward and place one of the numbers on the number line and explain why he or she placed the number in that location. Ask the class if they agree or disagree with the placement and the reasoning. Discuss as needed. Repeat this process for the other two numbers.
- Ask "Which number is closest to 50? Which two numbers are closest to each other? How far apart are 27 and 100? 62 and 100? 83 and 100?" With each question, give students time to think individually, then ask students to share their ideas and strategies for doing these comparisons. The methods that they use will be quite varied.
- Ask for responses from more than one student. Look for students who are breaking numbers apart and using benchmarks of fives and tens rather than simply subtracting numbers to find the difference.

Present the focus task to the class:

- You will need to choose three numbers for the students to compare. Numbers should be chosen purposefully to assess the understanding of a particular idea or to increase the likelihood that students will grapple with a particular idea or strategy. For example, if students have not yet explicitly used the notion of using hundreds as a benchmark, the numbers chosen might be 298, 402, and 318. Because 298 is so close to 300 and 402 is so close to 400, at least some students will use this idea to compare 298 and 402 to each other and the third number. For this lesson, we will use 219, 457, and 364. Write the numbers 219, 457, and 364 on the board with these questions:
  1. Which two are closest? Why?
  2. Which is closest to 300? To 250?
  3. About how far apart are 219 and 500? 219 and 5000?

Provide clear expectations:

- Tell students that they will need to explain how they determined their answers. Suggest that they use words, numbers, and/or a number line so that they can remember their thought processes and be ready to discuss their ideas with the class.

During

Initially:

- Observe that each student understands the questions and is in the process of attempting to answer them with some recording of their thoughts.

Ongoing:

- Observe students' work—notice the strategies they are using to compare numbers. See the "Assessment" section at the end of the lesson for details. Keep these details in mind when selecting who will share in the "After" phase of the lesson.

- As students work, ask them to tell you what the problem is asking and how they are thinking about solving it. See the "Assessment" section for details.

- If students are having difficulty, suggest that they use the number line as an aid to identify benchmarks. Ask them how they might use a benchmark to get closer to one of the numbers. Give no more assistance than is absolutely necessary to get students started. After making a suggestion, walk away and check back later.

- To differentiate for advanced learners, ask them questions about finding particular multiples between given numbers (e.g., "Name a multiple of 25 between 219 and 364").

After

Bring the class together to share and discuss the task:

- Ask students to share their strategies for responding to each question. Record ideas on the board in a manner that illustrates students' thinking.

- As students share, you might have to ask questions to either slow down a student's explanation so that classmates have a chance to process the ideas or to make explicit a subtle idea that you want students to think about.

- Do not evaluate the strategy, but ask students if they agree and understand the strategy and if they have questions. Allow other students to offer ideas for the same question.

- As new strategies emerge, ask students to compare and contrast them to strategies already shared. The discussion might pertain to which strategies seem quicker or more efficient and why or how various strategies use the notion of place value and/or benchmarks.

Assessment

Observe

- Look for students who are simply counting up or down by ones to determine how far away numbers are from each other. They likely need more work using fives and tens as benchmarks (which includes identifying multiples of 5 and 10).

- Are students using a variety of strategies depending on the numbers, or do they always use the same strategy? Being able to develop and use different strategies is evidence of number sense as well as the ability to think flexibly.

- Encourage students to find methods that do not involve subtraction.

Ask

- What strategy are you using?

- Can you show me your thinking (using an empty number line or hundreds chart)?

- Can you determine the answer without using paper and pencil to subtract?

- What benchmark might help you compare the numbers?

11

Building Strategies for Whole-Number Computation

Big IDEAS

1 Flexible methods of computation for all four operations involve taking apart (decomposing) and combining (composing) numbers in a variety of ways.

2 Flexible methods for computation require deep understanding of the operations and the properties of the operations (commutative property, the associative property, and the distributive property of multiplication over addition). How addition and subtraction, as well as multiplication and division, are related as inverse operations is also critical knowledge.

3 Invented strategies provide flexible methods of computing that vary with the numbers and the situation. Students must understand the strategies in order to successfully use them. Students must grasp that the process and the outcome of that process are related.

4 The standard algorithms are clever strategies for computing that were developed over time. Unfortunately, if introduced too early, standard algorithms tend to make students think in terms of digits rather than the composite number that the digits make up, so students often lose the actual place value of a digit.

5 Multidigit numbers can be built up or taken apart in a variety of ways. These parts can be used to create estimates in calculations rather than using the exact numbers involved.

6 Nearly all computational estimations involve using easier-to-handle parts of numbers or substituting difficult-to-handle numbers with close compatible numbers so that the resulting computations can be done mentally.

Toward Computational Fluency

Much of the public sees computational skill as the hallmark of what it means to know mathematics in grades 3 through 5. Although that is far from the whole story, learning computational skills with whole numbers is, in fact, a critical component of the curriculum.

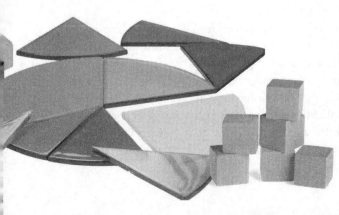

The *Principles and Standards for School Mathematics* define computational fluency as "having and using efficient and accurate methods for computing" (NCTM, 2000, p. 32). In grades 3 through 5, students continue work with addition and subtraction of large numbers, but they focus on whole-number computation strategies with multiplication and division. Teachers must create an instructional environment that rewards flexibility in solving problems so that students can successfully explore and test new ideas (Verschaffel et al., 2007). Students who only have knowledge of the standard algorithm often have difficulty following procedural steps they do not fully understand (Biddlecomb & Carr, 2011). When students can compute multidigit addition, subtraction, multiplication, and division problems in a variety of ways, complete written records of their work, explain their thinking, and discuss the merits of one strategy over another, they are developing into independent learners of mathematics.

Consider the following problem.

The school auditorium has 24 rows of seats. There are 39 seats in each row. How many students can be seated in the auditorium?

Stop and Reflect

Try solving this problem using some method other than the one you were taught in school. If you are drawn to begin by multiplying the 9 and the 4, try a different approach. How can you solve the problem mentally by thinking of the place values of the numbers? What is another way you can solve the problem? Work on this before reading further. ■

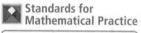

Standards for
Mathematical Practice

2 Reason abstractly
and quantitatively ▶

Here are just three of the many ways students thought about solving this computation:

- "24 is close to 25, and 25×4 is 100, so 25×39 is 25 less than 25×40 or 1000 (975) and because I rounded the 24 up, the answer is 39 less or 936."

- "39 is close to 40, and if I add 20 rows of 40 seats I get 800. Then I have 4 more rows for 160 more seats. That's 960. Then I have to take 24 away to fix the bump up to 40 from 39, so it is 936."

- "20×30 is 600, 20×9 is 180, so that is 780. Then, 30×4 is 120, so that's 900. And 9×4 is 36. The answer is 936."

Every day students and adults use these more meaningful methods, which can be done mentally, are often faster than the standard algorithm, and make more sense to the person using them and therefore are less susceptible to error.

◆ Direct Modeling

The developmental step that usually precedes invented strategies, and takes place in the primary grades for addition and subtraction and in grades 3 and 4 for multiplication and division, is called *direct modeling*. This is the use of manipulatives or drawings along with counting to directly represent the meaning of an operation or story problem. Students in grade 3 who consistently count by ones in additive situations most likely have not developed base-ten grouping concepts. As you work with students who are still struggling with seeing ten as a unit (or in multiplication seeing a factor as a unit), suggest that they group counters. Some students may need to write down the corresponding numbers for memory support (perhaps as they complete intermediate steps).

Students will soon move from direct modeling to invented strategies derived from number sense and the properties of the operations. Invented strategies no longer rely on materials or counting. However, some students may need encouragement to move away from the direct modeling process. Here are some ideas to foster the fading of direct modeling:

- Record students' verbal explanations on the board in ways that they and others can follow.

- Ask students who have just solved a problem with manipulatives to see whether they can do it in their heads.

- Ask students to make a written numeric record of how they solved the problem with physical models. Then have them try to use the same written method on a new problem.

◆ Student-Invented Strategies

Carpenter and colleagues (Carpenter, Franke, Jacobs, Fennema, & Empson, 1998) refer to an *invented strategy* as any strategy other than the standard algorithm that does not involve the use of physical materials or counting by ones. At times, invented strategies become mental methods after the ideas have been explored, used, and understood. For example, $847 + 256$ can be done mentally ($850 + 250$ is 1100, add 3 more is 1103). Some students may write down intermediate steps (such as adding 6 more and then taking 3 less to compensate) to aid in memory as they work through the problem. In the classroom, some written support is often encouraged as strategies develop because they are more easily shared and help students focus on the ideas.

There is cumulated evidence from research and practice that students can construct multiple methods for adding, subtracting, multiplying and dividing multidigit numbers (Ambrose, Baek, & Carpenter, 2003; Carpenter et al., 1998; Fosnot & Dolk, 2001; Keiser, 2010; Rittle-Johnson, Star, & Durkin, 2010; Van Putten, van den Brom-Snijders, & Beishuizen, 2005). These methods strengthen your students' understanding of the properties of numbers, such as in multiplication in which the ability to flexibly break numbers apart hinges on the use of the distributive property of multiplication over addition.

One of the best ways for students to grow their repertoire is to listen during discussions to the strategies invented by class members as they are shared, explored, and tried out by others. However, students should not be permitted to use any strategy without understanding it (Campbell, Rowan, & Suarez, 1998).

Creating an Environment for Inventing Strategies

Invented strategies are developed from a strong understanding of numbers. The development of place-value concepts must begin to prepare students for the challenges of inventing computational strategies. For example, the *Common Core State Standards* (CCSSO, 2010, p. 27) suggest that fourth graders should be able to "develop fluency with efficient procedures for multiplying whole numbers; understand and explain why the procedures work based on place value and properties of operations." (© Copyright 2010. National Governors Association Center for Best Practices and Council of Chief State School Officers. All rights reserved.)

When students in your classroom attempt to investigate new ideas in mathematics, they should find your classroom a safe and nurturing place for expressing naïve or rudimentary thoughts. Some of the characteristics described earlier in this book regarding the development of a problem-solving environment need to be reiterated here to establish the climate for taking risks, testing conjectures, and trying new approaches. Here are some factors to keep in mind:

- Avoid immediately identifying the right answer when a student states it. Give other students a chance to consider whether they think it is correct.

- Expect and encourage student-to-student interactions, questions, discussions, and conjectures. Allow plenty of time for discussion.

- Encourage students to clarify previous knowledge and make attempts to construct new ideas.
- Promote curiosity and openness to trying new things.
- Talk about both right and wrong ideas in a nonevaluative and nonthreatening way.
- Move unsophisticated ideas to more sophisticated thinking through coaching and strategic questioning.

- Use familiar contexts and story problems to build background and connect to students' experiences. Avoid using "naked numbers" as a starting point, as they do not encourage strategy development.

▶ • Show samples of anonymous students' work and allow students to critique the reasoning of others.

When encouraging students to develop their own methods, select numbers in your problems with care. For example, with subtraction tasks such as $417 - 103$ or $417 - 98$, the numbers used may encourage students to subtract 100 and then adjust. For multiplication, multiples of 5, 10, and 25 are good starting points. Even 325×4 may be easier than 86×7, even though there are three digits in the former example. For division, it is the divisor that requires attention. And, because most invented strategies for division rely on multiplication, the same comment applies. For example, $483 \div 75$ is easier than $483 \div 67$, and not much harder than $327 \div 6$.

Contrasts with Standard Algorithms

There are significant differences between invented strategies and the standard algorithms.

1. *Invented strategies are number oriented rather than digit oriented.* For example, one invented strategy for 68×7 begins 60×7 is 420 and 56 more is 476.

Teaching Tip

Note that the first product is 60×7, not the 7 times 6, as would be the focus in the standard algorithm. Make sure you use language that recognizes the place value (e.g., sixty or six tens) when reviewing the process with students.

Using the standard algorithm for $416 + 329$, students think of $4 + 3$ rather than $400 + 300$. Kamii, a longtime advocate for invented strategies, claims that standard algorithms "unteach" place value (Kamii & Dominick, 1998).

2. *Invented strategies are left-handed rather than right-handed.* Invented strategies often begin with the largest parts of numbers (left-most digits) because they focus on the entire number. For 26×47, many invented strategies begin with 20×40 is 800, providing some sense of the size of the eventual answer in just one step. In contrast, the standard algorithm begins with 7×6 is 42. By beginning on the right with a digit orientation, the result is hidden until the end. The exception is the standard long-division algorithm.

3. *Invented strategies are a range of flexible options, rather than "one right way."* Invented strategies are dependent on the numbers involved so that students can make the computation easier. Try each of these mentally: $465 + 230$ and $526 + 98$. Did you use the same method? The standard algorithm suggests using the same tool on all problems. The standard algorithm for $7000 - 25$ typically leads to student errors, yet a mental strategy is relatively simple.

Benefits of Invented Strategies

The development of invented strategies delivers more than computational proficiency. The positive benefits are:

- *Students make fewer errors.* Research reveals that students using methods they understand make many fewer errors than when they use strategies that they learned without understanding (Gravemeijer & van Galen, 2003; Kamii & Dominick, 1998). Not only do students using poorly understood algorithms make errors but the errors are also often systematic and difficult to remediate because the underlying concepts are not clear. Errors with invented strategies are less frequent and almost never systematic.

- *Less reteaching is required.* You may initially be concerned when you find students' early efforts with invented strategies are slow and time consuming. But the extended struggle in these early stages builds a meaningful and well-integrated network of ideas that is robust and long lasting and significantly decreases the time required for reteaching.

- *Students develop number sense.* "More than just a means to produce answers, computation is increasingly seen as a window on the deep structure of the number system" (National Research Council, 2001, p. 182). Students' development and use of number-oriented, flexible algorithms offers them a rich comprehension of the number system. Students rarely use an invented strategy they do not understand. In contrast, students using standard algorithms are often unable to explain why they work.

- *Invented strategies are the basis for mental computation and estimation.* When invented strategies are the norm for computation, there is little need to discuss mental computation or estimation as separate skills. Often students who record their thinking with invented strategies or learn to jot down intermediate steps find they can do the procedures more efficiently mentally.

- *Flexible methods are often faster than standard algorithms.* Consider 761 + 467. A simple invented strategy might involve 700 + 400 = 1100 and 60 + 60 = 120. The sum of 1100 and 120 is 1220 and add 8 more for 1228. This is easily done mentally, or even with some recording, in much less time than the steps of the standard algorithm.

- *Algorithm invention is itself a significantly important process of "doing mathematics."* Students who select from a variety of strategies for computing, or who adopt a meaningful strategy shared by a classmate, are involved intimately in the process of reasoning and sense making. They also develop confidence in their ability to learn mathematics.

- *Invented strategies serve students well on standardized tests.* Evidence suggests that students using invented strategies do as well in computation on standardized tests as students using standard algorithms (Campbell, 1996; Carroll, 1997). As an added bonus, students tend to do well with word problems because they are the principal vehicle for developing invented strategies. Oftentimes students' abilities to estimate with invented strategies help them eliminate unreasonable multiple-choice items and move more rapidly through the test.

Mental Computation

A *mental computation strategy* is simply any invented strategy that is done mentally. What may be a mental strategy for one student may require written support by another. Initially, students should not be asked to do computations mentally, as this may intimidate those who have not yet developed a reasonable invented strategy or who are still at the direct modeling stage.

Try mental computation with this example:

$$342 + 153 + 481$$

Stop and Reflect

For this addition task, try this method: Begin by adding the hundreds, saying the totals as you go—3 hundred, 4 hundred, 8 hundred. Then add on to this the tens in a successive manner and finally the ones. Try it now. ■

◆ Standard Algorithms

The main focus in teaching the standard algorithm should not be as a memorized series of steps, but as making sense of the procedure as a process. The *Common Core State Standards* (CCSSO, 2010) require that students eventually have knowledge of the standard algorithms (addition and subtraction with multidigit whole numbers in grade 4, multiplication with multidigit whole numbers in grade 5, and division of multidigit whole numbers in grade 6). Notice that the grades in which this knowledge of standard algorithms is required is long after the computational work is introduced, pointing again to the need for full conceptual development to take place first. Importantly, the *Common Core State Standards* recognize that starting by teaching only the standard algorithm doesn't allow students to explore other useful approaches. Understanding how algorithms work and when they are the best choice (over an invented approach) is central to development of procedural proficiency.

Standard Algorithms Must Be Understood

Students may pick up the standard algorithms from siblings and other family members while you are still trying to teach a variety of invented strategies. Some of these students may resist learning more flexible strategies thinking that they already know the "right" approach. What do you do then?

First and foremost, apply the same rule to standard algorithms as to all strategies: If you use it, you must understand why it works and be able to explain it. In an atmosphere that says, "Let's figure out why this works," students can profit from making sense of standard algorithms just as they should be able to reason about other approaches. But the responsibility for the explanations should be theirs, not yours. Remember, "Never say anything a kid can say!" (Reinhart, 2000, p. 478).

Once the standard algorithm is understood, it is one more strategy to put in the student's toolbox of methods. Reinforce the idea that, just like the other strategies, it may be more useful in some instances than in others. For example, point out that for a problem such as $4568 + 12,813$, the standard algorithm has distinct advantages. Also, pose problems in which a mental strategy is much more useful than the standard algorithm, such as $504 - 498$. Discuss which method seems best in a variety of situations.

> **Standards for Mathematical Practice**
>
> **7** Look for and make use of structure

Delay! Delay! Delay!

Students are unlikely to invent the standard algorithms. You will need to introduce and explain them, and help students understand how and why algorithms work. No matter how carefully you introduce these algorithms into your classroom as simply another alternative, students may sense that "this is the one right way." So, first, spend a significant time with invented strategies—months, not weeks. Note that the *Common Core State Standards* (CCSSO, 2010) suggest that students learn a variety of strategies based on place value and properties of operations one or two years before the standard algorithms are expected. The understanding students gain from working with invented strategies will make it easier for you to meaningfully teach the standard algorithms. If you think you are wasting precious time by delaying, just think of how many years you (and others) teach the same standard algorithms over and over to students who are still unable to understand them and cannot use them without making errors.

Cultural Differences in Algorithms

Some people falsely assume that mathematics is universal and is easier than other subjects for students who are not native English speakers. In fact, there are many international differences in notation, conventions, and algorithms. Knowing more about the diverse algorithms students might bring to the classroom and their ways of recording symbols for "doing mathematics" will assist you in supporting students and responding to families. What the United States calls the "standard algorithm" may not be customary in other countries, so encouraging a variety of algorithms is important in valuing the experiences of all students.

For example, *equal addition* is a subtraction algorithm used in many Latin and European countries. It is based on the knowledge that adding the same amount to both the minuend and the subtrahend will not change the difference (answer). Let's start with a simple example. If the expression to be solved is $15 - 5$, there is no change to the answer (or the difference) if you add 10 to the minuend and subtrahend and solve $25 - 15$. There is still a difference of 10. Let's look at $62 - 27$ to think about this further. Using the familiar algorithm that you may think of as "standard," you would likely regroup by crossing out the 6 tens, adding the 10 with a small 1 to the 2 in the ones column (making 12), and then subtracting the 7 from the 12 and so forth. In the equal addition approach (see Figure 11.1), you can add 10 to 62 by just mentally adding a small 1 (to represent 10) to the 2 in the ones column and thereby having 12, and then you counteract the addition of 10 to the minuend by mentally adding 10 to the 27 (subtrahend), by increasing the tens column by one and subtracting 37. This may sound confusing to you—but try it. Especially when there are zeros in the minuend (e.g., $302 - 178$), you may find this is a productive option. More important, your possible confusion can give you the sense of how your students (and their families) may react to a completely different procedure from the one they know and find successful.

Figure 11.1 The equal addition algorithm.

6̸2̸ (with 12 above)
3̸7̸ (with 3 above)
3 5

7 is larger than 2 so add 10 ones to the 2 in 62 and 1 ten to the 2 in 27 (12 − 7 = 5)

6 tens − 3 tens = 3 tens

Teaching Tip

Mental mathematics is emphasized in other countries (Perkins & Flores, 2002). In fact, students are taught to pride themselves on their ability to do math mentally. Don't be surprised if students from other countries can produce answers without showing work.

Development of Invented Strategies in Addition and Subtraction

You will not be surprised to hear that students do not spontaneously invent wonderful computational methods while you sit back and watch. The following section discusses pedagogical methods that support students' development of invented strategies for multidigit addition and subtraction.

◆ Models to Support Invented Strategies

The *Common Core State Standards* require that students "fluently add and subtract within 1000" using strategies based on "place value, properties of operations and the relationship between addition and subtraction" (CCSSO, 2010, p. 24). Try seeing how you would do these without using the standard algorithms: $487 + 235$ and $623 - 247$. For subtraction, a counting-up strategy is usually the easiest. Occasionally, other strategies appear with larger numbers. For example, "chunking off" multiples of 50 or 25 is often a useful method. For $462 + 257$, pull out 450 and 250 to make 700. That leaves 12 and 7 more, for 719.

There are three common types of student-invented strategies to solve addition and subtraction situations that can be extended to higher numbers: split strategy (also thought of as decomposition), jump strategy (similar to counting on or counting back), and shortcut strategy (sometimes known as *compensation*) (Torbeyns, De Smedt, Ghesquiere, & Verschaffel, 2009). The notion of "splitting" a number into parts (often by place value) is a useful strategy for all operations. Both the word *split* and the use of a visual diagram help students

Figure 11.2

Two methods of recording students' thought processes on the board so that the class can follow the strategy.

(a) How much is 86 and 47?

S: I know that 80 and 20 more is 100.

T: Where do the 80 and the 20 come from?

S: I split the 47 into 20 and 20 and 7 and the 86 into 80 and 6.

T: (illustrates the splitting with lines)
So then you added one of the 20s to 80?

S: Yes, 80 and 20 is 100. Then I added the other 20 and got 120.

T: (writes the equations on the board)

S: Then I added the 6 and the 7 and got 13.

T: (writes this equation)

S: Then I added the 120 to the 13 and got 133.

T: Indicates with joining lines.

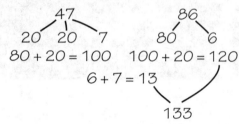

$$80 + 20 = 100 \quad 100 + 20 = 120$$
$$6 + 7 = 13$$
$$133$$

(b) What is 84 minus 68?

S: I started at 84. First, I jumped back 4 to make 80.

T: Why did you subtract 4 first? Why not 8?

S: It was easier to think about 80 than 84. I will save the other part of 8 until later. Then I jumped back 60 to get 20.

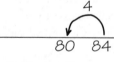

S: Then I jumped back 4.

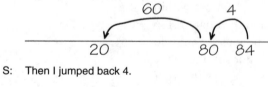

T: Why 4?

S: That was how much I still had left over from 68.

---

develop strategies (Verschaffel et al., 2007). Try using arrows or lines to indicate how two computations are joined together, as shown in Figure 11.2a, or an open number line as a visual, shown in Figure 11.2b.

Adding Multidigit Numbers

Although double-digit addition is taught in second grade, students in grades 3 and 4 may still be challenged by these computations. Problems involving the sum of 2 two-digit numbers will usually produce a wide variety of strategies, and it is these strategies that are the foundation for adding three-digit numbers. Some strategies will involve starting with one or the other number and working from that point, either by adding on to the next ten or by adding tens from one number to the other.

Figure 11.3 illustrates four different strategies for addition of 2 two-digit numbers, all of which can be adapted for three-digit numbers. For each of the examples, a possible recording method is offered as a suggestion to help students develop written techniques. Presenting problems to students in horizontal formats encourages them to think in terms of numbers instead of digits. Also, note the use of the empty number line.

The move to the shortcut or compensation strategies focusing on making a hundred is useful when one of the numbers is close to a multiple of 100. To promote that strategy, present problems with addends like 397 or 508. Note that it is only necessary to adjust one of the two numbers.

Formative Assessment Note

Try the following problem with a student in a diagnostic interview: 46 + 35. Notice how your student starts to solve this problem and ask questions about his or her thinking process. That is, for 46 + 35, a student may add on 4 to the 46 to get to 50 and then add 31 more, or first add 30 to 46 and then add 4 to get to 80 and then add 1 more. In either case, see if they are taking advantage of the utilization of place-value concepts. Another approach they may use involves splitting the numbers into parts and adding the easier parts separately. Usually the split will involve tens and ones, or students may use other parts of numbers, such as 50 or 25, as an easier compatible number. Students may use a counting by tens and ones technique. That is, instead of 46 + 30 is 76, they may use an open number line and count up "46, 56, 66, 76." These jumps can be written down to help students keep track. In each case, be mindful of how flexibly the students use place-value units or how they use the shortcut strategy. If they are not seeing the ten as a unit, more work on place value might be useful.

Stop and Reflect

Try adding 367 + 155 in as many different ways as you can. How many of your ways are like those in Figure 11.3? ∎

𝓕𝓲𝓰𝓾𝓻𝓮 11.3 Four different invented strategies for addition with 2 two-digit numbers.

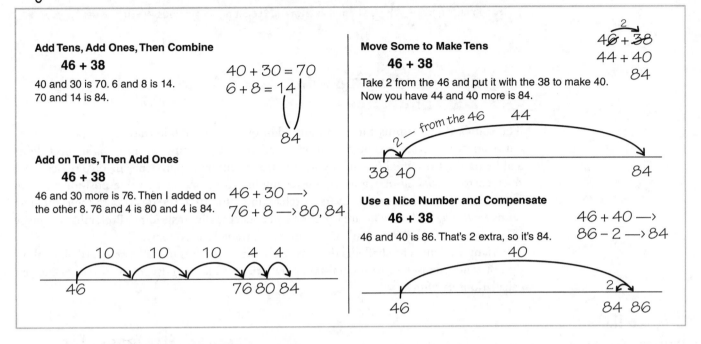

◆ Subtracting by Counting Up

This is an amazingly powerful way to subtract. Students who worked with the think-addition strategy for their basic facts can also use this strategy to solve problems with multidigit numbers. The concept is the same. For example, for 382 − 195, the idea is to think, "How much do I add to 195 to get 382?" This strategy is particularly successful with students with disabilities (Peltenburg, van den Heuvel-Panhuizen, & Robitzsch, 2011). Using join with change unknown problems or missing-part problems (discussed in Chapter 8) will encourage the counting-up strategy. Following is an example of each.

Sam had 467 baseball cards in his collection. A year later he had 735 cards. How many cards did Sam add to his collection that year?

Juanita counted all of the teacher's pencils. Some were sharpened and some not. She counted 743 pencils in all; 460 pencils were not sharpened. How many were sharpened?

The numbers in these problems encourage the use of multiple strategies that emphasize place value. Students can add hundreds to get close, then add tens and ones. They can add hundreds and overshoot, then come back by tens. You can emphasize the value of using place-value concepts by posing problems involving multiples of 10 or 100.

◆ Take-Away Subtraction

Take-away methods (particularly with three digits) are more difficult to do mentally or even with the help of paper and pencil. Exceptions involve problems such as 423 − 8 or 576 − 300 (subtracting a number less than 10 or a multiple of 10 or 100). Take away is very likely the strategy that will come to mind first for students who have previously been taught the standard algorithm. We suggest, however, that you emphasize adding-on methods whenever possible.

Stop and Reflect

Try computing 823 − 579. Use both take-away and counting-up methods. Which is easier for you? ■

◆ The Standard Algorithms for Addition and Subtraction

The standard algorithms for multidigit addition and subtraction are significantly different from nearly every invented method. In addition to starting with the right-most digits and being digit oriented (as already noted), the traditional approaches involve the concept referred to as *trading* or *regrouping*—exchanging 10 in one place-value position for 1 in the position to the left, or the reverse, exchanging 1 for 10 in the position to the right. The terms *borrowing* and *carrying* are obsolete and conceptually misleading. Preferable language is "10 ones are traded for a ten" or "a hundred is traded for 10 tens."

Many students are challenged to precisely record each trade. The standard algorithms do not lend themselves to mental computation, so tudents must learn to record interim calculations carefully.

Figure 11.4

Different ways to model 34 × 6 may support different computational strategies.

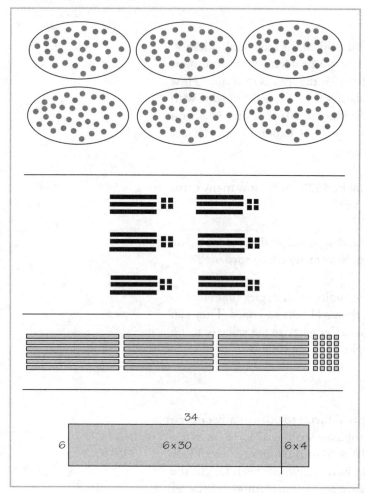

◢ Invented Strategies for Multiplication

For multiplication, the ability to break numbers apart in flexible ways is even more important than in addition or subtraction. This skill hinges on the full understanding of the distributive property of multiplication over addition. For example, to multiply 43 × 5, one might think about breaking 43 into 40 and 3, multiplying each by 5, and then adding the results. Students require ample opportunities to develop these concepts by making sense of their own ideas and those of their classmates.

◆ Useful Representations

The problem 6 × 34 may be represented in a number of ways, as illustrated in Figure 11.4. Often the choice of a model is influenced by a story problem. To determine how many oranges six classes need if there are 34 students in each class, students may model 6 sets of 34. If the problem is about a rectangle's area (6 cm × 34 cm), then some form of an array is likely. But each representation is appropriate for thinking about 6 × 34 regardless of the context, and students should get to a point at which they select meaningful ways to think about multiplication.

How students represent a product is directly related to their methods for determining answers. The equal groups of 34 students in a class might suggest repeated additions—perhaps taking the sets two at a time. Double 34 is 68 and there are three sets of those, so 68 + 68 + 68 = 204. Or the six sets of base-ten pieces might suggest breaking the numbers into tens and ones: 6 times 3 tens or 6 × 30 and 6 × 4. Or some students use the tens individually: 6 tens make 60. So that's 60 + 60 + 60 (180); then add on 24 more to make 204.

All of these ideas should be part of students' repertoire of models for multidigit multiplication computation. The NCTM *Principles and Standards for School Mathematics* suggest, "Having access to more than one method for each operation allows students to choose an approach that best fits the numbers in a particular problem" (NCTM, 2000, p. 155).

> *Teaching Tip*
>
> Although you may worry that sharing multiple methods to solve problems will overwhelm and confuse your students, researchers found when students compared a variety of methods from the start they gained flexibility and were more successful (Rittle-Johnson et al., 2010)!

◆ Multiplication by a One-Digit Multiplier

The types of strategies that students use for multiplication are more varied than for addition and subtraction. The three categories described here are strategies grounded in students' sense making, as described in research on multiplicative reasoning (Baek, 2006; Confrey, 2008; Petit, personal communication, September 2009).

Complete-Number Strategies (Including Doubling)

Students who are not yet comfortable decomposing numbers into parts will approach the numbers in the sets as single groups. Most likely, these early strategies will be based on repeated addition. Often students will list columns of the same number and add them up. In an attempt to shorten this process, students soon realize that if they add two numbers, the next two will have the same sum, and so on. This doubling can become the principal approach for many students (Flowers & Rubenstein, 2010–2011). Doubling capitalizes on the *distributive property*, whereby doubling 47 is double 40 + double 7, and the *associative property*, in which doubling 7 tens or 2 × (7 × 10) is the same as doubling 7 and then multiplying by 10 or (2 × 7) × 10. Figure 11.5 illustrates two methods students may use.

Partitioning Strategies

Students decompose numbers in a variety of ways that reflect an understanding of place value, at least four of which are illustrated in Figure 11.6. The "by decades" partitioning strategy (which can be extended to by hundreds, by thousands, etc.) is the same as the standard algorithm except that students always begin with the largest values. This is a very powerful mental math strategy. Another valuable strategy is to compute mentally with multiples of 25 and 50 and then add or subtract a small adjustment. All partitioning strategies rely on knowledge of the distributive property.

Compensation Strategies

Students look for ways to manipulate numbers so that the calculations are easy. In Figure 11.7, the problem 27 × 4 is changed to an easier one, and then an adjustment or compensation is made. The second example uses the "half-then-double strategy," in which one factor is cut in half and the other is doubled. This is often used when a 5 or a 50 is involved. Because these strategies are so dependent on the numbers involved, they can't be used

Figure 11.5

Students who use a complete-number strategy do not break numbers apart into decades or tens and ones.

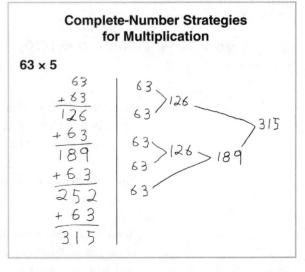

Complete-Number Strategies for Multiplication

63 × 5

Figure 11.6 Four different ways to make easier partial products.

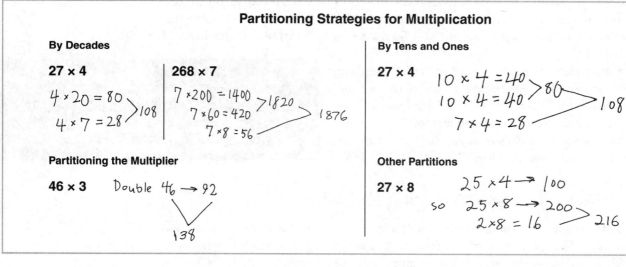

Figure 11.7

A compensation is made in the answer, or one factor is changed to compensate for a change in the other factor.

Compensation Strategies for Multiplication

27 × 4
$$27 + 3 \rightarrow 30 \times 4 \rightarrow 120$$
$$3 \times 4 = 12 \rightarrow -12$$
$$\overline{108}$$

250 × 5
I can split 250 in half and multiply by 10.
$$125 \times 10 = 1250$$

17 × 70
$$20 \times 70 \rightarrow 1400 - 210 \rightarrow 1190$$
$$3 \times 70$$

for all computations. However, they are powerful strategies, especially for mental math and estimation.

⬢ Multiplication of Multidigit Numbers

As you move students from one-digit to two-digit factors, there is value in exposing them to products involving multiples of 10 and 100. This supports the importance of place value and an emphasis on the number rather than the separate digits. Consider the following problem:

The Scout troop wanted to make 400 battery packs as a fundraising project. If each pack will have 12 batteries inside, how many batteries are the Scouts going to need?

Students can use $4 \times 12 = 48$ to figure out that 400×12 is 4800. Make sure you discuss how to say and write "forty-eight hundred." Be alert to students who simply tack on zeros without understanding why. Many students will say "to multiply by 10, just add a zero on the end." But very soon they will be solving 2.5×10, for which this rule will not work. Try problems such as 30×60 or 210×40 in which groups of tens are multiplied by groups of tens.

Then students should move to problems that involve any two-digit numbers, not just those that are multiples of 10. A problem such as this one can be solved in many different ways:

The parade had 23 clowns. Each clown carried 18 balloons. How many balloons were there altogether?

Some students might look for smaller products, such as 6×23, and then add that result three times. Another method is to do 20×23 and then subtract 2×23. Others will calculate and add four separate partial products: $10 \times 20 = 200$, $8 \times 20 = 160$, $10 \times 3 = 30$, and

$8 \times 3 = 24$. And still others may add up a string of 23s. Two-digit multiplication is both complex and challenging. Students can solve these problems in a variety of interesting ways, many of which will contribute to the development of the standard algorithm. Figure 11.8 shows the work of three fourth graders who had not yet been taught the standard algorithm. Kenneth's work shows how he is *partitioning* the factor 12 into $3 \times 2 \times 2$. Briannon is using a *complete-number strategy*. She may need to see and hear about strategies other classmates developed to move toward a more efficient approach. Nick's method is conceptually very similar to the standard algorithm. As students like Nick begin partitioning numbers by place value, the strategies are often like the standard algorithm but without the traditional recording schemes.

Figure 11.8

Three fourth-grade students at different levels solve a multiplication problem using their own invented strategies.

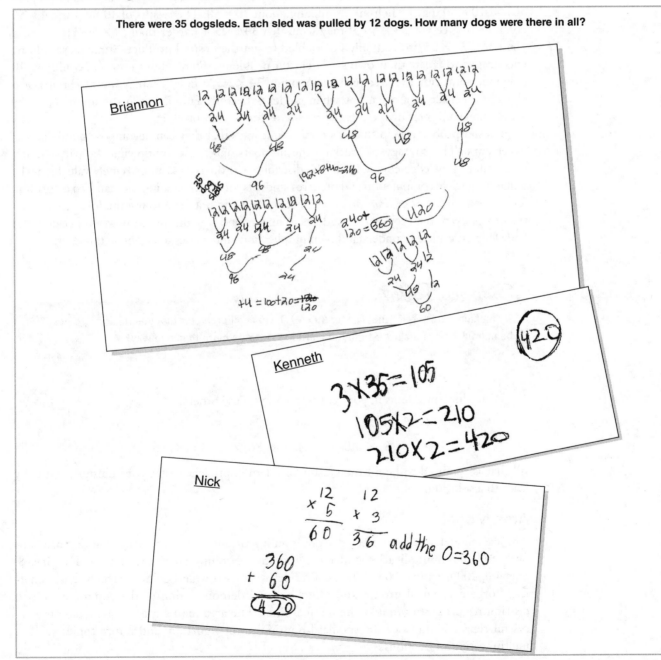

Cluster Problems

One approach to multidigit multiplication is called "cluster problems." This strategy encourages students to use facts and combinations they already know in order to figure out more complex computations. For example, to find 34×50, students might record the following cluster of known facts:

$$3 \times 50$$
$$10 \times 50$$
$$34 \times 25$$
$$30 \times 50$$

Using these problems as support, students can analyze to see which ones can be used in finding the product (there are multiple options). They can also consider adding other problems that might be helpful. In this case, have students make an estimate of the final product before doing any of the problems in the cluster. For example, in the cluster for 34×50, 3×50 and 10×50 may be helpful in thinking about 30×50. The results of 30×50 and 4×50 combine to give you 34×50. It may seem that 34×25 is harder than 34×50. However, if you know 34×25, it need only be doubled to get the desired product. Students should be encouraged to create their own set of cluster problems. Think about how you could use 10×34 (and some other related problems) to find 34×25. At first, you may want to brainstorm clusters together as a class, but when students become familiar with the approach, they should make up their own cluster of problems for a given product.

Cluster problems help students think about ways that they can decompose numbers into easier parts. The strategy of breaking the numbers apart and multiplying the parts—using place-value knowledge coupled with the distributive property—is an extremely valuable technique for flexible computation and prepares students for understanding the standard algorithm. The *Common Core State Standards* state that students do not have to use the formal term *distributive property*, but they expect students to understand why this property works because that knowledge is critical to understanding multiplication (and its ties to algebraic thinking).

Stop and Reflect

Try making a cluster of problems for 86×42. Include all problems that you think might possibly be helpful. Use your cluster to find the product. Is there more than one way? ■

Were these problems in your cluster? Did you use others?

$$2 \times 80 \qquad 4 \times 80 \qquad 2 \times 86 \qquad 40 \times 80$$
$$6 \times 40 \qquad 10 \times 86 \qquad 40 \times 86$$

All that is required to begin the cluster-problem approach is that your cluster eventually leads to a solution.

Area Model

The area model, or the connected array, is an important visual representation that can support students' multiplicative understanding and reasoning (Barmby, Harries, Higgins, & Suggate, 2009; Iszák, 2004). The area model with its row and column structure automatically organizes equal groups and offers a visual demonstration of the commutative and distributive properties (unlike the number line). The area model can also be linked to successful representations of the standard multiplication algorithm and future topics such as multiplication of fractions.

A valuable exploration with the area model uses large rectangles that have been precisely prepared with dimensions between 25 cm and 60 cm and square corners. Each group of students uses one of these rectangles to determine how many small ones pieces (base-ten materials) will fit inside the rectangle. Later, students can simply be given a rectangle on grid paper or be asked, "What is the area of a rectangle that is 47 cm by 36 cm?"

For a particular rectangle that is 47 cm by 36 cm, most students will fill the rectangle with as many hundreds pieces as possible. One obvious approach is to put the 12 hundreds in one corner. This will leave narrow regions on two sides that can be filled with tens pieces and a final small rectangle that will hold ones. Especially if students have had earlier experiences with finding products in arrays, figuring out the size of each subrectangle is not too difficult. The sketch in Figure 11.9 shows the four regions.

Standards for Mathematical Practice

◄ **5 Use appropriate tools strategically**

Figure 11.9

Ones, tens, and hundreds pieces fit exactly into the four sections of this 47 × 36 rectangle.

◆ *Activity 11.1* **BUILD IT AND BREAK IT**

Select a problem such as 23 × 18. Use base-ten blocks or grid paper to build the corresponding area model. Then, have students show and record as many ways as possible to "slice" the array into pieces. For example, they could cut the array into 23 × 10 + 23 × 8. What other vertical or horizontal slices can be made? What property does this link to? Before launching the activity, provide students, particularly ELLs, a labeled visual of an area model that includes the terms *array, area model, slice, vertical,* and *horizontal*. In wrap-up discussion, be sure to focus on the vocabulary of the key concepts (*distributive property, decompose, strategy,* etc.).

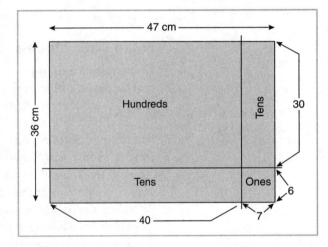

Research analyzed sixth graders' varied strategies for solving multiplication problems on the criteria of flexibility, accuracy, and efficiency. Given the problem 13 × 7, only 11 percent of the students used the standard algorithm. When multiplying 2 two-digit numbers, only 20 percent used the standard algorithm, with less than half of that 20 percent reaching the correct answer (Keiser, 2010). Interestingly, this work confirmed the researcher's prior observations that the standard algorithm for multiplication was not the most popular approach for two-digit factors when students had been taught other options. The array or area model was most often selected.

The Standard Algorithm for Multiplication

The standard multiplication algorithm is probably the most difficult of the four algorithms when students have not had numerous opportunities to explore their own strategies first. The multiplication algorithm can be meaningfully developed using either a repeated addition model or an area model. For two-digit multipliers in particular, the area model has advantages, so for that reason, the discussion here will emphasize that model.

◆ One-Digit Multipliers

As with the other algorithms, as much time as possible should be devoted to the conceptual development of the algorithm with the recording or written part coming later. In contrast, many textbooks spend less time on development and more time on memorizing steps.

Figure 11.10

A rectangle filled with base-ten pieces is a useful model for two-digit by one-digit multiplication.

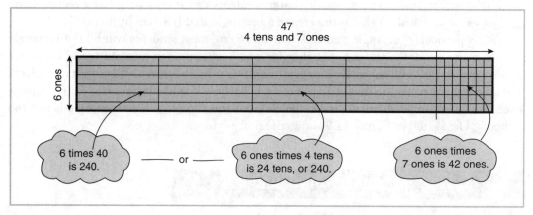

47
4 tens and 7 ones

6 ones

6 times 40 is 240.

or

6 ones times 4 tens is 24 tens, or 240.

6 ones times 7 ones is 42 ones.

Begin with Models

Give students a drawing of a rectangle that is 47 cm by 6 cm. How many small square centimeter pieces will fit in the rectangle? (What is the area of the rectangle in square centimeters?) Let students solve the problem in groups before discussing it as a class.

As shown in Figure 11.10, the rectangle can be "sliced" or separated into two parts so that one part will be 6 ones by 7 ones, or 42 ones, and the other will be 6 ones by 4 tens, or 24 tens. Notice that the base-ten language "6 ones times 4 tens is 24 tens" tells how many pieces of ten are in the section. To say "6 times 40 is 240" is also correct and tells how many units or square centimeters are in the section. Each section is referred to as a partial product. By adding the partial products, you get the total product or area of the rectangle.

Move from having students draw large rectangles and arrange base-ten pieces, to using the base-ten grid paper (see Blackline Master 19). On the grid paper, students can draw accurate rectangles showing all of the pieces. Do not impose any recording technique on students until they understand how to use the two dimensions of a rectangle to get a product.

BLM

technology
note

Computer versions of the area model can ease some of the difficulties of physically fitting base-ten blocks into rectangular grids. Go to the NLVM website and find the Rectangle Multiplication applet (http://nlvm.usu .edu/en/nav/frames_asid_192_g_2_t_1.html). Model a multiplication problem of your choice up to 30 × 30. See how the rectangle is split into two parts rather than four, corresponding to the tens and ones digits in the multiplier. How does this representation correlate to the standard algorithm? For students with disabilities, have a set of base-ten blocks nearby to show how the concrete version corresponds to the computer illustration.

Develop the Written Record

To help students develop a recording scheme, provide sheets with base-ten columns on which they can record problems. When the partial products are written separately, as in Figure 11.11, there is little new to learn. But, as illustrated in Figure 11.11a, it is possible to teach students how to write the first product with a regrouped digit so that the combined product is written on one line. This recording scheme is known to be a source of errors. The little regrouped digit is often the difficulty—it often gets added in before the subsequent multiplication, or is forgotten. Instead, to avoid errors, encourage students to record partial products. Then it makes no difference in which order the products are written. Figure 11.11b shows how students can record partial products, which mirrors how this computation can be done mentally.

◆ Two-Digit Multipliers

With the area model, the progression to a two-digit multiplier is relatively straightforward. Rectangles can be drawn on base-ten grid paper, or full-sized rectangles can be filled in with base-ten pieces. Now there will be four partial products, corresponding to four different sections of the rectangle.

Several variations in language might be used. Consider the product 47 × 36 as illustrated in Figure 11.12. In the

Figure 11.11

In the standard form, the product of ones is recorded first. (a) The tens digit of this first product is written as a "regrouped" digit above the tens column. (b) Partial products can be recorded in any order.

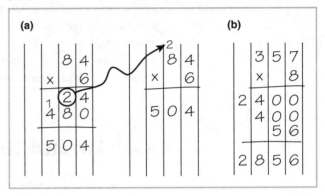

Figure 11.12

A 47 × 36 rectangle filled with base-ten pieces. Base-ten language connects the four partial products to the standard algorithm.

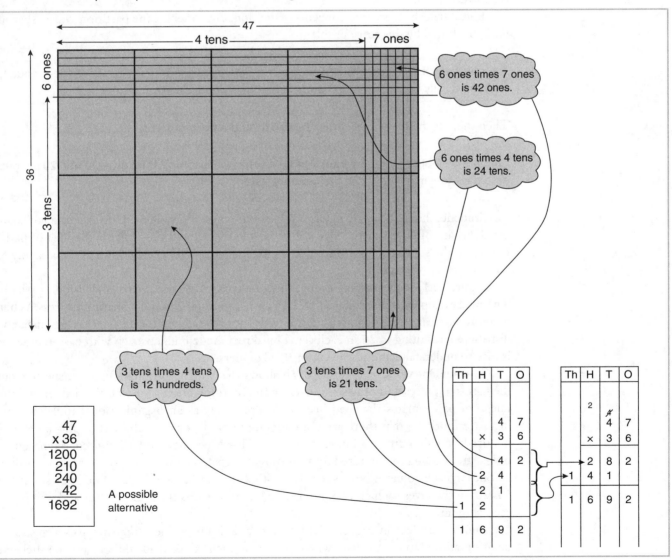

partial product 40×30, if base-ten language is used—4 tens times 3 tens is 12 hundreds—the result tells how many hundreds pieces are in that section. Again, avoid "four times three," which promotes thinking about digits rather than numbers. It is important to stress that a product of tens times tens is hundreds.

Figure 11.12 also shows the recording of four partial products in the traditional order and how these can be collapsed to two lines if small digits are used to record the trade. Here the second exchange technically belongs in the hundreds column, but it is often written elsewhere, which again is a source of errors. The lower left of the figure shows the same computation with all four products written in a different order. This is also acceptable. Using this approach, multiplying numbers such as 538×29 results in six partial products, but far fewer errors!

▲ Invented Strategies for Division

Even though many adults think division is the most onerous of the computational operations, some students find it considerably easier than multiplication. Division computation strategies with whole numbers are developed in third through fifth grades (CCSSO, 2010).

Recall that there are two concepts of division. First, there is the partition, or fair sharing idea, illustrated by this story problem:

The bag has 783 jelly beans, and Aidan and her four friends want to share them equally. How many jelly beans will Aidan and each of her friends get?

Then there is the measurement, or repeated subtraction, concept:

Jumbo the elephant loves peanuts. His trainer has 625 peanuts. If he gives Jumbo 20 peanuts each day, how many days will the peanuts last?

Students should be challenged to solve both types of problems. However, the fair share problems are often easier to solve with base-ten pieces, and they mirror the idea of partitioning in the standard algorithm. Eventually, students will develop strategies that apply to both types of problems.

Figure 11.13 shows strategies that three fourth graders used to solve division problems. The first example (a) illustrates $72 \div 3$ using base-ten blocks and a sharing process. When no more tens can be distributed, a ten is traded for ones. Then the 12 ones are grouped and distributed, resulting in 24 in each set. This direct modeling approach with base-ten pieces is easy to understand and use, even for third graders.

The student work in Figure 11.13b shows that for the problem $342 \div 4$, she sets out the base-ten pieces and draws a four-column recording chart to match the divisor and the image of paper plates that had been used previously as an organizational tool for sharing. After noticing that there are not enough hundreds for each child, she splits 2 of the 3 hundreds in half, putting 50 in each column. That leaves her with 1 hundred, 4 tens, and 2 ones. After trading the hundred for tens (now 14 tens), she gives 3 (tens) to each, recording 30 ones in each column. Now she is left with 2 tens and 2 ones, or 22. She knows that 4×5 is 20, so she gives each child 5, leaving 2. Then she splits the 2 into halves and writes $\frac{1}{2}$ in each column.

Another student in Figure 11.13c solves a division problem that involves a measurement situation: How many bags with 6 stickers in each can be made if there are 164 stickers? She wants to find out how many groups of six are in 164. As a first step she estimates and tries 6×20. She actually does this by multiplying 6×10 and doubling the answer. Then she tries adding another group of 10 and sees that is too high. So she knows the answer is more than 20 and less than 30. Then she thinks about how many sixes in 44, which she knows is 7 with 2 left over. So her answer is 27 bags with 2 stickers left over.

◆ Missing-Factor Strategies

In Figure 11.13c, the student is using a multiplicative approach. She is trying to find out what number times 6 will be close to 164 with less than 6 remaining.

Stop and Reflect

Before reading further, think about the quotient of $318 \div 7$ by trying to figure out what number times 7 (or 7 times what number) is close to 318 without going over. Do not use the standard algorithm. ■

There are several places to begin solving this problem. For instance, because 10×7 is 70 and 100×7 is 700, the answer is between 10 and 100. You might start with multiples of 10. Forty sevens are 280. Fifty sevens are 350. So 40 is not enough, and 50 is too many. It has to be forty-something. At this point, you could test numbers between 40 and 50 or add on groups of seven. Or you could notice that 40 sevens (280) leaves you with 20 plus 18 or 38. Five sevens will be 35 of the 38 with 3 remaining. In all, that's $40 + 5$ or 45 with a remainder of 3.

This missing-factor approach is likely to be invented by some students if they are solving measurement problems such as the following:

Grace can put 6 pictures on one page of her photo album. If she has 82 pictures, how many pages will she need?

Alternatively, you can simply pose a task such as $82 \div 6$ and ask students, "What number times 6 would be close to 82?"

Figure 11.13

Students use both models and symbols to solve division tasks.

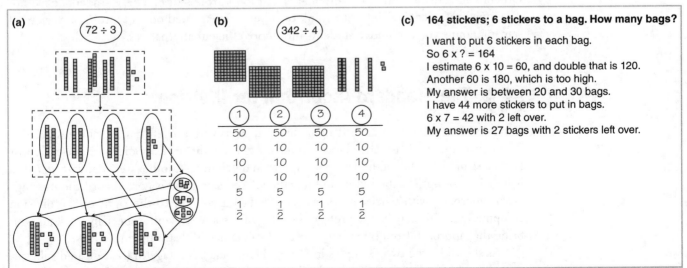

(a) $72 \div 3$

(b) $342 \div 4$

1	2	3	4
50	50	50	50
10	10	10	10
10	10	10	10
10	10	10	10
5	5	5	5
$\frac{1}{2}$	$\frac{1}{2}$	$\frac{1}{2}$	$\frac{1}{2}$

(c) **164 stickers; 6 stickers to a bag. How many bags?**

I want to put 6 stickers in each bag.
So 6 x ? = 164
I estimate 6 x 10 = 60, and double that is 120.
Another 60 is 180, which is too high.
My answer is between 20 and 30 bags.
I have 44 more stickers to put in bags.
6 x 7 = 42 with 2 left over.
My answer is 27 bags with 2 stickers left over.

◆ Cluster Problems

Another approach to developing missing factor strategies is to use cluster problems, as discussed for multiplication. Here are examples of two clusters for two different division problems:

Cluster 1	Cluster 2
4×100	10×72
$500 \div 4$	5×70
4×25	2×72
4×6	4×72
$527 \div 4$	5×72
	$381 \div 72$

Notice that the missing-factor strategy is equally good for one-digit divisors as for two-digit divisors. Also notice that it is useful to include division problems in the cluster. In the first example, $400 \div 4$ could easily replace 4×100 and 4×125 could replace $500 \div 4$. The idea is to capitalize on the inverse relationship between multiplication and division.

Cluster problems provide students with a sense that problems can be solved in different ways and with different starting points. Therefore, rather than cluster problems you can provide students with a variety of first steps for solving the problem.

Stop and Reflect

Solve 514 ÷ 8 in two different ways beginning with different first steps. Do your approaches converge before the solution? ■

For example, here are four possible starting points for $514 \div 8$:

$$8 \times 10 \qquad 400 \div 8 \qquad 8 \times 60 \qquad 80 \div 8$$

When you first ask students to solve problems using two strategies, they often use an inefficient method for their second approach (or revert to a standard algorithm). For example, to solve $514 \div 8$, a student might perform a very long string of subtractions ($514 - 8 = 506$, $506 - 8 = 498$, $498 - 8 = 490$, and so on) and count how many times he or she subtracted 8. Others will actually draw 514 tally marks and loop groups of 8. These students have not developed sufficient flexibility to think of other efficient methods. By posing a variety of starting points you can nudge students into more efficient alternatives.

▲ The Standard Algorithm for Division

Long division is the one standard algorithm that starts with the left-hand, or biggest, pieces. The conceptual basis for the algorithm most often taught in textbooks is the partition or fair-share method, the method we will explore in detail here. Another well-known algorithm is based on repeated subtraction and may be viewed as a good way to record the missing-factor approach with partial products recorded in a column to the right of the division computation. This may be the preferred strategy for some students, especially students who bring that approach from other countries and students with learning disabilities.

As shown by the two examples in Figure 11.14, one advantage of the repeated subtraction algorithm is that there is total flexibility in the factors selected at each step of the way.

This is important for students who struggle, as they can se-lect facts they know and work from that point.

One-Digit Divisors

The *Common Core State Standards* (CCSSO, 2010) suggest that the division algorithm with one-digit divisors is developed in the fourth grade, and it should provide the basis for the extension to two-digit divisors in the fifth grade. Students who are still struggling in grades 5 and beyond with single digit divisors can also benefit from the following conceptual development.

Begin with Models

Traditionally, if we were to do a problem such as 4)583, we might say, "4 goes into 5 one time." Initially, this is quite mysterious to students. How can you just ignore the "83" and keep changing the problem? Preferably, you want students to think of the 583 as 5 hundreds, 8 tens, and 3 ones, not as the independent digits 5, 8, and 3. One idea is to use a context such as candy bundled in boxes of 10, with 10 boxes (100 pieces) to a carton. Then the problem becomes as fol-lows: "We have 5 cartons, 8 boxes, and 3 pieces of candy to share evenly between 4 schools." In this context, it is reasonable to share the largest cartons first until no more can be shared. Those remaining cartons are "unpacked," and the boxes shared, and so on.

Figure 11.14

The numbers on the right side indicate the quantity of the divisor being subtracted from the dividend. The divisor can be subtracted from the dividend in groups of any amount.

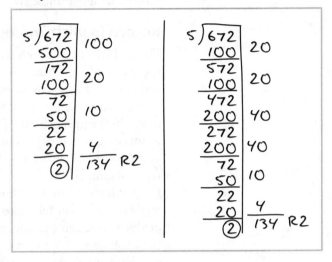

Stop and Reflect

Try the distributing or sharing process yourself using base-ten pieces, three paper plates (or pieces of paper), and the problem 524 ÷ 3. Try to talk through the process without using "goes into" language. Think sharing equally. ■

Language plays an enormous role in thinking conceptually about the standard division algorithm. Most adults are so accustomed to the "goes into" language that it is hard to let it go. For the problem 583 ÷ 4, here is some suggested language:

- I want to share 5 hundreds, 8 tens, and 3 ones among these 4 sets. There are enough hundreds for each set to get 1 hundred. That leaves 1 hundred that I can't share.

- I'll trade the remaining hundred for 10 tens. That gives me a total of 18 tens. I can give each set 4 tens and have 2 tens left over. Two tens are not enough to go around the four sets.

- I can trade the 2 tens for 20 ones and put those with the 3 ones I already had. That makes a total of 23 ones. I can give 5 ones to each of the four sets. That leaves me with 3 ones as a remainder. In all, I gave each group 1 hundred, 4 tens, and 5 ones, with 3 ones left over.

Develop the Written Record

The recording scheme for the long-division algorithm is not intuitive. You will need to be explicit in helping students learn to record the fair sharing with models. There are essen-tially four steps:

1. *Share* and record the number of pieces put in each group.
2. *Record* the number of pieces shared in all. Multiply to find this number.

3. *Record* the number of pieces remaining. Subtract to find this number.

4. *Trade* (if necessary) for smaller pieces, and combine with any of the same-sized pieces that are there already. Record the new total number in the next column.

When students model problems with a one-digit divisor, steps 2 and 3 seem unnecessary. Explain that these steps really help when you don't have the pieces there to count.

Record Explicit Trades

Figure 11.15 details each step of the recording process just described. On the left, you see the standard algorithm. To the right is an explicit-trade method that matches the actual action with the models by explicitly recording the trades. Instead of the "bring-down" step of the standard algorithm, the traded pieces are crossed out, as is the number of existing pieces in the next column. The combined number of pieces is written in this column using, in this case, a two-digit number. In the example, 2 hundreds are traded for 20 tens, combined with the 6 that were there, for a total of 26 tens. The 26 is, therefore, written in the tens column.

Students often find this explicit-trade method easier to follow. (The explicit-trade method is a successful approach invented by John Van de Walle and tested with students in grades 3 to 8. You will not find it in other textbooks.) Blank division charts with wide place-value columns are highly recommended for this method (see Blackline Master 9). By spreading out the digits in the dividend when writing down the problem, you help students avoid the common problem of leaving out a middle zero in a problem (see Figure 11.16 on page 194).

◆ Two-Digit Divisors

The *Common Core State Standards* state that fifth-grade students should be able to find "whole-number quotients of whole numbers with up to four-digit dividends and two-digit divisors, using strategies based on place value, the properties of operations, and/or the relationship between multiplication and division." The CCSS goes on to state that the student should "[i]llustrate and explain the calculation by using equations, rectangular arrays, and/or area models" (CCSSO, 2010, p. 35). In the past, a large part of fourth, fifth, and sometimes sixth grade was spent on "long division," with the result that many students did not master the skill and instead came away with negative attitudes toward mathematics.

An Intuitive Idea

Suppose that you were sharing a large pile of candies with 36 friends. Instead of passing them out one at a time, you conservatively estimate that each person could get at least 6 pieces. So you give 6 to each of your friends. Now you find there are more than 36 pieces left. Do you have everyone give back the 6 pieces so you can then give them 7 or 8? That would be silly! You simply pass out more.

The candy example provides two good ideas for sharing in long division. First, always underestimate how much can be shared. You can always pass out more. To do this, pretend there are more sets to share than there really are. For example, if you are dividing 312 by 43 (sharing among 43 sets or "friends"), pretend you have 50 instead. Round *up* to the next multiple of 10. You can determine that 6 pieces can be shared among 50 sets because 6 × 50 is an easy product. Therefore, because there are really only 43 sets, you can give *at least* 6 to each.

Using the Idea Symbolically

Using these ideas, both the standard algorithm and the explicit-trade method of recording are illustrated in Figure 11.17. The rounded-up divisor, 70, is written above in a little "think bubble." Rounding up has another advantage: It is easy to use the multiples of 70

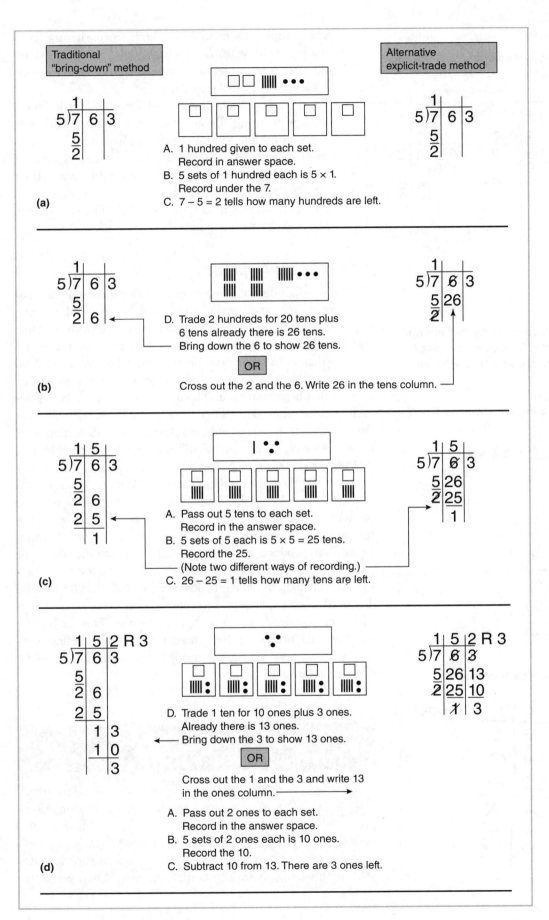

Figure 11.16

Using lines to mark place-value columns can help avoid forgetting to record zeros.

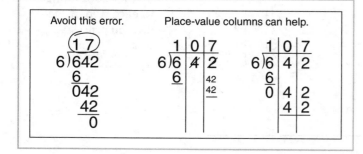

and compare them to 374. Think about sharing base-ten pieces (thousands, hundreds, tens, and ones). Work through the problem one step at a time, saying exactly what each recorded step stands for.

This approach has proved successful with fourth graders learning division for the first time, with students in middle school needing remediation, and with students with disabilities. It reduces the mental strain of making choices and eliminates the need to erase. If an estimate is too low, that's okay. And if you always round up, the estimate will never be too high. The same is true of the explicit-trade notation.

A Low-Stress Approach

With a two-digit divisor, it is harder to estimate the right amount to share at each step. Instead think back to repeated subtraction and the missing factor approach discussed previously. First, start by thinking about place value by asking students to estimate whether their answer will be in the thousands, hundreds, tens, and so on. Then create a "doubling" sidebar chart (Martin, 2009) that starts with a benchmark multiple of the divisor and then doubles each subsequent product. So, for 3842 ÷ 14, decide first whether the answer is in the thousands, hundreds, or tens. Selecting hundreds in this case, the students will then develop a chart of 100, 200, 400, and 800 times 14 (see Figure 11.18). Can you see how knowing 100 times 14 can help you figure out 200 times 14 and other products? Using this doubling chart helps students with the products of the divisor multiplied by 100 through 900 by adding the products in combinations. For example, to know 300 times 14, add the products of 100 times and 200 times the divisor or subtract 100 times 14 from 400 times 14. Knowing these products will logically help the student know what 10 through 90 times the divisor is! Then the division becomes focused on the equal groups within the dividend and, as such, lowers stress. This scaffolding will help students (particularly students who are struggling) estimate more successfully while allowing them to concentrate on the division process.

Figure 11.17

Round the divisor up to 70 to estimate, but multiply what you share by 63. In the ones column, share 8 with each set. Oops! There are 88 left over, so just give 1 more to each set.

Standard algorithm "bring down" method

$$
\begin{array}{r}
70 \\
63\overline{)3742} \\
315 \\
\hline
592 \\
504 \\
\hline
88 \\
63 \\
\hline
25
\end{array}
$$

58 = 59 R25

Alternative explicit-trade method

5 | 8 = 59 R25

70

63 | 3 | 7 | 4 | 2
37 | 374 | 592
315 | 504
59 | 88
63
25

with students with learning disabilities, you may need to progress in a structured way by first supplying them with the appropriate sidebar chart with the products filled in. Then, on the next day, supply them with the chart and have them fill in the products, moving toward their independent creation and completion of the chart. This "fading" of support moves students in an organized and systematic way to more responsibility for their learning.

When teaching a standard algorithm for any operation, you may give short assessments or use chapter-end tests. But can you really assess what students understand or do not understand from a strictly computational test? When students make a systematic error in an algorithm, it will likely be repeated in other problems. What you do not know is what conceptual knowledge students are using—or not using. Don't confuse correct use of a standard algorithm for conceptual understanding. Instead, consider an assessment that captures student reasoning.

Figure 11.18

A student uses doubling to generate useful estimates in a sidebar chart.

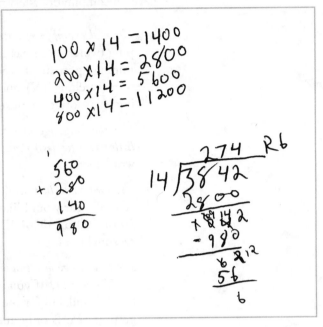

Formative Assessment Note

To assess understanding of algorithms, call on different students to explain individual steps using the appropriate terminology that connects to the concept of division. Use a checklist to record students' responses, indicating how well they seem to understand the algorithm. For struggling students, you may want to conduct a diagnostic interview to explore their level of understanding in more detail. Begin by having the students complete 115 ÷ 9 and ask them to talk about what they are thinking as they carry out specific steps in the process. If there is difficulty explaining, have the students use base-ten blocks to perform the computation. Then ask them to make connections between what was done with the models and what was done symbolically.

Introducing Computational Estimation

Whenever we face a computation in real life, we have a variety of choices to make concerning how we will find a reasonable answer. A first decision is: "Do we need an exact answer, or will an approximate answer be okay?" If precision is called for, we can use an invented strategy, a standard algorithm, or a calculator—but often, an estimate will suffice. How close an estimate must be to the actual computation is a matter of context, as was the original decision to use an estimate. The goal of computational estimation is to be able to flexibly and quickly produce an approximate result that will work for the situation and give a sense of reasonableness. The *Common Core State Standards* state that fourth graders should "Assess the reasonableness of answers using mental computation and estimation strategies including rounding" (CCSSO, 2010, p. 29).

⬢ Teaching Computational Estimation

Here are some general principles that are worth keeping in mind as you help your students develop computational estimation skills:

- *Use real examples of estimation.* Use common examples that include comparative shopping (which store has the item for less); adding up distances in planning a trip; determining approximate monthly totals (school supplies, haircuts, lawn-mowing income, time watching TV); and figuring the cost of going to a sporting event or movie including transportation, tickets, and snacks.

- *Use the language of estimation.* Words and phrases such as *about, close, just about, a little more (or less) than,* and *between* are part of the language of estimation. Avoid the word *guess.*

- *Use context to help with estimates.* For example, it is important to know whether the cost of a car would likely be $950 or $9500. Could attendance at the school play be 30 or 300 or 3000? Knowledge of the context can provide information to judge a reasonable range.

- *Accept a range of estimates, or offer a range as an option.* What estimate would you give for 270 + 325? If you use 200 + 300, you might say 500. Or you might use 250 for the 270 and 350 for the 325, making 600. You could also use 300 for 270 and add 325, getting 625. Is only one of these "right"? By sharing students' estimates and letting them discuss how and why different estimates resulted, they can see that estimates fall in a range around the exact answer. Another option is to offer a range of answers. For example, ask students whether the answer will be between 300 and 400, 450 and 550, or 600 and 700.

- *Do not reward or emphasize the one student's estimate that is the closest.* It is already very difficult for students to handle "approximate" answers; worrying about accuracy and pushing for the closest answer only exacerbates this problem. Instead, focus on whether the answers given are reasonable for the situation or problem at hand.

- *Focus on flexible methods, not answers.* Remember that your primary goal is to help students develop strategies for making computational estimates quickly. Reflection on the strategies therefore will lead to strategy development.

Here is an activity in which a specific number is not required to answer the questions.

◀ *Activity* 11.3 THAT'S GOOD ENOUGH

Present students with a computation that is reasonably difficult. For example: T-shirts with the school logo cost $6 wholesale. The Pep Club has saved $257. How many shirts can the club buy for a fundraiser? The task is to describe the steps they would take to get an exact answer without actually doing them. For students with disabilities, you may give them a series of examples of the steps (and counterexamples of steps) that they must choose from and put in order. Share students' ideas. Next, have students actually do one or two steps. Stop and see whether they come up with good estimates.

🔺 *Activity* 11.4 HIGH OR LOW?

Display a computation and three or more possible computations that might be used to create an estimate. The students' task is to decide whether the estimation will be higher or lower than the actual computation. For example, display the computation 736 × 18. For each of the following, decide whether the result will be higher or lower than the exact result and explain why you think so.

750 × 10	730 × 15
700 × 20	750 × 20

🔷 Computational Estimation Strategies

The NCTM *Principles and Standards for School Mathematics* suggest, "Instructional attention and frequent modeling by the teacher can help students develop a range of computational estimation strategies including flexible rounding, the use of benchmarks and front-end strategies" (NCTM, 2000, p. 156). Here are a few strategies to present to students.

Front-End Methods

This method aligns with invented strategies because it focuses on the leading, or left-most, digits in numbers. Once the first digit it identified, then students think about the rest of the number as if there were zeros in the other positions. Adjustments are made to correct for the digits or numbers that were ignored. The front-end method has been shown to be one of the easiest for students to learn (Star & Rittle-Johnson, 2009).

For example, a front-end estimation of 480 × 7 is 400 × 7, or 2800. Then in the case when both factors have more than one digit, the front ends of both are used. For 452 × 23, consider 400 × 20, or 8000. Because of the greater error that occurs in estimating with multiplication, it is important to adjust these estimates in a second step.

For division, one approach is to think multiplication. For a problem like 3482 ÷ 7, the front-end digit is determined by first deciding the correct position (100 × 7 is too low, 1000 × 7 is too high, so the answer must be in the hundreds). There are 34 hundreds in the dividend, so because 34 ÷ 7 is between 4 and 5, the front-end estimate is 400 or 500. In this example, because 34 ÷ 7 is almost 5, the closer estimate is 500.

> *Teaching Tip*
>
> Avoid presenting problems using the computational form 7)3482 because this format tends to suggest a computation rather than an estimate. Present problems in context or use the algebraic form 3482 ÷ 7.

Rounding Methods

The most familiar form of estimation is rounding, which is a way of changing the numbers in the problem to others that are easier to compute mentally. For example, you can round only the subtracted number (e.g., 6724 − 1863 becomes 6724 − 2000). You can stop here, or you can adjust. Adjusting might go like this: You took away a bigger number, so the result must be too small. Adjust to about 4800.

In multiplication, students can either round one number or round both (Star & Rittle-Johnson, 2009). The rounding strategy for multiplication is similar to the one for addition and subtraction, but the error involved from rounding in multiplication can be significant. This is especially true when both factors are rounded. In Figure 11.19, several multiplication situations are illustrated, and rounding is used to estimate each.

Figure **11.19** Rounding in multiplication.

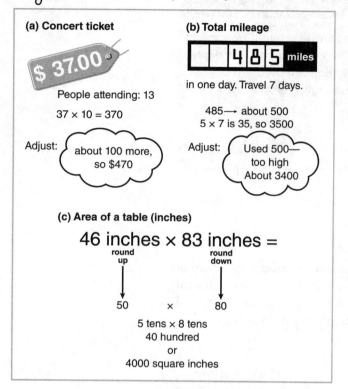

(a) Concert ticket

$ 37.00

People attending: 13

$37 \times 10 = 370$

Adjust: *about 100 more, so $470*

(b) Total mileage

4 8 5 miles

in one day. Travel 7 days.

485 → about 500
5 × 7 is 35, so 3500

Adjust: *Used 500— too high About 3400*

(c) Area of a table (inches)

46 inches × 83 inches =

round up   round down

↓   ↓

50   ×   80

5 tens × 8 tens
40 hundred
or
4000 square inches

If one number can be rounded to 10, 100, or 1000, the resulting product is easy to determine without adjusting the other factor. Figure 11.19a shows such a process.

When one factor is a single digit, round the other factor. Consider the product 7 × 485. If 485 is rounded to 500, the estimate is relatively easy, but is too high by the amount of 7 × 15. If a more precise result is required, subtract about 100 (an estimate of 7 × 15). See Figure 11.19b.

Another rounding strategy for multiplication is to round one factor up and the other down (even if that is not the closest round number). When estimating 86 × 28, 86 is between 80 and 90, but 28 is very close to 30. Try rounding 86 down to 80 and 28 up to 30. The actual product is 2408, only 8 off from the 80 × 30 estimate. If both numbers were rounded to the nearest 10, the estimate would be based on 90 × 30, with an error of nearly 300. See Figure 11.19c for another example.

When rounding in division, the key is to find two compatible numbers rather than rounding to the nearest benchmark. For example, 4325 ÷ 7 can be estimated by rounding to the close compatible number, 4200, to yield an estimate of 600.

Compatible Numbers

Here *compatible* is not a mathematical term. It refers to numbers that would make the problem easier to compute mentally. One of the best uses of the compatible-numbers strategy is in division. Adjusting the divisor or dividend (or both) to close numbers to create a division that results in a whole number is easy to do mentally. Many percent, fraction, and rate situations involve division, and the compatible numbers strategy is quite useful, as shown in Figure 11.20.

Figure **11.20**

Using compatible numbers in division.

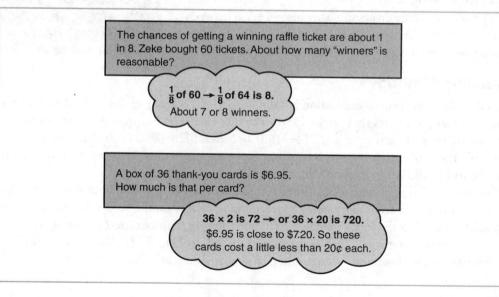

The chances of getting a winning raffle ticket are about 1 in 8. Zeke bought 60 tickets. About how many "winners" is reasonable?

$\frac{1}{8}$ of 60 → $\frac{1}{8}$ of 64 is 8.
About 7 or 8 winners.

A box of 36 thank-you cards is $6.95. How much is that per card?

36 × 2 is 72 → or 36 × 20 is 720.
$6.95 is close to $7.20. So these cards cost a little less than 20¢ each.

High or Low

Content and Task Decisions

Mathematics Goals

- To be able to explain that computational estimates are based on calculations of simpler related problems that can be computed mentally.

- To develop the concept that there are different estimates that can be made for a given computation and that some estimates can be better than others.

Grade Level Guide

NCTM Curriculum Focal Points	Common Core State Standards
In a Focal Point at grade 4 under Number and Operations and Algebra, students estimate products or use mental math to calculate multiplication problems with whole numbers.	At grade 4, students multiply whole numbers using strategies based on place value and the properties of operations.

Consider Your Students' Needs

Students' prerequisite knowledge needed for this lesson depends to a large degree on which operations the lesson addresses. Because this particular lesson focuses on multiplication, students should have some experience with mental math for multiplication. For example, they should have at least been working on determining products such as 34×6 or 80×40 mentally. However, the lesson does not require students to actually do these computations.

For English Language Learners

- In the *Before* phase, be sure to talk about what an estimate is, and discuss the meaning of the words *high* and *low*.

- Write "high" and "low" on the board, positioned to show what they mean. Practice saying the words, if needed.

- In the *During* phase, group students so that those needing language support are with others that speak their language or students who will be inclusive. Sometimes pairs are better than bigger groups.

For Students with Disabilities

- Instead of giving students who are struggling the three high/low comparisons, have one computation and three very different cards to compare. Have the students decide which of the three estimations would be a good one for the computation. After reaching success with this first step, then students can move on to more fine-tuned distinctions.

Materials

Each student will need:

- "High or Low?" recording sheet (see Blackline Master 23)

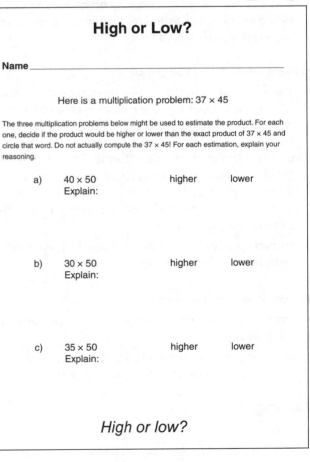

High or Low?

Name _____

Here is a multiplication problem: 37×45

The three multiplication problems below might be used to estimate the product. For each one, decide if the product would be higher or lower than the exact product of 37×45 and circle that word. Do not actually compute the 37×45! For each estimation, explain your reasoning.

a)	40×50 Explain:	higher	lower
b)	30×50 Explain:	higher	lower
c)	35×50 Explain:	higher	lower

High or low?

Lesson

Before

Begin with a simpler version of the task:

- On the board write 74×8. "Suppose you wanted to know the cost of eight snack bags that cost 74 cents. You don't really need to know the exact cost, just if $5.00 will be enough. How would you estimate this problem?"

- Ask students to share their strategies and discuss with students why they might want to round up or round down.

- Write 80×10 on the board. "Would your estimate be higher or lower than the exact answer to 74×8?"

- Explain that students are not to compute either 78×8 or 80×10 but only decide whether 80×10 is higher or lower than 78×8. Call on at least two students to share their reasoning.

- Repeat with 70×10 and 80×8 as possible estimates for the same product.

- Ask, "Is $5.00 enough?"

- State, "Today we will be working on estimating and deciding whether our estimates are higher or lower than the exact answer would be."

Present the focus task to the class:

- The handout consists of one multiplication problem (37×45) and three possible mental math multiplication problems that could be used to estimate the product of the original problem. For each mental math estimation problem the students' task is to decide whether that problem would yield a higher or lower product than the exact product of 37×45. Students circle "higher" or "lower" next to each and then explain why they think it is higher or lower.

- Students are not to actually compute the multiplication problems on the worksheet.

Provide clear expectations:

- Emphasize that students are not to perform any computation.

- Because students will be asked to share their responses, they should be prepared to explain their thinking.

During

Initially:

- Monitor students to be sure that they are not computing.

Ongoing:

- If a student has circled "lower" but is puzzled with what to write, ask, "How did you decide that it would be lower?" Listen to the student's thinking and encourage him or her to put those ideas, regardless of correctness or sophistication, in writing.

- Use the questions below to discuss the students' estimation skills.

After

Bring the class together to share and discuss the task:

- Examine each estimation multiplication problem separately. First ask who thinks the estimate is higher and who thinks it is lower.

- Call on students on both sides to explain their reasoning. Allow students to convince each other. Do not evaluate. Rather, ask other students if they understand the explanations. Do they have questions? Do they disagree and if so, why? The evaluation should come from the students' discussion.

- Note that for the problems on this worksheet, the first example is easier because both factors are greater than the factors in the original problem. Use this problem to call on students who may not be able to give explanations for the other two estimation problems.

- Ask, "Is there another estimation strategy that you might try?"

- Ask, "If the numbers were different, would these estimation strategies still work?"

Assessment

Observe

- When both factors have been adjusted in the same direction—either both up or both down—the explanation should be easy and reflect an understanding of what multiplication means. Students who have difficulty with these explanations may not have a good grasp of the concept of multiplication.

- When the two factors have been adjusted in opposite directions, the explanation is more difficult and students may have difficulty making their arguments without some assistance. Suggest that students break the numbers into partial products: 30×40, 7×40, 30×5, 5×7. Compare these pieces to 30×50. If students have difficulty with these ideas, they should probably investigate products using the area model for multiplication as described in Figure 11.12 on page 187 in the text.

Ask

- How did you decide whether an estimation problem would give a higher or lower product?

- Which estimation problem do you think would give a product closest to the exact product? Why?

- Why do you think 40×50 was used to estimate 37×45? Why was 35×50 used?

12

Exploring Fraction Concepts

Big IDEAS

1 Fractional parts are equal shares or parts (with equal measurements) of a whole or unit. The whole must be specified because it can be continuous (area or a measure) or discrete (collection of a set of objects). Examples of these wholes are area (e.g., a garden), measure (e.g., an inch), and set (e.g., students in the class).

2 Fractions are numbers with special names that tell how many parts of that size are needed to make the whole, written in the form $\frac{a}{b}$ (when b is not zero). For example, *thirds* require three parts to make a whole. And one of those parts would be *one-third*. By partitioning (thirds) and iterating the unit fraction (one-third, two-thirds, three-thirds, etc.) students understand the meaning of fractions, especially numerators and denominators.

3 When partitioning a whole into more equal shares the parts become smaller. For example, eighths are smaller than fifths.

4 Estimating with fractions is critical to understanding their magnitude or position on the number line.

5 When two fractions are equivalent that means there are two ways of describing the same amount by using different-sized fractional parts.

6 Fractions must be experienced using many interpretations, including part of a whole, ratios, and division.

 **Meanings of Fractions**

One of the major changes in emphasis in the *Common Core State Standards for Mathematics* is in the increased prominence of fractions in grades 3 through 5. Fractions present a considerable challenge, and when they are not learned well that can result in shortcomings. This is noted in the recent IES practice guide *Developing Effective Fractions Instruction for Kindergarten through 8th Grade*, in which the authors state, "A high percentage of U.S. students lack conceptual understanding of fractions, even after studying fractions for several years; this, in turn, limits students' ability to solve problems" (Siegler et al.,

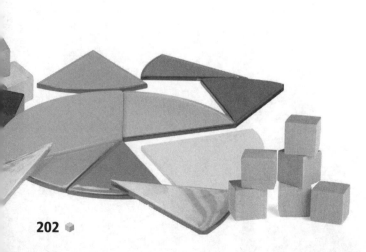

2010, p. 6). The topic of fractions is where students often give up trying to understand mathematics and instead resort to rules.

◆ Fractions as Equal Shares

The first goal in the development of fractions should be to help students construct the idea of *fractional parts of the whole*—the parts that result when the whole or unit has been partitioned into equal-sized portions or equal shares. This too is the progression established in the *Common Core State Standards* (CCSSO, 2012) when first and second graders begin to partition circular and rectangular shapes into equal parts as they use the language of fractions, such as halves, fourths, and thirds to describe those subdivisions. Students eventually make connections between the idea of partitioning into fair shares and fractional parts. Considerable research has been done with students from first through eighth grades to determine how they go about the process of forming fair shares and how the tasks posed to students influence their responses (e.g., Empson, 2002; Mack, 2004; Pothier & Sawada, 1983). To help students build on this research, Siegler and his colleagues state, "Build on students' informal understanding of sharing and proportionality to develop initial fraction concepts" (Siegler et al., 2010, p. 1). Students in the primary grades partition by thinking about fair shares (division); therefore sharing tasks are good places to begin.

You will generally pose sharing tasks as simple story problems: "Suppose there are four square brownies to be shared among three children so that each child gets the same amount. How much (or show how much) will each child get?" Task difficulty changes with the numbers involved, the types of things to be shared (regions such as brownies, discrete objects such as pieces of chewing gum), and the presence or use of a physical model.

Students initially perform sharing tasks (division) by distributing items one at a time. When this process leaves leftover pieces, it is much easier to think of sharing them fairly if the items can be subdivided or partitioned. Typical "regions" to share are brownies (rectangles), sandwiches, pizzas, crackers, quesadillas, candy bars, and so on. The problems and variations that follow are adapted from Empson (2002).

Problem difficulty is determined by the relationship between the number of things to be shared and the number of sharers. Because students' initial strategies for sharing involve halving, a good place to begin is with two, four, and then eight sharers. For ten brownies and four sharers, many students will deal out two to each child and then halve each of the remaining brownies (see Figure 12.1).

Consider these variations in numbers:

- 5 brownies shared with 2 children
- 4 brownies shared with 8 children
- 2 brownies shared with 4 children
- 5 brownies shared with 4 children
- 3 brownies shared with 4 children

The last example, three brownies shared with four children, is significantly more challenging. When the numbers allow for some items to be distributed whole (ten shared with four), some students will first share whole items and then partition the leftovers. Others will slice every piece in half

> **Teaching Tip**
>
> Note that when you use the word *equal*, make sure students realize that it means equal in amount, because the resulting equal shares may not be the same shape or have the same number of pieces.

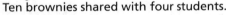

Figure 12.1

Ten brownies shared with four students.

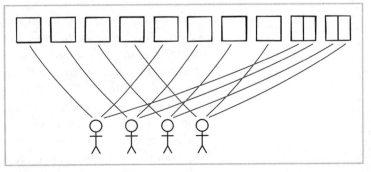

Figure 12.2

Three different sharing processes.

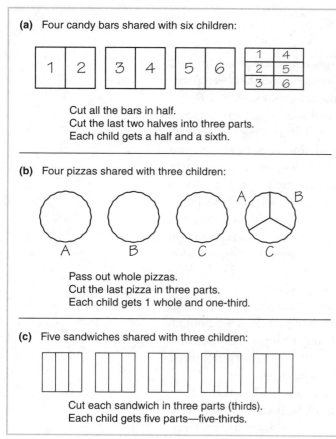

(a) Four candy bars shared with six children:

Cut all the bars in half.
Cut the last two halves into three parts.
Each child gets a half and a sixth.

(b) Four pizzas shared with three children:

Pass out whole pizzas.
Cut the last pizza in three parts.
Each child gets 1 whole and one-third.

(c) Five sandwiches shared with three children:

Cut each sandwich in three parts (thirds).
Each child gets five parts—five-thirds.

Teaching Tip

For all students, and particularly for ELLs, fraction parts often sound like whole numbers (e.g., fourths and fours). Be sure to emphasize the *th* on the end of the word and explicitly discuss the difference between four areas and a *fourth of* an area. Also, write and discuss the meaning of the words *whole* and *hole*.

and then distribute the halves. When there are more sharers than items, some partitioning must happen at the beginning of the solution process.

When students who are still using a halving strategy try to share five things among four children, they will eventually get down to two halves to give to four children. For some, the solution is to cut each half in half—that is, each child gets a whole (or two halves) and a half of a half.

When you think your students are ready, move them on the progression to three or six sharers. This will force students to confront their halving strategies as in the previous problem. To subdivide a region into a number of parts other than a power of two (four, eight, etc.) requires an odd number of subdivisions at some point. Several types of sharing solutions might be observed. Figure 12.2 shows three different approaches. Use a variety of representations for these problems. Start with paper circles (or squares) because some students may need to cut the paper and physically distribute the pieces.

During the discussions of students' solutions to the sharing tasks (and discussions are essential!) is a good time to reinforce the vocabulary of fractional parts. When a brownie or other area has been broken into four equal shares, simply say, "We call these fourths. The whole is cut into four parts. All of the parts are the same size—fourths."

As always, it is important to meet the needs of the range of learners in your classroom. The level of difficulty of the sharing tasks can vary depending on the background your students bring from the primary grades. A lesson geared to three ability ranges can be implemented to provide appropriate tasks for different students while still enabling all students to learn the important mathematics of the lesson (fair sharing as a meaning of fractions). Figure 12.3 shows how one teacher offers these three tiers (easy, middle, and advanced) for her lesson on sharing brownies.

◆ Fraction Interpretations

"The concept of unit is fundamental to the interpretation of rational numbers" (Barnett-Clarke, Fisher, Marks, & Ross, 2010, p. 19). Sometimes the words *whole* and *unit* are used interchangeably in discussing fractions, but the unit must be thought about to interpret all the possible concepts that fractions can represent. These interpretations appear to be developmental in nature.

One of the basic interpretations people immediately visualize is the part–whole relationship, including mental examples of part of a whole as shaded. Although the part–whole model is the one most used in textbooks, researcher suggest that students would understand fractions better if there were more emphasis across the different meanings or interpretations of fractions (Clarke, Roche, & Mitchell, 2008; Siebert & Gaskin, 2006). Let's look at some of the other meanings.

Figure 12.3

Examples of differentiating brownie sharing problems. Easy Tasks are for students who still need experiences with creating halves. Middle Tasks are for students comfortable with creating halves and ready to have experiences with other strategies. Advanced Tasks are for students who are ready to combine halving with new strategies.

Easy Tasks	Middle Tasks	Advanced Tasks
How can 2 people share 3 brownies?	How can 4 people share 3 brownies?	How can 3 people share 2 brownies?
How can 2 people share 5 brownies?	How can 3 people share 5 brownies?	How can 3 people share 7 brownies?
How can 3 people share 4 brownies?	How can 6 people share 4 brownies?	How can 5 people share 4 brownies?

Source: Adapted from Williams, L. (2008). Tiering and Scaffolding: Two Strategies for Providing Access to Important Mathematics. *Teaching Children Mathematics, 14*(6), 324–330.

Stop and Reflect

Beyond shading a region of a shape, how else are fractions represented? Before we move to the next section, try to name three other interpretations of fractions. ■

Part–Whole Relationship

Using the part–whole interpretation is an effective starting point for building meaning of fractions (Cramer & Whitney, 2010). But keep in mind that part–whole goes well beyond shading a region. For example, it could be part of a group of people ($\frac{3}{5}$ of the class went on the field trip), or it could be part of a length (we walked $3\frac{1}{2}$ of a 5-mile hike). Cramer, Wyberg, and Leavitt (2008) note that the circle model is particularly effective in illustrating the part–whole relationship.

Measurement

Measurement involves identifying an amount of a continuous unit (length, area, volume, or time), and then comparing that amount to a whole unit that is equal to 1. For example, in the fraction $\frac{1}{2}$ of a mile, you can use the amount as the subdivision and compare it to 1 mile. This concept focuses on how much rather than how many parts, which is the case in part–whole situations (Behr, Lesh, Post, & Silver, 1983; Martinie, 2007). The number line models a linear unit and is subdivided into equal amounts with the length between 0 and 1 as the unit.

Division

This interpretation links directly to the previous discussion about equal shares. Consider the idea of sharing $10 with 4 people. This is not a part–whole scenario, but it still means that each person will receive one-fourth ($\frac{1}{4}$) of the money, or $\frac{10}{4}$ or $2\frac{1}{2}$ dollars. Division is often not connected to fractions, which is unfortunate. Students should understand and feel comfortable with the example written as $\frac{10}{4}$, $4\overline{)10}$, $10 \div 4$, $2\frac{2}{4}$, and $2\frac{1}{2}$ (Flores, Samson, & Yanik, 2006).

Operator

Fractions can be used to indicate an operation, as in $\frac{4}{5}$ of 20 square feet, or $\frac{2}{3}$ of the audience was holding banners. In these situations the operator (fraction) changes the size or scale (e.g., shrinks, enlarges) through multiplication. Researchers note that this construct is not emphasized enough in school curricula (Usiskin, 2007). Just knowing how to represent fractions doesn't mean students will know how to operate with fractions, such as when working in other areas of the mathematics curriculum in which fractions are used (Johanning, 2008).

Ratio

The concept of ratio is yet another interpretation that comes into play in Grade 6 (CCSSO, 2010). A ratio "expresses a relationship between two (and sometimes more) quantities or parts of quantities and compares their relative measures or counts" (Barnett-Clarke et al., 2010, p. 25). Ratios can be part–part or part–whole. For example, the ratio $\frac{3}{4}$ could be the ratio of those wearing jackets (part) to those not wearing jackets (part), or it could be part–whole, meaning those wearing jackets (part) to those in the class (whole). Ratios can also be written as a percent.

Were these among the ideas you listed in responding to the Stop and Reflect?

◆ Why Students Find Fractions So Difficult

Although we want students to build on prior knowledge of whole numbers, fractions become more challenging when students misapply whole-number thinking to solve fraction situations. You need to find ways to help students see how fractions are like and different from whole numbers. The following list shows some common misapplications of whole-number knowledge to fractions that may assist you in pinpointing or heading off problems:

Teaching Tip

Avoid referring to the "top number" and the "bottom number" when speaking about fractions. This language reinforces the overgeneralization of whole-number thinking. Also, avoid the phrase "three *out of* four" (unless talking about ratios or probability) or "three *over* four" and instead say "three fourths" (Siebert & Gaskin, 2006).

1. Students think that the numerator and denominator are separate values and have difficulty seeing them as a single value (Cramer & Whitney, 2010). It is hard for them to see that $\frac{3}{4}$ is one number. Finding fraction values on a number line or ruler can help students develop this notion.

2. In thinking of the numbers separately, students may think that $\frac{2}{3}$ means any two parts, not equal-sized parts. For example, students may think that this shape shows $\frac{3}{4}$ shaded, rather than $\frac{1}{2}$ shaded:

3. Students think that a fraction such as $\frac{1}{5}$ is smaller than a fraction such as $\frac{1}{10}$ because 5 is less than 10. Many visuals and contexts that show parts of the same whole are essential in helping students understand. For example, ask students if they would rather have $\frac{1}{2}$ a pie, $\frac{1}{4}$ of a pie, or $\frac{1}{10}$ of a pie and have them explain why. Conversely, students may be told the bigger the denominator, the smaller the fraction. Teaching such rules, without providing concrete examples and reasons, may lead students to overgeneralize that $\frac{1}{5}$ is greater than $\frac{7}{10}$.

4. Students mistakenly use the operation "rules" for whole numbers to compute with fractions, for example, $\frac{1}{2} + \frac{1}{2} = \frac{2}{4}$. Explorations with actual fractional pieces will support students in reaching more generalizable "rules" and more reasonable answers.

Until students understand fractions meaningfully, they will continue to make errors by over-applying whole-number concepts (Cramer & Whitney, 2010; Lamon, 2012; Siegler et al., 2010). This chapter is designed to help your students acquire a deep understanding of fractions.

 Models for Fractions

Substantial evidence suggests that effectively using physical models in fraction tasks is important (Cramer & Henry, 2002; Empson & Levi, 2011; Siebert & Gaskin, 2006). Yet textbooks rarely encourage manipulatives, and when they do, they tend to use only area models (Hodges, Cady, & Collins, 2008). This means that students often do not explore fractions with a variety of models or do not have sufficient time to connect the models to the related concepts. In fact, what appears to be critical in learning is that the use of physical tools leads to the use of mental models, and this builds students' understanding of fractions (Cramer & Whitney, 2010; Petit, Laird, & Marsden, 2010). Properly used, tools can help students clarify ideas that are often confused in a purely symbolic form.

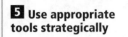

Standards for Mathematical Practice

5 Use appropriate tools strategically

Sometimes it is useful to do the same activity with two different representations as they offer different opportunities to learn. For example, an area model helps students visualize parts of the whole, and a linear model shows that there is always another fraction to be found between any two numbers.

Including real-world contexts that are meaningful to students is important (Cramer & Whitney, 2010) because often one representation is more aligned with the context over another. For example, if students are being asked who walked the farthest, a linear model is more likely to support their thinking than an area model. Let's look at three categories of models: area and length (which are both continuous models) and set (discrete units or objects).

◆ Area Models

In the discussion of the sharing tasks, all of the tasks involve sharing something that could be cut into smaller parts. The fractions are based on parts of an area. This is a good model to begin with and it is almost essential when doing sharing tasks. There are many good area models, as shown in Figure 12.4.

Teaching Tip

In initial development of the concepts, student-drawn area models of wholes with partitions have limitations because they may lead students to incorrect answers due to their lack of precision. When possible, start students with outlines to use in which the wholes are the same size and talk about how you think about partitioning same-sized units. Also show counterexamples, by sharing inaccurately drawn models so students can focus on important features to consider.

Figure 12.4 Area or region models for fractions.

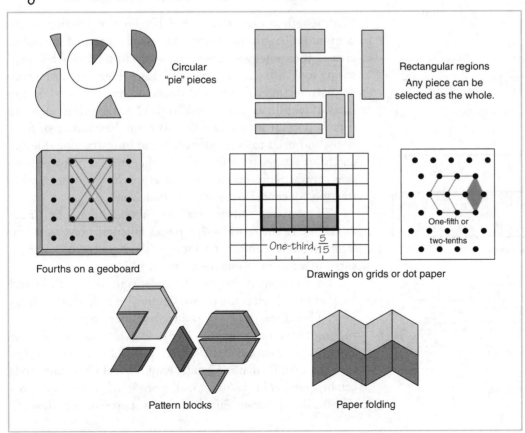

Circular fraction pieces are the most commonly used (see Blackline Masters 24, 25, and 26) as they emphasize the part–whole concept of fractions and the meaning of the relative size of a part to the whole (Cramer et al., 2008). The other models in Figure 12.4 demonstrate how different shapes can be the whole.

The following activity is an example of how area models can be used to help students develop concepts of equal shares.

Activity 12.1 PLAYGROUND FRACTIONS

Create this "playground" with your pattern blocks. It is the whole or unit. For each fraction below, find the pieces of the playground and draw it on your paper:

$\frac{1}{2}$ playground $\frac{1}{3}$ playground

$1\frac{1}{2}$ playground $\frac{2}{2}$ playground

2 playgrounds $\frac{4}{3}$ playground

Source: Adapted from Roddick & Silvas-Centeno (2007). Developing understanding of fractions through pattern blocks and fair trade. *Teaching Children Mathematics, 14*(3), 140–145. Reprinted with permission. Copyright 2007, by the National Council of Teachers of Mathematics. All rights reserved.

Figure 12.5
Length or measurement models for fractions.

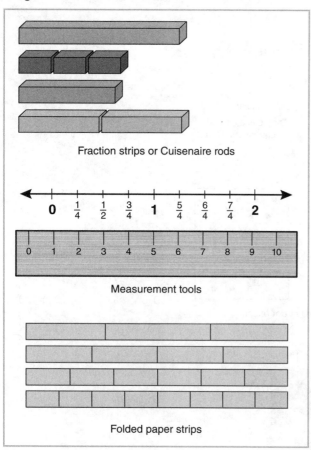

Fraction strips or Cuisenaire rods

Measurement tools

Folded paper strips

◆ Length or Measurement Models

With length models such as number lines or fraction strips, continuous lengths or measurements are compared instead of areas. Either lines are drawn on paper and subdivided, a measuring tool with a scale is used (such as a ruler, measuring cup, or thermometer), or physical materials are compared on the basis of length, as shown in Figure 12.5. Length models are very important in developing student understanding of fractions, and need to be used more often in instruction. Siegler and his colleagues (2010) advise teachers to "use number lines as a central representational tool in teaching this and other fraction concepts from the early grades on" (p. 1).

To prepare students for the number line, one linear model—Cuisenaire rods—has pieces in lengths of 1 to 10 cm long, each one a different color (e.g., the 2 cm rod is red) measured in terms of the smallest strip or rod.

For example, if you wanted students to work with $\frac{1}{4}$ s and $\frac{1}{8}$ s, you would select the brown Cuisenaire rod, which is 8 cm long. Therefore, the 4-cm rod (purple) becomes $\frac{1}{2}$, the 2-cm rod (red) becomes $\frac{1}{4}$, and the 1-cm rod (white) becomes $\frac{1}{8}$. For exploring twelfths, put the orange rod and red rod together to make a whole that is 12 units long. Virtual Cuisenaire rods can be found at http://nrich.maths.org/4782. These rods provide flexibility because any length can represent the whole.

Another linear model can be made from strips of paper or cash register tape which can be folded to produce student-made fraction strips. This too supports the eventual use of the number line and bar diagrams to think about fractional problems.

The number line is a significantly more sophisticated measurement model and a powerful tool for thinking about fractions (Bright, Behr, Post, & Wachsmuth, 1988). In fact, many researchers have found it to be an essential model that should be heavily emphasized in the teaching of fractions (Clarke et al., 2008; Flores et al., 2006; Siegler et al., 2010; Usiskin, 2007). Furthermore, in the *Common Core State Standards* (CCSSO, 2010), third graders are expected to place fractions on the number line. This is one of the few places in the document where a specific instructional model is stipulated. Using the number line helps students define the unit fraction—particularly the length of the unit (from 0 to the labeled point) on the number line. You will find this model also serves as a bridge that links fractions back to whole numbers while preparing students for integers and algebra.

Linear models are closely connected to the real-world contexts in which fractions are commonly used—measuring. Dougherty and her colleagues (Dougherty, Flores, Louis, & Sophian, 2010) emphasize the value of incorporating measurement situations as a way for you to support student progression from whole numbers to rational numbers.

The number line also allows comparisons in a fraction's relative size to other numbers, which is not as clear when using area models. Importantly, the number line reinforces that there is always one more fraction to be found between two fractions. The following activity (adapted from Bay-Williams & Martinie, 2003) uses a real-world context to engage students in thinking about fractions through a linear model.

Teaching Tip

Students often have difficulty with positioning fractions on the number line. Make sure they recognize that each number on a line designates the distance of the identified point from zero, not the point itself.

Standards for Mathematical Practice

◄ **6** Attend to precision

Activity 12.2 WHO IS WINNING?

The friends below are playing "Red Light, Green Light" and the fractions next to their names represent how far they are from the start line. Who do you think is winning? Can you place these friends on a line to show where they are between the start and finish?

Emma—$\frac{3}{4}$	Meredith—$\frac{1}{2}$	Jack—$\frac{5}{6}$
Han—$\frac{5}{8}$	Miguel—$\frac{5}{9}$	Angelika—$\frac{2}{3}$

The game "Red Light, Green Light" may not be familiar to some students, especially ELLs. Modeling the game, with students in the class taking positions on a number line on the floor (clearly mark the starting point) and having the students talk about how they are estimating their location, is a good way to build background and support students with disabilities.

◆ Set Models

In set models, the whole is understood to be a set of individual (discrete) objects, and subsets of the whole make up fractional parts. For example, when a set of 12 objects represents 1 or the whole, 3 objects are one-fourth. The idea of referring to a collection of counters as a single unit makes set models difficult for some students. Students will frequently focus

Figure 12.6 Set models for fractions.

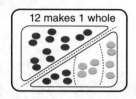
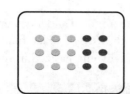

12 makes 1 whole

Two-color counters in sets showing $1\frac{1}{3}$ dark gray. The whole must be clearly indicated.

Two-color counters in arrays. Rows and columns help show parts. Each array makes a whole. Here $\frac{9}{15}$ or $\frac{3}{5}$ are light gray.

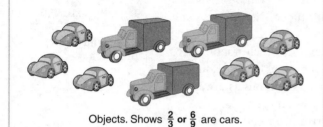

Objects. Shows $\frac{2}{3}$ or $\frac{6}{9}$ are cars.

on the size of the subset rather than the number of equal sets in the whole. For example, if 12 counters make a whole, then a set of 4 counters is one-third, not one-fourth, because 3 equal sets make the whole. Figure 12.6 illustrates several set models for fractions.

Counters in two colors on opposite sides are frequently used. They can easily be flipped to change their color to model various fractional parts of a whole set. Also, students with disabilities (and others) may be supported by putting a piece of yarn in a loop around the items in the set to help "see" the whole. The following activity can be done as an energizer.

Activity 12.3 CLASS FRACTIONS

Use a group of students as the whole—for example, six students. If you want to work on thirds, halves, and sixths, ask students, "What fraction of our group [are wearing tennis shoes, have brown hair, etc.]?" Change the number of people over time.

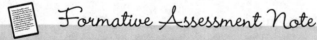

An increasing number of Web resources are available to help represent fractions. One excellent free source (although subscription based) is Conceptua Fractions at www.conceptuamath.com. This site offers area, set, and length models (including the number line).

Formative Assessment Note

Students must be able to explore fractions across the three categories of models because they will need to use the model that is most effective for a particular context. You will not know whether they really understand the meaning of a fraction unless you have seen a student represent a particular fraction using area, length, and set models. A straightforward way to assess students' knowledge of a fractional amount is to give them a piece of paper folded into thirds; write *area, length,* and *set* at the top of each section and observe as they draw a picture and write a sentence describing a context or example in all three ways for a selected fraction (e.g., $\frac{3}{4}$).

Fractional Parts of a Whole

A key idea about fractions that students must come to understand is that a fraction does not say anything about the size of the whole or the size of the parts. A fraction tells us only about the relationship between the part and the whole. Consider the following situation:

Mark is offered the choice of a third of a pizza or a half of a pizza. Because he is hungry and likes pizza, he chooses the half. His friend Jane gets a third of a pizza but ends up with more than Mark. How can that be?

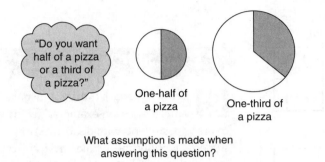

"Do you want half of a pizza or a third of a pizza?"

One-half of a pizza

One-third of a pizza

What assumption is made when answering this question?

The visual illustrates how Mark was misdirected in his choice. The point of the "pizza fallacy" is that whenever two or more fractions are discussed in the same context, one cannot assume (as Mark did in choosing a half of a pizza) that the fractions are all parts of the same size whole. Comparing two fractions with any representation can be made only if both fractions are parts of the same size whole.

Make it a point to use the terms *whole*, *one whole*, or simply *one* so that students have a language that they can use regardless of the model involved.

◆ Partitioning

Sectioning a whole into equal-sized pieces is called *partitioning*, a major part of developing fraction concepts. When partitioning a whole into fractional parts, students need to be aware that (1) the fractional parts must be the same size, though not necessarily the same shape, and (2) the number of equal-sized parts that can be partitioned within the unit determines the fractional amount (e.g., partitioning into 4 parts means each part is $\frac{1}{4}$ of the unit). You can partition regions or shapes (area models), a number line, paper strips, or sets of objects such as coins, counters, or baseball cards.

Partitioning with Area Models

Too often, when students are asked questions about what fraction is shaded, they are shown regions that are portioned into pieces of the same size and shape. The result is that students think that equal shares need to be the same shape, which is not the case. On the other hand, sometimes visuals do not show all the partitions. For example, consider the following picture:

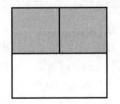

Referring back to the two criteria, a student might think, "If I partitioned the whole so that all pieces are the same size, then there will be four parts; therefore, the smaller partitioned region represents one-fourth." Many students without a conceptual understanding might suggest one-third. Again, emphasize that the number of equal parts that make up a whole determines the name of the fractional parts or shares.

The following activity focuses on partitioning, having examples that are (1) same shape, same size; (2) different shape, same size; (3) different shape, different size; and

Figure 12.7

Students should be able to tell (1) which of these figures are correctly partitioned in fourths and (2) why the other figures are not showing fourths.

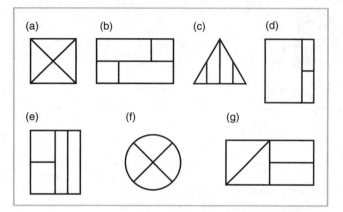

(4) same shape, different size. The first two categories are examples of fair shares, or equivalent shares. It is important that students can tell when an area has been separated into a particular type of fractional part.

Activity 12.4 CORRECT SHARES

Draw regions like those in Figure 12.7, showing examples and non-examples (which are very important to use with students with disabilities) of fractional parts. Have students identify the wholes that are correctly partitioned into requested fractional parts and those that are not. For each response, have students explain their reasoning.

Formative Assessment Note

The "Correct Shares" task is a good diagnostic interview to assess whether students understand that it is the *size* that matters, not the shape. Have students explain why they do or do not think the shape is partitioned correctly. The most important part is the discussion of the non-examples. If students identify all the wholes that are correctly portioned except (e) and (g), they do not understand this concept and you need to plan future tasks that focus on equivalence— for example, asking students to take a square on a geoboard or dot paper and partition it into halves, fourths, or other fractional parts.

Partitioning with Length Models

On a number line, students may ignore the distance or length of each part (McNamara & Shaughnessy, 2010; Petit, Laird, & Marsden, 2010), which challenges them in recognizing and creating accurately partitioned length models. As with the area models, providing examples in which the partitioning isn't already illustrated can help students develop a stronger understanding of equal parts. Students can develop these skills by folding their own paper strips.

Activity 12.5 provides another option for students to explore number lines that are not fully partitioned.

Activity 12.5 HOW FAR DID SHE GO?

Give students number lines partitioned such that only some of the partitions are showing. Use a context such as walking to school. For each number line, ask, "How far has Nicole gone? How do you know?"

Students can justify their reasoning by measuring the size of the sections that have been partitioned. Student with disabilities may need to work on this diagram in a larger scale, such as made with tape or chalk on the classroom floor. Once the lines are marked and labeled, students can move to the various points to consider the size of the segments from zero.

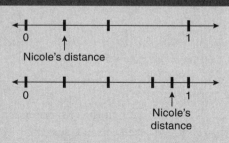

Partitioning with Set Models

When partitioning sets, students frequently confuse the number of counters in a share with the name of the share. In the example in Figure 12.8, the 12 counters are partitioned into six sets, or sixths. Each share or part has two counters, but each section should not to be mistaken as halves—it is the number of shares that makes the partition show sixths. As with the other models, when the equal parts are not already figured out, students may not see how to partition. Students seeing a picture of two cats and four dogs might think $\frac{2}{4}$ are cats (Bamberger, Oberdorf, & Schultz-Ferrell, 2010). Consider the following problem:

Figure 12.8

Given a whole, find fractional parts.

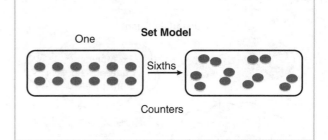

Eloise has 6 trading cards, Andre has 4 trading cards, and Lu has 2 trading cards. What fraction of the trading cards does Lu have?

As discussed previously, a student who answers "one-third" is not thinking about equal shares but about the number of people with trading cards.

Understanding that parts of a whole must be partitioned into equal-sized shares across different models is an important step in conceptualizing fractions and provides a foundation for exploring equivalence tasks, which are prerequisite to performing fraction operations (Cramer & Whitney, 2010).

◆ Iterating

In whole-number learning, counting precedes and helps students compare the size of numbers and later to add and subtract. This is also true with fractions. Counting fractional parts, initially unit fractions, to see how multiple parts compare to the whole helps students understand the relationship between the parts (the numerator) and the whole (the denominator). (A *unit fraction* is a single fractional part. The fractions $\frac{1}{3}$ and $\frac{1}{8}$ are unit fractions.) Students should come to think of counting fractional parts in much the same way as they might count apples or other objects. If you know the kind of part you are counting, you can tell when you get to one whole, when you get to two wholes, and so on. Students should be able to answer the question, "How many fifths are in one whole?" just as they know how many ones are in ten. However, in the 2008 National Assessment of Education Progress (NAEP) only 44 percent of fourth grade students answered that question correctly (Rampey, Dion, & Donahue, 2009).

This counting or repeating a piece is called iterating. Like partitioning, iterating is an important part of being able to understand and use fractions. Understanding that $\frac{3}{4}$ can be thought of as a count of three parts called fourths is an important idea for students to develop (Post, Wachsmuth, Lesh, & Behr, 1985; Siebert & and Gaskin, 2006; Tzur, 1999). The iterative concept is most clear when focusing on these two ideas about fraction symbols:

- The numerator *counts*.
- The denominator tells what fractional part is being counted.

Fraction symbols are just a shorthand for saying *how many* and *what*.

Iterating makes sense with length models because iteration is much like measuring. What if you have $2\frac{1}{2}$ feet of ribbon and are trying to figure out how many fourths of a foot you have? You can draw a strip and start iterating (counting) the fourths:

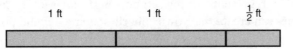

Figure 12.9

Iterating fractional parts using an area model (see Blackline Masters 24, 25, and 26).

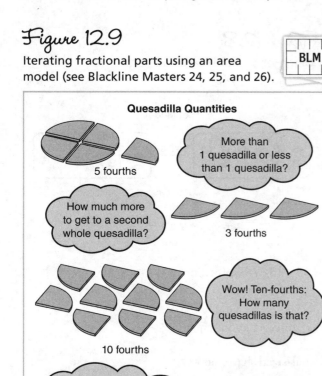

Using a ribbon that is $\frac{1}{4}$ of a foot long as a measuring tool, a student marks off ten fourths:

Then have students simply count them together: "*one-fourth, two-fourths, three-fourths, four-fourths, five-fourths.*" Pause and ask, "If we have five-fourths, is that more than one whole, less than one whole, or the same as one whole?" Then continue counting. To reinforce the piece size even more, you can slightly alter your language to emphasize the unit fraction saying, "One one-fourth, two one-fourths, three one-fourths," and so on.

Students can participate in many tasks that involve iterating lengths, progressing in increasing difficulty. For example, give the students a strip of paper and tell them that it is $\frac{3}{4}$ of the whole. Then ask them to find $\frac{1}{2}$, $1\frac{1}{2}$, $2\frac{1}{4}$, and 3. To find these, students should partition the paper strip into three sections to first find $\frac{1}{4}$ and then iterate the $\frac{1}{4}$ to find the fractions listed.

Iterating can be done with area models as well. Display some circular fractional pieces in groups as shown in Figure 12.9. For each collection, tell students what type of piece is being shown and simply count them together. See the bubbles in the figure for some great questions to ask as your students are counting each collection of parts. Also discuss the relationship to one whole. Make informal comparisons between different collections: "Why did we get more than two wholes with ten-fourths, and yet we don't even have one whole with ten-twelfths?"

Now is the time to lay verbal groundwork for mixed fractions. "What is another way that we could say ten-fourths?" (Two wholes and two more fourths or one whole and six fourths). With this background, students are ready for the following activity.

◢ Activity 12.6 MORE, LESS, OR EQUAL TO ONE WHOLE

Give students a collection of fractional parts (all the same size pieces) and tell them the kind of fractional part they have. Parts can be drawn on a worksheet, or physical models can be placed in plastic baggies with an identifying card. For example, if using Cuisenaire rods or fraction strips, the collection might have seven light green rods/strips with a note indicating "each piece is $\frac{1}{8}$." The task is to decide whether the collection is less than one whole, equal to one whole, or greater than one whole. Ask students to draw pictures or use symbols to explain their answer. Then try the activity with several different fraction models and then with no model, using mental imagery only.

Iteration can also be done with set models, although it tends to be more difficult for students. For example, show a collection of two-color counters and ask questions such as, "If 5 counters is one-fourth, how much is 15 counters?" These problems can be framed as engaging puzzles for students. For example: "Three counters represent $\frac{1}{8}$ of my set; how big is my set?" "Twenty counters represent $\frac{2}{3}$ of my set; how big is my set?" Students who are skillful at doing these puzzles can create their own "puzzle statements" and pose them to the class.

Activity 12.7 CALCULATOR FRACTION COUNTING

Calculators that permit fraction entries and displays are now quite common in schools. Many, like the TI-15, now display fractions in correct fraction format and offer a choice of showing results as mixed numbers or simple fractions. Counting by fourths with the TI-15 is done by first storing $\frac{1}{4}$ in one of the two operation keys: Op1 + I n 4 d Op1. To count, press 0, Op1, Op1, Op1, repeating to get the number of fourths wanted. The display will show the counts by fourths and also the number of times that the Op1 key has been pressed. Ask students questions such as: "How many $\frac{1}{4}$s to get to 3?" "How many $\frac{1}{5}$s to get to 5?" These can get increasingly more challenging: "How many $\frac{1}{4}$s to get to $4\frac{1}{2}$?" "How many $\frac{2}{3}$s to get to 6? Estimate and then count by $\frac{2}{3}$s on the calculator." Students, particularly students with disabilities, should coordinate their counts with fraction models, adding a new fourths piece to the pile with each count. At any time the display can be shifted from mixed number form to simple fractions with a press of a key. The TI-15 can be set so that it will not simplify fractions automatically, the appropriate setting prior to the introduction of equivalent fractions.

Stop and Reflect

Work through the exercises in Figures 12.10 and 12.11. If you do not have access to Cuisenaire rods or counters, just draw lines or circles. What can you learn about student understanding if they are able to solve problems in Figure 12.10 but not 12.11? If students are stuck, what contexts for each model can be used to support their thinking? ■

As noted throughout this text, it is a good idea to create simple story problems or contexts that ask the same questions.

Mr. Samuels has finished $\frac{2}{5}$ of his patio. It looks like this:

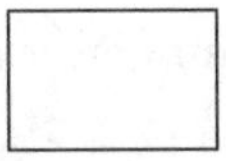

Draw a picture like this one on your paper. Then draw another that might be the size of the finished patio.

Questions involving unit fractions are generally the easiest. The hardest questions usually involve fractions greater than one. For example, problems such as the following will generally be more difficult for students: "If 15 chips are five-thirds of one whole set, how many chips are in a whole set?" However, in these kinds of

Figure 12.10
Given the whole, find the part.

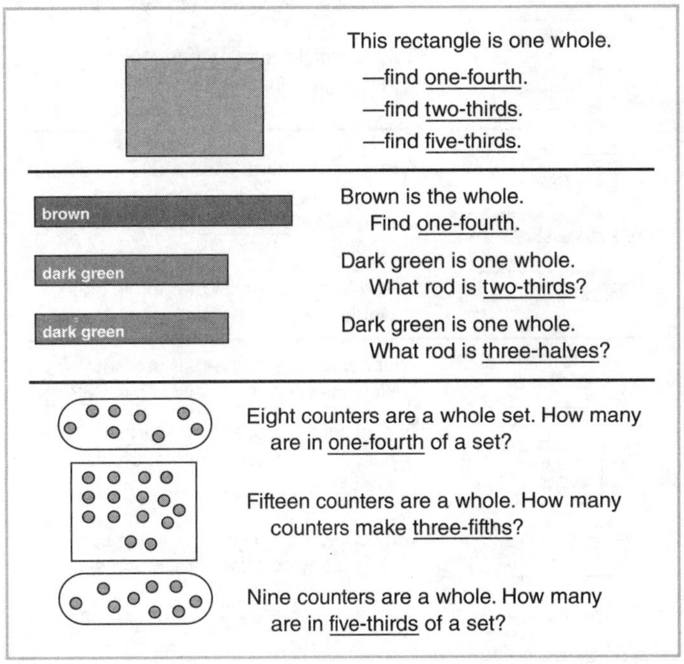

questions, the unit fraction plays a significant role (found through partitioning). If you have $\frac{5}{3}$ and want the whole, you first need to find $\frac{1}{3}$.

The parts-and-whole questions are challenging, yet very effective at helping students reflect on the meanings of the numerator and denominator.

Formative Assessment Note

The tasks in Figures 12.10 and 12.11 can be used as performance assessments. If students are able to solve these tasks, they can partition and iterate. That means they are ready to do comparison and equivalence tasks. If they are not able to solve problems such as these, provide a range of similar tasks, using real-life contexts and involving area, length, and set models.

◆ Fraction Notation

The way that we write fractions with a top component and a bottom component and a bar between is a *convention*—an agreement for how to represent fractions.

Teaching Tip

Always write fractions with a horizontal bar, not a slanted one. This is a historic convention (an accepted practice that can just be told to students) and is used because the horizontal bar will be the format consistently used in formal algebra. Write $\frac{3}{4}$, not ¾. Most word processing programs have an equation writing feature that will help you write them in this format.

We just need to tell students about conventions. However, understanding of the convention can be clarified by giving explicit attention to the meaning of the numerator and the denominator as part of activities such as those discussed previously for iterating with the ribbon and with quesadillas (Figure 12.9). Always include sets that are more than one, but write them at first as "improper" fractions and not as mixed numbers. After the class has counted and you have written the fraction for at least six sets of fractional parts, pose the following questions:

- What does the denominator in a fraction tell us?
- What does the numerator in a fraction tell us?

Here are some likely explanations from third graders:

- Numerator: This is the counting number. It tells how many shares or parts we have. It tells how many have been counted. It tells how many parts we are talking about. It counts the parts or shares.
- Denominator: This tells what is being counted. It tells how big the part is. If it is a 4, it means we are counting fourths; if it is a 6, we are counting sixths.

Figure 12.11

Given the part, find the whole.

This rectangle is one-third. What could the whole look like?

This rectangle is three-fourths. Draw a shape that could be the whole.

This rectangle is four-thirds. What rectangle could be the whole?

purple

Purple is one-third. What rod is the whole?

dark green

Dark green is two-thirds. What rod is the whole?

yellow

Yellow is five-fourths. What rod is one whole?

Four counters are one-half of a set. How many counters are in the set?

Twelve counters are three-fourths of a set. How many counters are in the full set?

Ten counters are five-halves of a set. How many counters are in one set?

This formulation of the meanings of the numerator and denominator may seem unusual to you. It is often said that the numerator tells "how many." (How many *what*?) The denominator is said to tell "how many parts it takes to make a whole." This is correct but can also be misleading. For example, a $\frac{1}{6}$ piece is often cut from a cake without making any slices in the remaining $\frac{5}{6}$ of the cake. That the cake is only in two pieces does not change the fact that the piece taken is $\frac{1}{6}$. Or if a pizza is cut in 12 pieces, two pieces still make $\frac{1}{6}$ of the pizza. So in these two examples, the denominator does not tell how many pieces make the whole.

Smith (2002) points out a slightly more "mathematical" definition of the numerator and denominator. For Smith, it is important to see the denominator as the *divisor* and the numerator as the *multiplier*. That is, $\frac{3}{4}$ is three *times* what you get when you *divide* a whole into 4 parts. This multiplier and divisor idea is especially useful when students are asked later to think of fractions as division; that is, $\frac{3}{4}$ also means $3 \div 4$.

◆ Fractions Greater Than One

Throughout this chapter, fractions less than and greater than one were mixed together. This was done intentionally and should similarly be done with students as they are learning fractions. The *Common Core State Standards* state that in third grade, students should be able to write whole numbers as fractions and identify fractions that are equivalent to whole numbers (CCSSO, 2010). Too often, students aren't exposed to fractions greater than one (e.g., $\frac{5}{2}$ or $4\frac{1}{4}$), so when they are, they find them confusing.

The term *improper fraction* is used to describe fractions such as $\frac{5}{2}$ that are greater than one.

Note that the term is *mixed number* when $\frac{5}{2}$ is in the form of $1\frac{1}{4}$.

Students must understand the many ways to represent fractions greater than one. In the fourth NAEP exam, about 80 percent of seventh graders could change a mixed number to an improper fraction, but less than half knew that $5\frac{1}{4}$ was the same as $5 + \frac{1}{4}$ (Kouba, Brown, Carpenter, Lindquist, Silver, & Swafford, 1988). This indicates that many students are using procedures without understanding them.

If you have consistently counted fractional parts beyond a whole, as in the previous section, your students already know how to write $\frac{13}{6}$ or $\frac{13}{5}$. Ask students to use a physical model to illustrate these values and find equivalent representations using wholes and fractions (mixed numbers). Neumer (2007), a fifth-grade teacher, found that using connecting cubes was the most effective way to help students see both forms for recording fractions greater than one. Figure 12.12 illustrates how to use connecting cubes to show $\frac{12}{5}$. Students identify one cube as the unit fraction $\left(\frac{1}{5}\right)$ for the problem. They count out 12 fifths and build wholes. Conversely, they could start with the mixed number, build it, and find out how many total cubes (or fifths) were used. This is an example of a length model. Repeated experiences in building and solving these tasks will lead students to see a pattern of multiplication and division that closely resembles the algorithm for moving between these two forms.

Teaching Tip

The term *improper* can be a source of confusion because it implies that this representation is not acceptable, which is false. Instead it is often the preferred representation in algebra. Avoid using this term and instead use "fraction" or "fraction greater than one." If you must use the term *improper* (due to local standards, for example), then share with students that it is really not improper at all.

Figure 12.12

Connecting cubes are used to represent the equivalence of $\frac{12}{5}$ and $2\frac{2}{5}$.

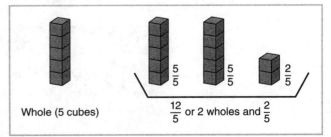

Whole (5 cubes) $\frac{5}{5}$ $\frac{5}{5}$ $\frac{2}{5}$

$\frac{12}{5}$ or 2 wholes and $\frac{2}{5}$

Context can help students understand the equivalence of these two ways to record fractions, which is the focus of Activity 12.8.

◆ *Activity* 12.8 PITCHERS AND CUPS

Show students a pitcher that can hold enough to fill six cups with juice. You can even use an actual pitcher and actual cups for sharing with the class. Ask questions such as the following: "If I have $3\frac{1}{2}$ pitchers, how many cups will I be able to fill?" and "If we have 16 students in our class, how many pitchers will I need?" Alter the amount the pitcher can hold to involve other fractions.

Help students move from models to mental images by reminding them of their experiences with iteration. Challenge students to figure out the two equivalent forms without using models. A good explanation for $3\frac{1}{4}$ might be that there are 4 fourths in one whole (they counted them), so there are 8 fourths in two wholes and 12 fourths in three wholes. The extra fourth makes 13 fourths in all, or $\frac{13}{4}$.

Delay presenting the standard algorithm (multiply the denominator by the whole number and add the numerator), because it can interfere with students making sense of the relationship themselves. This procedure can readily be developed by the students in their own words and with complete understanding by looking at patterns in their work.

◆ Estimating with Fractions

The focus on fractional parts is an important beginning, but number sense with fractions demands more—it requires that students have some intuitive feel for fractions. They should know "about" how big a particular fraction is and should be able to tell easily which of two fractions is larger.

As with whole numbers, students are often less confident and less capable of estimating than they are at computing exact answers. Therefore, you need to provide many opportunities for students to estimate. Even in daily classroom conversations, you can work on estimation with fractions, asking questions like "About what fraction of your classmates are wearing sweaters?" Or after tallying survey data about favorite dinners, ask, "About what fraction of our class picked spaghetti?"

The number line is a good model for helping students develop a better understanding for the relative size of a fraction (Petit, Laird, & Marsden, 2010). Activity 12.9 offers some examples of visual estimating activities using a rope as a number line, and it aligns with the *Common Core State Standards* third-grade standard (CCSSO, 2010) of representing fractions on a number line.

◆ *Activity* 12.9 ON THE LINE

Have two students stand and form the end points of a number line using a piece of rope. One stands at zero and the other student to the right at one whole (about 10 feet apart). Each student holding the rope will have a clothespin attached to the rope with a card marked 0 or 1 for the class to use as a guide. Give out a variety of fractions on cards with clothespins—one to each team of two students. Then ask for a volunteer team to place their fraction on the number line. The likely respondents to start may have a card with $\frac{1}{2}$ or $\frac{1}{4}$. Place those and then call on others to come up and locate their fraction on the number line. This activity can be played repeatedly with cards that include equivalent fractions (placed at the exact same point), cards with fractions greater than one (use larger pieces of rope and more holding points), and eventually decimals. Make sure students talk to each other as they agree or disagree on a location or as they think aloud about their decision making. Ask students who are watching a placement why an estimate of a location is a good one. At first, you may want to give students with disabilities unit fractions. That will help them estimate the distances (even by folding the rope if needed).

As suggested in Activity 12.9 important reference points or benchmarks for fractions are $0, \frac{1}{2}$, and 1. For fractions less than one, simply comparing them to these three numbers gives quite a lot of information. For example, $\frac{3}{20}$ is small, close to 0, whereas $\frac{3}{4}$ is between $\frac{1}{2}$ and 1. The fraction $\frac{9}{10}$ is quite close to 1. Because any fraction greater than one is a whole number plus an amount less than one, the same reference points are just as helpful: $3\frac{3}{7}$ is almost $3\frac{1}{2}$.

Activity 12.10   ZERO, ONE-HALF, OR ONE

Create sets of cards for each student team. The set should include a collection of 10 to 15 fractions, one per card. A few should be greater than one ($\frac{9}{8}$ or $\frac{11}{10}$), with the others ranging from 0 to 1. Let the teams sort the fractions into three groups: those close to 0, close to $\frac{1}{2}$, and close to 1. For those close to $\frac{1}{2}$, have them decide whether the fraction is greater or less than half. The difficulty of this task largely depends on the fractions you select. The first time you try this, use fractions such as $\frac{1}{20}, \frac{53}{100}$, or $\frac{9}{10}$ that are very close to the three benchmarks. On subsequent days, mostly use fractions with denominators less than 20. You might include one or two fractions such as $\frac{2}{8}$ or $\frac{3}{4}$ that are exactly in between the benchmarks. Ask students to explain how they are using the numerator and denominator to decide. Be sure that ELLs understand the term *benchmark*, and encourage illustrations as well as explanations.

The next activity is also aimed at developing the same three reference points. In "Close Fractions," however, the students must come up with the fractions rather than sort fractions already provided.

Activity 12.11   CLOSE FRACTIONS

Have students name a fraction that is close to 1 but not more than 1. Next, have them name another fraction that is even closer to 1 than the first. For the second response, they have to explain why they believe the fraction is closer to 1 than the previous fraction. Continue for several fractions in the same manner, each one being closer to 1 than the previous fraction. Similarly, try fractions close to 0 or close to $\frac{1}{2}$ (either under or over). The first several times you try this activity, let the students use models to help with their thinking. Later, have them fade the use of models to see how well their explanations work.

This activity emphasizes the *density of fractions*—that is, there are an infinite number of fractions, so you can always find one in between. This "betweenness property" (Petit, Laird, & Marsden, 2010) links to measurement—there is always a more accurate measurement by using smaller fractional partitions.

🔺 Equivalent Fractions

Equivalent fractions are two different names for the same point on a number line and the same-sized number. Every fraction is equal to an infinite number of other fractions. Having an understanding of equivalent fractions supports students' fraction sense because it helps them grasp fraction size (magnitude), relationships (comparing and ordering), and eventually computation (Johanning, 2011).

🔷 Conceptual Focus on Equivalence

Stop and Reflect

How do you know that $\frac{4}{6} = \frac{2}{3}$? Before reading further, think of at least two different explanations. ∎

Compare these possible answers to your answers:

1. They are the same because you can simplify $\frac{4}{6}$ and get $\frac{2}{3}$.

2. If you have a set of 6 items and you take 4 of them, that would be $\frac{4}{6}$. But you can put the 6 items into 3 groups, and the 4 items would then be 2 groups of the 3 groups. That means it's $\frac{2}{3}$.

3. If you start with $\frac{2}{3}$, you can multiply the numerator and the denominator by 2, and that will give you $\frac{4}{6}$, so they are equal.

4. If you had a square cut into 3 parts and you shaded 2, that's $\frac{2}{3}$ shaded. If you cut all 3 of these parts in half, that would be 6 parts with 4 parts shaded, or $\frac{4}{6}$.

All of these answers are correct, but they reflect different thinking. Responses 2 and 4 are conceptual, although not as efficient. The procedural responses (1 and 3) are efficient, but do not indicate conceptual understanding. Students need a balance with a clear understanding of both the meaning of the concepts and procedures. Consider how different the procedure and the concept appear to be:

Concept: Two fractions are equivalent if they are representations for the same amount or quantity—if they are the same number.

Procedure: To get an equivalent fraction, multiply (or divide) the numerator and denominator by the same nonzero number.

In a problem-based classroom, students can develop an understanding of equivalent fractions and also develop from that understanding a conceptually based algorithm. As with most algorithms, delay sharing "a rule." Be patient! Intuitive methods using drawings and manipulatives support student understanding.

◆ Equivalent-Fraction Models

Starting with a context and physical models is a perfect starting point for helping students create an understanding of equivalent fractions. Consider that this is the first time in their mathematics experience that a fixed quantity can have multiple names (actually an infinite number of names). Again, let's start with area models.

Activity **12.12** **DIFFERENT FILLERS**

Using an area model for fractions that is familiar to your students, prepare a worksheet with two or three outlines of different fractions, as in Figure 12.13. For example, if the model is circular fraction pieces, start with an outline for $\frac{2}{3}$, $\frac{1}{2}$, and $\frac{3}{4}$. The students' task is to use their own fraction pieces to find as many equivalent fractions for the area as possible (using other pieces of the same size or color). Have students record their findings.

Figure **12.13** Area models for equivalent fractions.

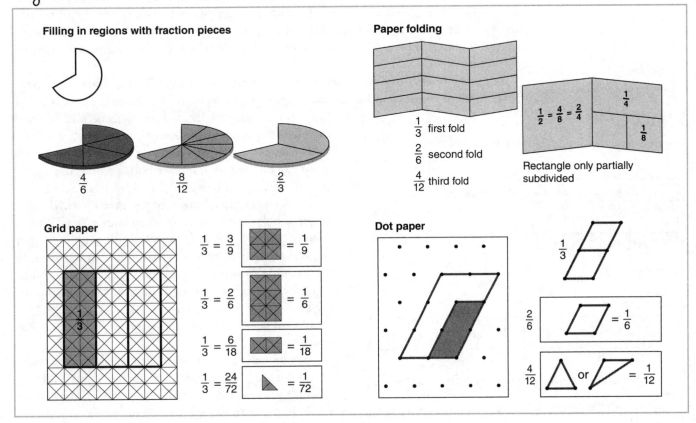

After completing the three examples, have students write about the ideas or patterns they may have noticed about the fractions equivalent to the original outline.

In the class discussion following the "Different Fillers" activity, a good question to ask involves what names could be found if students had other sized pieces. For example, ask students, "What equivalent fractions could you find if we had sixteenths in our fraction kit? What names could you find if you could have a piece of any size at all?"

The following activity is a variation of "Different Fillers." Instead of using a manipulative, the task is constructed on dot paper.

◤ *Activity* 12.13 DOT-PAPER EQUIVALENCES

Create a worksheet using a portion of either isometric or square dot grid paper (see Blackline Masters 13 and 15). On the grid, draw the outline of an area and designate it as one whole. Draw a part of the area within the whole. The task is to compare the part to the whole to find names for the part, and then find equivalent fractions. See Figure 12.13, which includes an example drawn on an isometric grid. Notice how the $\frac{1}{3}$ piece is also equivalent to $\frac{2}{6}$. As in the figure, students should draw a picture of the unit fractional part that they use for each fraction name. The larger the size of the whole, the more names the activity will generate.

The "Dot-Paper Equivalences" activity is a form of what Lamon (2012) calls *unitizing*—that is, given a quantity, finding different ways to chunk the quantity into parts in order to name it. She points out that this requires students to mentally organize the number of pieces and the size of the pieces, which are important components of "fraction sense."

Length models should be used in activities similar to the "On the Line" task. Asking students to locate $\frac{2}{5}$ and $\frac{4}{10}$ on the number line, for example, can help them see that the two fractions are located in the same position and therefore represent the same number and are equivalent (Siegler et al., 2010). Cuisenaire rods or paper strips can be used to designate both a whole and a part, as illustrated in Figure 12.14. Students use smaller rods to find fraction names for the given part. To have larger wholes and, thus, more possible parts, use a train of two or three rods for the whole. Folding paper strips is another method of creating fraction names. In the example shown in Figure 12.14, one-half is subdivided by successive folding in half. If students do not try to fold the strip in an odd number of parts, you should suggest it because these possibilities should be discussed.

Set models can also be used to develop the concept of equivalence. The following activity highlights unitizing, in which students look for different units or chunks of the whole in order to name a part of the whole in different ways.

Figure 12.14

Length models for equivalent fractions.

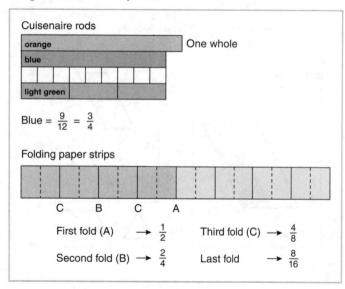

Activity 12.14 APPLES AND BANANAS

Have your students set out a specific number of two-color counters—for example, 24 counters, with 16 of them red (apples) and 8 of them yellow (bananas). The 24 counters make up the whole. The task is to group the counters into different fractional parts of the whole and use the parts to create fraction names for part of the whole that is apples and the part that is bananas. Use Figure 12.15 as a model for how to group the counters in different ways. Students with disabilities might need to start with arrays that can be arranged in ways that emphasize the equivalences. ELLs may not know what is meant by the term *group* because, when used in classrooms, the word usually refers to arranging students. Spend time before the activity modeling what it means to group objects. Ask questions such as, "If we make groups of four, what part of the set is red?" With these prompts, you can suggest fraction names that students are unlikely to suggest.

The following activity moves a bit closer to an algorithm for finding equivalent fractions.

Activity 12.15 MISSING-NUMBER EQUIVALENCES

Give students an equation expressing an equivalence between two fractions, but with one of the numbers missing. Ask them to draw a picture to solve the equation. Here are four different examples:

$$\frac{5}{3}=\frac{\Box}{6} \qquad \frac{2}{3}=\frac{6}{\Box} \qquad \frac{8}{12}=\frac{\Box}{3} \qquad \frac{9}{12}=\frac{3}{\Box}$$

The missing number can be either a numerator or a denominator. Furthermore, the missing number can either be larger or smaller than the corresponding part of the equivalent fraction. (All four of these possibilities are represented in the examples.) The task is to find the missing number and to explain your solution. Figure 12.16 illustrates how Zachary represented the equivalences with equations and partitioned rectangles. The examples shown involve simple whole-number multiples between equivalent fractions. Next, consider pairs such as $\frac{6}{8}=\frac{\Box}{12}$ or $\frac{9}{12}=\frac{6}{\Box}$. In these equivalences, one denominator or numerator is not a whole-number multiple of the other.

When doing "Missing-Number Equivalences" you may want to specify a particular model, such as sets or area.

Figure 12.15
Set models for illustrating equivalent fractions.

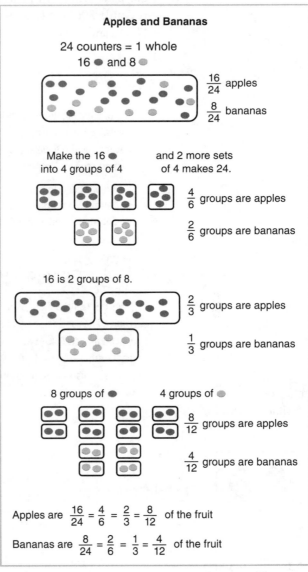

Figure 12.16
A student illustrated equivalent fractions by partitioning rectangles.

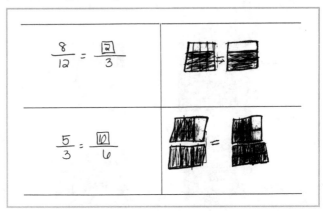

Alternatively, you can allow students to select whatever methods they wish to solve these problems. Students who have learning disabilities and other students who struggle may benefit from using clocks to think about equivalence (Chick, Tierney, & Storeygard, 2007). Students were able to use the clocks to find equivalent fractions for $\frac{10}{12}, \frac{3}{4}, \frac{4}{6}$, and so on.

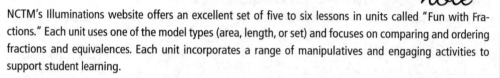

NCTM's Illuminations website offers an excellent set of five to six lessons in units called "Fun with Fractions." Each unit uses one of the model types (area, length, or set) and focuses on comparing and ordering fractions and equivalences. Each unit incorporates a range of manipulatives and engaging activities to support student learning.

- Area Model Unit: http://illuminations.nctm.org/LessonDetail.aspx?id=U113
- Length Model Unit: http://illuminations.nctm.org/LessonDetail.aspx?id=U152
- Set Model Unit: http://illuminations.nctm.org/LessonDetail.aspx?id=U112

Formative Assessment Note

Consider using a diagnostic interview to see whether your students are making the connection between equivalence and a variety of models. For example, use Figure 12.17 to see examples of area and set models you might use. Ask, "Which of these fractions are equivalent to $\frac{2}{3}$?" Ask students what they know about the fraction they selected. Students should be able to explain that they are equivalent fractions and that they are fractions that represent the same quantity.

Figure 12.17
Possible figures for diagnostic interview.

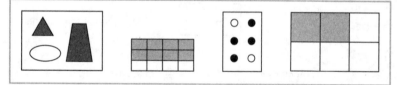

Figure 12.18
Jack partitions a garden to model equivalent fractions.

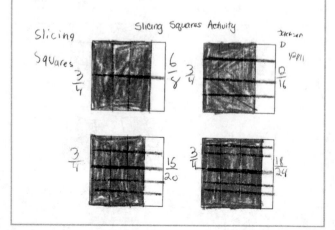

Developing an Equivalent-Fraction Algorithm

When students understand that fractions can have different (but equivalent) names, they are ready to develop a method for finding equivalent names for a particular value. An area model is a good visual for connecting the concept of equivalence to the standard algorithm for finding equivalent fractions (multiply both the numerator and the denominator by the same number to get an equivalent fraction). The approach suggested here is to look for a pattern in the way that the fractional parts in both the part and the whole are counted.

Activity 12.16 GARDEN PLOTS

Give students an outline of four square "gardens" on blank paper (or a set of cut out squares to fold). Begin by explaining that the garden is divided into rows of various vegetables. In the first example, you might illustrate four vertical partitions (fourths) and designate $\frac{3}{4}$ as corn. Ask students to partition their square into four rows and shade three-fourths as shown in Jack's work in Figure 12.18. For students with disabilities, you may want them prepartitioned so their efforts are focused on shading and the equivalence activity rather than on equally dividing the square accurately. Then explain that the garden is going to be shared with family and friends in a way that each person's share of the harvest is three-fourths corn. Show how the garden can now be partitioned horizontally to represent two people sharing the corn (i.e., $\frac{6}{8}$). Ask what fraction of the newly divided garden is corn. Next, tell students to come up with other ways that other numbers of friends can share the garden (they can choose how many friends, or you can). For each newly divided garden, ask students to record an equation showing the equivalent fractions.

Figure 12.19

How can you count the fractional parts if you cannot see them all?

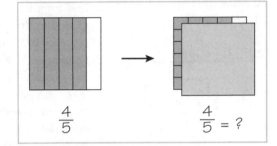

$$\frac{4}{5} \qquad \frac{4}{5} = ?$$

After students have prepared their own examples, provide time for them to look at their fractions and gardens and notice patterns about the fractions and the diagrams. Once they have time to do this individually, ask students to share. Some students will notice the multiplicative relationship between the numerators and denominators. But you can also assist in helping students make the connection from the partitioned square to the procedure by displaying a square, for example, partitioned to show $\frac{4}{5}$ (see Figure 12.19). Have another version of the same square with $\frac{4}{5}$ shaded, but adding six equal partitions horizontally. Cover most of the square as shown in the figure. Ask, "What is the new name for my $\frac{4}{5}$?"

The reason for this exercise is that students must move away from simply counting the small regions and think of the multiplicative relationship. This also helps students develop mental images of models that are critical to understanding equivalence. With the partially covered square, students can see that there are four columns and six rows to the shaded part, so there must be 4×6 parts shaded. Similarly, there must be 5×6 parts in the whole. Therefore, the new name for $\frac{4}{5}$ is $\frac{4 \times 6}{5 \times 6}$, or $\frac{24}{30}$. This thinking will also lay the groundwork for multiplication of fractions.

Using this idea, have students return to their fractions from the "Garden Plots" activity to see if the pattern works for other fractions.

Look at examples of equivalent fractions that have been generated with other models, and see if the rule of multiplying the numerator and denominator by the same number holds. If the rule is correct, how can $\frac{6}{8}$ and $\frac{9}{12}$ be equivalent?

Writing Fractions in Simplest Terms

The multiplication scheme for equivalent fractions produces fractions with larger denominators. To write a fraction in *simplest terms* means to write it so that numerator and denominator have no common whole-number factors. (Some texts use *lowest terms* instead of simplest terms.)

One meaningful approach to this task of finding simplest terms is to reverse the earlier process, as illustrated in Figure 12.20. The search for a common factor or a simplified fraction should be connected to grouping.

Teaching Tip

Use the language "simplify" or put into "lowest terms." Avoid using the language "reducing fractions" as the fraction is not getting smaller or going on a "diet" as some students will mistakenly explain.

Teaching Tip

Avoid telling students that fraction answers are incorrect if not in simplest or lowest terms. When students add $\frac{1}{6} + \frac{1}{2}$, both $\frac{2}{3}$ and $\frac{4}{6}$ are correct and equivalent answers. Sometimes students will be asked on a test to write their answer in lowest terms, so do share that as a task so they know how to respond.

Multiplying by One

Many textbooks and websites use a strictly symbolic approach to equivalent fractions. It is based on the multiplicative identity property of 1 that any number multiplied by 1 remains unchanged. Any fraction of the form $\frac{n}{n}$ can be used as the identity element. Therefore, $\frac{3}{4} = \frac{3}{4} \times 1 = \frac{3}{4} \times \frac{2}{2} = \frac{6}{8}$. Furthermore, the numerator and denominator of the identity element can also be fractions. In this way, $\frac{6}{12} = \frac{6}{12}\left(\frac{1/6}{1/6}\right) = \frac{1}{2}$.

◄ **Standards for Mathematical Practice**

2 Reason abstractly and quantitatively

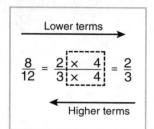

Figure 12.20

Using the equivalent-fraction algorithm to write fractions in simplest terms.

Developing the concept of equivalence can be supported with the use of technology. In the NCTM e-Examples, there is a fraction game (Fraction Track) for two players (www.nctm.org/standards/content .aspx?id=26975). The game uses a number-line model, and knowledge of equivalent fractions plays a significant role. Also explore "Equivalent Fractions" at NCTM's Illuminations website (http://illuminations .nctm.org). This activity is designed to help students create equivalent fractions by dividing and shading square or circular areas and then matching each fraction to its location on a number line. Students can use the computer-generated fraction or build their own. Once the rectangular or circular shape is divided, the student fills in the parts or fractional region and then builds two models equivalent to the original fraction. The three equivalent fractions are displayed in a table and in the same location on a number line.

The *Common Core State Standards* (CCSSO, 2010) suggest that students in third grade should understand the properties of multiplication (shown in Table 3 of that document), which includes the identity property of 1. This explanation relies on the procedure for multiplying two fractions. A reasonable conclusion may be to delay this algorithm until at least fifth grade, when students learn about multiplication of fractions, rather than teaching it earlier as a rote procedure.

Comparing Fractions

When two fractions are not equivalent but are parts of the same whole or unit, there are several ways to find which is greater through comparison. The ideas described previously for equivalence across area, length, and set models are therefore also appropriate for comparing fractions. Remember that students should be moving from real models to mental images to reasoning strategies. Just as students can become overreliant on the calculator when they could solve a problem mentally, they can become overreliant on a model (such as circle pieces) and not be reasoning about the size of the fraction. Instead, the use of contexts, models, and mental imagery can help students build a strong understanding of the relative size of fractions (Bray & Abreu-Sanchez, 2010; Petit, Laird, & Marsen, 2010).

Using Number Sense

In the National Assessment of Educational Progress (NAEP) test, only 21 percent of fourth-grade students could explain why one unit fraction was larger or smaller than another—for example, $\frac{1}{5}$ and $\frac{1}{4}$ (Kloosterman, Warfield, Weame, Koc, Martin, & Strutchens, 2004). For eighth graders, only 41 percent were able to correctly put in order three fractions given in simplified form (Sowder, Wearne, Martin, & Strutchens, 2004). As these researchers note, "How students can work meaningfully with fractions if they do not have a sense of the relative size of the fractions is difficult to imagine" (p. 116).

Comparing Unit Fractions

As noted earlier, whole-number knowledge can interfere with comparing fractions. Students think, "Seven is more than four, so sevenths should be bigger than fourths" (Mack, 1995). You need to create a variety of experiences so each student can create his or her own thinking regarding the inverse relationship between the number of parts and the size of parts in fractions compared.

Activity 12.17 ORDERING UNIT FRACTIONS

List a set of unit fractions such as $\frac{1}{3}$, $\frac{1}{8}$, $\frac{1}{5}$, and $\frac{1}{10}$. Ask students to use reasoning to put the fractions in order from least to greatest. Challenge students to explain their reasoning with an area model (e.g., circles) *and* on a number line. Ask students to connect the two representations with questions such as "What do you notice about $\frac{1}{3}$ of the circle and $\frac{1}{3}$ on the number line?" Students with disabilities may need to use clothes-pins with the fractions written on them and place them on the line first.

Students may notice that given the same whole, larger denominators mean smaller fractions, but this is not a rule to be memorized. Revisit this basic idea periodically to assess whether students are mistakenly returning to whole-number thinking. Repeat Activity 12.17 with fractions other than unit fractions. You may be surprised to see that this is much harder for students.

Comparing Any Fractions

You have probably learned several rules or algorithms for comparing two fractions. The usual approaches are finding common denominators and using cross-multiplication. These rules can be effective in getting correct answers but require no thought about the size of the fractions—no "fraction sense." Students need opportunities to think about and experiment with the relative sizes of various fractions because the goal is reflective thought, not the memorization of an algorithmic method of choosing the correct answer.

Stop and Reflect

Assume for a moment that you do not know the common denominator or cross-multiplication techniques. Now examine the pairs of fractions in Figure 12.21 and select the larger of each pair using a reasoning approach that a fourth grader might use. ■

Fourth graders trying this task used reasoning such as, "$\frac{4}{5}$ is only one away from being a whole" and "$\frac{4}{9}$ is closer to $\frac{1}{2}$" and "$\frac{5}{7}$ is greater than $\frac{4}{7}$ because the denominator is the same, but the numerator of $\frac{5}{7}$ is greater, making it a bigger fraction."

The list here summarizes ways that the fractions in Figure 12.21 might be compared:

1. *More of the same sized parts (denominators are the same).* To compare $\frac{3}{8}$ and $\frac{5}{8}$, think about having 3 parts of something and also 5 parts of the same thing. (This method can be used for problems B and G.)

2. *Same number of parts (numerators are the same) but parts of different sizes.* Consider the case of $\frac{3}{4}$ and $\frac{3}{7}$. If a whole is divided into 7 parts, the parts will certainly be smaller than if divided into only 4 parts. (This strategy can be used with problems A, D, and H.)

3. *More than/less than one-half or one whole.* The fraction pairs $\frac{3}{7}$ compared to $\frac{5}{8}$ and $\frac{5}{4}$ compared to $\frac{7}{8}$ do not lend themselves to either of the previous thought processes. In the first pair, $\frac{3}{7}$ is less than half of the number of sevenths needed to make a whole, and so $\frac{3}{7}$ is less than a half. Similarly, $\frac{5}{8}$ is more than a half. Therefore, $\frac{5}{8}$ is the larger fraction. The second pair is determined by noting that one fraction is greater than one and the other is less than one. (This method could be used on problems A, D, F, G, and H.)

Figure 12.21

Comparing fractions using concepts.

Which fraction in each pair is greater? Give one or more reasons. Try not to use drawings or models. <u>Do</u> not use common denominators or cross-multiplication. Rely on concepts.

A. $\frac{4}{5}$ or $\frac{4}{9}$	G. $\frac{7}{12}$ or $\frac{5}{12}$
B. $\frac{4}{7}$ or $\frac{5}{7}$	H. $\frac{3}{5}$ or $\frac{3}{7}$
C. $\frac{3}{8}$ or $\frac{4}{10}$	I. $\frac{5}{8}$ or $\frac{6}{10}$
D. $\frac{5}{3}$ or $\frac{5}{8}$	J. $\frac{9}{8}$ or $\frac{4}{3}$
E. $\frac{3}{4}$ or $\frac{9}{10}$	K. $\frac{4}{6}$ or $\frac{7}{12}$
F. $\frac{3}{8}$ or $\frac{4}{7}$	L. $\frac{8}{9}$ or $\frac{7}{8}$

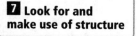

4. *Closeness to one-half or one whole.* Why is $\frac{9}{10}$ greater than $\frac{3}{4}$? Each is one fractional part away from one whole, and tenths are smaller than fourths. Similarly, notice that $\frac{5}{8}$ is smaller than $\frac{4}{6}$ because it is only one-eighth more than a half, while $\frac{4}{6}$ is a sixth more than a half. Can you use this basic idea to compare $\frac{3}{5}$ and $\frac{5}{9}$? (*Hint:* Each is half of a fractional part more than $\frac{1}{2}$.) Also try $\frac{5}{7}$ and $\frac{7}{9}$. (This is a good strategy for problems C, E, I, J, K, and L.)

Did your reasons for choosing fractions in Figure 12.21 match these ideas? It is important that you are comfortable with these informal comparison strategies as a major component of your own fraction sense, as well as for helping students develop theirs. Notice that some of the comparisons, such as problems D and H, could have been solved using more than one of the strategies listed.

Tasks you design for your students should assist them in developing these and possibly other methods of comparing two fractions. It is important that the ideas come from your students and their discussions. To teach "the four ways to compare fractions" would be adding four more mysterious rules and defeats the purpose of encouraging students to apply their own fraction sense. As you develop these tasks, make sure you strategically select pairs of fractions that will likely elicit desired comparison strategies.

For students who struggle, you may need to use an area or number-line model so a direct comparison can be made. Place greater emphasis on students' reasoning and connect it to the visual models.

◆ Using Equivalent Fractions

Equivalent-fraction concepts can be used in making comparisons. Smith (2002) suggests that the comparison question to ask is, "Which of the following two (or more) fractions is greater, or are they equal?" (p. 9). He points out that this question leaves open the possibility that two fractions that may appear different can, in fact, be equal. In addition to this point, with equivalent-fraction concepts, students can adjust how a fraction looks so that they can use ideas that make sense to them. Burns (1999) describes how fifth graders compared $\frac{6}{8}$ to $\frac{4}{5}$. (You might want to stop for a moment and think how you would compare these fractions.) One student changed the $\frac{4}{5}$ to $\frac{8}{10}$ so that both fractions would be two parts away from the whole and he reasoned from there. Another changed both fractions to a common numerator of 12. Revisit the comparison activities and include pairs such as $\frac{8}{12}$ and $\frac{2}{3}$ in which the fractions are equal but do not appear to be.

▲ Teaching Considerations for Fraction Concepts

Because the teaching of fractions is so important, and because fractions are often not well understood even by adults, a recap of the big ideas is needed. Hopefully you now recognize that one reason fractions are not well understood is that there is a lot to know about them. Another reason is that most people were taught procedures with fractions that are not based on fraction sense. Clarke and colleagues (2008) and Cramer and Whitney (2010), researchers of fraction teaching and learning, offer several research-based recommendations that provide an effective summary of this chapter and direction for your instruction:

1. Give a greater emphasis to number sense and the meaning of fractions, rather than rote procedures for manipulating them.

2. Provide a variety of physical models and contexts to represent fractions.

3. Emphasize that fractions are numbers, making extensive use of number lines in representing fractions.

4. Spend whatever time is needed for students to understand equivalences (concretely and symbolically), including flexible naming of fractions.

5. Link fractions to key benchmarks and encourage estimation.

Expanded Lesson

Dot-Paper Fraction Equivalences

Content and Task Decisions

Grade Level: 3

Mathematics Goals

- To develop a conceptual understanding of equivalent fractions; the same quantity can have different fraction names
- To look for patterns in equivalent fractions

Grade Level Guide

NCTM Curriculum Focal Points	Common Core State Standards
Developing fraction concepts is one of three Focal Points in grade 3: "*Number and Operations:* Developing an understanding of fractions and fraction equivalence" (NCTM, 2006, p. 15).	Fractions are one of four critical themes in grade 3. Specifically, third graders should be able to "solve problems that involve comparing fractions by using visual fraction models and strategies based on noticing equal numerators or denominators" (CCSSO, 2010, p. 21).

Consider Your Students' Needs

Students should have a good understanding of what the numerator and denominator in a fraction represent.

For English Language Learners

- As you are telling the story, write the fractions next to the diagram and point to the representations during the story.
- Focus on the terms *numerator* and *denominator.* These have Latin roots, so ELLs whose first language has a Latin root will benefit from this. Specifically, *nom* means name (the denominator is the *name* of the fraction). And *numerare* means "to number." In other words, the numerator is the numberer. The denominator is the name of pieces. This conceptual connection is a benefit to all learners.
- In observing and assessing, encourage students to illustrate or explain or both.

For Students with Disabilities

- If students are challenged by the dot-paper representations, you may need to use one-inch grid paper with color tiles to represent the fractions.
- As you are showing the fraction in the first example, use a think-aloud to describe how you are thinking as you decide whether the fractions are equivalent.

Materials

Each student will need:

- "Fraction Names" worksheet (Blackline Master 27)

Teacher will need:

- Transparency of or way to display centimeter dot grid (Blackline Master 13)
- Transparency of or way to display "Fraction Names" worksheet (Blackline Master 27)

Lesson

Before

Begin with a simpler version of the task:

- On the dot transparency, outline a 3×3 rectangle and shade it in as shown here.
- Tell this story: "Two students looked at this picture. Each saw a different fraction. Kyle saw $\frac{6}{9}$, but Terri said she saw $\frac{2}{3}$." Ask, "How can they see the same drawing and yet each see different fractions? Which one is right? Why?"
- Have students come to the front of the class and offer explanations for how Kyle saw the picture and how Terri saw it. When students in the class agree on and also understand a correct explanation, draw the corresponding unit fraction to aid in understanding. For example, you can explain, "Terri saw a column of three squares as $\frac{1}{3}$." Draw a column of 3 squares to the side of the rectangle. "If a column of 3 squares is $\frac{1}{3}$, then there are two columns of 3 squares shaded. Therefore, the shaded portion is $\frac{2}{3}$." Similarly, be sure that students see that one square is $\frac{1}{9}$ of the whole. "Since there are 6 squares shaded, the shaded part is $\frac{6}{9}$."

Present the focus task:

- Distribute the "Fraction Names" worksheet.

- For each shaded region on the worksheet, students are to find as many fraction names as possible.

- For each fraction name, students draw a picture of a fractional part and use words to tell how they partitioned the region. For example, if a shaded area is $\frac{4}{12}$, the student should show how the region could be partitioned into twelfths.

During

Initially:

- For students who are having difficulty getting started, draw a fractional part for them. For example, for problem 1, draw a two-square rectangle. Ask, "How many rectangles like this make up the whole? How many of the two-square rectangles are shaded? What fraction of the two-square rectangles are shaded?" Allow time for students to investigate these questions, rather than just showing them how to do it.

Ongoing:

- Students who do not seem to understand counting the fractional parts may need more development of the meaning of numerator and denominator.

- Be sure to ask questions that focus students' attention on connecting the visual to the symbols and explaining how they know whether a fraction is equivalent to another fraction.

- For students who seem to have finished quickly, make sure that their explanations reflect their capabilities. Also, consider challenging them to find even more names. In problem 2, for example, a small triangle can be used as a unit to produce $\frac{12}{24}$.

After

- Use a document camera to display students' completed Blackline Masters so that others can see. For each drawing on the worksheet, record a list of all of the fraction names that students have found for the shaded region.

- Ask students to show how they got the fractions, asking one student to explain one fraction, and a second student to explain a different fraction. For some fractions, students may have used a differently shaped unit fraction. For example, in problem 1, 4 squares of each

row of 6 squares can be used to name the shaded region as $\frac{4}{6}$ or columns of the 6 columns may have been used to name $\frac{4}{6}$.

- Problem 1 can be partitioned to show $\frac{2}{3}$, $\frac{4}{6}$, $\frac{8}{12}$, and $\frac{16}{12}$. A 1×1 square could be halved to produce $\frac{32}{48}$. Also, note that three squares are $\frac{1}{10}$ of the whole. Say, "Can the shaded region be named with tenths? Yes! The shaded region contains $6\frac{2}{3}$ tenths; $6\frac{2}{3}$ is in the numerator." Students often do not think of this.

- Problem 2 can be named $\frac{1}{2}$, $\frac{2}{4}$, $\frac{3}{6}$, and $\frac{6}{12}$. If a small triangle is used, it can be seen as $\frac{12}{24}$. If a trapezoid of three triangles is used, it is $\frac{4}{8}$. Students may divide it up in other ways as well.

- Problem 3 also has many equivalencies, from $\frac{1}{4}$ to $\frac{8}{32}$.

- If time permits, you may want to focus attention on all of the names for one region and discuss any patterns that students may observe.

Assessment
Observe

- Watch to see whether students connect the visual with the fraction notation. For example, there may be students who do not connect the denominator (unit) with the name of the parts in the *whole*. For example, in Problem 3 on the Blackline Master, if the full shaded region is used as the unit (fourths), some students may write $\frac{1}{3}$ (1 region to 3 regions). These students will need further foundational work with fraction concepts, in particular the meaning of denominator and numerator.

- See how many equivalencies students find. Do not expect all students to find all of the fraction names—in this way the activity is differentiated. It is, however, critical that every student finds some equivalencies and makes the connection of why two fractions are equivalent, both in the visual and in the symbols.

Ask

- How can the same quantity (shaded area) have different fraction names?

- What patterns do you see among the equivalent fractions?

- How did you determine whether two fractions name the same region?

13

Building Strategies for Fraction Computation

Big IDEAS

1 The meanings of the operations on fractions are the same as the meanings for the operations on whole numbers. Operations with fractions should begin by applying these same meanings to fractional parts.

2 For addition and subtraction, an essential understanding is that the numerator tells the number of parts and the denominator the type of part (what unit is being used). When denominators are different, an adaptation of the problem takes place.

3 For multiplication by a fraction, an essential understanding is that the denominator is a divisor. This idea allows us to find parts of the other factor.

4 For division by a fraction, there are two ways of thinking about the operation—partition and measurement.

5 Estimation should be an integral part of computation development to keep students' attention on the meanings of the operations and the expected size of the results.

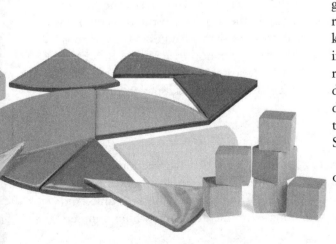

A fifth-grade student asks, "Why is it when we times 29 times two-ninths that the answer goes down?" (Taber, 2002, p. 67). Although incorrect generalizations from whole numbers can confuse students, you should realize that their ideas about fraction operations will be linked to their knowledge of whole-number operations and build on that understanding. The properties of the whole number operations align with those for rational numbers (Barnett-Clarke et al., 2010). Using students' prior understanding of the whole-number operations, combined with a firm understanding of fractions (including relative size and equivalence), provides the foundation for fraction computation (Petit, Laird, & Marsden, 2010; Siegler et al., 2010).

As with other topics in this book, we will discuss the importance of incorporating meaningful contexts and examples using appropriate models and manipulatives, valuing numerous invented strategies, using estimation, and addressing misconceptions explicitly.

⬛ Understanding Operations with Fractions

Students must be able to flexibly and accurately compute with fractions. Success with fractions, in particular computation in all four operations, is directly related to success in algebra (Brown & Quinn, 2007). The inverse is also true, that students with a poor understanding of operations with fractions are at risk for difficulty in algebra and that weakness will have long-term impact affecting college majors and career opportunities (National Mathematics Advisory Panel, 2008).

◆ Conceptual Development Takes Time

Students require ample opportunity to develop fraction number sense, and instruction should not immediately start with common denominators and other rules of computation. This aligns with the *Common Core State Standards* (CCSSO, 2010), which suggest the following:

- Grade 3: Students add equal-sized units (in this case unit fractions) to understand that a fraction $\frac{a}{b}$ is the quantity formed by a parts of size $\frac{1}{b}$. This is demonstrated by $\frac{3}{4} = \frac{1}{4} + \frac{1}{4} + \frac{1}{4}$. (This is foundational knowledge for addition of fractions.)
- Grade 4: Students add and subtract fractions with like denominators and multiply fractions with whole numbers.
- Grade 5: Students add and subtract fractions fluently with like and unlike denominators, multiply fractions, divide unit fractions by whole numbers, and divide whole numbers by unit fractions.

Developing understanding and gaining procedural proficiency for operations with fractions are priorities in grades 4 and 5, and they require significant time to evolve. This progression is significantly different from what you may have experienced as a student and from what many elementary school textbooks employ; therefore, this chapter will be an important resource as you consider ways to help students deeply understand the operations with fractions.

As with whole-number operations, sharing standard algorithms early as a quick approach leaves students without any means of assessing their results for reasonableness and any grasp of when they should use these procedures. When these four algorithms are mixed together, the rules of fraction computation soon become a meaningless jumble. Students ask, "Do I need a common denominator, or do you just add the bottom numbers like when we multiply the denominators in multiplication?" and "Which fraction do you invert, the first or the second number?" and "When can I change the sign in the problem, just in division or in multiplication too?" Additionally, often students can't adapt to slight changes in the fractions. For example, if a mixed number is used, students are unsure as to how to apply the algorithm. This can be a very confusing experience for even previously strong mathematics students, and becomes a point when their confidence in their mathematics abilities may start to falter.

◆ A Problem-Based, Number Sense Approach

Students should understand and have access to a variety of ways to solve fraction computation problems—knowing what they are doing and why. Just as with whole numbers, a mental or invented strategy can be applied and a standard algorithm can develop over time. And just as with whole numbers, "Rushing past reasoning with operations on whole numbers to teach answer-getting calculations leaves huge gaps in the foundations of algebra" (Daro et al., 2011, p. 49), the same results occur with fractions.

The *Principles and Standards for School Mathematics* (NCTM, 2000) state, "The development of rational-number concepts . . . should lead to informal methods for calculating with fractions. For example, a problem such as $\frac{1}{4} + \frac{1}{2}$ should be solved mentally with ease because students can picture $\frac{1}{2}$ and $\frac{1}{4}$ or can use decomposition strategies, such as $\frac{1}{4} + \frac{1}{2} = \frac{1}{4} + \left(\frac{1}{4} + \frac{1}{4}\right)$" (p. 35)*. In a summary of research on fraction learning, the authors suggest that teachers "help students understand why procedures for computations with fractions make sense" (Siegler et al., 2010). This research suggests four steps to effective fraction computation instruction:

1. *Use tasks in meaningful contexts.* If this sounds familiar, this recommendation applies to nearly every topic in this book. Huinker (2002) makes an excellent case for using meaningful contextual problems and for letting students develop their own methods of computation with fractions. Problems or contexts need not be elaborate. What you want is a context that addresses both the meaning of the operation and the fractions involved.

2. *Explore each operation incorporating a variety of models.* Have students defend their solutions using models, including drawings. Make sure they connect the models to the symbolic operations because that will provide a useful background for developing the standard algorithm.

3. *Include estimation and informal methods as the foundation for the development of strategies.* "Estimate $2\frac{1}{2} \times \frac{1}{4}$. Should it be more or less than 1? More or less than 2?" Can you reason to get an exact answer without using the standard algorithm? One way is to apply the distributive property, split the mixed number, and multiply the whole number and the fraction by $\frac{1}{4}$: $\left(2 \times \frac{1}{4}\right) + \left(\frac{1}{2} \times \frac{1}{4}\right)$. Two $\frac{1}{4}$s are $\frac{2}{4}$ or $\frac{1}{2}$ and a half of a fourth is $\frac{1}{8}$. So add an eighth to a half and you have $\frac{5}{8}$. Estimation and informal methods keep the focus on the meanings of the numbers and the operations, encourage reflective thinking, and build informal number sense with fractions.

4. *Address common misconceptions.* Teachers should present well-known misconceptions to students and discuss openly why some approaches lead to right answers and why other approaches do not (Siegler et al., 2010). For example, students often misapply their prior knowledge—in this case, computation with whole numbers—to their early experiences with operations with fractions. This results in their adding the denominators when combining fractions. In this case you could show students actual physical models to reason and prove the best method to add fractions. But the concepts of each operation are the same, and benefits can be had by purposefully connecting these ideas.

In the discussions that follow, estimation and informal exploration is encouraged for each operation. There is also a guided development of each standard algorithm.

◆ Computational Estimation

Estimation is one of the most effective ways to build understanding and procedural fluency with fractions. A mental image or awareness of the size of a fraction helps students assess their answers for reasonableness. There are different ways to estimate fraction computations (Siegler et al., 2010):

1. *Benchmarks.* Decide whether the fractions are closest to 0, $\frac{1}{2}$, or 1 (or 3, $3\frac{1}{2}$, or 4, for example, for mixed numbers). After making the determination for each fraction, mentally add or subtract.

---

*Reprinted with permission from *Principles and Standards*, by the National Council of Teachers of Mathematics. All rights reserved.

Example: $\frac{7}{8} + \frac{1}{10}$. Think, "$\frac{7}{8}$ is close to 1, $\frac{1}{10}$ is close to 0, the sum is about $1 + 0$ or close to 1."

Example: $5\frac{1}{3} \div \frac{3}{5}$. Think, "I am finding how many $\frac{3}{5}$s are in $5\frac{1}{3}$. $5\frac{1}{3}$ is close to five, and $\frac{3}{5}$ is close to $\frac{1}{2}$. So how many $\frac{1}{2}$s in 5? About 10. The answer is close to 10."

---

2. *Relative size of unit fractions.* Decide how big the fraction is, based on its unit (denominator), and apply this information to the computation.

Example: $\frac{7}{8} + \frac{1}{10}$. Think, "$\frac{7}{8}$ is just $\frac{1}{8}$ away from a whole (one) and that $\frac{1}{8}$ is close to (but larger than) $\frac{1}{10}$, so the sum will be close to, but less than, 1."

Example: $\frac{1}{3} \times 3\frac{4}{5}$. Think, "I need a third of $3\frac{4}{5}$. A third of 3 is 1 and $\frac{1}{3}$ of $\frac{4}{5}$ is going to be a little more than $\frac{1}{5}$ (because there are four parts), so about $1\frac{1}{5}$."

Addition and Subtraction

Estimation is a "thinking tool" that should be highlighted as students build meaning for addition and subtraction with fractions (Johanning, 2011). Here estimation requires two components: estimating fractions within the problem, and estimating the size of the overall answer. Students must bring a sense of a fraction's size to the process of addition and subtraction of fractions. Without that background, they can be asked to estimate the answer to $\frac{8}{9} + \frac{11}{12}$ and instead of finding an approximate answer, will make heroic efforts to locate common denominators and identify a precise answer. Even so, they may not grasp how that answer relates to the problem. For example, Petit and her colleagues (Petit, Laird, & Marsden, 2010, p. xi) discuss a piece of student work that asks the fifth grader to determine which number from a group of answers [20, 8, $\frac{1}{2}$, 1] is closest to the sum of $\frac{1}{12} + \frac{7}{8}$. The student carries out the full process of selecting a common denominator, creating equivalent fractions and adding to get the correct answer of $\frac{23}{24}$. But, when selecting from the multiple choices as to which one is closest to the sum, the student chooses 20. In response, the teacher stated, "In the past I would have been excited that a beginning 5th-grade student could add fractions using a common denominator. I would have thought my work was done. It never occurred to me to ask the student the value of the sum" (cited in Daro et al., 2011, p. 37*). Following is an activity that exemplifies the necessary emphasis on the size of the answer.

◤ *Activity* 13.1 MORE THAN OR LESS THAN ONE

Tell students that they are going to estimate a sum or difference of two fractions. Their job is to decide only whether the exact answer is greater than one or less than one. Display or project a problem for about 10 seconds, then hide, cover, or remove it. Ask students to hold up a card (with "More than one" and "Less than one" on either side). Do several problems (Figure 13.1 offers options). Have students discuss how they decided on each estimate. Students with disabilities may need more time and should have a number line marked with benchmark fractions available to assist them in visualizing the amounts.

---

*Originally in Ongoing Assessment Project. The Vermont Institutes (OGAP) 2005. Reprinted with permission.

Here are several variations on the same activity:

- Use a target answer that is different from one. For example, estimate more or less than $\frac{1}{2}$, $1\frac{1}{2}$, 2, or 3.
- Adapt to multiplication or division problems.
- Choose fraction pairs in which both are less than one or both are greater than one. Estimate sums or differences to the nearest half.
- Encourage students to create their own problems and targets. They can trade equations with other students, who in turn need to decide whether the sum or difference is greater than one or less than one (or another value).

Stop and Reflect

Test your own estimation skills with the sample problems in Figure 13.1. Look at each computation for about 10 seconds and write down an estimate. After writing down all six of your estimates, look at the problems and decide whether your estimate is greater than or less than the actual computation. ■

Figure 13.1

Examples for estimating addition and subtraction of fractions.

Estimate

1. $\frac{1}{8} + \frac{4}{5}$

2. $\frac{9}{10} + \frac{7}{8}$

3. $\frac{3}{5} + \frac{3}{4} + \frac{1}{8}$

4. $\frac{3}{4} - \frac{1}{3}$

5. $\frac{11}{12} - \frac{3}{4}$

6. $1\frac{1}{2} - \frac{9}{10}$

> Number your papers 1 to 6. Write only answers.
>
> Estimate!
>   Use whole numbers and familiar fractions.

Multiplication

In the real world, there are many instances when whole numbers and fractions must be multiplied and mental estimates are quite useful. For example, sale items are frequently listed as "half off," or we read of a "one-third increase" in the number of registered voters. Also, fractions are excellent substitutes for percents, as you will see in the next chapter. To get an estimate of 60 percent of $36.69, it is useful to think of 60 percent as $\frac{3}{5}$ or a little less than $\frac{2}{3}$.

Products of fractions and whole numbers can be calculated mentally by thinking of the meanings of the numerator and denominator. For example, $\frac{3}{5}$ is 3 one-fifths. So, if the problem is to find $\frac{3}{5}$ of 350, first think about one-fifth of 350, or 70. If one-fifth is 70, then three-fifths is 3×70, or 210. Start with compatible numbers, determine the unit fractional part (like a identifying a rate), and then multiply by the number of parts you want.

With challenging numbers, encourage students to use the estimation strategies they know from whole-number operations: front end, rounding, and compatible numbers. For example, to estimate $\frac{3}{5}$ of $36.69, a useful compatible number is $35. One-fifth of 35 is 7, so three-fifths is 3×7, or 21. Then make your adjustment—perhaps add an additional 50 cents, for an estimate of $21.50.

Division

Use estimation to support understanding of division of fractions. Consider the problem $12 \div 4$. This can mean "How many fours in 12?" Similarly, $12 \div \frac{1}{4}$ means "How many fourths in 12?" There are 48 fourths in 12. With this basic idea in mind, students should be able to estimate problems like $4\frac{1}{3} \div \frac{1}{2}$. Ask students to first use words to describe what these equations are asking (e.g., "How many halves in $4\frac{1}{3}$?"). This can help them think about the meaning of division and then develop a reasonable estimate.

As with the other operations, using contexts is important in providing mental images that support estimation with division. An example is: "We have five submarine sandwiches.

A serving for one person is $\frac{2}{5}$ of a sandwich. About how many people can we serve?" Activity 13.2 uses a context of servings to address the common student misconception that dividing results in an answer that is a smaller number.

▲ *Activity* 13.2 SANDWICH SERVINGS

Super Sub Sandwiches is starting a catering business. The employees know that a child's serving is one-sixth of a Super Sub, and an adult serving can be either one-third (if the customer orders a small serving) or $\frac{1}{2}$ (if the customer orders a medium) of a Super Sub. The employees must be quick at deciding the number of subs for an event based on numbers of guests wanting a particular serving size. See how you do—make a decision without computing.

Which of the following portion sizes serves the most people—child size, small, or medium? Why?

$$6 \div \tfrac{1}{6} \qquad 6 \div \tfrac{1}{3} \qquad 6 \div \tfrac{1}{2}$$

Which serves the most people—a child's serving of 8 sandwiches, 5 sandwiches, or 9 sandwiches? Why?

$$8 \div \tfrac{1}{6} \qquad 5 \div \tfrac{1}{6} \qquad 9 \div \tfrac{1}{6}$$

Which combination of sandwiches and portion sizes serves the most people? Why?

$$8 \div \tfrac{1}{3} \qquad 5 \div \tfrac{1}{2} \qquad 9 \div \tfrac{1}{6}$$

Standards for Mathematical Practice

8 Look for and express regularity in repeated reasoning

▶

▲ Addition and Subtraction

The idea of fostering invented strategies for fractions beginning with contextual problems is similar to the approach described in Chapter 11 for whole-number computation. As with whole numbers, set the expectation that students will use a variety of methods and that these methods will vary widely with the fractions encountered in the problems. Students should find ways to solve problems with fractions, and their invented strategies will contribute to the development of the standard algorithms (Huinker, 2002; Schifter, Bastable, & Russell, 1999).

In grade 3, students should be working with building fractions out of unit fractions. In the same way your students learned that $3 = 1 + 1 + 1$ they learn, $\frac{3}{4} = \frac{1}{4} + \frac{1}{4} + \frac{1}{4}$. This focus on rational number units will support students' ability to flexibly work with decomposing and composing fractions with the same denominators (Common Core Standards Writing Team, 2011), which is one essential component of both adding and subtracting fractions.

◆ Contextual Examples and Models

In the real world, most students first encounter the need to add or subtract fractions in measurement situations. Whether seeing how much they've grown, adding a half and a quarter hour of time, building a frame for a picture, combining amounts of ribbon needed for a costume, calculating how far they've jogged and how much more to run, students naturally see the need to combine and compare portions of units.

One early example emerges from doubling (repeated addition) or halving (repeated subtraction) using recipes. A junior cookbook or a book such as *Civil War Recipes* (George, 2010) can provide a context for these problems with links to social studies. Be sure to have a measuring cup available for reference. Consider the following problems based on recipes from the Civil War period: Robert and his brother were eating Northern brown bread. Robert had $\frac{3}{4}$ of his loaf left. His brother had $\frac{7}{8}$ of his loaf. How much brown bread do the boys have together? Many students will draw a simple rectangle for the two brown bread loaves, as in Figure 13.2. The drawing of $\frac{7}{8}$ suggests that if you had one more eighth it would be a whole. So the combined amount of brown bread it is the same as $1\frac{3}{4}$ with $\frac{1}{8}$ taken off. Or the drawing might suggest taking a fourth (in the form of $\frac{2}{8}$ from the $\frac{7}{8}$ and putting it with the $\frac{3}{4}$ to make a whole. That would leave $\frac{5}{8}$ for a total of $1\frac{5}{8}$.

Here are other problems based on the recipes:

Hardtack is a hard, dry bread often baked in a circular pan. A group of soldiers had $4\frac{1}{2}$ loaves of hardtack. One soldier ate $\frac{7}{8}$ of a loaf. How much was left for the others?

Josephine was making gingerbread and cornbread to share with the troops. She needed $2\frac{1}{2}$ cups of buttermilk for the one recipe and $6\frac{1}{4}$ cups for the other recipe. How much buttermilk did she need to complete both recipes?

Groundnut soup requires $\frac{2}{3}$ of a cup of crushed peanuts for one serving. How much would be needed if you were going to make two servings (using repeated addition)?

Notice that these contextual problems use a mix of models—both area and length or measurement (using a scale on a measuring cup). Encouraging students to model each of these problems is critical to developing the concept of addition and subtraction of fractions.

Starting with finding common denominators and jumping to algorithms would not provide the same opportunities to create mental models. Notice too that it is sometimes possible to find the sum or difference of two fractions without splitting pieces into smaller parts. Often the answer is determined by looking at the part left over.

Most of your initial problems should involve fractions with denominators no greater than 12. There is little need in the first phase of instruction to add fifths and sevenths, or even fifths and twelfths. The results involve numbers that cannot be handled easily with any model or drawing. At the same time, include mixed numbers and unlike denominators.

Cramer, Wyberg, and Leavitt (2008), well-known researchers in the area of rational numbers, have found circles to be the most effective model for adding and subtracting fractions. The circles allow students to develop mental images of the sizes of different pieces (fractions). Figure 13.3 shows how students estimate first (including marking a number line) and then explain in pictures and symbols how they added the fractions. Notice how the recording of their symbolic version is very close to the standard algorithm.

There are other effective area models that can be used, such as rectangles, as shown in Figure 13.4 and pattern blocks.

Pattern blocks have pieces such that the yellow hexagon can be one whole, the blue parallelogram $\frac{1}{3}$, the green triangle $\frac{1}{6}$, and the red trapezoid $\frac{1}{2}$. The following activity adapted from McAnallen and Frye (1995) uses the pattern blocks to informally explore ideas about subtraction of fractions.

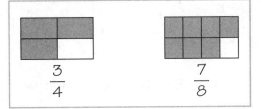

Figure 13.2

How could you combine these two quantities to determine the sum?

$$\frac{3}{4} \qquad \frac{7}{8}$$

◀ **Standards for Mathematical Practice**

1 Make sense of problems and persevere in solving them

Figure 13.3

A student estimates and then adds fractions using fraction pieces.

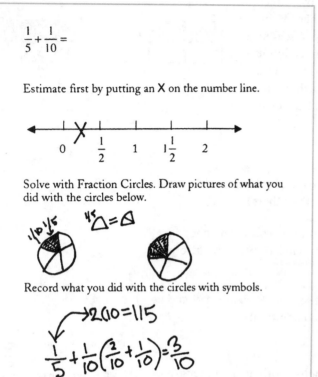

Source: Cramer, K., Wyberg, T., & Leavitt, S. (2008). "The Role of Representations in Fraction Addition and Subtraction." *Mathematics Teaching in the Middle School, 13*(8), p. 495. Reprinted with permission. Copyright 2008 by the National Council of Teachers of Mathematics. All rights reserved.

Teaching Tip

Notice that we didn't use the set model for introducing these ideas. Set models can initially be confusing and they can accidentally reinforce the adding of the denominator.

Figure 13.4

Using area models to subtract fractions.

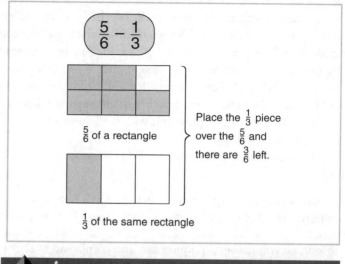

Activity 13.3 THE GOLD PRIZE

Use the pattern blocks to play a game that reinforces subtraction of fractions. All students need a collection of pattern blocks to work with. Start with each pair of students having three yellow hexagon pieces and name each yellow as one unit or whole (starting with the three wholes). Then roll a die that has the following fractions on its faces: $\frac{1}{6}, \frac{1}{3}, \frac{1}{2}, \frac{2}{6}, \frac{2}{3}, \frac{5}{6}$. Let's say one student rolls a $\frac{1}{3}$. They must take the third from one of the yellow pieces. Students might find trading one of the yellows for three blue thirds and then removing one of the thirds a useful strategy. Other students may try trading the yellow for two blues and subtracting the third in the process. The idea is to roll and subtract down to zero. At random points in the game, call a stop and ask students to note what they have left (such as $2\frac{1}{6}$ and later in the game $1\frac{1}{3}$). This game is actually reinforcing the finding of common denominators if students make equivalent trades before subtracting a piece.

Formative Assessment Note

The following can be used with an individual student in a diagnostic interview or paired with a checklist with the whole class. Share with your students the sample of Kieran's work shown here that provides his justification through words, pictures, and numbers to show that $\frac{1}{2} + \frac{1}{3} = \frac{2}{5}$.

As you will note, Kieran's work highlights a common misconception to combine the fractions: simply adding the numerators and the denominators. And he has provided a picture that seems to support his answer. Ask your students to try the problem on their own first. Then ask, "What do you think of Kieran's answer?" See whether your students are able to talk about how the whole changes with each fraction $\left(\frac{1}{2}, \frac{1}{3}, \frac{2}{5}\right)$. You will hope they notice the need for the wholes (or units) to be alike. But what if they don't see an issue?

$\frac{1}{2}$ $\frac{1}{3}$

add

Therefore, $\frac{1}{2} + \frac{1}{3} = \frac{2}{5}$.

Add tops and bottoms.

Standards for Mathematical Practice

1 Construct viable arguments and critique the reasoning of others

Students who have naïve understandings of addition of fraction concepts, coupled with Kieran's picture that appears to support this flawed approach, can cause students to doubt what they "know for sure." Placing these same fractions into a context and using visual models can help students begin to critically examine Kieran's approach. Say, for example, "Suppose you had $\frac{1}{2}$ of a small pizza and $\frac{1}{3}$ of a large pizza (using a visual of two different sized circles). When you put the two amounts together, you will have part of a pizza. But what is the size of that pizza?" This approach will support their critiquing of the different sized wholes used in Kieran's response.

The number line is another important model for adding and subtracting fractions (Siegler et al., 2010). The number line can be connected to the ruler, which for students is perhaps one of the most common real contexts for adding or subtracting fractions. The number line requires that the students understand $\frac{3}{4}$ as 3 parts of 4, and also as a value between 0 and 1 (Izsák, Tillema, & Tunc-Pekkam, 2008). Using the number line in addition to area representations can strengthen student understanding of fractions (Cramer et al., 2008; Petit, Laird, & Marsden, 2010).

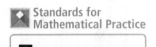
Teaching Tip

Remind students that when given a problem with fractions when no context is used (a "naked number" problem) they should assume the wholes (units) are equal.

Activity 13.4 JUMPS ON THE RULER

Using the ruler as a visual, find the results of these three problems without applying the common denominator algorithm. ELLs may not be as familiar with inches, so be sure to spend time prior to the activity discussing how the inch is partitioned and consider adding labels for fourths as a reminder.

$$\frac{3}{4} + \frac{1}{2} \qquad 2\frac{1}{2} - 1\frac{1}{4} \qquad 1\frac{1}{8} + 1\frac{1}{2}$$

In the first problem of Activity 13.4, students might use 1 as a benchmark and use $\frac{1}{4}$ from the $\frac{1}{2}$ to make one whole and then have $\frac{1}{4}$ more to add on, so $1\frac{1}{4}$. Similarly, they could use $\frac{1}{2}$ from the $\frac{3}{4}$ to make a whole and then add on the $\frac{1}{4}$, or they might just know that $\frac{1}{2} = \frac{2}{4}$, then add to get $\frac{5}{4}$ (or $1\frac{1}{4}$).

Standards for Mathematical Practice

◀ **2** Reason abstractly and quantitatively

◆ Developing the Algorithms

Students can build on their knowledge of equivalence and invented strategies to develop a meaningful grasp of the common-denominator approach for adding and subtracting fractions. The more fluent students are with exchanging one fractional unit for other equivalent units, the more easily they will be able to adapt problems into equivalent forms, a foundational skill for developing the algorithms.

Like Denominators

The *Common Core State Standards* (CCSSO, 2010) suggest that students in the fourth grade should add and subtract fractions with like denominators. If students have a good foundation with fraction concepts, they should be able to add or subtract like fractions immediately. Students who are not confident in solving problems such as $\frac{3}{4} + \frac{2}{4}$ or $3\frac{7}{8} - 1\frac{3}{8}$ may lack the understanding of the underlying fraction concepts and need additional experiences with concrete materials and relevant contexts. The idea that the numerator counts and the denominator tells what is counted makes addition and subtraction of like fractions the same as adding and subtracting whole numbers. When working on adding with like denominators, it is important to be sure that students are focusing on the key idea—the units are the same, so they can be combined (Mack, 2004).

Formative Assessment Note

Show a student the following problem in a diagnostic interview: $\frac{2}{3} + \frac{1}{2}$. Have a collection of fraction materials available. When your student is convinced that the sum is $1\frac{1}{6}$, substitute $\frac{16}{24}$ for the $\frac{2}{3}$ and $\frac{7}{14}$ for the $\frac{1}{2}$ and ask the student, "What is this sum $\left(\frac{16}{24} + \frac{7}{14}\right)$?" A student who understands that the two problems are equivalent should not hesitate and state that the answer remains the same—$1\frac{1}{6}$. If your student expresses any doubt about the equivalence of the two problems, that should be a clue that the concept of equivalent fractions is not well understood.

Unlike Denominators

Figure 13.5

Rewriting addition and subtraction problems involving fractions.

When starting to teach addition and subtraction with unlike denominators, begin by considering a task such as $\frac{5}{8} + \frac{2}{4}$, in which only one fraction needs to be changed. Let students use fraction pieces. Many will note that the models for the two fractions make one whole and there is $\frac{1}{8}$ extra. The key question to ask at this point is, "How can we change this problem into one in which the parts are the same?" For this example, it is relatively easy to see that fourths could be changed into eighths. Write the adapted equation on the board. Have students use models (manipulatives or drawings) to explain why the original problem and the converted problem are equivalent. The main idea is to see that $\frac{5}{8} + \frac{2}{4}$ is exactly the same problem as $\frac{5}{8} + \frac{4}{8}$ and that the reason for making the change is so that equal-sized units can be combined.

Next try some examples in which both fractions need to be changed—for example, $\frac{2}{3} + \frac{1}{4}$ (or $\frac{2}{3} - \frac{1}{4}$). Again, focus attention on using models to trade units and show with the corresponding symbols how the problem was *adapted* to a form in which the parts of both fractions are the same. As students discuss solutions, be sure they articulate clearly that the new form of the problem is the same problem. This process of finding common denominators is illustrated in Figure 13.5.

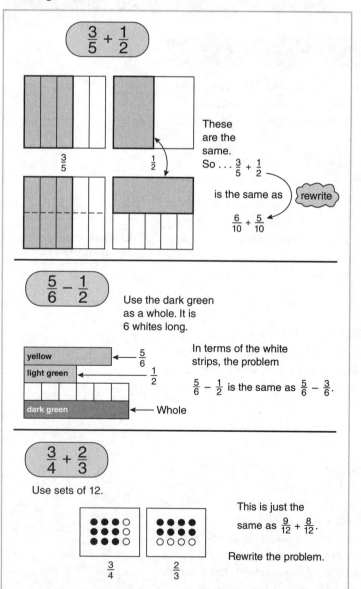

◆ Fractions Greater Than One

Include mixed numbers in all of your activities with addition and subtraction, and let students solve these problems in ways that make sense to them. Naturally, students will begin with what is familiar and add the whole numbers first and then deal with the fractions. The challenge arises in subtraction, when the need for regrouping across the whole number occurs.

For subtraction, dealing with the whole numbers first still makes sense. Consider this problem: $5\frac{1}{8} - 3\frac{5}{8}$. Ask students to estimate first. Will the answer be 2 or less than 2? After subtracting 3 from 5, students will need to address the $\frac{5}{8}$. Some will take $\frac{5}{8}$ from the whole part 2, leaving $1\frac{3}{8}$, and then $\frac{1}{8}$ more is $1\frac{4}{8}$. Others may take away the $\frac{1}{8}$ that is there and then $\frac{4}{8}$ from the remaining 2. A third but less likely method is to trade one of the wholes for $\frac{8}{8}$, add it to the $\frac{1}{8}$, and then take $\frac{5}{8}$ from the resulting $\frac{9}{8}$. This last method is the same as the standard algorithm.

◆ Addressing Misconceptions

Explicitly discuss common misconceptions with your students. This is particularly important with fraction operations because students incorrectly generalize rules from whole-number operations.

Adding Both Numerators and Denominators

The most common error in adding fractions is to add both numerators and denominators. Given the task, $\frac{3}{8} + \frac{2}{8}$, about half of students will write $\frac{5}{16}$, even after drawing the model correctly (Bamberger et al., 2010). Even when shown the discrepancy in their model and answer, students were not bothered by the difference. In such a case, ask students to defend which is right and justify why the other answer is not right—the key is for them to be able to overcome their misconceptions.

Ignoring the Denominators

Less common, but still prevalent, is the tendency to just ignore the denominator and add the numerators (Siegler et al., 2010). For example, $\frac{4}{5} + \frac{4}{10} = \frac{8}{10}$. This is an indication that students do not understand that the different denominators indicate different-sized pieces. Using fraction pieces, a number line, or a fraction strip to highlight the relative size of the fraction can help develop a stronger understanding of the role of the denominator.

Difficulty Finding Common Multiples

Many students have trouble finding common denominators because they are not able to quickly identify common multiples of the denominators. Activity 13.5 is aimed at practicing the skill of finding least common multiples or common denominators. Students will quickly find that least common denominators are preferred because the computation is more manageable with smaller numbers, and there is less simplifying to do. But *any* common denominator will work, whether it is the smallest or not.

 Activity 13.5 COMMON MULTIPLE CARDS

Give students (in teams of two) a deck of cards with pairs of numbers that are potential denominators (see Figure 13.6). First one student turns over a card and states a common multiple (e.g., for 6 and 8, a student might suggest 48). If possible, the partner can suggest a smaller common multiple (e.g., 24). The student suggesting the least common multiple (LCM) keeps the card. Be sure to include pairs in which both are prime, where one is a multiple of the other, and those that have a common divisor. Start students with disabilities with the card on which one member of the pair is a multiple of the other (color code the cards for easy identification).

Figure 13.6

Least common multiple (LCM) cards.

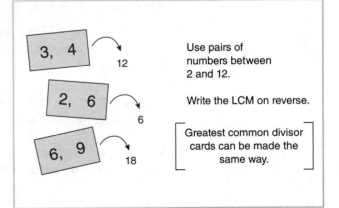

Difficulty with Mixed Numbers

Too often, instruction with mixed numbers is not well integrated into fraction instruction, and therefore students find these values particularly troubling. Here are three misconceptions described in the research (Petit, Laird, & Marsden, 2010; Siegler et al., 2010):

1. When given a problem like $3\frac{1}{4} - 1\frac{3}{8}$, students subtract the smaller fraction from the larger. Although this occurs with whole-number subtraction, it is more prevalent with mixed numbers.

2. When given a problem like $4 - \frac{7}{8}$, students don't know what to do with the fact that one number is not a fraction. They will even place an 8 as a denominator for the whole number $\left(\frac{4}{8} - \frac{7}{8}\right)$ in order to find a solution.

3. When given a problem like $14\frac{1}{2} - 3\frac{1}{8}$, students focus on the whole numbers and don't know what to do with the fractional part.

One way to avoid and to address these misconceptions, and other misconceptions, is to make them a part of public discussions about whether an approach is correct (or not) and why.

 **Multiplication**

Can you think of a situation that requires using multiplication of whole numbers? Those are familiar and come up almost every day. But can you think of a situation that requires multiplication of fractions? If not, why might that be? Many times the algorithm is presented early and as a result building the conceptual understanding never provides the background needed to answer "When do I use this?" Beginning with problems in everyday contexts supports students' ability to gain fluency in not only carrying out the algorithm, but also modeling problems, estimating, and seeing where this computation can be applied in a variety of real-world events.

◆ Contextual Examples and Models

When working with whole numbers, we would say that 3×5 means "3 sets of 5" (equal sets) or "3 rows of 5" (area or array) or "3 lengths of 5" (number line). The first factor tells how much of the second factor you have or want. This is a good place to begin. Using these ideas, we transition to language such as "$\frac{1}{2}$ of 5" or "$\frac{1}{2}$ of an area/array of 5" or "$\frac{1}{2}$ of a length of 5." The story problems that you use to pose multiplication tasks to your students need not be elaborate, but it is important to think about the numbers that you use in the problems. A possible progression of problem difficulty is developed in the sections that follow.

Fractions of Whole Numbers

As in the connection built previously to multiplication with whole numbers, this should be where you begin with multiplying fractions. Consider these two problems that can serve as a starting point:

There are 15 cars in Michael's toy car collection. Two-thirds of the cars are red. How many red cars does Michael have?

Suzanne has 11 cookies. She wants to share them with her three friends. How many cookies will Suzanne and each of her friends get?

Finding the fractional part of a whole number, which is the task in both problems, is not unlike the task of finding a fractional part of a whole. In Michael's car problem, think of the 15 cars as the whole and you want $\frac{2}{3}$ of the whole. First, find thirds by dividing 15 by 3. Multiplying by thirds, regardless of how many thirds, involves dividing by 3. The denominator is a divisor.

Suzanne's cookie problem is the same as the sharing problems discussed in the last chapter. Dividing by 4 is the same as multiplication by $\frac{1}{4}$. Or think of the 11 cookies as the whole. How many in one-fourth? Cookies are used so that the items can be subdivided.

Problems in which the first factor or multiplier is a whole number are also important.

Wesley filled 5 glasses with $\frac{2}{3}$ liter of soda in each glass. How much soda did Wesley use?

This problem may be solved in different ways. Some students will put the thirds together, making wholes as they go. Others will count all of the thirds and then find out how many whole liters are in 10 thirds.

Fractions of Fractions, without Subdivisions

To expand on the ideas just presented about fractions of a whole, the next step is to introduce fractions of fractions. At first we will use tasks in which no additional partitioning is required. Consider these three problems using the area, length, and set models:

You have $\frac{3}{4}$ of a pizza left. If you give $\frac{1}{3}$ of the leftover pizza to your brother, how much of a whole pizza will your brother get?

Someone ate $\frac{1}{10}$ of the bread, leaving only $\frac{9}{10}$. If you use $\frac{2}{3}$ of the bread that is left of the loaf to make sandwiches, how much of a whole loaf will you have used?

Gloria used $2\frac{1}{2}$ tubes of blue paint to paint the sky in her picture. Each tube holds $\frac{4}{5}$ ounce of paint. How many ounces of blue paint did Gloria use?

Notice that the units or fractional parts in these problems do not need to be subdivided or partitioned further. The first problem is $\frac{1}{3}$ of three things, the second is $\frac{2}{3}$ of nine things, and the last is $2\frac{1}{2}$ of four things. The focus remains on the number of unit parts in all, and then the size of the parts determines the number of wholes. Figure 13.7 shows how problems of this type might be modeled. However, it is very important to let students model and solve these problems in their own way, using whatever models or drawings they choose as long as they can explain their reasoning.

Subdividing the Unit Parts

When the pieces must be subdivided into smaller unit parts, the problems become more challenging.

Zack had $\frac{2}{3}$ of the lawn left to cut. After lunch, he cut $\frac{3}{4}$ of the grass he had left. How much of the whole lawn did Zack cut after lunch?

The zookeeper had a huge bottle of the animals' favorite liquid treat, Zoo Cola. The monkey drank $\frac{1}{5}$ of the bottle. The zebra drank $\frac{2}{3}$ of what was left. How much of the bottle of Zoo Cola did the zebra drink?

Figure **13.7** Connecting representations to the procedure for three problems involving multiplication of fractions.

Task	Finding the starting amount	Showing the fraction of the starting amount	Solution
Pizza Find $\frac{1}{3}$ of $\frac{3}{4}$ (of a pizza) or $\frac{1}{3} \times \frac{3}{4}$			$\frac{1}{3}$ of the $\frac{3}{4}$ is $\frac{1}{4}$ of the original pizza. $\frac{1}{3} \times \frac{3}{4} = \frac{1}{4}$
Bread Find $\frac{2}{3}$ of $\frac{9}{10}$ (of a loaf of bread) or $\frac{2}{3} \times \frac{9}{10}$			$\frac{2}{3}$ of the $\frac{9}{10}$ is 6 slices of the loaf or $\frac{6}{10}$ of the whole. $\frac{2}{3} \times \frac{9}{10} = \frac{6}{10}$
Paint Find $2\frac{1}{2}$ of $\frac{4}{5}$ (ounces of paint) or $2\frac{1}{2} \times \frac{4}{5}$			$2\frac{1}{2}$ of the $\frac{4}{5}$ is $\frac{4}{5} + \frac{4}{5} + \frac{2}{5} = \frac{10}{5}$

In Zack's lawn problem, it is necessary to find fourths of two things, the two-thirds of the grass left to cut. In the Zoo Cola problem, you need thirds of four things, the four-fifths of the cola that remains. Again, the concepts of the numerator counting and the denominator naming what is counted play an important role. Figure 13.8 shows two possible solutions for Zack's lawn problem. A similar approach can be used for the Zoo Cola problem. You may have used different drawings, but the ideas should be the same.

If students use counters to model problems in which the units require subdivision, an added difficulty arises. Figure 13.9 illustrates what might happen solving the problem $\frac{3}{5} \times \frac{2}{3}$. (Three-fifths of two-thirds of a whole is how much of a whole?) Here the representation of a whole must be changed so that the thirds can be subdivided. Do not discourage students from using counters, but be prepared to help them find ways to show thirds using larger sets. For example, because there is no context to the problem, why not use the commutative property—turn the factors around and consider $\frac{2}{3}$ of $\frac{3}{5}$. Wow! Now it reads as two-thirds of three-fifths! Do you immediately see that the answer is $\frac{2}{5}$?

Scaling

As students move to middle grades, they will learn about ratios and proportional thinking. Yet, the *Common Core State Standards* expect that fifth graders start to prepare for this work by

Figure **13.8**

Solutions to a multiplication problem in which the parts must be subdivided.

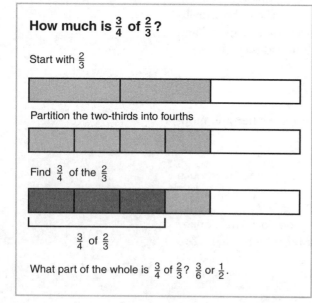

How much is $\frac{3}{4}$ of $\frac{2}{3}$?

Start with $\frac{2}{3}$

Partition the two-thirds into fourths

Find $\frac{3}{4}$ of the $\frac{2}{3}$

$\frac{3}{4}$ of $\frac{2}{3}$

What part of the whole is $\frac{3}{4}$ of $\frac{2}{3}$? $\frac{3}{6}$ or $\frac{1}{2}$.

thinking of multiplication of fractions from a perspective of scaling or resizing. Connect the fact that multiplication by one leaves the amount unchanged (identity property of multiplication), to multiplying a given number by numbers larger than one as producing a larger quantity, and multiplying a given number by numbers smaller than one (fractions, for example) as producing smaller quantities. This reasoning about the logical structure of multiplication will enhance your students' ability to decide whether their answers are reasonable while providing building blocks for the mathematics ahead.

◆ Developing the Algorithms

If you have spent adequate time (weeks working with multiple representations) with your students exploring multiplication of fractions as just described, students will begin to notice a pattern. Then, the standard multiplication algorithm will be relatively simple to develop. Shift from contextual problems to a straight computation. Have students use a square or a rectangle as the model.

To make the development problem-based and to connect it back to multiplication of whole numbers using an array, provide students with a drawing of $\frac{3}{4}$ of a square as shown in Figure 13.10. The task is to use the drawing to determine the product $\frac{3}{5} \times \frac{3}{4}$ (three-fifths of three-fourths of a whole) and explain the result. Remember, you want to find a fractional part of the shaded part. The *unit*—the way the parts are measured—must remain the whole.

Figure **13.9**

Modeling multiplication of fractions with counters.

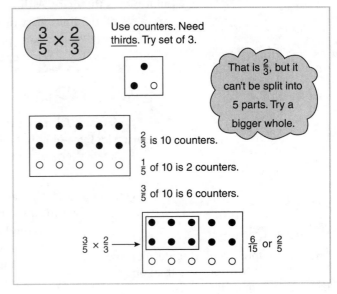

Figure **13.10** Development of the algorithm for multiplication of fractions.

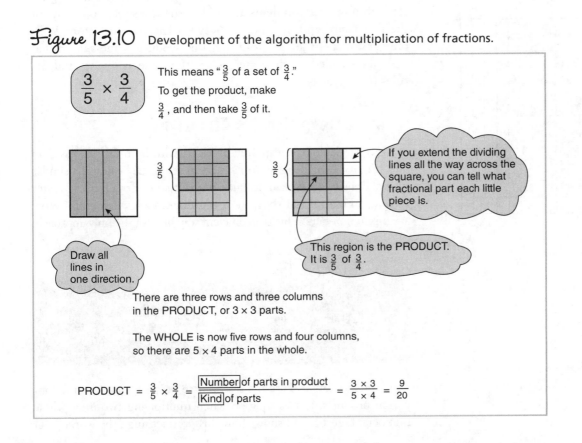

Drawn as shown, the easiest way to get $\frac{3}{5}$ of the shaded region is to partition it into fifths using lines in the opposite direction. Then the problem is to determine what types of unit pieces these are. Although students may not think of it, an easy method of doing this is to extend the lines, partitioning the entire whole into fifths. Then the product of the denominators tells how many pieces are in the whole (the kind of unit), and the product of the numerators tells the number of pieces in the product.

Stop and Reflect

Why is it reasonable to extend the lines to subdivide the entire whole into fifths when we are looking for three-fifths of three-fourths, not three-fifths of a whole? ■

Keep in mind that we are finding three-fifths of three-fourths *of a whole*, or $\frac{3}{5}$ of $\frac{3}{4}$ of 1. Extending the lines to subpartition the entire whole is maintaining the relationship between the fractional parts and the whole.

Avoid rushing students to formalize the rule or algorithm of multiplying numerators and denominators. At first, students will simply count each small part in the drawings and not notice that the numbers of rows and columns are actually the two numerators and the two denominators, respectively. Then, you might steer students in this direction by posing a problem with the initial sketch but asking them to determine the product without additional drawing. Try this with $\frac{7}{8} \times \frac{4}{5}$, in which the numbers make it almost mandatory that you multiply.

A cautionary note: Many textbooks make this sliced-square approach mechanically, such that it actually becomes a meaningless algorithm in itself. Students are told to shade a square one way for the first factor and the opposite way for the second factor. Without a rationale, they are told that the product is the region that is double-shaded. Such strategies are the same as giving students rules to memorize.

Figure 13.11

The same approach used to develop the algorithm for fractions less than one can be expanded to mixed numbers.

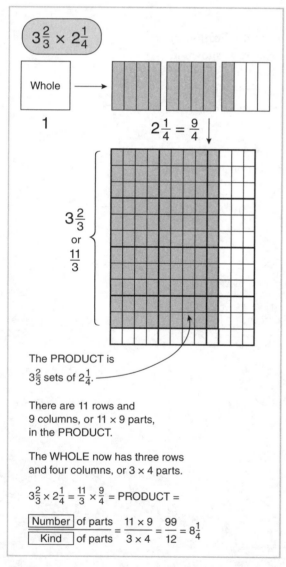

The PRODUCT is $3\frac{2}{3}$ sets of $2\frac{1}{4}$.

There are 11 rows and 9 columns, or 11 × 9 parts, in the PRODUCT.

The WHOLE now has three rows and four columns, or 3 × 4 parts.

$3\frac{2}{3} \times 2\frac{1}{4} = \frac{11}{3} \times \frac{9}{4} = \text{PRODUCT} =$

$\frac{\boxed{\text{Number}} \text{ of parts}}{\boxed{\text{Kind}} \text{ of parts}} = \frac{11 \times 9}{3 \times 4} = \frac{99}{12} = 8\frac{1}{4}$

◆ Factors Greater Than One

Once students have explored products with both factors less than one, it may be challenging to have them see if they can use a similar type of drawing to explain products with either or both factors greater than one. Figure 13.11 shows how this might look when both factors are mixed numbers. This is an efficient way but not the only approach.

Teaching Tip

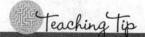

Have students estimate and consider the reasonableness of results so that they can notice the pattern that multiplying a given number by a fraction less than one results in a product smaller than the given number.

Students can also use the distributive property and find the four partial products, just as they do when multiplying two-digit whole numbers. Figure 13.12 shows how this product might be worked out by multiplying the individual parts. In most cases, the partial products can be solved mentally. More important, the process is more conceptual and also lends itself to estimation, either before the partial products are determined or after. Notice that the same four partial products of Figure 13.12 can be found in the rectangle in Figure 13.11. As mentioned in the previous section on scaling, the *Common Core State Standards* expect that student should be able to explain the impact of a product when the fraction is greater than one or less than one.

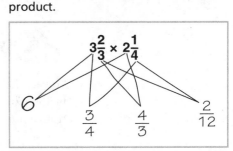

Figure 13.12

When multiplying two mixed numbers, there will be four partial products that need to be added to get the total product.

🔷 Addressing Misconceptions

Misconceptions can be intensified when students are too quickly pressed to memorize rules, such as "multiply both the bottom and the top," and are not given adequate time to explore multiplication of fractions conceptually. The result is an inability to solve multiplication problems, which is a significant barrier for solving proportions and algebraic expressions.

Treating the Denominator the Same as in Addition/Subtraction Problems

Why does the denominator stay the same when adding fractions and get multiplied when multiplying fractions? Do you have a conceptual explanation for this? In adding, the process is counting parts of a whole, so those parts must be the same size. In multiplication, you are finding a part of a part, so the part may change size. Compare the two operations with an area model or number line to see how they are conceptually different.

Inability to Estimate Approximate Size of the Answer

Some students have been told that "multiplication makes bigger." They also have difficulty deciding whether their answers make sense. On one hand, they may never even think about fraction size, so any answer looks reasonable (e.g., $\frac{1}{2} \times 6\frac{1}{4} = 12\frac{1}{8}$). On the other hand, they might see the answer $\left(\frac{1}{2} \times 6\frac{1}{4} = 3\frac{1}{8}\right)$, but become concerned that this can't be right because the answer should be bigger. Estimation, using contexts, and visuals help students think about whether answers are reasonable.

Matching Multiplication Situations with Multiplication (and Not Division)

Multiplication and division are closely related, and our language is sometimes not as precise as it needs to be. In the question, "What is $\frac{1}{3}$ of \$24?" students may correctly decide to divide by 3 or multiply by $\frac{1}{3}$. But they may (incorrectly) divide by $\frac{1}{3}$, confusing the idea that they are finding a fraction of the whole. This is particularly true for ELLs, who may become confused by language such as "divide it *in* half " and "divide it *by* half " (Carr, Carroll, Cremer, Gale, Lagunoff, & Sexton, 2009). Estimation can help students. Ask, "Should the result be larger or smaller than the original amount?"

Using a Key Word Strategy

When students decide which operation is appropriate for solving a word problem with fractions, a key word strategy is not useful. In a research study, when students were asked to explain their selection of an operation, 56 percent of students stated that when dealing with fractions, when you see the word *of,* it is always times. Ironically, 51 percent in explaining their choice of division said *of* means divide, and 33 percent said *of* helped them decide to subtract (Prediger, 2011). Students went on to state their reasoning for the "of" rule as "Our teacher has said . . ." (p. 81). When students are presented with word problems, the best strategy is to make meaning of the situation and not use one or two words in the entire problem to determine a direction for solution. One way to do this is to focus students' attention on the situation qualitatively (without a focus on the actual numbers): Should the result be more or less than the initial amount? What language in the story are you using to make your decision?

 # Division

"Invert the divisor and multiply" is probably one of the most mysterious rules in elementary mathematics. To avoid this mystery, students should first examine division with fractions from a more familiar perspective.

◆ Contextual Examples and Models

As with the other operations, go back to the meaning of division with whole numbers. Recall that there are two meanings of division: partition and measurement (Cramer, Monson, Whitney, Leavitt, & Wyberg, 2010; Kribs-Zaleta, 2008). Although you will present both types of division as you teach, for clarity let's review each meaning separately and look at some story problems in each problem type.

Stop and Reflect

Try to make up a word problem that would go with $2\frac{1}{2} \div \frac{1}{4}$. ■

Measurement Division

We start with this model because this is the interpretation of division of fractions that is almost always seen in textbooks, it can be used later to develop an algorithm for dividing fractions, and, as Cramer and colleagues found (2010), it is able to be effectively represented with pictures to show the measures. In these situations, an equal group is repeatedly subtracted from the total. Here is a contextual situation: "If you have 13 quarts of lemonade, how many pitchers holding 3 quarts each can you fill?" So the resulting problem, 13 ÷ 3, means "How many sets of 3 are in 13?" A key idea to get from this example involves repeatedly subtracting equal groups from the whole amount. The challenge arises when you deal with that last quart after filling the first four pitchers. If you continue to fill a fifth pitcher, it will get only one quart. It will be only one-third full. So the answer is $4\frac{1}{3}$ pitchers.

Students readily understand problems such as the following (adapted from Schifter et al., 1999, p. 120):

You are going to a birthday party. You order 6 pints of ice cream from Mitch and Bob's Ice Cream Factory. If you serve $\frac{3}{4}$ of a pint of ice cream to each guest, how many guests can be served?

Students typically draw pictures of six things partitioned into fourths and count out how many servings of $\frac{3}{4}$ can be found. The difficulty is in seeing this as $6 \div \frac{3}{4}$, and that part will require some direct guidance on your part. One idea is to relate the problem to one involving whole numbers (e.g., 6 pints, 1 pint per guest) and make a comparison.

Using servings is helpful in developing these ideas, and Gregg and Gregg (2007) propose a logical sequence of tasks in Figure 13.13 of how this might develop.

As you will note, students build on their whole-number understandings to move to more complex tasks such as the following problem:

Farmer Brown found that he had $2\frac{1}{4}$ gallons of liquid fertilizer concentrate. It takes $\frac{3}{4}$ gallon to make a tank of mixed fertilizer. How many tankfuls can he mix?

Try solving this problem yourself. Use any model or drawing you wish to help explain what you are doing. Notice that you are trying to find out how many sets of three-fourths are in a set of nine-fourths. Your answer should be three tankfuls (not three-fourths).

As the numbers increase in difficulty, students will begin to change all of the numbers to the same fractional unit. That is, both the dividend or given quantity and the divisor are expressed in the same type of fractional parts. This, in essence, results in a whole-number division problem, as you will find when we discuss the common denominator algorithm later.

Partition Division

Just as with whole-number division, this interpretation asks us to partition or find "fair shares" of the whole. Although we often think of the partition problems strictly as sharing problems ("If there are 24 apples to be shared with 4 friends, how many will each friend get?"), this same sharing structure applies to rate problems. A rate problem is, "If you walk 12 miles in 3 hours, how many miles do you walk per hour?" Both of these problems, ask the questions "How much is *one*?" and "How much is the amount for *one* friend?" and "How many miles are walked in *one* hour?"

Whole-Number Divisors.

Having the total amount be a fraction, with the divisor being a whole number, is not really a big leap. These problems still are easy to think of as sharing situations. However, as you work through these questions, notice that you are answering the questions "How much is the whole?" or "How much for one?"

Figure 13.13

Tasks that use the measurement interpretation of "How many servings?" to develop the concept of division.

1. A serving is $\frac{1}{2}$ cookie. How many servings can I make from 2 cookies?

2. A serving is $\frac{1}{2}$ cookie. How many servings can I make from 1 cookie?

3. A serving is $\frac{1}{2}$ cookie. How many servings can I make from $\frac{3}{4}$ cookie?

4. A serving is $\frac{1}{2}$ cookie. How many servings can I make from $\frac{3}{8}$ cookie?

5. A serving is $\frac{1}{2}$ cookie. How many servings can I make from $\frac{5}{8}$ cookie?

Source: Gregg, J., & Gregg, D. U. (2007). Measurement and fair-sharing models for dividing fractions. *Mathematics Teaching in the Middle School, 12*(9), p. 491. Reprinted with permission. Copyright © 2007 by the National Council of Teachers of Mathematics. All rights reserved.

Cassie has $5\frac{1}{4}$ yards of ribbon to make three bows for birthday packages. How much ribbon should she use for each bow if she wants to use the same length of ribbon for each?

When the $5\frac{1}{4}$ is thought of as fractional parts, there are 21 fourths to share, or 7 fourths for each ribbon. Alternatively, one might think of first allotting 1 yard per bow, leaving $2\frac{1}{4}$ yards, or 9 fourths. These 9 fourths are then shared, 3 fourths per bow, for a total of $1\frac{3}{4}$ yards for each bow. Regardless of the particular process, the unit parts required no further subdivision in order to do the division. In the following problem, the parts must be split into smaller parts.

Figure 13.14 Three models of partition division with a whole-number divisor.

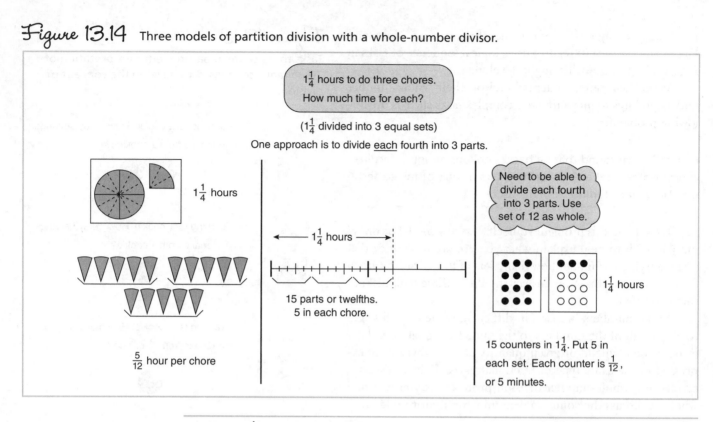

Marik has $1\frac{1}{4}$ hours to finish his three household chores. If he divides his time evenly, how many hours can he give to each?

Note that the question is "How much for one chore?" which considers the rate. The five-fourths of an hour that Marik has to complete this work does not split neatly into three parts. So some or all of the parts must be subdivided. Figure 13.14 shows three different models for figuring this out. In each case, all of the fourths are subdivided into three equal parts, producing twelfths. There are a total of 15 twelfths, or $\frac{5}{12}$ hour for each chore. (Test this answer against the solution in minutes: $1\frac{1}{4}$ hours is 75 minutes, which divided among 3 chores is 25 minutes per chore.)

Fractional Divisors. The sharing concept appears to break down when the divisor is a fraction. However, it is enormously helpful to keep in mind that for partition and rate problems, the fundamental question is "How much is *one*?" Interestingly, this connects back to the "given the part, find the whole" tasks shown in Figure 12.11. For example, if a set of 18 counters is $2\frac{1}{4}$ sets, how much is a whole set? In solving these part–whole problems, the first task is to find the number in one-fourth, and then multiply by 4 to get four-fourths, or one. Let's see if we can see the same process in the following activity:

Activity 13.6 **HOW MUCH FOR ONE?**

Pose problems with a context in which the question is, "How much for one?"

- Lisbeth bought $3\frac{1}{4}$ pounds of tomatoes for $2.50. How much did she pay per pound?
- Micah paid $2.40 for a $\frac{3}{4}$-pound box of cereal. How much is that per pound?
- Aidan found out that if she walks quickly during her morning exercise, she can cover $2\frac{1}{2}$ miles in $\frac{3}{4}$ of an hour. How fast she is walking in miles per hour?

For students with disabilities, support them by supplying them a possible picture they can use as a starting point.

For all three problems in the activity, first find the amount of one-fourth (equal partitioning) and then the value of one whole (iterating).

◆ Developing the Algorithms

There are two different algorithms for division of fractions. Methods of teaching both algorithms are discussed here.

The Common-Denominator Algorithm

The common-denominator algorithm relies on the measurement or repeated subtraction concept of division, and is most advantageous when you want to use a visual model (Cramer et al., 2010). Additionally, it links to what students have already learned in adding and subtracting fractions with common denominators and is aligned with whole-number division ($25 \div 5$ is how many groups of 5 are in 25?). "The concept of unit plays a central role in this measurement scenario" (Barnett-Clarke et al., 2010, p. 53).

Initially start by using problems without remainders, such as $1\frac{3}{4} \div \frac{1}{8}$. Look at Figure 13.15 to see a student's use of a number line to think about this problem. First, the student labels the number line in fourths and then makes jumps in eighths to count out the number of groups.

After trying other problems like this one, you can transition to problems with remainders, such as the following problem that includes a remainder (see Figure 13.16):

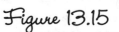

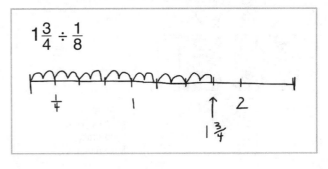

Figure 13.15
A student uses a number line to think about division of fractions.

Rory has $\frac{5}{3}$ of a pound of fudge. If she wants to cut the candy into $\frac{1}{2}$-pound pieces for her friends, how many friends will get a piece of fudge?

Cramer and colleagues (2010) discuss the importance of estimation in thinking about the remainders. They suggest you ask questions like, "Do you think you will have 2 servings of fudge? Could you have 4 friends who get the fudge pieces?" They also highlight the need to carefully identify the unit; otherwise meaning is lost in interpreting the remainder.

As shown in Figure 13.16, once each number is expressed in terms of the same fractional part, the answer is exactly the same as the whole-number problem $10 \div 3$. Then the problem becomes one of dividing the numerators—but let the students note this pattern.

As students begin to notice patterns in their solutions, connect that discussion to the common denominator algorithm. The resulting algorithm, therefore, is as follows: "To divide fractions, first get common denominators, and then divide numerators." For example, if the same amount of fudge would be divided into fourths of a pound, $\frac{5}{3} \div \frac{1}{4} = \frac{20}{12} \div \frac{3}{12} = 20 \div 3 = \frac{20}{3} = 5\frac{2}{3}$.

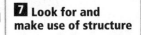
Standards for Mathematical Practice

7 Look for and make use of structure

 *Teaching Tip*
Make sure you carry out a discussion of what the remainder means. In this case, your students should be able to state that the remainder represents a portion of another serving (not a portion of the whole).

Invert-and-Multiply Algorithm

To invert the divisor and multiply may be one of the most commonly taught, but poorly understood, mathematical procedures in the elementary curriculum. (Were you taught why invert-and-multiply works?)

In an effort to help students see patterns that link to the algorithm, start with a unit fraction as a divisor.

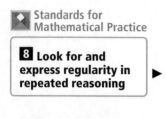

Standards for Mathematical Practice

8 Look for and express regularity in repeated reasoning ▶

$3 \div \frac{1}{2} =$ (How many servings of $\frac{1}{2}$ in 3 containers?)

$5 \div \frac{1}{4} =$ (How many servings of $\frac{1}{4}$ in 5 containers?)

$3\frac{3}{4} \div \frac{1}{8} =$ (How many servings of $\frac{1}{8}$ in $3\frac{3}{4}$ containers?)

In looking across a collection of these problem types students will notice they are multiplying by the denominator of the second fraction. For example, in the first example, a student might say, "You get two for every whole container, so 2×3 is 6."

Then move to similar problems, but with a second fraction that is not a unit fraction:

$$8 \div \frac{2}{5} =$$
$$3\frac{3}{4} \div \frac{3}{8} =$$

Figure 13.16

Models for the common-denominator method for fraction division.

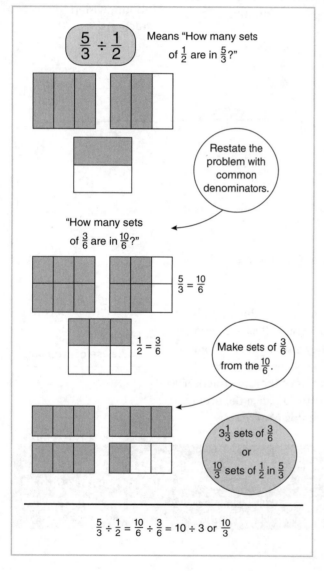

Have students think about what they know from the unit fraction problems to solve these problems. For example, in the first problem, think first of "per unit"—in this case, the unit fraction. Only after identifying that amount should you go back to consider the actual divisor. So, if there are 40 one-fifths in 8, then when you group the fifths in pairs (two-fifths), you will have half as many—20. Stated in servings, if the serving is twice as big, you will have half the number of servings. Similarly, if the divisor is $\frac{3}{4}$, after finding how many fourths, you will group in threes, which means you will get $\frac{1}{3}$ of the number of servings. You can see that this means you must divide by 3 or multiply by $\frac{1}{3}$. This gets at the heart of the definition of division as having an inverse relationship with multiplication; therefore, dividing by a number is equivalent to multiplying by the reciprocal. (Sound familiar?)

Partitioning or sharing examples effectively illustrates the standard algorithm. Consider this example:

You have $1\frac{1}{2}$ oranges, which is $\frac{3}{5}$ of an adult serving. How many oranges (and parts of oranges) make up 1 adult serving? (Kribs-Zaleta, 2008)

You may be thinking that because you know that $1\frac{1}{2}$ oranges is $\frac{3}{5}$ of a serving, you first need to find what a fifth would be. Logically that would be one-third of the oranges you have, or $\frac{1}{2}$ an orange (notice you are dividing by the numerator). Then, to get the whole serving, you multiply $\frac{1}{2}$ by 5 (the denominator) to find that there are $2\frac{1}{2}$ oranges in 1 adult serving. This process links to the algorithm.

In either the measurement or the partition interpretations, the denominator leads you to find out how many fourths, fifths, or eighths you have, and the numerator tells you the size of the serving, so you group according to how many are in the serving. So the process is multiply by the denominator and divide by the numerator. As you can see from the pattern identified above, this represents the reasoning of the well-known "invert and multiply" algorithm. However, there is actually no reason that the fraction needs to be inverted; instead just multiply by the denominator and divide by the numerator.

◆ Addressing Misconceptions

The biggest misunderstanding with division of fractions is when the algorithm is taught too quickly and students just don't know what the algorithm means. Once students realize the meaning of division, they are able to estimate, find different ways to approach problems, and decide whether their answers make sense. Within division of fractions there are some common misconceptions that need to be addressed.

Thinking the Answer Should Be Smaller

Based on their experiences with whole-number division, students think that when dividing by a fraction, the answer should be smaller. For example, Petit and her colleagues (Petit, Laird, & Marsden, 2010) describe a student who rules out the whole-number answers in a multiple choice for $\frac{1}{2} \div \frac{1}{4}$ because they are "bigger numbers" (p. 164). Although the answers to division with fractions can be smaller if the divisor is a fraction greater than one (e.g., $\frac{5}{3}$), that is not true if the fraction is less than one.

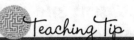

One way to help students address the misconception that "division always makes smaller" is to ask students to estimate first to help think about a reasonable answer.

Connecting the Representation with the Answer

Students may understand that $1\frac{1}{2} \div \frac{1}{4}$ means "How many fourths are in $1\frac{1}{2}$?" So they may set out to count how many fourths and get 6. But in recording their answer, they can get confused as to what the 6 refers to and think it should be a fraction and thus record it as $\frac{6}{4}$ (Cramer et al., 2010).

Remainders

As noted above, knowing what the unit is (the divisor) is critical and must be understood in giving the remainder (Coughlin, 2010/2011; Cramer et al., 2010; Lamon, 2012). In the problem $3\frac{3}{8} \div \frac{1}{4}$, students are likely to count 4 fourths for each whole (12 fourths) and one more for $\frac{2}{8}$ but then not know what to do with the remaining eighth. It is important to be sure they understand the measurement concept of division. Ask, "How much of the next piece do you have?" Context can also help—in particular, servings. In this case, if the problem were about pizza servings, there would be 13 full servings and $\frac{1}{2}$ of the next serving.

Another issue with remainders is that students mistakenly use the original unit (how the whole was divided) instead of using the denominator of the divisor to name the remainder. So, in the case of this last problem with one-eighth as a remaining piece (half of another serving), instead of thinking of what portion of another unit of the serving, they might say $\frac{1}{8}$ is the remainder, using the thinking that it must be labeled in terms of the whole.

Students need to carry out all four operations with fractions meaningfully and accurately in a reasonably efficient manner. Each of the algorithms has value. Regardless of which algorithm is your goal, you are strongly advised to build on informal work with story problems, concrete materials, and invented strategies. Find the Fraction Bars activity on the National Library of Virtual Manipulatives at http://nlvm.usu.edu/en/nav/frames_asid_203_g-2-t-1.html. Here is an applet (using a representation much like Cuisenaire rods), in which the step size can be adjusted, thereby providing a flexible model for all four operations with fractions.

You may find it surprising that only about 5 percent of mistakes made in fraction computation problems by students in the upper elementary grades involve miscalculations (errors in basic fact computations) (Hecht, Vagi, & Torgesen, 2007). Instead, most errors were based on misconceptions and naïve understandings about the size of fractions and how the computations must be adapted from the former whole-number algorithms. Working toward building the "fraction sense" and "operation sense" that underpins students' thinking is worth the time you spend on these important foundations.

Expanded Lesson

Multiplication of Fractions Stories

Content and Task Decisions

Grade Level: 5–6

Mathematics Goals

- To develop the meaning of multiplication of fractions through various area models

- To explore how different sized wholes affect area models

- To apply area models in solving real-world problems

Grade Level Guide

NCTM *Curriculum Focal Points*	*Common* *Core State Standards*
Multiplying fractions is part of a grade 6 Focal Point: "Number and Operations: Developing an understanding of and fluency with multiplication and division of fractions and decimals" (NCTM, 2006, p. 18).	Fraction computation, including multiplication, is one of three critical areas in grade 5. Specifically, fifth graders should be able to "Apply and extend previous understandings of multiplication and division to multiply and divide fractions" (CCSSO, 2010, p. 36).

Consider Your Students' Needs

Students understand that multiplication can be thought of as repeated addition; that is, 3×6 means 3 sets of 6. They understand that in the context of part-whole fractions, the whole is divided into equivalent parts. They also understand the symbolic notation of fractions. Students know that the bottom number in the fraction (denominator) names the size or number of the parts they are counting. The denominator indicates how many pieces make a whole unit. They know the top number in the fraction (numerator) is the number of parts they have.

For English Language Learners

- In the car example, use real toy cars or pictures of toy cars to provide both visual support for the language and a concrete way to solve the problem.

- Focus on the terms *numerator* and *denominator*. Both of these words have partial cognates that will help ELLs of Latin languages. Specifically, *nom* means name (the denominator is the name of the fraction), and

numerare meaning "to number." In other words, the numerator is the numberer (how many parts).

- Be sure the contexts in the stories are familiar to students. If they are not, change to something that is. Also, you can modify the handout by using the same context for each story so that students don't get bogged down in different contexts.

For Students with Disabilities

- Instead of having the students draw the fractional model, give them grid paper or color tiles to support the creation of the representation.

- To help students prepare for sharing their thinking, make sure you do a think aloud and share your thinking when discussing the first example. Students who are struggling need explicit demonstrations of what is important to share as they talk about their approaches to the problem.

Materials

Each student will need:

- "Solving Problems Involving Fractions" worksheet (Blackline Master 28)

Teacher will need:

- Transparency of or way to display "Solving Problems Involving Fractions" worksheet (Blackline Master 28)

Lesson

Before

Begin with a simpler version of the task:

- Ask students what 3×4 means. Have them either draw a picture or say/write a word problem to show what 3×4 means. Listen to students' ideas. Capitalize on ideas that emphasize that 3×4 means 3 groups of 4.

- Pose the following word problem to students: "There are 15 cars in Michael's toy car collection. Two-thirds of the cars are red. How many red cars does Michael have?"

- Encourage students to draw pictures not only to help them think about how to solve the problem but also as a way to explain how they did the problem. Have students share their work with the class. Many students will draw 15 rectangles (cars) and then divide the 15 into three equal parts. At this point, make sure to have the students explain why they divided the 15 into three equal parts (e.g., looking for thirds because $\frac{2}{3}$ are red). Once they have three equal parts (thirds), they count two of those sets because they need $\frac{2}{3}$.

- Help students connect this situation with multiplication with whole numbers. Just as 3×4 means 3 groups of 4, $\frac{2}{3} \times 15$ means $\frac{2}{3}$ of a group of 15.

Present the focus task to the class:

- Students are to solve the three problems on the worksheet and be ready to explain their thinking. They should use both words and pictures to help them think through the problems and to show how they solved them. They should be prepared to explain their thinking.

- To differentiate for students ready for more challenging problems, pose the following task in which the pieces must be subdivided into smaller unit parts: "Zack had $\frac{2}{3}$ of the lawn that needed to be cut. If he cuts $\frac{3}{4}$ of the grass that needs to be cut, how much of the whole lawn that needs to be cut will be cut? How much will still need to be cut?"

During

Initially:

- Observe that each student understands the question and is in the process of attempting to solve the first situation.

- If students have difficulty getting started, have them represent the information in the first sentence of the task. Have them explain why their picture represents this information. Then have them read the first part of the "if?" statement in the second sentence and identify what part of their original picture this amount is. Have them color the part they just identified with a different color to make it stand out. Now have them read the question at the end of the task and think about how the part they just colored can help them answer this question.

Ongoing:

- Look for students who use different representations to think about the problems. Highlight those different ways in the *After* portion of the lesson.

- If you notice an error, rather than correct it, ask the student to explain how he or she solved the problem.

(Students often catch their mistakes while explaining and showing.)

- As they work, ask students to tell you what the problem is asking and how they are thinking about solving it. See "Assessment" below for details.

After

Bring the class together to share and discuss the task:

- Starting with the first problem, ask a student to come to the board to explain his or her strategy for thinking about the problem. Ask questions about why the student drew what he or she did to make sure everyone in the class follows the rationale. Encourage the class to comment or ask questions about the student's representation or thinking.

- Help students make explicit what the whole is at each stage of the problem.

- Ask if others solved the problem in a different way. If so, have the students come forward to share their solutions.

- As students share their solutions, it is important to have them compare and contrast the different solutions. Some solutions that at first appear to be different are actually equivalent. Through questioning, help students make these connections.

- Help students connect fraction multiplication with the meaning of multiplication: $\frac{1}{3} \times \frac{3}{4}$ means $\frac{1}{3}$ of a group of $\frac{3}{4}$.

Assessment

Observe

- Look for students who struggle when the whole changes in the problem. These students need more experience working with part-and-whole tasks.

- Are students correctly using the meaning of the numerator and denominator? These problems are easily solved by thinking of the fractional parts as discrete units. For example, $\frac{2}{3}$ of $\frac{3}{4}$ is $\frac{2}{3}$ of three things called fourths.

- Are students answering the question that is being asked?

Ask

- How does your drawing show the situation in the task?

- What is the whole unit in the problem?

14

Developing Decimal and Percent Concepts and Decimal Computation

Big IDEAS

1 The base-ten place-value system extends infinitely in two directions: to very small values and to very large values. Between any two place values, the 10-to-1 ratio remains the same.

2 Decimals are simply another way of writing fractions, and are also called *decimal fractions.* Maximum flexibility is gained by understanding how the two symbol systems are related.

3 The decimal point is a convention that has been developed to indicate the units position. The position to the left of the decimal point marks the location of the units place.

4 Percents are simply hundredths, and as such are a third way of writing both fractions and decimals.

5 Addition and subtraction with decimals are based on the fundamental concept of adding and subtracting the numbers in like position values—an extension from whole numbers.

6 Multiplication and division of two numbers will produce the same digits, regardless of the positions of the decimal point. As a result, multiplicative computations with decimal fractions can be performed as whole numbers with the decimal placed by way of estimation.

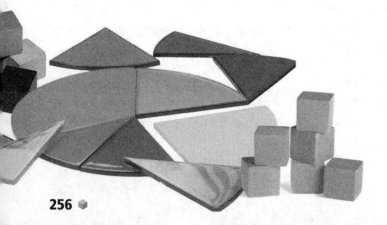

People need to be able to interpret decimals for such varied needs as reading precise metric measures, calculating distances, interpreting output on a calculator, and understanding sports statistics such as those at the Olympics for which winners and losers are separated by hundredths of a second. Decimals are critically important in many occupations such as for nurses, pharmacists, and workers building airplanes; in each case the level of precision affects the safety of the general public. Because students and teachers have been shown to have a greater difficulty understanding decimals than fractions (Martinie, 2007; Ubuz & Yayan, 2010), conceptual understanding of decimals and their connections to fractions must be carefully developed.

Developing Concepts of Decimals

Traditionally, decimals are typically introduced in the fourth grade and most of the computation work with decimals begins in the fifth grade and is continued in grades 6 and 7. This is also aligned with the *Common Core State Standards* (CCSSO, 2010), which state the following:

> Grade 4: Students see the link to fractions with denominators of 10 and 100 rewritten in decimal notation and they compare the size of decimal fractions up to hundredths by reasoning about place value.

> Grade 5: Students apply their understanding of decimal fractions to compare decimals to thousandths as they begin to add, subtract, multiply, and divide decimals to hundredths. They also use their knowledge of multiplication and division to explain patterns of decimal placement in answers.

The phrase *decimal fractions* is often shortened to *decimals* and in this chapter we will use these terms interchangeably.

Explicitly linking the ideas of fractions to decimals can be extremely useful, both from a pedagogical view as well as a practical view. Much of this chapter focuses on that connection.

◈ Extending the Place-Value System

Before exploring decimal numerals with students, it is advisable to review ideas of whole-number place value. One of the most basic of these ideas is the 10-to-1 multiplicative relationship between the values of any two adjacent positions. In terms of a base-ten model, such as paper strips and squares, 10 of any one piece will make 1 of the next larger (to the immediate left), and movement of a piece to the immediate right involves division by 10 (1 divided by 10 is one-tenth).

A Two-Way Relationship

The 10-makes-1 relationship continues indefinitely to larger and larger pieces or positional values. As you learned in Chapter 10, if you are using the paper strip-and-square model, for example, the strip and square shapes alternate in an infinite progression as they get larger. Likewise, each piece to the right in this continuum gets smaller by one-tenth. The critical question becomes, "Is there ever a smallest piece?" In the students' experience, the smallest piece is the centimeter square or unit piece. But couldn't that piece be divided into 10 small strips? And couldn't those small strips be divided into 10 very small squares, and so on?

The goal of this discussion is to help students see that a 10-to-1 relationship can extend infinitely in two directions. There is no smallest piece and no largest piece. The symmetry of the system is around the ones place, not the decimal point (tens to the left of the ones place, tenths to the right, and so on). The relationship between adjacent pieces is the same regardless of which two adjacent pieces are being considered. Figure 14.1 illustrates this idea.

Regrouping

Even at this stage, students need to be reminded of the powerful concept of regrouping. Flexible thinking about place values should be practiced prior to exploring decimals. Having students revisit not only making one 10 from ten units, but thinking about regrouping 2,451

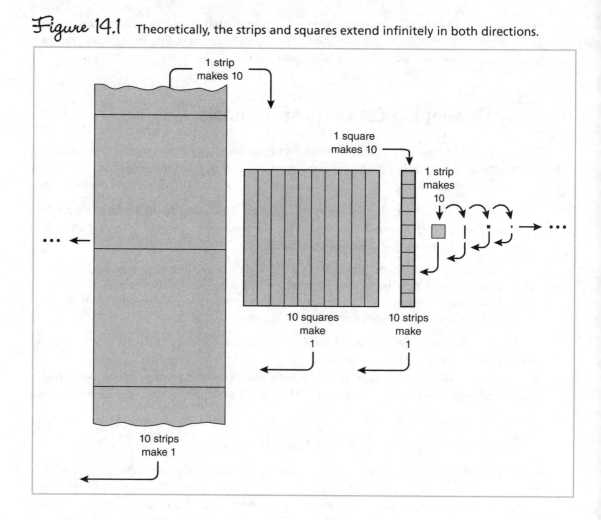

Figure 14.1 Theoretically, the strips and squares extend infinitely in both directions.

into 24 hundreds, 5 tens, and 1 unit; or 245 tens and 1 unit; or 2,451 ones. As you can see, this process will be essential in thinking about 0.6 as 0.60, and so on.

The Role of the Decimal Point

Students must know that the decimal point marks the location of the ones (or units) place. That is why on a calculator, when there is a whole number answer, no decimal point appears. Only when the ones place needs to be identified will the decimal point show in the display. Students also need to see that adding zeros to the left of a whole number will have no consequence and adding zeros to the right of a decimal fraction will not change the number.

An important idea to be realized is that there is no built-in reason why any one position (or base-ten piece) should be chosen to be the unit or ones position. In terms of strips and squares, for example, which piece is the ones piece? The small centimeter square? Why? Why not a larger or a smaller square? Why not a strip? *Any* piece could effectively be chosen as the ones piece. As shown in Figure 14.2, a given quantity can be written in different ways, depending on the choice of the unit or what piece is used to count the entire collection.

The decimal point is placed between two positions with the convention that the position to the left of the decimal is the units or ones position. Thus, the role of the decimal

> ### *Teaching Tip*
>
> The decimal notation of a 0 in the ones place, such as 0.60, is the accepted way to write decimal fractions. This is a convention and a way to indicate that the number is less than 1.

Standards for Mathematical Practice

6 Attend to precision ▶

point is to designate the units position, and it does so by sitting just to the right of that position. A reminder to help students think about the decimal point is shown in Figure 14.3 with the "eyes" focusing up at the name of the units or ones.

▲ *Activity* **14.1 THE DECIMAL POINT NAMES THE UNIT**

Have students display a certain number of base-ten pieces on their desks. For example, put out six squares, two strips, and four tinies, as in Figure 14.2. For this activity, refer to the pieces as *squares, strips,* and *tinies,* and reach an agreement on names for the theoretical pieces both smaller and larger. To the right of tinies can be *tiny strips* and then *tiny squares.* To the left of squares can be *super strips* and *super squares.* For ELLs, it is particularly important that you write these labels with the corresponding visuals in a prominent place in the classroom (and in student notebooks), so they can refer to this terminology as they participate in the activity. Each student should also have a "smiling" decimal point. Now ask students to write and say how many squares they have, how many super strips, and so on. The students position their decimal point accordingly and both write and say the amounts.

Activity 14.1 illustrates the convention that the decimal indicates the named unit and that the unit can change without changing the quantity.

The Decimal Point with Measurement and Monetary Units

The notion that the decimal identifies the units place is useful in a variety of contexts. For example, in the metric system, seven place values have special names. As shown in Figure 14.4, the decimal point can be used to designate any of these places as the unit without changing the actual measure. Our monetary system is also a decimal system. In the amount $172.95, the decimal point designates the dollars position as the unit. There are 1 hundred (dollars), 7 tens, 2 singles, 9 dimes (one-tenth of a dollar), and 5 pennies (one-hundredth of a dollar) in this amount of money, regardless of how it is written. If pennies were the designated unit, the same amount would be written as 17,295 cents or 17,295.0 cents. It could just as correctly be 0.17295 thousands of dollars or 1729.5 dimes.

Figure **14.2**

The decimal point indicates which position is the units.

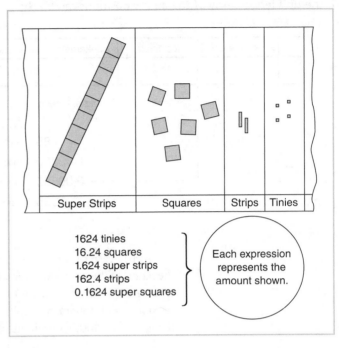

| Super Strips | Squares | Strips | Tinies |

1624 tinies
16.24 squares
1.624 super strips
162.4 strips
0.1624 super squares

Each expression represents the amount shown.

Figure **14.3**

The decimal point always "looks up at" the name of the units position. In this case we have 16.24.

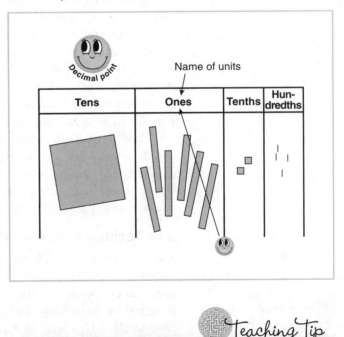

| Tens | Ones | Tenths | Hundredths |

Teaching Tip

Note that it is incorrect to write .50¢, as that would indicate $\frac{1}{2}$ of a cent! Instead write $0.50 or 50¢.

Figure 14.4

In the metric system, each place-value position has a name. The decimal point can be placed to designate which length is the unit length. Any of the metric positions can be the unit length, as illustrated here.

kilometer	hectometer	dekameter	meter	decimeter	centimeter	millimeter
			3	8	5	

3 meters, 8 decimeters, and 5 centimeters =

3.85	meters	
3850	millimeters	
0.00385	kilometers	Unit names
385	centimeters	

In the case of measures such as metric lengths or weights or the U.S. monetary system, the name of the unit is written after the number rather than above the digit as on a place-value chart. In the newspaper, we may read about Congress spending $7.3 billion. Here the units are billions of dollars, not dollars. A city may have a population of 2.4 million people. That is the same as 2,400,000 individuals.

 ## Connecting Fractions and Decimals

The symbols 3.75 and $3\frac{3}{4}$ represent the same quantity, yet on the surface the two appear quite different. And for students, the world of fractions and the world of decimals are very distinct. Even adults tend to think of fractions as sets or regions (e.g., three-fourths of something), whereas we think of decimals as values or numbers (e.g., weight). When we tell students that 0.75 is the same as $\frac{3}{4}$, this can be especially confusing because the denominators are hidden in decimal fractions. Even though these are different ways of writing the numbers, the amounts themselves are not different. A significant goal of instruction in decimal and fraction numeration should be to help students see that both systems represent the same concepts.

There are two important ways to help students see the connection between fractions and decimals. First, we can use familiar fraction concepts and models to explore rational numbers that are easily represented by decimals: tenths, hundredths, and thousandths. Then, we can help students use models to make meaningful translations between fractions and decimals. These components are discussed in turn.

Say Decimal Fractions Correctly

You must make sure you are reading and saying decimals in ways that support students' understanding. Always say "five and two tenths" instead of "five point two." Using the *point* terminology results in a disconnect to the fractional part that exists in every decimal. This is not unlike the ill-advised reading of fractions as "two over ten" instead of correctly saying "two-tenths." This level of precision in language will provide your students with the opportunity to *hear* the connections between decimals and fractions, so that when they hear "two-tenths," they think of both 0.2 and $\frac{2}{10}$.

Standards for
Mathematical Practice

6 Attend to precision

Decimal Fraction Models

Many fraction manipulatives do not lend themselves to depicting decimal fractions because they cannot show hundredths or thousandths. It is important to provide models for decimal

Figure 14.5 A rational number wheel for modeling decimal fractions.

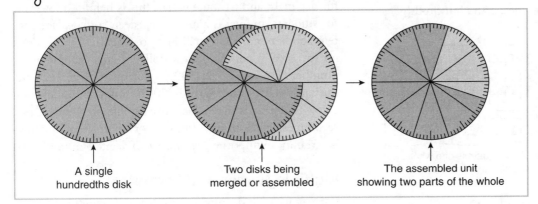

A single
hundredths disk

Two disks being
merged or assembled

The assembled unit
showing two parts of the whole

fractions using the same conceptual approaches that were used for fractions such as thirds and fourths.

Area Models. Two area models that can be used as representations of tenths and hundredths are circular disks and a square 10×10 grid. Circular disks such as the one shown in Figure 14.5 can be printed on cardstock (see Blackline Master 20). Each disk is marked with 100 equal intervals around the edge and is cut along one radius. Two disks of different colors, slipped together as shown, can be used to model any fraction less than one. Fractions modeled on this rational number wheel can be read as decimal fractions by noting the spaces around the edge, but can also be stated as three-fourths, helping students further make the connection between fractions and decimals.

The most common area model for decimal fractions is a 10×10 grid (see Figure 14.6 and Blackline Master 21). Another variation is to use base-ten place-value strips and squares. As a fraction model, the 10-cm square that was used as the hundreds model for whole numbers can be the unit or 1. Each strip is then one-tenth, and each small square (now referred to as a *tiny*) is one-hundredth.

Try using the Base Blocks—Decimals at http://nlvm.usu.edu. These base-ten blocks can be placed on a place-value chart to represent decimals. The number of decimal places can be selected, thus designating any of the four blocks as the unit. Later when students are working on decimal computation with addition and subtraction, problems can be created or can be generated randomly.

Length Models. One of the best length models for decimal fractions is a meter stick. Each decimeter is one-tenth of the whole stick, each centimeter is one-hundredth, and each millimeter is one-thousandth. Any number-line model broken into 100 subparts is likewise a useful model for hundredths.

Empty number lines like those used with whole-number computation are also useful in helping students compare decimals and think about scale and place value (Martinie & Bay Williams, 2003). Given two or more decimals, students can use an empty number line to position the values, revealing what they know about the size of these decimals by using zero, one, other whole numbers, or other decimal values as benchmarks. Again, the use of multiple representations will broaden not only students' understanding, but also your understanding of their level of performance.

Figure 14.6

These 10 × 10 squares model tenths and hundredths.

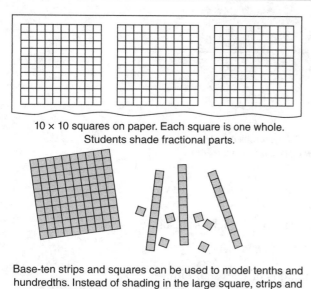

10 × 10 squares on paper. Each square is one whole. Students shade fractional parts.

Base-ten strips and squares can be used to model tenths and hundredths. Instead of shading in the large square, strips and small squares are placed on it to show a fractional part.

Set Models. Many teachers use money as a model for decimals, and to some extent this is helpful. However, for students, money is almost exclusively a two-place system and is nonproportional (e.g., one-tenth, a dime, does not physically compare to a dollar in that proportion). Numbers like 3.2 or 12.1389 do not relate to money and can cause confusion (Martinie, 2007). Students' initial contact with decimals should be more flexible, so money is not recommended as an initial model for decimals, although it is certainly an important *application* of decimal numeration.

Multiple Names and Formats

Early work with decimal fractions is designed to acquaint students with the visual models to help them begin to think of quantities in terms of tenths and hundredths, and to learn to read and write decimal fractions in different ways.

Have students show a decimal fraction using any base-ten model. Once a fraction (for example, $\frac{65}{100}$) is modeled, the following ideas can be explored:

- Is this fraction more or less than $\frac{1}{2}$? Than $\frac{2}{3}$? Than $\frac{3}{4}$? Some familiarity with decimal fractions can be developed by comparison with fractions that are easy to think about.

- What are some different ways to say this fraction using tenths and hundredths? ("6 tenths and 5 hundredths" or "65 hundredths") Include thousandths when appropriate.

- Show two ways to write this fraction ($\frac{65}{100}$ or $\frac{6}{10} + \frac{5}{100}$).

The last two questions are very important in building the connection to decimal fractions. Decimals are usually read as a single value. That is, 0.65 is read "sixty-five hundredths." But to understand them in terms of place value, the same number should be thought of as 6 tenths and 5 hundredths. A mixed number such as $5\frac{13}{100}$ is usually read the same way as a decimal: 5.13 is "five and thirteen-hundredths." For purposes of place value, it should also be understood as $5 + \frac{1}{10} + \frac{3}{100}$.

Expanded forms will be helpful in translating fractions to decimals. Given a model or a written or oral fraction, students should be able to give the other two forms of the fraction, including equivalent forms where appropriate.

Teaching Tip

Please note that it is accurate to use the word *and* when reading the decimal, which represents the decimal point.

▶ Activity 14.2 FRACTIONS TO DECIMALS

For this activity, have students use paper place-value strips and squares (see Blackline Master 4) agreeing that the large square represents one. Have students cover a fractional amount of the square using their strips and tinies (remember to call the pieces "tenths" and "hundredths"). For example, have them cover $2\frac{35}{100}$ of the square. Whole numbers will require additional squares. The task is to decide how to write and say this fraction as a decimal and demonstrate the connection using their physical models. For students with disabilities, you may want to have the amount shaded rather than have the students try to cover the exact amount, and then ask them to name and write the decimal fraction.

For the last activity, a reason why $2\frac{35}{100}$ is the same as 2.35 is that there are 2 wholes, 3 tenths, and 5 hundredths. It is important to see this physically. The same materials that are used to represent $2\frac{35}{100}$ of the square can be rearranged or placed on a place-value chart with a paper decimal point used to designate the units position as shown in Figure 14.7.

Although these translations between decimals and fractions are rather simple, the main agenda is for students to learn from the beginning that decimals are simply fractions.

The calculator can also play a significant role in developing decimal concepts.

Figure 14.7

Translation of a fraction to a decimal.

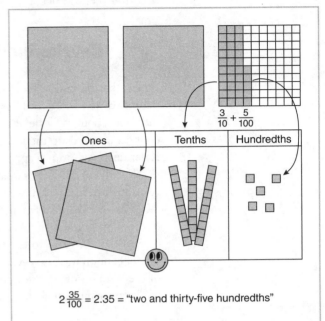

$$\frac{3}{10} + \frac{5}{100}$$

Ones	Tenths	Hundredths

$2\frac{35}{100}$ = 2.35 = "two and thirty-five hundredths"

Activity 14.3 CALCULATOR DECIMAL COUNTING

Recall how to make the calculator "count" by pressing + 1 = = and so on. Now have students press + 0.1 = = ... When the display shows 0.9, stop and discuss what this means and what the display will look like with the next count. Many students will predict 0.10 (thinking that 10 comes after 9). This prediction is even more interesting if, with each press, the students have been accumulating base-ten strips as models for tenths. One more press would mean one more strip, or 10 strips. Why doesn't the calculator show 0.10? When the tenth press produces a display of 1 (calculators are not usually set to display trailing zeros to the right of the decimal), the discussion should revolve around trading 10 strips for a square. Continue to count to 4 or 5 by tenths. How many presses to get from one whole number to the next? For students with disabilities and for ELLs, counting out loud along with the calculator "one tenth, two tenths . . . " supports the concept (e.g., ten-tenths being the same as one whole) while reinforcing appropriate mathematical language. Students may need to be reminded that a place is "full" when it has 9 of any unit and the addition of another unit will push to the position that is one place to the left (like the mileage in a car). Once students are working well with tenths, try counting by 0.01 or by 0.001. These counts illustrate dramatically how small one-hundredth and one-thousandth really are. It requires 10 counts by 0.001 to get to 0.01 and 1000 counts to reach 1.

The fact that the calculator counts 0.8, 0.9, 1, 1.1 instead of 0.8, 0.9, 0.10, 0.11 should give rise to the question "Does this make sense? If so, why?"

Calculators that permit entry of fractions also have a fraction–decimal conversion key. Some calculators will convert a decimal such as 0.25 to the fraction $\frac{25}{100}$ and allow for either manual or automatic simplification. The ability of fraction calculators to go back and forth between fractions and decimals makes them a valuable tool for connecting fraction and decimal symbolism. However, students should be challenged to explain why 0.25 and $\frac{25}{100}$ are equivalent and not simply rely on the calculator to do the conversion.

Precision and Equivalence

The *Common Core State Standards* Mathematical Practice "Attend to Precision" states, "[Mathematically proficient students] express numerical answers with a degree of precision appropriate for the problem context" (CCSSO, 2010, p. 7). Consider the two values 0.06 and 0.060. They are equivalent in terms of numerical value, but the latter communicates a greater level of *precision*. By adding the additional zero, it signals

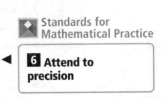

Standards for
Mathematical Practice

6 Attend to precision

that the measurement was done to the nearest thousandth and that there were 60 thousandths. In the first case, the measurement was completed only to the nearest hundredth. Precision becomes important when measuring very small things.

Developing Decimal Number Sense

So far, the discussion has focused on the connection of decimals to fractions with denominators related to 10 and 100. Number sense with decimals implies more. It means having intuition about, or a flexible understanding of, decimal numbers. To this end, it is useful to connect decimals to the fractions with which students are familiar, to be able to compare and order decimals, and to approximate decimals using useful benchmarks.

Results of NAEP exams reveal that students have difficulties with the fraction–decimal relationship. In 2004, fewer than 30 percent of high school students were able to translate 0.029 as $\frac{29}{1000}$ (Kloosterman, 2010). In 2009, Shaughnessy found that more than 46 percent of the sixth graders she studied could not write $\frac{3}{5}$ as a decimal. Instead, many wrote $\frac{3}{5}$ as 3.5, 0.35 or 0.3. She also found that more than 25 percent could not write $\frac{3}{10}$ as a decimal. This misconception was also reversed when students wrote the decimal 4.5 as the fraction $\frac{4}{5}$. Division of the numerator by the denominator may be a means of converting fractions to decimals, but it contributes little to understanding the resulting equivalence.

◆ Familiar Fractions Connected to Decimals

Chapter 12 discussed how to help students develop a conceptual familiarity with common fractions, especially halves, thirds, fourths, fifths, and eighths. We should extend this familiarity to the same concepts expressed as decimal fractions. One way to do this is to have students translate familiar fractions to decimals in a conceptual manner, which is the focus of the next two activities.

Figure 14.8

A 10 × 10 square can be used to convert familiar fractions to decimals.

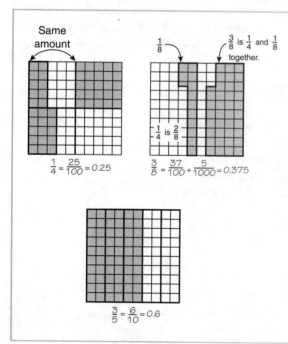

▲ *Activity 14.4* FAMILIAR FRACTIONS TO DECIMALS

Students are given a "familiar" or commonly used fraction to convert to a decimal. They first model the fraction using a 10 × 10 square grid and strips and tinies. Covering the grid with the materials, they model then write the fraction and decimal equivalent. A good sequence is to start with halves and fifths, then fourths, and possibly eighths.

Figure 14.8 shows how translations in the last activity might work with a 10 × 10 grid. For fourths, students will often cover a 5 × 5 section (half of a half). The question then becomes how to translate this to a decimal. Ask these students how they could think about each half strip as 0.05 and then use the models to reason that 2 of the half strips (0.05) would make one-tenth (0.1), so you'd have 0.1 + 0.1 + 0.05, or 0.25. This approach would start where the students' prior knowledge is and work toward a solution. The fraction $\frac{3}{8}$ represents a wonderful challenge. A hint might be to find $\frac{1}{4}$ first and then notice that $\frac{1}{8}$ is half of a fourth. Remember that the next smaller pieces are tenths of the tinies (or thousands). Therefore, half of a tiny is $\frac{5}{1000}$. Note how the shaded grid shows that $\frac{2}{8} + \frac{1}{8} = \frac{37}{100} + \frac{5}{1000} = 0.375$.

Because the circular model carries such a strong mental link to fractions, it is worth the time to do some fraction-to-decimal conversions with the rational number wheel shown in Figure 14.5 (see Blackline Master 20).

Standards for Mathematical Practice

2 Reason abstractly and quantitatively

BLM

Activity 14.5   ESTIMATE, THEN VERIFY

With the blank side of the wheel facing them, have students adjust the wheel to show a common fraction, for example $\frac{3}{4}$. Next, they turn the wheel over and record how many hundredths they estimate were in the section. Finally, they should make an argument for the correct number of hundredths and the corresponding decimal equivalent. Repeat with other fractions.

The number line is another good model to connect decimals and fractions. The following activity continues the development of fraction–decimal equivalences.

Activity 14.6   DECIMALS AND FRACTIONS ON A DOUBLE NUMBER LINE

Give students five decimal numbers that have common fraction equivalents. Keep the numbers between two consecutive whole numbers. For example, use 3.5, 3.125, 3.4, 3.75, and 3.66. Show a number line from 3.0 to 4.0 with subdivisions on the number line of only fourths, only thirds, or only fifths, but without labels. The students' task is to locate each of the decimal numbers on the fraction number line and to provide the fraction equivalent for each.

Formative Assessment Note

A simple yet powerful performance assessment to evaluate decimal understanding has students represent two related decimal numbers, such as 0.6 and 0.06, by using multiple representations: an empty number line, a 10 × 10 grid, and base-ten materials (Martinie & Bay-Williams, 2003). Ask students to describe their representations and see if they have significantly more difficulty with one model over another. Placement of decimals on an empty number line is perhaps the most interesting task, and it provides the most revealing information (see Figure 14.10).

Teaching Tip

If students struggle to find a decimal equivalent for their rational number wheel fraction, cut up some wheels into tenths and hundredths so that these parts of the fraction could be placed on a chart (see Figure 14.9).

Figure 14.9

Fraction models could be decimal models.

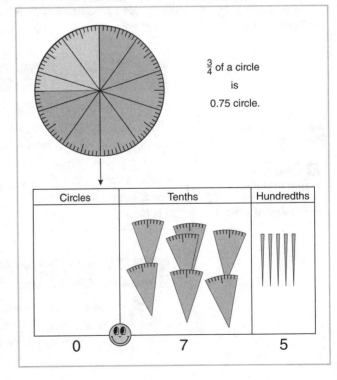

$\frac{3}{4}$ of a circle
is
0.75 circle.

Circles	Tenths	Hundredths
0	7	5

Figure 14.10

Three different students attempt to draw a number line and show the numbers 0.6 and 0.06.

Source: Reprinted with permission from Martinie, S. L., & Bay-Williams, J. (2003). "Investigating Students' Conceptual Understanding of Decimal Fractions Using Multiple Representations." *Mathematics Teaching in the Middle School, 8,* p. 246. Copyright © 2003 by the National Council of Teachers of Mathematics. All rights reserved.

Approximation with a Compatible Fraction

In the real world, decimal fractions are rarely those with exact equivalents to common fractions. What fraction would you say approximates the decimal 0.52? In the sixth NAEP exam, only 51 percent of students in the eighth grade selected $\frac{1}{2}$. The other choices were $\frac{1}{50}$ (29 percent), $\frac{1}{5}$ (11 percent), $\frac{1}{4}$ (6 percent), and $\frac{1}{3}$ (4 percent) (Kouba, Zawojewski, & Strutchens, 1997). Again, a possible explanation for this performance is a reliance on rules. Students need to wrestle with the size of decimal fractions and begin to develop a sense of familiarity with them.

As with fractions, the first benchmarks that should be developed are 0, $\frac{1}{2}$, and 1. For example, is 7.3962 closer to 7 or 8? Why? (What would need to be added to make this response acceptable: "Closer to 7 because 3 is less than 5"?) Is it closer to 7 or $7\frac{1}{2}$? Often the 0, $\frac{1}{2}$, or 1 benchmarks are good enough to make sense of a situation. If a closer approximation is required, encourage students to consider other common fractions (thirds, fourths, fifths, and eighths). In this example, 7.3962 is close to 7.4, which is $7\frac{2}{5}$. A good number sense with decimals entails the ability to quickly think of a fraction that is a close equivalent.

To develop this type of familiarity with decimals, students do not need new concepts or skills. They need opportunities to apply and discuss the related concepts of fractions, place value, and decimals in activities such as the following.

Activity 14.7 CLOSE TO A FAMILIAR FRACTION

Standards for Mathematical Practice

3 Construct viable arguments and critique the reasoning of others

Make a list of about five decimals (e.g., 24.80, 6.59, 0.973, 124.35, and 7.7) that are close to but not exactly equal to a familiar or commonly used fraction equivalent. The students' task is to decide on a decimal number that is close to each of these decimals and that also has a common fraction equivalent that they know. For example, 6.59 is close to 6.6, which is $6\frac{3}{5}$. They should write an explanation for their choices. Different students may select different equivalent fractions, providing for a discussion of which is closer.

Activity 14.8 BEST MATCH

Create a deck of cards with familiar fractions on half of the cards and the decimals that are close to the fractions, but not exact, on the other half. Students are to pair each fraction with the decimal to make a match in a memory-like game. The difficulty is determined by how close the various fractions are to one another. For students with disabilities, you may need to have them reflect whether what they've turned over is close to 0, close to $\frac{1}{2}$, or close to 1, to help support their match-making.

In Activities 14.7 and 14.8, students will have a variety of reasons for their answers. Sharing their thinking with the class provides a valuable opportunity for all to learn. Do not focus on the answers but on the rationales.

✍ *Formative Assessment Note*

The connections between models and the two-symbol systems for rational numbers—fractions and decimals—are a good topic for a **diagnostic interview.** Provide students with a number represented in any one of these three ways (fraction, decimal, or physical model) and have them provide the other two representations along with an explanation. Here are a few examples:

- Write the fraction $\frac{5}{8}$ as a decimal. Use a drawing or a physical model (meter stick or 10 × 10 grid) and explain why your decimal equivalent is correct.
- What fraction is represented by the decimal 2.6? Use an example and a physical model to explain your answer.
- Use a fraction and a decimal to tell the name of this marked point on the number line. Explain your reasoning.

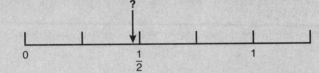

In the last example, it is especially interesting to see which representation students select first—fraction or decimal. Furthermore, do they then translate this number to the other representation or make a second independent estimate?

Other Fraction–Decimal Equivalents

Recall that the denominator is a divisor and the numerator is a multiplier. Therefore, $\frac{3}{4}$, for example, means the same as $3 \times (1 \div 4)$ or $3 \div 4$. So how would you express $\frac{3}{4}$ on a simple four-function calculator? Simply enter $3 \div 4$. The display will read 0.75.

Too often students think that dividing the denominator into the numerator is simply an algorithm for converting fractions to decimals, and they have no understanding of why this might work. Use the opportunity to help students develop the idea that in general $\frac{a}{b} = a \div b$ where b is not 0. (See Chapter 12.)

◆ Comparing and Ordering Decimal Fractions

Comparing decimal fractions and putting them in order from least to greatest is a skill closely related to comparing fractions and decimals. In the real world, we rarely think about the order of "ragged" decimals—decimals of unequal length. The real purpose of these exercises is to create a better understanding of decimal numeration and place-value concepts.

Formative Assessment Note

Consider the following list: 0.36, 0.05, 0.375, 0.97, 0, 2.0, and 0.4. Ask students to order these decimals from least to greatest. There are six common errors and misconceptions that students exhibit when comparing and ordering decimals (Desmet, Gregoire, & Mussolin, 2010; Steinle & Stacey, 2004a; 2004b). Knowing these will help you pinpoint ways to improve students' conceptual understanding as they overcome these misconceptions.

1. *Longer is larger.* This is the most common initial error, when students select the number with more digits as the largest. This is an incorrect application of whole-number ideas as students just look at the number beyond the decimal point and judge it as they would a whole number. So, under this misconception, they would say that 0.375 is greater than 0.97.

2. *Shorter is larger.* Here the students think that because the digits far to the right represent very small numbers, the longer numbers must be smaller. For example, they would choose 0.4 as larger than 0.97 because "a tenth is larger than a hundredth." This error is very persistent.

3. *Internal zero.* In this case, students are confused by a zero in the tenths position, as in 0.078. Here they would see 0.58 as less than 0.078 thinking that "zero has no impact" when written to the left, as is the case with a whole number. This has also been shown to be an issue when decimals are placed on the number line.

4. *Less than zero.* This misconception with zero is that when some students compare 0.36 with 0, they choose 0 as larger. This is due to thinking that zero is a whole number positioned in the ones column (to the left of the decimal point) and therefore is greater than a decimal fraction (to the right of the decimal point). They are unsure if a decimal fraction is greater than zero.

5. *Reciprocal thinking.* This error usually takes teachers by surprise. If students are asked to compare 0.4 and 0.6, they incorrectly select 0.4 as larger. Using their knowledge that decimals are like fractions, they connect 0.4 to $\frac{1}{4}$ and 0.6 to $\frac{1}{6}$ and erroneously decide 0.4 is greater.

6. *Equality.* Another surprise is that students don't integrate the idea of regrouping decimals, and that 4 tenths is equal to 40 hundredths or 400 thousandths. This misconception has them thinking that 0.4 is not close to 0.375 and/or that 0.3 is smaller than 0.30.

All of these common errors reflect a lack of conceptual understanding of how decimal fractions are constructed. The following activity helps promote discussion about the relative sizes of decimal fractions.

Activity 14.9 LINE 'EM UP

Prepare a list of four or five decimal fractions that students might have difficulty putting in order. Use a context such as the height of plants. The decimals should all be between two consecutive whole numbers. Have students first predict the order of the numbers, from least to greatest. Require students to use a model of their choice to defend their ordering. As students wrestle with representing the numbers with a physical model (perhaps a number line with 100 subdivisions or a 100 × 100 [10,000] grid (see Blackline Master 22), they will necessarily confront which digits contribute the most to the size of a decimal.

For students who are struggling, some explicit instruction might be helpful. Write a five-digit decimal on the board, such as 3.0917. Start with the whole numbers: "Is it closer to 3 or to 4?" Then go to the tenths: "Is it closer to 3.0 or to 3.1?" Repeat with hundredths and thousandths. At each answer, challenge students to defend their choices with the use of a physical model or other conceptual explanation. A large, empty number line, shown in Figure 14.11, is useful.

Figure 14.11 Decimal fractions on an empty number line.

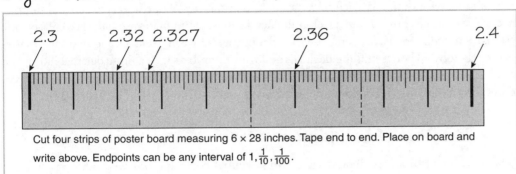

Cut four strips of poster board measuring 6 × 28 inches. Tape end to end. Place on board and write above. Endpoints can be any interval of $1, \frac{1}{10}, \frac{1}{100}$.

Density of Decimals

When students only see decimals rounded to two places, this may reinforce the notion that there are no numbers between 2.37 and 2.38 (Steinle & Stacey, 2004b). Finding the decimal located between any two decimals requires that students understand the density of decimals. Using a linear model helps to show that there is always another decimal to be found between any two decimals, an important concept that is emphasized in the following activity.

Activity 14.10 **CLOSE DECIMALS**

Have your students name a decimal between 0 and 1.0. Next have them name another decimal that is even closer to 1.0 than the first. Continue for several more decimals in the same manner, each one being closer to 1.0 than the previous decimal. Similarly, try close to 0 or close to 0.5. For students with disabilities, let them use physical models or a number line to help them with their decision making. Later, see how they can explain their thinking without those representations.

Confusion over the density of decimals also plays out when students try to find the nearest decimal (Ubuz & Yayan, 2010). Many times when students are asked to find which decimal is closer to a given decimal, they revert to thinking that tenths are only comparable to tenths and that there are no hundredths between. So, given the question which decimal is closer to 0.19—0.2 or 0.21—they are likely to incorrectly select 0.21. They also are not sure that 0.513 is near 0.51, but just a little larger. They may also think that 0.3 is near 0.4 but far away from 0.31784. These examples are evidence that students are in need of additional experiences and probably not yet ready for operations with decimals.

 Computation with Decimals

Students should develop computational fluency with decimal fractions. In the past, decimal computation was dominated by the following rules: Line up the decimal points (addition and subtraction), count the decimal places (multiplication), and shift the decimal point in the divisor and dividend so that the divisor is a whole number (division). Some textbooks continue to emphasize these rules, but specific rules for decimal computation are not always necessary if computation is built on a firm understanding of place value and a connection between decimals and fractions.

The *Common Core State Standards* state that fifth graders should "apply their understandings of models for decimals, decimal notation, and properties of operations to add and subtract decimals to hundredths. They develop fluency in these computations, and make reasonable estimates of their results. Students use the relationship between decimals and fractions, as well as the relationship between finite decimals and whole numbers (i.e., a finite decimal multiplied by an appropriate power of 10 is a whole number), to understand and explain why the procedures for multiplying and dividing finite decimals make sense" (CCSSO, 2010, p. 33).

◆ The Role of Estimation

Students should become adept at estimating decimal computations well before they learn to compute with pencil and paper. For many decimal computations, rough estimates can be made by rounding the numbers to whole numbers or simple fractions. A minimum goal for your students should be to have the estimate contain the correct number of digits to the left of the decimal—the whole-number part. Start your instruction by selecting problems for which estimates are not terribly difficult.

Stop and Reflect

Before continuing, what would be reasonable whole-number estimates of the following computations?

1. $4.91 + 123.01 + 56.123$
2. $459.8 - 12.345$
3. 24.67×1.84
4. $514.67 \div 3.59$

Your estimates might be in the following ranges. ■

1. Between 175 and 200
2. More than 400, or about 425 to 450
3. More than 25, closer to 50 (1.84 is more than 1 and close to 2)
4. More than 125, less than 200 ($500 \div 4 = 125$ and $600 \div 3 = 200$)

In these examples, an understanding of decimal numeration and basic whole-number estimation skills can produce a reasonable range for answers. When estimating, focus on the meanings of the numbers and the operations and not on counting decimal places. Many students who are taught to focus on poorly understood rules for decimal computation do not even consider the actual values of the numbers, much less estimate.

Begin computation with decimals is as soon as a conceptual background in decimal numeration is developed. As with fractions, until students have a sound understanding of place value, equivalence, and relative size of decimals, they are not ready to develop understanding of the operations (Cramer & Whitney, 2010). Many students who rely on rules for decimals make mistakes without being aware, as they are not using number sense.

◆ Addition and Subtraction

Consider this problem:

Jessica and Tiana each timed their own quarter-mile run with a stopwatch. Jessica says that she ran the quarter mile in 74.5 seconds. Tiana was more accurate in her timing, reporting that she ran the quarter mile in 81.34 seconds. Who ran it the fastest and how much faster was she?

Students who understand decimal numeration should be able to estimate approximately what the difference is—close to 7 seconds. Only then should they be challenged to figure out the exact difference. The estimate will help them avoid the common error of lining up the 5 under the 4. A variety of student strategies are possible. For example, students might note that 74.5 and 7 more is 81.5 and then figure out how much extra that is. Others may count on from 74.5 by adding 0.5 and then 6 more seconds to get to 81 seconds and then add on the remaining 0.34 second. These and other strategies will eventually push students to confront the difference between the 0.5 and 0.34. Students can resolve this issue by returning to their understanding of place value. Similar story problems for addition and subtraction, some involving different numbers of decimal places, will help develop students' understanding.

After students have had several opportunities to solve addition and subtraction story problems, see if they can reason without a context, as in the next activity.

◢ *Activity* 14.11 **EXACT SUMS AND DIFFERENCES**

Give students a sum involving addends with different numbers of decimal places, for example, 73.46 + 6.2 + 0.582. The first task is to make an estimate and explain how the estimate was made. The second task is to compute the exact answer and explain how that was done (no calculators allowed!). In the third and final task, students devise a method for adding and subtracting decimal numbers that they can use with any two numbers.

When students have completed these three tasks, have students share their strategies for computation and test them on a new computation that you provide. The same task can be repeated for subtraction.

Formative Assessment Note

As students complete Activity 14.11, use a checklist to record whether they are showing evidence of having an understanding of decimal concepts and the role of the decimal point. Note whether students get a correct sum by using a rule they learned but are challenged to give an explanation. Rather than continue a focus on how to add or subtract decimals, for struggling students, shift attention to basic decimal concepts until those are understood.

The earlier estimation practice will focus students' attention on the meanings of the numbers. Remember, students can rewrite decimals as fractions with the same denominator to make connections. It is reasonable to expect that students will develop an algorithm that is essentially the same as aligning the decimal points.

◆ Multiplication

Explore multiplication of decimals by using problems in a context and by returning to a model that was successful with multiplying whole numbers—the area model (Rathouz, 2011). Take a situation such as this one:

A gardener can plant flowers in 1.5 m² of her garden. She decides to plant bluebells on 0.6 of the garden. On how many square meters can she plant bluebells?

Figure 14.12

A student's use of grids to reason about 1.5 × 0.6.

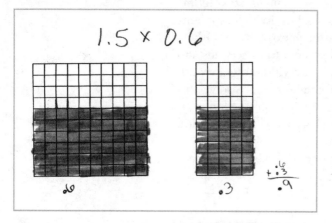

See a student's solution (Figure 14.12) using a grid diagram to model the problem. Each large square represents 1 square meter, with each row of 10 small squares as 0.1 of a square meter and each small square as 0.01 of a square meter. The shaded section shows 0.6 m² + 0.3 m² = 0.9 m². Notice that this is a proportional model allowing students to "see" the values of the factors.

Estimation should play a significant role in developing a multiplication algorithm. As a beginning, consider this problem:

The farmer fills each jug with 3.7 liters of cider. If you buy 4 jugs, how many liters of cider is that?

Begin with an estimate. Is the answer more than 12 liters? What is the most it could be? Could it be 16 liters? Once an estimate of the result is decided on, let students use their own methods for determining an exact answer. Many will start with repeated addition: 3.7 + 3.7 + 3.7 + 3.7. Others may begin by multiplying 3 × 4 and then adding up 0.7 four times. Eventually, students will agree on the exact result of 14.8 liters. Explore other problems involving whole-number multipliers. Multipliers such as 3.5 and 8.25 that involve common fractional parts—here, one-half and one-fourth—are also good choices.

As a next step, have students compare a decimal product with one involving the same digits but no decimal. For example, how are 23.4 × 6.5 and 234 × 65 alike? Interestingly, both products have exactly the same digits: 15210. (The zero may be missing from the decimal product.) Using a calculator, have students explore other products that are alike except for the location of the decimals. The digits in the answer are always alike. After seeing how the digits remain the same for these related products, do the following activity.

Activity 14.12 WHERE DOES THE DECIMAL GO?: MULTIPLICATION

Have students compute the following product: 24 × 63. Using the result of this computation and estimation, have them give the exact answer to each of the following:

  0.24 × 6.3   24 × 0.63   2.4 × 63   0.24 × 0.63

For each computation they should write a rationale for how they placed the decimal point. They can double check their results with a calculator. It is also important to have a class discussion about possible errors and how to avoid them.

Stop and Reflect

The product of 24 × 63 is 1512. How can you use this information to give the answer to each of the products in the previous activity? (Do *not* count decimal places. Use your fractional equivalents.) ■

Another way to support full understanding of the algorithm is to rewrite the decimals in their fraction equivalents. So, if you are multiplying 3.4 × 1.7, that is the same as $\frac{34}{10} \times \frac{17}{10}$. When multiplied, you would get $\frac{578}{100}$. When this is rewritten as a decimal it is 5.78, which corresponds to moving the decimal two places to the left (Rathouz, 2011).

The method of placing the decimal point in a product by way of estimation is more difficult as the product gets smaller. For example, knowing that 37×83 is 3071 does not make it easy to place the decimal in the product 0.037×0.083. Even the product 0.37×0.83 is challenging. A reasonable algorithm for multiplication is: "Ignore the decimal points, and do the computation as if all numbers were whole numbers. When finished, place the decimal point by estimation." Even if students have already learned the standard algorithm, they need to know the conceptual rationale that is centered on place value and the powers of ten for "counting" and shifting the decimal places. By focusing on rote applications of rules, students lose out on opportunities to understand the meaning and effects of operations and are more prone to misapply procedures (Martinie & Bay-Williams, 2003).

Questions such as the following keep the focus on number sense and provide useful information about your students' understanding.

> **Standards for Mathematical Practice**
>
> **3 Construct viable arguments and critique the reasoning of others**

1. Consider these two computations: $3\frac{1}{2} \times 2\frac{1}{4}$ and 2.276×3.18. Without doing the calculations, which product do you think is larger? Provide a reason for your answer that can be understood by someone else in this class.

2. How much larger is 0.76×5 than 0.75×5? How can you tell without doing the computation (Kulm, 1994)?

Students' discussions and explanations as they work on these or similar questions can provide insights into their decimal and fraction number sense and the connections between the two representations.

◆ Division

Like multiplication of decimals, division of decimals is often poorly understood, and estimation and concrete experiences are needed to build a strong understanding. In fact, the best approach to a division estimate generally comes from thinking about multiplication rather than division. Consider the following problem:

The trip to Washington was 282 miles. It took exactly 4.5 hours to drive. What was the average rate in miles per hour?

To make an estimate of this quotient, think about what times 4 or 5 is close to 280. You might think $60 \times 4.5 = 240 + 30 = 270$, so maybe about 61 or 62 miles per hour.

Here is a second example without context.

Make an estimate of $45.7 \div 1.83$. Think only of what times $1\frac{8}{10}$ is close to 46.

Stop and Reflect

Will the answer be more or less than 46? Why? Will it be more or less than 20? Now think about 1.8 being close to 2. What times 2 is close to 46? Use "think multiplication" to produce an estimate. ■

Because 1.83 is close to 2, the estimate is near 23. And since 1.83 is less than 2, the answer must be greater than 23—say 25 or 26. (The actual answer is 24.972677.)

Figure 14.13

Extension of the division algorithm.

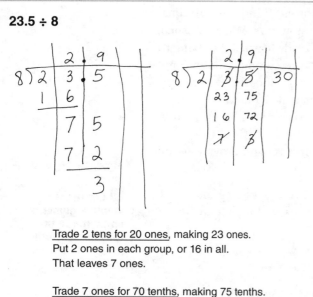

23.5 ÷ 8

Trade 2 tens for 20 ones, making 23 ones.
Put 2 ones in each group, or 16 in all.
That leaves 7 ones.

Trade 7 ones for 70 tenths, making 75 tenths.
Put 9 tenths in each group, or 72 tenths in all.
That leaves 3 tenths.

Trade the 3 tenths for 30 hundredths.

(Continue trading for smaller pieces as long as you wish.)

As you see, estimation can produce a reasonable result, but you may still require a standard algorithm to produce the precise digits, as was done for multiplication. Figure 14.13 shows division by a whole number and how that can be carried out to as many places as you wish. (The explicit-trade method described in Chapter 11 is shown on the right.) Through reasoning, you are placing the decimal point—that is, trade 2 tens for 20 ones, then put 2 ones in each group—so you know the 2 in the quotient is in the ones place.

> ◆ *Activity* **14.13 WHERE DOES THE DECIMAL GO?: DIVISION**
>
> Provide a quotient such as 146 ÷ 7 = 20857, correct to five digits but without the decimal point. The task is to use only this information and estimation to give a fairly precise answer to each of the following:
>
> 146 ÷ 0.7   1.46 ÷ 7   14.6 ÷ 0.7   1460 ÷ 70
>
> For each computation students should write a rationale for their answers and then double check their results with a calculator. Any errors should be acknowledged, and the rationale that produced the error adjusted. Engage students in explicit discussions of common errors or misconceptions and how to fix them.

A reasonable algorithm for division is parallel to that for multiplication: Ignore the decimal points, and do the computation as if all numbers were whole numbers. When finished, place the decimal by estimation. This is reasonable for divisors greater than 1 or close to a familiar value (e.g., 0.1, 0.5, 0.01). If students have a method for dividing by 45, they can divide by 0.45 and 4.5. So, for example, if the students were solving 24 ÷ 0.45, they might think, "I can think of the 45 as 50, or the 45 hundredths as 50 hundredths or five-tenths. So how many halves (rounding the 0.45) are in 24? About 48."

 **Introducing Percents**

The term *percent* is simply another name for hundredths and, as such, is a standardized ratio with a denominator of 100. If students can express fractions and decimals as hundredths, the term *percent* can be substituted for the term *hundredth*. Consider the fraction $\frac{3}{4}$. As a fraction expressed in hundredths, it is $\frac{75}{100}$. When $\frac{3}{4}$ is written in decimal form, it is 0.75. Both 0.75 and $\frac{75}{100}$ are read in exactly the same way: "seventy-five hundredths." When used as operators, $\frac{3}{4}$ of something is the same as 0.75 or 75 percent of that same thing. Thus, percent is merely a new notation and terminology, not a new concept.

The results of the 2005 NAEP exam revealed that only 30 percent of eighth graders could accurately calculate the percent of the tip when given the cost of the meal and the amount of the tip left by the diners. A reason for this weak performance is a failure to meaningfully develop percent concepts.

◆ Models and Terminology

Physical models provide the main link among fractions, decimals, and percents, as shown in Figure 14.14 (see Blackline Masters 20 and 21). Base-ten models are suitable for fractions, decimals, and percents, since they all represent the same idea. The rational number wheel (Figure 14.5) with 100 markings around the edge is a model for percents as well as a fraction model for hundredths. The same is true of a 10×10 grid in which each little square inside is 1 percent of the grid. Each row or strip of 10 squares is not only a tenth, but also 10 percent of the grid.

Zambo (2008) suggests linking fractions to percent with a 10×10 grid. By marking one out of every four squares or shading a 5×5 region in the corner of the grid, students can discover the link between $\frac{1}{4}$ and $\frac{25}{100}$ or 25 percent. Zambo goes on to suggest that even more complex representations such as $\frac{1}{8}$ can lead to interesting discussions about the remaining squares left at the end, resulting in $12\frac{1}{2}$ out of 100 squares or $12\frac{1}{2}$ percent. Similarly, the common fractions (halves, thirds, fourths, fifths, and eighths) should become familiar in terms of percents as well as decimals. Three-fifths, for example, is 60 percent as well as 0.6. One-eighth of an amount is $12\frac{1}{2}$ percent or 12.5 percent of the quantity. These ideas should be explored with base-ten models and with contexts rather than with poorly understood rules about moving decimal points.

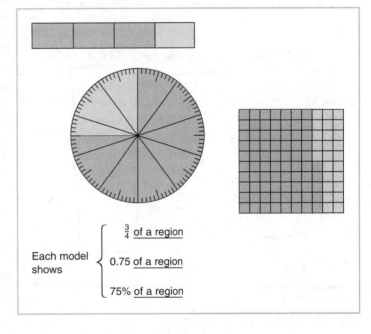

Figure 14.14

Models connect three different notations.

Each model shows
- $\frac{3}{4}$ of a region
- 0.75 of a region
- 75% of a region

One representation that can be used to link percentages with data collection is a percent necklace. Using fishing cord or sturdy string, link 100 same-sized beads and knot them in a tight, circular necklace. Anytime a circle graph is displayed in class, the percent necklace can provide an estimation tool. Given any circle graph, place the necklace in a circle so that its center coincides with the center of the circle graph (don't try to align the necklace with the outside edge of the circle graph). If the necklace makes a wider concentric circle, to distinguish the different categories, students use a straight edge to extend the lines straight out to meet the necklace. If the circle graph is larger than the necklace, merely use the radial lines to mark off the categories. Have students count the number of beads between any two lines that represent a category. For example, they might find 24 beads are in the section of the circle graph that shows how many students selected blue as their favorite color. That becomes an estimate that approximately 24 percent of the students favor blue. Counting the beads in a given category gives students an informal approach to estimating percent, while investigating a meaningful physical model for thinking about the per-100 concept.

Activity 14.14 MEMORY MATCH

Create a deck of cards of circle graphs with a percentage shaded in and matching percents (like a circle with $\frac{1}{2}$ shaded and 50%). Students are to pair each circle graph with the percent that best matches it in a memory game in which they must flip over matching cards to make a pair. For students with disabilities, you may need to have rational number wheels (Figure 14.5) as a moveable representation to help support their match-making. For a virtual game that has the same goal, see the NCTM Illuminations virtual "Concentration" game (http://illuminations.nctm.org/ActivityDetail.aspx?ID=73), which uses representations of percents and fractions and a regional model.

Figure 14.15

A student uses a model for reasoning about percent.

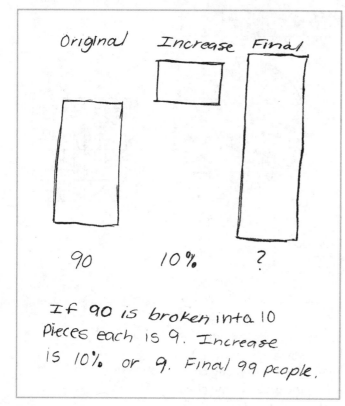

Percent concepts can be developed through other powerful visual representations that link to proportional thinking. One option is the use of a three-part model to represent the original amount, the decrease/increase, and the final amount (Parker, 2004). Using three rectangles that can be positioned and divided, students can analyze components of a situation and then consider each piece of the model. The rectangles can be a particularly useful representation for the often confusing problems that include a percentage increase to find an amount greater than the original. In a 2005 NAEP item, students were asked to calculate how many employees there were at a company whose workforce increased by 10 percent over the previous level of 90. Using Parker's approach, you can see in Figure 14.15 how a student used the proportional rectangle model to come up with a correct solution.

Another helpful approach to the terminology of percent is through the role of the decimal point. Recall that the decimal point identifies the units position. When the unit is ones, a number such as 0.659 means a little more than 6 tenths of 1. The word *ones* is understood (6 tenths of 1 *one* or one *whole*). But 0.659 is also 6.59 tenths and 65.9 hundredths and 659 thousandths. The name of the unit must be explicitly identified. Because *percent* is another name for *hundredths*, when the decimal point identifies the hundredths position as the units, the word *percent* can be specified as a synonym for *hundredths*. Thus, 0.659 (of some whole or 1) is 65.9 hundredths or 65.9 percent of that same whole. As illustrated in Figure 14.16, the notion of placing the decimal point to identify the percent position (i.e., hundredths) is conceptually more meaningful than the rule: "To change a decimal to a percent, move the decimal two places to the right." A more conceptually focused idea is to equate hundredths with percent both orally and in notation.

Figure 14.16

Hundredths are also known as percents.

Ones	Tenths	Percent Hundredths	Thousandths
	3	6	5

0.365 (of 1) = 36.5 percent (of 1)

◆ Percent Problems in Context

Some teachers may talk about "the three percent problems." The sentence "_____ is _____ percent of _____" has three spaces for numbers. For example, "20 is 25 percent of 80." The classic three percent problems come from this sterile expression; two of the numbers are given, and the students are asked to produce the third. Students tend to set up proportions, but are not quite sure which numbers to put where. In other words, they are not connecting understanding with the procedure. Furthermore, commonly encountered percent situations, such as sales figures, taxes, food composition (percent of fat) and economic trends, are almost never in the "_____ is _____ percent of _____" format. Instead of these short, decontextualized prompts, engage students in more realistic contextual problems.

Chapter 12 explored equivalent fractions in which one part was unknown. Developmentally, then, it makes sense to help students make the connection between the exercises done with fraction equivalencies and percents. How? Emphasize equivalency, but add on that you are seeking the equivalency for hundredths. Connect hundredths to percent and replace fraction language with percent language. In Figure 14.17, the three part-whole fraction exercises demonstrate the link between fractions and percents.

Though students must have some experience with the noncontextual situations in Figure 14.17, it is important to have them explore percent relationships in real contexts. Find or create percent problems, and present them in the same way that they appear in newspapers, on television, and in other real contexts. In addition, follow these guidelines for your instruction:

- Limit the percents to familiar fractions (halves, thirds, fourths, fifths, and eighths) or easy percents ($\frac{1}{10}$, $\frac{1}{100}$), and use numbers compatible with these fractions. The focus of these exercises is the relationships involved, not complex computational skills.

- Require students to use physical models, drawings, and contexts to explain their solutions. It is wiser to assign three problems requiring a drawing and an explanation than to give 15 problems requiring only computation and answers.

- Do not rush to developing rules or procedures for different types of problems—encourage students to notice patterns.

- Use the terms *part*, *whole*, and *percent* (or *fraction*). Help students see these percent exercises as the same types of exercises they did with simple fractions.

- Encourage mental computation.

The following problems meet these criteria for familiar fractions and compatible numbers. Try working each problem, identifying each number as a part, a whole, or a fraction. Draw bar diagrams to explain or work through your thought process. Examples of student reasoning using bar diagrams are illustrated in Figure 14.18.

1. The PTA reported that 75 percent of the total number of families were represented at the meeting. If students from 320 families go to the school, how many families were represented at the meeting?
2. The baseball team won 80 percent of the 25 games it played this year. How many games were lost?
3. In Mrs. Carter's class, 20 students, or $66\frac{2}{3}$ percent of the class, were on the honor roll. How many students are in her class?

Figure 14.17

Part–whole fraction exercises can be translated into percent exercises.

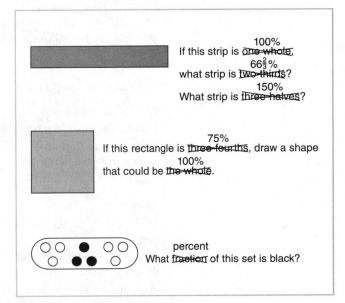

Figure 14.18

Students use bar diagrams to solve percent problems.

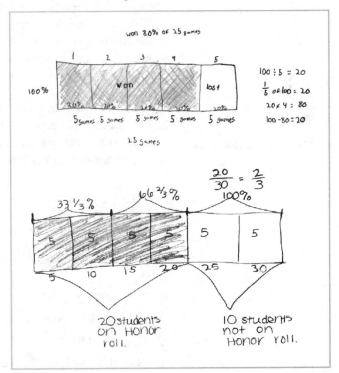

4. Zane bought his new computer at a $12\frac{1}{2}$ percent discount. He paid $700. How many dollars did he save by buying it at a discount?

5. If Nicolas has read 60 of the 180 pages in his library book, what percent of the book has he read so far?

6. The hardware store bought widgets at 80 cents each and sold them for $1 each. What percent did the store mark up the price of each widget?

Stop and Reflect

Look at the examples in Figure 14.18. Notice how each problem is solved with simple fractions and mental math. Then try each of the six problems just listed. Can each be done using familiar fraction equivalents? What are some models or drawings that you think your students might use? ■

Formative Assessment Note

These context-based percent problems can be an effective performance assessment to evaluate students' understanding. Assign one or two, and have students explain why they think their answer makes sense. You might take a percent problem and substitute fractions for percents (e.g., use $\frac{1}{8}$ instead of 12.5 percent) to see how students handle these problems with fractions compared to percents.

If your focus is on reasoning and justification rather than number of problems correct, you will be able to collect all the assessment information you need.

◆ Estimation

Many percent problems do not have simple (familiar) numbers. Frequently, in real life, an approximation or estimate in percent situations is enough to help one think through the situation. An estimate based on an understanding of the relationship confirms that a correct operation has been performed or that the decimal point is positioned correctly.

To help students with estimation in percent situations, consider these two ideas: (1) when the percent is not a simple one, substitute a close percent that is easy to work with, and (2) select numbers that are compatible with the percent involved, to make the calculation easy to do mentally. Here are some examples.

1. The 83,000-seat stadium was 73 percent full. How many people were at the game?

2. The treasurer reported that 68.3 percent of the dues had been collected, for a total of $385. How much more money can the club expect to collect if all dues are paid?

3. Max McStrike had 217 hits in 842 at-bats. What was his batting average?

Stop and Reflect

Use familiar percents, fractions, and compatible numbers to estimate solutions to each of these last three problems. Do this before reading on. ■

Here are some possible estimates:

1. (Use $\frac{3}{4}$ and 80,000) → about 60,000

2. (Use $\frac{2}{3}$ and $380; will collect $\frac{1}{3}$ more) → about $190

3. $(4 \times 217 > 842; \frac{1}{4}$ is 25 percent, or 0.250$)$ → a bit more than 0.250

There are several common uses for estimating percentages in real-world situations. As students gain full conceptual understanding and flexibility, there are ways to think about percents that are useful in a variety of situations:

- *Tips:* To figure a tip, you can find 10 percent of the amount and then half of that again to make 15 percent.

- *Taxes:* The same approach for finding tips is used for figuring sales tax. Depending on the amount, you can find 10 percent, take half of that, and then find 1 percent and add or subtract that amount as needed. Students should also realize that finding percents is a process of multiplication; therefore, finding 8 percent (tax) of $50 will generate the same result as finding 50 percent (half) of 8, or $4.

- *Discounts:* A 30 percent discount is the same as 70 percent of the original amount, and depending on the original amount, using one of those percents may be easier to use in mental calculations than the other. If a $48 outfit is 30 percent off, for example, you are paying 70 percent. Round $48 to $50. And you have 0.70×50 (think 7×5) and your cost is less than $35.

Again, these are not rules to be taught; they are real-world reasoning activities to be developed that require a full understanding of percent concepts and the commutative property.

Expanded Lesson

Friendly Fractions to Decimals

Content and Task Decisions

Grade Level: 4

Mathematics Goals

- To connect equivalent decimals to familiar fractions in a conceptual manner
- To reinforce the notion of the 10-to-I relationship between adjacent digits in our numeration system

Grade Level Guide

NCTM *Curriculum Focal Points*	Common *Core State Standards*
Understanding of fractions is applied to learning about decimals in grade 4 as one of the three focal points: "*Number and Operations:* Developing an understanding of decimals, including the connections between fractions and decimals" (NCTM, 2006, p. 16).	Understanding decimals (decimal fractions) and how they relate to fractions is part of the critical area on Fractions in grade 4. Specifically, fourth graders should be able to "Understand decimal notation for fractions, and compare decimal fractions" (CCSSO, 2010, p. 31).

Consider Your Students' Needs

Students are familiar with the 10-to-I relationship between adjacent digits in our numeration system. Students must understand the part–whole meaning of fractional parts and fraction equivalence.

For English Language Learners

- Be sure instructions are clear. For example, when asking for different ways to show $\frac{1}{10}$, it will be helpful to hold up two different ways and point to each to show that they are different.
- You will be introducing the term *decimal*. The term should be discussed (with all students) in the *After* phase. *Deci-* means tens. Connect to other words they may know with this term (decagon, decade, etc.).

For Students with Disabilities

- Have some pre-shaded 10×10 grids with different fractions and ask the student to find the grid that shows $\frac{1}{2}$.

Once they identify the representation of $\frac{1}{2}$ then have them skip count to show the equivalent $\frac{50}{100}$ grid.

Materials

Each student will need:

- Two copies of the 10×10 grids sheets (Blackline Master 27)
- Base-ten materials (Blackline Master 4)

Teacher will need:

- Transparency of or way to display the 10×10 grids (Blackline Master 18)
- Base-ten materials (Blackline Master 4)

BLM

Lesson

Before

Begin with a simpler version of the task:

- Ask students what it means to have $\frac{1}{2}$ of something. Highlight the idea that the whole is divided into 2 *equal* parts and you have one of those parts. Showing students the 10×10 grid, ask them to shade $\frac{1}{2}$ of the grid. Ask students to share different ways to shade the grid. It might be helpful to illustrate using base-ten materials as one way to think about this task (i.e., the hundreds square is used as the whole, the tens strip is used as a tenth, and the unit square is used as a hundredth).

- Ask students to look at what they have covered and see what other names they might have for that amount (e.g., $\frac{2}{4}$, $\frac{4}{8}$, etc.). If someone does not offer $\frac{50}{100}$, then ask students what the fraction would be if they were using the unit square as the name of the fraction (How many hundredths?). Highlight the fact that these are all equivalent names.

Present the focus task to the class:

- Using a 10×10 grid, determine equivalent names for each of the following fractions, including a fraction with the name "hundredths." $\frac{3}{4} \frac{2}{5} \frac{3}{8}$ *(adapt or add fractions, as appropriate, based on student needs)*

Provide clear expectations:

- Ask students to work with their own Blackline Master and base-ten blocks, but to work with a partner to share and compare their ideas. Explain that during the *After* phase, they will need to justify how they know the original fraction and the new fraction (hundredths) are equivalent.

During

Ongoing:

- Look for students who are shading their 10 × 10 grids differently. Highlight those different ways in the *After* phase of the lesson.

- If students have shaded their grid in a way that does not use long rows of ten, ask students how they could cover the area using as many strips and as few individual squares as possible.

- The $\frac{3}{8}$ task is the most challenging. A useful hint is to ask students how they would find $\frac{1}{8}$ if they had $\frac{1}{4}$.

- You may need to remind students that as they need something smaller than the smallest square on the grid, that the next smaller pieces are tenths of the little squares. Since a small square is $\frac{1}{100}$, one-tenth of it would be $\frac{1}{1000}$ and half of it would be $\frac{5}{1000}$.

After

Bring the class together to share and discuss the task:

- Introduce the decimal fraction notation at the beginning of this phase. Connect to students' experiences with tens and hundreds to now be tenths and hundredths. As students share their solutions, ask students how they can write the hundredths fraction as a decimal fraction. As students use the new notation, ask students to relate the symbols back to the diagrams.

- Students are likely to shade their grids differently. It is important to compare and contrast between different shadings so that students see that they have shaded an equivalent amount. For example, for fourths, students might shade a 5 × 5 section (half of a half). Others may shade two and a half rows of ten. Ask students to determine how these both show one-fourth.

Assessment

Observe

- Some students will be very successful with shading equal parts but will have difficulty connecting this to hundredths. As you suggest to them to use strips of 10 and individual squares, make sure they can explain why they are using these groupings rather than, say, strips of 5.

- Listen for students using the appropriate terminology (e.g., fourths, eighths, hundredths). This helps develop the concepts of the size of the parts and will be important in the discussion in the *After* phase.

Ask

- How do you know that the fraction name and decimal name apply to the same region?

- If you are given a fraction, how do you determine how to shade a 10 × 10 grid to show that fractional amount?

15

Promoting Algebraic Thinking

Big IDEAS

1 Algebra is a useful tool for generalizing arithmetic and representing patterns and relationships in the world. Explaining the regularities and consistencies across many problems gives students the chance to generalize.

2 Symbols, especially involving equations and variables, are used to express generalizations of patterns and relationships.

3 Variables are symbols that take the place of numbers or sets of numbers. They have different meanings depending on whether they are being used as representations of quantities that vary or change, representations of specific unknown values, or placeholders in a generalized expression or formula.

4 Equations and inequalities are used to express relationships between two quantities. Symbolism on either side of an equation or inequality represents a quantity. Thus, $3 + 8$ and $5n + 2$ are both expressions for numbers, not something "to do."

5 Methods we use to compute and the structures in our number system can and should be generalized. For example, the generalization that $a + b = b + a$ tells us that $83 + 27 = 27 + 83$ without computing the sums on each side of the equal sign.

6 Patterns, both repeating and growing, can be recognized, extended, and generalized through the identification of rules and relationships.

7 Functional relationships uniquely associate members of one set with members of another set. For every input, there is a unique output.

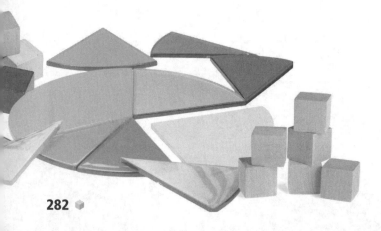

Algebra is sometimes referred to as *generalized arithmetic*. Arithmetic and algebraic thinking are closely connected, and this is captured in the *Common Core State Standards* kindergarten through fifth-grade content standards, in which numbers and algebra are combined in clusters and standards under the CCSS domain of "Operations and Algebraic Thinking." In middle school (grades 6 through 8), students will begin to extend what was learned in kindergarten through grade 5 to a study of algebra in more abstract and symbolic ways.

Algebraic Thinking

Algebra is an established content strand in kindergarten through grade 12. Although the level of sophistication changes across grade levels, one thing is clear: The algebra envisioned for grades 3 through 5—and for middle and high school as well—is not the algebra that you most likely experienced. Therefore, the elementary grades become the launching pad for important algebra ideas. Let's look at the critical topics suggested by the *Common Core State Standards* (CCSSO, 2010), at grades 3 through 5:

Grade 3: Students determine unknowns in multiplication and division equations, apply properties of operations (i.e., commutative, associative and distributive), represent problems with equations including those with variables and identify arithmetic patterns as they solve problems.

Grade 4: Students use symbols to represent the unknown quantity and they generate patterns using both numbers and shapes that follow a rule.

Grade 5: Students write, interpret and evaluate expressions using symbols (including grouping symbols) and generate and analyze patterns.

These expectations illustrate the explicit infusion of algebraic thinking in the four operations as a way to develop students who are not only mathematically proficient in addition, subtraction, multiplication, and division with whole and rational numbers, but who are also able to experience the beginnings of algebraic thinking. The connection to formal algebra begins with the identification of patterns and regularities and moves to more sophisticated generalizations (especially with the properties of operations) and an understanding of symbols. Although algebra is a separate strand of the curriculum, it is also embedded in all areas of mathematics.

Algebraic reasoning includes three major components (Blanton, 2008; Kaput, 2008) that infuse the central notions of generalization and symbolization:

1. Study of structures in the number system, including those arising in arithmetic (algebra as generalized arithmetic)
2. Study of patterns, relations, and functions
3. Process of mathematical modeling, including the meaningful use of symbols

These three strands provide the organization for this chapter. In each section, we share developmentally appropriate tasks and effective instructional activities across the grades 3 through 5 curriculum.

Generalized Arithmetic

The process of creating generalizations from arithmetic is central to learning algebra and begins as students explore all aspects of number and computation, including basic facts and behaviors of the four major operations (Russell, Schifter, & Bastable, 2011).

◆ Generalization with Number and Operations

Even the most basic arithmetic situation can be extended to look at generalizations about numbers and operations. Exploring patterns in numerical situations, rather than just computing with standard algorithms, is algebraic thinking, and it strengthens understanding of numbers in all the operations (and with all types of numbers)! Here students use what they know about how to decompose and recompose numbers to perform operations and, while doing so, identify generalizable characteristics or behaviors of the process. Using a context such as the story in *Guinea Pigs Add Up* (Cuyler, 2010) consider the example below:

Ten guinea pigs are housed in two different cages in the classroom. What are all the different ways the 10 guinea pigs can be in the two cages?

Stop and Reflect

Can you list all the ways for this to occur? If there were only 8 guinea pigs, how many different ways would be possible? What if there were 25 guinea pigs? Is there a generalizable rule for how many different ways the guinea pigs could be arranged in the two cages? ■

The significant algebraic thinking comes when you ask students, "How do you know that you've found all the different ways?" They should find that in this situation there are 11 ways to put 10 guinea pigs in two cages, 9 ways for 8 guinea pigs, and 26 ways for 25 guinea pigs. Have students explain this pattern. Can they begin to generalize and suggest why this is the case?

Generalizing can be described using symbols, something that students should do in grades 4 and 5. To move them to that thinking, you might ask, "If I have some guinea pigs in one cage, how might you describe how many guinea pigs are in the other cage?" Students might answer "Subtract from 10 what is in the first cage and you get what is in the second cage." Record this for the students as 10 − amount of pigs in the first cage = amount of pigs in the second cage. Then you can move from an equation in words to a more generalizable equation like $10 - n = ?$

Formative Assessment Note

Although younger students can use materials to figure out the guinea pig problem, this is a good performance assessment to use with the whole class or small groups to see to what extent students notice patterns. In this problem, students are trying to identify multiple solutions. As stated, the significant algebra lies in deciding when all of the solutions have been found, so notice what they do. At the most basic level, students will just say they cannot think of any more ways. At the next level, students will strategically use each number from 0 to 10 for one addend (and the corresponding number for the other addend). The final level is reached when a student explains that for each number there is one and only one solution based on reasoning rather than on finding possible solutions. At this final level, the student is making a ***generalization*** for how to determine the number of possible solutions. The student might say, "There is always one more way than the number of guinea pigs."

Standards for Mathematical Practice

8 Look for and express regularity in repeated reasoning

You can help students begin to understand symbols by asking how they might say the generalizations by using the letter n to be the number of guinea pigs. The number of ways to be in the two cages will be $n + 1$ because there can be 0, 1, 2 . . . n guinea pigs in the first cage. Finding that there is always one more way to arrange the pets in the cages than there are guinea pigs is a *generalization* for how to determine the number of solutions without listing them. Starting with a problem that is concrete and begins with listing numeric possibilities is a way to help students learn to generalize and use variables. To extend the discussion, ask students questions such as, "What if there were 120 guinea pigs—would the rule still be true?

How do you know? What if you knew there were 34 different ways the guinea pigs could be in the cages; could you figure out how many guinea pigs there were? Is there a rule for that?"

Slight shifts in how arithmetic problems are presented can open up opportunities for generalizations (Blanton, 2008). For example, instead of a series of unrelated two-digit multiplication problems, consider the following list:

$$\begin{array}{cccc} 35 & 52 & 23 & 46 \\ \times 52 & \times 35 & \times 46 & \times 23 \end{array}$$

Once students have solved these problems, you can focus attention on the factors, asking questions like "What do you notice?" and "Will this always be true?" and "How could we write that using symbols?" In their own words, students will explain that the numbers can be multiplied in any order. Although students may already understand the commutative property from learning their basic facts, they may not recognize the generalizability of the property, and this interaction can help them recognize the power of this important property.

When working on multiplication concepts and related facts, ask students to decide whether the following conjectures are true or false: "If you multiply any whole number by 2, the answer will be an even number" or "If you multiply any whole number by 9, the answer has digits that add up to 9" or "If a factor is doubled then the product is doubled."

Encourage students to make their own generalizations. For example, Figure 15.1 is the work of student in a fourth-grade classroom who suggests that if a factor is doubled, then the product is also doubled. Notice how she illustrates this conjecture by sketching rectangular arrays to show why it worked. This proof without words shows how this doubling and halving strategy will be true for $D \times H$ by moving the bottom set of the smaller squares (from dividing the rectangular array) and moving it to a position at the end of the top set of squares. This shows through a representation that $D \times H = \frac{1}{2}D \times 2H$ using a powerful image. This proof can also be then linked to the associative property, in which students can compose or decompose numbers to find solutions. To demonstrate this with first with simple numbers such as 4×16, we can show $4 \times 16 = 4 \times (2 \times 8) = (4 \times 2) \times 8 = 8 \times 8 = 64$. Then this can be eventually modeled for $D \times H$ where $D \times H = D \times (\frac{1}{2} \times 2)H = (D \times \frac{1}{2}) \times (2 \times H) = \frac{1}{2}D \times 2H$.

If students are to be successful in algebra, which is more abstract and symbolic, such discussions must be a part of the daily experience (Mark, Cuoco, Goldenberg, & Sword, 2010). This explicit focus on noticing patterns, seeking generalizations, and identifying structures using symbols is important in supporting the learning of those who struggle, as well as those who excel (Schifter et al., 2009). To do so requires thinking in advance of what questions you can ask to help students think about generalized characteristics within the problem they are working, such as representing relationships (e.g., when the number of guinea pigs in one cage goes down by 1, the number in the other goes up by 1) and to think about other problems that follow the same pattern.

The next activity is an interesting exploration for students in grades 3 through 5 and encourages students to notice patterns and move to generalizations.

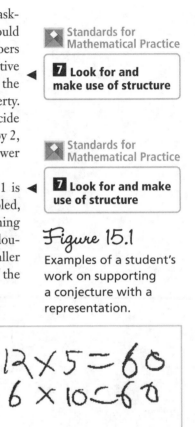

Standards for Mathematical Practice

◀ **7 Look for and make use of structure**

Standards for Mathematical Practice

◀ **7 Look for and make use of structure**

Figure 15.1

Examples of a student's work on supporting a conjecture with a representation.

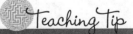 *Teaching Tip*

You can help students see relationships and think algebraically by using well-planned, strategic questions. Collect the questions suggested throughout this chapter on note cards and keep them handy for lesson planning or classroom discussions.

Figure 15.2

What happens when you begin with a number times itself (7 × 7), and then make one factor one greater and the other factor one less?

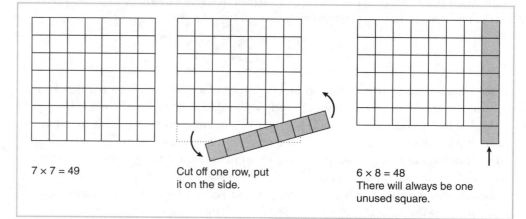

7 × 7 = 49

Cut off one row, put it on the side.

6 × 8 = 48
There will always be one unused square.

Activity 15.1 ONE UP AND ONE DOWN: MULTIPLICATION

Show students that when you begin with 7 × 7 = 49 and then raise one factor and lower the other factor, each by one, the product is one less than the original: 8 × 6 = 48. Their task is to explore this for other numbers multiplied by themselves (squares). To help with their exploration, suggest that they cut out the square array from grid paper. How can they change the square array into the new rectangle using scissors and tape? Students should use words, pictures, and numbers to tell what they have found. Does this only work for square numbers? Students with disabilities will benefit from creating the array with 1-inch square tiles and manipulating the rows to match other students' work with grid paper.

The results of this activity are quite interesting and not obvious. The new product will be one less if the original product is a square—a number multiplied by itself. Figure 15.2 illustrates how an array changes in the case of a square. When the original factors are not alike (increase the larger number and decrease the smaller), the difference can be related to the difference in the original factors.

Here is an activity adapted from Russell, Schifter, and Bastable (2011) that develops the same thinking strategies, this time with decimals.

Activity 15.2 DON'T PUSH THE POINT

Start with a simple problem involving multiplication of decimals in which students can analyze the answer without computing. Once they agree that it is a true statement, then follow that equation with a series of related problems that can be solved by thinking about the relationships between the expressions rather than computing the answers to each. Try a series such as the following:

$$34 \times 1 = 3.4 \times 10$$

$$34 \times 10 = 3.4 \times ?$$

$$34 \times 100 = 0.34 \times \;?$$
$$34 \times 0.1 = 3.4 \times \;?$$
$$34 \times 0.01 = 0.34 \times \;?$$

By exploring patterns and noticing the repetition in reasoning, the students begin to link the meanings of the operations with whole numbers to those with decimal fractions.

Behavior of the Operations

If we look back at the previous chapters on operation sense, as well as whole-number computation to develop algebraic thinking, these ideas need to be infused with seeing the structure and generalizations inherent in the operation. Let's explore the use of the compensation strategy in adding numbers. So, given the problem $67 + 28$, students might suggest adding 3 to the 67 to make it 70 and either subtract the 3 from the 28 to add 25 for a total of 95, or add the 28 to the 70 to get a total of 98 and then subtract the 3. This "doing and undoing" approach (Cai, Ng, & Moyer, 2011, p. 34) of course also works with multiplication and division, capitalizing on their inverse relationships. These investigations of the operations provide opportunities for conversations that emphasize the generalizations. So to think about this addition problem differently, $x + y$ or $67 + 28$ is the same as $(x + a) + (y - a)$ or $(67 + 3) + (28 - 3)$.

For students in grades 3 through 5, these ideas of drawing relationships to algebraic thinking with whole-number operations need to be extended to operations with fractions. As stated by Empson, Levi, and Carpenter (2011), students must begin to anticipate moves they will need to make numerically with fractions that will allow them to transform the numbers (as done previously with two-digit whole numbers) into easier numbers with which to operate. For example, in adding $\frac{1}{2} + \frac{7}{8}$, a student can think ahead and say "$\frac{1}{2} + \frac{7}{8}$ is the same as $\frac{1}{2} + (\frac{4}{8} + \frac{3}{8})$." Then using relationships already known, the student can add $(\frac{1}{2} + \frac{4}{8}) + \frac{3}{8}$ for a total of $1\frac{3}{8}$ using the associative property. Empson and colleagues go on to say "to understand arithmetic is to think relationally about arithmetic" (p. 412).

Generalization in the Hundreds (and Thousands) Chart

Even in grades 3 through 5, the hundreds chart remains a valuable way for students to notice patterns and develop generalizations. There are many interesting patterns in the hundreds chart that can be discovered with a focus on operations.

You can use a hard copy or an interactive virtual hundreds chart (see, for example, Crickweb at www.crickweb.co.uk/ks2numeracy-tools.html). In connecting arithmetic to algebra in the operations, you can ask students, "What did I add to get from 72 to 82? From 5 to 15? From 34 to 44?" When students stop counting and note the generalized idea that they are adding 10 and moving exactly one row down, they are deepening their understanding of number concepts and generalizing the idea of what +10 looks like. In the hundreds chart, moves can be represented with symbols—in this case arrows (for example, → means right one column or plus 1, and ↑ means up one row or less 10). Consider asking students to complete these problems:

$$14 \rightarrow \rightarrow \leftarrow \leftarrow \qquad 63 \uparrow \uparrow \downarrow \downarrow \qquad 4 \rightarrow \uparrow \leftarrow \downarrow$$

What do you anticipate students will do? At the most basic level, students may count up and back using a counting by ones approach. Or they may know to jump 10 (up or down) but still carry out all four arrow moves. Students who are reasoning and moving toward generalizations may recognize that a downward arrow "undoes" an upward arrow (Blanton, 2008). In other words, $+10 - 10$ results in a zero change. Students can write the equations for the arrow moves with numbers or with variables—for example, for the first problem, $n + 1 + 1 - 1 - 1 = n + (1 - 1) + (1 - 1) = n$.

Here are some additional tasks you might explore on the hundreds chart.

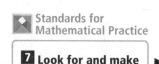

Formative Assessment Note

Observe students as they work on such tasks, and record your thoughts using a checklist. Note which students are solving by counting by ones, by rotely jumping, or by noticing the "doing" and "undoing." What you observe can help focus your discussion as you begin with students sharing the more basic strategies and then have students who have generalized the situation share how they think about it.

- When skip counting, which numbers make diagonal patterns? Which make column patterns? Can you describe a rule for explaining when a number will have a diagonal or column pattern?

- If you move down two and over one on the hundreds chart, what is the relationship between the original number and the new number?

- Can you find two skip-count patterns with one color marker "on top of" the other (that is, all of the shaded values for one pattern are part of the shaded values for the other)? How are these two skip-count numbers related? Is this relationship true for any pair of the numbers you found?

- Find a value on the hundreds chart. Add it to the number to the left of it and the one to the right; then divide by 3. What did you get? Why?

These examples extend number concepts to algebraic thinking. "When will this be true?" and "Why does this work?" questions require students to generalize (and strengthen) the number concepts they are learning. Note that when students focus on patterns in skip counting, those identified relationships support their use of invented strategies for multiplication. In fact, the key to exploring patterns in the upper elementary curriculum is not for patterns' sake; it is to strengthen students' understanding of number relationships and properties. The more often you can ask students "Did you notice a pattern?" the more they are considering and making sense of the mathematics they are doing.

Try this more complex hundreds chart activity.

◆ Standards for
Mathematical Practice

7 **Look for and make use of structure** ▶

◤ *Activity* 15.3 **DIAGONAL SUMS**

Have students select any four numbers in the hundreds chart that form a square. Add the two numbers on each diagonal as in the example shown here.

47	48	49	50
57	58	59	60
67	68	69	70
77	78	79	80

Have students explore other diagonal sums on the chart. Expand their search to diagonals of any rectangle. For example, the numbers 15, 19, 75, and 79 form four corners of a rectangle. The sums $15 + 79$ and $19 + 75$ are equal. Challenge students to figure out why this is so.

Meaningful Use of Symbols

Perhaps one reason that students are unsuccessful in algebra is that they do not have a strong understanding of the symbols they are using. For many adults, the word *algebra* elicits memories of simplifying long strings of variable-filled equations with the goal of finding *x*. These experiences of manipulating symbols were often devoid of meaning and resulted in such a strong dislike for mathematics that algebra has become a favorite target of cartoonists and the media. In reality, symbols represent real events and values and should be seen as useful tools for solving important problems that aid in decision making (e.g., calculating how many boxes of cookies we need to sell to make *x* dollars or at what rate a given number of employees need to work to finish the project on time). Looking at equivalent expressions that describe a context while encouraging generalization from a growing pattern is an effective way to bring meaning to numbers and symbols starting with concrete materials. The classic task (Boaler & Humphreys, 2005; Burns & McLaughlin, 1990) in Activity 15.4 involves such reasoning.

One method of identifying the pattern is to examine only one growth step and ask students to find a method of counting the elements without simply counting each by one.

Activity 15.4 THE BORDER TILES PROBLEM

Ask students to build an 8 × 8 square array representing a swimming pool, using color tiles such that a different color of tile is used around the border (see Figure 15.3). Challenge students to find at least two ways to determine the number of border tiles used without counting them one by one. Students should use their model, words, and number sentences to show how they counted the squares. Ask students to illustrate their solution on centimeter grid paper. For ELLs, the drawing will be a useful support, but be sure the instructions are clear and that they understand that they are counting the outside tiles and need to find more than one way. There are at least five different methods of counting the border tiles around a square other than counting them one at a time.

A great tool to help students explore the border tiles problem is the site Plan Your Room (www.planyourroom.com). Input your dimensions (e.g., 8' 0" × 8' 0") and click "Start with a Room."

Figure 15.3

How many different ways can you find to count the border tiles of an 8 × 8 pool without counting them one at a time?

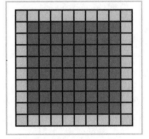

Stop and Reflect

See if you can find four or five different counting schemes for the border tiles problem. Can you see how the different expressions are equivalent? What questions might you pose to students in order to help them focus on the role of the equal sign in recording the equivalent expressions? What questions might you pose to emphasize variables and how this pattern could be generalized? ■

A very common solution to the border tiles problem is to notice that there are 10 squares across the top and also across the bottom, leaving 8 squares on either side. This might be written as:

$$10 + 10 + 8 + 8 = 36 \text{ or } (2 \times 10) + (2 \times 8) = 36$$

Each of the following expressions can likewise be traced to looking at the squares in various groupings:

$$4 \times 9$$
$$4 \times 8 + 4$$
$$4 \times 10 - 4$$
$$100 - 64$$

More equivalent expressions are possible, because students may use addition instead of multiplication. In any case, once the generalizations are created, students need to justify how the elements in the expression map to the physical representation.

Another approach to the border tiles problem is to have students build a series of pools in growth steps, each with one more tile on the side (3×3, 4×4, 5×5, etc.). Then students can find a way to count the elements of each step using an algorithm that handles the step numbers in the same manner. Students can find, for example, number sentences parallel to what they wrote for the 8×8 to find a 6×6 pool and a 7×7 pool. Eventually, this can result in a generalized statement, for example, taking the original $(2 \times 10) + (2 \times 8)$ and generalizing it to $2 \times (n + 2) + 2 \ (n)$.

This task involved a start to mapping ideas that can be verbalized by students into equivalent expressions with symbols. Let's explore two types of symbols that are very important (and poorly understood): the use of the equal sign and variables.

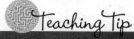

Standards for Mathematical Practice

8 Look for and express regularity in repeated reasoning

◆ The Meaning of the Equal Sign

The equal sign is one of the most important symbols in elementary arithmetic, in algebra, and in all mathematics using numbers and operations. At the same time, recent research, as well as studies dating as far back as 1975, clearly indicate that = is a very poorly understood symbol (Kieran, 2007; RAND Mathematics Study Panel, 2003). The equal sign is rarely represented in textbooks in a way that encourages students to understand the equivalence relationship—an understanding that is critical to understanding algebra (McNeil et al., 2006). Although the *Common Core State Standards* require first graders to "understand the meaning of the equal sign," there are many students in grades 3 through 5 who do not fully understand the relationship that the equal sign describes.

Stop and Reflect

Students were asked, "In the following expression, what number do you think belongs in the box?"

$$8 + 4 = \square + 5$$

How do you think students typically answer this question? ■

Teaching Tip

When writing multiple equations in a string of addition, for example, do not attach them with equal signs unless they are equal. For example, when adding 6 and 6 and then adding 3 more to that answer and 7 more to that sum, do *not* write that as $6 + 6 = 12 + 3 = 15 + 7 = 22$. Doing this incorrectly reinforces that the equal sign means "and the answer is" rather than the correct meaning of linking quantities that are equal.

In a classic study, not even one sixth grader out of 145 put a 7 in the box (Falkner, Levi, & Carpenter, 1999). Try it with your students! The most common responses were 12 and 17. (How did students get these answers?)

Where do such misconceptions come from? Most, if not all, equations that students encounter in elementary school look like this: $5 + 7 =$ ___ or $8 \times 45 =$ ____. Naturally, students come to see = as signifying "and the answer is," rather than a symbol to indicate the relationship of equivalence (Carpenter et al., 2003; McNeil & Alibali, 2005; Molina & Ambrose, 2006). Subtle shifts in the way you approach teaching computation can alleviate this major misconception.

One option that encourages reasoning about the equal sign is instead of asking students to solve a problem (like 45 + 61 or 4 × 26), ask them to find an equivalent expression and use that expression to write an equation (Blanton, 2008). So, for 45 + 61, students might write 45 + 61 = 40 + 66. For a multiplication problem, students might write 4 × 26 = 4 × 25 + 4 or 4 × 26 = 2 × (2 × 26). Activity 15.5 is a way to apply this idea.

Teaching Tip

The *Common Core State Standards* require that students in first grade see and interpret equations in a variety of forms such as 7 = 7, 3 + 5 = 7 + 1, and 13 = 5 + 8. Make sure you are offering all of these options to your students.

Activity 15.5 EQUAL TO THE CHALLENGE

Make a collection of cards with a variety of expressions on each (e.g., 42 + 7, 7 × 7). Make sure for each card there is a corresponding card that is equal. Have a pair of students lay them out on their desks. One student selects a card and together the partners decide which card is equivalent and they put the pair together. You can ask students to verbally state the answer, but that is not necessary. Students can also play independently. The game can be modified for students with disabilities by creating easier combinations or only using a single operation, such as addition.

Why is it so important that students correctly understand the equal sign? First, it is important for students to understand and symbolize relationships in our number system. The equal sign is a principal method of representing these relationships. For example, 6 × 7 = 5 × 7 + 7 shows a basic fact strategy linked to the distributive property of multiplication over addition. When these ideas, initially and informally developed through arithmetic, are generalized and expressed symbolically, powerful relationships are available for working with other numbers in a generalized manner.

A second reason is that when students fail to understand the equal sign, they typically have difficulty with algebraic expressions (Knuth, Stephens, McNeil, & Alibali, 2006). Consider the equation $5x - 24 = 81$. It requires students to see both sides of the equal sign as equivalent expressions. It is not possible to "do" the left-hand side. However, if both sides are understood as being equivalent, students will see that $5x$ must be 24 more than 81 or $5x = 81 + 24$.

Teaching Tip

When reading equations to students, use the language "equals" or "is the same as" when reading the equal sign. This reinforces that it is a relationship sign, rather than a sign signaling an operation.

Conceptualizing the Equal Sign as a Balance

Helping students understand the idea of equivalence can be developed concretely. The next two activities illustrate how kinesthetic approaches, tactile objects, and visualizations can reinforce the "balancing" notion of the equal sign (ideas adapted from Mann, 2004).

Activity 15.6 SEESAW STUDENTS

Ask students to raise their arms to look like a seesaw (make sure all students, particularly ELLs, know what a seesaw is—use an online image or video to show how it works). To start, explain that you have numbers that weigh the same amount as their value. Ask students to imagine (or give them cards with a visual) that you have placed nine hamsters in each of their left hands (students should tip to lower the

Teaching Tip

Remember, this activity can be used for various types of numbers, such as fractions and decimal equivalents, as a way to compare and find equivalencies. Still maintain the emphasis on the equivalence and the equal sign by having students record the equations.

left side). Ask students to imagine that you've placed another nine hamsters on the right side (students level off). Next, with the nine hamsters still there in each hand, ask students to imagine another 5 hamsters added to the left hand.

Now that students have the idea, give them numbers, multiplication facts, or other expressions either verbally or on cards for each side and ask them to show how the seesaw reacts. This is a particularly important activity for students with disabilities, who may be challenged with the abstract idea of balancing values of expressions, especially in the form of $15 \times 8 = 8 \times 15$.

Then use facts that are equal such as 9×4 and 6×6. When they are in the balanced position, ask them to add an amount such as 5 to one side, then the other. How does the seesaw react? Ask the students, "What if we take away 5 from each side?"

After acting out the seesaw movement several times, ask students to write Seesaw Findings (e.g., "If you have a balanced seesaw and add something to one side, it will tilt to that side," and "If you take away the same amount from both sides of the seesaw, it will still be balanced"). These generalizations are critical to developing algebraic thinking.

Formative Assessment Note

You may be surprised at how common it is for students to interpret the equal sign as a symbol separating the problem from the answer. Ask students in a diagnostic interview to tell you what the equal sign means in an equation such as $5 \times 8 = 40$. Then ask the same question for $8 \times 2 = 15 + 1$ (an equation with an expression on each side.) Students often believe that there must be an "answer" or single number on one side of the equal sign. Finally, ask whether it is acceptable to write something such as this: $5 = 5$. Here students sometimes believe that there must be an operation involved if there is an equal sign. The ways in which students answer these questions will depend a lot on how well you have taught the *balance* meaning of equality. After early introductions to the equal sign in first grade, the assumption is that students understand what you mean by "equals." This interview will help uncover any misunderstandings.

Figure 15.4

Latisha's work on the shapes problem.

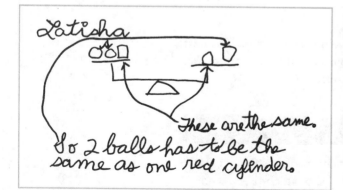

Activity 15.7 **WHAT DO YOU KNOW ABOUT THE SHAPES?**

Present a balance scale with objects on both sides. Here is an example:

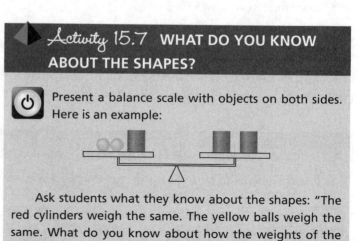

Ask students what they know about the shapes: "The red cylinders weigh the same. The yellow balls weigh the same. What do you know about how the weights of the balls and the cylinders compare?" Figure 15.4 illustrates how a third grader explained what she knew. For more explorations like this, see "Pan Balance—Shapes" on NCTM's Illuminations website (http://illuminations.nctm.org/ActivityDetail.aspx?id=33).

These two tasks provide a strong foundation for relational thinking that will be discussed later in the chapter.

After students have experiences with these shapes, they can then explore numbers and eventually move on to variables. Figure 15.5 offers examples that connect the balance to the related equation. This two-pan balance model also illustrates that the expressions on each side represent a number.

Activity 15.8 TILT OR BALANCE?

Draw or project a simple two-pan balance. In each pan, write a numeric expression and ask which pan will tilt down or whether the two sides will balance (see Figure 15.5a). Challenge students to write number sentences (equations and inequalities). Note that when the scale "tilts," indicate the relationship by either a "greater than" or "less than" symbol ($>$ or $<$) or, if it is balanced, an = symbol is used. Include examples (like the third and fourth balances) for which students can make the determination by analyzing the relationships on both sides rather than doing the computation. For students with disabilities, instead of having them write expressions for each side of the scale, share a small collection of cards with expressions and have them identify the ones that will make the scale balance.

As an alternative or extension, use missing value expressions. Ask students to find a number that will result in each side tilting, and it being balanced (see Figure 15.5b).

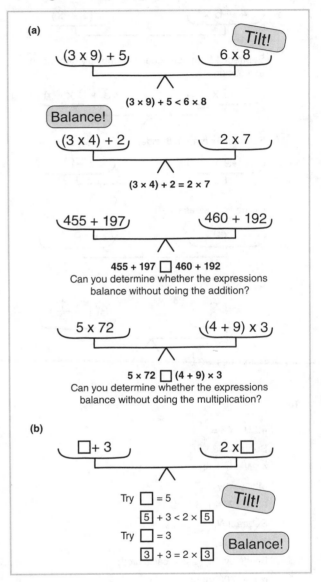

Figure 15.5

Using expressions and variables in equations and inequalities. The two-pan balance helps develop the meaning of the equal sign.

(a)

$(3 \times 9) + 5$ 6×8 Tilt!

$(3 \times 9) + 5 < 6 \times 8$ Balance!

$(3 \times 4) + 2$ 2×7

$(3 \times 4) + 2 = 2 \times 7$

$455 + 197$ $460 + 192$

$455 + 197 \square 460 + 192$
Can you determine whether the expressions balance without doing the addition?

5×72 $(4 + 9) \times 3$

$5 \times 72 \square (4 + 9) \times 3$
Can you determine whether the expressions balance without doing the multiplication?

(b)

$\square + 3$ $2 \times \square$

Try $\square = 5$ Tilt!
$5 + 3 < 2 \times 5$

Try $\square = 3$ Balance!
$3 + 3 = 2 \times 3$

technology note

The balance scale is a concrete tool that can help students understand that if you add or subtract a value from one side, you must add or subtract a like value from the other side to keep the equation balanced. An NCTM Illuminations applet titled "Pan Balance—Expressions" (http://illuminations.nctm.org/ActivityDetail.aspx?id=10) provides a virtual balance scale in which students can enter what they believe to be equivalent expressions (with numbers or symbols) each in a separate pan to see whether, in fact, the expressions balance.

Figure 15.6 shows solutions for two equations, one in a balance and the other without. Even after you have stopped using the balance, it is a good idea to refer to the pan-balance concept of equality and the idea of keeping the scales balanced. This use of concrete (actual balance) or semiconcrete (drawings of a balance) representations supports the abstract concept of how to preserve equivalence when moving numbers or variables across the equal sign. Students with intellectual disabilities, as well as other students, benefit from this approach to learning.

◆ Standards for Mathematical Practice

2 Reason abstractly and quantitatively

Figure 15.6

Using a balance scale to think about solving equations.

(a)

$$4 - 6x \qquad 3(1 + x)$$

Subtract 4 from both sides and multiply right-hand expression.

$$-6x \qquad 3 + 3x - 4$$

Subtract 3x from both sides.

$$-9x \qquad -1$$

Divide both sides by –9.

$$x \qquad \frac{1}{9}$$

Check:

$$4 - \frac{6}{9} \qquad 3\left(1 + \frac{1}{9}\right)$$

Both sides = $3\frac{1}{3}$.

(b)

$4.2N + 63 = \dfrac{N}{2}$

Subtract 63.

$4.2N = \dfrac{N}{2} - 63$

Multiply by 2.

$8.4N = N - 126$

Subtract N.

$7.4N = -126$

Divide by 7.4. (Use a calculator!)

$N = -17.03$ (about)

True/False and Open Sentences

Carpenter and colleagues (2003) suggest that a good starting point for helping students with the equal sign is to explore equations as either true or false. Clarifying the meaning of the equal sign is just one of the outcomes of this type of exploration, as seen in the following activity.

Activity 15.9 TRUE OR FALSE

Introduce true/false sentences or equations with simple examples to explain what is meant by a true equation and a false equation. Then put several simple equations on the board, some true and some false. Keep the computations simple so that the focus is on equivalence. Ask students to decide which of the equations are true and which are false. For each response, they must explain their reasoning. Here are some examples, but you should fit the problems you use to what your students are studying:

$$120 = 60 \times 2 \qquad 1 = \frac{3}{4} + \frac{4}{3} \qquad 318 = 318$$

$$\frac{1}{2} = \frac{1}{4} + \frac{1}{4} \qquad 345 + 71 = 70 + 344$$

$$210 - 35 = 310 - 45 \qquad 0.4 \times 15 = 0.2 \times 30$$

Listen to the types of reasons that students use to justify their answers and plan additional equations accordingly. ELLs and students with disabilities will benefit from first explaining (or showing) their thinking to a partner (a low-risk speaking opportunity) and then sharing with the whole group. For false statements, ask students to rewrite the statement using > or < to make the statement true. "Pan Balance—Numbers" on NCTM's Illuminations website (http://illuminations.nctm.org/ActivityDetail.aspx?id=26) can be used to model and/or verify equivalence.

An equation with no operation (318 = 318) can raise questions for students who have not seen the equal sign without an operation on one side. Reinforce that the equal sign is a relational symbol. In other words, expressions can be related in one of three ways: an expression is less than, the same as, or greater than another expression.

After students have experienced true/false sentences, introduce an open sentence—one with a box to be filled in or letter to be replaced. To develop an understanding of open sentences, encourage students to look at the number sentence holistically and discuss in words what the equation represents.

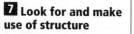

◆ **Standards for Mathematical Practice**

7 Look for and make use of structure

Activity 15.10 OPEN SENTENCES

Pose several open sentences. Here is a sampling for operations with fractions and decimals:

$$\frac{1}{2} + \square = 5 \qquad \square + 0.4 = 0.6 \qquad \frac{1}{4} + \frac{1}{2} = \square - 1$$

$$0.3 \times 7 = 7 \times \square \qquad \square \times 4 = 4 \div 2 \qquad 2.4 \div \square = 4.8 \div 6$$

Discuss how students solved the problems. After using open boxes, begin to mix in variables in place of the open box so that students can see the variable as representing a missing value.

Relational Thinking

Once students understand that the equal sign means that the quantities on both sides are the same, they can use relational thinking in solving problems. Relational thinking takes place when a student observes and uses numeric relationships between the two sides of the equal sign rather than actually computing the amounts. Relational thinking of this sort is a first step toward generalizing from relationships found in arithmetic to relationships used when variables are involved.

Consider two distinctly different explanations for placing an 8 in the box for the open sentence $7 + \square = 6 + 9$. Students might explain:

1. Because $6 + 9$ is 15, I need to figure out 7 plus what equals 15. It is 8, so the 8 goes in the box.

2. Seven is one more than the 6 on the other side. That means that the box should be one less than 9, so it must be 8.

The first student computes the result on one side and adjusts the result on the other to make the sentence true. The second student uses a relationship between the expressions on either side of the equal sign. This student does not need to compute the values on each side. When the numbers are large, relational thinking is much more useful.

Stop and Reflect

How are the two students' correct responses for $7 + \square = 6 + 9$ different? How would each of these students solve this open sentence? Note that the $\square$ can shift to a letter variable such as *n* when your students are ready.

$$534 + 175 = 174 + n \qquad ■$$

The first student will do the computation and will perhaps have difficulty finding the correct addend. The second student will use relational thinking to reason that 174 is one less than 175, so the number in the box must be one more than 534.

Formative Assessment Note

You can use these tasks as a diagnostic interview (for those students from whom you need to gather more data). Listen for whether they are using relational thinking. If they are not, ask, "Can you find the answer without actually doing any computation?" This questioning helps nudge students toward relational thinking and helps you decide what instructional steps are next.

In order to nurture relational thinking and the meaning of the equal sign, explore this series of true/false and open sentences with your class. Select challenging equations designed to elicit relational thinking rather than computation. Use large numbers that make computation difficult (not impossible) as a means to push them toward relational thinking. Here are some examples. (One of the true/false statements is false; can you explain why?)

TRUE/FALSE:

$674 - 389 = 664 - 379$	$5 \times 84 = 10 \times 42$
$37 + 54 = 38 + 53$	$64 \div 14 = 32 \div 28$

OPEN SENTENCES:

$73 + 56 = 71 + n$	$126 - 37 = n - 40$
$20 \times 48 = n \times 24$	$68 + 58 = 57 + 69 + n$

Stop and Reflect

How might you use true/false or open sentences with fractions or decimals? Why is it important to have students think about the relationship of these ideas with rational numbers? ∎

◆ The Meaning of Variables

Expressions or equations with variables are a means for expressing patterns and generalizations. Variables enable us to use mathematical symbolism as a tool to think and help better understand mathematical ideas in the same way physical objects and drawings are used. Unfortunately, students often think that the variable is a placeholder for one exact number and not that a variable could represent multiple, even infinite values. In both fourth and fifth grade, the *Common Core State Standards* content standards discuss using a symbol to represent the unknown value.

 *Teaching Tip*

Variables should be written as lowercase letters in italics. This will also help support students' challenges with seeing the difference between x as a multiplication operation and as the variable *x*.

Three uses of variables are commonly encountered in school mathematics:

1. *As a specific unknown.* Initially this is the use found in equations such as $8 + \square = 12$. Later, we see exercises such as this: If $3x + 2 = 4 \times 14$, solve for x.

2. *As a pattern generalizer.* Variables are used in statements that are true for all numbers. For example, $a \times b = b \times a$ for all real numbers.

3. *As quantities that vary.* Sometimes two variables are used within an equation to communicate a relationship, such as $y = 3x$ to represent x items that cost \$3 each (y would be the total cost). This is called joint variation because when one quantity (x) changes so does another (y). Formulas are also an example of joint variation. In $A = L \times W$, as L (length) and W (width) change, so does A, the area.

Variables as Unknowns

In the open sentence explorations, the $\square$ is a precursor of a variable used as an unknown or missing value. In the elementary grades, open boxes, as well as letters, can be used in open sentences or missing value problems. So beginning with boxes and then transitioning to variables helps make this connection explicit.

Initial work with finding the value of the variable that makes the sentence true should initially rely on relational thinking (reasoning).

Context can help students develop meaning for variables. Many story problems involve a situation in which the variable is a specific unknown, as in the following basic example:

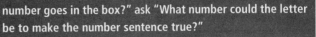

Begin to shift your language. Rather than ask students "What number goes in the box?" ask "What number could the letter be to make the number sentence true?"

Standards for Mathematical Practice

◀ **6 Attend to precision**

Gary ate 14 strawberries and Jeremy ate some, too. The container of 25 strawberries was gone! How many did Jeremy eat?

Although students can solve this problem mentally without using algebra, they can begin to learn about variables by expressing it in symbols: $5 + n = 12$, where the n represents the strawberries that Jeremy ate. These problems can grow in difficulty over time.

The following activity is a reasonable way for students to experience the meaning of a variable within a context.

Activity 15.11 STORY TRANSLATIONS

Read a simple story problem to students but omit the question. Their task is to write an equation that means the same thing. For example: "There are 3 full boxes of pencils and 5 extra pencils; there are 41 pencils in all" can be written as $(3 \times n + 5 = 41)$. Be sure to include stories for all four operations. The activity can be reversed by providing an equation with an unknown and letting students make up a story to go with it. Once equations are agreed on, students should try different strategies to find values that make the sentences true.

Teaching Tip

Avoid using the first letter of the word as a variable in problems (for example, using s for strawberries in this example instead of the better choice of n). Many students confuse those "first letter in a word" variables with shortened versions of the word (more like a label) instead of thinking of the variable as a quantity.

Sometimes students will write what may look like different equations. Consider this situation: Al has 3 times as many baseball cards as Mark. If Mark has 75 cards, how many does Al have? Some students may write $x = 3 \times 75$ while others may write $x \div 3 = 75$. Students can then discuss how these equations are alike and different. The result will be a better understanding of the relationship between multiplication and division.

Other times drawings can help represent the ideas and help support the use of variables in equations. Look at the following example.

Roberto has a 54-page book. He wants to read the book in three days. If he wants to read the same number of pages each day, how many pages should he read on the first day?

If you look at Figure 15.7 you will see how two students approached the problem by using drawings to help them decide on an operation. By representing the unknown amounts with variables they were able to reason about the situation.

The following activity illustrates how an unknown can be manipulated or treated just like a number.

Figure 15.7

Drawings that incorporate unknown amounts help students understand what operations to use.

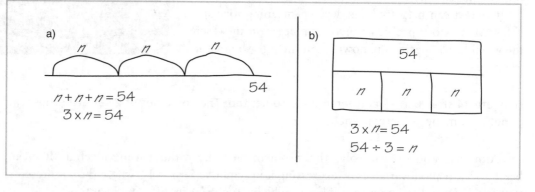

Activity 15.12 NUMBER TRICKS

Have students do the following sequence of operations:

- Write down any number.
- Add to it the number that comes after it.
- Add 9.

- Divide by 2.
- Subtract the number you began with.

Now you can "magically" read their minds. Everyone ended up with 5!

The task is to see if students can discover how the trick works. If students need a hint, suggest that instead of using an actual number, they use a box or a letter to begin with. The box or letter represents a number, but even they do not need to know what the number is. Start with n. Add the next number: $n + (n + 1) = 2n + 1$. Adding 9 gives $2n + 10$. Dividing by 2 leaves $n + 5$. Now subtract the number you began with, leaving 5.

Figure 15.8

Number tricks can be modeled using a block or a box for the unknown. Additional numbers are shown with counters or base-ten pieces.

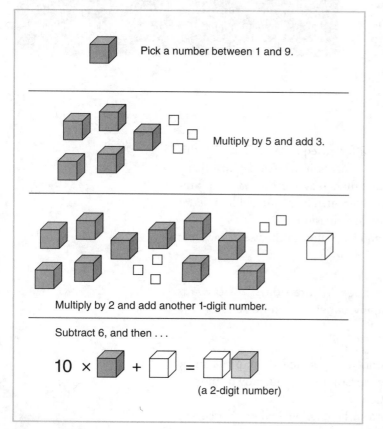

There are endless trick sequences like the one in this activity. Here are two more:

- Pick a number between 1 and 9, multiply by 5, add 3, multiply by 2, add another number between 1 and 9, subtract 6. What do you notice?
- Pick a number, multiply by 6, add 12, take half of the result, subtract 6, divide by 3. What do you notice?

These tricks can also be explored with physical models by using a small box or a cube for the unknown. Figure 15.8 shows how the first of the two preceding tricks might be modeled. Notice the place-value component required to understand the result.

Extend student thinking beyond concrete models by using and discussing the value of variables as a tool for exploring relationships.

Variables as Pattern Generators

Variables are often used to illustrate rules or regularities that exist in our number system. We often write down these rules using variables without giving much thought to the fact that students may not understand the variables involved. The next two activities focus on this topic.

Activity 15.13 WHAT'S TRUE FOR ALL NUMBERS?

Ask students how they know that $465 + 137 = 137 + 465$ without doing the computation. Students' explanations should show evidence of understanding the commutative property for addition, although the name of the property is not important.

How can this be written to show that it's a rule that is true for every number, even fractions and decimals? If students do not suggest it, offer the idea that letters or shapes could be used like this:

$$\triangle + \square = \square + \triangle \qquad \text{or} \qquad n + m = m + n$$

Be sure students understand that the choice of letter or shape is totally arbitrary, as long as it is understood that each stands for any number and that when the same letter or shape appears in the same equation, it must represent the same value.

With this introduction, challenge students to find other statements that are true for all numbers. Students with disabilities may need support with some visual examples such as the divided rectangle shown in Figure 15.9. Ask, "What are two ways to calculate the area?" This can lead to the generalized version of the distributive property: $a(b + c) = (a \times b) + (a \times c)$.

Standards for
Mathematical Practice

◄ **7** **Look for and make use of structure**

Activity 15.14 SPECIAL QUANTITIES

What numeric expression would tell the number of chair legs on 376 chairs? (376×4) What about 195 chairs? (195×4) How would you write the number of legs on any number of chairs? ($n \times 4$) Using this as an example, challenge students to write expressions for other types of quantities: fingers on students, eggs in a carton, crayons in boxes, wheels on tractor trailers, hours in a day, inches in feet, quarts in gallons, and so on. Similarly, use variables to express these special numbers: any odd number, any even number, any multiple of 7, a multiple of 3 plus a different multiple of 5, any two-digit number, any power of 2. Once students get the idea, have them make up their own special quantities and see whether others can describe them verbally. An adaptation for students with disabilities would be to have these ideas, such as eggs in a carton, on one set of cards and then have a set of expressions with variables on another set. The student with disabilities must match the expression to the quantity.

Figure 15.9

The distributive property of multiplication over addition is just one of many ideas that can be generalized using variables.

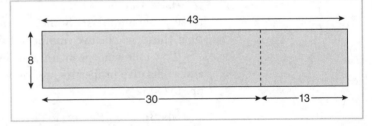

Variables as Quantities That Vary

Whenever students develop charts that list the corresponding values of two related quantities, they are exploring the idea of joint variation; the value in one row varies according to the value in the other row. Think back to the guinea pigs problem earlier in this chapter.

As one cage gets more guinea pigs, the other gets fewer (joint variation), and as the total number of guinea pigs increases, the ways they can be in the two cages also increases. Students can also make charts relating cost to the number of units purchased or relating miles driven to gallons of gasoline used. In measurement, charts are made that relate perimeter of a square to the length of a side. These are also examples of functions.

Making Structure in the Number System Explicit

In grades 3 through 5, students apply the properties of addition and the properties of multiplication as they learn basic facts and computational strategies. For example, understanding the commutative property for both addition and multiplication substantially reduces the number of facts to be memorized. In third grade, as part of a critical area, the *Common Core State Standards* specify that students should understand properties of multiplication and the relationship between multiplication and division. This standard goes beyond just expecting that students memorize or state the properties; instead the expectation is that students will use the properties to solve problems.

Students should examine these properties explicitly and begin to see they can be written in general terms. For example, a student solving $394 + 176 = n + 394$ may say that n must be 176 because $394 + 176$ is the same as $176 + 394$. This is a specific instance of the commutative property. To articulate this (and other structural properties of our number system) in a general way, either in words or symbols (e.g., $a + b = b + a$), noting that it is true for all numbers, is what making structure explicit means. When made explicit and understood, these structures not only add to students' tools for computation but also enrich their understanding of the number system, providing a base for even higher levels of abstraction (Carpenter et al., 2003).

◆ Making Sense of Properties

Properties of the number system can be built into students' explorations with true/false and open number sentences. For example, elementary students will generally agree that the true/false sentence $41 \times 3 = 3 \times 41$ is true. The pivotal algebraic question asks, "Is this true for any two numbers?" Some students will argue that although it seems to be true all of the time, there may be two numbers that haven't been tried yet for which it does not work.

The following problem and discussion was focused on investigating the distributive and associative properties, not on whether the equation was true or false (from Baek, 2008, pp. 151–152*):

Ms. J:	[*Pointing at* $(2 \times 8) + (2 \times 8) = 16 + 16$ *on the board*] Is it true or false?
LeJuan:	True, because two 8s is 16 and two 8s is 16.
Lizett:	$(2 \times 8) + (2 \times 8)$ is 32 and $16 + 16$ is 32.
Carlos:	8 plus 8 is 16, so 2 times 8 is 16, and 8 plus 8 is 16, and 2 times 8 is 16.
Ms. J:	[*Writing* $4 \times 8 = (2 \times 8) + (2 \times 8)$ *on the board*] True or false?
Students:	True.
Ms. J:	What does the 2 stand for?
Reggie:	Two boxes of eight.
Ms. J:	So how many boxes are there?

---

*Reprinted with permission from *Algebra and Algebraic Thinking in School Mathematics*, copyright 2008, by the National Council of Teachers of Mathematics. All rights reserved.

Students: Four.

Ms. J: [*Writing* $32 + 16 = (4 \times 8) + (a \times 8)$ *on the board*] What is a?

Michael: Two, because 4 times 8 is 32, and 2 times 8 is 16.

Ms. J: [*Writing* $(4 \times 8) + (2 \times 8) = (b \times 8)$ *on the board*] What is b?

Students: 6

Notice how the teacher is developing the aspects of these properties in a conceptual manner—focusing on exemplars to guide students to generalize, rather than asking students to memorize the properties as they appear in Table 15.1 as their first experience, which can be a meaningless, rote activity.

The structure of numbers can sometimes be illustrated geometrically. For example, as noted previously in Figure 15.9, 43×8 can be illustrated as a rectangular array. That rectangle can be partitioned into two rectangles (e.g., $(40 \times 8) + (3 \times 8)$), preserving the quantity.

Again, challenge students to think about this idea *in general*, first described in words, and then as symbols: $a \times b = (c \times b) + (d \times b)$, where $c + d = a$. Be sure students can connect the examples to general ideas and the general ideas back to examples. This is the distributive property, and it is perhaps the most important central idea in arithmetic (Goldenberg, Mark, & Cuoco, 2010).

◀   Standards for Mathematical Practice

7 Look for and make use of structure

◀   Standards for Mathematical Practice

7 Look for and make use of structure

Table 15.1   Properties of the Operations

Name of Property	Symbolic Representation	How Students Might Describe the Pattern or Structure
Addition		
Commutative	$a + b = b + a$	"When you add two numbers in any order, you'll get the same answer."
Associative	$(a + b) + c = a + (b + c)$	"When you add three numbers, you can add the first two and then add the third or add the last two numbers and then add the first number. Either way, you will get the same answer."
Additive Identity	$a + 0 = 0 + a = a$	'When you add zero to any number, you get the same number you started with."
	$a - 0 = a$	"When you subtract zero from any number, you get the number you started with."
Additive Inverse	$a - a = 0$*	"When you subtract a number from itself, you get zero."
Inverse Relationship of Addition and Subtraction	If $a + b = c$ then $c - b = a$ and $c - a = b$	"When you have a subtraction problem you can 'think addition' by using the inverse."
Multiplication		
Commutative	$a \times b = b \times a$	"When you multiply two numbers in any order, you will get the same answer."
Associative	$(a \times b) \times c = a \times (b \times c)$	"When you multiply three numbers, you can multiply the first two and then multiply the answer by the third or multiply the last two numbers and then multiply that answer by the first number. Either way, you will get the same answer."
Multiplicative Identity	$a \times 1 = 1 \times a = a$	"When you multiply one by any number, you get the same number you started with."
Multiplicative Inverse	$a \times \frac{1}{a} = \frac{1}{a} \times a = 1$	"When you multiply a number by its reciprocal, you will get one."
Inverse Relationship of Multiplication and Division	If $a \times b = c$ then $c \div b = a$ and $c \div a = b$	"When you have a division problem, you can 'think multiplication' by using the inverse."
Distributive (Multiplication over Addition)	$a \times (b + c) = a \times b + a \times c$	"When you multiply two numbers, you can split one number into two parts (5 can be 2 + 3), multiply each part by the other number, and then add them together."

*The additive inverse property is usually written as $a + (-a) = 0$, but the symbolic representation $a - a = 0$ will make more sense to elementary children.

◆ Making Conjectures Based on Properties

Most of the properties are ones students have experienced in their work with numbers. A great way to make these properties explicit is to pursue student ideas on what they notice to be always true. A good way to start is to ask students to try to state an idea in words of something they think is always true. For example, when multiplying a number by a second number, you can split the first number and multiply each part by the second number, and you will get the same answer. If a generalization is not clear or entirely correct, have students discuss the wording until all agree that they understand. Write this verbal statement of the property on the board. Call it a *conjecture*, and explain that it is not necessarily a true statement just because we think that it is true. Until someone either proves it or finds a counterexample—an instance for which the conjecture is not true—it remains a conjecture.

Activity 15.15 CONJECTURE CREATION

Post the following on the board: $2 \times 5 + 5 = 3 \times 5$. Ask students, "Could I trade 5 for another number and still have a true statement?" and "What other numbers will work?" Allow time for students to explore and then have them share their ideas. They will share that it works for any number (even fractions and decimals). Explain that a conjecture is $2 \times n + n = 3 \times n$. It is best to have them state the conjectures in words. The full class should discuss the various conjectures, asking for clarity or challenging conjectures with counterexamples. Conjectures can be added to a class list written in words and in symbols. All students, but particularly ELLs, may struggle with correct and precise terms. You can "revoice" their ideas using appropriate phrases to help them learn to communicate mathematically, but be careful to not make this the focus—the focus should be on the ideas presented. Importantly, students with disabilities are helped by the presentation and discussion of counterexamples. They cement their thinking by focusing on the critical elements.

Attempting to justify or prove that a conjecture is true is a significant form of algebraic reasoning and is at the heart of what it means to do mathematics (Ball & Bass, 2003; Carpenter et al., 2003; Schifter, 1999; Schifter, Monk, Russell, & Bastable, 2007). Researchers and recent standards (*Curriculum Focal Points* and *Common Core State Standards*) argue that making conjectures and justifying that they are always true is central to reasoning and sense making.

The most common form of justification is the use of examples. Students will try lots of specific numbers in a conjecture. "It works for any number you try." They may try very large numbers as substitutes for "any" number and they may try fractions or decimal values. Proof by example will hopefully lead to someone asking, "How do we know there aren't some numbers that it doesn't work for?"

Second, students may reason with physical materials or illustrations to show the reasoning behind the conjecture (like the rectangular arrays demonstrating the distributive property). What moves this beyond "proof by example" is an explanation such as, "It would work this way no matter what the numbers are." Activity 15.16 explores properties of odd and even numbers using the calculator and can lead to proof using physical materials or variables.

Activity 15.16 **BROKEN CALCULATOR: CAN YOU FIX IT?**

Explore these two challenges. Afterward, ask students for conjectures they might make about odds and evens.

1. If you cannot use any of the even keys (0, 2, 4, 6, 8), can you create an even number in the calculator display? If so, how?
2. If you cannot use any of the odd keys (1, 3, 5, 7, 9), can you create an odd number in the calculator display? If so, how?

 ## Patterns and Functional Thinking

Patterns are found in all areas of mathematics. Learning to look for patterns and how to describe, translate, and extend them is part of thinking algebraically. Two of the eight mathematical practices actually begin with the phrase "look for," implying that students who are mathematically proficient pay attention to patterns as they do mathematics.

Identifying and extending patterns is an important process in algebraic thinking. The development of this recognition of regularity usually begins in kindergarten. Students typically use materials such as color tiles, pattern blocks, toothpicks, or simply drawings to both copy and extend patterns that repeat. A few examples of repeating patterns are shown in Figure 15.10.

By third grade, students will have had numerous experiences with repeating patterns. Besides simply extending the patterns using materials or drawings, they should also have translated patterns from one medium to another. For example, a pattern made with triangles and circles can be translated to one involving red and yellow circular counters. The essence of both patterns remains the same. When two patterns made with very different materials are each read in the same manner, how they are mathematically alike becomes obvious—they have the same pattern structure.

Figure 15.10

Examples of repeating patterns using manipulatives.

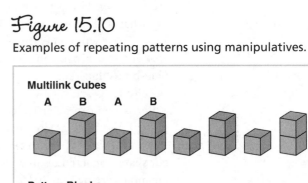
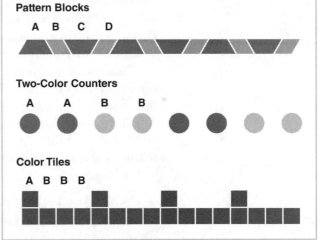

If you find that your students have not had experiences with repeating patterns, it may be worthwhile to spend a few days exploring them. After even a brief exposure, the next activity will be a useful challenge. It is a forerunner to looking at the function aspect of patterns.

Activity 15.17 **PREDICT DOWN THE LINE**

For most repeating patterns, the elements of the pattern can be numbered 1, 2, 3, and so on (often referred to as *terms* or *steps*). Provide students with a pattern to extend. Before students begin to extend the pattern, have them predict exactly what element will be in, say, the fifteenth step. Students should be required to provide a reason for their prediction, preferably in writing.

Notice in an ABC pattern that the third, sixth, ninth, and twelfth terms are the C element. Students can use their developing concepts of multiplication and division to predict what the eighteenth and twenty-fifth term would be. Ask them to predict what the element will be in the hundredth term. Because 100 ÷ 3 = 33 remainder 1, it would be the A element in the pattern. If predicting the hundredth element, students will not be able to check the prediction by extending the pattern. Justification focuses on students' knowledge of multiplication and division (Warren & Cooper, 2008).

A variation of the prediction activity adds yet another challenge. Suppose that you are working with a red-blue-blue-red-blue-blue pattern made of blocks. Instead of asking what will be in position 38, ask in what position the thirty-eighth blue block will be. What color will come after it? Notice that it is more difficult to locate the position of an element that repeats in the pattern. The same question is more difficult for this pattern: blue-blue-blue-red.

Students are surrounded by patterns in the world around them. Keep a look out for patterns that can be analyzed and used to make predictions. Encourage students to do the same. This can be as simple as asking students to look for numerical patterns and when they spot one, bring it back to class to share. Or, they can be assigned to look for patterns in the newspaper or activities in which they participate. One context is the Olympics. The Summer Olympics are held in 2016, 2020, and every four years after that. The Winter Olympics are held in 2014, 2018, and so on. Ask students to create a way to determine if x year will be an Olympic year (in general), a Summer Olympic year, and/or a Winter Olympic year (Bay-Williams & Martinie, 2004).

Hurricanes also are named in a repeating manner and can be analyzed and generalized. For each letter of the alphabet, there are six names that are used cyclically (except a name that is retired when a major hurricane, like Katrina, occurs) (Fernandez & Schoen, 2008). The six A names, for example, will be used as follows: Andrea in 2013, Arthur in 2014, Ana in 2015, Alex in 2016, Arlene in 2017, and Alberto in 2018. (Did you notice the pattern regarding gender?) Assuming the names do not get retired, students can answer questions such as these:

- In what year in the 2020s will the first hurricane of that year be named Alex?
- What will be the first hurricane's name be in the year 2020? 2050?
- Can you describe in words or symbols how to figure out the name of a hurricane, given the year?

◆ Growing Patterns

Third-grade students can explore patterns that grow by a factor, such as "times four," which can reinforce their multiplication facts and the relationship between multiplication and division. In technical terms, these are called *sequences*. We will simply call them *growing patterns*. With these patterns, students not only extend patterns, but also look for a generalization or an algebraic relationship that will tell them what the pattern will be at any point along the way. Growing patterns also demonstrate the concept of function and can be used as an entry point to this important mathematical idea.

Figure 15.11 illustrates some growing patterns that are built with various materials or drawings. The patterns consist of a series of separate steps, with each new step related to the previous one according to the pattern.

First, focus on building them and talking about how they can be extended in a logical manner. Building the patterns with physical materials such as tiles, counters, blocks, or flat toothpicks allows students to make changes if necessary and to build onto one step to make a new step. It is also more fun! Some growing patterns quickly get quite large and can require more materials than you have. One solution to this dilemma is to have students make a step with materials and then record it on grid paper. In this way, they will only need enough materials to make one step at a time.

When discussing a pattern, students should try to determine how each step in the pattern differs from the preceding step. The focus of the discussion should be how to operate on the value of the current step to get to the next step. Examples should encourage students to use both additive and multiplicative strategies.

Growing patterns also have a numeric component—the number of objects in each step. One row of the table or chart is always the number of steps, and the other is for recording how many objects are in that step. This leads to the following activity, based on Figure 15.11a.

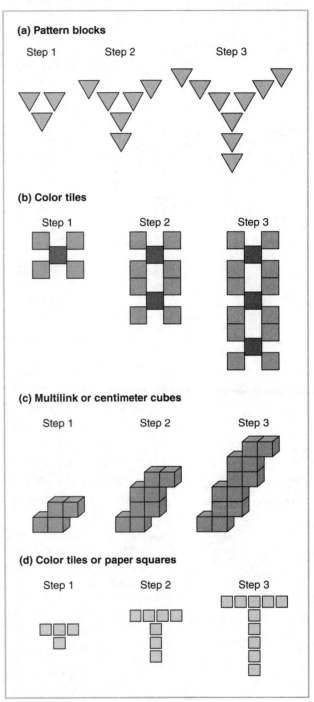

Figure 15.11

Geometric growing patterns using manipulatives.

(a) Pattern blocks

Step 1 Step 2 Step 3

(b) Color tiles

Step 1 Step 2 Step 3

(c) Multilink or centimeter cubes

Step 1 Step 2 Step 3

(d) Color tiles or paper squares

Step 1 Step 2 Step 3

Activity 15.18 PREDICT HOW MANY

Working in pairs or small groups, have students explore a pattern and respond to these questions:

- Complete a table that shows the number of triangles for each step.

Step Number (Term)	1	2	3	4	5	10	20
Number of Triangles (Element)							

- How many triangles are needed for step 10? Step 20? Step 100? Explain your reasoning.
- Write a rule (in words and/or symbols) that gives the total number of pieces to build any step number (n).

Keep in mind that ELLs need clarification on the specialized meanings of *step* and *table* because these words mean something else outside of mathematics.

Analyzing growing patterns should include the developmental progression of reasoning by looking at the visuals, then reasoning about the numerical relationships, and then extending to a larger (or nth) case (Friel & Markworth, 2009). Students' experiences with growing patterns should start with fairly straightforward patterns in grade 3 (such as in Figure 15.11) and continue with patterns that are somewhat more complicated (look at Figure 15.12) as they are asked in grades 4 and 5 to generate and analyze patterns.

Figure 15.12

Two different ways to analyze relationships in the "dot pattern."

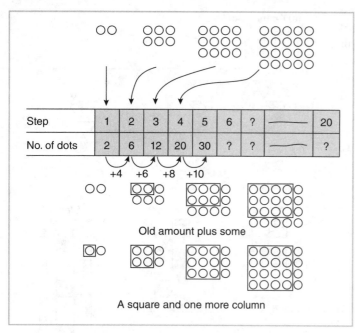

A square and one more column

Figure 15.13

NAEP item that includes fractions and decimals.

Term	1	2	3	4
Fraction	$\frac{1}{2}$	$\frac{2}{3}$	$\frac{3}{4}$	$\frac{4}{5}$

If the list of fractions above continues in the same pattern, which term will be equal to 0.95?

Ⓐ The 100th

Ⓑ The 95th

Ⓒ The 20th

Ⓓ The 19th

Ⓔ The 15th

Source: Lambdin, D. V., & Lynch, K. (2005). "Examining Mathematics Tasks from the National Assessment of Educational Progress." *Mathematics Teaching in the Middle School, 10*(6), 314–318. Reprinted with permission. Copyright © 2005, by the National Council of Teachers of Mathematics. All rights reserved.

Including fractions and decimals in working with growing patterns is very important. In 2003, the National Assessment of Educational Progress (NAEP) tested middle school students on the item in Figure 15.13. Only 27 percent of students answered correctly (Lambdin & Lynch, 2005). With the shift to the heavy focus on fractions in grades 3 through 5, this is a crucial algebra connection to foster.

When looking for relationships, some students will focus on the table and others will focus on the physical pattern. It is important for students to be able to use both forms. If a relationship is found in a table, challenge students to see how that plays out in the physical model, and vice versa.

The patterns discussed so far, repeating and growing patterns, are far from the only patterns in mathematics (not even all the options in growing patterns). Students not only need opportunities to explore patterns, but also to learn to expect, see, and use patterns in all of mathematics.

Standards for Mathematical Practice

5 Use appropriate tools strategically ▶

◆ Functional Thinking

Functions are relationships that describe situations that demonstrate joint variation (see previous section) or covariance. Although functions and function notation is the focus of eighth grade (CCSSO, 2010), experiences with functional thinking situations must begin with meaning-making experiences in the elementary grades (Blanton & Kaput 2011). First, geometric growing patterns provide a concrete and engaging way to introduce functions. Second, contexts build meaning for functions and for the relevance of algebra in general. Third, thinking of functions in an input–output manner helps students develop meaning of function.

Algebraic thinking also involves learning different ways to represent functions. As we saw with growing patterns, functional relationships can be represented in a real context, in a chart or table, with a graph, with an equation,

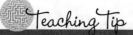

Teaching Tip

Asking questions will help your students analyze specific examples in order to determine the general relationship: What is changing? What is staying the same? What is changing will become the variable.

and with words. Each different representation offers a different way to think about relationships and, thus, helps us to better understand them.

Activity 15.19 TWO OF EVERYTHING

Two of Everything: A Chinese Folktale (Hong, 1993) is a story about Mr. and Mrs. Haktak, who discover a pot that doubles whatever goes in it, including Mrs. Haktak! Begin by exploring the doubling pattern in the story. Use tables of data labeled with "input" and "output" at the top of the two columns to help students generalize and write an equation to describe the pattern. Ask students questions like, "What if 200 pencils were dropped in the pot? If 60 tennis balls were pulled out, how many were dropped in the pot?" Second (the next day), explain that the Magic Pot has been acting up! It is not just doubling, but each day it is using a different rule. Give students partially completed tables that represent different rules (e.g., three rows completed for the rules such as $+5$, $4x$, $\frac{1}{2}x$, and so on). For each, ask students to add examples to the table and explain the rule in words and as an equation. This lesson is good for ELLs because it brings in another culture through the book, it has a concrete situation that is easily acted out or illustrated, completing the tables for the different rules does not involve a great deal of vocabulary, and there are great opportunities for student communication (speaking and listening) within the lesson. This also works well for students with disabilities because using an image of a pot and concrete representations combined with a table of values can assist in their thinking about an input–output relationship.

Notice the explicit connection in this story to the input–output concept of patterns and relationship. Something goes in the pot, and then something came out of the pot (in-pot, out-pot).

When students examine real-world functions or explore growing patterns, the relationship is found in the context—for example, horses in a race. Students should be engaged in conversations in which they link the multiplicative relationship to the context. For example, they can make statements such as "for every one horse in the race, there are four legs." Another student may say "six legs for every horse if you are counting the jockey."

The students' task is to represent relationships in a variety of ways besides words, pictures, and numbers that include charts, graphs, and equations. Another important type of activity is to determine the relationship or the rule by simply observing the numbers that are paired up without a context involved. This could be done by giving students a partially filled in chart and asking them to determine the rule. A completely equivalent format that is generally more fun is a "function machine" as described in the next activity.

Figure 15.14

A simple function machine is used to play "Guess My Rule." Students suggest input numbers and the operator records the output value.

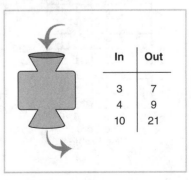

In	Out
3	7
4	9
10	21

Activity 15.20 GUESS MY RULE

Draw a simple in–out "machine" on the board, as shown in Figure 15.14. The machine "operator" knows the secret that is stored in the machine. For example, a rule might be "double the input number and add 1." Students try to guess the rule by putting numbers into the machine and observing what comes out. A list of in–out pairs is kept on the board in a table. Students who think they have guessed the rule raise their hands. As more numbers are put into the machine, those students who think they know the rule tell what comes out. Continue until most have guessed the rule.

"Guess My Rule" can be played with the whole class, or students can play in small groups, perhaps as a learning station activity. Provide a collection of rules on cards. Include at least two examples so that the machine operator is sure to understand the rule. Eventually students can make up their own rules to try to stump their classmates.

There are numerous websites that offer input–output machine investigations. These activities focus on the operations and continue to link addition, subtraction, multiplication, and division to algebraic thinking. Here are two:

- NLVM: http://nlvm.usu.edu/en/nav/frames_asid_191_g_3_t_1.html
- Math Playground: www.mathplayground.com/functionmachine.html

There is no single best method for students to find the relationship between numbers in the first column and numbers in the second. At first, some students gain insights by simply "playing around" with the numbers and asking, "What operation can I use on the number in the first column to get the corresponding number in the table?" Most will benefit from examining the physical pattern for regularities. For example, at the bottom of Figure 15.12, a square array is outlined for each step. Each successive square is one column larger on a side. What relationship might exist between this subset of the pattern and the step numbers? In this example, the side of each square is the same as the step number. The column to the right of each square is also the same as the step number.

Formative Assessment Note

Students need to connect the numbers in the tables or charts they build with the actual patterns and with the graphs. After students have constructed a graph for their physical pattern, conduct a diagnostic interview and ask them to select different numbers in the graph and ask them to explain where these numbers came from in the pattern or chart (or both). If your students have been able to find a general rule related to the pattern, they should be able to use the rule to determine the number associated with any set of numbers in the table with any point in the graph.

Figure 15.15

Graphs of two growing patterns.

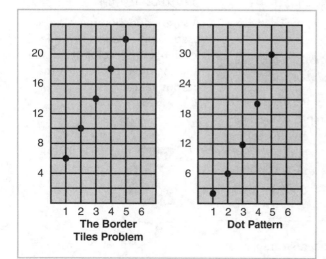

So far, patterns have been represented by (1) physical materials or drawings, (2) tables, (3) words, and (4) symbols. A graph adds a fifth representation. In the *Common Core State Standards*, coordinate graphs are introduced in fifth grade, in which students represent real-world data and solve mathematical problems in the first quadrant (CCSSO, 2010). Figure 15.15 provides a graph of the border tiles problem (presented in Figure 15.3 on page 289) and shows a graph for the dot pattern (presented in Figure 15.12 on page 306).

Here are some other examples of real-world situations that give rise to graphs for intermediate-grade students.

- The length of a row of students holding arms outstretched. The *x*-axis can represent the number of students; the *y*-axis the length of the row.
- Weight of jellybeans in increments of 10 jellybeans. The weight of jellybeans is a function of the number of jellybeans.

- Height of liquid in a glass determined by the number of units poured in. Liquid is measured into the bottle using a small container, such as a medicine cup. The height of the liquid in the glass is a function of the quantity of liquid poured in.

- Height of bean plants compared to the days since they sprouted. The height of the bean plant is a function of the number of days since it was planted.

These real-world examples provide the chance to connect the graphing of points on the coordinate axis with algebra. Ask questions about what they notice about their data on the graph. What might they predict for an x value they did not plot on the graph? Why? How does the graph provide insights into the situation?

Try this with fifth graders who are exploring the volume of solids. Consider the task of creating a tower of 1-inch cubes. The base of the tower is 2 inches by 3 inches. As the height of the tower changes from 1 inch to 10 inches, the volume of the tower will increase in 6-cubic-inch increments for each inch added. The equation would be $V = H \times 6$, and the graph will be a series of points that are in a straight line. The graph or the equation can be used to predict how many cubes would be needed for a tower of any height or, if the number of cubes is known, to be able to determine how tall a tower could be built.

◀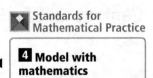

Standards for
Mathematical Practice

4 Model with mathematics

Expanded Lesson

Tilt or Balance

Content and Task Decisions

Grade Level: 5

Mathematics Goals

- To connect the symbols =, <, and > to the concept of equality, less than, and more than
- To develop the notion of variables as unknowns

Grade Level Guide

NCTM Curriculum Focal Points	Common Core State Standards
In fifth grade, as an Algebra Connection, students use models and relationship as contexts for writing and solving simple equations and inequalities (NCTM, 2006).	Students in Grade 4 should be able to represent and solve problems using equations with a letter standing for the unknown quantity. In fifth grade, students "Use parentheses, brackets, or braces in numerical expressions, and evaluate expressions with these symbols" (CCSSO, 2010, p. 35).

Consider Your Students' Needs

Students have been challenged to find different ways to express the relationship between numbers and expressions as in Activity 15.6, "Seesaw Students." Students also know how to apply the order of operations for grouping symbols to an expression and are familiar with the symbols =, <, and >.

For English Language Learners

- Make sure all students, particularly ELLs, know what a see-saw is. Use an online image or video to show how it works.
- ELLs and students with disabilities will benefit from first explaining (or showing) their thinking to a partner (a low-risk speaking opportunity) and then sharing with the whole group.

For Students with Disabilities

- Modify the game for students with disabilities by creating easier combinations or only using a single operation, such as addition.

- Instead of having students with disabilities write expressions for each side of the scale, share a small collection of cards with expressions and have them identify the ones that will make the scale balance.

Materials

Each student will need:

- "Tilt or Balance Challenge" worksheet for each student (Blackline Master 32)

Teacher will need:

- Transparency of "Tilt or Balance?" (see Blackline Master 31)

Lesson

Before

Begin with a simpler version of the task:

- Show students the transparency "Tilt or Balance?" Explain that the drawing is a representation of a pan balance, and because the drawing cannot tilt when the quantities are unequal, we can indicate the inequality by using < or >. Ask them to determine whether the first scale tilts or balances. Have a volunteer explain his or her thinking and which symbol (<, >, or =) he or she would use to indicate the relationship between the quantities.
- Have students consider and discuss the next two balance scales in a similar manner. Be sure that students understand the correct use of < and >.

Present the focus task to the class:

- Given the "Tilt or Balance Challenge" worksheet, substitute numbers for the □ symbol to create a numeric expression on each side of the scales to make them balance.

Provide clear expectations:

- Make it clear to students that the □ represents the same value on both sides of the scale. Their goal is to write expressions for each side of the scale to make it balance by substituting a number for the □. If they try a number that results in an unbalanced scale, they should write a corresponding inequality using < or > to indicate the relationship. For each successful attempt at balancing the scales, they should write a corresponding equation to illustrate the meaning of =.

During

Ongoing:

- Look for students who are mistakenly using different numbers for the variable on each side of the scale. The variable or unknown should be the same number on both sides of the scale.

- Look for different strategies used by students to determine the unknowns. Capitalize on these differences in the *After* portion of the lesson.

After

Bring the class together to share and discuss the task:

- Ask for volunteers to share their thinking in determining the solution for the first scale problem. Do not evaluate students' ideas, but encourage other students to comment on and question their classmates' thinking. Ask for other ways to think about the task. Repeat for the next two scale problems.

- Ask students to write down what they think the symbol = means. Have students share with a partner and then

discuss ideas as a class. It is important for the students to come to the consensus that = means *is the same as.*

Assessment

Observe

- Are students using a systematic approach to determine the solutions? In other words, are they using the results of their attempts to inform their next attempt? Or are they haphazardly trying numbers?

- Do students have a clear sense that = means that the expressions on either side of it are equivalent amounts? Do they understand this in equations without a reference to a scale?

Ask

- What happens when each shape on the scales represents a different value? How can you solve that kind of problem?

- Can you change an amount on each side of the balance and maintain the balance? What is the key consideration in making that work?

16

Building Measurement Concepts

Big IDEAS

1 Measurement involves a comparison of an attribute of an item or situation with a unit that has the same attribute. Lengths are compared to units of length, areas to units of area, time to units of time, and so on.

2 Estimation of measures and the development of benchmarks for frequently used units of measure help students increase their familiarity with units, preventing errors and aiding in the meaningful use of measurement.

3 Measurement instruments (e.g., rulers) group multiple units so that you do not have to iterate a single unit multiple times.

4 Area and volume formulas provide a method of measuring these attributes by using only measures of length.

5 Area, perimeter, and volume are related. For example, as the shapes of regions or three-dimensional objects change while maintaining the same areas or volumes, there is an effect on the perimeters and surface areas.

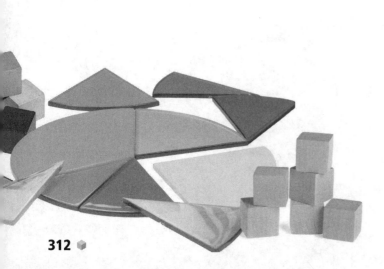

Measurement is one of the most useful mathematics content strands because it is an important component in everything from occupational tasks to life skills for the mathematically literate citizen. From gigabytes that measure amounts of information, to font size on computers, to miles per gallon, to recipes for a meal, people are surrounded daily with measurement concepts that apply to a variety of real-world contexts and applications. However, measurement is not an easy topic for students to understand. Data from international studies consistently indicate that U.S. students are weaker in the area of measurement than any other topic in the mathematics curriculum (Thompson & Preston, 2004).

The *Common Core State Standards* (CCSSO, 2010) expect that not only will measurement be an important context for other mathematical ideas such as number and geometry, but there are also other grade-level goals for measurement that are critical:

Grade 3: Students estimate and measure using units of time, liquid volumes, weight in metric units as well as understand area (including its relationship to multiplication and addition) and perimeter.

Grade 4: Students convert measurement units in the same system by expressing a larger unit in the form of a smaller unit, solve problems using the four operations with measurement contexts such as with units of time, liquid volume, weights of objects, money, area (using the formula) and perimeter (using the formula). Students understand the concept of angles and how to measure them in degrees using a protractor.

Grade 5: Students continue to convert measurement units in the same system and use the conversions to solve problems (including multistep problems). They also understand the concept of volume (including its relationship to multiplication and addition) to solve a variety of problems.

In this chapter you will learn how to help students develop a conceptual understanding of the measurement process and the tools of measurement. You will also learn about nonstandard units (what *Common Core State Standards* refers to as *improvised units*) and standard units of measurement, estimation in measurement including the use of benchmarks, and the development of measurement formulas.

The Meaning and Process of Measuring

Suppose that you asked your students to measure an empty bucket, as in Figure 16.1. The first thing they would need to know is *what* about the bucket is to be measured. They might measure the height, depth, diameter (distance across), or perimeter (distance around). All of

Figure 16.1 Measuring different attributes of a bucket.

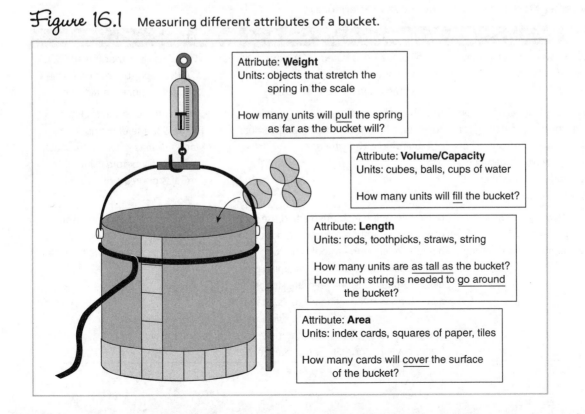

Attribute: **Weight**
Units: objects that stretch the spring in the scale

How many units will pull the spring as far as the bucket will?

Attribute: **Volume/Capacity**
Units: cubes, balls, cups of water

How many units will fill the bucket?

Attribute: **Length**
Units: rods, toothpicks, straws, string

How many units are as tall as the bucket?
How much string is needed to go around the bucket?

Attribute: **Area**
Units: index cards, squares of paper, tiles

How many cards will cover the surface of the bucket?

these are length measures. A bucket also has volume (or capacity) and weight. Each aspect that can be measured is an *attribute* of the bucket. Notice that these are continuous quantities.

Once students determine the attribute to be measured, they then choose a unit that has the same attribute being measured. Length is measured with units that have length, volume with units that have volume, and so on.

Technically, a *measurement* is a number that indicates a comparison between the attribute of the object (or situation, or event) being measured and the same attribute of a given unit of measure. We commonly use small units of measure to determine a numeric relationship (the measurement) between what is measured and the unit. For example, to measure a length, the comparison can be done by lining up copies of the unit directly against the length being measured. For most attributes measured in schools, we can say that to measure means that the attribute being measured is "filled" or "covered" or "matched" with a unit of measure with the same attribute.

In summary, to measure something, one must perform three steps:

1. Decide on the attribute to be measured.

2. Select a unit that has that attribute.

3. Compare the units, by filling, covering, matching, or using some other method, with the attribute of the object being measured. The number of same-sized units required to match the object is the measure.

Measuring instruments, such as rulers, scales, and protractors, are devices that make the filling, covering, or matching process easier. For example, a ruler lines up the units of length and numbers them, and a protractor lines up the unit angles and numbers them.

◆ Concepts and Skills

The skill of measuring with a unit must be explicitly linked to the concept of measuring as a process of comparing attributes, using measuring units and using measuring instruments as outlined in Table 16.1.

Table 16.1 Measurement Instruction—A Sequence of Experiences

Step	Goal	Type of Activity	Notes
1—Making comparisons	Students will understand the attribute to be measured.	Make comparisons based on the attribute. For example, longer/shorter, heavier/lighter. Use direct comparisons whenever possible.	When it is clear that the attribute is understood, there is no further need for comparison activities.
2—Using physical models of measuring units	Students will understand how filling, covering, matching, or making other comparisons of an attribute with measuring units produces a number called a *measure*.	Use physical models of measuring units to fill, cover, match, or make the desired comparison of the attribute with the unit.	Begin with nonstandard units. Progress to the direct use of standard units when appropriate, and certainly before using formulas or measuring tools.
3—Using measuring instruments	Students will use common measuring tools with understanding and flexibility.	Make measuring instruments and use them in comparison with the actual unit models to see how the measurement tool is performing the same function as the individual units. Make direct comparisons between the student-made tools and the standard tools. Standard measuring instruments, such as rulers, scales, and protractors, are devices that make the filling, covering, or matching process easier.	Without a careful comparison with the standard tools, much of the value in making the tools can be lost.

Making Comparisons

Sometimes with a measure such as length, a direct comparison can be made in which one object can be lined up and matched to another. But often an indirect method using a third object must be used. For example, if students compare the volume of one box to another, they must devise an indirect way to compare. They may fill one box with beans and then pour the beans into the other box. Another example using length would use a string to compare the height of a wastebasket to the distance around the top. The string is the intermediary, as it is impossible to directly compare these two lengths.

When students compare objects on the basis of some measurable attribute, that attribute becomes the focus of the activity. For example, is the size of one angle more than, less than, or about the same as the size of another angle? No measurement is required, but some manner of comparing one angle to the other must be devised. The attribute of "angular spread" (the spread of the rays of the angle) is inescapable.

Remember, when helping students make comparisons you should use precise language in your instruction. Avoid using the phrases "bigger than" and "smaller than" and instead use more precise language such as "longer than" or "holds more than."

Standards for Mathematical Practice

◄ **6** Attend to precision

Using Physical Models of Measuring Units

For most attributes measured in grades 3 through 5, it is possible to have physical models of the units of measure. Time and temperature are exceptions. Many other attributes not commonly measured in school also do not have physical units of measure, such as light intensity, speed, and loudness. Unit models can be found for both nonstandard (sometimes referred to as *informal*) units and standard units. For length, for example, drinking straws that are all the same arbitrary length (nonstandard) or 1-foot-long card stock strips (standard) might be used as units.

To help make the notion of unit explicit, use as many copies of the unit as are needed to fill or match the attribute measured (this is called *tiling* and it involves equal partitioning). To measure the area of the desktop with an index card (nonstandard) as your unit, you can literally cover the entire desk with cards. Somewhat more difficult is to use a single copy of the unit (this is called *iteration*). That means measuring the same desktop with a single index card by repeatedly moving it from position to position and keeping track of which areas the card has covered.

It is useful to measure the same object with units of different size to help students understand that the unit used is important. For each different-sized unit, estimate the measure in advance and discuss the estimate afterward. They also must start to observe that smaller units produce larger numeric measures, and vice versa. This is a concept related to converting units and it is hard for some students to understand. This inverse relationship can only be mentally constructed by estimating, then experimenting, and finally reflecting on the measurements.

Using Measuring Instruments

On the 2003 NAEP exam (Blume, Galindo, & Walcott, 2007), only 20 percent of fourthgraders could give the correct measure of an object not aligned with the end of a ruler, as in Figure 16.2. Even at the middle school level, only 56 percent of eighth graders answered the same situation accurately (Kloosterman, Rutledge, & Kenney, 2009). These results point to the difference between using a measuring device and understanding how it works. Students on the same exam also experienced difficulty when the increments on a measuring device were not one unit.

Figure 16.2   "How long is this crayon?"

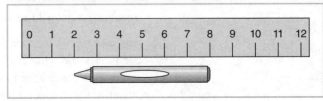

If students construct simple measuring instruments using unit models with which they are familiar, it is more likely that they will understand how an instrument measures. A ruler is a good example. If students line up individual physical units along a strip of card stock and mark them off, they can see that it is the spaces on rulers and not the hash marks or numbers that are important. It is essential that students discuss how measurement with iterating individual units compares with measurement using an instrument. Without this comparison and discussion, students may not understand that these two methods are essentially the same. Then they are ready to compare their "ruler" with standard rulers (or other instruments like scales) and can compare the use of these devices.

◆ Introducing Nonstandard Units

It is common in primary grades to use nonstandard units to measure length, but unfortunately, measurement activities in grades 3 through 5, in which other attributes are measured, often do not begin with this important first step. The use of nonstandard units for measurement activities with new units is beneficial at all grade levels for the following reasons:

- Nonstandard units make it easier to focus directly on the attribute being measured. For example, when discussing how to measure the area of an irregular shape, units such as square tiles or circular counters may be suggested. Each unit covers area and each will give a different result. The discussion can focus on what it means to measure area.

- The use of nonstandard units avoids conflicting objectives in introductory lessons. Is your lesson about what it means to measure area, or about understanding square centimeters?

- Nonstandard units provide a good rationale for using standard units. The need for a standard unit has more meaning when your class has measured the same objects with their own collections of nonstandard units and arrived at different and sometimes confusing answers.

The amount of time that should be spent using nonstandard units varies with students' age, level of understanding, and the attributes being measured. Some students need many experiences over multiple days with a variety of nonstandard units of area, weight, and capacity. Conversely, fourth graders may only need to work with nonstandard units for a day or two when they learn to measure angles. When nonstandard units have served their purpose, move on.

◆ Developing Standard Units

Measurement sense demands that students be familiar with standard measurement units, be able to make estimates in terms of these units, and meaningfully interpret measures depicted with standard units.

Teaching Tip

Remember as you teach the standard units to review necessary words and symbols and include these on your math word wall.

Perhaps the biggest error in measurement instruction is the failure to recognize and separate two types of objectives: (1) understanding the meaning and technique of measuring a particular attribute, and (2) learning about the standard units commonly used to measure that attribute.

Teaching standard units of measure can be organized around three broad goals:

1. *Familiarity with the unit.* Students should have a basic idea of the size of commonly used units and what they measure. Knowing approximately how much 1 liter of water is or being able to estimate a shelf as 5 feet long is as important as measuring either of these accurately.

2. *Ability to select an appropriate unit.* Students should know both what is a reasonable unit of measure in a given situation and the precision that is required. (Would you measure your lawn to purchase grass seed with the same precision as you would use in measuring a window to buy a pane of glass?) Students need practice in selecting appropriate standard units and judging the level of precision.

3. *Knowledge of relationships between units.* Students should know the relationships that are commonly used, such as those between inches, feet, and yards, or between milliliters and liters.

Developing Unit Familiarity

Two types of activities can develop familiarity with standard units: (1) comparisons that focus on a single unit, and (2) activities that develop personal referents or benchmarks for single units or easy multiples of units.

Activity 16.1   FAMILIAR MEASURES

Use the book *Measuring Penny* (Leedy, 2000) to get students interested in the variety of ways familiar items can be measured. In this book, the author bridges between nonstandard units (e.g., dog biscuits) and standard units to measure Penny the pet dog. Have students use the idea of measuring Penny to find something at home (or in class) to measure in as many ways as they can think using standard units. The measures should include the adding of fractional units to be more precise. Discuss in class the familiar items chosen and their measures so that different ideas and benchmarks are shared.

Of special interest for length are benchmarks found on our bodies. These become quite familiar over time and can be used in many situations as approximate rulers.

Activity 16.2   PERSONAL BENCHMARKS

Measure your body. About how long is your foot, your stride, your hand span (stretched and with fingers together), the width of your finger, your arm span (finger to finger and finger to nose), the distance around your wrist and around your waist, and your height to waist, to shoulder, and to head? (There are wonderful proportional relationships to be found between these measures too!) Some of these measures may prove to be useful benchmarks for standard units, and some may be excellent physical models for single units. (The average person's fingernail width is about 1 cm, and most people can find a 10-cm length somewhere on their hands.)

Choosing Appropriate Units

Should the area of the room be measured in square feet or square inches? Should the concrete blocks be weighed in grams or kilograms? The answers to questions such as these involve more than simply knowing how large units are, although that is certainly required. Another consideration involves the need for precision. If you were measuring your wall in order to cut a piece of molding to fit, you would need to measure it very precisely. The smallest unit would be an inch or a centimeter, and you would also use small fractional parts. But if you were determining how many 8-foot molding strips to buy, the nearest foot would probably be sufficient.

Standards for
Mathematical Practice

◄ **6** Attend to precision

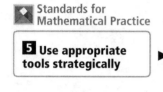

Activity 16.3 GUESS THE UNIT

Find examples of measurements of all types in newspapers, on signs, or in other everyday situations. Present the context and measures but without units. For example, you may consider ads for carpeting, articles about gas prices, and so forth. The task is to predict what units of measure were used. Have students discuss their choices. For students with disabilities, you may want to provide the headings for the possible units so they can sort the real-world measures into groups (i.e., area, capacity, weight, time, length). If you have a hard time finding such contexts from the newspaper, write some ideas on cards, such as the amount of sugar needed to make a cake, the amount of medicine that needs to be taken, and the amount of paper needed to wrap a gift, and have students sort those instead.

◆ Standards for
Mathematical Practice

5 Use appropriate
tools strategically ▶

⬢ Important Standard Units and Relationships

NCTM's position statement on the metric system (2011) clearly states, "Because the metric system is an effective, efficient, base-ten measurement system used throughout the world, students need to develop an understanding of its units, and their relationship as well as fluency in its application to real world situations." The statement goes on to say that because we are still using customary measures in day-to-day life, students must work in that system as well. The *Common Core State Standards* state directly in the third, fourth, and fifth grade expectations that units such as meters, centimeters, cubic centimeters, grams, kilograms, and liters are expected.

Countries worldwide have passed laws stating that international commerce must use metric units. So if U.S. students are going to be prepared for the global workplace, they must be knowledgeable and comfortable with metric units. Results of the 2004 NAEP reveal that only 40 percent of fourth graders were able to identify how many kilograms a bicycle weighed given the choices of 1.5, 15, 150, and 1500 kg. Even among eighth graders, only 37 percent knew how many milliliters were in a liter (Perie, Moran, & Lutkus, 2005). Interestingly, U.S. students do better on metric units than customary units (Preston & Thompson, 2004).

Stop and Reflect

Why do you think U.S. students are more successful with metric units than the more familiar customary units? ■

The relationships between units within either the metric or customary systems are conventions. As such, students must simply be told what the relationships are, and instructional experiences must be devised to reinforce them. It can be argued that initially knowing about how much liquid makes a liter, or being able to pace off 3 meters—unit familiarity—is more important than knowing how many cubic centimeters are in a liter. Another approach to unit familiarity is to begin with common items and use their measures as references or benchmarks. A doorway is a bit more than 2 meters high, and a doorknob is about 1 meter from the floor. A bag of flour is a good reference for 5 pounds. A paper clip weighs about a gram, and is about 1 centimeter wide. A gallon of milk weighs a little less than 4 kilograms. However, in the intermediate grades, knowing basic relationships becomes important.

The customary system has few patterns or generalizable rules to guide students in converting units. In contrast, the metric system was systematically created around powers of ten.

Understanding of the role of the decimal point as indicating the units position is a powerful concept for making metric conversions (see Figure 14.4). As students grasp the structure of decimal notation, develop the metric system with all seven places: three prefixes for smaller units (*deci-, centi-, milli-*) and three for larger units (*deka-, hecto-, kilo-*). Avoid mechanical rules such as "To change centimeters to meters, move the decimal point two places to the left." Instead, create conceptual, meaningful methods for conversions rather than rules that are often misused, misunderstood, and forgotten.

◆ The Role of Estimation and Approximation

Measurement estimation is the process of using mental and visual information to measure or make comparisons without using measuring instruments. It is a practical skill used by people almost every day. Do I have enough sugar to make cookies? Can you throw the ball 15 meters? Is this suitcase over the weight limit or the size limit? Will my car fit into that parking space? Here are several reasons for including estimation in measurement activities:

- Estimation helps students focus on the attribute being measured and the measuring process. Think about how you would estimate the area of the cover of this book using playing cards as the unit. To do so, you have to think about what area is and how the units might be placed on the book cover.

- Estimation provides intrinsic motivation to measurement activities. It is interesting to see how close you can come in your estimate to the actual measure.

- When standard units are used, estimation helps develop familiarity with the unit. If you estimate the height of the door in meters before measuring, you must think about the size of a meter.

- The use of a benchmark to make an estimate promotes multiplicative reasoning. The width of the building is about one-fourth of the length of a football field—perhaps 25 yards.

In all measuring activities, emphasize the use of approximate language. The front of the math book is covered by *about* 8 index cards and the sidewalk in front of the school is *about* 15 newspaper sheets in area. Approximate language is very useful for students because many measurements do not result in whole numbers. As they become more sophisticated, students will begin to search for smaller units and use fractional units to be more precise, which is an opportunity to develop the idea that all measurements include some error. Acknowledge that each smaller unit or subdivision produces a greater degree of *precision*.

Stop and Reflect

A length measure can never be more than one-half unit in error. Why is this the case? ■

Suppose you are measuring a length of ribbon with a ruler that only shows quarter inches—so the unit is a quarter of an inch. If the length of ribbon falls between $3\frac{3}{4}$ and 4 inches, we would usually round to whichever number is closer to the length of ribbon. If the length of ribbon is more than halfway towards the 4-inch mark, we would say it's 4 inches long. However, if the length of ribbon is less than halfway from $3\frac{3}{4}$, we say it is closer to $3\frac{3}{4}$ inches long. In either case, we are within $\frac{1}{8}$ of an inch or one-half of the unit and are essentially ignoring the difference, and this constitutes our "error." If we need more precision in our measurement, we use smaller units to ensure that our measurement rounding or error is within an acceptable range.

Because mathematically there is no "smallest unit," there is always some error in measurement. The *Common Core Standards for Mathematical Practice* (CCSSO, 2010) include "Attend to Precision." Under that practice, they expect that students "are careful about specifying units of measure" and that they "express numerical answers with a degree of precision appropriate for the problem context" (p. 7).

◆ Strategies for Estimating Measurements

Always begin a measurement activity with students making an estimate. This is true with both nonstandard and standard units. Just as for computational estimation, specific strategies exist for estimating measures. Here are four strategies that can be taught:

1. *Develop and use benchmarks or referents for important units.* Research shows that students who have both acquired mental benchmarks or reference points for measurements *and* have practiced using them in class activities are much better estimators than students who have not learned to use benchmarks (Joram, 2003). Students must pay attention to the size of the unit to estimate well (Towers & Hunter, 2010). Referents should be things that are easily envisioned by the student. One example is the height of an average child (see Figure 16.3). Students should have a good referent for single units and also useful multiples of standard units.

2. *Use "chunking" when appropriate.* Figure 16.3 shows an example. It may be easier to estimate the shorter chunks along the wall than to estimate the whole length. The weight of a stack of books is easier if some estimate is given to the weight of an average book.

3. *Use subdivisions.* This is a strategy similar to chunking, with the chunks imposed on the object by the estimator. For example, if the wall length to be estimated has no useful chunks, it can be mentally divided in half and then in fourths or even eighths by repeated halving until a more manageable length is found. Length, volume, and area measurements all lend themselves to this technique.

Figure 16.3 Estimating measures using benchmarks and chunking.

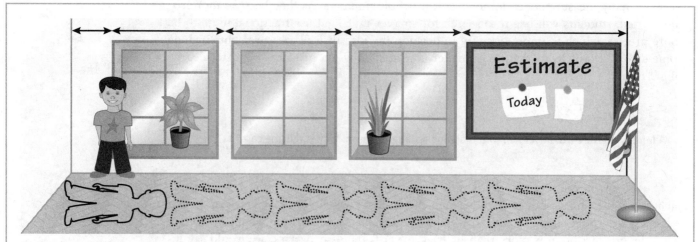

Estimate the room length.

Use: windows, bulletin board, and spaces between as "chunks."

Use: mental benchmark—"My height is about 5 feet long. I could get 5 kids lying down in here plus maybe 3 more feet. Say, 28 feet."

4. *Iterate a unit mentally or physically.* For length, area, and volume, it is sometimes easy to mark off single units visually. You might use your hands or make marks or folds to keep track as you go. If you know, for example, that your stride is about $\frac{3}{4}$ meter long, you can walk off a length and then multiply to get an estimate. Hand and finger widths are useful for shorter measures.

◆ Tips for Teaching Estimation

Each strategy just listed should be explicitly taught and discussed with students. Suggested benchmarks for useful measures can be developed and recorded on a class chart. Include items found at home. But the best approach to improving estimation skills is to have students do a lot of estimating. Keep the following tips in mind:

1. *Help students learn strategies by having them first try a specified approach.* Later activities should permit students to choose whatever techniques they wish.

2. *Discuss how different students made their estimates.* This will confirm that there is no single right way to estimate while reminding students of other useful approaches.

3. *Accept a range of estimates.* Think in relative terms about what is a good estimate. Within 10 percent for length is quite good. Even 30 percent "off" may be reasonable for weights or volumes.

4. *Encourage students to give a range of estimates that they believe includes the actual measure* (e.g., the door is between 7 and 8 feet tall). This is not only a practical approach in real life, but it also helps focus on the approximate nature of estimation.

Teaching Tip

Do not promote a "winning" estimate. It discourages estimation and promotes only seeking the exact answer.

5. *Make measurement estimation an ongoing activity.* Post a daily measurement to be estimated. Students can record their estimates and discuss them in a five-minute period. Students can take turns determining the daily measurements to estimate, with a student or team of students assigned this task each week.

6. *Be precise with your language.* Do not use the word *measure* interchangeably with the word *estimate* (Towers & Hunter, 2010). Randomly substituting one word for the other will cause uncertainty and possibly confuse students.

◆ Measurement Estimation Activities

Estimation activities need not be elaborate. Any measurement activity can have an "estimate first" component. For more emphasis on the process of estimation itself, simply think of measures that can be estimated, and have students estimate. Here are two suggestions.

◤ *Activity* 16.4 **ESTIMATION QUICKIE**

Select a single object such as a box, a painting on the wall of the school, a jar, or even the principal! Each day, select a different attribute or dimension to estimate. For the painting, for example, students can estimate its height, perimeter, weight, and area.

◀ *Activity* 16.5 ESTIMATION SCAVENGER HUNT

Conduct estimation scavenger hunts. Give teams a list of either nonstandard or standard measurements, and have them find things that are close to having those measurements. Do not permit the use of measuring instruments. A list might include the following items:

- A length of 3.5 meters
- Something that has an area about the same as the cover of your mathematics book
- Something that weighs more than 1.5 kg but less than 2 kg
- A container that holds about 200 mL
- An angle of 45 degrees or 135 degrees

Let students suggest how to judge results in terms of accuracy.

Formative Assessment Note

Estimation tasks are a good way to assess students' understanding of both measurement and units. Use a checklist while students estimate measures of real objects inside and outside the classroom. Prompt students to explain how they arrived at their estimates to get a more complete picture of their measurement knowledge. Asking only for a numeric estimate and not asking for an explanation can mask a lack of understanding and will not give you the information you need to provide appropriate remediation.

In this chapter, each kind of measurement in the grades 3 through 5 curriculum is discussed, infusing ideas of teaching measurement and estimation using activities as examples.

 Length

Length is usually the first attribute students learn to measure. Length measurement is not immediately understood by young students, and students in grades 3 through 5 may be challenged with the concept of length as they investigate problems that include perimeter.

Teaching Tip

Remind students that the units are what they are counting, not the lines or hash marks.

Length is an attribute of an object that is found by locating two endpoints and examining how far it is between those points. We measure lengths by selecting a unit and repeatedly matching that unit to the object.

Formative Assessment Note

When considering length instruction in the third or fourth grade, a quick performance assessment may be in order to be sure that students have gained the ideas that are often taken for granted at this level. Here are some ideas that will not take too much time.

- Provide students with a supply of toothpicks or another suitable informal unit of length. Prepare a paper with two dots at diagonally opposite sides of the paper. Have students determine how far apart the dots are in terms of toothpicks. If students know to line up the toothpicks in a straight line between the dots without any significant gaps or overlapping units, and not use any broken toothpicks as a unit, then it may be assumed that they understand the process of using units to measure.

- Demonstrate in the classroom how a fictitious second grader used a ruler to measure the length of the board using gaps in his placement of the ruler, overlaps, and a wavy line of alignment. The students' task is to explain to the second grader why his measurement may be inaccurate.
- Have students measure two different objects. Then ask how much longer the longer object is. Observe whether students can use the measurements to answer or whether they need to make a third measurement to find the difference.
- Have students measure a line with small paper clips and then again with large paper clips. Can they identify the inverse relationship between the measures they find and the size of the units?

In their explanations you are looking for the same issues as stated earlier: use of units with equal length, straight alignment of units without overlap or gaps (or mismatching the beginning or endpoint of the line), and that the size of the unit is important in understanding the measurement.

If your assessment of students indicates that there is some confusion about how length is measured, then the results of the assessment will undoubtedly produce different ideas and answers. Rather than correcting inappropriate ideas or techniques, use the class discussion of these results so that students will self-assess and come to deeper understanding.

Standards for Mathematical Practice

◄ **3** Construct viable arguments and critique the reasoning of others

Linked to the assessment above, and as required in the standards (CCSSO, 2010), students must be able to convert measures in the same system to larger or smaller units. Yet, it is a challenge to explain to students that larger units will produce a smaller measure and vice versa. Instead, engage students in activities like the following, in which this issue is emphasized.

Activity 16.6 CHANGING UNITS

Have students measure a length with a specified unit. Then provide them with a different unit that is either twice as long or half as long as the original unit. Their task is to predict the measure of the same length using the new unit. Students should write down their estimations and discuss how they made their estimations. Then have them make the actual measurement. Cuisenaire rods are excellent for this activity. Some students can be challenged with units that are more difficult multiples of the original unit.

Standards for Mathematical Practice

◄ **2** Reason abstractly and quantitatively

In "Changing Units," you are looking first for the basic idea that when the unit is longer, the measure is smaller, and when the unit is smaller, the measure is larger.

This is a good activity to do just prior to introducing unit conversion with standard units, and is an excellent proportional thinking task.

Fractional Parts of Units

Students are sometimes initially perplexed when measurements do not result in a whole number, but measurement is an excellent context for students to apply their developing concepts of fractions. Students can relate the idea of unit to the whole, and partition to see half units or other fractional parts. The use of fractional units helps students understand subdivision marks on a ruler.

Students should use their rulers to measure lengths that are longer than their rulers and discuss how that can be done. If they simply read the last mark on the ruler they may not understand how a ruler is a representation of a continuous row of units. Another challenge is to find more than one way to measure a length with a ruler. Do you have to begin at the end? What if you begin at another unit in the center of the ruler?

All of these ideas can be pulled together in large-scale measuring activities that involve whole and fractional units using rulers, measuring tapes, or even trundle wheels that measure and count meter lengths. An example of such an activity is described by Kurz (2012), in which different large water shooters were tested to assess whether the manufacturers' claims on how far they can shoot water were actually accurate. Another option is testing the distance paper airplanes can travel (Reeder, 2012).

There are other measures of length, such as perimeter and circumference. Perimeter will be discussed later in this chapter.

Area

Area is the two-dimensional space inside a region. As with other attributes, students must first understand the attribute of area before measuring. Data from the 2003 NAEP suggest that fourth- and eighth-grade students have an incomplete understanding of area (Blume, Galindo, & Walcott, 2007). Estimating and measuring area is one of the critical areas in third grade (CCSSO, 2010).

Comparison Activities

One purpose of comparison activities with areas is to help students distinguish between size (or area) and shape, length, and other dimensions. A long, skinny rectangle may have less area than a triangle with shorter sides. This is an especially difficult concept for students to understand. Many 8- or 9-year-olds do not understand that rearranging areas into different shapes does not affect the amount of area.

Direct comparison of two areas is frequently impossible, except when the shapes involved have some common dimension or property. For example, two rectangles with the same width can be compared directly (see Blackline Master 48). Comparison of these special shapes, however, fails to deal with the attribute of area. Instead, activities in which one area is rearranged (conservation of area) are suggested. Cutting a shape into two parts and reassembling it in a different shape can show that the before and after shapes have the same area, even though they are different shapes. This idea is not at all obvious to students.

◢ *Activity* 16.7 TWO-PIECE SHAPES

Cut out a large number of rectangles of the same area, about 3 inches by 5 inches, or use blank index cards with those dimensions. Each pair of students will need six rectangles. Have students fold and cut the rectangles on the diagonal, making two identical triangles. Next, have them rearrange the triangles into different shapes, including back into the original rectangle. The rule is that only sides of the same length can be matched up and must be matched exactly. Have pairs of students find all the shapes that can be made this way, gluing the triangles on paper as a record (see Figure 16.4). Discuss the area and shape of the different responses. Does one shape have a greater area than the rest? How do you know? Did one take more paper to make? Help students conclude that although each figure is a different shape, all the figures have the same area.

Tangrams, an ancient puzzle, can be used for the same purpose (see Figure 17.8 in the next chapter). The standard set of seven tangram pieces is cut from a square, as shown in Figure 16.5 (Blackline Master 40), or an online version at http://nlvm .usu.edu/en/nav/frames_asid_268_g_1_t_3.html?open=activities. The two smallest triangles can be used to make the parallelogram, the square, and the medium triangle. This permits a similar discussion about the pieces having the same size (area) but different shapes.

Figure 16.4   Different shapes, same area.

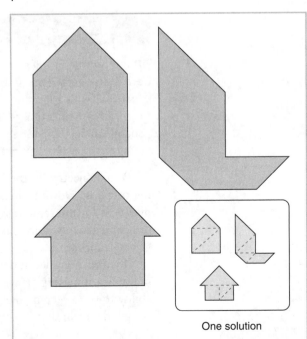

Activity 16.8   TANGRAM AREAS

Draw the outline of several shapes made with tangram pieces, as in Figure 16.6, and duplicate them and give them to groups of students. Ask groups to estimate which one they think has the largest (or smallest) area. Then let students use tangrams to decide which shapes are the same area, which are larger, and which are smaller. Let students explain how they came to their conclusions. Use the animal shapes from *Grandfather Tang's Story* (Tompert, 1997) for additional investigations. Are all the animals the same area?

Figure 16.5

Tangrams provide an opportunity to investigate area concepts (see Blackline Master 40).

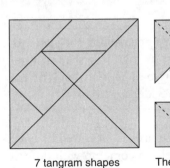

7 tangram shapes

These two make

The two small triangles make each of the medium shapes.

Two small triangles with any of the medium pieces will make the large triangle.

Figure 16.6

Compare the area of shapes made of tangram pieces.

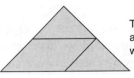

One solution

◆ Using Physical Models of Area Units

Although squares are the most common area units, any tile that conveniently fills up a plane region can be used. Nonstandard units, such as index cards or playing cards, can be used initially to explore the concept of area. Here are some suggestions for nonstandard area units:

- Cardboard squares. Squares (about 20 cm on a side) work well for large areas. Smaller units should be about 5 cm to 10 cm on a side.
- Sheets of newspaper make excellent units for very large areas.

In addition, standard units can be used:

- Color tiles (one-inch on a side)
- White Cuisenaire rods or base-ten blocks unit cubes (the dimension of the face is 1 cm on a side).

Figure 16.7

Measuring the area of a large shape drawn with tape on the floor. Units are cardstock squares of the same size.

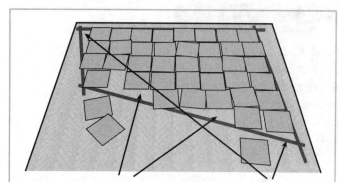

These spaces can each count as one square.

There is about one-half of a square in this corner and in the opposite corner that together can count as one square.

Students can use units to measure surfaces in the room such as desktops, bulletin boards, and books. Large regions can be outlined with masking tape on the floor. Small regions can be duplicated on paper so that students can work at stations. Surfaces such as the surface of a watermelon or the outside of a wastebasket provide a connection of area in two dimensions to area in three dimensions (surface area).

In area measurements, there may be lots of units that only partially fit. You may wish to begin with shapes in which the units fit by building a shape with units, and drawing the outline. According to the *Common Core State Standards* (CCSSO, 2010), in third grade, students should begin to wrestle with partial units and mentally put together two or more partial units to count as one unit. Figure 16.7 shows one possible measurement exercise.

The following activity is a good starting point to see what ideas your students have about units of area.

Activity 16.9 COVER AND COMPARE

Draw two rectangles and a blob shape on a sheet of paper. Make it so that the three areas are not the same, but with no area that is clearly largest or smallest. The students' first task is to estimate which is the smallest and the largest of the three shapes. After recording their estimate, they should trace or glue the same two-dimensional unit on the shapes to decide. Students should explain in writing what they discovered.

Your objective in the beginning is to develop the idea that area is measured by covering or tiling. Do not introduce formulas yet. Groups are likely to come up with different measures for the same region. Discuss these differences with the students and point to the difficulties involved in making estimates around the edges. Avoid the idea that there is one "right" approach.

By fourth grade, students should begin to use spatial reasoning to apply the concept of multiplication using arrays to the area of rectangles. This requires that students develop the ability to see a rectangular region as rows and columns. The following comparison activity is a good step in that direction.

Activity 16.10 RECTANGLE COMPARISON—SQUARE UNITS

Students are given a worksheet showing a pair of rectangles that are the same or very close in area (see Blackline Master 49). They are also given a physical model of a single square unit and a ruler that measures the appropriate unit. The students are not permitted to cut out the rectangles, but they may draw on them if they wish. The task is to use their rulers to determine, in any way that they can, which rectangle is larger or whether they are the same. They should use words, pictures, and numbers to explain their conclusions. Some suggested pairs are as follows:

4×10 and 5×8 5×10 and 7×7 4×6 and 5×5

Some students with disabilities may need to have modified worksheets of the figures on grid paper that matches the square units to be used.

The goal of this activity is not to develop an area formula, but to apply students' developing concepts of multiplication to the area of rectangles. Not all students will use a multiplicative approach. In order to count a single row of squares along one edge and then multiply by the length of the other edge, the first row must be thought of as a single unit that is then replicated to fill in the rectangle (Outhred & Mitchelmore, 2004). Many students will attempt to draw in all the squares. However, some may use their rulers to determine the number of squares that will fit along each side and, from that, use multiplication to determine the total area (see Figure 16.8). By having students share strategies, more students can be exposed to the use of multiplicative reasoning in this context.

Have students try the following example to carry their reasoning to the next level.

A rectangular garden has an area of 120 square feet. If the garden is 8 feet wide, how long is it?

Grids of various types can be thought of as "area rulers." A grid of squares does for area what a ruler does for length. It lays out the units for you. Square grids on transparencies can be made from Blackline Masters 10 through 12. Have students place the clear grid over a region to be measured and count the units inside. An alternative method is to trace around a region on a paper grid.

Figure 16.8 Some students use multiplication to tell the total number of square units.

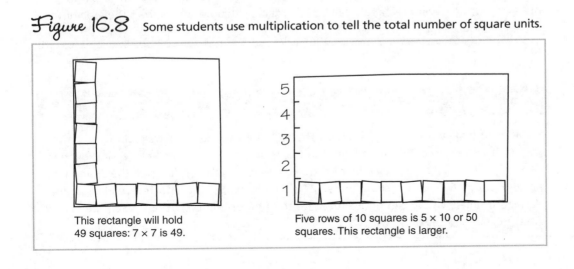

This rectangle will hold
49 squares: 7 × 7 is 49.

Five rows of 10 squares is 5 × 10 or 50
squares. This rectangle is larger.

◆ The Relationship between Area and Perimeter

Area and perimeter (the distance around a region) are a continual source of confusion for students. Although perimeter is a content standard (CCSSO, 2010) and a focal point (NCTM, 2006) at grade 3, eighth grade students on the NAEP exam were given an illustration of a rectangle with side lengths and only 71 percent could accurately identify the perimeter. Perhaps it is because both area and perimeter involve regions to be measured or because students are taught formulas (possibly too soon) for both concepts at about the same time that they tend to get formulas confused. Teaching these two concepts during a close time frame is particularly challenging for students with disabilities (Parmar, Garrison, Clements, & Sarama, 2011). Whatever the reason, expect that even fifth and sixth grade students will confuse these two ideas.

A good hint for helping students remember the concept of perimeter is that the word *rim* is in pe**rim**eter.

Perimeter is a length measure and, as such, it is additive. Students should be able to calculate perimeter given side measures as well as identify missing side lengths.

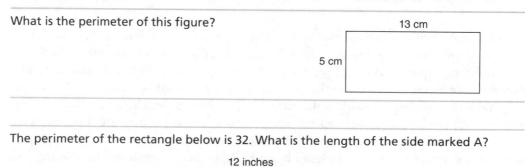

What is the perimeter of this figure?

13 cm

5 cm

The perimeter of the rectangle below is 32. What is the length of the side marked A?

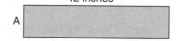

12 inches

A

An interesting approach to alleviating the confusion between area and perimeter is to contrast the two ideas as in the next activities.

◢ Activity 16.11 FIXED PERIMETERS

Give students a loop of non-stretching string that is 24 centimeters in circumference (fold the string in half and at 12 cm tie a knot) and 1-cm grid paper, or just use the grid paper alone. The task is to decide what different-sized rectangles can be made with a perimeter of 24 cm. Each different rectangle can be recorded on the grid paper with the area noted inside the figure (e.g., area = 20 cm²).

◢ Activity 16.12 FIXED AREAS

Provide students with 1-cm grid paper. The task is to see how many rectangles can be made with an area of 36 squared cm—that is, to make filled-in rectangles, not just borders. Each new rectangle should be recorded by sketching the outline and the dimensions on grid paper. For each rectangle, students should determine and record the perimeter measurement inside the figure (because the figures will be cut out). (See the "Fixed Areas" Expanded Lesson.)

Stop and Reflect

Let's think about the two previous activities. For "Fixed Areas," will all of the perimeters be the same? If not, what can you say about the shapes with longer or shorter perimeters? For "Fixed Perimeters," will the areas remain the same? Why or why not? Which rectangle creates the largest area? The smallest area? ▪

When students complete Activities 16.11 and 16.12, have them cut out all the figures. Label either two charts or locations on the board with "perimeter" and "area," and have the teams come up and place their figures (left to right) from the shortest perimeter (or area) to the largest perimeter (or area) on the appropriate chart. Ask students to state what they observe, make conjectures, and see if any conclusions can be drawn. Students may be surprised to find out that rectangles having the same areas do not necessarily have the same perimeters, and vice versa. And, of course, this fact is not restricted to rectangles.

Students will notice an interesting relationship. When the area is fixed, the shape with the shortest perimeter is "square-like," as is the rectangle with the largest area. If you allowed for any shapes whatsoever, the shape with the shortest perimeter and a fixed area is a circle. Students will also notice that the fatter a shape, the shorter its perimeter and the skinnier a shape, the longer its perimeter. (These relationships are also true in three dimensions—replace perimeter with surface area and area with volume.)

Standards for
Mathematical Practice

◀ **2 Reason abstractly and quantitatively**

Math Playground at www.mathplayground.com/area_perimeter.html provides a great activity in which two students explore the relationship between area and perimeter of rectangles. After the lesson, you can measure the lengths and widths of a variety of rectangles and calculate the area and perimeter of each.

◆ Developing Formulas for Perimeter and Area

When students *develop* formulas, they gain conceptual understanding of the ideas and relationships involved and they engage in "doing mathematics." Also, there is less likelihood that students will confuse area and perimeter or that they will select the incorrect formula on an assessment.

Begin by having students generate ways that perimeter problems can be solved. As in the rectangle shown previously, it is common for students to be given a perimeter problem in which only one length and one width are included. So if students are only considering adding these two numbers, discussing the formula $P = l + w + l + w$ will help point out that there are four length dimensions that should be added. This connection to the equation will help avoid the common error of only adding the two given dimensions. An alternative perimeter formula for rectangles that might emerge from the conversations would be $P = 2 (l + w)$, which will reinforce the multiplication of the pair of sides, or $P = 2l + 2w$, which emphasizes that the perimeter involves combining lengths.

Standards for
Mathematical Practice

◀ **8 Look for and express regularity in repeated reasoning**

Students form general relationships when they see how all area formulas are related to one idea: length of the base times the height. And students who understand where formulas come from tend to remember them or are able to derive them, and this reinforces the idea that mathematics makes sense.

Figure 16.9

Understanding the attribute of area.

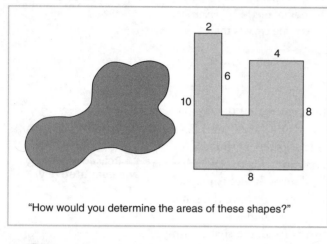

"How would you determine the areas of these shapes?"

Teaching Tip

"Length times width" is not a definition of area.

Figure 16.10

Heights of two-dimensional figures are not always measured along an edge.

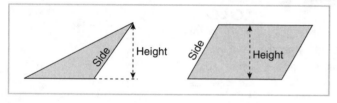

Teaching Tip

A good way to strengthen students' understanding of height is to have them identify the height for every base of a quadrilateral (be sure to vary the shapes so that the height falls inside and outside of the shape).

The results of NAEP testing clearly indicate that students do not have a very good understanding of area formulas. For example, in the 2007 NAEP, only 39 percent of fourth-grade students were able to give the area of a carpet 15 feet long and 12 feet wide. As mentioned previously, a common student error is to confuse formulas for area and perimeter. Such results are largely due to an overemphasis on formulas with little or no conceptual background. The tasks in Figure 16.9 cannot be solved with simple formulas; they require an understanding of concepts and how formulas work.

Another common error when students use area formulas comes from failure to conceptualize the meaning of height and base in two-dimensional geometric figures. The shapes in Figure 16.10 each have a slanted side and a height given. Students tend to confuse these two. Any side of a figure can be called a base. For each base that a figure has, there is a corresponding height. If the figure were to slide into a room on a selected base, the height would be the height of the shortest door it could pass through without tipping—that is, the perpendicular distance to the base. Perhaps because students have a lot of early experiences with the length-times-width formula for rectangles, in which the height is exactly the same as the length of a side, this is the source of the confusion. Before formulas involving heights are discussed, students should identify where a height could be measured for any base on a figure.

The formula for the area of a rectangle is one of the first that is developed and is usually given as $A = L \times W$, "area equals length times width." Thinking ahead to other area formulas, an equivalent but more unifying idea might be $A = b \times h$, "area equals *base* times *height*." The base-times-height formulation can be generalized to all parallelograms (not just rectangles) and is useful in developing the area formulas for triangles and trapezoids. Furthermore, the same approach can be extended to three dimensions, in which volumes of cylinders are given in terms of the area of the base times the height. Therefore, base times height connects a large family of formulas that otherwise must be mastered independently.

Research suggests that it is a significant leap for students to move from counting squares inside of a rectangle to a conceptual development of a formula. Battista (2003) found that students often try to fill in empty rectangles with drawings of squares and then count the result one square at a time.

An important concept to review is the meaning of multiplication as seen in arrays. Show students the structure of rows and columns of squares and discuss why multiplication tells the total amount. We count either a single row or column and then find out how many columns or rows there are in all. This is the same concept that they will apply to the area of a rectangle. When we multiply a length times a width, we are not multiplying "squares times squares." Rather, the *length* of one side indicates how many squares will fit on that side. If this set of squares is taken as a unit, then the *length* of the other side (not a number of squares) will determine how many of these *rows of squares* can fit in the rectangle. Then the amount of square units covering the rectangle is the product of the length of a row and the number of rows (column × row = area).

A good activity to begin your exploration of area formulas is to revisit Activity 16.10, "Rectangle Comparison—Square Units." Students who draw in all of the squares and count them have not thought about a row of squares as a single row that can be replicated.

When your students have formulated an approach to area based on the idea of a row of squares (determined by the length of a side) multiplied by the number of these rows that will fit the rectangle (determined by the length of the other side), it is time to consolidate these ideas (see Figure 16.11). Explain to students that you like the idea of measuring one side to tell how many squares will fit in a row along that side. You would like them to call or think of this side as the *base* of the rectangle, even though some people call it the length or the width. Then the other side you can call the *height*. But which side is the base? Be sure that students conclude that either side could be the base. If you use the formula $A = b \times h$, then the same area will result using either side as the base.

Stop and Reflect

Do you think that students should learn special formulas for the area of a square? Why or why not? Do you think students need formulas for the perimeters of squares and rectangles? ■

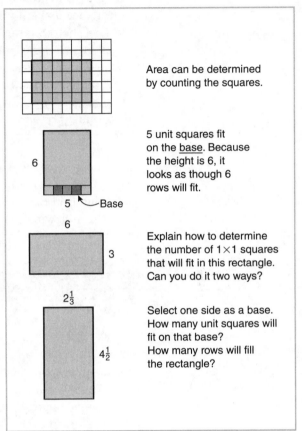

Figure 16.11

Activities leading to the development of the formula for the area of a rectangle.

Area can be determined by counting the squares.

5 unit squares fit on the **base**. Because the height is 6, it looks as though 6 rows will fit.

Explain how to determine the number of 1×1 squares that will fit in this rectangle. Can you do it two ways?

Select one side as a base. How many unit squares will fit on that base? How many rows will fill the rectangle?

Volume and Capacity

Volume and *capacity* are both terms for measures of the "size" of three-dimensional regions, and are an important topic for fifth grade (CCSSO, 2010). The term *capacity* is generally used to refer to the amount that a container will hold. Standard units of capacity include quarts, gallons, liters, and milliliters. The term *volume* can be used to refer to the capacity of a container, but is also used for the size of three-dimensional objects. This addition of a third dimension challenges students' spatial reasoning. Standard units of volume are expressed in terms of length units, such as cubic inches or cubic centimeters.

◆ Comparison Activities

Comparing the volumes of solid objects can be challenging. A simple method of comparing capacity is to fill one container with something and then pour this amount into the comparison container. By third grade, most students understand the concept of "holds more" with reference to containers. The concept of volume for solid objects may not be as readily understood.

Do not expect students to accurately predict which of two containers holds more because even adults have difficulty making this judgment. Try the following activity.

◀ *Activity* 16.13 **SILOS**

Have pairs of students take two sheets of the same-sized construction paper. With one sheet they make a tube shape (cylinder) by taping the two long edges together. They make a shorter, fatter cylinder from the other sheet by taping the short edges together. Then ask, "If these models were two silos, which cylinder holds more, or do they have the same capacity?" Ask students to write down their predictions. Most student groups will split roughly in thirds: short and fat, tall and skinny, or same capacity. To test the conjectures, use a filler such as beans or pasta. Place the skinny cylinder inside the fat one. Fill the inside tube and then lift it up, allowing the filler to empty into the fat cylinder.

The goal of these activities is for students to realize that surface area (the size of the paper) does not determine the volume, but that there is a relationship between surface area and volume, just as there is between perimeter and area.

The following activity is a three-dimensional adaptation of Activity 16.12, "Fixed Areas."

◀ *Activity* 16.14 **FIXED VOLUME: COMPARING PRISMS**

Give each pair of students a supply of centimeter cubes or wooden cubes. Their task is to use 64 (or 36) cubes to build different rectangular prisms and record the surface area for each prism formed in a table. If you have ELLs, provide a visual of a rectangular solid, labeling all the key words they will need for the lesson (*length, width, height, surface area, cube, volume, side*). Using the tables students construct, they should observe any patterns that occur. Eventually compare the dimensions of the prisms they have recorded to the surface area of each as the prism becomes less like a tall, skinny box and more like a cube.

The eventual goal here is for students to realize that volume does not dictate surface area and to recognize that the pattern between surface area and volume is similar to the one found between area and perimeter. Namely, prisms that are more cube-like have less surface area than prisms with the same volume that are long and narrow.

◆ Using Physical Models of Volume and Capacity Units

Two types of units can be used to measure volume and capacity: solid units and containers. Solid units are objects like wooden cubes that can be used to fill the container being measured. The other type of unit model is a small container that is filled with liquid and poured repeatedly into the container being measured. The following are a few examples of units that you might want to collect:

- Liquid medicine cups
- Plastic jars and containers of almost any size
- Wooden cubic blocks or blocks of any shape (as long as you have a lot of the same size)
- Styrofoam packing peanuts (which still produce conceptual measures of volume despite not packing perfectly)

The following activity is similar to Activity 16.10, "Rectangle Comparison—Square Units."

Activity 16.15 BOX COMPARISON—CUBIC UNITS

Provide students with a pair of small boxes that you have folded up from cardstock board (see Figure 16.12). Use unit dimensions that match the blocks that you have for units. Students are given two boxes, exactly one block, and an appropriate ruler. (If you use 2-cm cubes, make a ruler with the unit equal to 2 cm.) The students' task is to decide which box has the greater volume or if the boxes have the same volume.

Here are some suggested box dimensions ($L \times W \times H$):

6 × 3 × 4   5 × 4 × 4   3 × 9 × 3   6 × 6 × 2   5 × 5 × 3

Students should use words, drawings, and numbers to explain their conclusions.

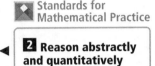

Standards for Mathematical Practice

◀ **2 Reason abstractly and quantitatively**

A useful hint in the last activity is to first figure out how many cubes will fit on the bottom of the box. Some students will discover a multiplicative rule for the volume. The boxes can be filled with cubes to confirm conclusions. No formulas should be used unless students can explain them.

Instruments for measuring capacity are generally used for pourable materials such as rice or water. These tools are commonly found in kitchens and laboratories. Students should use measuring cups to explore recipes (e.g., foods, papier-mâché, or Oobleck for science experiments—Google "making Oobleck" for recipes). Books such as the *Better Homes and Gardens New Junior Cookbook* (Better Homes and Gardens, 2012) provide student-friendly recipes and multiple opportunities to use units of capacity.

The following two activities encourage the understanding of liquid volume.

Activity 16.16 THAT'S COOL!

Give teams of students beakers marked with a scale in milliliters. Tell the students they will receive three ice cubes. First they must estimate how many milliliters of water will fill the beaker when the ice melts. Then after the ice is placed in each team's container, they wait until the ice warms and turns to water. What was the difference between their estimates and their actual answers? Students can use a line plot to record and discuss the different measures (see Chapter 18).

Figure 16.12 Make small boxes by starting with a rectangle and drawing a square on each corner as shown. Cut on the solid lines and fold the box up, wrapping the corner squares to the outside and tape them to the sides as shown.

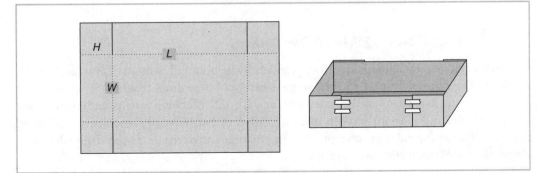

Activity 16.17 **SQUEEZE PLAY**

Students should work in teams, with each team having access to a measuring cup or beaker marked in milliliters. Have several stations set up with buckets and different sized sponges. Have students first estimate how much water they can squeeze from each sponge using the hand they do not write with. Does a sponge that is two times larger than another sponge provide two times the water? What do the students notice?

Developing Formulas for Volumes of Common Solid Shapes

Figure 16.13

Heights of figures are not always measured along an edge or a surface.

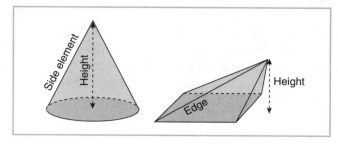

A common error that repeats from two- to three-dimensional shapes is when students confuse the meaning of height and base in their use of formulas. Note that the shapes in Figure 16.13 each have a slanted side and a height given. The base of the figure can be any flat surface of the figure. As mentioned before, to visualize the height, have students think of the figure sliding under a doorway and the *height* would be the height of the shortest door it could pass through. Keep this in mind as you work to use precise language to develop formulas for volume.

The relationships between the formulas for volume are completely analogous to those for area. As you read, notice the similarities between rectangles and prisms. Not only are the formulas related, but the process for developing the formulas is similar.

A *cylinder* is a solid with two congruent parallel bases and sides with parallel elements that join corresponding points on the bases. There are several special classes of cylinders, including *prisms* (with polygons for bases), *right prisms*, *rectangular prisms*, and *cubes* (Zwillinger, 2011). Interestingly, all of these solids have the same volume formula.

Figure 16.14

Volume of a right prism: Area of the base times height.

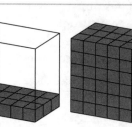

Base is 3 × 5. Area of base is 15 squares.

Base holds a set of 15 cubes.

Six layers of 15 cubes fills the box. $V = 6 \times 15$ cubes.

Review Activity 16.15. The development of the volume formula from this box exploration is parallel to the development of the formula for the area of a rectangle, as shown in Figure 16.14. The area of the base (instead of length of the base for rectangles) determines how many cubes can be placed on the base forming a single unit—a layer of cubes. The height of the box then determines how many of these layers will fit in the box just as the height of the rectangle determined how many rows of squares would fill the rectangle.

The volume, as just discussed, is $V = A \times h$, with A equal to the *area of the base* and h the *height*.

Connections between Formulas

The connectedness of mathematical ideas can hardly be better illustrated than with the connections of all of these formulas to the single concept of base times height.

A conceptual approach to the development of formulas helps students understand they are meaningful and efficient ways to measure different attributes of the objects around us. After developing formulas in conceptual ways, students can derive formulas from what they already know. Mathematics does make sense!

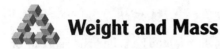

Weight and Mass

Weight is a measure of the pull or force of gravity on an object. *Mass* is the amount of matter in an object and a measure of the force needed to accelerate it. On the moon, where gravity is much less than on Earth, an object has a smaller weight but the identical mass as on Earth. For practical purposes, on Earth, the measures of mass and weight will be about the same. In this discussion, the terms *weight* and *mass* will be used interchangeably.

◆ Comparison Activities

The most conceptual way to compare weights of two objects is to hold one in each hand, extend your arms, and experience the relative downward pull on each. Which one weighs more? This personal experience can then be transferred to one of two basic types of scales—balances and spring scales.

When students place the objects in the two pans of a balance, the pan that goes down can be understood to hold the heavier object. Even a relatively simple balance will detect small differences. If two objects are placed one at a time in a spring scale, the heavier object pulls the pan down farther. Both balances and spring scales have real value in the classroom. (Technically, spring scales measure weight and balance scales measure mass. Why?)

◆ Using Physical Models of Weight or Mass Units

Any collection of uniform objects with the same mass can serve as weight units. For very light objects, large paper clips, wooden blocks, or plastic cubes work well. You can also use coins for weight units. For example, all U.S. nickels weigh 5 grams and pennies weigh 2.5 grams. Large metal washers found in hardware stores are effective for weighing slightly heavier objects. You will need to rely on standard weights to weigh things as heavy as a kilogram or more.

Weight cannot be measured directly, so either a two-pan balance or a spring scale must be used. In a balance scale, place an object in one pan and weights in the other until the two pans balance. In a spring scale, first place the object in and mark the position of the pan on a piece of paper taped behind the pan. Remove the object and place just enough weights in the pan to pull it down to the same level. Discuss how equal weights will pull the spring with the same force.

Although the concept of heavier and lighter begins to be explored in kindergarten, the notion of units of weight or mass appears in third grade standards (CCSSO, 2010). At any grade level, experiences with informal unit weights are good preparation for standard units and scales.

Angles

Understanding the concept (or attribute) of angle and measuring angles is one of the standards in the *Common Core State Standards* (CCSSO, 2010), beginning at grade 4 and developing through middle school and high school. Angle measurement can be a challenge for two reasons: The attribute of angle size is often misunderstood, and protractors are commonly introduced and used without understanding how they work.

Figure 16.15 Which angle is larger?

Trace over angle *A*.

Place tracing on angle *B*.

Teaching Tip

Some students think that the length of the rays has an effect on the size of the angle. Explicitly show them that this is not the case, and in fact it is the spread between the rays (be they long or short) that defines the angle.

Figure 16.16

Using a small wedge cut from an index card as a unit angle, this angle measures about $7\frac{1}{2}$ wedges. Accuracy of measurement with these nonstandard angles is less important than the idea of how an angle is used to measure the size of another angle.

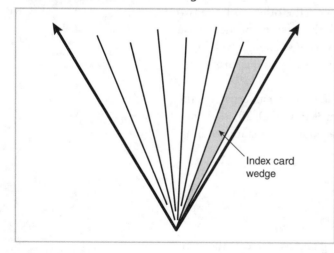

Index card wedge

Standards for Mathematical Practice

5 Use appropriate tools strategically ▶

⬢ Comparison Activities

The attribute of angle size might be called the "spread of the angle's rays." Angles are composed of two rays that are infinite in length with a common vertex. The only difference in their size is how widely or narrowly the two rays are spread apart or rotated about the vertex.

To help students conceptualize the attribute of the spread of the rays, two angles can be directly compared by tracing one and placing it over the other (see Figure 16.15). Be sure to have students compare angles with the rays represented with different lengths. A student might think a wide angle with short rays is less than a narrow angle with long rays. This is a common misconception (Munier, Devichi, & Merle, 2008). As soon as students can tell the difference between a wide angle and a narrow one, regardless of the length of the rays, you can move on to measuring angles.

⬢ Using Physical Models of Angular Measure Units

A unit for measuring an angle must be an angle. Nothing else has the same attribute of spread that we want to measure. (Contrary to what many people think, you do not need to use degrees to measure angles.)

Activity 16.18 A UNIT ANGLE

BLM

Give each student an index card. Have students draw a narrow angle on the card using a straightedge and then cut it out (or use wedges made from Blackline Master 51). The resulting wedge can then be used as a unit of angular measure by counting the number of wedges that will fit in a given angle as shown in Figure 16.16. Distribute a worksheet with assorted angles on it, and have students use their unit to measure them. Because students made their own unit angles, the results will differ and can be discussed and compared in terms of unit size.

Activity 16.18 illustrates that measuring an angle is the same as measuring length or area; unit angles are used to cover the spread of an angle just as unit lengths cover a length. Once this concept is well understood, move on to the use of measuring instruments.

⬢ Using Protractors and Angle Rulers

The two tools commonly used for measuring angles are angle rulers and protractors (see Figure 16.17). According to the *Common Core State Standards*, fourth-grade

Figure 16.17 Different tools to measure angles.

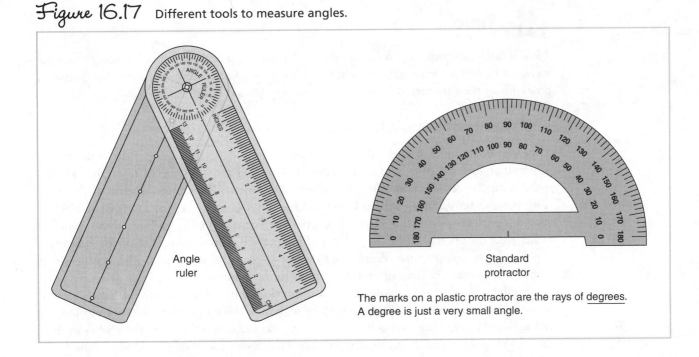

Angle ruler

Standard protractor

The marks on a plastic protractor are the rays of <u>degrees</u>. A degree is just a very small angle.

students need to begin to learn to use protractors accurately. Yet the protractor is one of the most poorly understood measuring instruments. Part of the difficulty arises because the units (degrees) are so small. It would be physically impossible for students to cut out and use a single degree to measure an angle accurately. In addition, the numbers on most protractors run clockwise and counterclockwise along the edge, making the scale hard to interpret without a strong conceptual foundation. Note that the units of degrees are based on an angle in which the vertex of the rays is located at the midpoint of a circle creating an arc. A "one degree" angle is one in which the arc is $\frac{1}{360}$ of the circle (see Blackline Master 51). These small angles are the units used to measure larger angles. Angle rulers are a good choice for measuring angles, but also require experience in order to understand how to set the tool on the angle to be measured and how to read the scale.

BLM

Students can make nonstandard waxed-paper protractors (see Figure 16.18), but soon move them to standard instruments. To understand measures on a protractor or angle ruler, students need an approximate mental image of angle size. Then false readings of the protractor scale will be eliminated. One approach is to use an angle maker. You can cut and merge two different colored paper dessert plates in the same way as the rational number wheel in Figure 14.5 on page 261. You can then rotate the plates to match angles observed or to estimate important benchmark angles such as 30, 45, 60, 90, 135, 180, 270, and 360 degrees. If students have a strong grasp of the approximate sizes of angles, this "angle sense" will give them the background needed to move to standard measuring tools such as the protractor or angle ruler.

Have students try their measuring skills with pattern blocks. Using one of each piece in the collection of pattern blocks, they answer these questions: What is the measure of each angle? Which angles are equal?

Figure 16.18

Measuring angles in a polygon using a waxed-paper protractor.

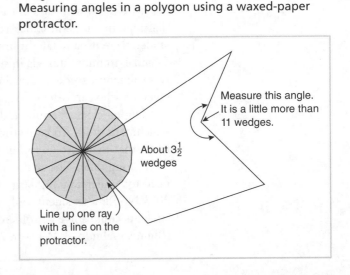

Measure this angle. It is a little more than 11 wedges.

About $3\frac{1}{2}$ wedges

Line up one ray with a line on the protractor.

 **Time**

Time is different from most other attributes that are commonly measured in school because it cannot be seen or felt and because it is more difficult for students to comprehend units of time or how they are matched against a given time period or duration.

◆ Comparison Activities

Time can be thought of as the duration of an event from its beginning to its end. As with other attributes, for students to adequately understand the attribute of time, they should make comparisons of events that have different durations. If two events begin at the same time, the shorter duration will end first and the other last longer. For example, which top spins longer? However, this form of comparison focuses on the ending of the duration rather than the duration itself. In order to think of time as something that can be measured, it is helpful to compare two events that do not start at the same time. This requires that some form of measurement of time be used from the beginning.

Students need to learn about seconds, minutes, and hours and to develop some concept of how long these units are. You can help by making a conscious effort to point out the duration of short and long events during the day. Have students time familiar events in their daily lives: brushing teeth, eating dinner, riding to school, spending time doing homework.

Timing small events of $\frac{1}{2}$ minute to 2 minutes is fun and useful and can be adapted from the following activity.

▶ *Activity* 16.19 **READY FOR THE BELL**

 BLM

Give students a recording sheet with a set of clock faces (see Blackline Master 50). Secretly set a timer to go off at the hour, half hour, or minute. When the bell rings, students should look up and record the time on the clock face and in numerals on the recording sheet. This highly engaging activity motivates students to not only think about telling time, but to consider the relationship between the analog clock reading and digital recording. Elapsed time can also be explored by discussing the time between timer rings.

◆ Reading Clocks

The common instrument for measuring time is the clock. However, learning to tell time has little to do with time measurement and more to do with the skills of learning to read a dial-type instrument. Clock reading can be a difficult skill to teach. Starting in first grade, students are usually taught first to read clocks to the hour, then the half hour, and finally to 5- and 1-minute intervals in second and third grades (CCSSO, 2010). In the early stages of this sequence, students are shown clocks set exactly to the hour or half hour. Thus, many students who can read a clock at 7:00 or 2:30 are initially challenged by 6:58 or 2:33.

Digital clocks permit students to read times easily, but do not relate times very well to benchmark times. To know that a digital reading of 7:58 is nearly 8 o'clock, the student must know that there are 60 minutes in an hour, that 58 is close to 60, and that 2 minutes is not a very long time. The analog clock (with hands) shows "close to" times visually without the need for understanding large numbers or even how many minutes are in an hour. On the 2003 NAEP assessment, only 26 percent of fourth graders and 55 percent of eighth-grade students could solve a problem involving the conversion of one measure of time to another (Blume, Galindo, & Walcott, 2007).

◆ Elapsed Time

Determining combinations and comparisons of time intervals in minutes is a skill required starting in grade 3 (CCSSO, 2010). If given the digital time or the time after the hour, students must be able to tell how many minutes to the next hour. This should certainly be a mental process of counting on for multiples of 5 minutes, possibly using an analog clockface as a mental image to support the skip counting. Avoid having students use pencil and paper to subtract 25 from 60. This links to elapsed time, which is a skill that students can find challenging, especially when the period of time includes noon or midnight. The problem is due less to the fact that students don't understand what happens on the clock at noon and midnight as it is that they have trouble counting the interval that spans those times.

Figuring the time from 8:15 a.m. to 11:45 a.m., for example, is a multistep task that requires deciding what to do first and keeping track of the intermediate steps. In this case, you could count hours from 8:15 to 11:15 and add on 30 minutes. But then what do you do if the endpoints are 8:45 and 11:15?

There is also the task of finding the end time given the start time and elapsed time, or finding the start time given the end time and the elapsed time. In keeping with the spirit of problem solving and the use of models, consider the following.

Figure 16.19

A sketch of an empty time line can be useful in solving elapsed time problems.

(a) School began late today at 10:45 a.m. If you get out at 3:30, how much time will you be in school today?

10:45   3:30

11   12 noon   3

Four hours from 11 to 3. Then 15 minutes in front and 30 minutes at the end—45 minutes. Three hours 45 minutes in all.

(b) The game begins at 11:30 a.m. If it lasts 2 hours and 15 minutes, when will it be over?

11:30   12:30   1:45

12 noon   1:30

One hour after 11:30 is 12:30 and a second hour gets you to 1:30 and then 15 minutes more is 1:45. It's p.m. because it is after noon.

As a general model for all of these elapsed time problems, suggest that students sketch an empty time line (similar to the empty number line discussed for computation). This is also the physical model suggested in the *Common Core State Standards*. It is important not to be overly prescriptive in telling students how to use the time line because there are various alternatives (Dixon, 2008). For example, in Figure 16.19a, a student might count by full hours from 10:45, 11:45, 12:45, 1:45, 2:45, 3:45, and then subtract 15 minutes, whereas another student might count 15 minutes to get to 11:00 and then count by full hours 11:00, 12:00, 1:00, 2:00, 3:00, and finally add on 30 minutes.

note

Also explore What Time Will It Be? at http://nlvm.usu.edu/en/nav/frames_asid_318_g_2_t_4.html to find elapsed time word problems.

 Money

The names of our coins are conventions of our social system. Students learn these names the same way that they learn the names of physical objects in their daily environment—through exposure and repetition.

The value of each coin is also a convention that students must simply be told. For these values to make sense, students must understand 5, 10, and 25, and think of these quantities without seeing countable objects. Where else do we say "this is 5," while pointing to a single item? A student who remains tied to counting objects will be challenged to understand the values of coins. Coin value lessons should focus on purchase power—a dime can buy the same thing that 10 pennies can buy.

◆ Counting Sets of Coins

To name the total value of a group of coins is the same as mentally adding their values. Students should have learned this prior to entering third grade. Make sure students sort their coins and start counting from the highest values. Even though it is actually mental computation, the numbers are fortunately restricted to multiples of 5 and 10 with some 1s added at the end. The next activity is a preparation for counting money.

Activity 16.20 HUNDREDS CHART MONEY COUNT

Have student take out their hundreds chart and a collection of play money. Begin with only two different amounts, say, a quarter and a dime. Count down to represent the 25 cents in the same way students have used the hundreds chart (two rows down and over five more spaces). Put the quarter on the 25 point on the chart and then count 10 more (down one row) and place the dime on 35. The total is 35 cents. Use other collections of coins and what students already know about patterns on the hundreds chart to figure out how to count collections of money.

When discussing solutions to situations involving counting of coins, pay special attention to students who put combinations together utilizing thinking with tens.

◆ Making Change

Because adding on to find a difference is such a valuable skill, it makes sense to give students experiences with "think addition" as mentioned in Chapter 11, which uses adding on to find differences before asking them to make change. As students become more skillful at adding on, they can see the process of making change as an extension of a skill already acquired.

This sequence of suggested activities is not a surefire solution to the difficulties students experience with money. It is designed to build on prerequisite number and place-value skills and concepts without or before using coins.

Expanded Lesson

Fixed Areas

Content and Task Decisions

Grade Level: 3–4

Mathematics Goals

- To contrast the concepts of area and perimeter
- To develop an understanding of the relationship between area and perimeter of different shapes when the area is fixed
- To compare and contrast the units used to measure perimeter and those used to measure area

Grade Level Guide

NCTM Curriculum Focal Points	Common Core State Standards
Perimeter is a grade 3 connection within measurement. Area is a grade 4 focal point in Measurement: "Developing an understanding of area and determining the areas of two-dimensional shapes" (NCTM, 2006, p. 16).	Area is one of four critical themes in grade 3: "developing understanding of the structure of rectangular arrays and of area." Specifically, students will be able to "recognize perimeter as an attribute of plane figures and distinguish between linear and area measures" (CCSSO, 2010, p. 22).

Consider Your Students' Needs

Students have worked with the ideas of area and perimeter. Some, if not the majority of, students can find the area and perimeter of given figures and may even be able to state the formulas for finding the perimeter and area of a rectangle. However, they may become confused as to which formula to use.

For English Language Learners

- Build background for the terms *rectangle, length, width, area,* and *perimeter.* Ask students if they have heard of these words and use their ideas to talk about their mathematical meaning.
- Use visuals (tiles) as you model the mathematical terms.

For Students with Special Needs

- Students who struggle may need to use a computer-based program to model different areas or a geoboard.
- Sometimes the large number of color tiles used for an area of 24 or 26 can be distracting. Students may focus more on the construction than the mathematical concept. Consider using a smaller total, like 16 and one color.
- If you are using color tiles to model smaller areas, create a special set with the word *area* written with a permanent marker on each. The use of these tiles to create the shapes with an area will reinforce the difference between area and perimeter. Also note for students who confuse these two measures that the word "rim" is in the word *perimeter*—this mnemonic can jog the memory of students who struggle.

Materials

Each student will need:

- 36 square tiles, such as color tiles
- Two or three sheets of "Rectangles Made with 36 Tiles" grid paper (Blackline Master 52)
- "Fixed Area" recording sheet (Blackline Master 53)

Teacher will need:

- Color tiles
- "Rectangles Made with 36 Tiles" grid paper (Blackline Master 52)
- "Fixed Area" recording sheet (Blackline Master 53)

Lesson

Before

Begin with a simpler version of the task:

- Have students build a rectangle using 12 tiles at their desks. Explain that the rectangle should be filled in, not just a border. After eliciting some ideas, ask a student to come to the document camera and make a rectangle as described.

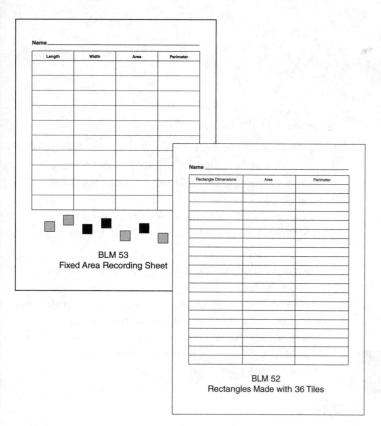

BLM 53
Fixed Area Recording Sheet

BLM 52
Rectangles Made with 36 Tiles

- Model sketching the rectangle on a grid. Record the dimensions of the rectangle in the recording chart—for example, "2 by 6."

- Ask, "What do we mean by *perimeter*? How do we measure perimeter?" After helping students define *perimeter* and describe how it is measured, ask students for the perimeter of this rectangle. Ask a student to come to the document camera to measure the perimeter of the rectangle. (Use either the rectangle made from tiles or the one sketched on grid paper.) Emphasize that the units used to measure perimeter are one-dimensional, or linear, and that perimeter is just the distance around an object. Record the perimeter in the chart.

- Ask, "What do we mean by *area*? How do we measure area?" After helping students define *area* and describe how it is measured, ask for the area of this rectangle. Here you want to make explicit that the units used to measure area are two-dimensional and, therefore, cover a region. After counting the tiles, record the area in square units on the chart.

- Have students make a different rectangle using 12 tiles at their desks and record the perimeter and area as before. Students will need to decide what "different" means. Is a 2×6 rectangle different from a 6×2 rectangle? Although these are congruent, students may wish

to consider these as being different, which is okay for this activity.

Present the focus task to the class:

- See how many different rectangles can be made with 36 tiles.

- Determine and record the perimeter and area for each rectangle.

Provide clear expectations:

- Write the following directions on the board:
  1. Find a rectangle using *all* 36 tiles.
  2. Sketch the rectangle on the grid paper.
  3. Measure and record the perimeter and area of the rectangle on the recording chart.
  4. Find a new rectangle using *all* 36 tiles and repeat steps 2–4.

- Place students in pairs to work collaboratively, but require that each student draw his or her own sketches and use his or her own recording sheet.

During

Initially:

- Question students to be sure they understand the task and the meaning of *area* and *perimeter*. Look for students who are confusing these terms.

- Be sure students are both drawing the rectangles and recording them appropriately in the chart.

Ongoing:

- Observe and ask the assessment questions, posing one or two to a student and moving to another student (see the "Assessment" section of this lesson).

After

Bring the class together to share and discuss the task:

- Ask students what they have found out about perimeter and area. Ask, "Did the perimeter stay the same? Is that what you expected? Which shapes have a longer perimeter and which shapes have a shorter perimeter?

- Ask students how they can be sure they have all of the possible rectangles.

- Ask students to describe what happens to the perimeter as the length and width change. ("The perimeter gets shorter as the rectangle gets fatter." "The square has the shortest perimeter.") Provide time to pair-share ideas.

Assessment

Observe

- Are students confusing perimeter and area?

- As students form new rectangles, are they aware that the area is not changing because they are using the same number of tiles each time? These students may not know what area is, or they may be confusing it with perimeter.

- Are students looking for patterns in how to find the perimeter?

- Are students stating important concepts or patterns to their partners?

Ask

- What is the area of the rectangle you just made?

- What is the perimeter of the rectangle you just made?

- How is area different from perimeter?

- How do you measure area? Perimeter? How are the units different? How are the units similar?

17

Developing Geometric Thinking and Concepts

Big IDEAS

1 What makes shapes alike and different can be determined by an array of geometric properties. Shapes can be classified into a hierarchy of categories according to the properties they share.

2 Transformations provide a significant way to think about the ways properties change or do not change when a shape is moved on the plane. Line symmetry is a component of the transformation called a reflection.

3 Shapes can be described in terms of their location in a plane or in space. Coordinate systems can be used to describe these locations precisely. In turn, the coordinate view of shape offers another way to understand certain properties of shapes.

4 Visualization provides the ability to create mental images that support the identification of properties and help link noticed likenesses to more formal definitions.

Geometry is a "network of concepts, ways of reasoning and representation systems" used to explore and analyze shape and space (Battista, 2007, p. 843). This critical area of mathematics appears in everything from global positioning systems to computer animation. Unique to the *Common Core State Standards*, geometry appears as a domain across grades kindergarten through 8.

Geometry Goals for Your Students

Let's think about the major geometry objectives across the grades in terms of two related frameworks: (1) spatial sense and geometric reasoning about shape and space,

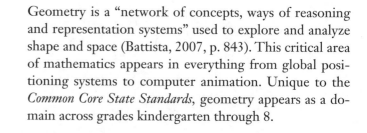

and (2) specific geometric content such as knowing about symmetry, triangles, parallel lines, and so forth. These frameworks align with the *Common Core State Standards* (CCSSO, 2010), which suggest the following:

Grade 3: Students understand that shapes in different categories (rectangles, squares, and rhombi for example) may share attributes (four sides) which sometimes put them in a more inclusive category like quadrilaterals.

Grade 4: Students identify two-dimensional figures based on the types of lines (perpendicular or parallel for example) and size of angles (acute, obtuse, or right). They also can identify line symmetry and draw a line of symmetry in two-dimensional figures.

Grade 5: Students classify two-dimensional figures based on their properties in large categories and subcategories. They also locate points in the first quadrant of the coordinate plane.

◆ Spatial Sense

Spatial sense can be defined as an intuition about shapes and the relationships among shapes. Spatial sense includes the ability to mentally visualize objects and spatial relationships, including being able to turn objects around in one's mind. It also includes a familiarity with geometric descriptions of objects and position. People with well-developed spatial sense appreciate geometric form in art, nature, and architecture, and they use geometric ideas to describe and analyze their world.

Some people say that you either are or are not born with spatial sense. This is simply not true! Meaningful experiences with shape and spatial relationships, when provided consistently over time, can and do develop spatial sense. Between 1990 and 2000, NAEP data indicated a steady, continuing improvement in students' geometric reasoning (Sowder & Wearne, 2006). However, students did not just get smarter. Instead, there has been an increasing emphasis on geometry at all grades, particularly in the elementary grades. The NCTM *Principles and Standards for School Mathematics* support "The notion of building understanding in geometry across the grades, from informal to more formal thinking, is consistent with the thinking of theorists and researchers" (NCTM, 2000, p. 41).

Stop and Reflect

Consider your own beliefs concerning an individual's abilities in the area of spatial sense. What do you think causes some people to have better spatial sense than others? ■

◆ Geometric Content

For too long, the geometry curriculum in the United States emphasized the learning of terminology in low-level tasks (such as "this is a right triangle"). Geometry is much more than vocabulary and naming shapes. Now the attention has shifted to geometric experiences and this heightened importance has led to the creation of a huge assortment of meaningful tasks for students. As with each of the *Common Core State Standards* content standards, the geometry domain has a number of goals that apply to grades 3 through 5:

- *Shapes* and *properties* include a study of the properties of shapes, as well as a study of the relationships built on properties.

- *Transformations* refer to such things as translations, reflections, rotations, and dilations, but in grades 3 through 5, the focus is on reflections through examining line symmetry.

- *Location* refers to coordinate geometry and other ways of specifying how objects are located in a plane or in space.

- *Visualization* includes the recognition of shapes in the environment, the development of relationships between two- and three-dimensional objects, and the ability to recognize, construct, and draw figures from different viewpoints.

The content in this chapter is organized around these four categories, with each category beginning with experiences that are foundational and moving toward those that are more challenging. You will note that more attention is devoted to the topic of shapes and properties because that also aligns with the emphasis of the *Common Core State Standards* for grades 3 through 5.

Developing Geometric Thinking

All learners in your classroom are capable of growing and developing in the ability to think and reason in geometric contexts. Recently there has been an emphasis in mathematics education on identifying learning progressions and trajectories as a way to move students forward on different topics. Fortunately, in geometry such a progression has been well documented. The research of two Dutch educators, Pierre van Hiele and Dina van Hiele-Geldof (husband and wife), provides insights into the differences in individuals' geometric thinking through the description of different levels of thought. The van Hiele (1986) theory significantly influences geometry curricula worldwide and can help all teachers understand developmentally appropriate next steps for their students' geometry instruction.

◆ The van Hiele Levels of Geometric Thought

The most prominent feature of the van Hiele model is described as a five-level hierarchy of ways of understanding spatial ideas (see Figure 17.1). Each level describes the thinking processes used in geometric contexts. Specifically, the levels describe what types of geometric ideas we think about (called *objects of thought*) and how we think about those ideas.

Figure 17.1

At each level of geometric thought, the ideas created become the focus or object of thought at the next level.

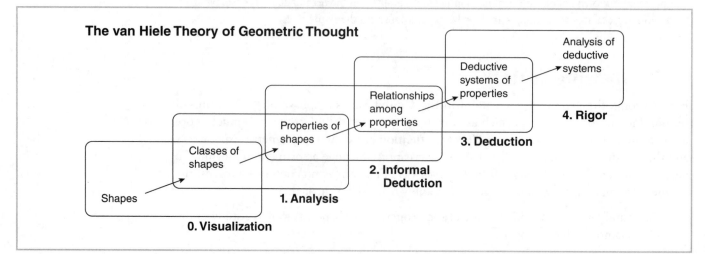

Level 0: Visualization

The objects of thought at level 0 are shapes and what they "look like."

Students at level 0 recognize and name figures based on the global visual characteristics of the figure. For example, a square is defined by a level 0 student as a square "because it looks like a square." Although we expect students to demonstrate higher level geometric thinking by grade 3, there are many students in grades 3 through 5 who are still level 0 thinkers. Students at this level will sort and classify shapes based on their appearances—"I put these together because they are all pointy" (or "fat," or "look like a house," and so on). Therefore, students are starting to see how shapes are alike and different. As a result, students at this level can create and begin to understand classifications of shapes.

> ### Teaching Tip
>
> Appearance is dominant at level 0 and can therefore overpower students' thinking about the properties of a shape. A level 0 thinker, for example, may see a square with sides that are not horizontal or vertical (it appears tilted) and believe it is a diamond and no longer a square.

The products of thought at level 0 are classes or groupings of shapes that seem to be "alike."

The emphasis at level 0 is on shapes that students can observe, feel, build, take apart, or work with in some manner. The general goal is to explore how shapes are alike and different and to use these ideas to create classes of shapes (both physically and mentally). Some of these classes of shapes have names—rectangles, triangles, rhombi, and so on. Properties of shapes, such as parallel sides, perpendicular lines, symmetry, right angles, and so on, are included at this level but only in an informal, observational manner.

Although the van Hiele theory applies to students of all ages learning any geometric content, it may be easier to apply the theory to the shapes-and-property category. The following is a good representation of an activity appropriate for level 0 learners.

◣ Activity 17.1 SHAPE SORTS

BLM Have students work in groups of four with a set of two-dimensional shapes comparable to those in Figure 17.2 (see Blackline Masters 33–39), doing the following related activities in order:

- Each student selects a shape. In turn, the students tell one or two things they find interesting about their shape.
- Students each randomly select two shapes and try to find something that is alike about their two shapes and something that is different.
- The group selects one target shape at random and places it in the center of the workspace. Their task is to find all other shapes that are like the target shape according to the same rule. For example, if they say "This shape is like the target shape because it has a curved side and a straight side," then all other shapes that they put in the collection must have these properties. Challenge them to do a second sort with the same target shape but use a different property.
- Do a "secret sort." You (or one of the students) create a collection of about five shapes that fit a secret rule. Leave others that belong in your group in the pile. The other students try to find additional pieces that belong to the set and/or guess the secret rule.

Figure 17.2

A collection of shapes for sorting.

Stop and Reflect

Why might you have students choose their own rules rather than saying, "Find all the pieces with straight sides" or "Find the triangles"? ■

These find-a-rule activities will elicit a wide variety of ideas as students examine the shapes. They may start describing the shapes with ideas such as "curvy" or "looks like a rocket" rather than typical geometric properties. But as students notice more sophisticated attributes, you can attach appropriate names to them. For example, students may notice that some shapes have corners "like a square" (explain that those are also called right angles) or that "these shapes match on both sides" (suggest that is called line symmetry).

What clearly makes this a level 0 activity is that students are operating on the shapes that they see in front of them and are beginning to see ways they are alike and ways they are different. By forming groups of shapes, students begin to identify shapes belonging to these classes that are not present in their collection.

Formative Assessment Note

How do you discover the van Hiele level of each student? Once you know, how will you select the right activities to match your students' levels? As you conduct an activity such as "Shape Sorts," listen to the types of observations that students make and record them on a checklist. Can your students talk about shapes as classes? Do they refer, for example, to "rectangles" rather than talking only about a particular rectangle? Do they generalize that certain properties are attributable to a type of shape or simply the shape at hand? Do they understand that shapes do not change when the orientation changes? With simple observations such as these, you will soon be able to distinguish between levels 0 and 1. By grade 5, if students are not able to understand logical arguments, are not comfortable with conjectures, and are unsure of if–then reasoning, these students are likely still at level 1 or below.

Level 1: Analysis

Level 1 is where the greatest proportion of grades 3 through 5 content in the *Common Core State Standards* curriculum falls (see list at the beginning of this chapter).

The objects of thought at level 1 are classes of shapes rather than individual shapes.

You will know your students are at the analysis level if they are able to consider all shapes within a class rather than just the single shape on their desk. Instead of talking about *this* particular rectangle, they can talk about properties of *all* rectangles. By focusing on a class of shapes, students are able to think about what makes a rectangle a rectangle (four sides, opposite sides parallel, opposite sides same length, four right angles, congruent diagonals, etc.). The irrelevant features (e.g., size, color, or orientation) fade into the background and students begin to understand that if a shape belongs to a particular class, such as cubes, it has the corresponding properties of that class. "All cubes have six congruent faces, and each of those faces is a square." These properties were unspoken at level 0. Students operating at level 1 may be able to list all the properties of squares, rectangles, and parallelograms, but may not see that these are subclasses of one another (e.g., that all squares are rectangles and all rectangles are parallelograms). In defining a shape, level 1 thinkers are likely to list as many properties of a shape as they know.

The products of thought at level 1 are the properties of shapes.

Although your level 1 students will continue to use manipulatives and drawings of shapes, they begin to see individual shapes as representatives of classes of shapes. Their understanding of the properties of shapes—such as symmetry, perpendicular and parallel lines, and so on—continues to be refined. This identification of geometric properties is an important cognitive activity (Yu, Barrett, & Presmeg, 2009).

In the following activity, students use the properties of shapes, such as symmetry, angle classification (right, obtuse, acute), parallel and perpendicular, and the concept of congruent line segments and angles.

Activity 17.2 PROPERTY LISTS FOR QUADRILATERALS

Prepare handouts for parallelograms, rhombi, rectangles, and squares (see Blackline Masters 43–46 and Figure 17.3). Assign groups of three or four students to work with one type of quadrilateral (for ELLs and students with disabilities, post labeled shapes as a reference). Ask students to list as many properties as they can that apply to all of the shapes on their sheet. They will need tools such as index cards (to check right angles, to compare side lengths, and to draw straight lines), mirrors (to check line symmetry), and tracing paper (for angle congruence). Encourage students to use the terms "at least," "only," and "at most" when describing how many of something: for example, "rectangles have at least two lines of symmetry," because squares—included in the category of rectangles—have four.

Have students prepare their property lists under these headings: Sides, Angles, Diagonals, and Symmetries. Groups then share their lists with the class and eventually a class list for each category of shape will be developed. For ELLs, placing emphasis on these words, having students say the words aloud, and having students point to the word as you say it are ways to reinforce meaning and support their participation and comprehension during the sharing time. For students with disabilities, provide the recording sheet with the table listing the headings above. This will help organize their thinking around the diverse possibilities.

Figure 17.3

Shapes for "Property Lists for Quadrilaterals" worksheets can be found in Blackline Masters 43–46.

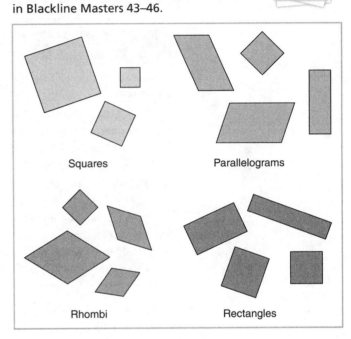

What distinguishes this activity from the earlier level 0 activity is the object of students' thinking. Now, students must assess whether the properties apply to all shapes in the category. If they are working on the squares, for example, their observations must apply to a square mile as well as a square centimeter.

Level 2: Informal Deduction

The objects of thought at level 2 are the properties of shapes.

As students begin to think about properties of geometric objects without focusing on one particular object (shape), they are able to develop relationships between these properties. "If all four angles are right angles, the shape must be a rectangle. If it is a square, all angles are right angles. If it is a square, it must be a rectangle." Once students have a greater ability to engage in "if–then" reasoning, they can classify shapes using only a minimum set of defining characteristics. For example, four congruent sides and at least one right angle are sufficient to define a square. Rectangles are parallelograms with a right angle. Observations go beyond properties themselves and begin to focus on logical arguments about the properties. When your students are at level 2, they will be able to follow and comprehend informal deductive arguments about shapes and their properties. "Proofs" may be more intuitive than deductive; however, there is the ability to follow a logical argument. An understanding of a formal deductive system, however, remains under the surface.

The products of thought at level 2 are relationships among properties of geometric objects.

The hallmark of level 2 activities is the inclusion of informal logical reasoning. Because your students have developed an understanding of the various properties of shapes, it is now time for you to encourage conjecture and to ask "Why?" or "What if?"

◢ *Activity* 17.3   MINIMAL DEFINING LISTS

This activity is a sequel to Activity 17.2, "Property Lists." Once the class has agreed on property lists for the parallelogram, rhombus, rectangle, and square (and possibly the kite and trapezoid), post the lists. Have students work in groups to find "minimal defining lists," or MDLs, for each shape. An *MDL* is a subset of the properties for a shape that is defining and "minimal." The term *defining* here means that any shape that has all the properties on the MDL must be that shape. *Minimal* means that if any single property is removed from the list, the list is no longer defining. For example, one MDL for a square is a quadrilateral with four congruent sides and one right angle. Another minimal defining list for a square is that is has four sides of the same length and perpendicular diagonals. Students should try to find at least two or three MDLs for their shape. A proposed list can be challenged as being either not minimal or not defining. A list is not defining if a counterexample—a shape other than one being described—can be produced by using only the properties on the list.

The hallmark of this and other level 2 activities is the emphasis on logical reasoning. "*If a quadrilateral has these properties, then it must be a square.*" Logic is also involved in proving that a list is faulty—either not minimal or not defining. Here students begin to learn the nature of a definition and the value of counterexamples. In fact, any minimal defining list (MDL) is a potential definition. The other aspect of this activity that clearly involves level 2 thinking is that students focus on the lists of properties of the shapes—the very factors that were products of the earlier level 1 activity. As a result of the MDL activity, students are creating a collection of new relationships that exist between properties.

Level 3: Deduction

The objects of thought at level 3 are relationships between properties of geometric objects.

At level 3, students analyze informal arguments; the structure of a system complete with axioms, definitions, theorems, corollaries, and postulates begins to develop; and they begin to grasp the necessary means of establishing geometric truth. The student at this level is usually in high school and is able to work with abstract statements about geometric properties and make conclusions based on logic.

The products of thought at level 3 are deductive axiomatic systems for geometry.

Level 4: Rigor

The objects of thought at level 4 are deductive axiomatic systems for geometry.

At the highest level of the van Hiele hierarchy, the objects of attention are axiomatic systems themselves, not just the deductions within a system. This is generally the level of a college mathematics major who is studying geometry as a branch of mathematical science.

The products of thought at level 4 are comparisons and contrasts among different axiomatic systems of geometry.

We have given brief descriptions of all five levels to illustrate the scope of the van Hiele theory. Most students in grades 3 through 5 will be at level 0 or 1, moving to 2.

Characteristics of the van Hiele Levels

Here are some important things to know about the van Hiele levels of geometric thought:

- The products of thought at each level are the same as the objects of thought at the next level (see Figure 17.1). The ideas must be developed at one level so that the relationships between these ideas can become the focus of the next level.

- The levels are sequential. To arrive at any level above level 0, students must move through all prior levels.

- The levels are not age dependent. Although a third grader should be working at level 1, he could be at level 0. Indeed, some students and adults remain forever at level 0, and a significant number of adults never reach level 2.

- Advancement through the levels requires geometric experiences (the third grader operating at level 0 needs carefully selected activities to help him move to level 1). Students should explore, talk about, and interact with content at the next level, while increasing their experiences at their current level.

- When instruction or language is at a level higher than that of the students, students will be challenged to understand the concept being developed. A student can, for example, memorize a fact (e.g., all squares are rectangles) but not mentally construct the actual relationship of how the properties of a square and rectangle are related.

Implications for Instruction

The van Hiele theory and the developmental perspective of this book highlight the necessity of teaching at the student's level of thought. However, almost any activity can be modified to span two levels of thinking, even within the same classroom.

Moving from Level 0 to Level 1

Instructional activities that support students' movement are as follows:

The collection of geometric experiences you provide are the single most important factor in moving students up the developmental ladder.

- *Challenge students to test ideas about shapes by using a variety of examples from a particular category.* Say to them, "Let's see if that is true for other rectangles" or "Can you draw a triangle that does *not* have a right angle?" In general, question students to see whether the observations they make about a particular shape apply to other shapes of the same category.

- *Focus on the properties of figures rather than on simple identification.* As new geometric concepts are learned, students should be challenged to use these features to classify shapes.

- *Provide ample opportunities to draw, build, make, put together (compose), and take apart (decompose) shapes in both two and three dimensions.* These activities should be built around the understanding and use of specific characteristics or properties.

- *Apply ideas to entire classes of figure (e.g., all rectangles, all prisms) rather than to individual shapes in a set.* For example, find ways to sort all possible triangles into groups. From these groups, define types of triangles.

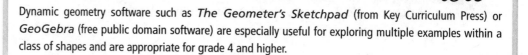

Dynamic geometry software such as *The Geometer's Sketchpad* (from Key Curriculum Press) or *GeoGebra* (free public domain software) are especially useful for exploring multiple examples within a class of shapes and are appropriate for grade 4 and higher.

Moving from Level 1 to Level 2

Level 2 thinking is expected to begin in grade 5, when students start to classify two-dimensional figures based on their properties in large categories and subcategories. Students transitioning from level 1 to level 2 can be supported as follows:

- Challenge students to explore or test examples. Ask questions such as "If the sides of a four-sided shape are all congruent, will you always have a square?" and "Can you find a counterexample?"

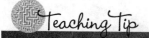

Teaching Tip

Consistently use the language of informal deduction: *all, some, none, if–then, what if,* and so on. Place these words on your math word wall.

- *Encourage the making and testing of hypotheses or conjectures.* "Do you think that will work all the time?" and "Is that true for all triangles or just equilateral triangles?"

- *Examine the properties of shapes to determine the necessary and sufficient conditions for a shape to be a particular shape.* "What properties must diagonals have to guarantee that a quadrilateral with these diagonals will be a square?"

- *Encourage students to attempt informal proofs.* As an alternative, require them to make sense of informal proofs that you or other students have suggested.

Task Selection and Levels of Thought

The remainder of this chapter offers a sampling of activities organized around four content goals of the NCTM *Principles and Standards for Mathematics*: shapes and properties, vocation, transformations, and visualization. Within each of these content groupings, activities are further organized in a progression of difficulty and sophistication. Understand that all of these subdivisions are quite fluid; that is, the content areas overlap and build on each other. Activities in one section may help develop geometric thinking in another content area.

Learning about Shapes and Properties

This content area is most often associated with geometry in pre-K through grade 8 classrooms and is the time when students begin to "perceive, say, describe/discuss, and construct objects in 2-D space" (National Research Council Committee, 2009, p. 177).

Students need experience with a wide variety of two- and three-dimensional shapes. Triangles should be shown in more than just equilateral forms and not always with the vertex at the top. (If you have students say a triangle is upside down, it is because they have rarely seen triangles illustrated differently.) Shapes should have curved sides, straight sides, and combinations of these. Along the way, as students describe the shape or property, the terminology can be introduced.

Sorting and Classifying

In grades 3 through 5, sorting and classifying shapes can be a good formative assessment to see whether students are beginning to notice properties of shapes (level 1) rather than just what the shape "looks like." For variety in two-dimensional shapes, create your own materials (see Blackline Masters 33–39). Make multiple copies so that groups of students can all work with the same shapes. Once you have your sets constructed, try Activity 17.1, "Shape Sorts."

In any sorting activity, the students—not the teacher—should decide how to sort. This allows students to do the activity using ideas they own and understand. By listening to the kinds of attributes that they use to sort, you will be able to tell what properties they know and use and how they think about shapes. Figure 17.4 illustrates a few of the many possible ways a set of shapes might be sorted.

The secret sorting activity (in Activity 17.1) is one option for introducing a new property. For example, sort the shapes so that all have at least one right angle or "square corner." When students discover your rule, you have an opportunity to talk more about that property and name the property "right angle."

The following activity is also done with the two-dimensional shapes.

Activity 17.4 WHAT'S MY SHAPE?

From Blackline Masters 33–34, cut out a double set of two-dimensional shapes on cardstock. Glue each shape from one set of the shapes inside a file folder to make "secret shape" folders. The other set should be glued on cards and placed on the table for reference. Designate one student in a group the leader; he or she holds the secret shape folder. The other students are to find the shape that matches the shape in the folder by asking the leader only yes or no questions. The group can eliminate shapes (turning over the cards) as they ask questions about properties. They are not allowed to point to a card and ask, "Is it this one?" Once they've reduced the choices through questioning, the final shape card is checked against the shape in the leader's folder. Students with disabilities may need a list of possible properties and characteristics (e.g., number of sides) to help support their question asking.

The difficulty of Activity 17.4 largely depends on the shape in the folder. The more shapes in the collection that resemble the secret shape, the more difficult the task.

Formative Assessment Note

Adapt "Shape Sorts" (Activity 17.1) using three-dimensional shapes and conduct a diagnostic interview. Make sure you have a collection of solids that has a lot of variation (curved surfaces, etc.). Power solids and other collections of three-dimensional shapes are available commercially, or collect real objects such as cans, boxes, and balls. Figure 17.5 illustrates some classifications of solids.

The ways students describe these three-dimensional shapes is good evidence of their level of geometric thinking. Level 0 thinkers are generally limited to the shapes that they have in front of them. Level 1 thinkers will begin to create categories based on properties, and their language will indicate that there are many more shapes in the group than those present. Students may say things like "These shapes have sides with square corners sort of like rectangles" or "These look like boxes. All the boxes have square [rectangular] sides."

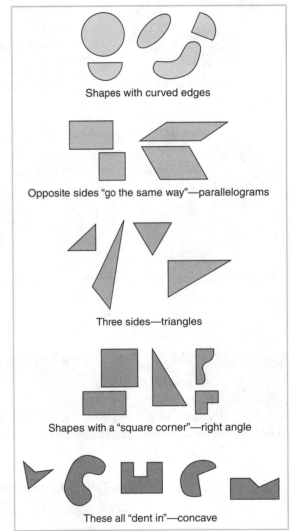

Figure 17.4

By sorting shapes, students begin to recognize properties.

Shapes with curved edges

Opposite sides "go the same way"—parallelograms

Three sides—triangles

Shapes with a "square corner"—right angle

These all "dent in"—concave

Figure 17.5

Classifications of three-dimensional shapes.

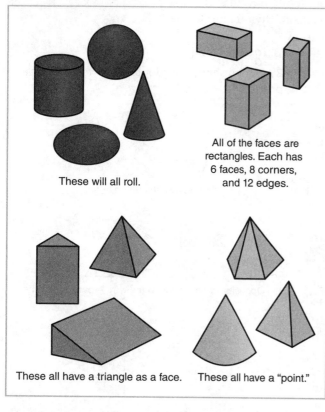

These will all roll.

All of the faces are rectangles. Each has 6 faces, 8 corners, and 12 edges.

These all have a triangle as a face.

These all have a "point."

Teaching Tip

Have lots of geoboards available in the classroom. It is better for two or three students to have 10 or 12 boards at a station than for each to have only one. That way, a variety of shapes can be made and compared before they are changed.

Activity 17.5 CAN YOU MAKE IT?

Create a collection of challenges in which students take the descriptions of one or more properties of a shape, and then create a corresponding shape on the geoboard. The list that follows is only a sample of possible descriptions. Try combining two or more properties to create new challenges. Also have students create challenges for others to try.

- A shape with only one square corner and four sides
- A shape with two square corners (or three, four, five, or six square corners)
- A shape with one or two lines of symmetry
- A shape with two pairs of parallel lines
- A shape with two pairs of parallel lines and no right angles

If the class keeps track of solutions to the challenges in the last activity, there is an added possibility of creating classes of shapes possessing certain properties that may result in definitions of new classes of shapes. The activity can also include impossible tasks, such as a four-sided shape with exactly three right angles. Also, a triangle with three congruent sides (equilateral) is not possible on a geoboard. Finally, a connection to measurement can be added by including the requirement of having a particular area or having a particular perimeter, or both.

Once students are able to describe aspects of shapes, they are ready to explore categories of shapes, moving to higher level geometric thinking. Activity 17.6 targets definitions of two-dimensional shapes.

Activity 17.6 MYSTERY DEFINITION

Standards for Mathematical Practice

3 Construct viable arguments and critique the reasoning of others

▶

Use a projector to show a collection of shapes that have one or more properties in common and another collection of shapes that do not share this commonality, such as the example in Figure 17.6. With your first collection, be certain that you have allowed for all possible variables. Notice in the figure that a square is included in the set of rhombi. Also, choose non-examples to be as close to the positive examples as is necessary to help develop a more precise definition. The third or mixed set should also include those with which students are most likely to be confused. Students should justify their choices in a class discussion. Note that the use of non-examples is particularly important for students with disabilities.

The value of the "Mystery Definition" activity is that students develop ideas and definitions based on their own concept development. After their definitions have been discussed, compare their ideas to the common definition for that shape. Determine whether their definitions captured the necessary aspects of the shape and stated them precisely.

For defining types or categories of triangles, the next activity is especially good.

◄ *Activity* 17.7 **TRIANGLE SORT**

Make copies of the Assorted Triangles sheet (see Blackline Master 42). Note the examples of right, acute, and obtuse triangles; examples of equilateral, isosceles, and scalene triangles; and triangles that represent every possible combination of these categories. Have students cut them out. Ask students to sort the entire collection into three groups so that no triangle belongs to two groups. When this is done and descriptions of the groups are recorded, students should then find a second criterion for creating three different groups. Students with disabilities may need a hint to look only at angle sizes or only at the issue of congruent sides, but delay giving these hints if you can.

Once the groups have been determined, provide appropriate terminology. For ELLs and other students who may struggle with the vocabulary, it is important to focus on the specialized meaning of the terms (e.g., contrasting *acute pain* and *acute angle*) as well as on root words (e.g., *equi-* meaning equal and *-lateral* meaning side). As a follow-up activity, challenge students to sketch a triangle in each of the nine cells of the chart.

As a way to extend this to a level 2 activity, repeat the process using kites and trapezoids or introduce three-dimensional shape definitions.

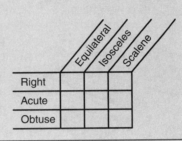

	Equilateral	Isosceles	Scalene
Right			
Acute			
Obtuse			

Stop and Reflect

Of the nine cells in the chart, two of them are impossible to fill. Can you tell which ones and why? ■

Quadrilaterals (polygons with four sides) are an especially rich source of investigations. Once students are familiar with the concepts of right, obtuse, and acute angles; congruence of line segments; and line symmetry, Activity 17.2 "Property Lists for Quadrilaterals" is a good way to bring these ideas together.

The "Property Lists for Quadrilaterals" activity may take several days, but it addresses important geometry content for grade 5 and is worth the time invested. Share lists beginning with parallelograms, then rhombi, then rectangles, and finally squares. Have one group present its list. Then others who worked on the same shape should add to or subtract from it. The class must agree with everything placed on the list. Like the "Mystery Definition" activity, it is important to generate definitions and compare them to the common definition for that shape. In addition, students can explore

Figure 17.6   A mystery definition.

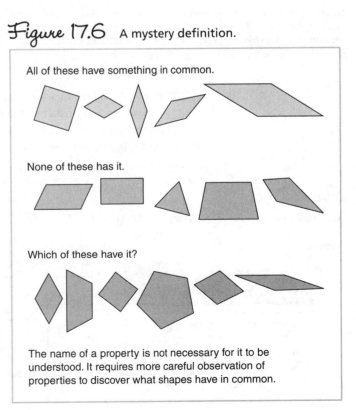

All of these have something in common.

None of these has it.

Which of these have it?

The name of a property is not necessary for it to be understood. It requires more careful observation of properties to discover what shapes have in common.

Figure **17.7** Assorted materials for activities.

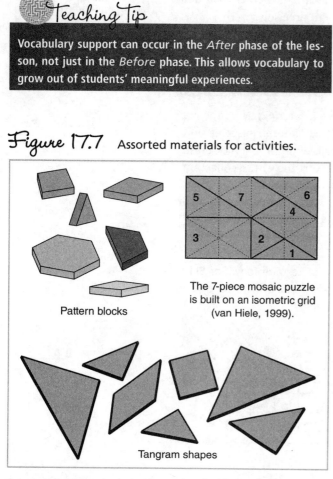

Pattern blocks

The 7-piece mosaic puzzle is built on an isometric grid (van Hiele, 1999).

Tangram shapes

Source: Van Hiele mosaic puzzle reprinted with permission from Developing Geometric Thinking through Activities That Begin with Play, *Teaching Children Mathematics,* 5(6), copyright 1999, by the National Council of Teachers of Mathematics. All rights reserved.

which of these shapes are subcategories of other shapes (e.g., squares are a subset of rectangles).

As new relationships are presented, you can introduce proper terminology. For example, if two diagonals intersect in a square corner, then they are *perpendicular*. Other terms such as *parallel, congruent, bisect, midpoint,* and so on can be clarified as you help students write their descriptions. This is also a good time to introduce symbols such as ≅ for "congruent" or ‖ for "parallel."

Composing and Decomposing Shapes

Students need to freely explore how shapes fit together to form larger shapes (compose) and how larger shapes can be taken apart into smaller shapes (decompose). This ability to compose and decompose supports geometric measurement such as finding area, surface area, and volume.

Among two-dimensional shapes for these activities, pattern blocks and tangrams (see Blackline Master 40) are the best known. Pierre van Hiele (1999) also describes an interesting set of tiles he calls the mosaic puzzle (see Figure 17.7 and Blackline Master 40). The value of the mosaic puzzle is that it contains five different angles (lending itself to discussions of types of angle measures such as right, acute, and obtuse). Notice that initially students can and should make these geometric distinctions without measuring angles or even mentioning degrees.

Figure 17.8 shows a collection of tangram puzzles in order of increasing difficulty. These puzzle pieces can also be used to measure area and model fractional parts. Students gain geometric experiences by exploring ways that the tangram shapes fit together. Beware: Finding the full-sized square using all seven tangram pieces can be difficult! Challenge students to create a puzzle using an illustration that is smaller than the actual tangram pieces. This reduced-size format involves proportional reasoning because the student must mentally enlarge the shape in order to create it with the tangrams.

Figure **17.8**

Four tangram puzzles (see Blackline Master 40).

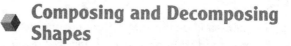

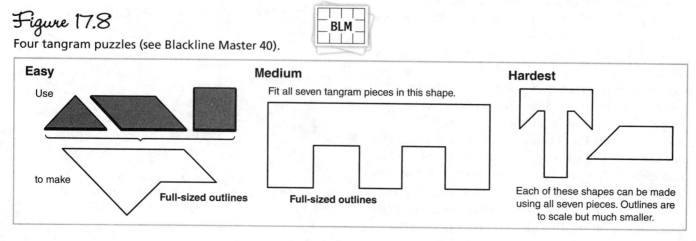

Easy

Use

to make

Full-sized outlines

Medium

Fit all seven tangram pieces in this shape.

Full-sized outlines

Hardest

Each of these shapes can be made using all seven pieces. Outlines are to scale but much smaller.

The National Library of Virtual Manipulatives (http://nlvm.usu.edu/en
/nav/frames_asid_268_g_1_t_3.html?open=activities&from=topic_t_3
.html) has a tangram applet with a set of 14 puzzle figures that can
each be made using all 7 tangram pieces. The e-version of tangrams has
the advantage of motivation and the fact that you must be much more
deliberate in arranging the shapes.

The geoboard is one of the best devices for "constructing" two-dimensional shapes. Following are just a few of the many possible activities appropriate for thinking about composing and decomposing shapes.

Activity 17.8 GEOBOARD COPY

Prepare small cards on which you have drawn designs that can be made on a geoboard (see Figure 17.9). Project the shapes onto a screen. Students copy shapes, designs, and patterns. Begin with one band and then create more complex designs with multiple bands that show a shape composed of other smaller shapes. Students with disabilities may need to have a copy of the card at their desk for closer reference.

"Geoboard Copy" has an element of proportional thinking in it, just as the tangram puzzles in which students worked from small designs. This concept of scaling (or resizing) is particularly important for fifth graders (CCSSO, 2010).

In addition, the use of the geoboard supports the study of area, particularly of compound shapes. Students also begin to understand that rectangles can be decomposed into equal rows or columns, which connects area to multiplication.

With the next activity, the concept of spatial reasoning can be introduced or reinforced.

Activity 17.9 CONGRUENT PARTS

You can also connect geometry to fractions by displaying shapes and asking students to copy the shape on the geoboard and partition the shape into equal parts (see Figure 17.10). Then they can write the fraction of the whole for each part within the composed whole. You can also specify the fractional value and have them create the corresponding number of smaller shapes.

Figure 17.9

Shapes that can be enlarged on geoboards (see Blackline Master 41).

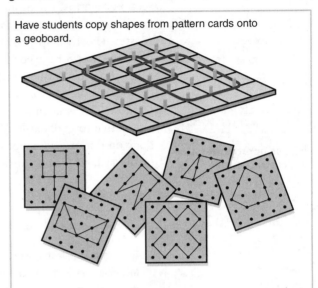

Have students copy shapes from pattern cards onto a geoboard.

Besides pattern cards with and without dots, have students copy <u>real</u> shapes—tables, houses, letters of the alphabet, etc.

Figure 17.10

Subdividing shapes.

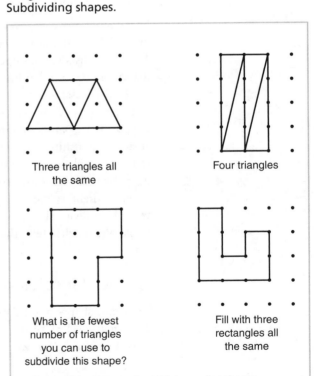

Three triangles all the same

Four triangles

What is the fewest number of triangles you can use to subdivide this shape?

Fill with three rectangles all the same

Start with a shape and cut it into smaller shapes. Add special conditions to make the activity challenging.

In the next activity, students are challenged to create shapes that have specific properties. This is a good way to begin to shift the focus to the properties of shapes that have important geometric significance. Line symmetry is discussed later in this chapter in the section on transformations.

Teach students from the very beginning to record their geoboard designs (use Blackline Master 41). To help your students who struggle with this transfer, suggest that they first mark the dots for the corners of their shape ("second row, end peg"). With the corners identified, it is much easier for them to draw lines between the corners to make the shape. These drawings can be placed in groups for classification and discussion or sent home to families to show what students are learning in geometry. Assorted dot and grid papers provide an alternative to geoboards. Virtually all of the activities suggested for geoboards can also be done on dot or grid paper (see Blackline Masters 10–13). Allow students to choose the tool (geoboard, grid paper, or dot paper) that best supports their thinking for the given problem.

Standards for Mathematical Practice

5 Use appropriate tools strategically ▶

---

technology note

There are excellent electronic geoboards. One of them is found at the National Library of Virtual Manipulatives (http://nlvm.usu.edu) and includes the instant calculation of perimeter and area of a shape on the geoboard by clicking the "measures" button. Another is the Geoboard applet at the University of Illinois Office for Mathematics, Science, and Technology Education website (http://mste.illinois.edu/users/pavel/java/geoboard), which has an option that shows the lengths of the sides of the figure.

◈ Categories of Two-Dimensional Shapes

As students move to level 1 thinking and beyond, the important definitions of two- (and three-) dimensional shapes support the exploration of the relationships between shapes. Table 17.1 lists some important categories of two-dimensional shapes. Examples of these shapes can be found in Figure 17.11 (p. 360).

In the classification of quadrilaterals and parallelograms, some subsets overlap. For example, a square is a rectangle and a rhombus. All parallelograms are trapezoids, but not all trapezoids are parallelograms.* Students at level 1 commonly have difficulty seeing this type of subrelationship. They may quite correctly list all the properties of a square, a rhombus, and a rectangle and still identify a square as a "nonrhombus" or a "nonrectangle." Encourage your students to be more precise in their classifications. Burger (1985) points out that upper elementary students correctly use such classification schemes in other contexts. For example, individual students in a class can belong to more than one club. A square is an example of a quadrilateral that belongs to two other clubs.

◈ Categories of Three-Dimensional Shapes

Important shapes and relationships also exist in three dimensions, and it is these relationships that will link to students' understanding of how to find the volume of these shapes. This is what the *Common Core State Standards* document recommends as part of what fifth

---

*Some definitions of trapezoid specify *only one* pair of parallel sides, in which case parallelograms would not be trapezoids. The University of Chicago School Mathematics Project (UCSMP) uses the "at least one pair" definition, meaning that parallelograms and rectangles are trapezoids.

$Table$ 17.1 Categories of Two-Dimensional Shapes

Shape	Description
Simple Closed Curves	
Concave, convex	An intuitive definition of *concave* might be "having a dent in it." If a simple closed curve is not concave, it is *convex.* A more precise definition of *concave* may be interesting to explore with older students.
Symmetrical, nonsymmetrical	Shapes may have one or more lines of symmetry and may or may not have rotational symmetry. These concepts will require more detailed investigation.
Polygons	Simple closed curves with all straight sides.
Concave, convex	
Symmetrical, nonsymmetrical	
Regular	All sides and all angles are congruent.
Triangles	
Triangles	Polygons with exactly three sides.
Classified by sides	
Equilateral	All sides are congruent.
Isosceles	At least two sides are congruent.
Scalene	No two sides are congruent.
Classified by angles	
Right	Has a right angle.
Acute	All angles are smaller than a right angle.
Obtuse	One angle is larger than a right angle.
Convex Quadrilaterals	
Convex quadrilaterals	Convex polygons with exactly four sides.
Kite	Two opposing pairs of congruent adjacent sides.
Trapezoid	At least one pair of parallel sides.
Isosceles trapezoid	A pair of opposite sides is congruent.
Parallelogram	Two pairs of parallel sides.
Rectangle	Parallelogram with a right angle.
Rhombus	Parallelogram with all sides congruent.
Square	Parallelogram with a right angle and all sides congruent.

graders will explore (CCSSO, 2010). Table 17.2 (p. 361) describes classifications of solids. Figure 17.12 (p. 362) shows examples of cylinders and prisms. Note that prisms are defined here as a special case of a cylinder—a cylinder with a polygon for a base (Zwillinger, 2011). Figure 17.13 (p. 362) shows a comparable grouping of cones and pyramids.

Figure 17.11 Classification of two-dimensional shapes.

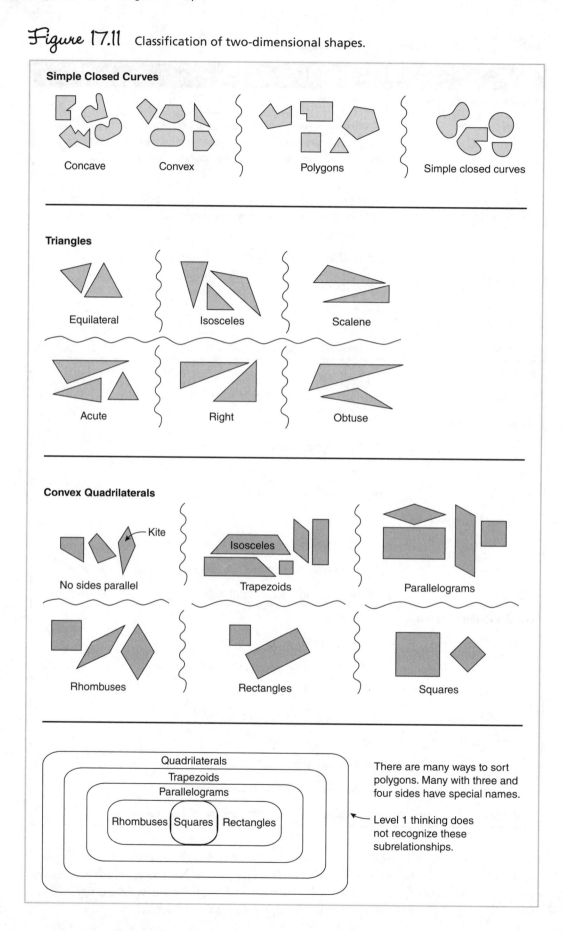

There are many ways to sort polygons. Many with three and four sides have special names.

Level 1 thinking does not recognize these subrelationships.

Table 17.2   Categories of Three-Dimensional Shapes

Shape	Description
Sorted by Edges and Vertices	
Sphere and "egglike" shapes	Shapes with no edges and no vertices (corners). Shapes with edges but no vertices (e.g., a flying saucer). Shapes with vertices but no edges (e.g., a football).
Sorted by Faces and Surfaces	
Polyhedron	Shapes made of all faces (a *face* is a flat surface of a solid). If all surfaces are faces, all the edges will be straight lines. Some combination of faces and rounded surfaces (cylinders are examples, but this is not a definition of a cylinder). Shapes with curved surfaces. Shapes with and without edges and with and without vertices. Faces can be parallel. Parallel faces lie in places that never intersect.
Cylinders	
Cylinder	Two congruent, parallel faces called *bases.* Lines joining corresponding points on the two bases are always parallel. These parallel lines are called *elements* of the cylinder.
Right cylinder	A cylinder with elements perpendicular to the bases. A cylinder that is not a right cylinder is an oblique cylinder.
Prism	A cylinder with polygons for bases. All prisms are special cases of cylinders.
Rectangular prism	A cylinder with rectangles for bases.
Cube	A square prism with square sides.
Cones	
Cone	A solid with exactly one face and a vertex that is not on the face. Straight lines (*elements*) can be drawn from any point on the edge of the base to the vertex. The base may be any shape at all. The vertex need not be directly over the base.
Circular cone	Cone with a circular base.
Pyramid	Cone with a polygon for a base. All faces joining the vertex are triangles. Pyramids are named by the shape of the base: *triangular* pyramid, *square* pyramid, *octagonal* pyramid, and so on. All pyramids are special cases of cones.

Stop and Reflect

Explain the following: Prisms are to cylinders as pyramids are to cones. How is this relationship helpful in learning volume formulas? ■

Many textbooks limit the definition of cylinders to just circular cylinders. These books do not have special names for other cylinders. Under that definition, the prism is not a special case of a cylinder. This illustrates that mathematical definitions are not universally agreed upon. If you return to the development of the volume formulas in Chapter 16, you will see that the more inclusive definition of cylinders and cones given here allows one formula for any type of cylinder—hence, prisms—with a matching statement that is true for cones and pyramids.

Standards for
Mathematical Practice

7 Look for and make use of structure

Figure 17.12 Cylinders and prisms.

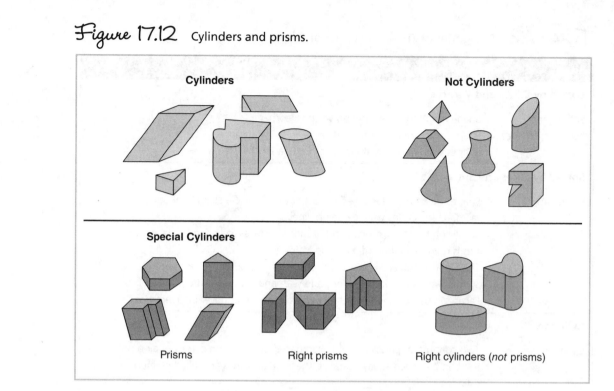

Figure 17.13 Cones and pyramids.

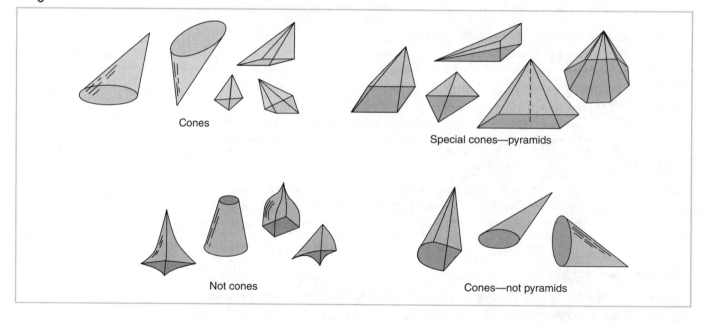

◆ Construction Activities

Students building or drawing shapes, lines, and angles continues to be important to helping them think about the properties and defining features of shapes (CCSSO, 2010). Through the making of these physical models, students can focus on the properties and components that are important in each shape. In the next activity, students examine the diagonals of various classes of quadrilaterals. Rather than beginning with the shapes, it begins with the diagonals.

Figure 17.14   Diagonals of quadrilaterals.

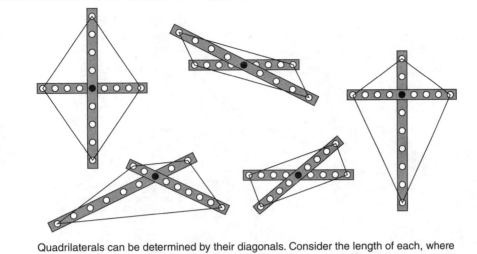

Quadrilaterals can be determined by their diagonals. Consider the length of each, where they cross, and the angles between them. What conditions will produce parallelograms? Rectangles? Rhombi? Challenge: What properties will produce a nonisosceles trapezoid?

◄ *Activity* 17.10   **DIAGONAL STRIPS**

For this activity, students need three strips of card stock about 2 cm wide. Two strips should be the same length (about 30 cm) and the third shorter (about 20 cm). Punch nine holes equally spaced along the strip. (Punch a hole near each end. Divide the distance between the holes by 8. This will be the distance between the remaining holes.) Use a brass fastener to join two strips. A quadrilateral is formed by joining the four end holes as shown in Figure 17.14.

Provide students with the list of possible relationships for angles and lengths. Their task is to use the strips to explore and determine the properties of diagonals that will produce different quadrilaterals. Students may also want to make drawings on dot grids to test the various hypotheses.

Standards for
Mathematical Practice

◄ **5** **Use appropriate tools strategically**

Every type of quadrilateral can be uniquely described in terms of its diagonals using only the conditions of length, proportional comparison of parts, and whether they are perpendicular. Some students will work with the diagonal relationships to see what shapes can be made. Others will begin with examples of the shapes and observe the diagonal relationships.

Because fifth graders focus a great deal of attention on learning about volume, there is good reason to explore three-dimensional shapes. Building three-dimensional shapes is a little more difficult compared with two-dimensional shapes. A variety of commercial materials permit fairly creative construction of geometric solids, including Geoshapes and Polydron. These materials consisting of plastic polygons that can be snapped together to make three-dimensional models. Another is the Zome System, a stick and connector set used to form skeletal shapes. The following are three excellent homemade approaches to constructing skeletal models.

- *Plastic coffee stirrers with pipe cleaners.* Plastic stirrers can be easily cut to different lengths. To connect the corners, cut the pipe cleaners into 2-inch lengths and insert them into the ends of the stirrers.

Figure 17.15 Large skeletal structures.

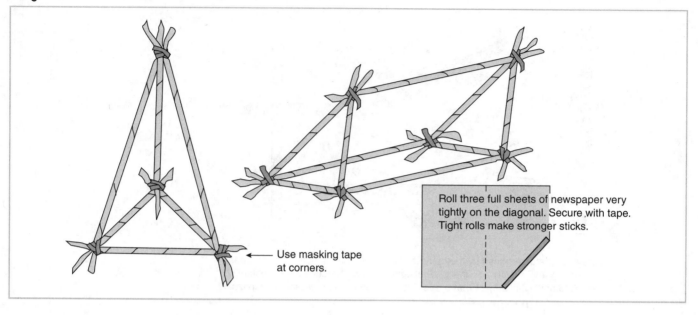

Roll three full sheets of newspaper very tightly on the diagonal. Secure with tape. Tight rolls make stronger sticks.

← Use masking tape at corners.

- *Plastic bendable drinking straws.* With scissors, cut the straws lengthwise from the top down to the flexible joint. These slit ends can then be inserted into the uncut bottom ends of other straws, making a strong but flexible joint. Three or more straws are joined in this fashion to form two-dimensional polygons. To make skeletal solids, use wire twist ties to join polygons side to side.

- *Rolled newspaper rods.* Fantastic large three-dimensional shapes can be built using newspaper and masking or duct tape. Roll three large sheets of newspaper on the diagonal to form a rod. The more tightly the paper is rolled, the less likely the rod is to bend. Secure the roll at the center with a piece of tape. The ends of the rods are thin and flexible for about 6 inches, where there is less paper. Connect rods by bunching and taping (use a lot of tape!) these thin parts together. Additional rods can be joined after two or three are already taped (see Figure 17.15).

The newspaper rod method is exciting because the structures quickly become large. Let students work in groups of four or five. They will soon discover what makes a structure rigid (triangular components) and ideas of balance and form (they can also find the volume of these structures).

⬡ Integrating Technology

In a dynamic geometry program, points, lines, and geometric figures are easily constructed on the computer using only the mouse. Once drawn, the geometric objects can be moved about and manipulated in an endless variety. As the figures are changed, the measurements of distances, lengths, areas, angles, and perimeters update instantly! Additionally, lines can be drawn perpendicular or parallel to other lines or segments. Angles and segments can be drawn congruent to other angles and segments. A figure can be produced that is a reflection of another figure, which can be linked to line symmetry. The most significant thing is that when a geometric object is created with a particular relationship to another, that relationship is maintained no matter how either object is moved or changed.

Three of the best-known dynamic geometry programs are *The Geometer's Sketchpad* from Key Curriculum Press, *GeoGebra* (free public domain software at www.geogebra.org/cms) and *Cabri Geometry II* from Texas Instruments. Originally designed for high school students, all can be used starting about grade 4. To appreciate the potential (and the fun) of dynamic geometry software, you really need to experience it.

In Figure 17.16, the midpoints of a freely drawn quadrilateral ABCD have been joined to explore the properties of quadrilaterals. The diagonals of the resulting quadrilateral (EFGH) are also drawn and measured. No matter how the points A, B, C, and D are dragged around the screen, even inverting the quadrilateral, the other lines will maintain the same relationships (joining midpoints and diagonals), and the measurements will be instantly updated on the screen.

Remember that at level 1, the objects of thought are *classes* of shapes. In a dynamic geometry program, if a quadrilateral is drawn, only one shape is observed, as would be the case on paper or on a geoboard. But now that the quadrilateral can be stretched and altered in endless ways, students actually explore not one shape but an enormous number of examples from that class of shapes. If a property does not change when the figure changes on the dynamic geometry program, the property is attributable to the class of shapes. This is critical as students move to level 2 thinking that includes informal logical reasoning.

Figure 17.16

A Sketchpad construction illustrating an interesting property of quadrilaterals.

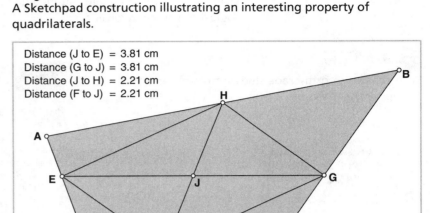

Distance (J to E) = 3.81 cm
Distance (G to J) = 3.81 cm
Distance (J to H) = 2.21 cm
Distance (F to J) = 2.21 cm

Source: Used by permission of Key Curriculum Press.

◆ Definitions and Proofs

To really understand the difference between levels 1 and 2 of the van Hiele theory, let's revisit the pair of activities "Property Lists for Quadrilaterals" (Activity 17.2) and "Minimal Defining Lists" (Activity 17.3).

The parallelogram, rhombus, rectangle, and square all have at least four MDLs. One of the most interesting MDLs for each shape consists only of the properties of its diagonals. For example, a quadrilateral with diagonals that bisect each other and are perpendicular (intersect at right angles) is a rhombus.

Notice that the MDL activity is actually more involved with logical thinking than with examining shapes. Students say, "*If* a quadrilateral has these properties, *then* it must be a square." Logic is also involved in disproving a faulty list. A second feature is the opportunity to discuss what constitutes a definition. In fact, any MDL could be the definition of the shape. We usually choose MDLs based on the ease with which we can understand them. A quadrilateral with diagonals that bisect each other (MDL) does not immediately call to mind a parallelogram, even though we can understand them. Recall that when students created their property lists, no definition was given, only a collection of shapes and a label. Theoretically, the lists could have been created without ever having heard of these shapes.

Teaching Tip

It does little good to simply push students to learn definitions when they are not ready to develop the relationship.

Stop and Reflect

Use the property list for squares and rectangles to prove that "All squares are rectangles." Notice that you must use logical reasoning to understand this statement. ■

The next activity is also a good follow up to Activities 17.1 and 17.2, because it is not restricted to quadrilaterals and can include three-dimensional shapes as well. Notice again the logical reasoning involved.

Figure 17.17

True or false? A fifth-grade student presents an argument to support her decision.

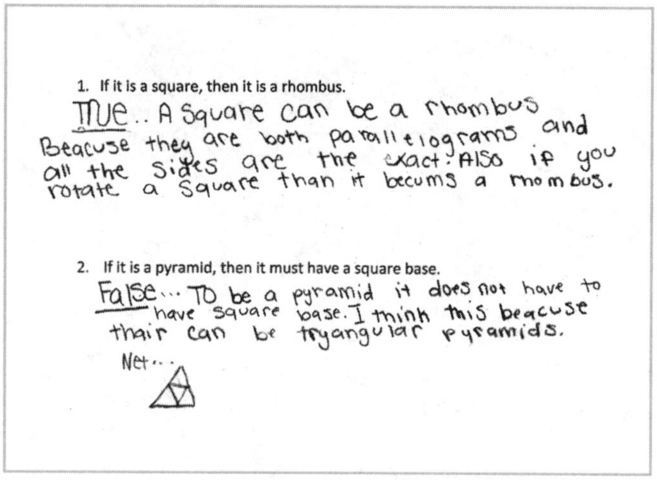

> 1. If it is a square, then it is a rhombus.
>
> TRUE.. A square can be a rhombus Beacuse they are both parallelograms and all the sides are the exact! Also if you rotate a Square than it becums a rhombus.
>
> 2. If it is a pyramid, then it must have a square base.
>
> False... To be a pyramid it does not have to have square base. I think this beacuse thair can be tryangular pyramids.
>
> Net...

Teaching Tip

When a student makes an observation or statement about a geometric concept, it can be written on the board with a question mark as a *conjecture*—a statement whose truth has not yet been determined. You can ask, "Is it true? Always? Can we prove it? Can we find a counterexample?"

Activity 17.11 TRUE OR FALSE?

Prepare statements such as the following: "If it is a _____, then it is also a _____." "All are _____." "Some are _____." A few examples are suggested here but numerous possibilities exist.

- If it is a square, then it is a rhombus.
- All squares are rectangles.
- Some parallelograms are rectangles.
- All parallelograms have congruent diagonals.
- If it has exactly two lines of symmetry, it must be a quadrilateral.
- If it is a cylinder, then it is a prism.
- All pyramids have square bases.

Students determine whether the statements are true or false and, in the *After* phase of the lesson, present an argument to support the decision (see Figure 17.17). Four or five true-or-false statements will make a good lesson. Once this format is understood, let students challenge their classmates by making their own lists of a mixture of true and false statements. Students' lists can be used in subsequent lessons with a focus on informal ways to prove whether a statement is true or false.

Standards for Mathematical Practice

3 Construct viable arguments and critique the reasoning of others

▶

Formative Assessment Note

The "True or False?" activity is also a good diagnostic assessment. Note how the student's response shown in Figure 17.17 gives insights into her fully formed ideas and representations. She also reveals her emerging conceptions as she attempts to make arguments for her answers of true or false.

Learning about Transformations

Transformations are changes in position or size of a shape. Traditionally the study of *translations* (slides), *reflections* (flips), and *rotations* (turns) were initiated in the elementary grades, but in the *Common Core State Standards* these topics have largely moved to middle school (CCSSO, 2010). The study of *line symmetry* is included under the study of transformations due to its link to reflections.

If a shape can be folded on a line so that the two halves match exactly, then it is said to have *line symmetry* (or mirror symmetry). Notice that the fold line is actually a *line of reflection*—the portion of the shape on one side of the line is reflected onto the other side. Again, that is the connection between line symmetry and transformations.

One way to introduce line symmetry to students is to show examples and non-examples using an all-of-these/none-of-these approach, as in Figure 17.18. Here's another possibility:

Fold a sheet of paper in half and cut out a shape of your choosing on the side with the fold. When you open the paper, what do you notice?

Another novel approach is to use mirrors. When you place a mirror on a picture or design so that the mirror is perpendicular to the table, you see a shape with symmetry when you look in the mirror. See http://illuminations.nctm.org/ActivityDetail.aspx?ID=24 for a wonderful symmetry activity with a virtual mirror.

Figure 17.18

All of these, none of these: a mystery definition.

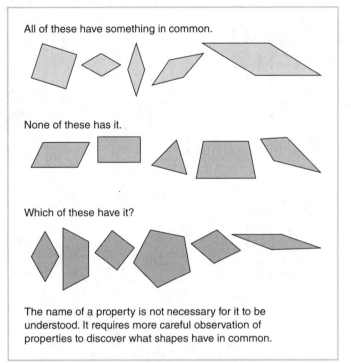

All of these have something in common.

None of these has it.

Which of these have it?

The name of a property is not necessary for it to be understood. It requires more careful observation of properties to discover what shapes have in common.

Activity 17.12 PATTERN BLOCK MIRROR SYMMETRY

Students need a plain sheet of paper with a straight line drawn through the middle. Ask students to use about six to eight pattern blocks to make a design completely on one side of the line that touches the line in some way. When the one side is finished, students try to make the mirror image of their design on the other side of the line. When finished, they use a mirror to check their work. They place the mirror on the line and look into it from the side of the original design. With the mirror in place they should see exactly the same image as they see when they raise the mirror. You can also challenge students to make designs with more than one line of symmetry.

Teaching Tip

Building symmetrical designs with pattern blocks tends to be easier if the line is "pointing" at the student, that is, with a left and a right side. With the line oriented horizontally or diagonally, the task is harder.

The same task can be done with tangrams or can be created on a geoboard. If students wish to try the geoboard, first they stretch a band down the center or from corner to corner. Then they make a design on one side of the line and its mirror image on the other. Check with a mirror. This can also be done with dynamic geometry software or on either isometric or rectangular dot grids as described in the following activity.

Activity 17.13 DOT GRID LINE SYMMETRY

BLM

For this activity, students need to use either isometric or rectangular dot grid paper (see Blackline Masters 13 and 15). Students should draw a line through several dots. This line can be horizontal, vertical, or diagonal. Students

Figure 17.19

Exploring line symmetry on dot grids.

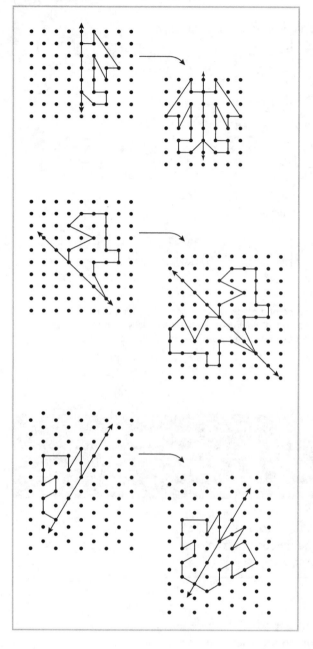

should make a design completely on one side of the drawn line that touches the line in some way (see the left-hand drawings in Figure 17.19). Now the task is to make the mirror image of their design on the other side of the line. Students can exchange designs and make the mirror image of each other's design. When finished, they can use a mirror to check their work. They place the mirror on the line and look into it from the side of the original design. With the mirror in place, they should see exactly the same image as they see when they lift the mirror. You can also challenge them to make designs with more than one line of symmetry.

Have students try these two problems:

A shape with one line of symmetry has exactly 6 sides and two 90 degree angles. Can you draw the shape?

A quadrilateral has diagonals that do not form lines of symmetry, but the quadrilateral is symmetrical (one line). Can you draw the quadrilateral?

These exercises combine several key areas of geometry such as line symmetry, properties of shapes, and visualization with reasoning. Try to have students come up with other problems for their classmates to draw.

Learning about Location

Location activities begin early, when young children develop positional descriptions for actual events that describe how objects are located with respect to other objects. They say "the ball is under the table," or "that street intersects with the road the school is on." In the same way we use a map to analyze paths from point to point, the use of coordinate systems helps locate places and positions. The *Common Core State Standards* for grade 5 state that students should "[g]raph points on the coordinate plane to solve real-world and mathematical problems" (CCSSO, 2010, p. 34).

Imagine that a visitor who doesn't know the way wants to walk from our classroom to the gym. What are the exact directions you would give to the visitor? Be specific about distance and turns.

Using coordinate systems helps students refine the way they think and reason about direction, distance, and location while enhancing spatial understanding. Geometry, measurement, and algebra are all supported by the use of a grid system with numbers or coordinates attached that can specify location. As students become more sophisticated thinkers, their use of coordinates progresses.

The next activity can serve as a readiness task for coordinates and help students see the value of having a way to specify location without pointing.

Figure 17.20

The "Hidden Positions" game.

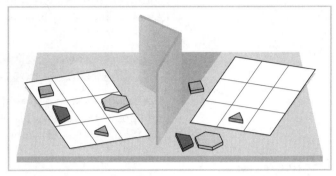

Activity 17.14 HIDDEN POSITIONS

For the game boards, draw an 8-inch square on card stock. Subdivide the squares into a 3 × 3 grid. Two students sit with a "screen" separating their desktop space so that neither student can see the other's grid (see Figure 17.20). Each student has four different pattern blocks. The first player places a block on four different sections of the grid. He then tells the other player where to put blocks on her grid to match his own. When all four pieces are positioned, the two grids are checked to see that they are alike. Then the players switch roles. Model the game once by taking the part of the first student. Use words such as *top row, middle, left,* and *right.* Students can play in pairs as a station activity. For students with disabilities, consider starting with just one shape. Then move to two and so on. For gifted students, extend the grids up to 6 × 6. As the grid size increases, notice how the need for a system of labeling positions increases.

To introduce a coordinate system, project a grid with coordinates on the board (see Figure 17.21). Explain how to use two numbers (positive whole numbers) to designate an intersection point on the grid. The first number tells how far to move to the right. The second number tells how far to move up. In the beginning, use the words along with the numbers: right 3 and up 0. Be sure to include 0 in your introduction. Then select a point on the grid and have students decide what two numbers name that point. If your point is at (2, 4) and students incorrectly say "four, two," then simply indicate where the point is that they named. Emphasize that when they say or write the two numbers, the first number is the number of units (or steps) to the right and the second is the number of units up.

Activity 17.15 STEP RIGHT UP

Create a coordinate grid on the floor of the gymnasium using painter's tape, or on the school playground with paint (with permission of course). Give each student a small whiteboard for recording. Select a student and secretly give her a set of coordinates. Then the student moves to that location. Other students write the coordinates for that location and display their answers. If you repeatedly call this activity "Step Right Up," that can act as a mnemonic for students with disabilities as they will remember to first step right, then up, to locate the position for coordinates of positive whole numbers.

Figure 17.21

A simple coordinate grid. The X is at (3,2) and the O is at (1,3). Use the grid to play "Three in a Row" (like Tic-Tac-Toe). Put marks on intersections, not spaces.

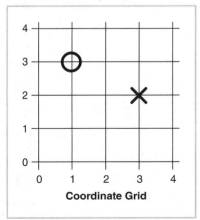

Once a coordinate system has been introduced, students may want to try NCTM's applet (www .nctm.org/standards/content.aspx?menu_id=1155&id=26868). In this activity, students move a ladybug by issuing a list of directions to hide the ladybug beneath a leaf. When the directions are complete, the ladybug is set in motion to follow them. The ladybug can also be directed to draw shapes such as a rectangle in a tilted position or to travel through mazes.

At this level, students are simply using coordinates to describe positions. Although important, by grade 5, students will be able to use coordinates to describe reflections on a coordinate grid. Note that at this beginning level it is important to restrict the lines of reflection to the *x*- or *y*-axis, as in the following activity.

> ### ◢ *Activity* 17.16 COORDINATE REFLECTIONS
>
> Have students draw a five-sided shape in the first quadrant on coordinate grid paper using grid points for vertices. Label the figure ABCDE and call it Figure 1 (see Figure 17.22). Use the *y*-axis as a line of symmetry and draw the reflection of the shape in the second quadrant. Call it Figure 2 (for second quadrant) and label the reflected points A'B'C'D'E'. Now use the *x*-axis as the line of symmetry. Reflect both Figure 2 and Figure 1 into the third and fourth quadrants, respectively, and call these Figures 3 and 4. Label the points of these figures with double and triple primes (A'' and A''', and so on). Write in the coordinates for each vertex of all four figures.
>
> - How is Figure 3 related to Figure 4? How else could you have gotten Figure 3? How else could you have found Figure 4?
> - How are the coordinates of Figure 1 related to its image in the *y*-axis, Figure 2? What can you say about the coordinates of Figure 4?
> - Make a conjecture about the coordinates of a shape reflected in the *y*-axis and a different conjecture about the coordinates of a shape reflected in the *x*-axis.
> - Draw lines from the vertices of Figure 1 to the corresponding vertices of Figure 2. What can you say about these lines? How is the *y*-axis related to each of these lines?

Figure 17.22

Exploring reflections on the coordinate grid.

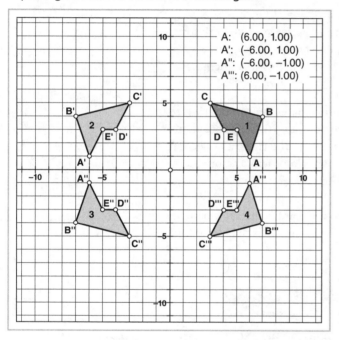

A: (6.00, 1.00)
A': (−6.00, 1.00)
A'': (−6.00, −1.00)
A''': (6.00, −1.00)

Students who have done this activity should have a general way to describe reflection across an axis in terms of coordinates. Soon fifth graders will be combining this knowledge with their understanding of scaling and resizing to learn about dilations at the middle school level.

◢ Learning about Visualizations

Visualization might be called "geometry done with the mind's eye." It involves being able to create mental images of shapes and then turn them around, thinking about how they look from different viewpoints—in some cases predicting the results of various transformations. It includes the mental coordination of two and three dimensions—predicting the unfolding of a box (called a *net*) by understanding a two-dimensional drawing of a three-dimensional shape. Any activity that requires students to think about, manipulate, or transform a shape mentally or to represent a shape as it is seen visually will contribute to the development of their visualization skills.

Remember that at level 0, students are thinking about shapes in terms of the way they look. Visualization activities at this level will have students using a variety of physical shapes and drawings and will challenge them to think about these shapes in different orientations.

Finding out how many different shapes can be made with a given number of simple tiles demands that students mentally flip and turn shapes in their minds and find ways to decide whether they have found them all. That is the focus of the next activity.

Activity 17.17 PENTOMINOES

A *pentomino* is a shape formed by joining five squares as if cut from a square grid. Each square must have at least one side in common with another. Provide students with five square tiles and a sheet of square grid paper for recording. Challenge them to see how many different pentomino shapes they can find. Shapes that are flips or turns of other shapes are not considered different. Do not tell students how many pentomino shapes there are. Good discussions will come from deciding whether some shapes are really different and if all shapes have been found.

Once students have decided that there are just 12 pentominoes (see Figure 17.23), the 12 pieces can then be used in a variety of activities. For example, try to fit all 12 pieces into a 6×10 or 5×12 rectangle. Another task is to examine each of the 12 pentominoes and decide which will fold up to make an open box. For those that are "box makers," which square is the bottom?

It is also fun to explore the number of shapes that can be made from six equilateral triangles or from four 45-degree right triangles (halves of squares). With the right triangles, sides that touch must be the same length. How many of each of these "ominoes" do you think there are? These variations work well for a class that has worked previously with pentominoes and wants additional visualization experiences.

A flat shape that folds up to make a solid figure is called the *net* of that solid. The process of envisioning a three-dimensional shape from the flattened two-dimensional version is important in developing students' visualization skills (as well as noticing relationships between surface area and volume). The following activity suggests several different challenges involving nets.

Figure 17.23

Pentominoes.

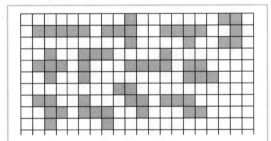

There are 12 pentominoes.

Finding all possible shapes made with five squares—or six squares (called "hexominoes") or six equilateral triangles and so on—is a good exercise in spatial problem solving.

Activity 17.18 NET CHALLENGES

The following tasks involve using nets of solids.

- For each of the pentomino "box makers," see how many different places a sixth square can be attached to create a net for a closed cube. Are there other nets for a cube that do not begin with a pentomino?
- Begin with a solid, such as a rectangular prism or a square pyramid. Sketch as many nets as possible for this shape. For students with disabilities, give them a solid with a set of nets—some that work for that solid and some that are non-examples. Let them decide which will be successful nets of the shape and which are not.
- Use Polydrons or 3-D Geoshapes to create a flat figure that you think will fold up into a solid. Test the result. Challenge a gifted student by setting the number of pieces they can use or the type of shape. In that way, the task can be made more difficult.

The following activity also provides students with experiences in the three-dimensional world but in a rather different manner. Here students also must mentally manipulate shapes and predict the results. The activity combines ideas of line symmetry (reflections) as well as visualization and spatial reasoning.

Activity 17.19   NOTCHES AND HOLES

Use a half-sheet of paper that can be projected on a document camera. Fold it in half. With the paper folded, cut notches in one or two sides and/or cut off one or two corners. While still folded, place the paper on the projector showing the notches and holes (see Figure 17.24). The task is for students to predict and draw what they think will appear when you open the paper.

To extend this activity, make two folds (with the second fold in the opposite direction from the first). This will provide a more difficult challenge.

In "Notches and Holes," students will eventually learn which cuts create holes and how many, and which cuts make notches in the edges or on the corners. Notice how line symmetry, or reflection, plays a major role in the activity. Symmetry determines the position, the shape, and the number of holes created by each cut.

Figure 17.24   An example showing the "Notches and Holes" activity.

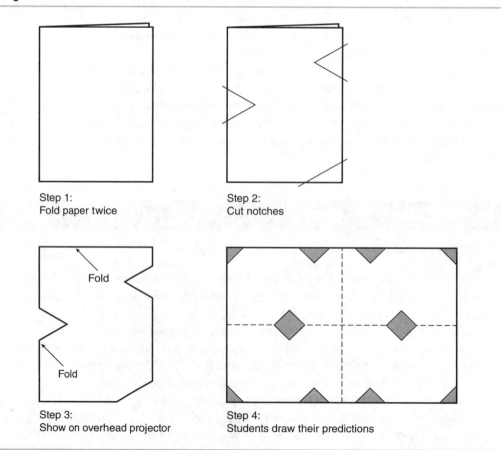

Step 1:
Fold paper twice

Step 2:
Cut notches

Step 3:
Show on overhead projector

Step 4:
Students draw their predictions

Activity 17.20 BUILDING VIEWS

For this activity, students will need paper for drawing a building plan and 1-inch blocks for constructing a building.

- Version 1: Students begin with a building made of the blocks and draw the left, right, front, and back views (these are called *elevations*). In Figure 17.25, the building plan shows a top view of the building and the number of blocks in each position. After students build a building from a plan like this, they draw the elevations (views) of the front, right, left, and back as shown in the figure.
- Version 2: Students are given the right and front elevations. Ask students to build the corresponding building. To record their solution, they draw a building plan (top elevation with numbers).

Figure 17.25 "Building Views" task.

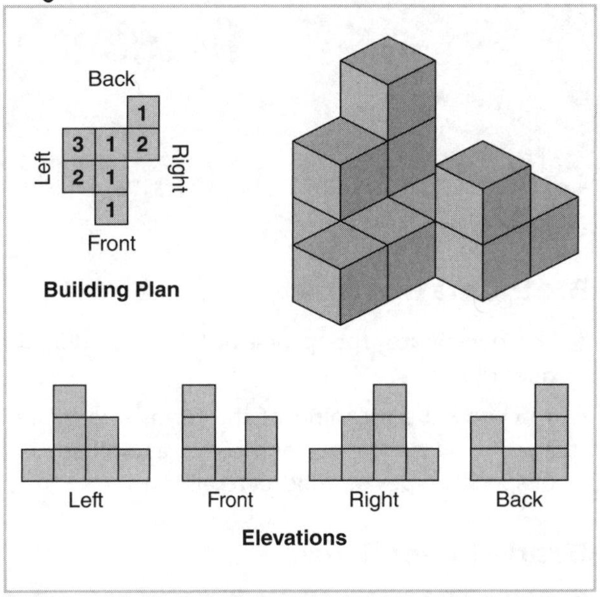

Notice that the front and back elevations are symmetric, as are the left and right elevations. That is why only one of each is given in the second part of the activity.

Expanded Lesson

Diagonals of Quadrilaterals

Content and Task Decisions

Grade Level: 3–5

Mathematics Goals

- To investigate the properties of the diagonals of quadrilaterals
- To clarify the meaning of the terms *quadrilateral, diagonal, perpendicular,* and *bisect,* as well as the names of specific types of quadrilaterals

Grade Level Guide

NCTM Curriculum Focal Points	Common Core State Standards
Students in third grade describe and analyze properties of two-dimensional shapes to classify and connect attributes to definitions of shapes. They are able to build and draw shapes to better understand the properties of two-dimensional space.	Fifth-grade students are able to use the properties of two-dimensional shapes to group them into categories.

Consider Your Students' Needs

Students should be able to identify different types of quadrilaterals (rectangle, parallelogram, trapezoid, kite, rhombus) and talk about their properties in terms of the lengths of sides and the angles formed by the sides. They should also understand the terms *quadrilateral, diagonal, congruent, perpendicular,* and *bisect.*

For English Language Learners

- While all students will need special attention to these terms, using cognates and visuals will be essential for ELLs. For example, *quad-* in quadrilateral (*quadra* means square in Spanish) and *bi-* as in bilingual or biannual, with *sect* meaning section. However, do not take so much time on language that students are not able to focus on and engage in the higher level thinking of the lesson.

- Add visuals for each term in the table on Blackline Master 54 (or have students do this).

For Students with Disabilities

- It might be helpful to brainstorm a list of the possible quadrilaterals and have students work from each to explore the diagonals.

- For students who struggle, you may want to have cards with a pictorial representation of each quadrilateral and its name. Having them available will support students in completing the Diagonals of Quadrilaterals chart. You may need to have enough cards so students can write on them and draw in the diagonals. Then they can model the drawings they made of the diagonals with matching tagboard strips and fasteners.

Materials

Each student will need:

- Three strips of cardstock or tagboard about 2 cm wide (two strips should be about 30 cm long and one about 20 cm long). Punch a hole near each end. Divide the distance between the holes by 8 and use this distance to evenly space 7 holes between the ends. (One set per pair of students)
- Brass fasteners
- "Diagonals of Quadrilaterals" recording sheet (Blackline Master 54)
- 1-cm square dot-grid paper (Blackline Master 13)

Teacher will need:

- Transparency of or way to display Blackline Master 54 and at least two transparencies of Blackline Master 13 or copies for use with a projection device.

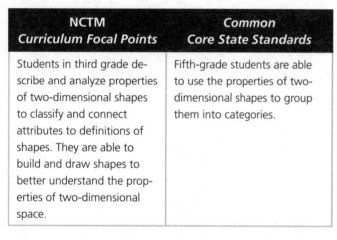

Lesson

Before

Begin with a simpler version of the task:

- On the board, write the terms *diagonal, congruent, bisect,* and *perpendicular.*

- Using the two diagonal strips that are equal in length, show students how to join them in the middle of each with the brass fastener. Join the diagonals so that they bisect each other at a right angle. Lay the diagonals on the overhead and ask students to tell what they can about how the two are related. Refer to the terms on the board. As students share their observations, record the properties on the first line of the transparency by checking the "Yes" column under Congruent Diagonals, checking the "Both" column under Diagonals Bisected, and checking the "Perpendicular" column under Intersections of Diagonals. Clarify the meaning of terminology as necessary. Now ask students to think about what quadrilateral would be formed if the ends of the diagonals were connected. On the overhead, mark the vertices through the holes at the end of each diagonal on the dot-grid paper. Use a straightedge to connect the vertices and, thus, form a square.

- On the dot-grid transparency, show students how they can draw two intersecting lines with the same properties (congruent, bisecting each other, and perpendicular). Then connect the endpoints of these lines to form the quadrilateral. Have students draw a pair of intersecting congruent lines on their own paper. Have them use lines that are either shorter or longer than the two on the transparency. When they connect the endpoints, all students should get squares regardless of the lengths of their diagonals.

- Together generate a list of possible types of quadrilaterals that might be formed. You may wish to put this list on the board.

Present the focus task to the class:

- Students are to use the three strips of tagboard to determine the properties of diagonals that will produce different types of quadrilaterals.

- Before giving students the task, remind them that they can use the third, shorter diagonal with one of the longer diagonals to form a quadrilateral with noncongruent diagonals.

- Make clear to students that they are to work in pairs to identify the properties of the diagonals and the quadrilateral formed by the diagonals. They are to record their findings on their own worksheets and also draw a corresponding pair of diagonals and the quadrilateral on their dot grid. They should put the name of the quadrilateral on each drawing.

Provide clear expectations:

- Students will work with partners, but each student needs to complete his or her own worksheets.

During

Initially:

- If students are having difficulty getting started, suggest that they try creating diagonals with one set of properties from the worksheet.

Ongoing:

- Observe how students are determining the properties of diagonals that produce different quadrilaterals. Do they start with the diagonal relationships to see what shapes can be made? Or do they start with examples of the shapes and determine the diagonal relationships? Either approach is fine.

- Do they have a systematic way of generating different quadrilaterals? For example, do they use the same two diagonals, keep one property constant (e.g., diagonals are perpendicular), and then look for ways to vary the other property (e.g., diagonals bisect or do not bisect each other)?

- For students who are ready for a challenge, have them determine the properties that will produce a non-isosceles trapezoid.

After

Bring the class together to share and discuss the task:

- As students share their findings, have them draw the diagonals and quadrilateral on your dot-grid transparency (Blackline Master 13).

- Referring to the descriptions (properties) of the diagonals, ask students whether *all* quadrilaterals of a given type have the same diagonal properties. For example, will all rhombuses have these same diagonal properties? Use the transparency of the dot-grid paper to have students make drawings to test various hypotheses regarding the quadrilateral type and the properties of the diagonals.

- Ask students to look at the quadrilaterals that have a diagonal property in common (e.g., all quadrilaterals whose diagonals bisect each other) and to make conjectures about other properties in the quadrilaterals that happen as a result of the common diagonal property.

Assessment

Observe

- Are they testing their hypotheses with different sizes of quadrilaterals using the grid paper? Or are they convinced without using the grid paper? If so, how are they convinced? Are they even questioning what might happen with different examples of the same quadrilateral? The answers to these questions will provide evidence that students are or are not beginning to think at van Hiele level 2.

Ask

- What is a *diagonal*?
- What does *perpendicular* mean?

- What does *bisect* mean?
- What do you know about the diagonals of (name a specific quadrilateral)?
- When naming a quadrilateral, does the length of the diagonals matter if the properties remain the same?
- Does the size of the quadrilateral change the properties of the diagonals of a specific quadrilateral?

18

Helping Students Represent and Interpret Data

Big IDEAS

1 Statistics is its own field and different from mathematics; one key difference is the focus on variability of data in statistical reasoning.

2 Doing statistics involves a four-step process: formulating questions, collecting data, analyzing data, and interpreting results.

3 Data are gathered and organized in order to answer questions about the populations from which the data come. With data from only a sample of the population, inferences are made about the population.

4 Different types of graphs and other data representations provide different information about the data and, hence, the population from which the data were taken. The choice of graphical representation can impact how well the data are understood.

5 Graphs can provide a sense of the shape of the data, including how spread out or how clustered the data are. Having a sense of the shape of data is having a big picture of the data rather than the data being a collection of numbers.

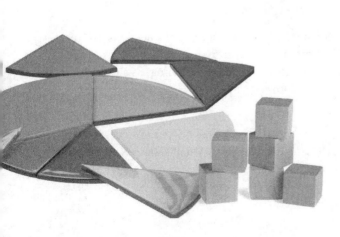

Graphs and statistics bombard the public in areas such as advertising, opinion polls, population trends, health risks, and progress of students in schools. We hear that the average amount of rainfall this summer is more than it was last summer or that the average U.S. family consists of 3.19 people. We read on the U.S. Census website (www.census.gov) that the median home price in May 2000 was $164,700, and in May 2011 it was $222,000. The mean home price in May 2011 was $262,700. Knowing these statistics should raise an array of questions: How were these data gathered? What was the purpose? What does it mean to have an average of 3.19 people? Why are the median and the mean for home sales so different? Which statistic makes more sense for communicating about the prices of homes?

Statistical literacy is critical to understanding the world around us, essential for effective citizenship, and vital for developing the ability to question information presented in the media (Shaughnessy, 2007). Misuse of statistics occurs even in trustworthy sources like newspapers, in which graphs are often designed to exaggerate a finding.

Students in grades 3 through 5 should have meaningful experiences with basic concepts of statistics throughout their school years. The *Common Core State Standards* (CCSSO, 2010) expect the following grade-level goals:

Grade 3: Students represent and interpret data through creating scaled picture graphs and bar graphs (categorical data) and line plots (numerical data) gathered through measurement activities (with fractional units).

Grade 4: Students make line plots to display numerical data from measurements (with fractional units) and interpret the data to solve problems involving addition and subtraction of fractions.

Grade 5: Students continue to use line plots to display numerical measurement-based data and use operations with fractions to solve problems using information from the graphs.

What Does It Mean to Do Statistics?

Doing statistics is, in fact, a different process from doing mathematics, a notion that has received much attention in standards documents and research (Burrill & Elliott, 2006; Franklin et al., 2005; Shaughnessy, 2003). As Richard Scheaffer, past president of the American Statistics Association notes:

Mathematics is about numbers and their operations, generalizations and abstractions; it is about spatial configurations and their measurement, transformations, and abstractions. . . . Statistics is also about numbers—but numbers in context: these are called data. Statistics is about variables and cases, distribution and variation, purposeful design or studies, and the role of randomness in the design of studies, and the interpretation of results. (Scheaffer, 2006, pp. 310–311)

Statistical literacy is needed by all students to interpret the world. This section describes some of the big ideas and essential knowledge regarding statistics and explains a general process for doing statistics. Each of the four steps in the process is used as a major section in the organization of this chapter.

◆ Is It Statistics or Is It Mathematics?

Statistics and mathematics are two different fields; however, statistical questions are often asked in assessments with questions that are mathematical in nature rather than statistical. The harm in this is that students are not focusing on statistical reasoning, as shown by the following excellent exemplars from Scheaffer (2006).

Stop and Reflect

Read the questions that follow and label each as "doing mathematics" or "doing statistics." ■

---

1. The average weight of 50 prize-winning tomatoes is 2.36 pounds. What is the combined weight, in pounds, of these 50 tomatoes? (NAEP sample question)

   a. 0.0472   b. 11.8   c. 52.36   d. 59   e. 118

2. The following table gives the times each girl has recorded for seven trials of the 100-meter dash this year. Only one girl may compete in the upcoming track meet. Which girl would you select for the meet and why?

			Race				
Runner	**1**	**2**	**3**	**4**	**5**	**6**	**7**
Suzie	15.2	14.8	15.0	14.7	14.3	14.5	14.5
Tanisha	15.8	15.7	15.4	15.0	14.8	14.6	14.5
Dara	15.6	15.5	14.8	15.1	14.5	14.7	14.5

Which of these problems involves statistical reasoning? Both? Neither? As explained by Schaeffer, only the second one is statistical in nature. The first requires computing with multiplication—mathematical thinking, not statistical thinking. The second question is statistical in nature because the situation requires analysis—graphs or averages might be used to determine a solution. The mathematics here is basic; the focus is on statistics. Notice the context is central to responding to the question, which is an indication that it is statistical reasoning.

◆ The Shape of Data

A big conceptual idea in data analysis can be referred to as the *shape of data:* a sense of how data are spread out or grouped, what characteristics about the data set as a whole can be described, and what the data tell us in a global way about the population from which they are taken.

There is no single technique that can tell us what the shape of the data is. Across the elementary curricula, students begin looking at the shape of data by examining various graphs. Different graphing techniques or types of graphs can provide a different snapshot of the data as a whole. For example, bar graphs and circle graphs (percentage graphs) each show how the data cluster in different categories. The circle graph focuses more on the relative values of the clusters, whereas the bar graph adds a dimension of quantity. The choices of which graph and how many categories to use in a graph will cause different shapes to emerge.

Part of understanding the shape of data is being aware of how spread out or clustered the data are. In grades 3 through 5, this can be discussed informally by looking at almost any graph (see Figure 18.1).

Figure 18.1 Graphs help us consider the shape of the data.

Figure **18.2** Process of doing statistics.

1. Formulate Questions
   • Clarify the problem at hand.
   • Formulate one (or more) questions that can be answered with data.
2. Collect Data
   • Design a plan to collect appropriate data.
   • Employ the plan to collect the data.
3. Analyze Data
   • Select appropriate graphical and numerical methods.
   • Use these methods to analyze the data.
4. Interpret Results
   • Interpret the analysis.
   • Relate the interpretation to the original question.

Source: Franklin, C., Kader, G., Mewborn, D., Moreno, J., Peck, R., Perry, M., & Scheaffer, R. (2005, August). *Guidelines for Assessment and Instruction in Statistics Education (GAISE) Report: A Pre-K–12 Curriculum Framework,* p. 11. Reprinted with permission. Copyright 2005 by the American Statistical Association. All rights reserved.

The Process of Doing Statistics

To engage students meaningfully in learning and doing statistics, they should be involved in the full process, from asking and defining questions to interpreting results. This broad approach provides a framework and purpose under which students learn how to create graphs, compute the mean, and analyze data in other ways. This chapter is organized around this process, which is presented in Figure 18.2.

Formulating Questions

Statistics is about more than making graphs and analyzing data. It includes both asking and answering questions about our world. The first goal in the Data Analysis and Probability standard of the *Principles and Standards for School Mathematics* says that students should "formulate questions that can be addressed with data and collect, organize, and display relevant data to answer them" (NCTM, 2000, p. 48). Notice that data collection should be for a purpose, to answer a question, just as in the real world. Then the analysis of data actually adds information about some aspect of our world, just as political pollsters, advertising agencies, market researchers, census takers, wildlife managers, medical researchers, and hosts of others gather data to answer questions and make informed decisions.

According to *Curriculum Focal Points* (NCTM, 2006) and the *Common Core State Standards* (CCSSO, 2010) students should be given opportunities to generate their own questions, decide on appropriate data to help answer these questions, and determine methods of collecting the data. Whether the question is teacher initiated or student initiated, students should engage in conversations about how well-defined the question is. When students formulate the questions the data they gather become more meaningful.

Ideas for Questions

Often the need to gather data will come from the class naturally in the course of discussion or from questions arising in other content areas. Science, of course, is full of measurements and, thus, abounds in data analysis possibilities. Social studies is also full of opportunities to pose questions requiring data collection. The next few sections suggest some additional ideas.

Classroom Questions

Students want to learn about themselves (what does the "typical" student look like or what is she interested in?), their families and pets, measures such as arm span or time to get to school, their likes and dislikes, and so on. The easiest questions to begin with are those that can be answered by each class member contributing one piece of data. Here are a few ideas:

• *Favorites:* TV shows, games, movies, ice cream, video games, sports teams, music

• *Numbers:* Number of pets, siblings; hours watching TV or hours of sleep; bedtime; time spent on the computer

• *Measures:* Height, arm span, area of foot, long-jump distance, shadow length, seconds to run around the track, minutes spent traveling to school

Teaching Tip

When there are lots of possibilities, start by restricting the number of choices. Give a "forced" choice of the top-five TV shows after taking a quick poll.

Beyond One Classroom

The questions in the previous section are designed for students to contribute data about themselves. These questions can be expanded by asking, "How would this compare to another class?" Comparison questions are a good way to help students focus on the data they have collected and the variability within that data (Russell, 2006). As students get older, they can begin to think about various populations and differences between them. For example, how are fifth graders similar or different from middle school students? Students might examine questions where they compare responses of boys versus girls, or adults/teachers versus students. These situations involve issues of sampling and making generalizations and comparisons. In addition, students can ask questions about things beyond the classroom. Discussions about communities provide a good way to integrate social studies and mathematics. Here is an example followed by an activity.

Tally the number of cars (or the number of people) that pass your home from 4:30 to 5:30 p.m. Compare your data to your classmates. How busy is your street? How would you classify your neighborhood into a grouping such as urban, suburban, or rural?

◤ *Activity 18.1* **FIND ME**

Have students go to a site such as Google Earth to find the school's neighborhood, their neighborhood, or another area of your choice (maybe a location you are studying). Zoom down to locate approximately a one-block area. Decide in advance items to tally such as cars, garages, sheds, pools, play equipment, and so forth. See what you can identify. Then select another neighborhood and compare. Ask, what do you notice? What can you tell about the area from knowing the number of pieces of backyard play equipment?

The newspaper also is a source for answers to data-related questions. For example, how many full-page ads occur on different days of the week? What types of stories are on the front page? Which comics are really for children and which are not?

Science is another area where questions can be asked and data gathered.

- What is the width of leaves that fall to the ground? Can you identify the tree by knowing the width of the leaf?

- How many times do different types of balls bounce when each ball is dropped from the same height?

- How many days does it take for different types of bean, squash, and pea seeds to germinate when kept in moist paper towels?

- Also, observations on a zoo fieldtrip (or any fieldtrip) can be preceded with the development of questions that are used to gather data on the trip (Mokros & Wright, 2009).

technology *note*

Because context is particularly important, and is particularly supportive when it is culturally meaningful (McGlone, 2008), the Web is an important resource. Students may have interests about various sports, nature, or international events. Whatever their interests, data can be located on the Web. For example, students may wonder how athletes are chosen for the Olympics. Data can be gathered on swimmers' times at various meets and then students can analyze which swimmers should be selected.

Data Collection

There are two main types of data—*categorical* and *numerical*. NCTM suggests that by the sixth grade students should be able to sort these two data types (NCTM, 2000), making the time frame of grades 3 through 5 important in that process. Categorical data refer to information that can be collected about such things that can be grouped by labels, such as favorite vacation sites, colors of cars in the school parking lot, and the most popular name to give the class guinea pig. Categorical data may not have any order—the bars in a bar graph could be put in any arrangement or they could be in an order when you rank something on a scale from 1 to 10. Numerical data, on the other hand, count or measure on a continuous scale. This includes how many miles to school, the temperature in your town over a one-week period, or the weight of the students' backpacks.

How students organize the data and the techniques for analyzing them have a purpose. But gathering data is not easy for students without a plan. After receiving a question for which they need to collect data, eager students can't just ask others their question and record answers. They may want to start by just hand raising, using a tally, or by a ballot using both limited (narrowing the range of possible answers) or unlimited response options (Hudson, Shupe, Vasquez, & Miller, 2008). The problem is that they typically have no idea whom they have asked more than once or whom they have not asked at all. This provides an excellent entry into a discussion about how statisticians gather data. Ask your students to brainstorm ways to gather the data in an organized manner from their classmates.

> ### Teaching Tip
>
> Note that the word *data* is plural, hence the use of "data are." The singular is *datum*.

Gathering data also must take into consideration *variability*. Students can understand that asking a group of first graders their favorite TV show will produce different answers from a group of fifth graders. Answers also may vary based on the day the question is asked or whether a particular show has been recently discussed.

Data can also be collected through observation. This creates a shared context for students, in that they will all be a part of observing phenomena. For example, set up a bird feeder outside the classroom window and collect data at different times during the day to either count the number or type of birds, which can be recorded on a line plot. Students can also collect observational data on fieldtrips, such as the zoo, where they can record frequencies of animal behaviors such as preening, eating, or playing (Mokros & Wright, 2009). They can also report on data from evening, weekend, or vacation activities with their families.

As you plan to collect data, make sure to include gathering data from more than one classroom to seek a more representative sample, or even use random sampling. In fact, as an extension for some students, it is important that they engage in the whole process including designing an experiment in which most variables are kept the same (controlled) so that one variable can be analyzed (plant growth under a variety of conditions). These experiences dovetail nicely with the science fairs that many elementary schools have.

Using Existing Data Sources

Data do not have to be collected by survey; existing data abound in various places, such as the following sources of print and Web data.

Print Resources

Newspapers, almanacs, sports record books, maps, and various government publications are possible sources of data that may be used to answer student questions. Children's literature is an excellent and engaging resource. Nonfiction literature can be a source of data, especially for older students. For example, the *Book of Lists: Fun Facts, Weird Trivia, and Amazing Lists on Nearly Everything You Need to Know!* (Buckley & Stremme, 2006) reports on various statistics and includes surveys at the end of every section. Books on sports, such as *A Negro League Scrapbook* (Weatherform, 2005), can have very interesting statistics about historic periods that students can explore and compare.

Internet Sources

Students may be interested in facts about another country as a result of a social studies unit or a country in the news. Olympic records in various events over the years or data related to environmental issues are other examples of topics around which student questions may be formulated. For these and hundreds of other questions, data can be found on the Web. Below are several websites with a lot of interesting data.

- Economic Research Service, USDA (www.ers.usda.gov/data-products/commodity-consumption-by-population-characteristics.aspx): Here you can find wonderful data sets on the availability and consumption of hundreds of foods. Annual per capita estimates often go back to 1909.

- Google Public Data Explorer (www.google.com/publicdata/home): This site makes large datasets available to explore, visualize, and interpret.

- Internet Movie Database (www.imdb.com): This website offers information about movies of all genres.

- State Data Map (http://illuminations.nctm.org/ActivityDetail.aspx?ID=151): This is a source that displays state data on population, land area, political representation, gasoline use, and so forth.

- World Fact Book (www.cia.gov/library/publications/the-world-factbook/index.html): This website provides demographic information for every nation in the world, including population, age distributions, death and birth rates, and information on the economy, government, transportation, and geography.

- U.S. Census Bureau (www.census.gov): This website contains copious statistical information by state, county, or voting district.

◭ Data Analysis: Classification

Classification involves making decisions about how to categorize things, a basic activity that is fundamental to data analysis. In order to formulate questions and decide how to represent data that have been gathered, decisions must be made about how things might be categorized based on some attribute or characteristic of the data.

Attribute activities start in as early as kindergarten, yet the reasoning involved can be expanded as students move to grades 3 through 5. At least initially, attribute activities are best done by grouping students in a large circle on the floor or around an area where all students can see and have access to the materials to be sorted in Venn diagrams. With the use of words such as *and, or,* and *not,* the loop activities become quite challenging, even for fifth graders.

Standards for Mathematical Practice

1 **Make sense of problems and persevere in solving them**

Activity 18.2 WHAT ABOUT "BOTH"?

Give students two large loops of string and attribute pieces (these are usually blocks of two dimensional shapes that are red, blue, or yellow, large or small, and sometimes thick or thin). Direct them to put all the red pieces inside one string and all triangles inside the other. Let the students try to resolve the difficulty of what to do with the red triangles. When the notion of overlapping the strings to create an area common to both loops is clear, more challenging activities can be explored. Students with disabilities will need to use written labels on each loop of string.

As shown in Figure 18.3, the labels need not be restricted to single attributes. If a piece does not fit in any region, it is placed outside all of the loops.

As students progress, it is important to introduce labels for negative attributes such as "not red" or "not small." Also important is the eventual use of *and* and *or* connectives to form two-value rules such as "red and square" or "big or happy." This use of *and, or,* and *not* significantly widens students' classification schemes.

Figure 18.3

A Venn diagram activity with attribute pieces. A rule is written on each card.

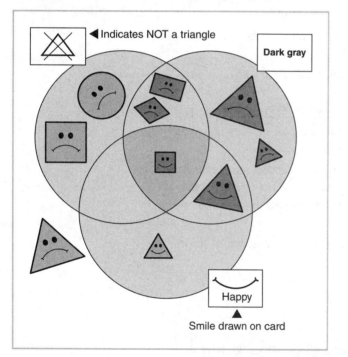

An engaging and challenging activity is to infer how things have been classified when the loops are not labeled. The following activities require students to make and test conjectures about how things are being classified.

Activity 18.3 GUESS MY RULE

For this activity, try using students instead of shapes as attribute pieces. Decide on an attribute such as has blue jeans or stripes on clothing, but do not tell your rule to the class. Silently look at one student at a time and move the student to the left or right according to this secret rule. After a number of students have been sorted, have the next student come up and ask students to predict in which group he or she belongs. Before the rule is articulated, continue the activity for a while so that others in the class will have an opportunity to determine the rule. This same activity can be done with virtually any materials that can be sorted, such as students' shoes, or shells, or buttons. Encourage ELLs to use their native language and English to describe the rule.

Activity 18.4 HIDDEN LABELS

Create label cards for the loops of string. Select two of the cards and place the cards face down next to the two circles of the Venn diagram. Ask students to select an attribute piece for you to place. For ELLs and students with disabilities, provide a list of the possible labels with pictures and/or translations for each as a reference. Begin to sort the attribute pieces according to the hidden rules. As you sort, have students try to determine what the labels are for each of the loops. Let students who think they have guessed the labels try to place a piece in the proper loop, but avoid having them guess the labels aloud. Students who think they know the labels can also be asked to "play teacher" and respond to the guesses of the others. Point out that one way to test an idea about the labels is to select a piece that you think might go in a particular section. Wait to turn the cards up until most students have figured out the rule. Then hide the rules for three Venn areas!

"Guess My Rule" can and should be repeated with real-world materials connected to other content areas and to students' experiences. The class can "graph" data about themselves by first placing information in loops with labels. A graph of "Our Pets" might consist of a picture of each student's pet, or a picture from the Internet of an animal the student would like to have (if he or she doesn't have a pet), affixed to a wall display showing how the pets or animals were classified.

Data Analysis: Graphical Representations

How data are organized should be directly related to the question that caused you to collect the data in the first place. For example, suppose students want to know how many siblings their classmates have. Data collection involves each student counting his or her own family members.

Stop and Reflect

If your third-grade class had collected these data, what methods might you suggest they use for organizing and graphing them? Is one of your ideas better than others for answering the question about how many siblings? ■

A bar graph with one bar per student will certainly tell how many siblings each student has. However, is it the best way to answer the question? If the data were categorized by number of siblings, then a line plot showing the number of students with no siblings, one sibling, two siblings, and so on will easily show which number of siblings is most common and how the number of siblings varies across the class.

Students should be involved in deciding how they want to represent their data. However, for students lacking experience with the various methods of picturing data, you will need to introduce options.

Once students have made the display, they can discuss its value. If, for example, a line plot has seven sticky notes above the five, students may think that five people have seven siblings or seven people have five siblings. How can this be remedied? Analyzing data that are numerical (number of siblings) versus categorical (color of hair) is an added challenge for students as they struggle to make sense of the graphs (Russell, 2006).

The goal is to help students see that graphs and charts tell information and that different types of representations tell different things about the same data. The value of having students actually construct their own graphs is not so much that they learn the techniques, but that they are personally invested in the data and that they learn how a graph conveys information. Once a graph is constructed, the most important activity is discussing what it tells the people who see it, especially those who were not involved in making the graph. Discussions about graphs of real data that the students have themselves been involved in gathering will help them analyze and interpret other graphs and charts that they see in newspapers and on TV.

What we should *not* do is only concentrate on the details of graph construction. Your objectives should focus on the issues of analysis and communication, which are much more important than the technique! In the real world, technology will take care of details.

Students should construct graphs or charts by hand and with technology. First, encourage students to make charts and graphs that make sense to them and that they feel communicate the information they wish to convey. The intent is to get the students involved in accurately communicating a message about their data.

◆ Bar Graphs

Bar graphs are some of the first ways to group and present data. In grade 3, students should be able to create their own displays (CCSSO, 2010). Initially, bar graphs should be made so that each bar consists of countable parts such as squares, objects, tallies, or pictures of objects. Then students move to bar graphs in which a picture or symbol represents a "many-to-one" relationship—for example, one star represents five books that a student has read. The scale of a bar graph (located on the axis without the bars) is merely a measuring tool like a ruler—sometimes with nonstandard units and other times linking to standard units as in the next activity.

◢ *Activity* 18.5 STORM CHASER

This activity involves students collecting data over time about the amount of rainfall (or snowfall) right outside their classroom. Install a rain (or snow) gauge outside the classroom in a location where it can be easily accessed. After a heavy rain (or snow) storm, send a pair of students outside with a piece of cash register tape. Their task is to cut the tape as long as the height of the rain on the scale (and empty the gauge). Then they should mark the tape with the date of the storm. Place the strips chronologically on a base line labeled with the month and day. These strips form a bar graph that can be added to and analyzed over the year. For example, if it rained 2 inches on October 5, $\frac{1}{2}$ inch on October 10, and 1 inch on October 23, there would be three bars with the indicated heights (2 inches, $\frac{1}{2}$ inch, 1 inch), each labeled with the corresponding date. If the storm occurred over the weekend, the students can problem solve how they want to record that observation (one strip of paper for the whole weekend if it is one storm, cut the piece in half if there are two storms [average], or consult the news for approximate rain or snow falls). Again, the important components are combining and comparing the data: How does the storm total in October compare to the total in April? Note that this paper strip to bar graph approach can also be used with monitoring plant growth, and other measurable things.

A "real graph" uses the actual objects being graphed and is a precursor to the picture graph. Examples include types of shoes, favorite apple, energy bars (wrappers), and books. Each item can be placed in a square or on a floor tile so that comparisons and counts are easily made.

Picture graphs use a drawing that represents what is being graphed. Students can make their own drawings (on the same-sized paper), or you can duplicate drawings to be colored or cut out to suit particular needs.

Symbolic graphs use something like squares, blocks, tallies, or Xs to represent the items being counted in the graph. An easy approach is to use sticky notes as elements of a graph. These can be stuck directly to the board or chart paper and rearranged if needed.

Once a graph has been constructed, engage the class in a discussion of what information the graph tells or conveys. "What can you tell about how you cared for the plants or our classroom conditions by looking at this plant growth graph? Where was the best location to put our plants?" Graphs convey factual information (students with their plants regularly fertilized had greater growth than any other variable) and also provide opportunities to make inferences that are not directly observable in the graph (placing the plant next to the window was not as important for growth as fertilizer).

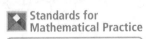

Standards for
Mathematical Practice

2 Reason abstractly
and quantitatively

The difference between actual facts and the inferences that go beyond the data is an important idea in graph construction. Students can examine graphs found in newspapers or magazines and discuss the *facts* in the graphs and the *message* that may have been intended by the person who made the graph.

Students' conceptual ability to analyze data and draw conclusions and interpretations is often weak (Tarr & Shaughnessy, 2007), so work to emphasize this higher-level skill.

◆ Circle Graphs

Typically, we think of circle graphs as showing percentages and fractional parts. As such, these are well-suited for students in the intermediate grades. However, notice in Figure 18.4 that the circle graph could be set up to only indicate the number of data points (in that case, students) in each of five categories.

Figure 18.4

Circle graphs show
ratios of part to whole.

Notice also that the circle graph shows information that is not as easily available from the other graphs. In Figure 18.4, the two graphs show the percentages of students with different numbers of siblings. One graph is based on classroom data and the other on school-wide data. Because circle graphs display proportions rather than quantities, the small set of class data can be compared to the large set of school data, which could not be done with bar graphs.

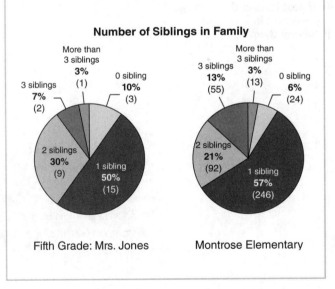

Easily Made Circle Graphs

There are several fun and simple ways to make a circle graph. First, use students. Suppose, for example, that each student picked his or her favorite basketball team in the NCAA tournament's Final Four. Line up all of the students in the room so that students favoring the same team are together. Now form the entire group into a circle of students. Tape the ends of four long strings to the floor in the center of the circle, and extend them to the circle at each point where the teams change. Voila! A life-sized circle graph with no measuring and no percentages. If you copy and cut out a rational number wheel (see Blackline Master 20) and place it on the center of the circle, the strings will show approximate percentages for each part of your graph (see Figure 18.5).

A second easy approach is to convert bar graphs into a circle graph. Once a bar graph is complete, cut out the bars themselves, and tape them together end to end into

BLM

Figure 18.5

A human circle graph: Students are arranged in a circle, with string stretched from the center to show the divisions.

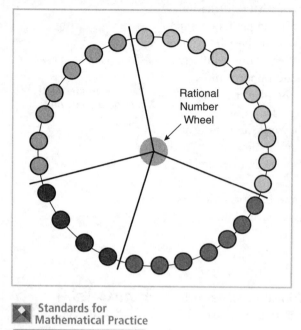

Rational
Number
Wheel

**Standards for
Mathematical Practice**

**1 Make sense
of problems and
persevere in
solving them** ▶

a single strip. Next, tape the two ends of the strip together to form a loop. Trace around the loop onto a piece of paper. Estimate where the center of the circle is and draw lines from the center point to the points where different bars meet. You can estimate percentages using the rational number wheel or percent necklace as described in Chapter 14.

Determining Percentages

If students have experienced the methods just described, using their own calculations to make circle graphs will make more sense. The numbers in each category are added to form the total or whole. (That's the same as taping all of the bar graphs together into a strip or lining up all the students.) By dividing each of the parts by the whole, students will find the decimals and convert to percents. It is an interesting proportional problem for students to convert between percents and degrees (considering the angle measure), because one is out of 100 and the other out of 360. It is helpful to start students with obvious values, like 50 percent ($\frac{1}{2}$), 25 percent ($\frac{1}{4}$), and 10 percent ($\frac{1}{10}$), before moving to more difficult values. A table with one column for percent and one column for degrees can serve as an important tool to help students reason about the conversions.

Percent	Degrees
25	90
50	180
60	?
10	?

Formative Assessment Note

Students should write in a **journal** about their graphs, explaining what the graph tells and why they selected that type of graph to illustrate the data. As you evaluate students' responses, it is important not to focus undue attention on the skills of constructing a graph, but instead to focus on whether they chose an appropriate representation and have provided a good rationale for its selection that connects back to their question (step 1).

◆ Continuous Data Graphs

Bar graphs or picture graphs are useful for illustrating categories of data that have no numeric ordering—for example, favorite musical performers or TV shows. On the other hand, when data are grouped along a continuous scale, they should be ordered along a number line. Examples of such information include temperatures that occur over time, height or weight over age, and percentages of test takers scoring in different intervals along the scale of possible scores.

Line Plots

Line plots are counts of things along a numeric scale. To make a line plot, a number line is drawn and an X (or other marker) is made above the corresponding value on the line for every corresponding data element. One advantage of a line plot is that every piece of data is shown on the graph. It is also a very easy type of graph for students to make. It is essentially a bar graph arranged along a continuous scale with a potential bar for every indicated value on the horizontal scale. A simple example is shown in Figure 18.6.

The line plot is so central to the curriculum in grades 4 and 5 that there are several activities to develop this representation of numerical information.

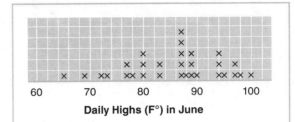

Figure **18.6** Line plot of temperatures.

Activity 18.6 STAND BY ME

Create a line plot on the floor of the classroom. Use masking tape to mark a line and label it with numbers ranging from 2 minutes to 20 minutes (or whatever is appropriate for your students). Have students write on a small sticky note how many minutes it takes them to come to school by car or bus. Then they are to stand on the location above that number on the line. Use the small sticky notes to recreate the line plot above a long piece of cash register tape (labeled with the range of minutes) on the board. Then students can better interpret the data. If there is great variability in the transportation times, you may need to cluster the times into intervals such as 1 to 3 minutes, 4 to 6 minutes, and so on.

Ask students to draw some conclusions about the different travel times of students in the class. What are the differences in times? What is the total of the five longest trips? How long does Emma travel over the five days during the school week (back and forth)? Use the data to create word problems that involve all of the four operations.

> **Teaching Tip**
>
> Having students be "in the graph" is an important experience that will enable them to better understand the more abstract representation.

Activity 18.7 COMPARING CUBITS

A cubit is an ancient measure used to note the length of the forearm from the crook of the elbow to the end of the fingers. Have students use a tape measure to find the length of their cubit to the nearest half or quarter inch. Then using a cash register tape with measures to the half or quarter inch labeled (and spaced far enough apart to allow for the width of a small sticky note), have students mark the location of their measurement on a line plot. Send students to other classes to get measures of other students' cubits from different grades. Use a different color sticky note to mark other classes' measures. What do students notice? Can they predict the grade levels for each of the "mystery" students? Can they broadly state if a particular mystery student is in a grade above or below their grade? Can students find the differences between two values (use fractional measures)?

> **Teaching Tip**
>
> Note that when you are trying to find appropriate data for a line plot, you want numerical values that are similar so the range of numbers on the scale is reasonable.

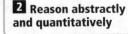 Standards for Mathematical Practice

◄ **2 Reason abstractly and quantitatively**

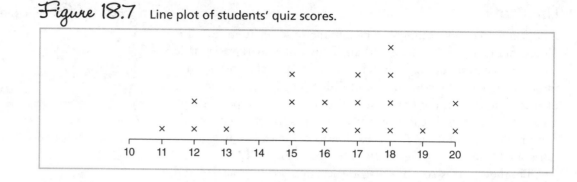

Figure 18.7 Line plot of students' quiz scores.

Activity 18.8 GROSS!

Collect data from the Web or a nonfiction book about a topic of interest to the students, such as the length of insects (especially large ones). Use a field guide about insects to collect data (which is likely to be in a decimal form, such as the largest cockroach, which is 8.3 cm). Then create a line plot to record these lengths, asking students to round to the nearest 0.5 cm. Again, create word problems so that the students can engage in using the data to answer questions that require them to add, subtract, multiply, and divide decimals.

Standards for Mathematical Practice

3 Construct viable arguments and critique the reasoning of others

Activity 18.9 TEST ANXIETY

Show students this line plot of a set of fictitious quiz scores (a perfect score was 20) (see Figure 18.7). Have students make decisions from the data asking such questions as: Was this a surprise pop quiz? Was this a quiz at the end of a series of lessons on the topic? What can you conjecture about the data? Which students may need extra help? How can you justify your responses?

Line Graphs

A *line graph* is used to represent two related pieces of continuous data, and a line is drawn to connect the points. For example, a line graph might be used to show the length of a flagpole shadow as it changed from one hour to the next during the day. The horizontal scale would be time, and the vertical scale would be the length of the shadow. Data can be gathered at specific points in time (e.g., every 15 minutes), and these points can be plotted.

A straight line can be drawn to connect these points because time is continuous and data points do exist between the plotted points. Although line graphs are not the focus in grades 3 through 5, we bring them up here as they are so often misused. Because they are often a choice on a computer graphing program, elementary students can mistakenly choose this format. In fact, line graphs need to be used for identifying trends over time, such as growth in height, an increasing bank account, or temperature change. The assumption is that the points on the line between the identified values are real and that at some timeframe between those values those points were feasible

Teaching Tip

Have students explicitly note the difference between a line plot and a line graph. A line plot uses a set of points representing amounts and labels the frequency of the occurrence of that amount directly above the point on the scale. A line graph shows the relationship between two variables on two axes.

(for example, those temperatures were passed through on the way to the heat wave). That doesn't work for some data, and students need to learn which graphs are best to display different kinds of data.

Computer programs can provide a variety of graphical displays. Use the time saved by technology to focus on the discussions about the information that each display provides. Students can make their own selections among different graphs and justify their choice based on their own intended purposes. Create a graph at NCES Kids Zone (http://nces.ed.gov/nceskids/createagraph), which provides tools for creating five different graphical displays. Data Grapher and Advanced Data Grapher (Illuminations, http://illuminations.nctm.org/ActivityDetail.aspx?ID=204 and http://illuminations.nctm.org/ActivityDetail.aspx?ID=220) analyze data from bar graphs, line graphs, circle graphs, and pictographs. Users can enter data, select which sets to display, and choose the type of representation.

 Interpreting Results

Interpretation is the fourth step in the process of doing statistics. As seen in the sample test items shown in the Stop and Reflect at the beginning of the chapter, sometimes questions focus on mathematical ideas rather than statistical ideas. Although it is helpful to ask mathematical questions, it is essential to ask questions that are statistical in nature. That means the questions focus on the context of the situation and seeing what can be learned or inferred from the data. During interpretation, students might want to loop back and create a different data display to get a different look at the data, or gather data from a different population to see if their results are representative.

Standards for Mathematical Practice

◄ **5 Use appropriate tools strategically**

Different researchers have recommended questions that focus on statistical thinking (Franklin et al., 2005; Friel, O'Conner, & Mamer, 2006; Russell, 2006; Shaughnessy, 2006). Here are some ideas from their lists to get you started on having meaningful discussions about interpreting data:

- What do the numbers (symbols) tell us about our class (or other population)?
- If we asked another class (population), how would the data look? What if we asked a larger group, how would the data look?
- How do the numbers in this graph (population) *compare* to this graph (population)?
- Where are the data "clustering"? Where are the data that are not in the cluster? About what percent is or is not in the cluster?
- Would the results be different if . . . [change of sample, population, or setting]? (Example: Would gathered data on word length in a third-grade book be different from a fifth-grade book? Would a science book give different results from a reading book?)
- What does the graph *not* tell us?
- What new questions arise from these data?
- What is the maker of the graph trying to tell us?

These prompts apply across many data displays. It certainly should be a major focus of your instruction. Consider it the *After* phase of your lesson, though some of these questions will

Figure **18.8** Graphs for journey stories.

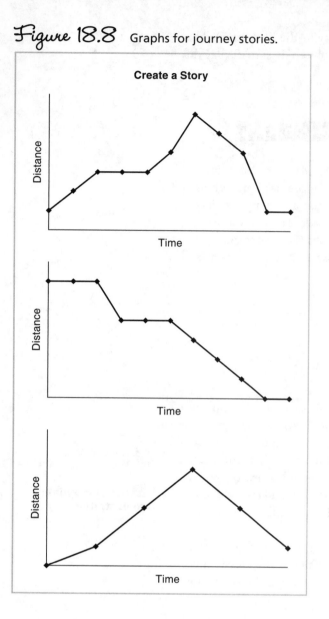

Create a Story

be integrated in the *During* phase as well. The emphasis of the questions in this phase is on getting students to notice differences in the data and provide possible reasons for those differences (Franklin & Mewborn, 2008).

Activity **18.10** **JOURNEY STORIES**

Give students a collection of graphs with a variety of different profiles, as in Figure 18.8. What is the story behind the graph? How can they make sense of the information? You may want to have them start by thinking of each graph as a walk, with the steeper the line the faster the walk. Make sure you pair your ELLs with another student who might be able to assist in the translation. For students with disabilities, create a set of stories for several of the graphs and see if they can match the correct graph to the story.

Our world is inundated with data, from descriptive statistics to different graphs. It is essential that we prepare students to be literate about what can be interpreted from data and what cannot be interpreted from data, what is important to pay attention to and what can be discarded as misleading or poorly designed statistics. This is important for success in school, as well as for being a mathematically literate citizen.

Expanded Lesson

Bar Graphs to Circle Graphs

Content and Task Decisions

Grade Level: 4–5

Mathematics Goals

- To introduce the use of a circle graph (pie chart) to display data
- To explore the concept of percent

Grade Level Guide

NCTM Curriculum Focal Points	Common Core State Standards
In grades 4 and 5, students construct and analyze a variety of graphs to solve problems. Also in the fifth grade students begin to apply their understanding of whole numbers and fractions to construct and analyze graphs.	In grades 4 and 5, student construct a variety of graphs to answer questions and solve problems.

Consider Your Students' Needs

Students have previously made a variety of graphs, such as bar graphs, line plots, and tally charts, but have limited or no experience with circle graphs. They have not been introduced formally to the idea of percentage. If students have explored the connections between decimals and fractions, this lesson can be used to both expand that connection and also introduce the concept of percent.

For English Language Learners

- In thinking of topics for which students will gather data, be sure to consider topics that are culturally relevant. (Eye color would not be in a largely Hispanic population, for example.)
- When explaining the problem, use language/categories that would be familiar to the ELL.
- Provide illustrations of bar graphs and circle graphs as a reference for students.

For Students with Disabilities

- Some students with disabilities may have a difficult time analyzing or "seeing" the circle graph when they are standing in the circle. You may need to have a

visual of a circle graph to show the overhead view of what is taking place.

Materials

Each student will need:

- Rational number wheel (Blackline Master 20)
- 2-cm grid paper (Blackline Master 10)
- Access to scissors, tape, and crayons

Teacher will need:

- Rational number wheel (Blackline Master 20) cut out for use
- Transparency of or way to display 2-cm grid paper (Blackline Master 10)
- Five pieces of yarn or string, each about 10 to 12 feet long
- Heavy weight such as a brick or large book (the ends of the string will be anchored to this weight as the center of a class-sized circle graph)

Lesson

This lesson may take two days. Prior to this lesson, students must have gathered data to answer a question of their own. This can be a common data set for the class or individual students, or groups can gather their own data sets from different questions. Use questions that lend themselves to being grouped in three to five categories. The following are offered as examples:

- What are the favorite _____ (e.g., TV shows) of students in the fourth grade? (Gather data by listing four shows and "other.")
- What are the populations of the top 50 cities in our state? (Get data from the Internet. Group the data into three categories.)
- How many students buy lunch at our school on each day of the school week? (Get data from the cafeteria staff.)

Before

Begin with a simpler version of the task:

- Ask a question in which each student will have one of three to five choices. For example: What are the colors of our eyes? Write the choices on the board (brown, blue, green, other).

- Create a bar graph on the 2-cm grid, coloring in one square for each student as he or she tells you the color of his or her eyes.

- Have the students form a human bar graph by aligning themselves in rows for each color. Next, help the students rearrange their rows into a circle formed of all the students in the class. In the center of the circle place the weight with the strings attached. Extend a string to be held by students between each different color of eyes (between the brown and green, the green and blue, and so on). To explore the idea of percents, place a rational number wheel at the center where the strings come together. With the strings fairly straight you can estimate the percentage of students in each category by counting the number of hash marks in-between the two strings on the rational number wheel. See Figure 18.5 for a visual of this arrangement.

Present the focus task to the class:

- Decide on an appropriate way to graph the data gathered prior to this lesson to answer the students' question(s).

- Students are to make one or more graphs to illustrate the data they collected to answer their question. Allow students to use whatever graphing technique(s) they choose.

Provide clear expectations:

- You may want to do the *Before* portion of the lesson somewhere other than the classroom so that there is room to form a circle of all your students.

During

Initially:

- This is an example of a lesson in which students are introduced to a new convention. The circle graph does not arise out of a problem or task. Rather, you are showing students how such a graph is made.

- Because you are introducing a convention—how to make a circle graph—you are mainly looking for students who are having difficulty understanding how the graph is made. Students who need help making their graphs can get help from peers or from you.

Ongoing:

- Discuss with individual students or groups how their graphs will help others answer their question. Keep their focus on good ways to answer the question.

After

Bring the class together to share and discuss the task:

- Have several students or groups display their graphs and have the class decide if the graphs help answer the question the data were collected to answer.

- If students have not made a bar graph of their data, have them do so. Each bar should be colored differently or marked with pencil to distinguish the bars. Have students cut the bars from the graph and tape them end to end to form a long strip. The two ends of the strip are then taped together to form a loop. This loop is similar to the circle students made by rearranging their rows at the start of the lesson.

- Have students place the loop on the paper with the rational number wheel and form the loop into a circle. The center of the circle should be the center of the wheel. Next they draw straight lines from the center of the wheel to the divisions between the different bars, as they did earlier with the strings in their human graph. If the loop is smaller than the wheel, extend the lines to the edge of the wheel. Demonstrate all of this on a projection device using the number wheel and one of the students' bar graph loops. Show how the first line drawn should align with one of the major subdivisions on the wheel.

- Project the wheel (using projector). Examine the wheel and note that it has ten large subdivisions, each with ten smaller divisions, for a total of 100 sections. Each is *1 percent of the whole*. Explain that 1 percent is the same as $\frac{1}{100}$.

- With this information, students can now label their own circle graphs as another representation of the data they collected. Have a discussion about which graph, the bar graph or the circle graph, is best for answering their question.

Assessment

Observe

- Once the circle graphs have been made, see how well students seem to understand how the circle graph represents the data.

Ask

- How are the bar graph and circle graph the same? How are they different?

- Which graph (bar or circle) is easier to use to answer our question(s)? Why?

- If we asked 100 people our question, about how many do you think would answer the way you did (if the circle graph is based on survey data)?

Common Core State Standards

Standards for Mathematical Practice

The Standards for Mathematical Practice describe varieties of expertise that mathematics educators at all levels should seek to develop in their students. These practices rest on important "processes and proficiencies" with longstanding importance in mathematics education. The first of these are the NCTM process standards of problem solving, reasoning and proof, communication, representation, and connections. The second are the strands of mathematical proficiency specified in the National Research Council's report *Adding It Up*: adaptive reasoning, strategic competence, conceptual understanding (comprehension of mathematical concepts, operations and relations), procedural fluency (skill in carrying out procedures flexibly, accurately, efficiently and appropriately), and productive disposition (habitual inclination to see mathematics as sensible, useful, and worthwhile, coupled with a belief in diligence and one's own efficacy).

1 Make sense of problems and persevere in solving them.

Mathematically proficient students start by explaining to themselves the meaning of a problem and looking for entry points to its solution. They analyze givens, constraints, relationships, and goals. They make conjectures about the form and meaning of the solution and plan a solution pathway rather than simply jumping into a solution attempt. They consider analogous problems, and try special cases and simpler forms of the original problem in order to gain insight into its solution. They monitor and evaluate their progress and change course if necessary. Older students might, depending on the context of the problem, transform algebraic expressions or change the viewing window on their graphing calculator to get the information they need. Mathematically proficient students can explain correspondences between equations, verbal descriptions, tables, and graphs or draw diagrams of important features and relationships, graph data, and search for regularity or trends. Younger students might rely on using concrete objects or pictures to help conceptualize and solve a problem. Mathematically proficient students check their answers to problems using a different method, and they continually ask themselves, "Does this make sense?" They can understand the approaches of others to solving complex problems and identify correspondences between different approaches.

Source: © Copyright 2010. National Governors Association Center for Best Practices and Council of Chief State School Officers. All rights reserved.

2 Reason abstractly and quantitatively.

Mathematically proficient students make sense of quantities and their relationships in problem situations. They bring two complementary abilities to bear on problems involving quantitative relationships: the ability to *decontextualize*—to abstract a given situation and represent it symbolically and manipulate the representing symbols as if they have a life of their own, without necessarily attending to their referents—and the ability to *contextualize*, to pause as needed during the manipulation process in order to probe into the referents for the symbols involved. Quantitative reasoning entails habits of creating a coherent representation of the problem at hand; considering the units involved; attending to the meaning of quantities, not just how to compute them; and knowing and flexibly using different properties of operations and objects.

3 Construct viable arguments and critique the reasoning of others.

Mathematically proficient students understand and use stated assumptions, definitions, and previously established results in constructing arguments. They make conjectures and build a logical progression of statements to explore the truth of their conjectures. They are able to analyze situations by breaking them into cases, and can recognize and use counterexamples. They justify their conclusions, communicate them to others, and respond to the arguments of others. They reason inductively about data, making plausible arguments that take into account the context from which the data arose. Mathematically proficient students are also able to compare the effectiveness of two plausible arguments, distinguish correct logic or reasoning from that which is flawed, and—if there is a flaw in an argument—explain what it is. Elementary students can construct arguments using concrete referents such as objects, drawings, diagrams, and actions. Such arguments can make sense and be correct, even though they are not generalized or made formal until later grades. Later, students learn to determine domains to which an argument applies. Students at all grades can listen or read the arguments of others, decide whether they make sense, and ask useful questions to clarify or improve the arguments.

4 Model with mathematics.

Mathematically proficient students can apply the mathematics they know to solve problems arising in everyday life, society, and the workplace. In early grades, this might be as simple as writing an addition equation to describe a situation. In middle grades, a student might apply proportional reasoning to plan a school event or analyze a problem in the community. By high school, a student might use geometry to solve a design problem or use a function to describe how one quantity of interest depends on another. Mathematically proficient students who can apply what they know are comfortable making assumptions and approximations to simplify a complicated situation, realizing that these may need revision later. They are able to identify important quantities in a practical situation and map their relationships using such tools as diagrams, two-way tables, graphs, flowcharts and formulas. They can analyze those relationships mathematically to draw conclusions. They routinely interpret their mathematical results in the context of the situation and reflect on whether the results make sense, possibly improving the model if it has not served its purpose.

5 Use appropriate tools strategically.

Mathematically proficient students consider the available tools when solving a mathematical problem. These tools might include pencil and paper, concrete models, a ruler, a protractor, a calculator, a spreadsheet, a computer algebra system, a statistical package, or dynamic geometry software. Proficient students are sufficiently familiar with tools appropriate for their grade or course to make sound decisions about when each of these tools might be helpful, recognizing both the insight to be gained and their limitations. For example, mathematically proficient high school students analyze graphs of functions and solutions generated using a graphing calculator. They detect possible errors by strategically using estimation and other mathematical knowledge. When making mathematical models, they know that technology can enable them to visualize the results of varying assumptions, explore consequences, and compare predictions with data. Mathematically proficient students at various grade levels are able to identify relevant external mathematical resources, such as digital content located on a website, and use them to pose or solve problems. They are able to use technological tools to explore and deepen their understanding of concepts.

6 Attend to precision.

Mathematically proficient students try to communicate precisely to others. They try to use clear definitions in discussion with others and in their own reasoning. They state the meaning of the symbols they choose, including using the equal sign consistently and appropriately. They are careful about specifying units of measure, and labeling axes to clarify the correspondence with quantities in a problem. They calculate accurately and efficiently, express numerical answers with a degree of precision appropriate for the problem context. In the elementary grades, students give carefully formulated explanations to each other. By the time they reach high school they have learned to examine claims and make explicit use of definitions.

7 Look for and make use of structure.

Mathematically proficient students look closely to discern a pattern or structure. Young students, for example, might notice that three and seven more is the same amount as seven and three more, or they may sort a collection of shapes according to how many sides the shapes have. Later, students will see 7×8 equals the well remembered $7 \times 5 + 7 \times 3$, in preparation for learning about the distributive property. In the expression $x^2 + 9x + 14$, older students can see the 14 as 2×7 and the 9 as $2 + 7$. They recognize the significance of an existing line in a geometric figure and can use the strategy of drawing an auxiliary line for solving problems. They also can step back for an overview and shift perspective. They can see complicated things, such as some algebraic expressions, as single objects or as being composed of several objects. For example, they can see $5 - 3(x - y)^2$ as 5 minus a positive number times a square and use that to realize that its value cannot be more than 5 for any real numbers x and y.

8 Look for and express regularity in repeated reasoning.

Mathematically proficient students notice if calculations are repeated, and look both for general methods and for shortcuts. Upper elementary students might notice when dividing 25 by 11 that they are repeating the same calculations over and over again, and conclude they have a repeating decimal. By paying attention to the calculation of slope as they repeatedly check whether points are on the line through (1, 2) with slope 3, middle school students might abstract the equation $(y - 2)/(x - 1) = 3$. Noticing the regularity in the way terms cancel when expanding $(x - 1)(x + 1)$, $(x - 1)(x^2 + x + 1)$, and $(x - 1)(x^3 + x^2 + x + 1)$ might lead them to the general formula for the sum of a geometric series. As they work to solve a problem, mathematically proficient students maintain oversight of the process, while attending to the details. They continually evaluate the reasonableness of their intermediate results.

Connecting the Standards for Mathematical Practice to the Standards for Mathematical Content

The Standards for Mathematical Practice describe ways in which developing student practitioners of the discipline of mathematics increasingly ought to engage with the subject matter as they grow in mathematical maturity and expertise throughout the elementary, middle and high school years. Designers of curricula, assessments, and professional development should all attend to the need to connect the mathematical practices to mathematical content in mathematics instruction.

The Standards for Mathematical Content are a balanced combination of procedure and understanding. Expectations that begin with the word "understand" are often especially good opportunities to connect the practices to the content. Students who lack understanding of a topic may rely on procedures too heavily. Without a flexible base from which to work, they may be less likely to consider analogous problems, represent problems coherently, justify conclusions, apply the mathematics to practical situations, use technology mindfully to work with the mathematics, explain the mathematics accurately to other students, step back for an overview, or deviate from a known procedure to find a shortcut. In short, a lack of understanding effectively prevents a student from engaging in the mathematical practices.

In this respect, those content standards which set an expectation of understanding are potential "points of intersection" between the Standards for Mathematical Content and the Standards for Mathematical Practice. These points of intersection are intended to be weighted toward central and generative concepts in the school mathematics curriculum that most merit the time, resources, innovative energies, and focus necessary to qualitatively improve the curriculum, instruction, assessment, professional development, and student achievement in mathematics.

Common Core State Standards

Grades 3–5 Critical Content Areas and Overviews

CCSS Mathematics | Grade 3 Critical Areas

In Grade 3, instructional time should focus on four critical areas:

1. developing understanding of multiplication and division and strategies for multiplication and division within 100;
2. developing understanding of fractions, especially unit fractions (fractions with numerator 1);
3. developing understanding of the structure of rectangular arrays and of area;
4. describing and analyzing two-dimensional shapes.

1. *Students develop an understanding of the meanings of multiplication and division of whole numbers through activities and problems involving equal-sized groups, arrays, and area models; multiplication is finding an unknown product, and division is finding an unknown factor in these situations.* For equal-sized group situations, division can require finding the unknown number of groups or the unknown group size. Students use properties of operations to calculate products of whole numbers, using increasingly sophisticated strategies based on these properties to solve multiplication and division problems involving single-digit factors. By comparing a variety of solution strategies, students learn the relationship between multiplication and division.

2. *Students develop an understanding of fractions, beginning with unit fractions.* Students view fractions in general as being built out of unit fractions, and they use fractions along with visual fraction models to represent parts of a whole. Students understand that the size of a fractional part is relative to the size of the whole. For example, $\frac{1}{2}$ of the paint in a small bucket could be less paint than $\frac{1}{3}$ of the paint in a larger bucket, but $\frac{1}{3}$ of a ribbon is longer than $\frac{1}{5}$ of the same ribbon because when the ribbon is divided into 3 equal parts, the parts are longer than when the ribbon is divided into 5 equal parts. Students are able to use fractions to represent numbers equal to, less than, and greater than one. They solve problems that involve comparing fractions by using visual fraction models and strategies based on noticing equal numerators or denominators.

3. ***Students recognize area as an attribute of two-dimensional regions.*** They measure the area of a shape by finding the total number of same-size units of area required to cover the shape without gaps or overlaps, a square with sides of unit length being the standard unit for measuring area. Students understand that rectangular arrays can be decomposed into identical rows or into identical columns. By decomposing rectangles into rectangular arrays of squares, students connect area to multiplication, and justify using multiplication to determine the area of a rectangle.

4. ***Students describe, analyze, and compare properties of two-dimensional shapes.*** They compare and classify shapes by their sides and angles, and connect these with definitions of shapes. Students also relate their fraction work to geometry by expressing the area of part of a shape as a unit fraction of the whole.

Grade 3 Overview

Operations and Algebraic Thinking

- Represent and solve problems involving multiplication and division.
- Understand properties of multiplication and the relationship between multiplication and division.
- Multiply and divide within 100.
- Solve problems involving the four operations, and identify and explain patterns in arithmetic.

Number and Operations in Base Ten

- Use place value understanding and properties of operations to perform multi-digit arithmetic.

Measurement and Data

- Solve problems involving measurement and estimation of intervals of time, liquid volumes, and masses of objects.
- Represent and interpret data.
- Geometric measurement: understand concepts of area and relate area to multiplication and to addition.
- Geometric measurement: recognize perimeter as an attribute of plane figures and distinguish between linear and area measures.

Geometry

- Reason with shapes and their attributes.

CCSS Mathematics | Grade 4 Critical Areas

In Grade 4, instructional time should focus on three critical areas:

1. developing understanding and fluency with multi-digit multiplication, and developing understanding of dividing to find quotients involving multi-digit dividends;
2. developing an understanding of fraction equivalence, addition and subtraction of fractions with like denominators, and multiplication of fractions by whole numbers;

3. understanding that geometric figures can be analyzed and classified based on their properties, such as having parallel sides, perpendicular sides, particular angle measures, and symmetry.

1. ***Students generalize their understanding of place value to 1,000,000, understanding the relative sizes of numbers in each place.*** They apply their understanding of models for multiplication (equal-sized groups, arrays, area models), place value, and properties of operations, in particular the distributive property, as they develop, discuss, and use efficient, accurate, and generalizable methods to compute products of multi-digit whole numbers. Depending on the numbers and the context, they select and accurately apply appropriate methods to estimate or mentally calculate products. They develop fluency with efficient procedures for multiplying whole numbers; understand and explain why the procedures work based on place value and properties of operations; and use them to solve problems. Students apply their understanding of models for division, place value, properties of operations, and the relationship of division to multiplication as they develop, discuss, and use efficient, accurate, and generalizable procedures to find quotients involving multi-digit dividends. They select and accurately apply appropriate methods to estimate and mentally calculate quotients, and interpret remainders based upon the context.

2. ***Students develop understanding of fraction equivalence and operations with fractions.*** They recognize that two different fractions can be equal (e.g., $\frac{15}{9} = \frac{5}{3}$), and they develop methods for generating and recognizing equivalent fractions. Students extend previous understandings about how fractions are built from unit fractions, composing fractions from unit fractions, decomposing fractions into unit fractions, and using the meaning of fractions and the meaning of multiplication to multiply a fraction by a whole number.

3. ***Students describe, analyze, compare, and classify two-dimensional shapes.*** Through building, drawing, and analyzing two-dimensional shapes, students deepen their understanding of properties of two-dimensional objects and the use of them to solve problems involving symmetry.

Grade 4 Overview

Operations and Algebraic Thinking

- Use the four operations with whole numbers to solve problems.
- Gain familiarity with factors and multiples.
- Generate and analyze patterns.

Number and Operations in Base Ten

- Generalize place value understanding for multi-digit whole numbers.
- Use place value understanding and properties of operations to perform multi-digit arithmetic.

Number and Operations—Fractions

- Extend understanding of fraction equivalence and ordering.
- Build fractions from unit fractions by applying and extending previous understandings of operations on whole numbers.
- Understand decimal notation for fractions, and compare decimal fractions.

Measurement and Data

- Solve problems involving measurement and conversion of measurements from a larger unit to a smaller unit.
- Represent and interpret data.
- Geometric measurement: understand concepts of angle and measure angles.

Geometry

- Draw and identify lines and angles, and classify shapes by properties of their lines and angles.

CCSS Mathematics | Grade 5 Critical Areas

In Grade 5, instructional time should focus on three critical areas:

1. developing fluency with addition and subtraction of fractions, and developing understanding of the multiplication of fractions and of division of fractions in limited cases (unit fractions divided by whole numbers and whole numbers divided by unit fractions);

2. extending division to 2-digit divisors, integrating decimal fractions into the place value system and developing understanding of operations with decimals to hundredths, and developing fluency with whole number and decimal operations; and

3. developing understanding of volume.

1. ***Students apply their understanding of fractions and fraction models to represent the addition and subtraction of fractions with unlike denominators as equivalent calculations with like denominators.*** They develop fluency in calculating sums and differences of fractions, and make reasonable estimates of them. Students also use the meaning of fractions, of multiplication and division, and the relationship between multiplication and division to understand and explain why the procedures for multiplying and dividing fractions make sense. (Note: this is limited to the case of dividing unit fractions by whole numbers and whole numbers by unit fractions.)

2. ***Students develop understanding of why division procedures work based on the meaning of base-ten numerals and properties of operations.*** They finalize fluency with multi-digit addition, subtraction, multiplication, and division. They apply their understandings of models for decimals, decimal notation, and properties of operations to add and subtract decimals to hundredths. They develop fluency in these computations, and make reasonable estimates of their results. Students use the relationship between decimals and fractions, as well as the relationship between finite decimals and whole numbers (i.e., a finite decimal multiplied by an appropriate power of 10 is a whole number), to understand and explain why the procedures for multiplying and dividing finite decimals make sense. They compute products and quotients of decimals to hundredths efficiently and accurately.

3. ***Students recognize volume as an attribute of three-dimensional space.*** They understand that volume can be measured by finding the total number of same-size units of volume required to fill the space without gaps or overlaps. They understand that a 1-unit by 1-unit by 1-unit cube is the standard unit for measuring volume. They select appropriate units, strategies, and tools for solving problems that involve estimating and measuring volume. They decompose

three-dimensional shapes and find volumes of right rectangular prisms by viewing them as decomposed into layers of arrays of cubes. They measure necessary attributes of shapes in order to determine volumes to solve real world and mathematical problems.

Grade 5 Overview

Operations and Algebraic Thinking

- Write and interpret numerical expressions.
- Analyze patterns and relationships.

Number and Operations in Base Ten

- Understand the place value system.
- Perform operations with multi-digit whole numbers and with decimals to hundredths.

Number and Operations—Fractions

- Use equivalent fractions as a strategy to add and subtract fractions.
- Apply and extend previous understandings of multiplication and division to multiply and divide fractions.

Measurement and Data

- Convert like measurement units within a given measurement system.
- Represent and interpret data.
- Geometric measurement: understand concepts of volume and relate volume to multiplication and to addition.

Geometry

- Graph points on the coordinate plane to solve real-world and mathematical problems.
- Classify two-dimensional figures into categories based on their properties.

A Guide to the Blackline Masters

This appendix contains thumbnail sketches of all of the Blackline Masters that are referenced throughout the book. Each full-size master can easily be downloaded from the PDToolkit at http://pdtoolkit.pearson.com. Once downloaded, you may print as many copies as you need. Keep the files on your computer.

Tips for the Use of the Blackline Masters

When a Blackline Master is to be used either as a workmat for students or will be cut apart into smaller pieces, the best advice is to duplicate the master on card stock. Card stock is heavy paper that comes in a variety of colors and can be found at office supply stores.

With materials that require cutting into smaller pieces, we suggest that you laminate the card stock before you cut out the pieces. This will preserve the materials for several years and save valuable time in the future. Here are some additional, specific instructions for certain masters.

- Little Ten-Frames (BLMs 2 and 3): Make the full ten-frames on one color of card stock and the less-than-ten sheet on another. One set consists of the ten cards of each type, cut from a strip of ten on the master.

- Assorted Shapes (BLMs 33–39): Make each set of seven pages a different color. Otherwise, it is very difficult to tell to which set a stray shape belongs.

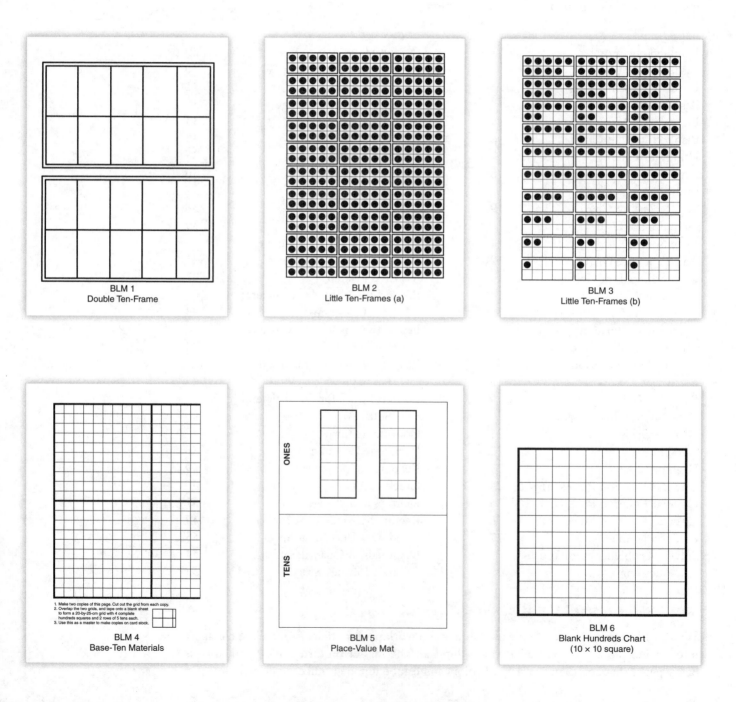

BLM 1
Double Ten-Frame

BLM 2
Little Ten-Frames (a)

BLM 3
Little Ten-Frames (b)

BLM 4
Base-Ten Materials

BLM 5
Place-Value Mat

BLM 6
Blank Hundreds Chart
(10 × 10 square)

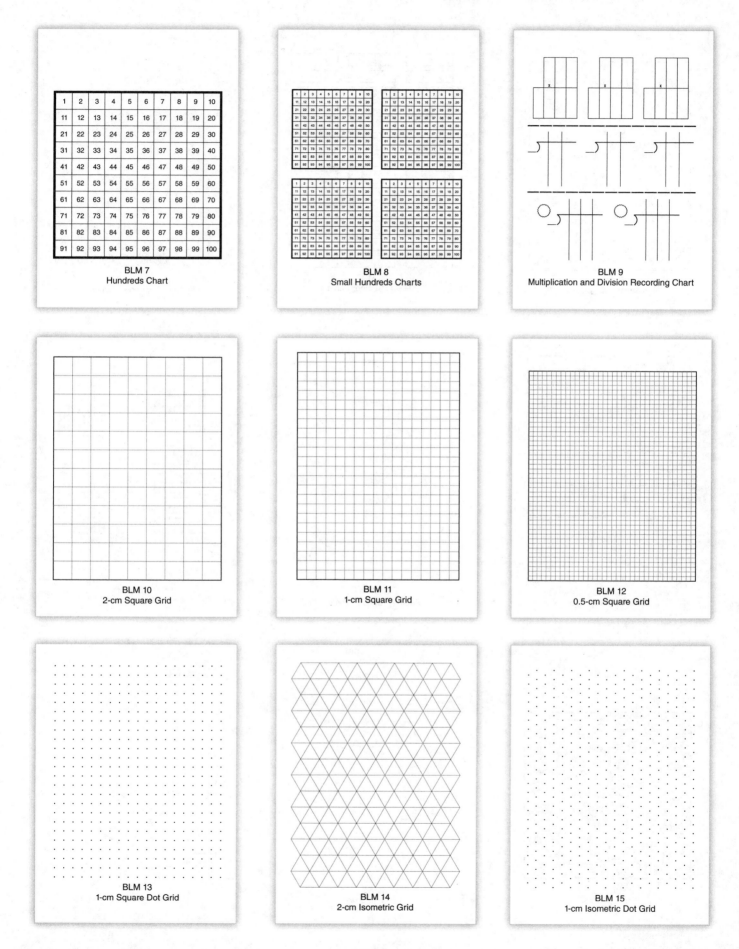

BLM 7
Hundreds Chart

BLM 8
Small Hundreds Charts

BLM 9
Multiplication and Division Recording Chart

BLM 10
2-cm Square Grid

BLM 11
1-cm Square Grid

BLM 12
0.5-cm Square Grid

BLM 13
1-cm Square Dot Grid

BLM 14
2-cm Isometric Grid

BLM 15
1-cm Isometric Dot Grid

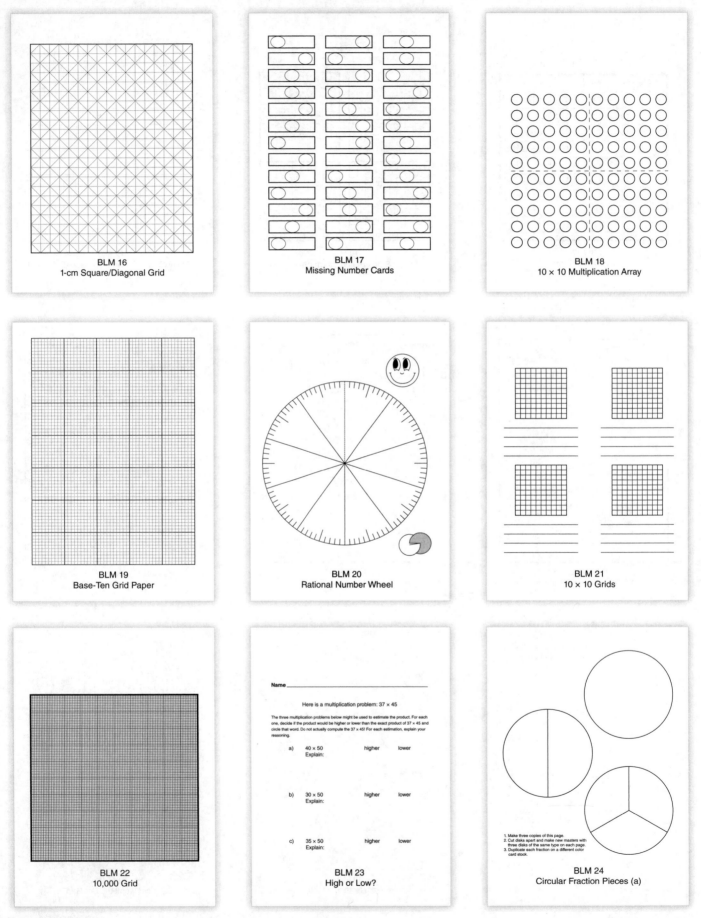

BLM 16
1-cm Square/Diagonal Grid

BLM 17
Missing Number Cards

BLM 18
10 × 10 Multiplication Array

BLM 19
Base-Ten Grid Paper

BLM 20
Rational Number Wheel

BLM 21
10 × 10 Grids

BLM 22
10,000 Grid

BLM 23
High or Low?

Name _____

Here is a multiplication problem: 37 × 45

The three multiplication problems below might be used to estimate the product. For each one, decide if the product would be higher or lower than the exact product of 37 × 45 and circle that word. Do not actually compute the 37 × 45! For each estimation, explain your reasoning.

a) 40 × 50   higher   lower
    Explain:

b) 30 × 50   higher   lower
    Explain:

c) 35 × 50   higher   lower
    Explain:

BLM 24
Circular Fraction Pieces (a)

1. Make three copies of this page.
2. Cut disks apart and make new masters with three disks of the same type on each page.
3. Duplicate each fraction on a different color card stock.

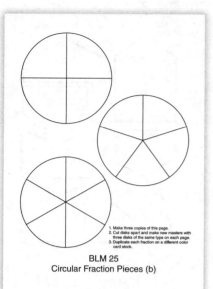

1. Make three copies of this page.
2. Cut disks apart and make new masters with three disks of the same type on each page.
3. Duplicate each fraction on a different color card stock.

BLM 25
Circular Fraction Pieces (b)

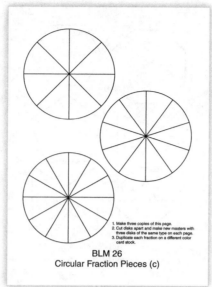

1. Make three copies of this page.
2. Cut disks apart and make new masters with three disks of the same type on each page.
3. Duplicate each fraction on a different color card stock.

BLM 26
Circular Fraction Pieces (c)

Name_____

Find fraction names for each shaded region. Explain how you saw each name you found.

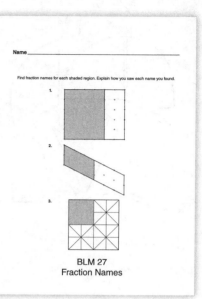

1.

2.

3.

BLM 27
Fraction Names

Name_____

Solve these problems. Use words and drawings to explain how you got your answer.

1. You have ⅔ of a pizza left. If you give ⅓ of the leftover pizza to your brother, how much of a whole pizza will your brother get?

2. Someone ate ⅛ of the cake, leaving only ⅞. If you eat ⅔ of the cake that is left, how much of a whole cake will you have eaten?

3. Gloria used 2½ tubes of blue paint to paint the sky in her picture. Each tube holds ⅔ ounce of paint. How many ounces of blue paint did Gloria use?

BLM 28
Solving Problems Involving Fractions

Windows

Name_____

Step	1	2	3	4	5	6	7		20
No. of sticks	4	7	10						

Describe the pattern you see in the drawing:

Describe the pattern you see in the table:

Use words to describe the rule for finding out how many sticks you need to make any length of window:

Use numbers and symbols to write an equation for your rule:

BLM 29
Predict How Many (a)

Name_____

Step	1	2	3	4	5	6	7	8	9	...	20
No. of dots	2	6	12	20						...	

Describe the pattern you see in the drawing:

Describe the pattern you see in the table:

Use words to describe the rule for finding out how many dots you need to make any dot array:

Use numbers and symbols to write an equation for your rule:

BLM 30
Predict How Many (b)

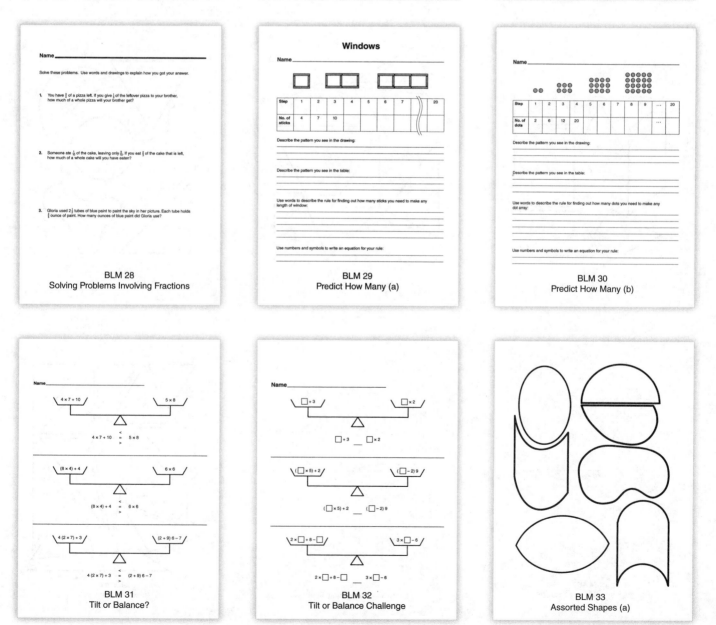

Name_____

4 × 7 + 10   5 × 8

4 × 7 + 10   <=>   5 × 8

(8 × 4) + 4   6 × 6

(8 × 4) + 4   <=>   6 × 6

4 (2 × 7) + 3   (2 + 9) 6 − 7

4 (2 × 7) + 3   <=>   (2 + 9) 6 − 7

BLM 31
Tilt or Balance?

Name_____

☐ + 3   ☐ × 2

☐ + 3 ___ ☐ × 2

(☐ × 5) + 2   (☐ − 2) 9

(☐ × 5) + 2 ___ (☐ − 2) 9

2 × ☐ + 8 − ☐   3 × ☐ − 6

2 × ☐ + 8 − ☐ ___ 3 × ☐ − 6

BLM 32
Tilt or Balance Challenge

BLM 33
Assorted Shapes (a)

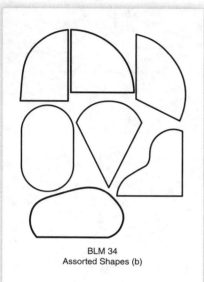

BLM 34
Assorted Shapes (b)

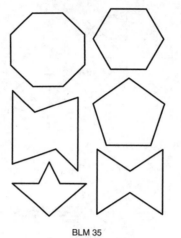

BLM 35
Assorted Shapes (c)

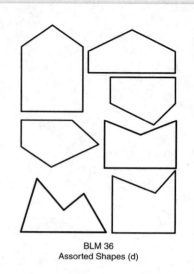

BLM 36
Assorted Shapes (d)

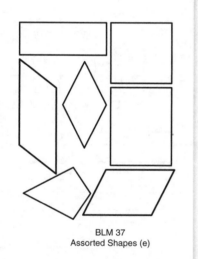

BLM 37
Assorted Shapes (e)

BLM 38
Assorted Shapes (f)

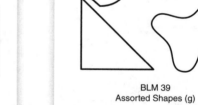

BLM 39
Assorted Shapes (g)

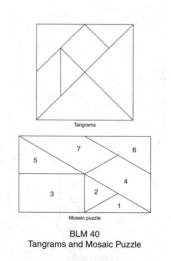

BLM 40
Tangrams and Mosaic Puzzle

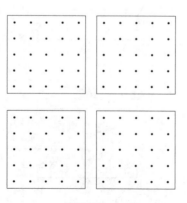

BLM 41
Geoboard Recording Sheets

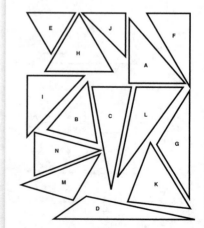

BLM 42
Assorted Triangles

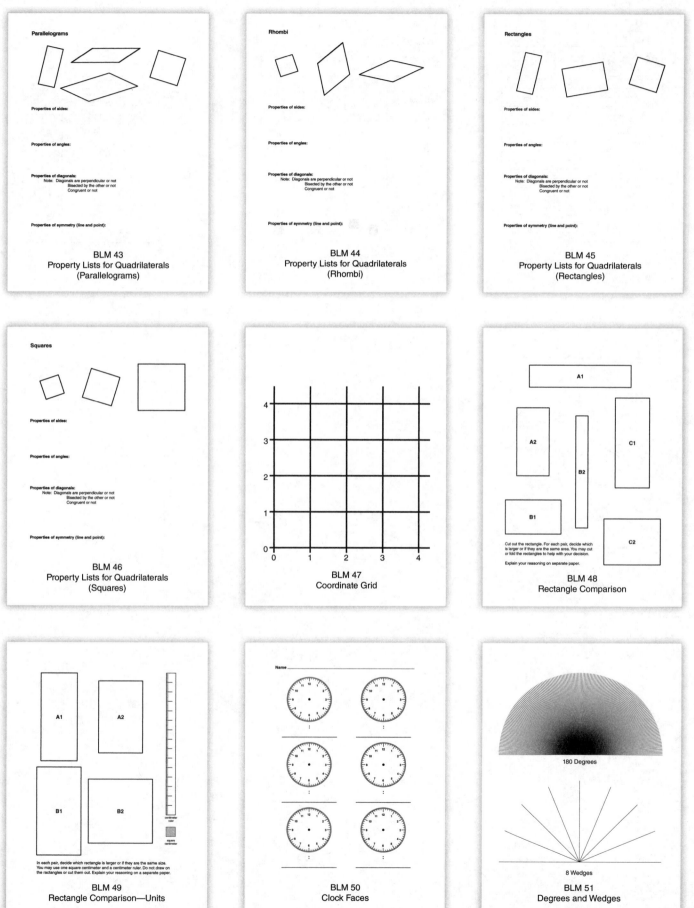

BLM 43
Property Lists for Quadrilaterals
(Parallelograms)

BLM 44
Property Lists for Quadrilaterals
(Rhombi)

BLM 45
Property Lists for Quadrilaterals
(Rectangles)

BLM 46
Property Lists for Quadrilaterals
(Squares)

BLM 47
Coordinate Grid

BLM 48
Rectangle Comparison

BLM 49
Rectangle Comparison—Units

BLM 50
Clock Faces

BLM 51
Degrees and Wedges

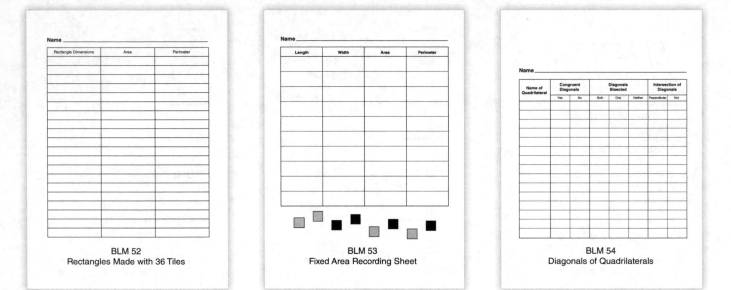

Name _____

Rectangle Dimensions	Area	Perimeter

BLM 52
Rectangles Made with 36 Tiles

Name _____

Length	Width	Area	Perimeter

BLM 53
Fixed Area Recording Sheet

Name _____

Name of Quadrilateral	Congruent Diagonals		Diagonals Bisected			Intersection of Diagonals	
	Yes	No	Both	One	Neither	Perpendicular	Not

BLM 54
Diagonals of Quadrilaterals

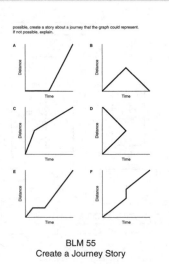

possible, create a story about a journey that the graph could represent. If not possible, explain.

BLM 55
Create a Journey Story

Ambrose, R. (2002). Are we overemphasizing manipulatives in the primary grades to the detriment of girls? *Teaching Children Mathematics, 9*(1), 16–21.

Ambrose, R., Baek, J., & Carpenter, T. P. (2003). Children's invention of multidigit multiplication and division algorithms. In A. J. Baroody & A. Dowker (Eds.), *The development of arithmetic concepts and skills: Constructing adaptive expertise* (pp. 305–336). Mahwah, NJ: Erlbaum.

Ashcraft, M. H., & Christy, K. S. (1995). The frequency of arithmetic facts in elementary texts: Addition and multiplication in grades 1–6. *Journal for Research in Mathematics Education, 26*(5), 396–421.

Aspiazu, G. G., Bauer, S. C., & Spillett, M. D. (1998). Improving the academic performance of Hispanic youth: A community education model. *Bilingual Research Journal, 22*(2), 1–20.

Assouline, S. G., & Lupkowski-Shoplik, A. (2011). *Developing math talent: A comprehensive guide to math education for gifted students in elementary and middle school* (2nd ed.). Waco, TX: Prufrock Press.

Averill, R., Anderson, D., Easton, H., Te Maro, P., Smith, D., & Hynds, A. (2009). Culturally responsive teaching of mathematics: Three models from linked studies. *Journal for Research in Mathematics Education, 40*(2), 157–186.

Baek, J. M. (2006). Children's mathematical understanding and invented strategies for multidigit multiplication. *Teaching Children Mathematics, 12*(5), 242–247.

Baek, J. M. (2008). Developing algebraic thinking through exploration in multiplication. In C. E. Greenes & R. Rubenstein (Eds.), *Algebra and algebraic thinking in school mathematics: 70th NCTM yearbook* (pp. 141–154). Reston, VA: NCTM.

Ball, D. L., & Bass, H. (2003). Making mathematics reasonable in school. In J. Kilpatrick, W. G. Martin, & D. Schifter (Eds.), *A research companion to Principles and Standards for School Mathematics* (pp. 27–44). Reston, VA: NCTM.

Bamberger, H. J., Oberdorf, C., & Schultz-Ferrell, K. (2010). *Math misconceptions: From misunderstanding to deep understanding*. Portsmouth, NH: Heinemann.

Barmby, P., Harries, T., Higgins, S., & Suggate, J. (2009). The array representation and primary children's understanding and reasoning in multiplication. *Educational Studies in Mathematics, 70*(3), 217–241.

Barnett-Clarke, C., Fisher, W., Marks, R., & Ross, S. (2010). *Developing essential understanding of rational numbers: Grades 3–5*. Reston, VA: NCTM.

Barney, L. (1970, April). Your fingers can multiply! *Instructor, 129–130*.

Baroody, A. J. (1985). Mastery of the basic number combinations: Internalization of relationships or facts? *Journal for Research in Mathematics Education, 16*(2), 83–98.

Baroody, A. J. (2003). The development of adaptive expertise and flexibility: The integration of conceptual and procedural knowledge. In A. J. Baroody & A. Dowker (Eds.), *The development of arithmetic concepts and skills: Constructing adaptive expertise* (pp. 1–34). Mahwah, NJ: Erlbaum.

Baroody, A. J. (2006). Why children have difficulties mastering the basic number combinations and how to help them. *Teaching Children Mathematics, 13*(1), 22–31.

Baroody, A. J. (2011). Learning; A framework. In F. Fennell (Ed.), *Achieving fluency in special education and mathematics* (pp. 15–58). Reston, VA: NCTM.

Baroody, A. J., Bajwa, N. P., & Eiland, M. (2009). Why can't Johnny remember the basic facts? *Developmental Disabilities Research Reviews, 15, 69–79*.

Battista, M. T. (2003). Understanding students' thinking about area and volume measurement. In D. H. Clements (Ed.), *Learning and teaching measurement* (pp. 122–142). Reston, VA: NCTM.

Battista, M. T. (2007). The development of geometric and spatial thinking. In F. Lester (Ed.), *Second handbook of research on mathematics teaching and learning* (pp. 843–908). Reston, VA: NCTM.

Bay, J. M., Reys, B. J., & Reys, R. E. (1999). The top 10 elements that must be in place to implement standards-based mathematics curricula. *Phi Delta Kappan, 80*(7), 503–506.

Bay-Williams, J. M. (2010). Influences on student outcomes: Teachers' classroom practices. In D. Lambdin (Ed.), *Teaching and learning mathematics: Translating research for elementary school teachers* (pp. 31–36). Reston, VA: NCTM.

Bay-Williams, J. M., & Martinie, S. L. (2003). Thinking rationally about numbers in the middle school. *Mathematics Teaching in the Middle School, 8*(6), 282–287.

Bay-Williams, J. M., & Martinie, S. L. (2004). What does algebraic thinking look like? *Mathematics Teaching in the Middle School, 10*(4), 198–199.

Bay-Williams, J. M., & Meyer, M. R. (2003). What parents want to know about standards-based mathematics curricula. *Principal Leadership, 3*(7), 54–60.

Beckmann, S. (2004). Solving algebra and other story problems with simple diagrams: A method demonstrated in grade 4–6 texts used in Singapore. *The Mathematics Educator, 14*(1), 42–46.

Behr, M. J., Lesh, R., Post, T. R., & Silver, E. A. (1983). Rational number concepts. In R. Lesh & M. Landau (Eds.), *Acquisition of mathematics concepts and processes* (pp. 91–126). New York, NY: Academic Press.

Better Homes and Gardens. (2012). *Better Homes and Gardens new junior cookbook*. New York, NY: Wiley and Sons.

Biddlecomb, B., & Carr, M. (2011). A longitudinal study of the development of mathematics strategies and underlying counting schemes. *International Journal of Science and Mathematics Education, 9*(1), 1–24.

Blanton, M. L. (2008). *Algebra in the elementary classroom: Transforming thinking, transforming practice*. Portsmouth, NH: Heinemann.

Blanton, M. L., & Kaput, J. (2011). Developing algebraic thinking in the context of arithmetic. In J. Cai & E. Knuth (Eds.), *Early algebraization: A global dialogue from multiple perspectives* (pp. 5–24). New York, NY: Springer.

Bley, N. S., & Thornton, C. A. (1995). *Teaching mathematics to students with learning disabilities* (3rd ed.). Austin, TX: Pro-Ed.

Blume, G., Galindo, E., & Walcott, C. (2007). Performance in measurement and geometry from the viewpoint of *Principles and*

Standards for School Mathematics. In P. Kloosterman & F. Lester, Jr. (Eds.), *Results and interpretations of the 2003 mathematics assessment of the National Assessment of Educational Progress* (pp. 95–138). Reston, VA: NCTM.

Boaler, J. (2006). Promoting respectful learning. *Educational Leadership, 63*(5), 74–78.

Boaler, J., & Humphreys, C. (2005). *Connecting mathematical ideas: Middle school video cases to support teaching and learning.* Portsmouth, NH: Heinemann.

Bray, W. S. (2009). The power of choice. *Teaching Children Mathematics, 16*(3), 178–184.

Bray, W. S., & Abreu-Sanchez, L. (2010). Using number sense to compare fractions. *Teaching Children Mathematics, 17*(2), 90–97.

Breyfogle, M., & Williams, L., (2008-2009). Designing and implementing worthwhile tasks. *Teaching Children Mathematics, 15*(5), 276–280.

Bright, G. W., Behr, M. J., Post, T. R., & Wachsmuth, I. (1988). Identifying fractions on number lines. *Journal for Research in Mathematics Education, 19*(3), 215–232.

Brown, G., & Quinn, R. J. (2007). Investigating the relationship between fraction proficiency and success in algebra. *Australian Mathematics Teacher, 63*(4), 8–15.

Brownell, W., & Chazal, C. (1935). The effects of premature drill in third grade arithmetic. *Journal of Educational Research, 29*(1), 17–28.

Bruner, J. (1966). *Toward a theory of instruction.* Cambridge, MA: Harvard University Press.

Buckley, J., Jr., & Stremme, R. (2006). *Book of lists: Fun facts, weird trivia, and amazing lists on nearly everything you need to know!* Santa Barbara, CA: Scholastic.

Burger, W. F. (1985). Geometry. *Arithmetic Teacher, 32*(6), 52–56.

Burns, M. (1999). *Making sense of mathematics: A look toward the twenty-first century.* Presentation at the annual meeting of the National Council of Teachers of Mathematics, San Francisco.

Burns, M., & McLaughlin, C. (1990). *A collection of math lessons from grades 6 through 8.* Sausalito, CA: Math Solutions Publications.

Burrill, G. F., & Elliot, P. (2006). *Thinking and reasoning with data and chance: 68th NCTM yearbook.* Reston, VA: NCTM.

Cai, J., Ng, S. F., & Moyer, J. (2011). Developing students' algebraic thinking in earlier grades: Lessons from China and Singapore. In J. Cai & E. Knuth (Eds.), *Early algebraization: A global dialogue from multiple perspectives* (pp. 25–42). New York, NY: Springer.

Campbell, P. F. (1996). Empowering children and teachers in the elementary mathematics classrooms of urban schools. *Urban Education, 30,* 449–475.

Campbell, P. F., Rowan, T. E., & Suarez, A. R. (1998). What criteria for student-invented algorithms? In L. J. Morrow (Ed.), *The teaching and learning of algorithms in school mathematics* (pp. 49–55). Reston, VA: NCTM.

Carpenter, T. P., & Moser, J. M. (1984). The acquisition of addition and subtraction concepts in grades one through three. *Journal for Research in Mathematics Education, 15*(3), 179–202.

Carpenter, T. P., Fennema, E., Franke, M. L., Levi, L., & Empson, S. B. (1999). *Children's mathematics: Cognitively guided instruction.* Portsmouth, NH: Heinemann.

Carpenter, T. P., Franke, M. L., Jacobs, V. R., Fennema, E., & Empson, S. B. (1998). A longitudinal study of invention and understanding in children's multidigit addition and subtraction. *Journal for Research in Mathematics Education, 29*(1), 3–20.

Carpenter, T. P., Franke, M. L., & Levi, L. (2003). Thinking mathematically: Integrating arithmetic and algebra in elementary school. Portsmouth, NH: Heinemann.

Carr, J., Carroll, C., Cremer, S., Gale, M., Lagunoff, R., & Sexton, U. (2009). *Making mathematics accessible to English learners, grades 6–12.* San Francisco, CA: WestEd.

Carroll, W. M. (1997). Results of third-grade students in a reform curriculum on the Illinois State Mathematics Test. *Journal for Research in Mathematics Education, 28*(2), 237–242.

Carter, S. (2008). Disequilibrium & questioning in the primary classroom: Establishing routines that help students learn. *Teaching Children Mathematics, 15*(3), 134–137.

Cassone, J. D. (2009). Differentiating mathematics by using task difficulty. In D. Y. White & J. S. Spitzer (Eds.), *Mathematics for every student: Responding to diversity, grades pre-K–5* (pp. 89–98). Reston, VA: NCTM.

Cayton, G. A., & Brizuela, B. M. (2007). First graders' strategies for numerical notation, number reading and the number concept. In J. H. Woo, H. C. Lew, K. S. Park, & D. Y. Seo (Eds.), *Proceedings of the 31st conference of the international group for the psychology of mathematics education* (Vol. 2, pp. 81–88). Seoul, South Korea: Psychology of Mathematics Education (PME).

CCSSO (Council of Chief State School Officers). (2010). *Common core state standards.* Retrieved from http://corestandards.org

CCSSO (Council of Chief State School Officers). (2011). *Common core state standards applications for English learners.* Retrieved from www.corestandards.org/assets/application-for-english-learners .pdf

Celedón-Pattichis, S. (2009). What does that mean? Drawing on Latino and Latina students' language and culture to make mathematical meaning. In M. W. Ellis (Ed.), *Responding to diversity: Grades 6–8* (pp. 59–74). Reston, VA: NCTM.

Celedón-Pattichis, S., & Ramirez, N. G. (2012). *Beyond good teaching: Advancing mathematics education for ELLs.* Reston, VA: NCTM.

Chapin, S. H., O'Conner, C., & Anderson, N. C. (2009). *Classroom discussions: Using math talk to help students learn* (2nd ed.). Sausalito, CA: Math Solutions.

Chick, C., Tierney, C., & Storeygard, J. (2007). Seeing students' knowledge of fractions: Candace's inclusive classroom. *Teaching Children Mathematics, 14*(1), 52–57.

Civil, M., & Menéndez, J. M. (2010). *NCTM research brief: Involving Latino and Latina parents in their children's mathematics education.* Retrieved from www.nctm.org/uploadedFiles/Research_News_ and_Advocacy/Research/Clips_and_Briefs/Research_brief_17-civil .pdf

Civil, M., & Planas. N. (2010). Latino/a immigrant parents' voices in mathematics education. In E. L. Grigorenko & Takanishi, R. (Eds.), *Immigration, diversity, and education* (pp. 130–50). New York, NY: Routledge.

Clark, F. B., & Kamii, C. (1996). Identification of multiplicative thinking in children in grades 1–5. *Journal for Research in Mathematics Education, 27*(1), 41–51.

Clarke, D., Roche, A., & Mitchell, A. (2008). 10 practical tips for making fractions come alive and make sense. *Mathematics Teaching in the Middle School, 13*(7), 373–380.

Clement, L. (2004). A model for understanding, using, and connecting representations. *Teaching Children Mathematics, 11*(2), 97–102.

Clement, L., & Bernhard, J. (2005). A problem-solving alternative to using key words. *Mathematics Teaching in the Middle School, 10*(7), 360–365.

Clements, D., & Sarama, J. (2009). *Learning and teaching early math: The learning trajectories approach.* New York, NY: Routledge.

Coates, G. D., & Mayfield, K. (2009). Families ask: Cooperative learning. *Mathematics Teaching in the Middle School, 15*(4), 244–245.

Common Core State Standards Writing Team. (2011). Progressions for the common core state standards in mathematics—3–5 number and operations—fractions. Retrieved from www.commoncoretools .wordpress.com

Confrey, J. (2008). *Student and teacher reasoning on rational numbers, multiplicative structures, and related topics.* Presentation at ICME–11, Monterrey, Mexico.

Cooper, H. (2007). *The battle over homework: Common ground for administrators, teachers, and parents* (3rd ed.). Thousand Oaks, CA: Corwin Press.

Coughlin, H. A. (2010/2011). Dividing fractions: What is the divisor's role? *Mathematics Teaching in the Middle School, 16*(5), 280–287.

CCSSO (Council of Chief State School Officers). (2010). *Common core state standards.* Retrieved from www.corestandards.org/the -standards/mathematics

Cramer, K., & Henry, A. (2002). Using manipulative models to build number sense for addition of fractions. In B. Litwiller (Ed.), *Making sense of fractions, ratios, and proportions* (pp. 41–48). Reston, VA: NCTM.

Cramer, K., Monson, D., Whitney, S., Leavitt, S., & Wyberg, T. (2010). Dividing fractions and problem solving. *Mathematics Teaching in the Middle School, 15*(6), 338–346.

Cramer, K., & Whitney, S. (2010). Learning rational number concepts and skills in elementary school classrooms. In D. V. Lambdin & F. K. Lester, Jr. (Eds.), *Teaching and learning mathematics: Translating research for elementary school teachers* (pp. 15–22). Reston, VA: NCTM.

Cramer, K., Wyberg, T., & Leavitt, S. (2008). The role of representations in fraction addition and subtraction. *Mathematics Teaching in the Middle School, 13*(8), 490–496.

Crespo, S., & Nicol, C. (2006). Challenging preservice teachers' mathematical understanding: The case of division by zero. *School Science and Mathematics, 106*(2), 84–97.

Cummins, J. (1994). Primary language instruction and the education of language minority students. In C. F. Leyba (Ed.), *Schooling and language minority students: A theoretical framework* (pp. 3–46). Los Angeles: California State University, National Evaluation, Dissemination and Assessment Center.

Cuyler, M. (2010). *Guinea pigs add up.* New York, NY: Walker.

Daro, P., Mosher, F., & Corcoran, T. (2011). *Learning trajectories in mathematics: A foundation for standards, curriculum assessment and instruction.* Philadelphia, PA: Consortium for Policy Research in Education.

Desmet, L. Gregoire, J., & Mussolin, C. (2010). Developmental changes in the comparison of decimal fractions. *Learning and Instruction, 20,* 521–532.

Ding, M., & Li, X. (2010, April). *The associative property: What do teachers know and how do textbooks help?* Paper presented at the annual meeting of the National Council of Teachers of Mathematics, San Diego, CA.

Dixon, J. (2008). Tracking time: Representing elapsed time on an open timeline. *Teaching Children Mathematics, 15*(1), 18–24.

Dougherty, B. (2008). Measure up: A quantitative view of early algebra. In J. Kaput, D. Carraher, & M. Blanton (Eds.), *Algebra in the early grades* (pp. 389–412). New York, NY: Lawrence Erlbaum.

Dougherty, B., Flores, A., Louis, E., & Sophian, C. (2010). *Developing essential understanding of number and numeration for teaching mathematics in prekindergarten–grade 2.* Reston, VA: NCTM.

Drake, J., & Barlow, A. (2007). Assessing students' level of understanding multiplication through problem writing. *Teaching Children Mathematics, 14*(5), 272–277.

Echevarria, J., Vogt, M. E., & Short, D. (2008). *Making content comprehensible for English learners: The SIOP model* (3rd ed.). Boston, MA: Allyn & Bacon.

Else-Quest, N. M., Hyde, J. S., & Hejmadi, A. (2008). Mother and child emotions during mathematics homework. *Mathematical Thinking and Learning, 10,* 5–35.

Empson, S. B. (2002). Organizing diversity in early fraction thinking. In B. Litwiller (Ed.), *Making sense of fractions, ratios, and proportions* (pp. 29–40). Reston, VA: NCTM.

Empson, S. B., & Levi, L. (2011). *Extending children's mathematics: Fractions and decimals.* Portsmouth, NH: Heinemann.

Empson, S. B., Levi, L., & Carpenter, T. P. (2011). The algebraic nature of fractions: Developing relational thinking in elementary school. In J. Cai & E. Knuth (Eds.), *Early algebraization: A global dialogue from multiple perspectives* (pp. 409–428). New York, NY: Springer.

Falkner, K. P., Levi, L., & Carpenter, T. P. (1999). Children's understanding of equality: A foundation for algebra. *Teaching Children Mathematics, 6*(4), 232–236.

Fernandez A., Anhalt, C., & Civil, M. (2009). Mathematical interviews to assess Latino students. *Teaching Children Mathematics, 16*(3), 162–169.

Fernandez, M. L., & Schoen, R. C. (2008). Teaching and learning mathematics through hurricane tracking. *Mathematics Teaching in the Middle School, 13*(9), 500–512.

Flores, A., Samson, J., & Yanik, H. B. (2006). Quotient and measurement interpretations of rational numbers. *Teaching Children Mathematics, 13*(1), 34–39.

Flowers, J. M., & Rubenstein, R. N. (2010–2011). Multiplication fact fluency using doubles. *Mathematics Teaching in the Middle School, 16*(5), 296–301.

Forbringer, L., & Fahsl, A. J. (2010). Differentiating practice to help students master basic facts. In D. Y. White & J. S. Spitzer (Eds.), *Responding to diversity: Grades pre-K–5* (pp. 7–22). Reston, VA: NCTM.

Fosnot, C., & Dolk, M. (2001). *Young mathematicians at work: Constructing number sense, addition, and subtraction.* Portsmouth, NH: Heinemann.

Fosnot, C., & Jacob, B. (2007). *Young mathematicians at work: Constructing algebra.* Portsmouth, NH: Heinemann.

Franklin, C. A., Kader, G., Mewborn, D., Moreno, J., Peck, R., Perry, M., & Scheaffer, R. (2005). *Guidelines for assessment and instruction in statistics education (GAISE) report.* Alexandria, VA: American Statistical Association.

Franklin, C. A., & Mewborn, D. S. (2008). Statistics in the elementary grades: Exploring distribution of data. *Teaching Children Mathematics, 15*(1), 10–16.

Frayer, D. A., Fredrick, W. C., & Klausmeier, H. J. (1969, April). *A schema for testing the level of concept mastery* (Working Paper No. 16). University of Wisconsin Center for Educational Research.

Friel, S. N., & Markworth, K. A. (2009). A framework for analyzing geometric pattern tasks. *Mathematics Teaching in the Middle School, 15*(1), 24–33.

Friel, S. N., O'Conner, W., & Mamer, J. D. (2006). More than "meanmedianmode" and a bar graph: What's needed to have a statistical conversation? In G. F. Burrill & P. C. Elliott (Eds.), *Thinking and reasoning about data and chance: 68th NCTM yearbook* (pp. 117–138). Reston, VA: NCTM.

Fuchs, L. S., & Fuchs, D. (2001). Principles for the prevention and intervention of mathematics difficulties. *Learning Disabilities Research and Practice, 16*(2), 85–95.

Fuchs, L. S., Fuchs, D., Prentice, K., Hamlett, C. L., Finelli, R., & Courey, S. J. (2004). Enhancing mathematical problem solving among third-grade students with schema based instruction. *Journal of Educational Psychology, 96*(4), 635–647.

Fuchs, L. S., Fuchs, D., Yazdian, L., & Powell, S. R. (2002). Enhancing first-grade children's mathematics development with peer-assisted learning strategies. *School Psychology Review, 31*(4), 569–583.

Fuson, K. C. (1984). More complexities in subtraction. *Journal for Research in Mathematics Education, 15*(3), 214–225.

Fuson, K. C. (1992). Research on whole number addition and subtraction. In D. A. Grouws (Ed.), *Handbook of research on mathematics teaching and learning* (pp. 243–275). New York, NY: Macmillan.

Fuson, K. (2003). Developing mathematical power in whole number operations. In J. Kilpatrick, W. G. Martin, & D. Schifter (Eds.), *A research companion to principles and standards in school mathematics* (pp. 68–94). Reston, VA: NCTM.

Fuson, K. C., & Kwon, Y. (1992). Korean children's single-digit addition and subtraction: Numbers structured by ten. *Journal for Research in Mathematics Education, 23*(2), 148–165.

Gagnon, J., & Maccini, P. (2001). Preparing students with disabilities for algebra. *Teaching Exceptional Children, 34*(1), 8–15.

Gallagher, J., & Gallagher, S. (1994). *Teaching the gifted child.* Boston, MA: Allyn & Bacon.

Garrison, L. (1997). Making the NCTM's Standards work for emergent English speakers. *Teaching Children Mathematics, 4*(3), 132–138.

Garza-Kling, G. (2011). Fluency with basic addition. *Teaching Children Mathematics, 18*(2), 81–88.

Gavin, M. K., & Sheffield, L. J. (2010). Using curriculum to develop mathematical promise in the middle grades. In M. Saul, S. Assouline, & L. J. Sheffield (Eds.), *The peak in the middle: Developing mathematically gifted students in the middle grades.* (pp. 51–76). Reston, VA: National Council of Teachers of Mathematics, National Association of Gifted Children, and National Middle School Association.

Geary, D. C., & Hoard, M. K. (2005). Learning disabilities in arithmetic and mathematics: Theoretical and empirical

perspectives. In J. Campbell (Ed.), *Handbook of mathematical cognition* (pp. 253–267). New York, NY: Psychology Press.

George, L. (2010). *Civil war recipes: Adding and subtracting simple fractions.* New York, NY: Rosen Publishing Group.

Gersten, R., Beckmann, S., Clarke, B., Foegen, A., Marsh, L., Star, J. R., & Witzel, B. (2009). *Assisting students struggling with mathematics: Response to Intervention (RtI) for elementary and middle schools* (NCEE 2009-4060). Washington, DC: National Center for Education Evaluation and Regional Assistance, Institute of Education Sciences, U.S. Department of Education. Retrieved from http://ies.ed.gov/ncee/wwc/publications/practiceguides

Gilbert, M. C., & Musu, L. E. (2008). Using TARGETTS to create learning environments that support mathematical understanding and adaptive motivation. *Teaching Children Mathematics, 15*(3), 138–143.

Goldenberg, E. P., Mark, J., & Cuoco, A. (2010). An algebraic-habits-of-mind perspective on elementary school. *Teaching Children Mathematics, 16*(9), 548–556.

Gómez, C. L. (2010). Teaching with cognates. *Teaching Children Mathematics, 16*(8), 470–474.

González, N., Moll, L.C., & Amanti, C. (Eds.). (2005). *Funds of knowledge: Theorizing practices in households and classrooms.* Mahwah, NJ: Lawrence Erlbaum.

Gravemeijer, K., & van Galen, F. (2003). Facts and algorithms as products of students' own mathematical activity. In J. Kilpatrick, W. G. Martin, & D. Schifter (Eds.), *A research companion to Principles and Standards for School Mathematics* (pp. 114–122). Reston, VA: NCTM.

Greenes, C., Teuscher, D., & Regis, T. (2010). Preparing teachers for mathematically talented middle school students. In M. Saul, S. Assouline, & L. J. Sheffield (Eds.), *The peak in the middle: Developing mathematically gifted students in the middle grades.* (pp. 77–91). Reston, VA: National Council of Teachers of Mathematics, National Association of Gifted Children, and National Middle School Association.

Greer, B. (1992). Multiplication and division as models of situations. In D. A. Grouws (Ed.), *Handbook of research on mathematics teaching and learning* (pp. 276–295). Old Tappan, NJ: Macmillan.

Gregg, J., & Gregg, D. U. (2007). Measurement and fair-sharing models for dividing fractions. *Mathematics Teaching in the Middle School, 12*(9), 490–496.

Griffin, L., & Lavelle, L. (2010). *Assessing mathematical understanding: Using one-on-one mathematics interviews with K–2 students.* Presentation given at the Annual Conference of the National Council of Supervisors of Mathematics, San Diego, CA.

Gutiérrez, R. (2009). Embracing the inherent tensions in teaching mathematics from an equity stance. *Democracy and Education, 18*(3), 9–16.

Haas, E., & Gort, M. (2009). Demanding more: Legal standards and best practices for English language learners. *Bilingual Research Journal, 32*(2), 115–135.

Hattie, J. (2009). *Visible learning: A synthesis of over 800 meta-analyses relating to achievement.* New York, NY: Routledge.

Hecht, S., Vagi, K., Torgesen, J. (2007). Fraction skills and proportional reasoning. In D. Berch & M. Mazzocco (Eds.), *Why is math so hard for some children? The nature and origins of mathematical learning difficulties and disabilities* (pp. 121–132). New York, NY: Brookes Publishing.

Heddens, J. (1964). *Today's mathematics: A guide to concepts and methods in elementary school mathematics.* Chicago, IL: Science Research Associates.

Henderson, A. T., Mapp, K. L., Jordan, C., Orozco, E., Averett, A., Donnelly, D., Buttram, J., Wood, L. Fowler, M., & Myers, M. (2002). *A new wave of evidence: The impact of school, family, and community connections on student achievement.* Austin, TX: Southwest Education Development Laboratory.

Henry, V. J., & Brown, R. S. (2008). First grade basic facts: An investigation into teaching and learning of an accelerated, high-demand memorization standard. *Journal for Research in Mathematics Education, 39*(2), 153–183.

Hiebert, J., Carpenter, T. P., Fennema, E., Fuson, K., Wearne, D., Murray, H., Olivier, A., & Human, P. (1997). *Making sense: Teaching and learning mathematics with understanding.* Portsmouth, NH: Heinemann.

Hiebert, J., & Grouws, D. A. (2007). The effects of classroom mathematics teaching on students' learning. In F. K. Lester (Ed.), *Second handbook of research on mathematics teaching and learning* (pp. 371–404). Charlotte, NC: Information Age Publishing.

Hodges, T. E., Cady, J., & Collins, R. L. (2008). Fraction representation: The not-so-common denominator among textbooks. *Mathematics Teaching in the Middle School, 14*(2), 78–84.

Hoffman, B. L., Breyfogle, M. L., & Dressler, J. A. (2009). The power of incorrect answers. *Mathematics Teaching in the Middle School, 15*(4), 232–238.

Hong, L. T. (1993). *Two of everything: A Chinese folktale.* New York, NY: Albert Whitman.

Howden, H. (1989). Teaching number sense. *Arithmetic Teacher, 36*(6), 6–11.

Hudson, P. J., Shupe, M., Vasquez, E., & Miller, S. P. (2008). Teaching data analysis to elementary students with mild disabilities. *Teaching Exceptional Children Plus, 4*(3), Article 5. Retrieved April 15, 2011, from http://escholarship.bc.edu/education/tecplus/vol4/iss3/art5

Huff, K., & Goodman, D. P. (2007). The demand for cognitive diagnostic assessment. In J. P. Leighton & M. J. Gierl (Eds.), *Cognitive diagnostic assessment for education: Theory and applications* (pp. 19–60). New York, NY: Cambridge.

Huinker, D. (1994, April). *Multi-step word problems: A strategy for empowering students.* Presented at the annual meeting of the National Council of Teachers of Mathematics, Indianapolis, IN.

Huinker, D. (2002). Examining dimensions of fraction operation sense. In B. Litwiller (Ed.), *Making sense of fractions, ratios, and proportions, 2002 yearbook* (pp. 72–78). Reston, VA: NCTM.

Izsák, A. (2004). Teaching and learning two-digit multiplication: Coordinating analyses of classroom practices and individual student learning. *Mathematical Thinking and Learning, 6*(1), 37–79.

Izsák, A., Tillema, E., & Tunc-Pekkam, Z. (2008). Teaching and learning fraction addition on number lines. *Journal for Research in Mathematics Education, 39*(1), 33–62.

Jacobs, V. R., & Ambrose, R. C. (2008). Making the most of story problems. *Teaching Children Mathematics, 15*(5), 260–266.

Janzen, J. (2008). Teaching English language learners in the content areas. *Review of Educational Research, 78*(4), 1010–1038.

Johanning, D. J. (2008). Learning to use fractions: Examining middle school students' emerging fraction literacy. *Journal for Research in Mathematics Education, 39*(3), 281–310.

Johanning, D. J. (2011). Estimation's role in calculations with fractions. *Mathematics Teaching in the Middle School, 17*(2), 96–102.

Joram, E. (2003). Benchmarks as tools for developing measurement sense. In D. H. Clements (Ed.), *Learning and teaching measurement* (pp. 57–67). Reston, VA: NCTM.

Jordan, N. C., Kaplan, D., Locuniak, M. N., & Ramineni, C. (2007). Predicting first grade math achievement from developmental number sense trajectories. *Learning Disabilities Research & Practice, 22*(1), 36–46.

Kamii, C. K. (1985). *Young children reinvent arithmetic.* New York, NY: Teachers College Press.

Kamii, C. K., & Anderson, C. (2003). Multiplication games: How we made and used them. *Teaching Children Mathematics, 10*(3), 135–141.

Kamii, C. K., & Dominick, A. (1998). The harmful effects of algorithms in grades 1–4. In L. J. Morrow (Ed.), *The teaching and learning of algorithms in school mathematics* (pp. 130–140). Reston, VA: NCTM.

Kaput, J. J. (2008). What is algebra? What is algebraic reasoning? In J. J. Kaput, D. W. Carraher, & M. L. Blanton (Eds.), *Algebra in the early grades* (pp. 5–17). Reston, VA: NCTM.

Karp, K., & Howell, P. (2004). Building responsibility for learning in students with special needs. *Teaching Children Mathematics, 11*(3), 118–126.

Keiser, J. M. (2010). Shifting our computational focus. *Mathematics Teaching in the Middle School, 16*(4), 216–223.

Kenney, J. M., Hancewicz, E., Heuer, L., Metsisto, D., & Tuttle, C. L. (2005). *Literacy strategies for improving mathematics instruction.* Alexandria, VA: Association for Supervision and Curriculum Development.

Kersaint, G., Thompson, D. R., & Petkova, M. (2009). *Teaching mathematics to English language learners.* New York, NY: Routledge.

Khisty, L. L. (1997). Making mathematics accessible to Latino students: Rethinking instructional practice. In M. Kenney & J. Trentacosta (Eds.), *Multicultural and gender equity in the mathematics classroom: The gift of diversity* (pp. 92–101). Reston, VA: NCTM.

Kieran, C. (2007). Learning and teaching algebra at the middle school through college levels: Building meaning for symbols and their manipulation. In F. K. Lester, Jr. (Ed.), *Second handbook of research on mathematics teaching and learning* (pp. 707–762). Charlotte, NC: Information Age Publishing.

Kilic, H., Cross, D. I., Ersoz, F. A., Mewborn, D. S., Swanagan, D., & Kim, J. (2010). Techniques for small-group discourse. *Teaching Children Mathematics, 16*(6), 350–357.

Kingore, B. (2006, Winter). Tiered instruction: Beginning the process. *Teaching for High Potential, 5–6.*

Kliman, M. (1999). Beyond helping with homework: Parents and children doing mathematics at home. *Teaching Children Mathematics, 6*(3), 140–146.

Kloosterman, P. (2010). Mathematics skills of 17-year-olds in the United States: 1978 to 2004. *Journal for Research in Mathematics Education, 41*(1), 20–51.

Kloosterman, P., Rutledge, Z., & Kenney, P. (2009). Exploring the results of the NAEP: 1980s to the present. *Mathematics Teaching in the Middle School, 14*(6), 357–365.

Kloosterman, P., Warfield, J., Wearne, D., Koc, Y., Martin, W. G., & Strutchens, M. (2004). Fourth-grade students' knowledge of mathematics and perceptions of learning mathematics. In P. Kloosterman & F. K. Lester, Jr. (Eds.), *Results and interpretations of the 1990–2000 mathematics assessments of the National Assessment of Educational Progress* (pp. 71–103). Reston, VA: NCTM.

Knuth, E. J., Stephens, A. C., McNeil, N. M., & Alibali, M. W. (2006). Does understanding the equal sign matter? Evidence from solving equations. *Journal for Research in Mathematics Education, 37*(4), 297–312.

Kouba, V. L., Brown, C. A., Carpenter, T. P., Lindquist, M. M., Silver, E. A., & Swafford, J. O. (1988). Results of the fourth NAEP assessment of mathematics: Number, operations and word problems. *Arithmetic Teacher, 35*(8), 14–19.

Kouba, V. L., Zawojewski, J. S., & Strutchens, M. E. (1997). What do students know about numbers and operations? In P. A. Kenney & E. Silver (Eds.), *Results from the sixth mathematics assessment of the National Assessment of Educational Progress* (pp. 87–140). Reston, VA: NCTM.

Kribs-Zaleta, C. (2008). Oranges, posters, ribbons, and lemonade: Concrete computational strategies for dividing fractions. *Mathematics Teaching in the Middle School, 13*(8), 453–457.

Kulm, G. (1994). *Mathematics and assessment: What works in the classroom.* San Francisco, CA: Jossey-Bass.

Kurz, T. (2012). A super way to soak in linear measurement, *Teaching Children Mathematics, 18*(9), 535–541.

Labinowicz, E. (1985). *Learning from children: New beginnings for teaching numerical thinking.* Menlo Park, CA: AWL Supplemental.

Lambdin, D. V., & Lynch, K. (2005). Examining mathematics tasks from the National Assessment of Educational Progress. *Mathematics Teaching in the Middle School, 10*(6), 314–318.

Lamon, S. J. (2012). *Teaching fractions and ratios for understanding: Essential content knowledge and instructional strategies for teachers.* New York, NY: Routledge.

Leedy, L. (2000). *Measuring penny.* New York, NY: Henry Holt and Company.

Lesh, R. A., Cramer, K., Doerr, H., Post, T., & Zawojewski, J. (2003). Model development sequences. In R. A. Lesh & H. Doerr (Eds.), *Beyond constructivism: A models and modeling perspective on mathematics teaching, learning, and problem solving* (pp. 35–58). Mahwah, NJ: Lawrence Erlbaum.

Lewis, T. (2005). Facts + fun = fluency. *Teaching Children Mathematics, 12*(1), 8–11.

Locuniak, M. N., & Jordan, N. C. (2008). Using kindergarten number sense to predict calculation fluency in second grade. *Journal of Learning Disabilities, 41*(5), 451–459.

Mack, N. K. (1995). Confounding whole-number and fraction concepts when building on informal knowledge. *Journal for Research in Mathematics Education, 26*(5), 422–441.

Mack, N. K. (2004). Connecting to develop computational fluency with fractions. *Teaching Children Mathematics, 11*(4), 226–232.

Mack, N. K. (2011). Enriching number knowledge. *Teaching Children Mathematics, 18*(2), 101–109.

Maldonado, L. A., Turner, E. E., Dominguez, H., & Empson, S. B. (2009). English language learning from, and contributing to, mathematical discussions. In D. Y. White & J. S. Spitzer (Eds.), *Responding to diversity: Grades pre-K–5* (pp. 7–22). Reston, VA: NCTM.

Mann, R. L. (2004). Balancing act: The truth behind the equals sign. *Teaching Children Mathematics, 11*(2), 68.

Mark, J., Cuoco, A., Goldenberg, E. P., & Sword, S. (2010). Developing mathematical habits of mind. *Mathematics Teaching in the Middle School, 15*(9), 505–509.

Martin, J. F. (2009). The goal of long division. *Teaching Children Mathematics, 15*(8), 482–487.

Martinie, S. L. (2007). *Middle school rational number knowledge.* (Unpublished doctoral dissertation, Kansas State University.)

Martinie, S. L., & Bay-Williams, J. M. (2003). Investigating students' conceptual understanding of decimal fractions using multiple representations. *Mathematics Teaching in the Middle School, 8*(5), 244–247.

Mathis, S. B. (1986). *The hundred penny box.* New York, NY: Puffin Books.

Mazzocco, M. M. M., Devlin, K. T., & McKenney, S. J. (2008). Is it a fact? Timed arithmetic performance of children with mathematical learning disabilities (MLD) varies as a function of how MLD is defined. *Developmental Neuropsychology, 33*(3), 318–344.

Mazzocco, M. M. M., & Thompson, R. E. (2005). Kindergarten predictors of math learning disability. *Learning Disabilities Research & Practice, 20*(3), 142–155

McAnallen, R., & Frye, E. (1995). *Action fractions with hexadrons and pattern blocks.* Boston, MA: Koplow Games, Incorporated.

McGlone, C. (2008). *The role of culturally-based mathematics in the general mathematics curriculum.* Paper presented at the Eleventh International Congress on Mathematics Education, Monterrey, Mexico.

McNamara, J., & Shaughnessy, M. M. (2010). *Beyond pizzas & pies: Ten essential strategies for supporting fraction sense (Grades 3–5).* Sausalito, CA: Math Solutions.

McNeil, N. M., & Alibali, M. W. (2005). Knowledge change as a function of mathematics experience: All contexts are not created equal. *Journal of Cognition and Development, 6,* 285–306.

McNeil, N. M., Grandau, L., Knuth, E. J., Alibali, M. W., Stephens, A. C., Hattikudur, S., & Krill, D. E. (2006). Middle school students' understanding of the equal sign: The books they read can't help. *Cognition & Instruction, 24*(3), 367–385.

Meyer, M., & Arbaugh, F. (2008). Professional development for administrators: What they need to know to support curriculum adoption and implementation. In M. Meyer, C. Langrall, F. Arbaugh, D. Webb, & M. Hoover (Eds.), *A decade of middle school mathematics curriculum implementation: Lessons learned from the Show-Me Project* (pp. 201–210). Charlotte, NC: Information Age Publishing.

Midobuche, E. (2001). Building cultural bridges between home and the mathematics classroom. *Teaching Children Mathematics, 7*(9), 500–502.

Mokros, J., & Wright, T. (2009). Zoos, aquariums and expanding students' data literacy. *Teaching Children Mathematics, 15*(9), 524–530.

Molina, M., & Ambrose, R. C. (2006). Fostering relational thinking while negotiating the meaning of the equals sign. *Teaching Children Mathematics, 13*(2), 111–117.

Moschkovich, J. (2009). *Using two languages when learning mathematics: How can research help us understand mathematics learners who use two languages?* NCTM Research Brief. Reston, VA: NCTM.

Munier, V., Devichi, C., & Merle, H. (2008). A physical situation as a way to teach angle. *Teaching Children Mathematics, 14*(7), 402–407.

Murata, A. (2008). Mathematics teaching and learning as a mediating process: The case of tape diagrams. *Mathematical Thinking and Learning, 10*, 374 –406.

Murray, M., & Jorgensen, J. (2007). *The differentiated math classroom: A guide for teachers, K–8.* Portsmouth, NH: Heinemann.

Murrey, D. L. (2008). Differentiating instruction in mathematics for the English language learner. *Mathematics Teaching in the Middle School, 14*(3), 146–153.

National Center for Education Statistics (NCES). (2011). *The condition of education 2011* (NCES 2011-033). Washington, DC: U.S. Department of Education.

National Center for Education Statistics. (n.d.). Retrieved from http://nces.ed.gov/nationsreportcard/itmrlsx/search .aspx?subject=mathematics

National Mathematics Advisory Panel. (2008). *Foundations for success.* Jessup, MD: U.S. Department of Education. (Also available online at www.ed.gov/MathPanel)

National Research Council. (2001). *Adding it up: Helping children learn mathematics.* Washington, DC: National Academy Press.

National Research Council Committee. (2009). *Mathematics learning in early childhood: Paths toward excellence and equity.* Washington, DC: The National Academies Press.

NCTM (National Council of Teachers of Mathematics). (2000). *Principles and standards for school mathematics.* Reston, VA: NCTM.

NCTM (National Council of Teachers of Mathematics). (2006). *Curriculum focal points for prekindergarten through grade 8 mathematics: A quest for coherence.* Reston, VA: NCTM.

NCTM (National Council of Teachers of Mathematics). (2007). Research brief: Effective strategies for teaching students with difficulties in mathematics. Retrieved from www.nctm.org/news /content.aspx?id=8452

NCTM (National Council of Teachers of Mathematics). (2008, January). *Equity in mathematics education.* Retrieved January 5, 2011, from www.nctm.org/about

NCTM (National Council of Teachers of Mathematics). (2011a, March). Position statement on interventions. Retrieved June 5, 2011, from www.nctm.org/about/content.aspx?id=30506

NCTM (National Council of Teachers of Mathematics). (2011b, March). Position statement on the metric system. Reston, VA: NCTM. Retrieved from www.nctm.org/about/content.aspx?id=29000

Nebesniak, A. L., & Heaton, R. M. (2010). Student confidence and student involvement. *Mathematics Teaching in the Middle School, 16*(2), 97–103.

Neumann, M. D. (2005). Freedom quilts: Mathematics on the underground railroad. *Teaching Children Mathematics, 11*(6), 316–321.

Neumer, C. (2007). Mixed numbers made easy: Building and converting mixed numbers and improper fractions. *Teaching Children Mathematics, 13*(9), 488–492.

Norton, A., & D'Ambrosio, B. S. (2008). ZPC and ZPD: Zones of teaching and learning. *Journal for research in mathematics education 39*(3), 220–246.

Outhred, L., & Mitchelmore, M. (2004). Students' structuring of rectangular arrays. In M. J. Hoines & A. B. Fuglestad (Eds.), *Proceedings of the 28th PME International Conference, 3*, 465–472.

Parker, M. (2004). Reasoning and working proportionally with percent. *Mathematics Teaching in the Middle School, 9*(6), 326–330.

Parker, R., & Breyfogle, L. (2011). Learning to write about mathematics. *Teaching Children Mathematics, 18*(2), 90–99.

Parmar, R., Garrison, R., Clements, D., & Sarama, J. (2011). Measurement. In F. Fennell (Ed.), *Achieving fluency in special education and mathematics* (pp. 197–216) Reston, VA: NCTM.

Patall, E. A., Cooper, H., & Robinson, J. C. (2008). Parent involvement in homework: A research synthesis. *Review of Educational Research, 78*(4), 1039–1101.

Peltenburg, M., van den Heuvel-Panhuizen, M., & Robitzsch, A. (2012). Special education students' use of indirect addition in solving subtraction problems up to 100—A proof of the didactical potential of an ignored procedure. *Educational Studies in Mathematics, 79*(3), 351–369.

Perie, M., Moran, R., & Lutkus, A. (2005). *NAEP 2004 trends in academic progress: Three decades of student performance in reading and mathematics.* Washington, DC: National Center for Education Statistics.

Perkins, I., & Flores, A. (2002). Mathematical notations and procedures of recent immigrant students. *Teaching Children Mathematics, 7*(6), 346–351.

Pesek, D., & Kirshner, D. (2002). Interference of instrumental instruction in subsequent relational learning. In J. Sowder & B. P. Schappelle (Eds.), *Lessons learned from research* (pp. 101–107). Reston, VA: NCTM.

Petit, M. M., Laird, R. E., & Marsden, E. L. (2010). *A focus on fractions: Bringing research to the classroom.* New York, NY: Taylor & Francis.

Petit, M., & Zawojewski, J. (2010). Formative assessment in elementary school mathematics. In D. Lambdin & F. K. Lester, Jr. (Eds.), *Teaching and learning mathematics: Translating research for elementary school teachers.* (pp. 73–79). Reston, VA: NCTM.

Philipp, R., & Vincent, C. (2003). Reflecting on learning fractions without understanding. *OnMath, 2*(7).

Piaget, J. (1976). *The child's conception of the world.* Totowa, NJ: Littlefield, Adams.

Post, T. R., Wachsmuth, I., Lesh, R. A., & Behr, M. J. (1985). Order and equivalence of rational numbers: A cognitive analysis. *Journal for Research in Mathematics Education, 16*(1), 18–36.

Pothier, Y., & Sawada, D. (1983). Partitioning: The emergence of rational number ideas in young children. *Journal for Research in Mathematics Education, 14*, 307–317.

Prediger, S. (2011). Why Johnny can't apply multiplication? Revisiting the choice of operations with fractions. *International Electronic Journal of Mathematics Education, 6*(2), 65–88.

Quinn, R., Lamberg, T., & Perrin, J. (2008). Teacher perceptions of division by zero. *Clearing House, 81*(3), 101–104.

Rampey, B. D., Dion, G. S., & Donahue, P. L. (2009). *NAEP 2008 trends in academic progress (NCES 2009–479).* Washington, DC: National Center for Education Statistics, Institute of Education Sciences, U.S. Department of Education.

RAND Mathematics Study Panel. (2003). *Mathematical proficiency for all students: Toward a strategic research and development program in mathematics education* (Issue 1643). Santa Monica, CA: Rand Corporation.

Rasmussen, C., Yackel, E., & King, K. (2003). Social and sociomathematical norms in the mathematics classroom. In H. L. Schoen & R. I. Charles (Eds.). *Teaching mathematics through problem solving: Grades 6–12* (pp. 143–154). Reston, VA: NCTM.

Rathmell, E. C. (1978). Using thinking strategies to teach the basic skills. In M. N. Suydam (Ed.), *Developing computational skills* (pp. 13–38). Reston, VA: NCTM.

Rathmell, E. C., Leutzinger, L. P., & Gabriele, A. (2000). *Thinking with numbers.* (Separate packets for each operation.) Cedar Falls, IA: Thinking with Numbers.

Rathouz, M. M. (2011). Making sense of decimal multiplication. *Mathematics Teaching in the Middle School, 16*(7), 430–437.

Ravenna, G. (2008). *Factors influencing gifted students' preferences for models of teaching.* Doctoral dissertation, University of Southern California.

Reeder, S. (2012). Cleared for takeoff: Paper airplanes in flight. *Mathematics Teaching in the Middle School, 17*(7), 402–409.

Reinhart, S. (2000). Never say anything a kid can say. *Mathematics Teaching in the Middle School, 5*(8), 478–483.

Reis, S., & Renzulli, J. S. (2005). *Curriculum compacting: An easy start to differentiating for high potential students.* Waco, TX: Prufrock Press.

Renzulli, J. S., Gubbins, E. J., McMillen, K. S., Eckert, R. D., & Little, C. A. (Eds.). (2009). *Systems & models for developing programs for the gifted & talented* (2nd ed.). Mansfield Center, CT: Creative Learning Press.

Rittle-Johnson, B., Star, J. R., & Durkin, K. (2010, April). *Developing procedural flexibility: When should multiple solution methods be introduced?* Paper presented at the Annual Conference of the American Educational Research Association, Denver, CO.

Robinson, J. P. (2010). The effects of test translation on young English learners' mathematics performance. *Educational Researcher, 39*(8), 582–590.

Roddick, C., & Silvas-Centeno, C. (2007). Developing understanding of fractions through pattern blocks and fair trade. *Teaching Children Mathematics, 14*(3), 140–145.

Rodríguez-Brown, F. V. (2010). Latino families: Culture and schooling. In E. G. Murillo, Jr., S. A. Villenas, R. T. Galván, J. S. Muñoz, C. Martínez, & M. Machado-Casas (Eds.), *Handbook of Latinos and education: Theory, research, and practice* (pp. 350–360). New York, NY: Routledge.

Ross, S. H. (1986). *The development of children's place-value numeration concepts in grades two through five.* Presented at the annual meeting of the American Educational Research Association, San Francisco. (ERIC Document Reproduction Service No. ED 2773–482).

Ross, S. R. (2002). Place value: Problem solving and written assessment. *Teaching Children Mathematics, 8*(7), 419–423.

Rotigel, J., & Fellow, S. (2005). Mathematically gifted students: How can we meet their needs? *Gifted Child Today, 27*(4), 46–65.

Russell, S. J. (2006). What does it mean that "5 has a lot"? From the world to data and back. In G. F. Burrill & P. C. Elliott (Eds.), *Thinking and reasoning about data and chance: 68th NCTM yearbook* (pp. 17–30). Reston VA: NCTM.

Russell, S. J., & Economopoulos, K. (2008). *Investigations in number, data, and space.* New York, NY: Pearson.

Russell, S. J., Schifter, D., & Bastable, V. (2011). Developing algebraic thinking in the context of arithmetic. In J. Cai & E. Knuth (Eds.), *Early algebraization: A global dialogue from multiple perspectives* (pp. 43–70). New York, NY: Springer.

Sadler, P., & Tai, R. (2007). The two pillars supporting college science. *Science, 317*(5837), 457–458.

Sarama, J., & Clements, D. H. (2009). *Early childhood mathematics education research: learning trajectories for young children.* New York, NY: Routledge.

Saul, M., Assouline, S., & Sheffield, L. J. (Eds.) (2010). *The peak in the middle: Developing mathematically gifted students in the middle grades.* Reston, VA: National Council of Teachers of Mathematics, National Association of Gifted Children, and National Middle School Association.

Scheaffer, R. L. (2006). Statistics and mathematics: On making a happy marriage. In G. F. Burrill & P. C. Elliott (Eds.), *Thinking and reasoning about data and chance: Sixty-eighth yearbook* (pp. 309–322). Reston, VA: NCTM.

Schifter, D. (1999). Reasoning about operations: Early algebraic thinking, grades K through 6. In L. Stiff & F. Curcio (Eds.), *Developing mathematical reasoning in grades K–12* (pp. 62–81). Reston, VA: NCTM.

Schifter, D., Bastable, V., & Russell, S. J. (1999). *Developing mathematical understanding: Numbers and operations, part 2: Making meaning for operations* (Casebook). Parsippany, NJ: Dale Seymour Publications.

Schifter, D., Bastable, V., & Russell, S. J. (2000). *Developing mathematical ideas: Numbers and operations, part 1: Building a system of tens.* (Casebook). Parsippany, NJ: Dale Seymour Publications.

Schifter, D., Monk, G. S., Russell, S. J., & Bastable, V. (2007). Early algebra: What does understanding the laws of arithmetic mean in the elementary grades? In J. Kaput, D. Carraher, & M. Blanton (Eds.), *Algebra in the early grades.* Mahwah, NJ: Lawrence Erlbaum.

Scott, T., & Lane, H. (2001). *Multi-tiered interventions in academic and social contexts.* Unpublished manuscript, University of Florida, Gainesville.

Secada, W. G. (1983). *The educational background of limited-English-proficient students: Implications for the arithmetic classroom.* Arlington Heights, IL: Bilingual Education Service Center. (ERIC Document Reproduction Service No. ED 237318).

Seeley, C. L. (2009). *Faster isn't smarter: Messages about math, teaching, and learning in the 21st century.* Sausalito, CA: Math Solutions.

Setati, M. (2005). Teaching mathematics in a primary multilingual classroom. *Journal for Research in Mathematics Education, 36*(5), 447–466.

Shaughnessy, J. M. (2003). Research on students' understanding of probability. In J. Kilpatrick, W. G. Martin, & D. Schifter (Eds.), *A research companion to Principles and Standards for School Mathematics* (pp. 216–226). Reston, VA: NCTM.

Shaughnessy, J. M. (2006). Research on students' understanding of some big concepts in statistics. In G. F. Burrill & P. C. Elliott (Eds.), *Thinking and reasoning about data and chance: 68th NCTM yearbook* (pp. 77–98). Reston, VA: NCTM.

Shaughnessy, J. M. (2007). Research on statistics learning and reasoning. In F. Lester, Jr. (Ed.), *Second handbook of research on mathematics teaching and learning* (pp. 957–1010). Reston, VA: NCTM.

Shaughnessy, M. (2009). *Students' flexible use of multiple representations for rational numbers: Decimals, fractions, parts of area and number lines.* Doctoral dissertation, University of California–Berkeley.

Sheffield, L. J. (Ed.). (1999). *Developing mathematically promising students.* Reston, VA: NCTM.

Shoecraft, P. (1982). Bowl-a-fact: A game for reviewing the number facts. *Arithmetic Teacher, 29*(8), 24–25.

Siebert, D., & Gaskin, N. (2006). Creating, naming, and justifying fractions. *Teaching Children Mathematics, 12*(8), 394–400.

Siegler, R., Carpenter, T., Fennell, F., Geary, D., Lewis, J., Okamoto, Y., et al. (2010). *Developing effective fractions instruction for kindergarten through 8th grade: A practice guide* (NCEE #2010-4039). Washington, DC: National Center for Education Evaluation and Regional Assistance, Institute of Education Sciences, U.S. Department of Education. Retrieved from www.whatworks.ed.gov /publications/practiceguides

Skemp, R. (1978). Relational understanding and instrumental understanding. *Arithmetic Teacher, 26*(3), 9–15.

Small, M. (2009). *Good questions: Great ways to differentiate mathematics instruction.* Reston, VA: NCTM.

Smith, J. P., III. (2002). The development of students' knowledge of fractions and ratios. In B. Litwiller (Ed.), *Making sense of fractions, ratios, and proportions* (pp. 3–17). Reston, VA: NCTM.

Smith, M., Hughes, E., Engle, R., & Stein, M. (2009). Orchestrating discussions. *Mathematics Teaching in the Middle School, 14*(9), 548–556.

Smith, M. S. & Stein, M. K. (1998). Selecting and creating mathematical tasks: From research to practice. *Mathematics Teaching in the Middle School, 3*(5), 344–350.

Sousa, D., & Tomlinson, C. (2011). *Differentiation and the brain: How neuroscience supports the learner-friendly classroom.* Bloomington, IN: Solution Tree Press.

Sowder, J. T., & Wearne, D. (2006). What do we know about eighth-grade student achievement? *Mathematics Teaching in the Middle School, 11*(6), 285–293.

Sowder, J. T., Wearne, D., Martin, W. G., & Strutchens, M. (2004). What do 8th-grade students know about mathematics? Changes over a decade. In P. Kloosterman & F. K. Lester, Jr. (Eds.), *Results and interpretations of the 1990–2000 mathematics assessments of the National Assessment of Educational Progress* (pp. 105–143). Reston, VA: NCTM.

Sowder, L. (1988). Children's solutions of story problems. *Journal of Mathematical Behavior, 7*(3), 227–238.

Star, J. R., & Rittle-Johnson, B. (2009). The role of prior knowledge in the development of strategy flexibility: The case of computational estimation. In S. Swars, D. Stinson, & S. Lemons-Smith (Eds.), *Proceedings of the 31st annual meeting of the North American Chapter of the International Group for the Psychology of Mathematics Education* (pp. 577– 584). Atlanta: Georgia State University.

Steinle, V., & Stacey, K. (2004a). Persistence of decimal misconceptions and readiness to move to expertise. *Proceedings of the 28th conference of the International Groups for the Psychology of Mathematics Education, 4*, 225–232.

Steinle, V., & Stacey, K. (2004b). A longitudinal study of students' understanding of decimal notation: An overview and refined results. In I. Putt, R. Faragher, & M. McLean (Eds.), *Mathematics education for the third millennium: Towards 2010. Proceedings of the 27th Annual Conference of the Mathematics Education Research Group of Australasia, 2*, 541–548.

Stephan M., & Whitenack, J. (2003). Establishing classroom social and sociomathematical norms for problem solving. In F. K. Lester, Jr., & R. I. Charles (Eds.), *Teaching mathematics through problem solving: Grades pre-K–6* (pp. 149–162). Reston, VA: NCTM.

Stiggins, R. (2009). Assessment for learning in upper elementary grades. *Phi Delta Kappan, 90*(6), 419–421.

Storeygard, J. (2010). *My kids can: Making math accessible to all learners, K–5.* Portsmouth, NH: Heinemann.

Sullivan, P., & Lilburn, P. (2002). *Good questions for math teaching: Why ask them and what to ask, K–6.* Sausalito, CA: Math Solutions.

Taber, S. B. (2002). Go ask Alice about multiplication of fractions. In B. Litwiller (Ed.), *Making sense of fractions, ratios, and proportions* (pp. 61–71). Reston, VA: NCTM.

Tarr, J. E., & Shaughnessy, J. M. (2007). *Data and chance. Results from the 2003 National Assessment of Educational Process.* Reston, VA: NCTM.

Thompson, C. S. (1990). Place value and larger numbers. In J. N. Payne (Ed.), *Mathematics for the young child* (pp. 89–108). Reston, VA: NCTM.

Thompson, T. D., & Preston, R. V. (2004). Measurement in the middle grades: Insights from NAEP and TIMSS. *Mathematics Teaching in the Middle School, 9*(9), 514–519.

Tobias, S. (1995). *Overcoming math anxiety.* New York, NY: W. W. Norton.

Tomlinson, C. (1999). Mapping a route towards differentiated instruction. *Educational Leadership 57*(1), 12–16.

Tomlinson, C. (2003). *Fulfilling the promise of the differentiated classroom: Strategies and tools for responsive teaching.* Alexandria, VA: Association of Supervision and Curriculum Development.

Tompert, A. (1997). *Grandfather Tang's story.* New York, NY: Dragonfly Books.

Torbeyns, J., De Smedt, B., Ghesquiere, P., & Verschaffel, L. (2009). Acquisition and use of shortcut strategies by traditionally schooled children. *Educational Studies in Mathematics, 71*, 1–17.

Torgesen, J. K. (2002). The prevention of reading difficulties. *Journal of School Psychology, 40*(1), 7–26.

Towers, J., & Hunter, K. (2010). An ecological reading of mathematical language in a grade 3 classroom: A case of learning and teaching measurement estimation. *The Journal of Mathematical Behavior, 29*, 25–40.

Turner, E. E., Celedón-Pattichis, S., Marshall, M., & Tennison, A. (2009). "Fijense amorcitos, les voy a contra una historia": The power of story to support solving and discussing mathematical problems among Latino and Latina kindergarten students. In D. Y. White & J. S. Spitzer (Eds.), *Responding to diversity: Grades pre-K–5* (pp. 23–42). Reston, VA: NCTM.

Tzur, R. (1999). An integrated study of children's construction of improper fractions and the teacher's role in promoting learning. *Journal for Research in Mathematics Education, 30*(4), 390–416.

Ubuz, B., & Yayan, B. (2010). Primary teachers' subject matter knowledge: Decimals. *International Journal of Mathematical Education in Science and Technology, 41*(6), 787–804.

Usiskin, Z. (2007). Some thoughts about fractions. *Mathematics Teaching in the Middle School, 12*(7), 370–373.

van Hiele, P. M. (1986). *Structure and insight: A theory of mathematics education.* Orlando, FL: Academic Press.

van Hiele, P. M. (1999). Developing geometric thinking through activities that begin with play. *Teaching Children Mathematics, 5*(6), 310–316.

van Putten, C. M., van den Brom-Snijders, P., & Beishuizen, M. (2005). Progressive mathematization of long division in Dutch primary schools. *Journal for Research in Mathematics Education, 36*(1), 44–73.

VanTassel-Baska, J., & Brown, E. F. (2007). Toward best practice: An analysis of the efficacy of curriculum models in gifted education. *Gifted Child Quarterly, 51*(4), 342–358.

Verschaffel, L., Greer, B., & DeCorte, E. (2007). Whole number concepts and operations. In F. Lester, Jr. (Ed.), *Second handbook of research on mathematics teaching and learning* (pp. 557–628). Charlotte, NC: Information Age Publishing.

Vygotsky, L. S. (1978). *Mind and society.* Cambridge, MA: Harvard University Press.

Wallace, A. (2007). Anticipating student responses to improve problem solving. *Mathematics Teaching in the Middle School, 12*(9), 504–511.

Wallace, A. H., & Gurganus, S. P. (2005). Teaching for mastery of multiplication. *Teaching Children Mathematics, 12*(1), 26–33.

Warren, E., & Cooper, T. J. (2008). Patterns that support early algebraic thinking in elementary school. In C. E. Greenes & R. Rubenstein (Eds.), *Algebra and algebraic thinking in school mathematics: 70th NCTM yearbook* (pp. 113–126). Reston, VA: NCTM.

Weatherform, C. B. (2005). *A Negro League scrapbook.* Honesdale, PA: Boyds Mills Press.

Whiteford, T. (2009/2010). Is mathematics a universal language? *Teaching Children Mathematics, 16*(5), 276–283.

Whitin, P., & Whitin, D. (2008). Learning to solve problems in the primary grades. *Teaching Children Mathematics, 14*(7), 426–432.

Wiggins, G., & McTighe, J. (2005). *Understanding by design* (2nd ed.). Alexandria, VA: Association for Supervision and Curriculum Development.

Wiliam, D. (2010). *Practical techniques for formative assessment.* Presentation given in Boras, Sweden, September 2010. Retrieved June 11, 2011, from www.slideshare.net/BLoPP /dylan-wiliam-bors-2010

Williams, L. (2008). Tiering and scaffolding: Two strategies for providing access to important mathematics. *Teaching Children Mathematics, 14*(6), 324–330.

Witzel, B. S. (2005). Using CRA to teach algebra to students with math difficulties in inclusive settings. *Learning Disabilities—A Contemporary Journal, 3*(2), 49–60.

Wood, T., & Turner-Vorbeck, T. (2001). Extending the conception of mathematics teaching. In T. Wood, B. S. Nelson, & J. Warfield (Eds.), *Beyond classical pedagogy: Teaching elementary school mathematics* (pp. 185–208). Mahwah, NJ: Erlbaum.

Wood, T., Williams, G., & McNeal, B. (2006). Children's mathematical thinking in different classroom cultures. *Journal for Research in Mathematics Education, 37*(3), 222–255.

Woodward, J. (2006). Developing automaticity in multiplication facts: Integrating strategy instruction with timed practice drills. *Learning Disability Quarterly, 29*(4), 269–289.

Xin, Y. P., Jitendra, A. K., & Deatline-Buchman, A. D. (2005). Effects of mathematical word problem-solving instruction on middle school students with learning problems. *Journal of Special Education, 39*(3), 181–192.

Yackel, E., & Cobb, P. (1996). Sociomathematical norms, argumentation, and autonomy in mathematics. *Journal for Research in Mathematics Education, 27*(4), 458–477.

Ysseldyke, J. (2002). Response to "Learning Disabilities: Historical Perspectives." In R. Bradley, L. Danielson, & D. Hallahan (Eds.), *Identification of learning disabilities: Research to practice* (pp. 89–98). Mahwah, NJ: Erlbaum.

Yu, P., Barrett, J., & Presmeg, N. (2009). Prototypes and categorical reasoning: A perspective to explain how children learn about interactive geometry objects. In T. Craine & R. Rubenstein (Eds.), *Understanding geometry for a changing world* (pp. 109–126). Reston, VA: NCTM.

Zambo, R. (2008). Percents can make sense. *Mathematics Teaching in the Middle School, 13*(7), 418–422.

Zwillinger, D. (Ed.). (2011). *Standard mathematical tables and formulae* (32nd ed.). Boca Raton, FL: CRC Press.